GOD'S WARRIOR

Father Albert Braun, OFM, 1889–1983
Last of the Frontier Priests

GOD'S WARRIOR
Father Albert Braun, OFM, 1889–1983
Last of the Frontier Priests

Dorothy Cave

SUNSTONE
PRESS

SANTA FE

Sunstone books may be purchased for educational, business, or sales promotional use.
For information please write: Special Markets Department, Sunstone Press,
P.O. Box 2321, Santa Fe, New Mexico 87504-2321.

Book and Cover design ▷ Vicki Ahl
Body typeface ▷ Adobe Garamond Pro
Printed on acid free paper

Library of Congress Cataloging-in-Publication Data

Cave, Dorothy, 1927-
 God's warrior : Father Albert Braun, OFM, 1889-1983, last of the frontier priests / by Dorothy Cave.
  p. cm.
 Includes bibliographical references (p.   ) and index.
 ISBN 978-0-86534-520-1 (softcover : alk. paper)
 1. Braun, Albert, 1889-1983. 2. Mescalero Indians--Missions--New Mexico--Mescalero Indian
Reservation. 3. Missionaries--New Mexico--Mescalero Indian Reservation--Biography. I. Title.
E99.M45B734 2011
978.9'6504092--dc22
[B]

                          2011002641

Published in
Santa Fe

WWW.SUNSTONEPRESS.COM
SUNSTONE PRESS / POST OFFICE BOX 2321 / SANTA FE, NM 87504-2321 /USA
(505) 988-4418 / ORDERS ONLY (800) 243-5644 / FAX (505) 988-1025

Father Albert Braun, OFM, 1889–1983. Courtesy of Saint Joseph's Apache Mission, Mescalero, New Mexico (SJAM).

Brother Peter Boegel, OFM. Courtesy of Mary Serna.

DEDICATION

For
Brother Peter Boegel, OFM
whose zeal in preserving St. Joseph's Mission
evokes the spirit of Father Al in building it.

CONTENTS

ILLUSTRATIONS

School. Courtesy of Prof. Pete Eidenbach and Mary Serna.

Page 349: Father Al with ex-POW comrades Juan Jr. and Pepe Baldonado, far left and right, and Bruce Klinekole, center, with Father Al. Courtesy of S JAM.

Page 360: God's Warrior. Father Albert speaks to his people. On the church wall hang the plaque and title bestowed on him by the Mescalero Apache tribe. Courtesy of SJAM.

Page 362: Father Al receives the Legion of Merit at Mescalero, November 1945. Courtesy of SJAM.

Page 362: Chaplain Albert Braun stands at head of formation with Major General John L. Homer, Commander at Fort Bliss, Texas, representing General Wainwright.

Page 363: Concluding the ceremony, Fred Pellman, on behalf of the Mescalero Apache tribe, presents a war bonnet to General Homer, who accepts it for General Wainwright. Courtesy of SJAM.

Page 363: Father Al with Mescalero friends after the ceremony. Courtesy of SJAM.

Page 374: General Jonathan Wainwright presents Chaplain Albert Braun with the Silver Star. "I guess Skinny felt he had to give me something. . . ." Photo source: US Signal Corps.

Page 387: "Just a Soldier." Courtesy of SBA.

Page 405: Children dressed for First Communion at Santa Rosa. Courtesy of Jeanne de Lue Marsteller.

Page 413: Father Al says mass in the roofless *ramada*. Courtesy of *The Way of St. Francis.*

Page 421: "You bring me bricks and we'll build a church together." Courtesy of SJAM.

Page 430: Awaiting the procession of the barrio's first celebration of Corpus Cristi Day, 23 June 1956. Courtesy of Jeanne de Lue Marsteller.

Page 437: Father Albert with some Bataan veterans, his 'New Mexico boys.' L to R: Calvin Graef, Tom Foy, Juan Baldonado, Father Al, unnamed 'Airman of the Year' (presumably from Holloman Air Force Base, Alamogordo, NM) and Jack Rupe. Courtesy of SJAM.

Page 440: Father Hubert Mounier, OFM, and Eric Tortilla. Photo courtesy of MUA.

Page 454: Father Al's Jubilee Mass at Saint Joseph's in Los Angeles, the church of his boyhood. June 1965. Courtesy of Barbara Brown.

Page 455: Father Al surrounded by members of his prolific family, following his Jubilee Mass in California. Courtesy of Barbara Brown.

Page 478: Father Al always enjoyed his occasional picnics with Jeanne Marsteller when she was in town. Courtesy of Jeanne de Lue Marsteller.

Page 485: Father Al with Father Sixtus Brambilla, OFM, visiting from Boston. Picture taken 12 November 1982, when the padre was recovering from the amputation of his left leg. Source unknown.

Page 492: Mescalero artist Ignacio Palmer's "Last Supper" adorns the altar of Saint Joseph's Mescalero Apache Mission. Courtesy of SJAM.

Page 494: Plaque above Father Albert's tomb. Courtesy of Brother Peter Boegel, OFM, photographer.

Page 500: This statue of Father Albert Braun, OFM, stands in the Wesley Bolin Memorial Plaza, Capitol Grounds, Phoenix, Arizona. Carlos Ayala, sculptor. Courtesy of Tony Valenzuela, Chairman of Fr. Braun Memorial Committee.

Page 504: Father Albert's apple trees still bloom. Courtesy of Brother Peter Boegel, OFM, photographer.

PREFACE

I seem to have grown up with Father Albert Braun, though I met him only once, when I was too young to remember. But I heard stories. Everyone who knew the padre had stories—adventure tales, inspiriting dramas, war sagas, comic yarns. Many of these were the recollections of Father Al's friend and admirer Ashton Hawkins, who was also my great-uncle, and a master raconteur. As a child I listened magnetized by his tales of the frontier New Mexico to which he had come as a young lawyer, and of the people he had known—cowboys, ranchers, railroad men, soldiers, Indians, outlaws—and Father Al, who was even then becoming a legend.

Through the years leading up to the Second World War my family motored frequently from our home in Roswell through the Mescalero Apache reservation, always noting the progress of the great stone mission church Father Albert was building for his beloved Mescaleros. Each year the walls grew taller. In time Saint Joseph's—'the Apache Cathedral' the countryside was calling it—towered on its hilltop against the firred slopes of the Sacramento Mountains. Then came Pearl Harbor, and the church, essentially complete, was boarded up for the duration as Father Al went off to war.

Years later a friend approached me regarding a coming benefit concert in Saint Joseph's, all funds to go toward its restoration. Would I help with a little publicity? I was delighted. Here was a chance to connect, however tenuously, with an intriguing chunk of history and with this priest who had piqued my curiosity for so long. We arranged to meet with Brother Peter Boegel, the Franciscan friar directing the restoration.

It was a seminal luncheon. We discussed the coming concert, the restoration, and Father Al himself. I was struck with Brother Peter's intense dedication to preserving the mission, buoyed by his enthusiastic energy. (A 'friar afire' I would soon be calling him—though not to his face.) We exchanged Father Al stories, and I admitted I'd always wanted to write a biography of this fascinating man.

"Well then," he said, "why not start now?"

I detailed the obstacles, chief among them the formidable difficulty of breaching the Franciscan archives, without which no creditable biography was possible: one doesn't just knock on the monastery door, a female stranger, non-Catholic as well, and say 'here I am.'

"Let me do some inquiring," he said.

That was the genesis of *God's Warrior*. I had gone to a meeting prepared to write a press release. I left fueled for a biographical journey.

It was a long journey, full of turns and twists and surprises, exciting all the way. Brother Peter introduced me to Franciscans I should know—those who had known the padre, or might have relevant records. He alerted Brother Timothy Arthur, archivist for the Franciscan Province of Santa Barbara, who began assiduously gathering material. In time he introduced me to Father Finian McGinn, then Provincial Minister, whose permission I needed to gain access to the closely guarded archives. Father Finian graciously granted the necessary authorization; additionally, having known the padre, he gave me a very perceptive interview.

Meanwhile I was meeting, interviewing, and making friends from Father Albert's world—his former parishioners, combat veterans with whom he had served, his fellow Franciscans, his migrant friends, and members of his own large family.

Capping it all were the days my husband and I spent as guests in Old Mission Santa Barbara, which houses the archives as well as a number of retired friars, many of whom had known Father Al and added to my stockpile of stories. We arose each dawn to the deep-toned bells, as Father Al had done as a young seminarian; we walked the grounds he had trod. I worked by day in the archives, with the invaluable help of Brother Tim, who had accrued boxes of material. I read letters—hundreds of letters, and passed them to Brother Peter who, having met us in Santa Barbara, did duty on the copy machine.

Days later I left with bags of material.

Lifting off the runway with the precious cargo, I knew then that this book could be written. More, I knew it must be written. The incredible unfolding story was both gift and command.

An individual must be seen in the context of the times, climes, and cultures in which he has lived. Father Al lived many lives in many worlds and made each of them his own. He entwined with the people, absorbed their traditions and their history, and became one with them.

This is the story of a man, and also of the times and places of which he is a part. Home was wherever he was—in the high mountain camps of the Mescalero Apache, the squalid slums of south Phoenix, or the old Franciscan missions of California. His tall figure looms large in the battlefields of France in 1918, the murderous chaos of revolutionary Mexico in the twenties, the bloody sieges of Bataan and Corregidor in 1942, the horrors of Japanese prison camps, and later among the scientists on a lonely atoll in the South Pacific at the fiery birth of the hydrogen bomb.

But the whole exceeds its parts. Though he absorbed these disparate worlds he was never absorbed by them. Braun was a man of singular nature whose very presence redefined the turf. His life was an action-packed drama. A man with a vision, he led strongly and changed lives; and always—to the consternation of some and the delight of many—spiced any situation with his feisty humor. "I've been in trouble all my life," he often chuckled. He strode into a landscape, saw its needs, rolled up his cassock sleeves, and changed the terrain. He welcomed challenges; he dismissed all obstacles as *'Insignificant!'* An inheritor of the ages, a begetter of tomorrows, Father Albert Braun, OFM, is a man of history.

He was called a living legend. Father Al stories abound—tales of his derring-do, his crusty wit, his spectacular temper, his terrible driving (he wrecked more than one vehicle), his mulish stubbornness, his courage and compassion and conviction. Stories told and retold almost certainly grow with the telling; but though the details may vary the nub is the same, and because they are consistent with his style and character they hold their own truths. However apocryphal—and some may be—they picture the padre as those who knew him saw him.

He left letters behind—reams of letters, to other friars, to friends and family, to and about the soldiers with whom he served during two wars. His handwriting, big and bold and solid like the man himself, penned with a blunt tip in black ink, marches across the pages—sometimes in well reasoned detail, other times impatient, rushed, and innocent of punctuation except for an adamant exclamation point or a heavily underlined opinion.

His spelling is often haphazard, a bit of trivia he doubtless deemed "insignificant" in life's larger context. I have taken the liberty of amending most of his irregularities to prevent a rash of 'sics' from erupting like measles and to prevent any perception some might gain that the padre was unlettered, which he certainly was not. (He spoke several languages, a niece reported, and "thought in Latin because it covers everything.")

The pen strokes grow shakier with age, infirmity, and failing eyesight; the lines begin to limp, but the strokes stand tall, determined to the end, and the messages they carry remain as strong, the humor as crisp and insouciant.

This profuse correspondence is the bedrock of the narrative. The padre lived in the whirlwind of his own energy; his archival letters vibrate with plans and projects and progress reports. He is impatient with bureaucratic dawdling and lazy people; his greatest fear is of idleness. His letters pulse with dreams, plans, frustrations, and strong opinions, always spiced with his puckish humor.

His personal letters deepen the portrait and add perspective. The warm relations with his family, his love for children, his devotion to his mother (whom as a small child he had often confused with the Blessed Virgin) all shine through. So does the close camaraderie with his military companions (he treasured his life as a soldier), and with his many friends among the laity, of any religion or none. He muses long, perceptively, analytically over the state of the world, his country, and the Church. He bluntly scolds one senator for a cowardly unprincipled policy, teases a congressman for a boisterous Saint Patrick's Day celebration they had shared; he delights in a picnic or a bottle of good red wine with a cohort, builds a snowman with the children, feeds a pack of dogs he has befriended.

Through his letters ring the sounds of bugles and church bells and the mariachi music he loved, of hammers and blasting powder, the roar of planes and the thunk of bombs before the explosions. We hear the beat of Apache drums, the cry of an infant at baptism, the barking of dogs and the shouts of children at play, the solemn intonations of the Mass; and—this from the memories of many friends—his hearty laugh overriding everything, a deep-from-the-belly laugh springing from pure delight.

The bulk of the padre's personal correspondence has, in the way of casual letters, been tossed or lost. Those that remain, thanks to the friends and relatives who have saved and shared them, are priceless morsels and, like tasty canapés, both please and tease.

There are gaps in his correspondence. During the padre's three and a half years as a Japanese POW during World War II, all communication ceased. That vital period is recounted from postwar memories—his own and those of men with whom he served—in his citations for valor in battle, and in his testimony for the War Crimes Tribunal. Details of his sub rosa sorties into revolutionary Mexico are likewise scant. Because priests were being exiled, executed, or driven underground, he wrote or spoke little, lest he endanger others. That fascinating episode is pieced together sketchily from external clues and from the padre's later reminiscences, sans names and dates. Much still remains a tantalizing mystery.

Of tremendous importance have been the oral recollections of those who knew him. Through their memories we glimpse him rooting lustily at a football game, breaking the ice to swim on a cold-winter dare, dancing a jig at a veterans' reunion, admonishing some august bishops to 'get off your butts and out among the people,' tippling merrily with Mexican officers (who, had they learned his identity, would have hauled him before a firing squad), plodding dustily through the barrios of south Phoenix, his mongrel dog at his side, riding a tough mountain pony through rough terrain to the Apache camps, or dodging bombs and bullets to say mass in the jungles of Bataan. Such recollections—vivid, kaleidoscopic, and entirely unofficial—flesh out the whole, and attest the value of oral history, each memory a unique tile in the grand mosaic of an extraordinary life.

Like the old Spanish padres before him, Father Albert blazed trails; he was truly the last of the western frontier priests. He was apostle, builder, secret agent, educator, war hero, humanitarian, drug-and-crime fighter. A superior chastised him as an adventurer. He called himself 'a rough old soldier' and hoped to be remembered only as 'a simple Franciscan friar.' To his beloved Apaches he was 'God's Warrior.'

"How does one sum up his life?" wrote Father Provincial Louis Vitale on Father Al's death. "The dozen manila folders in his file, plus a book and many articles about him call for a notable biography. He is a legend in his own time."

In the hope of answering Father Louis's call I have pursued the memory of Father Al for ten often frustrating but always inspiring years. I hope I have captured some small glimmer of the padre's vast and gleaming spirit.

ACKNOWLEDGMENTS

Father Albert always launched his many projects by enlisting its beneficiaries (and anyone else he could snag), incorporating each one into what quickly became a community effort. This solidarity has not only lived on, but has expanded into a widespread community of those whose lives he changed and those who followed and inherited the 'Braun tradition.' Without their healthy participation in telling the padre's story, *God's Warrior* would never have survived its long gestation. It, like Father Al's many projects, has become an ongoing community effort.

The tradition inspired the Schola Cantorum choir from Saint Francis Cathedral in Santa Fe to give a benefit concert in Mescalero for the restoration of Saint Joseph's. Choir member Camille Flores-Turney, in drafting me to help with publicity and introducing me to Brother Peter Boegel, lit the spark that impelled my search for the legend that was Father Al.

Brother Peter kept that fire burning throughout the ten-year journey. He worked at my side in the provincial archives; he connected me with key people in the Franciscan fraternity, the Mescalero-Apache tribe, the Braun/Brown family, the Phoenix connection, and the padre's widespread firmament of friends; and he uncovered reams of source material.

Father Finian McGinn, then Provincial Minister, granted me access to the archives in Old Mission Santa Barbara, thereby opening the means without which no definitive biography of the padre could have been written. There Brother Timothy Arthur, OFM, Provincial Archivist, worked with me closely, locating the reams of material that form the guts and backbone of the story. Then and throughout the writing he was always there to answer my many questions as they inevitably arose.

I am deeply indebted to the friars at Santa Barbara for the hospitality they accorded my husband and me during our stay. Those who guided us through the ancient monastery imparted the little stray waifs of history and tradition that breathe within its walls. Brother Joachim Grant and Fathers Kieran McCarty and Maurus Kelly added their share of 'Father Albert stories' to the mix. Our thanks go also to Jack Fletcher, Guestmaster of the Old

Mission Retreat, for hosting our stay—and especially for the cheerful notes he left on our door each morning.

Through the tolling of the mission bells, the serenity of the spacious grounds, and the friars with whom we ate and conversed, we beheld the deep Franciscan brotherhood the padre so cherished throughout his life, which afforded an important insight into Father Albert Braun.

For the illustrations in *God's Warrior*, I am indebted to Barbara Brown and Dorothy Brown Bumgarner for their treasured family photographs. To Mark Thiel, Archivist at Marquette University, thanks for the many images he furnished and authorized for publications in *God's Warrior*—along with providing, through Brother Peter, much information regarding Father Al. Likewise my thanks to Sharon Melberg, Managing Editor of *The Way of St. Francis,* for permission to reprint the picture from the magazine's November 1953 cover.

Dick and Sue Mackey, Mary Serna, and Brother Peter produced pictures from the padre's Mescalero years; Jeanne de Lue Marsteller and Tony Valenzuela furnished those from the Phoenix era. Sister Nancy Johnson sent snapshots from the Blazer-Jette family, along with letters her mother, Ruth Jette, had saved.

To Colonel Michael Rauer, my deepest thanks for acquiring and sending via Brother Tim the pictures of the war-torn French village of Cunel, Meuse district, where Father Al was serving when the armistice silenced the guns of World War I, and for the detailed documentation accompanying them.

To all who furnished pictures, my appreciation; I only wish space would have allowed the inclusion of them all.

A special thanks to John R. Aldrich for his dedicated work in upgrading the pictures—many old and worn—to professional quality, for 'burning' the discs, and for otherwise preparing them for publication.

Biography comprises many elements, among which letters and interviews loom largely. The contributors of both are named in my sources. Their help in portraying Father Albert, however, deserves special mention, not only for the considerable time and effort they spent, but for their enthusiasm in so doing. Gathering, organizing, and copying the numerous letters was time consuming; their willingness to grant interviews was compounded with their hospitality in opening their homes and offering their deeply personal memories. Each added factual information, new perspectives, and larger dimensions to the padre's many facets, imparted with a cordiality like his own: we became friends in a mutual project.

Brothers Timothy Arthur and Peter Boegel, Father Warren Rouse, and Mary Serna have all read and critiqued the manuscript in its entirety, corrected my many errors, and made many helpful suggestions. Dr. Erskine 'Bud' Burns, physicist, edited the section on the creation of the hydrogen bomb and patiently explained its mysteries in laymen's language that even I could understand. Mescaleros Bruce and Helen Klinekole, June Denny, and Clarice Rocha reviewed and amended my inaccuracies regarding the puberty ceremony. Jeanne de Lue Marsteller likewise read and set me right concerning the Workers of the Sacred Heart. To Jeanne I am deeply indebted also for the many papers she wrote and records she resurrected from her time as secretary of the group and aide to Father Al.

Each tile in the mosaic is important; my thanks go to all who supplied them to enrich and complete the whole. Antonio Serna Candelaria showed us the sites of the old *chozas* in Tularosa and explained the process by which his ancestors and the other original settlers had dug and utilized them. Fathers Blaise Cronin and Walter Holley, after giving their interviews, guided us through the beautiful Saint Mary's Basilica in Phoenix, enriching our tour with its history and the many stories behind it.

Jerry Leyva furnished me with the genealogy of his kinsman 'Old Tony' and their joint ancestor the leather-jacket soldier Juan Agustín de Leyba during the Spanish settling of California.

Donna Brown-Van Vandert spent hours in Strasbourg examining civic documents for clues in her search for John Brown (Johannes Braun) and his flight from Alsace.

Pete Dimas, Abe Arvisu, Jr., and Saint Mary's historian Gary Weiand, escorted us to the now endangered Sacred Heart Church—Sagrado Corazon—that the padre built 'brick by brick' in Phoenix. They too gave interviews and, during a delightful dinner, enlightened us on many facets of the Golden Gate barrio, Father Al's part in its transformation, and the building of the church.

Frank Barrios hosted us in Phoenix during one important visit and provided much information regarding Saint Mary's and Father Al's time in Arizona.

I must also thank friends in my hometown who have been especially helpful: To Denise Rawdon, owner and manager of Alpha-Omega Printers, for her always cheerful help in copying and helping preserve my manuscripts. To Jack Swickard and Ron McKay who furnished typewriters when mine was out of commission. To Susie Lee, who came to the rescue when time was pressing, with last-minute images to add to the master disc. And to my friend, attorney Jim Bruin, who relieved me of considerable legal legwork in tracking down Father Al's testimony at the sensational trial of Albert Fall, many thanks.

I am grateful, as always, to the trusty team at Sunstone Press for their patience and professionalism throughout the long and often frustrating production of *God's Warrior*. I am especially beholden to Kay Carlson for her eagle eye in ferreting out my many typos, her tolerance in deciphering my often messy manuscript, and, when time became of the essence, her persistence in the race to 'get the blooming thing done.'

Nor can I omit my eternal gratitude to my husband Jack Aldrich, who has been at my side throughout this journey, and without whose support I could never have completed this work.

Finally and importantly is my love and gratitude for the unending help, support, enthusiasm, and friendship of the crew at Saint Joseph's Mission in Mescalero—especially that of Brother Peter Boegel and Mary Serna, who were never too busy to answer my many questions, to find a missing link, an elusive fact, a necessary contact. They, with Father Paul Botenhagen, OFM, Tommy Spottedbird and his restoration crew—the 'mission gang'—have kept my spirits high and my typewriter clattering, with our many 'enchilada breaks' at the Old Road Café in Mescalero.

They and the larger widespread 'Father Al community' comprising the Braun/Brown clan, the Franciscan family, the Mescalero-Apache tribe, the former residents and parishioners of the barrio who built Sagrado Corazon, the padre's brothers-in-arms from wars and prison camps—these are the true community that Father Al engendered. Thanks to all of you for letting me be a part of it. This community, like Father Albert's apple trees, still bear the ever-ripening fruit.

I

THE MAVERICK

"I've been in trouble all my life."

1: THE HOUSE THAT JOHN BUILT

On an August afternoon in 1916 a young priest stepped from a horse-drawn buggy into the heart of the Mescalero Apache country in southern New Mexico. He had never met an Indian, and he knew nothing of Apaches beyond their reputed ferocity. He spoke not one word of their language, knew little of their history and less of their ways. He was twenty-seven years old.

He was a tall young man, six feet and something, and his hands and feet were enormous. His grin bisected his face and sent crinkles toward his ears. His eyes rippled with a humor that had often gotten him into trouble, and with an immense joy of being.

With Geronimo's surrender in 1886 the Apache wars had ended; the captives, following imprisonment in Florida, Alabama, and more recently in Oklahoma, had only three years earlier been released onto the reservation where he now stood. He doubtless sensed they might be bitter, even hostile. It was the sort of challenge the newly ordained Father Albert Braun relished.

He had traveled by rail from the California coast to the tiny village of Tularosa in the New Mexican desert, thence by buggy along the rutty trail that grew dustier and rougher and narrower as it climbed into the mountain beyond. He and his companion seemed the only two people on the planet, except for an occasional tepee that might or might not conceal dark eyes following their passage.

A challenge and an adventure lay before him, and he welcomed both. He had trails to blaze and he was impatient to begin, though he likely paused to look back on the paths that lay behind. If so, he would have grinned: he was in Mescalero, a brown-robed Franciscan priest, all quite by accident, the result of his own impulsive nature and a prank only he had thought funny.

Through the years he said, again and again, and always with a chuckle: "I've been in trouble all my life."

The population of Los Angeles, California, reaching toward fifty thousand, increased by one on 5 September 1889 with the birth of John William, the first son of John and Caroline Arzner Braun. Already blessed with two daughters, the Brauns were happily filling the large frame house on a hill along the city's eastern fringe, overlooking fertile fields of grain and groves of citrus. It was a time of transition, of energy and growth and restless optimism, for the city, for California. For the America into which John William—they called him Bud—was born.

Benjamin Harrison was President. America was exploding in high spirits and expansionist energy. Gunshot at high noon on 22 April had opened Oklahoma to non-Indian settlement, triggering the greatest land rush ever seen as some 200,000 land-hungry Americans raced hell-for-leather across the Texas and Kansas borders. Four new states—the Dakotas, Montana, and Washington—entered the Union that year; Idaho and Wyoming would soon follow; and Mark Twain had just published *A Connecticut Yankee in King Arthur's Court.*

Though still licking the wounds of civil war, America was again hearing the old siren song of Manifest Destiny. Stilled during the war, it rose once more, too seductive, too blood-stirring to have died completely. The Union had been saved and faith in a glorious future blazed again. Westward ho! charged America, led by the iron rails and rolling stock of the transcontinental railroads. The Central and Union Pacifics had joined a score of years earlier to link the coasts. The Northern and Southern Pacifics followed, the Great Northern, the Santa Fe, and a host of lesser titans, racing for the best routes, pounding, hustling, maneuvering, challenging distance, terrain, the elements, and each other—and incidentally but significantly peopling the West.

America had expanded to the continent's edge, but destiny still called and, poised on a Pacific coast now accessible, America heard the whole earth beckoning. The reunited States had acquired coaling privileges in Samoa and rights for a naval base in Hawaii's Pearl River harbor, when in 1990 Captain Alfred Thayer Mahan published his monumental *Influence of Sea Power in History, 1660-1783*. America, he argued, must build a first-class navy, a strong merchant marine, an isthmian canal guarded by American dominance in the Caribbean. America must expand commercially, must gain world markets for its swelling industrial production; and this called for coaling stations, naval bases, and colonies.

While Mahan looked toward expanded American sea power, historian Frederick Jackson Turner looked backward on the disappearing frontier which, though far from conquered, was officially declared closed in 1890. In his soon-to-be-famous thesis, Turner cited the frontier as the molding force of America, and believed the nation's forward-thrusting character would continue to look toward wider fields.

America poised restlessly between the roistering frontier ethos that had challenged a continent and won, and that of the larger world to be challenged by the financier, the entrepreneur, the barons of the new industrial age propelled by the steam-driven ships of commerce and the United States Navy.

California was on the cutting edge of the new era. As the railroads competed for land on which to build wharves, San Diego and Los Angeles, each vying to become the great southern terminus, courted the railroads. Los Angeles was a seething stewpot, surging like the Pacific just beyond, with the adventurous, the ambitious, the honest and the not-so, men in a hurry; and when the city and the neighboring shore-side community of San Pedro paid the Southern Pacific $600,000 to bring a line into the city and donated land for a depot, San Diego, despite the fine natural harbor Los Angeles lacked, was cut from the running.

A rate war between the Southern Pacific and the Santa Fe ensued, and the resulting low fares and intense propaganda touting the glories of the golden coast lured thousands to southern California. By 1884 the population of Los Angeles swelled to 100,000. Business boomed. Real estate prices soared, until the bubble burst. By 1888 the population of Los Angeles had stabilized to the 50,000 into which John William Braun was born. It was an exciting world for an adventurous boy to explore.

✟✟✟

But if the land and times into which he was born gave play to the boy's restless spirit, the story of his own father's passage to America gave as much to his imagination.

Johannes Pius Braun grew up in Alsace, in the long-fought-over French-German borderlands, where he began at an early age to work as a carpenter and cabinetmaker. He had probably learned the craft from his father, and would likely have lived out his life there, peacefully plying his trade where his family's roots grew deep, had not the events of 1871 thrust into his life.

In that year the Franco-Prussian War, fomented by Otto von Bismarck, the 'Iron Chancellor' of Prussia, ended with a German victory. France lost her emperor, five billion francs in indemnities, part of Lorraine, and all of Alsace. The province's population comprised a large percentage of south Germanic families whose ancestors had militantly opposed the north German Reformation in the seventeenth century. Now, in the nineteenth, their descendants resurged to oppose Bismarck's anti-Catholic 'Kulturkampf.' It was a time of apprehension in Alsace, and throughout all Europe. The Ottoman Empire was crumbling. The Balkans seethed. Catholic Poland tried to resist Russian domination on one side and eyed Prussia warily on the other. Friction brewed between the Papacy and the recently unified Italy. Nationalist parties teemed restively; and France, weakened and isolated, nursed a smoldering anti-German hostility.

At the center stood a militant Germany, the dominant power in Europe; and from Berlin Bismarck spun an elaborate spider web of alliances to ensnare the continent as he hardened German strength with his blood-and-iron policy. Prussian militarism became a way of life. And it extended to Alsace.

The Braun family, of staunchly Catholic south-German lineage, could have felt no allegiance to Bismarckian Germany, though there is no knowing what discussions may have transpired within the privacy of their home. But at age seventeen, and facing mandatory conscription in the German army, young Johannes made a decision, presumably with the backing of his family.

He fled Alsace. By what route or means of transit he went we know nothing. He may have had some funds, but it is doubtful he would have spent his reserves on fares. He likely hitched his way when he could and walked when he couldn't. He may have hired on with a railroad crew when there was a vacancy or hidden in the cars when there was not. At any rate, he crossed the greater length of Germany to the teeming port of Hamburg, where among the many ships in harbor he saw one whose stars and stripes flapped in the salt breeze with an energy like his own. He was young and sturdy and courageous. He was also agile and canny enough to steal aboard and stow away.

Johannes Braun was bound for America.

Through long days cramped in some niche, doubtless hungry much of the time, he knew each heave of the ship brought him nearer his shore of freedom. Within him he carried the strength of all his inheritance—the history and traditions and beliefs that had made him what he was.

No Statute of Liberty greeted him; that lady had not yet arrived. He did not need her: it was enough to step onto United States land. Once ashore, Alsatian Johannes Braun became American John Brown. So at least wrote the immigration clerk (Braun and Brown being pronounced alike), though the boy still spelled it Braun.

What happened next? We can only conjecture. He probably fled Alsace in 1877.[1] His son John William was born 5 September 1889. The period between is a blank page. How long he spent in New York is uncertain, but at some point he headed west, again by means unknown. Having arrived on the Golden Coast he earned enough money to buy land, build a large house, and establish a dairy farm. Meanwhile he married and fathered two daughters, Loretta and Mary, to be followed by Bud, Clarence, and Ray.

Why California drew him across the continent is another question. Like many others, John Braun was probably lured by the spate of leaflets with which promoters and railroads, advertising for immigrants, flooded the East, and the incredibly low rates offered by railroads engaged in rate wars and pushing to bring people west.

For whatever reason, John Braun crossed the forests and mountains and prairies, he saw the vitality of the burgeoning towns, and along the way he became an intensely patriotic American, a citizen in heart as well as name. Once in California, with work and will and solid faith, he built a life and a tradition, and served as a productive cog in his community. His is the quintessential American success story.

It is also a first-rate love story. While in New York John Braun had met a young woman who captured his eye and then his heart. Where they met is unclear, though it is likely they attended the same church. Caroline Arzner was, like John, of German Catholic lineage in an America where homesick immigrants clustered in parish communities with others of like blood, religion, and language.

The courtship was obviously intense, for both made the long journey to California—though separately. Perhaps John wanted to establish a living before he embarked on marriage. Perhaps Caroline's family objected, or thought them too young. Perhaps they quarreled and separated, only to follow the western star and find themselves reunited at journey's end.

John traveled overland. Caroline went by ship, around the storm-swept tip of South America and north to California. Did she sail with family? Was she the magnet that drew him west? Or did she follow him alone, defying family and propriety? However it happened, John and Caroline—he called her Carrie—met again on the opposite end of the continent, married, settled in the San Gabriel Valley on what was then the eastern fringe of Los Angeles, and reared a family. They looked to their God for eternal salvation, pledged full-hearted allegiance to their beloved new country, and depended on their own energy and ingenuity for their earthly progress.

John was a builder. Working with a sure hand and an artist's eye he built a house on a hill overlooking his farm and beyond it to the fertile valley. When the growing community between city and farmland became a parish in 1888 and began building a large church in 1901, he volunteered his skills, did much of the carpentry, and fashioned the pillars that graced the façade of Saint Joseph's. Most importantly, John and Carrie Braun were building a family.

✞ ✞ ✞

Central to Bud's early life was the large white clapboard home on the hill—tall storied, with wide porches, many windows, and Victorian fretwork, spacious enough for five high-spirited children and their expanding dreams. It was an enduring house, a solid house, one whose children and grandchildren would continue to return for frequent visits in years to come.

The family within was as solid. Reared with love, discipline, and strict Catholic piety ("though I was never taught to hate Protestants," the boy wrote many years later), young Bud's lively antics were tempered by strong parents and a firm patriarchal tradition. John Braun was the undisputed head of the household. He demanded honesty, loyalty, and useful endeavor of his children. Always by his side was Carrie, a born matriarch, as strong of will as he, and as devoted to her bumptious family. (As a young child, Bud later recalled, he often identified his mother with the Blessed Virgin, both of whom he adored intensely then and for the rest of his life.)

Dedication to church and country, a strong sense of duty, simple honesty, strength of purpose, and the will to work—these were the parental priorities passed on to their children. They were a happy family, sure of their values, comfortable in their parameters, loyal to one another. Papa and Mama were broad in their humor, large in their love, and secure in their faith. But they tolerated no nonsense.

The house in which Bud Braun spent his childhood seems symbolic of America as it approached the twentieth century, and of the boy as he grew. To the east it looked back toward rolling farmland; so did the nation, still primarily agricultural but rapidly urbanizing. As if anticipating the encroaching city and the industry it heralded, the house looked Janus-like from its hill, backward with nostalgia, forward toward the exciting energy of the city, and beyond to the surging Pacific. The boy too must have paused, as boys do, on the hillside of youth, all-impatient for the world he itched to conquer, but rooted always in the rich compost of blood, history, and tradition. Like Mahan and Turner, boy, nation, and world looked out from the old century into the new.

The Trabert and Braun families were close friends. "Since we were three years old," Bud later wrote, he and Willie "played and fought together,"[2] swam in the river, and roamed the countryside with the freedom of children in a still-rural setting. They committed their share of mischiefs, partook of the combined family picnics, fished and hunted, and attended church and school together (though Willie was a year ahead of Bud).

In September 1895 Bud entered the first grade at Saint Joseph's elementary school, where he prepared for his first communion, after which he transferred to public school for the next six years.

Bud was not yet nine years old when the jingoism of the Spanish-American War inflamed America. It was the age of yellow journalism, and Californian William Randolph Hearst led the pack with wildly exaggerated tales of Spanish cruelty in Cuba rolling off his presses. This was heady stuff for any spirited American boy. He and his classmates doubtless chanted "Remember the *Maine*" along with the rest of America, and whooped wildly when their nation declared war. War fever was in the air, it was contagious, and young minds were susceptible. What boy did not thrill when Dewey captured Manila? Wartime pride certainly boosted the already healthy patriotism of John William Braun.

The debate over annexation of the Philippines that followed the 'splendid little war' was in contrast dull stuff for young minds, and nine-year-old Bud Braun could not know that America's debut as a world power and her entrance into the far-eastern orbit would profoundly impact his life. The cry, however, to 'take up the white man's burden,' to extend America's civilizing hand to 'our little brown brothers' in the Philippines could well have hit a chord that would vibrate some years later when he and Willie Trabert, both studying for the priesthood, would press for a mission in the Orient. The possibility is speculative but plausible when examining the forces that molded the boyhood mind of the future Father Albert Braun.

In the early summer of 1902, having just completed the seventh grade in public school, and with summer's freedom ahead, Bud apparently got into some mischief, which Papa Braun would not tolerate. Reasoning that small misdeeds lead to larger ones, and that both stem from idleness, he headed with Bud in tow to nearby Alhambra to the sheep ranch of his good friend Sylvester Dupuy. Could Dupuy use a young farmhand?

He could: he was threshing hay for winter feed. Bud could start right away. And about wages—

Wages? *Wages?* Just teach the boy to work![3]

Dupuy did just that. In the fall, well tanned and muscled, Bud entered Saint Joseph's, where he could study for confirmation, complete the eighth grade, and "make up my mind for the future."[4]

By his second summer at Dupuy's ranch Bud was earning a small stipend. He was strong, a good worker, and generally good natured, though if pushed too far his stubborn German temper could flare quickly. Summer was nearing its end and he was looking toward high school, scheduled to open in a week or so, when the pivotal incident happened.

Except for Bud, the bailing crew were all Frenchmen. A foreman, who had throughout the summer irked young Braun, was napping in the shade of a hay bale during the lunch break, and had removed his heavy boots. At that sight (as the boy told it later) the devil entered Bud Braun. Into each empty boot went a glob of fresh horse dung.

The foreman failed to see the humor, a fight ensued, and Bud quit his job before he was fired. "Only a German," a crewmember reportedly said, "would do that to a Frenchman."[5]

Shortly afterward Bud came on his friend Willie Trabert, preparing to return for his second year at Saint Anthony's High School and Seminary in Santa Barbara.

"Is it any good?" he asked, and when Willie said it was okay and challenged him to "come along and try it out," the idea caught fire.[6] Bud Braun had never been able to resist a challenge.

There must have been more to the conversation than suggested in the above account, which Bud gave years later with his customary clipped humor. Willie must have inspired some sort of enthusiasm, which fell on the fertile soil of the staunchly Catholic boy, and at a time when he was facing parental censure for his recent escapade. It was nonetheless an impulsive decision. It would prove the most significant of his life.

"I'm going to Saint Anthony's," he announced to his startled parents that evening. "I'm going to be a priest."[7] John and Carrie must have been skeptical: a boy who couldn't even hold a farm job would never make it through the demanding discipline at the seminary. They knew too well their son's streak of mischief, his stubbornness, quick temper, often irreverent humor, and his tendency to resist authority. They certainly shared some doubts; on the other hand, it might be good for him.

Within a few days Bud and Willie were on their way to Santa Barbara on a small coastal boat. "I didn't ask our priest or anybody," he later recalled. "I just went."[8]

Father Peter Wallischeck, rector and high-school principal of Saint Anthony's, was welcoming new and returning students on that hot August day in 1903 when he noted an extra boy, gangling, big-boned, flashing a puckish grin that could mean good humor or devilment. From his first glimpse he seems to have suspected the latter.

And whence did he come? All other new boys were properly sponsored, had been interviewed and accepted. This boy simply appeared, as Braun told it, "unannounced and unapproved." The scene, as reconstructed, went roughly as follows:

"Who is this boy?" asked Father Peter.

Willie spoke up: Bud Braun was his friend; he'd brought him along "to try it out." He prudently failed to mention the circumstances behind his arrival. Willie had also forgotten another detail, namely that every boy needed a sponsor, usually his own parish priest—a detail of which Father Peter reminded him.

"I sponsor him," Willie answered breezily.

The priest, doubtless with a sharp look at Trabert (whose levity reputedly often tried his teachers) and then at Braun, threw the newcomer a few questions, and sized him up. Baptismal name: John William. Going on thirteen, voice still crackling with puberty, taller already than most of the sixteen-year-olds and as self-assured as any of them. A lively one, and—to judge by his unorthodox arrival—impulsive. The eyes hinted at mischief. If admitted to Saint Anthony's, would John William Braun prove a bonus? Or a maverick?

Several moments passed. Very well, Father Peter finally decided: young Braun could enroll—

On a strictly trial basis.

2: THE CHALLENGE

So here he was—uninvited, unannounced, unauthorized, and unperturbed. If not exactly wanted, he was tolerated, though by all accounts few on the teaching staff believed that either Bud Braun or his buddy and impromptu sponsor Willie Trabert would make it through Saint Anthony's. Father Peter Wallischeck was a strict disciplinarian and the rate of student attrition was steep. Scholastic standards were demanding, and Bud grew restless when confined to a desk—an impatience he would carry throughout his life. But a challenge was a call to combat, and he applied himself as necessary to keep his scholastic standing intact.

If combat on the field of academia was dull, that on the sports arena was pure joy. "The Fathers used to play baseball, tennis, and handball with us," he later recalled. "Handball was what we really liked. It gave us a chance to clip them behind the ear with a hard Irish handball."[1]

Years later he still chuckled remembering the time one Joe McKenzie aimed a peashooter at Father Peter and hit him squarely in the face, at which Bud exploded laughing and was instantly reprimanded as an accomplice. A few swats on his rear with a board quickly subdued Joe. Then it was Bud's turn. Still he could not stop laughing; it was too funny. Father Peter increased his punishment to thirty swats. "Count them," he ordered. Bud began: one, two, five, eight . . . . Father Peter was not amused. He started over. Bud counted properly this time, now in real pain but refusing to cry. He reached the end dry-eyed, stouthearted, blister-bottomed, and wiser. "That's how I learned not to cheat!"[2]

The day Herman Hobrecht arrived marked a new friendship. "We have been close all these years," Herman wrote in 1966. "I first met Bud . . . when I transferred from St. Joseph's Seminary in Teutopolis, Illinois to St. Anthony's in Santa Barbara."[3] Bud, Willie, and Herman quickly formed a lively triumvirate, and the teaching staff doubtless added a third name to their least-likely-to-succeed list.

Despite their shenanigans the trio pursued a serious purpose. For all his spirited humor, Bud Braun was sounding his own depths and discovering a new sobriety. That he had his troubling moments is suggested in Herman's memory years later of one of Bud's nightmares. One night in the dormitory "he let out a loud scream . . . . I jumped out of bed and shook him not gently. He did wake up; but it was only next morning that I got the details of his dream. He was being mauled by a brutal stranger."[4] Whether the chimera more nearly symbolized Father Peter, an overdue English essay, or Bud's own restless nature, probably even he could not have said.

Or perhaps it was the dawning enormity of the path he had chosen. At Saint Anthony's, literally and spiritually in the shadow of Old Mission Santa Barbara, the past surrounded him—in the deep-toned bells that ordered his hours, in the ancient litanies recited daily, in the shadowy halls where lingered the ghosts of many friars who had walked this way before. Did he dare to follow?

✞✞✞

The Franciscan Order, in whose midst Bud Braun now lived, was born in the dawning thirteenth century, when John 'Francesco' Bernardone—Francis of Assisi—praying in the crumbling little church of San Damiano, heard a voice that seemed to issue from the Christ figure behind the altar. *Francis, mend my church. . . .* Taking the words literally, he restored San Damiano, then began to rebuild other churches, and with them his own life, living as Christ's apostles had lived, in simplicity, prayer, and poverty. Finally, deploring the worldliness into which society, and many of the clergy, had fallen, he set out by example to repair the Church Universal. Others joined him; the Franciscan movement grew; in 1209 Pope Innocent III approved the innovative new Rule; and the Order of Friars Minor (OFM) was born.

The discovery of the New World in the waning fifteenth century revealed a vast landmass that sparked European imagination, Renaissance energy, and clerical zeal. Here were empires to be won, trade routes to be opened, and souls to be saved. Catholic Spain led the charge, and Mexico and Peru yielded riches for the Crown. Turning north, Spanish sailors probed the coasts of Florida, Texas, and California. Coronado's inland expedition (1540–42) penetrated Arizona and New Mexico, from which they explored seven thousand miles of North American wilderness.

But they found no gold. The Crown lost interest in further northern exploration, and after 1573 curtailed all expeditions into the interior except for small units of clergy protected by a handful of soldiers, their sole intent to spread the faith. But in 1579 Francis Drake, prowling along the California coast, sparked Spanish fears of English penetration. This, and the pleas of the friars not to abandon the Christianized northern Indians, however few, led the Crown to authorize a buffer settlement, which materialized in 1598 in Don Juan de Oñate's colony—the first in present New Mexico—and in time a string of missions along the Rio Grande.

California lay untouched for another century and a half except for the Baja peninsula, which the Jesuits entered in 1697, believing it an island. It would take the pioneering visionary Padre Eusabio Francisco Kino to prove otherwise.

Kino had established an outpost in the northwest Mexican frontier in 1687, from which he began to convert Indians and build missions. For the next quarter century he explored and mapped tremendous expanses, in the course of which he discovered the confluence of the Gila River with the Colorado, followed it to its mouth, and proclaimed Baja part of the mainland. He then began to envision a line of missions linking Sonora to Upper California.[5] Kino's dream lay fallow for years. Vast distances, hostile terrain, dwindling Spanish coffers, and a series of Indian wars were formidable realities; and California remained terra incognita.

In 1767 the Jesuits, losing a long power struggle with the Crown, were expelled from all Spanish territory. The Franciscans had barely replaced them in Baja when reports of Russian interest in California sent Spain hurriedly planning to take possession first. An expedition of soldiers and clerics was to proceed overland from Baja to rendezvous with supply ships in the bays of San Diego and Monterey. While the main group explored, the friars would build missions, convert the Indians, settle them into productive agricultural communities, and make of them good Christians and loyal Crown subjects. The Crown had long relied on this uniquely Spanish 'mission system' for New World colonization, by which Spain had created the world's most extensive empire, and for which she relied on her resolute frontier friars.

Fray Junípero Serra headed the Franciscan contingent. He was fifty-five years old and suffering a painful limp from an old injury; but he was strong of will and character, an experienced frontiersman, and a dynamic leader, often testy with the military but beloved by his fellow friars.

Preceded by a forward land party and two supply ships, Serra and overall commander Gaspar de Portolá set out on muleback with their party on 15 May 1769. Arriving in San Diego in July they found the lead group a chaos of starved and dying men. Portolá ordered the one ship *San Antonio* to return for provisions (the storm-swept *San Carlos* had not arrived) and journeyed on as ordered with the main group to find Monterey Bay. Fray Junípero, two friars, a small guard, and a few laborers stayed to tend the sick, bury the dead, begin to build, and await supplies.

The Indians soon attacked. Through waves of arrows, howling savages, and fire from their own guards, there shines the image of Fray Junípero crouching in a flimsy hut, calmly praying that no Indian be killed while yet unbaptized.

Supplies dwindled, men were still dying, and no ship hove in sight. Portolá returned in January. He had failed to find Monterey; his men were sick, discouraged, and ready to abandon the venture. Fray Junípero and the friars held firm. "Our needs are many," he wrote, ". . . but if we have health, a tortilla, and some vegetables, what more do we want?" He vowed to "hold out to the last breath."[6] The friars held a nine-day prayer vigil until—it seemed in answer—the *San Antonio*, laden with men and sustenance, sailed into the bay.

In time the *San Carlos* arrived, Portolá did find Monterey, and, having accomplished his mission, returned to Mexico. The new viceroy, heartened by the commander's report, soon dispatched more provisions and another two friars to build five more missions. But Fray Serra and Portolá's replacement Pedro Fages soon clashed. The padre's temper blew. After accusing Fages of obstructing his mission work, the testy friar mounted his mule, made the long journey to Mexico City, reported to the viceroy, and secured a new commander. He requested—and got—more friars. Detailing the defects of the supply system, he revived Kino's old dream for a Sonora route: the viceroy ordered immediate exploration for a possible passageway, and Fray Junípero returned to California expansive with accomplishment. The great Jesuit had dreamed the dream and paved the way; the great Franciscan would realize it.

On viceregal orders the seasoned frontiersman Juan Bautista de Anza and a small party left Tubac in present Arizona in January 1774, blazed a trail through the treacherous Sierras, and later brought thirty families and three friars over the route, arriving in Monterey in March 1775. He then headed north and scouted the great bay area, after which the families followed from Monterey to found San Francisco in September 1776.

Meanwhile Fray Junípero, truly California's founding father, continued to build thriving communities in the south, one being San

Gabriel, to which eleven families came in 1781 and founded the future city of Los Angeles. At the time of Junípero's death in 1784 he had built a chain of nine missions that would grow to twenty-one along the increasingly traveled *camino real.* Alta California was becoming a successful and growing borderland, largely due to the faith, courage, and persistent labor of Fray Junípero Serra and his fellow friars.

✞ ✞ ✞

The independent spirit of the youthful Bud Braun could relate to these frontier fathers—doers, buildings, explorers, civilizers, venturers into a challenging unknown. These were men saintly enough to forfeit their own lives in saving the souls of others, human enough to labor among them to better their earthly lives. That their fearlessness, dedication, and sheer energy made a deep imprint on the young seminarian is apparent; their influence would become increasingly evident throughout his life.

Still, the early missionaries may have seemed removed from Bud's immediate world of Latin conjugations, baseball games, teenage high jinks, and Father Peter's eagle eye. If so, he found a living link with the heroic past in the person of Antonio Maria Leyva—'Old Tony,' they called him at the mission. He was a stone mason by profession—chief mason for sandstone construction at Saint Anthony's during Bud's time there—and part-time companion to young seminarians by inclination.[7]

Tony's ancestor was one Juan Agustín de Leyba, a Basque *soldado de cuero*—a leather-jacket soldier—of the Royal Spanish Army in Mexico, part of a group that served as escort for colonizing expeditions. In 1781 Leyba was among those who accompanied the eleven families to San Gabriel; he was later present at the founding of San Buenaventura Mission and the founding of the presidio at Santa Barbara. There, according to family tradition, Juan retired, married a mission Indian, and founded the family into which Antonio Maria Leyva was eventually born.[8]

Bud Braun saw much of Tony during his years at Saint Anthony's, and later. The bond would grow into a deep and productive friendship that would last until Tony's death in 1936—"my dearest and most devoted friend," Braun called him.[9] During his years at Saint Anthony's the adolescent Braun found him a living link with the bold-spirited Junípero Serra.

John William Braun was confirmed on 29 June 1906 by the Right Reverend Thomas J. Conaty.[10] Doubtless the solemnity of the occasion was heightened by his growing awareness of the frontier friars, their history, and by extension all history, a keen interest kindled at Saint Anthony's, and one he would pursue throughout his life.

Despite that interest, however, neither he nor his two closest buddies broke any records for scholastic brilliance. Nor did Father Peter see in Bud Braun any latent Franciscan material. "You'll never be a priest," he said more than once. "You're too stubborn."

But if Trabert, Hobrecht, and Braun were less than ideal seminarians in certain eyes, neither were they among those who fell by the wayside. To the surprise of many, all three were among the eight left who remained in the ranks of the 1908 graduating class of Saint Anthony's.

"July 25, 1908," penned Braun in his usual terse prose, "entered the Novitiate at Fruitvale [later called Oakland], received Habit. Fr. Matthew Schmidt—Master of Novices." He had already, as required, assigned any property he might possess to his father, "until my solemn profession in the Order of St. Francis."[11]

His year of novitiate had begun—a year, Maynard Geiger explains, "required by canon law . . . before a novice takes his vows and becomes a full member of the Order." Much the same as in Serra's time, continues Geiger, it is "a year of strict seclusion and rigorous discipline during which the novice's vocation is tested and during which he imbibes the spirit of the Order. . . . During that year . . . the novice must prove to himself and to his superiors that he has a true vocation. . . ."[12]

At Saint Elizabeth's Friary in Fruitvale, Bud, Herman, and Willie received the names they would henceforth bear as Franciscans—provided they made it through. Though Bud had requested the name Sylvester (in honor of Sylvester Dupuy, his first employer and his father's friend), he was designated Albert. Herman and Willie became Augustine and Ambrose respectively. The triumvirate were thereafter known as "the three A's."

Herman—now Augustine—recalled that "we, the three A's, spent long hours chanting the office along with the Father Guardian Englebert Guy [Gey] who could just barely [see to] follow the words. . . . Matins and Lauds often kept us mumbling along for more than an hour."

When they entered their novitiate, he added, "there were six of us. Only three of us: Ambrose, Albert and Augustine were left after the retreat. . . ." On 26 July 1909, one year and a day after entering, the three took their simple vows, and in November received their tonsures and minor orders. Three years of intensive study and training would follow, the first three devoted to the humanities and philosophy.

"After our novitiate," Augustine continued, "the three A's remained in Oakland for another year with Father Joachim Meyer as lector. That year was a tough one. . . . The next year we spent studying Philosophy. . . . Three other clerics . . . were added to our class. Two of these three could not make it; one became a lay brother . . . [and] another left the Order because of lack of sufficient talent."[13]

At some time during their studies the three A's decided to request assignment to China after they were ordained. The Spanish-American War had aroused American awareness of the Orient back during the formative years of the young seminarians' imaginations; and memories of the Boxer Rebellion had stirred desires to 'civilize' and Christianize the 'heathen Chinee' that had obviously rubbed off on them. So had the example of Father Juniper Doolin, who went to Shensi in 1907 to become the first missionary in China from their province.[14] Anticipating such an assignment, Albert Braun, and presumably his buddies, began to study Chinese history and philosophy.

On 24 August 1912, having completed the three-year courses centering around philosophy, Albert Braun signed his will, naming his father as executor, and bequeathing all temporal goods he owned or might inherit to the Superior of Old Mission Santa Barbara "for the purpose of buying instruments or books necessary for . . . educating the Franciscan clerics studying on the Pacific Coast between Canada and Mexico."[15]

Two days later, "at the Old Mission in Santa Barbara, I took my solemn vows as a Franciscan."[16]

The three A's, by then the only remaining students in their class, prepared for their final three years in theology. "One of the lectors," Augustine commented, "was a former pastor, who . . . [when] he did not have enough material . . . would read from a periodical in a monotonous voice, which often put us to sleep."[17] Then suddenly theology classes were interrupted, Braun later wrote in his usual abbreviated style. "Because of a Dream an old lady had, . . . we Franciscan clerics we[re] sent to St. Louis, Missouri, to complete our studies in Theology."[18]

Father Blaise Cronin, a close friend of Father Albert's in later years, enlarged on this baffling statement: "Somewhere down the canyon," he related, "a lady was having visions—presumably. She dreamt or saw the fall of the clerical students in the mission. . . . They were coming off the tree like leaves, all going to hell. Well, the guardian, whoever that was, must've believed this gal—they moved the whole school back to St. Louis." There, Albert found the Provincial and Guardian "both tougher than any oldtime Army sergeants."[19]

On 2 July 1915 Fathers Albert, Ambrose, and Augustine were ordained in St. Louis by Archbishop John Joseph Glennon. The three who could never make it were the only three who, from the original class at Saint Anthony's and those later added, had survived the attrition. All three would become extraordinary priests. At the time of ordination, however, the new Father Albert Braun, OFM, "couldn't help wondering what the future would be."[20]

"We were allowed to go to California for our first holy mass," Augustine recorded, he to Saint Boniface in San Francisco, Albert and Ambrose to the church of their boyhood, Saint Joseph's in Los Angeles, "then returned to St. Louis for what was called our 'Simplex year.' Strangely enough, I was to spend the summer at Tularosa, New Mexico, with the Indian Mission at Mescalero as part of my charge. At the end of the summer I was told to start teaching at St. Anthony's Seminary in Santa Barbara."[21]

Father Albert spent that year at the mission in Santa Barbara while awaiting the assignment the three A's hoped for, the Franciscan Foreign Mission in China. ("He had really lobbied for that China job," an old friend commented. "That's the way he was. . . . He could be a real rascal."[22])

Father Provincial Hugolinus Storff, however, had other ideas. These three, about whom he seems to have entertained serious doubts, only wanted "to go where we cannot keep an eye on you." None would go to China. "I will send you to a foreign mission," he told a nonplussed Father Albert. "I am sending you to the Apache Indian Reservation at Mescalero, New Mexico."[23]

Father Albert on the occasion of his ordination, July 1915. Courtesy of SJAM.

The new priest with his family. Left to right, seated: Addie (Loretta's son), patriarch John Braun, Mary's children 'Curl' and Loretta, matriarch Caroline Arzner Braun. Standing: siblings Loretta, Father Al, Raymond, and Mary. Clarence is missing. Courtesy of Dorothy Brown Bumgarner.

Newly ordained, Father Albert stands ready to leave for his
first frontier at Mescalero, New Mexico. Courtesy of SJAM.

II

THE FRONTIERSMAN

"I used to go out and stay with the Indians all night.
They told me their stories many times."

3: RAILS AND TRAILS

"I didn't know where Mescalero, New Mexico, was," he later wrote, but "got a map and saw it was near Tularosa, New Mexico," where his superior, Father Ferdinand Ortiz, was pastor. He boarded a train dressed in the prescribed travel wear—cutaway coat, clerical collar, derby hat—and settled in for the dusty ride across the southern desert. It was August 1916.

Father Albert Braun, OFM, ordained but yet untried, approached the threshold of challenge. Mescalero was a far cry from China, but it seemed as foreign; and he doubtless wondered again, as at his ordination, what the future would be. He was crossing into a land of Spanish *conquistadores* and Franciscans whose trail stretched two centuries farther into the past than those of the California missions he had left. How much of their story he knew is impossible to say. He had doubtless studied the Franciscan saga in America and, given his penchant for history, had probably delved fairly deeply. That the dedication, courage, and faith of the early friars impacted him strongly is evident throughout his life. Those who had gone before both beckoned and dared the young Al Braun as he journeyed to the land of the frontier priests.

✞✞✞

The Franciscan story in early New Mexico is written in the blood of martyrs. Leading the procession was Fray Juan de Padilla. He came with Francisco Vásquez de Coronado's *entrada* in 1540, in the course of which he made the long trek to Quivira, far to the east. When the main expedition returned to Mexico in 1542, Fray Juan stayed behind, vowing to bring eternal salvation to the Quivirans, whom he believed ripe for conversion. Fray Luís de Escalona (also known as Luís de Úbeda) remained with him, along with the Portuguese soldier Andrés do Campo, two Indian oblates, a few servants, some sheep, mules, and a horse. Those departing prayed for the best, feared the worst, and heard no more of the friars—until Campos and the oblates appeared five years later in Mexico to tell their story:

Leaving Fray Luís at Cicuique (Pecos) pueblo, Fray Juan and his tiny cavalcade headed east. On reaching Quivira they were welcomed; but some weeks later, seeking new souls to save, they were attacked. Ordering his friends to flee, Fray Juan fell to his knees and began to pray. From where they hid, his friends beheld his gallantry: as arrows pierced his body he commended his soul to God and serenely met his fate.[1]

The centuries that followed saw a swelling line of blue-robed friars marching into history. In 1581 the small expedition of Fray Agustín Rodríguez blazed a river route to the Rio Grande pueblos. The nine soldiers returned to Mexico; the three friars did not. The grisly details of their murders, painted on kiva walls, were found by members of Don Juan de Oñate's colonizing expedition of 1598.

Ten Franciscans came with Oñate; seven trekked in as many directions into the wilderness, converting a reported seven thousand Indians. For nine years the tiny colony on the Rio Grande clung on the precipice of extinction until Oñate, his fortune gone, could no longer continue. The Crown was ready to abandon the unprofitable northern kingdom.

It was the friars, in the field and in Spain, who exhorted Philip III not to desert the Christianized Indians and persuaded him to proclaim New Mexico a royal colony, fund it, and appoint a royal governor. Under these terms Don Pedro de Peralta founded his new capital and named it Santa Fé.[2] The year was 1610. Nine friars came with Peralta. Ten years later another nine arrived, and from their ecclesiastical capital at Santo Domingo Pueblo a promise of permanence seemed to radiate to the missions that were the northern kingdom's reason for being.

But with Peralta also arrived a new *padre presidente.* The power-mad, corrupt Fray Isidro Ordoñez escalated a quarrel with the governor into major combat, alienated the colonists and even his own friars, and—most significantly—established a continuing pattern of conflict between church and state that would splinter the colony and define the seventeenth century in New Mexico—a divisiveness not unobserved by the Indians.

Despite Ordoñez, however, the friars went stoically about their labors. "Fifty churches," Horgan notes, "were built in New Mexico by twenty-six friars in the first quarter of the seventeenth century."[3]

These apostles of the desert were men of courage, persistence, and many skills. The frontier priest, alone in his assigned territory, was in himself a colony of men. He must first learn the native language and then build a church: as God gave each soul a body to inhabit, so must His friar provide a home for the pueblo's collective soul. He was surveyor, architect, engineer.

He was military planner, for the church complex must be a fortress against nomadic tribes. Its entirety rose from the earth of human mortality and, reaching for heaven, united the two. When possible he positioned the church atop a rise, for its spiritual effect and for military observation—a happy marriage of the symbolic and the practical.

The frontier priest taught European music to intone the chants, and enough Latin for proper responses at mass. He taught painting and weaving and blacksmithing. He was herdsman and farmer, laboring with his people in stable and field; and as he worked with them they worked with him to build and maintain their church. They became acolytes, bell ringers, sacristans. The church complex and its outlying fields became a nucleus for the growing mission family, its sanctuary promising eternal salvation, its thick walls affording protection from raiding enemies.

Such was the ideal toward which the padre labored, and which to a large degree he achieved; the mission system worked remarkably well in the early years. The padre found the Indians spiritual by nature, and the grandeur of the mass engaged their love of drama and ritual. That much of their Christianity was superficial he knew; but with time and partaking, he believed, would come grace. On his shoulders lay the burden, and the joy.[4]

These mission communities were not easily gained. Friars were too often hindered—even martyred—by anticlerical governors. When Fray Pedro de Ortega tried to build a needed church at Pecos, Juan de Eulate (1618–1625) forbade the Indians' working on pain of death. Assigned later to Taos, Fray Pedro, when refused lodging, found Eulate's malevolence had spread there also. He built a lean-to of piñon branches. When offered tortillas of corn meal, ground mice, and urine, he remarked cheerfully that "for a good appetite there is no bad bread," and ate with seeming relish.[5] When an Indian, about to loose an arrow at the padre, was attacked by a Spaniard's dog and mauled so severely that he died, Fray Pedro quickly baptized and absolved him. Believing the friar's God had intervened, many tribal members were converted.[6] Fray Pedro ultimately died among the Jumanos from exhaustion, or—some said—from poison.

Fray Esteban de Perea, as custos, requested help from the Holy Office in Mexico to fight the venom of Eulate and other governors of his ilk. He was rewarded: the governor was removed, and Fray Alonso de Benavides arrived in 1626 as agent for the Inquisition. The two dedicated friars erupted into a three-year whirlwind of mission-building, expanding their territory widely. They pressed east to the land of the Jumanos; they built missions at the Salinas pueblos overlooking the southern plains; they thrust westward to hostile Ácoma atop its high mesa, whose sheer walls Fray Juan Ramirez scaled in the face of flying arrows, and stayed to build a church. Three friars traveled farther west to the Zuñi villages and built three churches before the Zuñis brutally murdered Fray Francisco Letrado. Three others journeyed to the Hopi mesas, where one—possibly all three—died of poisoning.

Benavides left in 1629 armed with copious notes that became his *Memoir* of 1630, which, when presented at court in Madrid proved instrumental in reinforcing the Franciscans in New Mexico. Perea, named local agent for the Inquisition, kept governors in check until his death in 1638 or 1639. Then began a period of renewed gubernatorial corruption.

Governors Luís de Rosas (1637–1641), Bernardo López de Mendizábal (1659-1661), and Diego Peñalosa (1661-1664) routinely exploited and brutalized the natives. They dispatched soldiers to capture and enslave Plains Indians, which they sold to work in the Mexican mines. They forced labor and tributes from the Pueblos, incited hatred against the friars, and stirred revolts against them.

Rosas sold the children of Christianized Indians into slavery. He drove priests from their missions, expelled them from Santa Fé, clubbing two until the blood ran. At his instigation Fray Pedro Miranda was murdered as he prayed, his church sacked and burned.

López de Mendizábal was even more brutal, in which he was abetted by his *alcalde mayor* for the Salinas pueblos, Nicolás de Aguilar. When a group from Quarai prepared for a special mass, Aguilar had them seized, tied, and lashed mercilessly.[7] López was so abusive of the clergy, one friar reported, that the Franciscans would have to abandon New Mexico unless relief came soon.[8]

When a new priest arrived at Taos, Peñalosa threatened death to any who helped him rebuild the church, and appointed as pueblo governor the same Indian who had murdered Fray Pedro Miranda.[9]

But Peñalosa met his match in Fray Alonso de Posada, who arrived in 1660 as custos and agent of the Inquisition in response to charges against López. Armed with wide authority and a no-nonsense attitude, he managed to bring López, Aguilar, and Peñalosa to trial before the Holy Office.[10]

The power struggle between church and state marked the larger part of the seventeenth century, and tore constantly at the thin fabric of government in New Mexico. But still another terror threatened the colony: converging from the surrounding vastness swept the tribes of the savage Apaches. They were, Benavidez declared, the "crucible of Spanish valor."

The Apaches had long been the greatest external threat to Pueblos and Spaniards alike. Growing no crops, they attacked those who did and took what they wanted. The outer pueblos and the Spanish trade routes were the most vulnerable, most significantly the *camino real*, Santa Fé's only link to Mexico.

Apache fury intensified during the great drought of the 1660s. Streams and springs disappeared. Crops dried and died. Wild game migrated or starved. Herds perished. Food stores gave out and no supply wagons came. Hunger led to sickness, and many who had not starved died of disease. The Apaches rode wild, killing Spaniards and Christianized Indians, sacking and burning indiscriminately. By 1670 they had completely isolated the Salinas pueblos. Between 1672 and 1678, Fray Francisco de Ayeta reported, six southern pueblos were abandoned and their priests brutally murdered. "The whole land," Fray Juan Bernal wrote, "is at war with the . . . heathen nations of Apache Indians. . . . No road is safe; everyone travels . . . at the risk of his life, for the heathen are everywhere."[11]

The Pueblo Revolt of 1680, which left four hundred Spaniards dead—twenty-one of them friars—was not a sudden eruption. For nearly a century the Indians had watched the struggle between the empires of God and king that had eroded their trust in either. The Spaniards, weakened by years of internal strife, were helpless against the ravages of drought, famine, disease, and Apaches. The province was vast, the soldiers few. The Church grew more militant, demanding a strict monotheism that banned the kiva ceremonials, increased the Indians' resentment, and drove them underground.

Fray Francisco Ayeta, arriving in 1674 as Padre Quartermaster, saw the warning signs, made two arduous journeys to Mexico City, and returned both times with wagon trains of men, horses, and weapons to defend the colony. He had just reached the small outpost of El Paso del Norte with the second convoy when riders galloped in with the awful news:

The pueblos had revolted. Everyone upriver was believed dead; those farther down were fleeing. The river kingdom was lost.

Fray Ayeta took charge. He led the supply wagons across the flooding river, dispatched soldiers upriver to rescue survivors, organized a refugee camp, and sent men to Nueva Viscaya for help. He held the terrified masses at the post, thereby preventing a wholesale exodus that would have endangered the downriver missions and all Sonora. Ayeta then journeyed south again, pled that El Paso be made a permanent, strongly garrisoned fort, and returned in 1681 with supplies and a royal order to mount an offensive and retake New Mexico. Those orders would be realized in 1692 with the triumphant reentry of Don Diego de Vargas. The northern kingdom was again saved by a Franciscan friar.

The following century held its share of turmoil. But churches, homes, and civil structures were rebuilt, fields and orchards replanted, and the beginnings of order restored. De Vargas had left the kivas undefiled and the Church grew less militant. The common enemy were now the encroaching Utes and Comanches, the Navajos, and as ever, the Apaches.

✝✝✝

Truly the young Father Albert rolling toward his first mission field in August 1916 had sandal prints of daunting consequence to follow. Caught up in the hypnotic rhythm of heavy wheels on steel rails, it is safe to assume he would have pondered those who had gone before, wondered at his own place in the long procession, and contemplated the challenge. Of Apaches he knew little beyond their past savagery—some of it quite recent. But the wars were over, the warriors peaceful. Of how to approach them he had no idea. Their culture was a closed book. Of their traditions, beliefs, the habits of their material lives or the principles of their spiritual ones, he was ignorant. There was a church at Mescalero, he had been told, but to what extent it was attended he had no idea. Nor could he utter a word of their language.

Beyond the window of the sweltering car the southern desert stretched seamlessly into forever, a cactus-studded veil masking the Arizona-New Mexico boundary; and off to portside the Mexican border lay as seamless. Would his juncture with the Mescaleros be as smooth?

At length he reached El Paso, and with several hours between trains he paid his respects to Bishop Anthony Schuler, whose diocese included Tularosa and Mescalero. "'Good Bishop Schuler,'" Braun noted. "That's what everybody, even Protestants, called him. The most unusual Jesuit who ever lived. When I told him I don't know a thing about Indians, he said, 'You just go up there for a day or two, and come right back. I don't want to lose you.'"[12]

With that meeting there began a deep and lasting friendship, and what would become one of the greatest apostolates in the American Southwest. The two were not entirely separate.

4: INDIAN COUNTRY

But for the cinders flying past his window, the landscape showed no movement in the glaring August light. El Paso was behind and New Mexico lay before him like a newly opened book. North he rolled through the desert flatlands of the Tularosa Basin from which in contrast thrust mountains on either side—the Huecos and the MacGregor Range on his right, on his left the vertical peaks of the Organs, so named for their pipelike granite pinnacles in whose hidden bastions renegade Apaches had but recently lurked. The tracks of the little El Paso and Northeastern line—which itself had penetrated the basin a scarce eighteen years before—cut through the Jarillas, a desolate mass of boulders—dry, treeless, slashed with ravines of late the haunt of rustlers and outlaw gangs, a magnet for gold-seekers, a den for Apache war parties.

Here also on the western fringes had occurred the murder of prominent attorney and ex-Union soldier Colonel Albert Jennings Fountain and his eight-year-old son Henry. Bound for Las Cruces, Fountain had with him thirty-two indictments—"enough to convict" rancher Oliver Lee for cattle rustling, Fountain had told Dr. Joseph Blazer at whose mill he stopped overnight on 30 January 1896.[1]

He never reached Las Cruces. Coming on the lonely buckboard nearing San Agustín Pass, the searchers found a few relics of the sad tale— little Henry's hat, an unsigned threatening note, blood in the sand, and the trail of the murderers winding through a pass in the Jarillas. The indictments were gone. Neither the murderers nor the bodies were ever found. The mystery remained a subject on which everyone had an opinion and no one a proof. Many believed Lee guilty; among other suspects was Fountain's political opponent Albert B. Fall—soon to become Father Al's close friend.

Past the Jarillas and approaching Alamogordo he saw to the west the dazzling dunes of the White Sands, a rolling expanse of pure gypsum paralleling his route, and beyond them the purple peaks of the San Andres. To his right loomed the green-firred Sacramentos, home of the Mescalero Apaches.

It was tough country into which Al Braun detrained at Tularosa, a drought-ridden land—a land, it was said, where blood flowed more freely than water, and much of it spilled because of water. Tularosa seemed in contrast green, quiet, sleepy. Seeing no one near the little station house, he picked up his bag and began to walk; the church could not be far in the tiny village. Past large cottonwoods he wended, and small trees ripe with fruit, past flowering roses and neat plots of vegetables, past vines heavy with grapes—an oasis of growing things, a place of peace.

✝ ✝ ✝

Tularosa's was a peace hard won.

The land had been Indian country forever it seemed—*Apachería*, the Spaniards had called it—roving grounds of the Apache and the Lipans, who had violently and effectively kept out or wiped out all who might settle, or try to. Until 1862. That spring the Rio Grande flooded, sweeping away fields, homes, and *placitas* in the Mesilla Valley, forcing the desperate families to seek new land.

They looked east, beyond the San Andres, where lay the Tularosa Valley, water-fed but rife with Apache. Fort Stanton, established in 1855 in an attempt to control the Mescaleros, had for a while some limited success, and might have offered a measure of protection for the home-seeking settlers; but in the summer of 1861 the Civil War had pushed up the Rio Grande from Texas in a wash of Confederate gray, to be driven downriver by a tide of Union blue the following May. During the incursion Fort Stanton was twice evacuated, and the Apaches erupted in an orgy of murdering, pillaging, and burning, until the Union army reoccupied the fort in September 1862 and turned again toward trying to subdue the Mescaleros.

On learning this some fifty-three of the flooded-out families, all erstwhile Mexican citizens, dared to people the spot where only two years earlier the Indians had driven out another attempted settlement. The men left the Rio Grande in November to prepare for their families to follow. Posting armed sentries, they cleared fields and built crude adobe quarters. Indian raids were minor, until the women and children arrived in the spring signaling a permanence the Mescaleros would not peaceably tolerate. Raids increased in frequency and ferocity.

The settlers tunneled into *chozas*—dugouts, whose sod-covered roofs were proof against flaming arrows. A central square formed an underground passageway that opened onto separate living quarters, their dirt roofs rising slightly above ground level, enough for high narrow windows. From the excavated dirt they made adobe bricks with which they erected a protective wall around the square, with firing holes through which to shoot when attacked.[2] High adobe walls enclosed the livestock at night; guards were always posted. This walled excavation served until a proper town could be laid out.

Apaches, and often Comanches, galloped widely, attacked settlements and lone ranch houses, ambushed wagon trains and military units. But when Brigadier General James Carleton's California Column grew restless with no more Confederates to fight, the general directed them toward the Indians. Enlisting a reluctant Kit Carson, he ordered a ruthless war on the Mescaleros, who when subdued were sent to the Bosque Redondo, a forlorn area on the Pecos River. The army turned next on the Navajos, who as they surrendered were forced to make the infamous 'Long March' to the Bosque. Bad blood erupted between the tribes, and in 1865 the Mescaleros broke out of confinement en masse and returned to their homeland. Scattered widely, they continued to ride and raid until 1873, when a workable peace was finally negotiated. Although renegade bands continued to attack, the Mescaleros as a tribe ceased to be a threat.

The great necessity for the settlers was water. They had diverted a flow from Tularosa Creek by digging a large mother ditch—an *acequia madre*. The life-giving artery carried its first irrigation water on 2 April 1863, the feast day of Saint Francis de Paola, for whom they named their church.

But in May 1873 a group of ex-Union soldiers-turned-farmers dammed the creek, cutting off Tularosa's only source of water. The villagers formed a posse, rode upstream, destroyed the dam, and opened fire on those attempting to rebuild it. The farmers sent to Fort Stanton for help, and an already endemic racial hostility escalated rapidly when Captain Chambers McKibben, feeding his own animosity for 'Mexicans,' dispatched troops to protect the 'gringos' while they rebuilt the dam, and threatened Tularosa's *alcalde* against any armed retribution.

The posse regrouped, returned, reopened fire, and forced the defenders to flee to Blazer's Mill. McKibben galloped to the rescue with troops and a howitzer, dispersed the posse, and continued on to Tularosa, where forty armed men awaited him behind adobe walls. At the gate a delegation, headed by the parish priest Don Pedro Lassaigne, contested his authority to enter the village; but McKibben, backed by cavalry and cannon, thrust past them, threatening to hang the priest should one shot be fired.

McKibben was latter indicted in Doña Ana County; but the struggles for water continued. They were further complicated when the little stream flooded in 1895, cut a new channel, and destroyed the old bed. The days of easy-flowing water ended. The fight did not.

Meanwhile came the Texans—loud, crude, wild, and arrogant, with herds of cattle, a greed for land, and a supercilious attitude toward 'Mexicans.' There came lawless gangs, flotsam in the wake of civil war, prospectors and prostitutes, gunmen and gamblers, rustlers and renegades. (One did not have to come from Texas to be a *tejano*, though most of them did; merely to act like one merited the name.) The Tularosa Basin became a land of feuds—over water and cattle and open range, and they were usually lethal. It was a land where men debated politics at gunpoint and often argued court trials the same way.

Street brawls, saloon fights, range wars, rigged juries, political rings, waterhole shootouts had but recently been commonplace when Father Al arrived—so recently that his contemporaries remembered them well; many had been actors in the melodrama. It was a place to whet the adventurous young priest's gusto.

Most recently—a scarce five months before Al Braun arrived—the insouciant *bandito* Francisco 'Pancho' Villa, having murdered eighteen Americans at Santa Ysabel, had invaded United States soil at Columbus, New Mexico, laid waste the town, and killed seventeen more. Seeing smoke on the border and alerted by the lone telephone operator who manned her switchboard amid flying bullets and shattering glass, thirty National Guardsmen from nearby Deming rushed to the aid of the single squadron of regulars garrisoned there. Even as Father Albert rolled into Tularosa, 150,000 National Guardsmen from many states were on the border as General John Pershing's expedition fruitlessly chased Villa far into Mexico.

The Villa episode had come after three years of American meddling in Mexico, led by a president afflicted with misguided idealism and a secretary of state who never did figure out what was going on. Wilson had progressed from non-recognition of the Huerta regime (on moralistic grounds) to armed intervention on behalf of Carranza (who politely asked him to mind his own business) to wiggling out of the embarrassing spot (when South American mediators stepped in) to recognition of the Carranza government. Villa, breaking from his former allegiance to Carranza, and itching for a border war, drew Wilson once again into the fray with his attack.

✟✟✟

How Father Al viewed this muddle we can only guess. It certainly perked his interest; and it is entirely possible that his later involvement in the Mexican turmoil sprang from this episode, so near in time and place. Before it was over he would play his own strange part in it.

He spent his first night in New Mexico at the recently built Tularosa rectory. Father Ferdinand—now his immediate superior—was in Arizona, the housekeeper told him, but would return the next day. Meanwhile he was to make himself at home. He began immediately to familiarize himself with his surroundings, doubtless starting with the church, on whose wall he could read the names of Tularosa's first settlers. He would hear their story on Ferdinand's return.

Father Ferdinand Ortiz was a small man, slightly built, scholarly, graceful with the quiet courtesy of his distinguished Mexican-Spanish heritage and the proud bearing also of Aztec ancestry. He had spent a number of years at Old Mission Santa Barbara translating ancient handwritten documents. Because of resulting eyestrain and frail health his provincial had assigned him to a more bracing climate and less sight-taxing duties in the dry Southwest, first at San Xavier del Bac in Tucson and then in Tularosa.[3]

"He told me all about the Mescalero Apache Mission," Father Albert wrote, "and advised that I rest for a few days then on Saturday he will take me to Mescalero and leave me there till Monday when [he] would pick me up by horse and buggy and take me back to Tularosa."[4]

The Franciscans had been assigned responsibility for Saint Francis and Mescalero two years earlier, in 1914, at which time Father Ferdinand arrived to relieve the elderly Father Lucien Migeon, a French secular priest who had served there since 1902. Migeon had visited Mescalero monthly to hear confessions, say mass, and as needed to marry, bury, catechize, and baptize. He had held services in the home of James A. Carroll, reservation superintendent from 1902–1912, or in that of Samuel Miller, and later in the tiny adobe church he built in 1912. Father Ferdinand, assuming these duties along with those at Saint Francis, had built a small rectory and added a bell tower to the church. He also taught classes in Spanish, a service that proved useful to Anglos working in the agency office.

The arrival of the vigorous young Albert Braun would provide valuable assistance. The two Franciscans complemented each other in size, demeanor, and personality—the one large, athletic, bursting with youth and energy, the other small, quiet, ascetic. Theirs would be an amiable and productive alliance.

They set out a few days later as planned, over the worst road Al Braun had ever seen. Ferdinand, he recorded, "drove me in horse and buggy. . . . It took three hours to travel the 18 miles,"[5] along which Ferdinand doubtless acquainted him with the landmarks as they passed.

Outside Tularosa the dirt road began to rise toward the mountain home of the Mescalero Apache. Over a rocky stretch cut by deep ravines they bumped, and past Round Mountain, the site, the young priest learned, of a battle fought on 17 April 1868, during the height of the Indian depredations. A small detail from Fort Stanton, having escorted a supply wagon to Tularosa, was returning to the fort when they were confronted by an Apache band at Cottonwood Springs. Galloping ten miles back to town, one trooper spread the alarm and returned with twenty-six men. They joined battle near Round Mountain (also known tellingly as Dead Man's Hill) where the detachment had taken cover in a roofless one-time adobe fortification, from which they fought the surrounding Apaches.

In Tularosa the citizens gathered to pray: if Saint Francis would intercede and save their men and their colony, they vowed, they would replace the old ramshackle church. Their prayers were answered. All twenty-six returned, minus their mounts, but alive. The Indians, sighting a lone man who had crawled to the creek for water, and apparently thinking he was leading reinforcement troops, had rustled the horses and vanished. Both sides claimed victory. The Indians had lost only one man, and they had the horses. The colonists, believing they had stopped a murderous raid and saved the village, danced in the street, thanked Saint Francis, and began to rebuild the church.[6]

The air grew cooler as the two priests drove on, ascending into the pine-forested slopes from which branched small stream-fed valleys. Through the resinous air they continued, and past Blazer's Mill—another historic monument. The sawmill on Tularosa Creek—*La Maquina*, they called it—was quite old—no one knew how old, but it had furnished the lumber used in the earliest structures for miles around, for *vigas*, door frames, and furniture for the desert country below. The Apaches, despite their depredations elsewhere, had strangely left it alone.

During the war with Mexico, Mexican troops had used it as fort and garrison until defeated in the winter of 1846-47. Later American entrepreneurs, under military protection, rejuvenated the war-gutted mill to provide timber for forts, only to have it destroyed in 1855 and again four years later—not by Apaches, but by their plains enemies, the Comanches. *La Maquina* rose again from the ashes after each assault. The need for lumber outlived the tides of Civil War, Indian raids, and several changes of ownership.

In 1868—the same year as the Battle of Round Mountain—Joseph Hoy Blazer arrived. He had been a dentist until arthritis forced him from his profession. He had served as a Union soldier until wounded and discharged, and then became sutler for his old regiment until it was disbanded at war's end. On returning to Iowa he found his wife and oldest son ill with tuberculosis and looked to the dry Southwest for their cure. With wagons and mules he had acquired as a sutler, he started a freight business, in the course of which he stopped at Tularosa and saw it as a potential home. He became involved in the perennial fight for water, to be attacked by a knife-wielding would-be assassin. Unarmed, he fought off his assailant barehanded.[7] His plan for fair and efficient water usage was adopted, and he quickly became a respected member of the community.

He also acquired an interest in *La Maquina*, and within a year was head of operations; and when in 1869 the mill was again burned by Comanches, or by arsonists dressed as Comanches, Blazer quickly found a partner with whom he bought out the ruined owners.

In 1878 gun-blazing rivalry erupted in nearby Lincoln town between the Murphy-Dolan-Riley hegemony and the McSween-Chisum-Tunstall challengers. All-out war soon swept the countryside and exploded on 4 April at Blazer's Mill. One man was killed; and Billy Bonney (alias 'the Kid') threatened to kill the unarmed Blazer who, refusing to take sides, walked away unscathed.[8]

That the Mescaleros never attacked Blazer's Mill was the result of one of the strangest friendships in western history, that of the feared and ferocious Chief Santana and 'Doc' Blazer. After years of fighting, Santana, believing a peace treaty the only way to save his people from annihilation, covertly approached Blazer; sizing each other up, both saw the beginnings of trust, which grew to friendship and finally to brotherhood. It was Blazer who conveyed Santana's desire for peace to the military commanders and acted as his contact during the ensuing negotiations. In time Blazer and Santana were instrumental in securing the reservation in the Mescaleros' beloved mountain homeland, guarded by their sacred peak. Doc Blazer had died before Father Al arrived; but the padre would soon know the Blazer family well.

Nearing Mescalero, the two priests began to see small herds of goats in the clearings, and children, and the scattered tepees that marked Apacheland. Then, approaching the tiny settlement, Father Al first saw Sierra Blanca, towering twelve thousand feet, in whose aeries are said to dwell the mountain spirits that guard the sacred water, which is to say the lives of the Mescaleros. Girded on the south by the Sacramentos, whence rises Tularosa Creek, and on the north by the Sierra Blancas, the settlement lay in a widening canyon where the two branches joined. Both streams had once flowed constantly, though increasing population upstream had severely sapped the north fork by the time Father Albert arrived.

The creek's importance far outweighed its size. It nurtured the tribe above and the village below, and with the steepness of its drop it powered the mill. Below, running onto the flatlands, the Tularosa spread into the marshy delta whose cattails—*tules*—gave river, town, and basin their names. Approaching the White Sands the little river is lost in the parched desert.

Then they were there. In the cup of the canyon lay Mescalero, a tiny cluster of agency buildings—the government school, the trading post, a few houses for the agency personnel—and a Dutch Reformed chapel. On a rise between the dirt road and the stream perched the tiny adobe church that was now Father Albert's charge.

They had dinner with the Millers. 'Captain' Samuel Miller (born Mueller, of German parentage in Pennsylvania) had enlisted at age fourteen in the Union army, with which he came to New Mexico. Captivated like many others by the raw new country, he stayed. He seems to have done some prospecting; there was a "gambling sense about him," his grandson remembered. "He was looking for a pot of gold. I guess he was a good businessman, and he ended up owning some land down in the valley."[9] Captain Sam first went to work for Blazer, where he became known for his integrity and his great rapport with the Indians. Impressed with the young man, agency superintendent Carroll hired him to oversee tribal farming and herding, at which he proved very successful. In Mescalero he met and married Blasa Telles, a remarkable Apache woman, a fervent Catholic who ministered to the Mescaleros in the absence of a priest, served as community midwife, welcomed and fed visitors, and bore Samuel seven children. When an epidemic (probably typhoid) swept the reservation, six of the children died. Only a daughter, Katherine, lived.

Sam, Blasa, and fifteen-year-old Katherine greeted the two priests. There also, to Father Al's delight, was his old friend and classmate Augustine, who had spent the summer at the Mescalero mission pending Albert's arrival. Gus would leave immediately for their old seminary Saint Anthony's, where he had been assigned to teach. Braun "felt at home immediately," he wrote, with his old friend, his new superior, and the Millers, who would prove as close as family.

Also in the party that day was a young man about Father Al's age. He was Charles Mackey, an agency employee who boarded with the Millers, former friends of his deceased parents. Charlie had a lively air, an impish Irish grin, and a quick humor that matched Al Braun's; a friendship sparked quickly.

The new padre spent his first night in Mescalero in the tiny adobe rectory Father Ferdinand had built. Augustine returned to Tularosa with Father Ferdinand to catch the next train out; and Al Braun was alone at last, a padre with a mission, among a people of whom he knew nothing, who spoke a language he did not understand, honored traditions of which he had never heard, and worshiped mountain spirits. He must have felt the tug of brotherhood with those early Franciscans who had blazed the trail he now trod.

Father Albert Braun, OFM, who had always loved a challenge, had now found a worthy one. With morning he would inspect the little church, meet some of his parishioners, prepare to say his first mass in his first assignment. And he would certainly clean his spartan, dirt-floored quarters, which, separated from the sacristy by a tarpaulin, was furnished with an army cot, a desk, an ancient typewriter, and a wood-burning iron cookstove.

And, he soon learned, an army of bedbugs.

A cluster of agency buildings, ca. 1916, at Mescalero. Courtesy of Dick Mackey.

Father Al's first church, built of adobe in 1912 by Father Migeon. Father Ferdinand built the rectory behind it and added the bell tower (which high winds blew down shortly before Father Al arrived). Courtesy of SJAM.

5: MEN AND BRAVES

Possibly the very triviality of this first challenge reminded the tenderfoot priest of his own insignificance in the universal scheme. Almost certainly he saw the humor of it. Always one to laugh at his own comeuppance, he would have dismissed the bedbugs as *insignificant!*—his favorite adjective for any obstacle—fought back, and turned to larger matters.

Who were these people he had come among? We can imagine him tossing through a sleepless night, alternately pondering the large question and battling the tiny pests, as elusive (if not as deadly) as the Apaches who gave the United States Army a wild and bloody chase for forty years.

Who were the Mescaleros?

✞✞✞

The Apaches had always been nomads and predators. Tough, wily, fierce, and fearless, they lived off a harsh land that gave little. The whole Southwest was their hunting ground—the Spaniards had called it *Apachería*. Having preyed successively on Pueblos, Spaniards, and Mexicans, they initially accepted the Yankees who arrived in 1846 and fought the Apaches' Mexican enemies. Soon, however, alarmed by the sheer numbers of the invaders, they turned on them—first on the soldiers, then on the California-bound 'forty-niners' who followed in droves. They attacked mail wagons, travelers, and incoming settlers, whose threat of permanence was ominous.

The Mescaleros comprised nine small, loosely connected but independent bands which, along with their cousins the Chiricahuas and Lipans, ranged and raided widely on both sides of the border. With the land acquired by the Treaty of Guadalupe-Hidalgo the United States also acquired the Indians living on it and the responsibility for keeping them out of Mexico. When ordered to stop the Mexican raids, the chiefs answered with terse logic that they had to steal from someone. "If you will not permit us to rob the Mexicans, we must steal from you or fight you."[1]

The Mescaleros must starve, raid, or parley. The southern bands chose to raid, and fight. Perceiving the superiority of the *norteamericanos* in arms and numbers, those in the Sierra Blanca band chose to remain isolate in their mountain lairs until a fair treaty could be negotiated. Toward this end their three powerful chiefs Barranquito, Santana, and Josecito, along with several Jicarilla and Comanche chiefs, began to parley.

But that same month a detachment of United States troops on an exploring party blundered into the Sierra Blanca homeland. Santana was waiting. There were, he warned the lieutenant in charge, two thousand warriors assembled to attack. It was a colossal lie—he might have mustered two hundred—but it worked. The officer thought it "prudent to retire."[2]

By 1854 Santana had turned from bluff to battle. Treaties proved ephemeral. Peace was a fragile flower in a gale of mutual distrust, fear, and misunderstanding. The tribes never understood that treaties were invalid until ratified, and most were not, so that perceived promises went unhonored. Nor did they understand the changing personnel—and rationale—of the Great White Father's Indian policy. Governors and agents came and went, civil and military authorities wrangled constantly, and no officer could guarantee that commitments he made would not be brushed aside by another authority.

The *norteamericanos* were just as ignorant of the political structure of the nomadic tribes. No chief could guarantee the actions of any beyond his particular band, and was often hard put to control his own. The peaceful Apaches were therefore blamed for the depredations of the belligerents. To the military an Apache was an Apache, all were bad, and the Mescaleros were the worst of all the savage lot.

The Indians in turn saw all White Eyes as fork-tongued liars, and unscrupulous traders fanned these suspicions for their own bootlegging profits. Raid led to retaliation, strike to counterstrike, and the cycle accelerated. Good men, red and white, signed treaties and bad men of both races broke them.

Santana and his warriors had worked in good faith for peace; now they had had enough. Choosing Santana to lead them, the Mescaleros went on the warpath.

Late in December 1854 they made off with some 2,500 sheep stolen from near Santa Fe, thundered south, and set in motion a 450-mile chase which, under command of Captain (later Confederate General) Richard B. Ewell, penetrated the Sierra Blanca heartland. The Indians massed to fight, but failing to stop Ewell, melted into the crags and crannies known only to them. The only trace Ewell found was a hastily abandoned camp. There Captain Henry Whiting Stanton, leading a small scouting detachment, was ambushed and killed with two of his men.[3] Bitter winter ice and treacherous terrain prevented Ewell from further pursuit.

Brigadier General John Garland, commander of the Military District of New Mexico, reported fifteen Apaches killed, including Santana, for whose death he had "positive information."[4] Positive or not, it was unfounded—a ruse carefully planted by Santana himself. For the next fifteen years the great chief remained isolate from the white man's world, unseen, unheard, unsuspected. That he kept close contact with his own people there is no doubt.

Stanton's death stirred what would have become a war of extermination but for Dr. Michael Steck, government agent for the Mescaleros. Steck promised them protection and, after convincing the governor, a treaty whereby they would be allotted a reservation in their homeland, controlled by an agency at the newly established Fort Stanton (named for the recently killed captain) to which they were answerable and from which they would receive rations, blankets, and other necessities.

Garland fumed, but his hand had been stayed. The Senate as usual failed to ratify the treaty, but Steck upheld his promises as best he could, and, with Chief Cadete (son of Barranquito) managed to keep the Mescaleros out of trouble most of the time.

Santana had by disappearing made possible the truce and treaty, which, though unratified, filled the immediate purpose and kept the people alive. Cadete could negotiate while Santana lived with his small band in the wilds of his mountains, hunting, gathering, stealing, and forgotten by the white world. Almost certainly the power behind the parleys, the voice behind the peace, he stayed hidden for fifteen years until time and circumstance allowed him to reemerge and accomplish, through his strange friendship with Doc Blazer what Cadete had worked for so long.

His was the ultimate statesmanship.

In 1861 the Civil War came to New Mexico.

A number of territorial officers resigned their commissions to join the Confederacy. Others, loyal to the Union, were sent east with their units, thereby reducing the already thin ranks in the Southwest. Post commanders throughout Apache country were ordered to repair with their men to the Rio Grande to defend against the Confederate invasion then mustering near El Paso.

It was an open invitation to the tribes who, believing themselves the cause of the wholesale egress and determined to drive out the remainder, erupted widely. Indian relations in the Territory "are daily becoming more unsatisfactory," reported Colonel E. R. S. Canby, commanding the Union troops remaining in New Mexico. "The depredations of the Navajos are constant. The Mescalero Apaches are becoming more daring in their inroads. . . ."[5] Faced with the Confederate invasion Canby could do little.

The invading vanguard came up the Rio Grande in July, led by an Indian-hating Texan, Lieutenant Colonel (soon to be Brigadier General) John H. Baylor. Taking Mesilla, Baylor proclaimed himself governor of the "Confederate Territory of Arizona," captured Fort Fillmore, occupied Fort Stanton, and, while the main body of Confederates under command of General Henry H. Sibley marched up the river, turned his energy toward subduing Indians.[6]

This proved difficult. Apaches were everywhere. They swooped on Baylor's supply trains; they ambushed military details; they looted and burned and murdered; and they forced Baylor to abandon Fort Stanton. The Indians, he concluded, must be exterminated.

He organized two forces of volunteers. On learning that western Apaches were seeking a peace treaty in Tucson, he issued his infamous order of 20 March 1862: His troops, he ordered, would "use all means to persuade the Apaches . . . to come in for the purpose of making peace, and when you get them all together, kill the grown Indians and take the children prisoners and sell them to defray from the expenses of killing the Indians. . . . Let no Indian escape."[7]

Upon learning of this order Confederate President Jefferson Davis, appalled at this savagery, recalled Baylor. By this time Sibley's main Confederate invasion had been defeated at Glorieta Pass and was in retreat down the Rio Grande.

Canby had stopped the Confederates, but he faced chaos. Forts built to control Indians were largely destroyed, Indians were sweeping through the Territory, and his own ranks were decimated.

Into the breach in September rode Brigadier General James A. Carleton and the long-awaited California Column. Too late to fight Confederates, Carleton turned on the Indians. Assuming command in Santa Fe, he ordered Colonel Christopher 'Kit' Carson and five companies of New Mexico Volunteers to reoccupy Fort Stanton, from which they would fight "until [the Indians] had been punished for their recent aggressions."

Carson opposed this harsh retaliation. The elderly Chief Manuelito, he reported, had come to him with twenty braves seeking peace "in behalf of the entire Mescalero Nation." With other chiefs Manuelito planned to approach Superintendent of Indian Affairs James L. Collins, seek peace, and offer "to fight against the Navajos, Comanches, or any other enemies of the United States." Carson, who knew Indians as well as any man alive, believed Manuelito spoke in good faith and urged he be given a chance.[8]

But Carleton had already hardened his inflexible mind. No quarter would be given, he ordered the dismayed Carson. All Mescalero men would be killed "whenever and wherever you find them. . . ." To surrender, "their chiefs and twenty of their principle men" must go to Santa Fe.[9]

The order found its first victim on 18 October. Captain James 'Paddy' Graydon, 1st Mounted New Mexico Volunteers, came on Manuelito en route to Santa Fe with his people. Seeing the detachment, the old chief raised his hand in peace and started forward unarmed. Following orders, Graydon opened fire without warning, killing Manuelito, Chief José Largo, and a number of others, wounding many, and taking the rest captive. Carson protested vigorously. The general refused to modify his orders.

In November Cadete, trying to surrender, was attacked from the rear and badly defeated. He and the survivors fled to Carson, pursued by the Californians bent on unconditional surrender or total annihilation. Carson, against orders, gave the Indians protection and sent five of them, with the sympathetic agent Lorenzo Labadie and a military escort, to Santa Fe, where Cadete faced Carleton: "You are stronger than we," he began:

> We have fought you so long as we had rifles and powder; but your weapons are better than ours . . . [and] we are worn out; . . . we have no more provisions, no means to live; your troops are everywhere. . . . You have driven us from our last and best stronghold, and we have no more heart. Do with us as may seem good to you, but do not forget we are men and braves.[10]

Many were moved. Carleton was not. "They were remanded back to Fort Stanton," wrote Captain John C. Cremony, a California Volunteer, "and from thence sent to the Bosque Redondo . . . where they arrived after a long and painful march of one hundred and twenty miles, with short rations and much suffering."[11]

Then began what became for the Mescaleros a hell of burning heat or bitter cold, and constant wind; of brackish water, lack of firewood, poor shelter, and scanty rations of moldy flour and spoiled beef. The site afforded bare subsistence, though they tried to farm, until the eventual arrival of nearly nine thousand surrendered Navajos.

Inevitably there were fights. The tribes, Cremony wrote, "had never lived comfortably together. . . . At length the matter became so unbearable to the Apaches, who, . . . outnumbered nine to one, . . . applied to General Carleton to be placed on a separate reservation."[12] Carleton refused. During the night of 3 November 1865 the Mescaleros left en masse, scattered, passed from sight, and for several years seem to have been swallowed by the canyons and crests and crevasses only they could penetrate.

It was during these years of invisibility that Santana (who had escaped being sent to the Bosque) established his friendship with Doc Blazer. Still in contact with his people and working behind the scenes, he was able through Blazer to initiate dialogue with the military that eventually led to the return and rehabilitation of the Mescaleros on a reservation created under President Grant in 1873, in their own homeland.[13]

There was still friction. There were still poverty, scant rations, and raiding. There were still renegade bands and whiskey peddlers sowing discord and drunkenness. There was frequent turnover in agents. Some worked with the tribe, helped them grow crops, run cattle and sheep, cut and sell timber, and establish a viable community. There were also bad agents who tried to force their wills and ways: the Apache men must cut their hair; they must wear white men's clothes, and give up their ceremonial dances. They must live in houses. Their children must attend school or be forcibly seized. Agents and edicts came and went, and when such agents were gone the Mescaleros quietly went back to their own ways. Indian policy in Washington continued to shift; civil and military authorities continued to bicker. In 1870 Indian affairs were transferred from the War Department to Interior and the following years Congress declared Indians wards of the government, thereby ending their treaty-making status.

Meanwhile the Mescaleros lost their two great leaders. Cadete was murdered in 1872, presumably by some white bootleggers against whom he had just testified; and in 1876 Santana died of smallpox, despite the dedicated nursing of Doc Blazer, who stuck by his old comrade to the end.

Elsewhere the continuing Apache wars impacted on the Mescaleros. Warm Springs Apaches, unhappy at being pent at San Carlos, escaped, and arrived starving in Mescalero in two groups, one led by old Chief Nana, a second with Victorio.

All went well until a Mescalero was killed in a drunken brawl, bad blood resulted, and Victorio, having been indicted for rustling and murder, grew restless. The frightened agent sent for troops, whose arrival lit the fuse: Victorio, Nana, and a number of Mescaleros erupted into one of the bloodiest episodes in frontier history. The renegades cut a fiery swath through New and Old Mexico, murdering, burning, looting. The Indians— perhaps three hundred—eluded combined Mexican and American troops numbering some two thousand until 1880, when Victorio, surrounded and out of ammunition, was killed along with most of his band.

Nana and about thirty braves were in Mexico at the time and escaped annihilation. Seventy years old, partly blind, and bent with rheumatism, the old chief could still outride and outfight many younger warriors. Determined on revenge, he with a handful of braves crossed the border in the summer of 1881 and, joined by about twenty-five Mescaleros, swept through New Mexico on a rampage of death and destruction, covering over a thousand miles in six weeks, chased by a thousand soldiers and several hundred civilians, with whom they fought eight battles and won them all.

But numbers and logistics were against them. In 1883 they surrendered to General George Crook, whom they respected as a hard fighter and trusted as a man of his word. They lived peaceably for two years before Nana broke out again. With him were Geronimo, the dreaded Juh, Chatto (among the fiercest warriors, who would later become a trusted scout for the United States Army), and Naiche, son of Cochise and the real leader of Geronimo's warring band.

They held out until 27 March 1885, when they accepted Crook's humane terms. This would have ended the matter but for two mishaps. First, a bootlegging trader smuggled whiskey into the camp, and Geronimo, after a night of carousing, bolted with Naiche and several others. Second, President Cleveland repudiated Crook's terms, insisting on unconditional surrender. Crook, a man of honor, refused to break his word, asked to be relieved of his command, and was replaced immediately by the iron-fisted General Nelson A. Miles.

Geronimo, the hundred-plus who had fled with him, and some who had never surrendered were still at large. But time, tide, and five thousand United States troops wrote the end. By the close of 1886 the embattled warriors surrendered to inevitability and General Miles.

The Apache wars were over.

By history's necessity new civilizations supplant the old, by conflict or erosion, seldom without pain, at best with justice. The nation still bled from the wounds of civil war, reconstruction, and the Indian wars; and memories were bitter. It was not a climate that easily nurtured justice.

Carson, sickened at Carleton's ruthless inflexibility, had asked to be relieved of duty several times before the Mescalero and Navajo campaigns ended, only to have his integrity rebuffed and his requests denied. Crook, who had fought hard but always honorably, and who had dealt justly with a defeated enemy, was censured and undermined by his own superiors. And a number of Apaches who had served the United States honorably as scouts were sent with the others into captivity.

The Apaches were shipped in toto to Florida, where many died of hunger, cold, damp, and filth. Later they were transferred to Alabama, where for some reason one group of Mescaleros was released and returned to the homeland. In 1894—largely due to the continuing intercession of General Crook—the prisoners were taken to Fort Sill, Oklahoma. There the Kiowas and Comanches gave them a part of their lands, where they could live a decent life.

In 1913 the captives were finally released with the option of remaining in Oklahoma on lands they had settled and farmed, or settling permanently with the Mescaleros, who had agreed to welcome them to their mountain home. About a third stayed behind, among them Geronimo, who became quite a celebrity, a role he fell into gleefully and profitably. Old Nana also stayed, remaining to the end fierce, proud, and untamed.

The rest opted for New Mexico. Accordingly, in April one hundred eighty-seven Indians erupted from boxcars in the Tularosa depot—the fourteen Mescaleros who had not been released earlier, a scattering of Lipans and Comanches, the overwhelming rest Chiricahuas—to settle at last and permanently among their fellow Apaches in Mescalero.

These—the freed prisoners and the little mountain tribe who had clung so heroically to their homeland—were the durable people among whom Father Albert now, only three years after their release, had arrived, the people who would become his life for decades to come. These—tough, proud, and tenacious—were the survivors.

6: PADRE ON HORSEBACK

These things Father Albert learned in bits and pieces. He listened avidly to their stories, eager to learn their beliefs, traditions, attitudes. These he must absorb gradually. Meanwhile he prepared a carefully reasoned homily for his first mass in the tiny adobe church.

"When it came time," he often told chuckling, "I had all my notes, and I started this big sermon. The Indians had dogs. Dogs all over. Big dogs. And this was just a little church—no more than maybe eight or nine people in there, and the dogs. Suddenly this huge one—a monster of a dog—came running in the door, and he was barking at me, raising an awful fuss. I got so distracted I couldn't remember anything. So I just talked." Apparently soothed by Father Al's voice, the dog sat as if mesmerized, almost at the young priest's feet throughout the service.

That was the last time he relied on notes.[1]

He quickly learned the art of simple impromptu sermons. From the Mescaleros he learned their ways, medicine man Paul Ortega remembered, and conveyed his messages in terms that related to them, to their daily habits, to the way they lived.[2] He identified the universal with the simple, the everyday, the understandable. It was a technique he would perfect through the years, a dynamic style for which he became well known.

Father Al learned at this first mass how extremely poor these people were. "First Sunday collection—17 cents," he penned in his usual terse manner. On the collection rested his subsistence. "Immediately became a farmer—never went hungry."[3]

Neither, he vowed, would his Mescaleros. Although his first farming effort, begun late in the short growing season, was on a small scale, he planned for the next year a larger effort for the whole community. He would need tools, he wrote his father, and John Braun responded. Within weeks there arrived plow, harrow, and cultivator. Alice Weiss, who lived in the East and had some property just off the reservation, became fond of the enthusiastic young priest and contributed a hundred apple trees, which he planted in a clearing, blessed, and began instructing the Mescaleros in their proper care.

Alice would visit often in the coming years and contribute to his various efforts.

At his first mass, aside from the dogs, his congregation comprised only men. To his surprise, only women attended his second service. Apache tradition, it seemed, forbade any man to enter the presence of his mother-in-law. "A simple superstition," agent E. V. Stottler (determined to eradicate the 'heathen' customs of the Mescaleros) had sneered a few years earlier. "Just why it is no Indian has been able to explain to me, but an Indian cannot look at his mother-in-law. . . ."[4] One explanation suggests it forestalled any possibility of the man finding his wife's mother too attractive—or the other way around. Others said it was merely a mark of respect. For whatever reason, it was a practice resolutely observed, so that men and women attended masses on alternate weeks.

Insignificant! Al Braun quickly solved the problem by hanging a long red curtain down the center aisle, thereby dividing the sexes and doubling each Sunday's attendance.

At the Millers' home, where it was agreed Father Al would take his meals, he met Eric Tortilla. Within a few days of the padre's arrival Blasa arranged for several young Apaches who had learned English at the Carlisle Indian School in Pennsylvania to come and meet their new priest. "Felt at home immediately," he wrote, "because of Carlisle Indian School's famous football players [Eric among them] who had just returned to Mescalero—Carlisle had [the] most famous football team in the United States with Jim Thorpe starring and Pop Warner coaching. . . . [W]e talked football [all] night."[5] Eric would soon become his close friend, guide, and interpreter.

Respecting Mescalero traditions, the young priest adapted his ways to accommodate theirs and quickly became a working part of the tribal community. He was young, intoxicated with life, buoyant in his newfound mission. He made friends quickly and with Eric's help he was learning the people's ways. Unable to abide idleness in himself or anyone else, he soon enlisted the Mescaleros' aid in the community bean fields and the orchard and in patching and maintaining the shabby little church. Persuading the men to work in the fields, he found, was not easy: farming was women's work and beneath a brave's dignity. He would have to persuade by example.

The agency community greeted him also as a welcome adjunct to their own work with the Mescaleros.[6] The Millers and the Dorames, who lived close by the church, took him into their family lives. The Blazers and their work crew offered any help he might wish. So absorbed Father Albert became in his new life that the 'day or two' Bishop Schuler had suggested for the greenhorn padre's initial stay at Mescalero had stretched into several weeks before he belatedly reported to the bishop in El Paso. He had, he explained, "been talking football ever since I got there."[7] Schuler understood.

Returning to Mescalero he knew he must take the church to the people. It was a sturdy undertaking on a reservation of nearly half a million acres stretching south from Tularosa Canyon into the Sacramentos and north into the Sierra Blancas to cover over 720 square miles of rugged terrain, most of it accessible only by foot or horseback. Tribal lands ranged from some twenty-seven miles north-to-south and thirty-six east-to-west at their widest points. An extension at the northwest corner jutted to encompass a sizeable portion of the Sierra Blancas, including the sacred peak and the area below known as *Tres Ritos*—Three Rivers—where three streamlets drained from the mountain to come together in one of the loveliest valleys in nature. The brooks, like Tularosa Creek, disappear below the mountain to sink into the parched expanses of the White Sands.

The Mescaleros, still semi-nomadic, spread widely through this expanse in small camps, moving always to hunt the wild game or gather the usable plants. When not afield they tended to cluster in the small tribal communities of Whitetail, Elk Springs, Carrizo, Windmill, Silver Springs, or—the farthest from Mescalero—the Shanta community at Three Rivers. Widowed women lived apart in the 'Old Ladies' Village.' In all, it meant a lot of riding for one lone priest.

It was Eric Tortilla who, acting as interpreter, had first shown him the trails and taken him to the camps. On their first ride, the padre recounted, he noted the reluctance of anyone to speak, "and I said, 'Eric, why are the Indians so quiet?'

"'Well,' he said, 'they don't trust the white man. They want to get a look at you. Wait till the next time you go out.'

"The next time I couldn't get to bed. They talked all night."[8]

They continued to talk as he and Eric rode the hills and camped with them. Here was a white man who listened more than he talked, who was interested in them, in their stories and their culture.

With his mass vessels in his saddlebag, a rifle for possible wild game and Eric at his side, the rangy priest astride a stout Indian horse became a common figure as he probed the canyon-gouged slopes searching out clusters of tepees. In these small, far-flung enclaves each family tended its plot of corn, beans, and squash, herded its own sheep—some had cattle—and, looking ever toward the sacred peak, acknowledged their spirits and honored their traditions. They always welcomed Father Albert. He ate with them, slept on the ground with them, prayed with them.

He was still nominally living in Tularosa, but as the days began to shorten into autumn, his life among his scattered people must, he realized, emanate from Mescalero. Father Ferdinand lacked authority to grant his request to move permanently to the reservation, but the father provincial, Braun wrote, "gave me permission to stay at Mescalero one year." That year would stretch into many.

He moved into the spartan quarters where he had more or less camped before. From here he sallied widely, until he seemed forever on the trail. "I used to start out on Monday morning. . . . I'd stay with this family all night, and that family, and that family, and Thursday afternoon I had to go home and get ready for Sunday."[9] In this way he launched the last and most remarkable of the great frontier ministries to the Indians. "He'd visit the camps—go out and marry them," one recalled. "They didn't have to go to any marriage counselor like today. He just married them and baptized their babies," often simultaneously.[10]

Among Father Al's earliest acquaintances was Shanta Boy, patriarch of the colony at Three Rivers. The padre had not been long at Mescalero when Father Ferdinand drove him to that farthest corner of the reservation. No road went directly over the mountain; they must descend to Tularosa whence, bumping north in Ferdinand's buggy, he first saw the great black lava flow of the badlands—the *malpais* that commenced past where the glare of the White Sands leaves off and parallels the road some eighty miles, against the purple backdrop of the San Andres Mountains a hundred miles to the west. These cracked waterless wastes had in the not-too-distant past teemed with hostile Apaches.

At Three Rivers Station they turned east onto a trail that rises past a ridge strewn with petroglyphs chipped by the Mogollon peoples who predated the Mescaleros' ancestors by centuries. Beyond that they passed the outlying adobe *casitas* of the workmen and the irrigation ditches and parades of cottonwoods leading to the sumptuous Tres Ritos ranch house built by a wild Irish Texan grown rich on stolen cattle and a gunslinging saloon in Tularosa. Ten years before Father Al's arrival in Mescalero, New

Mexico's Senator Albert Bacon Fall had acquired that property along with the adjoining land of one-time 'Cattle Queen of New Mexico' Susan McSween Barber.

Beyond the Fall ranch they crossed back onto reservation land, where lay the Shanta community. Here the firred foothills rose toward the western flanks of the Sierra Blanca that commanded the lives of the Mescaleros. Here Father Albert met Shanta Boy, clan patriarch, whose spread abutted the Fall ranch, separated only by the reservation line. Together with their Hispanic workers, the two ranches constituted the Three Rivers community. The Shanta colony was among the most stable and progressive on the reservation, with one of the few houses among the Apaches. Shanta Boy farmed a number of well watered acres, ran many horses, some cattle, and three thousand sheep on the fine grazing land the canyon afforded, deposited his profits from lambs and wool in the Tularosa bank, and lifted his eyes to Sierra Blanca thrusting baldly above.

Shanta Boy, center, flanked by relatives. Courtesy of Department of Special Collections and University Archives, Marquette University Libraries (MUA).

The young priest was soon riding regularly to minister to those in this remote corner, a practice he would continue through the years. "He traveled straight across from Mescalero, which is about thirty miles by horseback over the mountain," Shanta Boy's granddaughter Virginia recalled. "He would stop at every Apache camp and stay overnight with them, share a meal, and then start to the next camp, all the way back to Three Rivers. He'd come over the hill on horseback, and he'd get with my grandfather. . . . They were very strong friends, and he would always stay with us, maybe a couple of days, and say mass every day. That's the reason why most of my family are Catholic—because of Father Al.

"That's the kind of person he was. He was with the people. . . . He didn't say, 'Well here is a catechism, we're going to learn about Catholic religion.' He was a person of God . . . a true Franciscan. He didn't care whether someone was another religion—he wanted them to know about God . . . and he visited families—Baptist or Dutch Reformed or whatever. He'd go in and visit, share a meal, talk."[11]

Father Al talked, and he listened. He listened to Eric as they rode, and sitting around the campfires with the families at night he listened to tribal history, lore, myths, and beliefs. Exploring their language, he began to glimpse their thoughts. Camping with them, he grew into their ways, and—unlike many—he had no wish to change those ways to conform with white man's ideas. His genuine respect for their beliefs garnered theirs for his.

A hearty trencherman, Al Braun quickly learned to relish Apache food. Meat was usually plentiful and formed a large part of the Mescalero diet. The mountains teemed with deer and wild turkey, sometimes bear and quail, and, in the flatlands, antelope. Lacking game, most families could slaughter a goat or a sheep from their herds, or, for special occasions, a steer.

Apache bread was traditionally made from ground mesquite beans or sunflower seeds. By Father Al's day the Mescaleros were also making tortillas from flour, which they cooked on hot flat stones or made into fry bread cooked in hot grease over an open fire.

Wild onions, potatoes, cattail, tumbleweed roots, berries, and piñon nuts all extended the Mescaleros' diet. Bee trees offered honey. Special delicacies in spring and summer were cactus blossoms and fruits of the various cacti. Their god Ussen created each plant for a reason—for food or clothing or shelter. Nothing created is useless.

Their great staple was—and is—mescal, from which the name *Mescalero* derives. Made from the heart and leaves of the century plant, or agave, mescal is quintessential to all feasts and their attendant rites. No puberty celebration is complete without it. Mescal in its dried form is a basic on the trail; and it had nourished families through years of drought and famine.

For generations mescal-gathering parties have set out each May or June when the central stalks are pushing skyward but not yet flowering. Mescal gathering is the women's province. Armed with hatchets and sharpened piñon sticks, they cut and chisel the tough spiked leaves to get at the central stalks and crowns, a rigorous operation of several days. The men dig the cooking pits and layer them with stones and wood carried from the timbered heights. Proper rites accompany the firing, the sacred cattail pollen being strewn in the cardinal directions and the torches applied at these points.

The harvested material is thrown into the pit with wet grass, covered with dirt, and steamed for the ceremonial four days. The whole process is grueling dawn-to-dark work, but evenings around the campfires are social gatherings, terminating in the feast when finally the mescal is cooked. Eaten in this state it is sweet, sticky, and satisfying, accompanied by any game the hunters might bring in. The women's last chore is to pound the remaining mescal with large rocks into flat sheets which, well dried in the sun, will keep indefinitely. The fibrous chunks can be softened in water and gnawed on alone or cooked into various pudding-like concoctions.

A potent liquor can be made from the juice of the mescal, but the drink is more common below the border; the Mescaleros prefer *talpai*, or *tiswin*, made from sprouted corn, on which many drunken orgies are blamed—unfairly, Father Al believed. He'd gone to some of their *tiswin* parties in the forest, sampled the brew, and found it "about like beer . . . [I]t took an awful lot of tiswin to get drunk, and they didn't have that much." The drunken orgies, he added, were usually "because some white man was bootlegging bad liquor to 'em."[12]

Whether Father Al ever participated in a mescal excursion is not on record; but given his tireless horseback ministry, he must have come more than once on a mescal camp, by accident or invitation. Meshing into their lives as he did, he would have joined the action, and would almost certainly have added his own prayer to the ceremony. "That's what made him different," one Mescalero averred. "He became part of the community."[13]

Sometimes Father Al went to the cow camps. Once a woman in camp "was about to have a baby," according to a friend. "The husband was off somewhere, and she wouldn't call him until it was over. The other women were bustling around—there were buckets of water heating in front of the tepee. . . . Finally the baby was born—a little girl and she was beautiful. So Father said to them, 'You say there is no God? See this beautiful little girl? God permitted her to be born.' They called her Rosa.

"Another time he was at a cow camp and it was night. Everybody was sleeping in a circle around the fire, and a guy was right behind him and all night long he kept spitting in the fire, right over Father Albert. He was so willing to live the way they lived, you know. And later, after he left for [World War II] and these other priests came in to take his place—it wasn't ever the same."

It was likely on a cattle drive that he met Pete Crawford, or maybe at Three Rivers where Crawford lived. "Pete was a black man, or part black. A wonderful man. . . . He was a cook on the cattle drives. We saw him take a twenty pound sack of flour and make biscuits right in the flour sack—he put liquid in the flour and lifted up the dough and made his biscuits. He didn't mess the rest of the flour—he had to do it that way on the range—just hand-gather enough to make the biscuits."[14]

Eating with the Apaches, camping with them, swapping yarns and philosophies around their campfires, matching their wry humor with jokes of his own, Al Braun by his own testimony learned as much as he taught.

He learned simplicity. So recently from seminary and steeped in theological doctrine, he was once trying to explain the reality of the transcendent God and having a difficult time. "He gave a pretty good explanation," as he later told it to Dick Mackey, "but when he finished they kind of sat there, so he tried again. 'Well,' he said, 'you know God is not visible, and you can't touch Him,' and he was explaining, and still they just sat. Finally one [reportedly Roman Chiquita] said, 'Yes, we know that—we go out and see tracks in the snow, and we don't see the turkey. But we know he's there.'"[15]

Father Al would later tell that story often, always grinning at the simple explanation that had shamed his academic one. Through the years he used the turkey-tracks illustration in his own sermons.

The miles he rode would have daunted lesser men. To him they were—*Insignificant!* He obviously loved life on the trails, sitting around their campfires, hearing the stories the Mescaleros loved to tell—their mythology, their beliefs and traditions, their explanations of the cosmos, their daily habits, and the symbolism that gave meaning to each simple task. He loved sleeping in their tepees, in cool summer breezes or frigid winter gales. He loved the Mescaleros.

The Mescaleros soon loved him. Passive acceptance became active friendship, smiles of polite acknowledgment became grins of joy when he rode into their camps. If there was work afoot, he pitched in to help. Sometimes he hunted with the men, and earned their respect: if he tired in the saddle he never showed it. He was, moreover, a crack shot—like an Apache.

On one occasion—he often laughed about it—"They were all around the fire, and they had their wives with them, and going into the tepees after a bit, the elders offered him one of the Indian girls for the night. He didn't quite know what to do, but he made some joke or other and wiggled out. He used to tell these stories on himself."[16]

Father Al administered the sacraments, brought his God to their camps, never trying to change their culture, but embracing it with the wide arms of his welcoming Church. He saved his sermons for the pulpit; at the campfire he preferred dialogue to oratory. He talked of his God, but he learned also of theirs.

He learned of Ussen,[17] the Apache god who had created the world and everything in it, and who, when evil monsters were devouring the people, sent to earth White-Painted-Woman and impregnated her with lightning and falling water, thereby begetting Child-of-Water. They told him how the child grew and went forth to slay the monsters, each in turn, and saved the people from destruction by evil. They told him how, when Child-of-Water died, he returned to his earthly form before ascending to be with his father Ussen.

The analogy is obvious to the Christian mind: the son, begotten on a virgin by extraordinary means to bring salvation, who dies, is resurrected, and returns briefly to earth—an analogy not lost on Father Albert.[18] Listening to this and other beliefs, he gained an immense respect for the inherent spirituality of these people who, however they differed in myth and method, worshipped a benevolent Creator not so very different from his own.

He learned too of the mountain spirits that Ussen sent to correct the people when they fell into error in their ways, to help and instruct them. Had not the saints—including the founder of his Order—come for like reasons? Was not Ussen, like his own Creator, a god of forgiveness? Could not he build on these similarities to bring Christ to his people?

Throughout his life Father Al had little use for rectories, or for priests who sat in them passively waiting for their parishioners to come to them. "I'd like to see every damned rectory blown to rubble," he wrote and said repeatedly throughout his life, often shocking his fellow Franciscans. "Christ told his disciples to go out into the world, not sit on their butts at a desk and move papers around."

Although a number of Mescaleros were nominally Catholic, he realized the Church had far to go to reach its potential among them. As late as 1881 Superintendent Llewellyn had reported that no missionary had ever appeared at the agency.[19] Two years later Father José Sambrano Tafoya visited the reservation, revived whatever Christian influence may have survived from early Spanish contacts, and baptized 173 Mescaleros. But the following year Padre Sambrano died from injuries suffered when he was thrown from his wagon and dragged through treacherous terrain by runaway horses. No missionary followed for another six years.

In 1887 clerics from Saint Francis de Paola in Tularosa began looking toward the Mescaleros and according to tradition made some horseback treks into the tribal mountains the following year. If so, they doubtless encountered some of those Padre Sambrano had baptized earlier; but any sorties they may have made were peremptory at best. Cummings notes that "no priest is known to have followed up on Padre Sambrano's work until after the turn of the century."[20]

In 1902 Henry Granjon, Bishop of Tucson, visited Tularosa (then in his diocese), noted the Mescaleros, and wrote it "would be a matter of building a small mission chapel here, the Indians showing themselves to be admirably disposed. . . ."[21] In that same year Father Lucien Migeon, the new pastor in Tularosa, began saying mass fairly regularly at Mescalero and 1912 built the small adobe church that Father Al found waiting.

In the meantime Dutch Reformed missionaries had arrived in 1907, erected a church, established residence, and were making considerable headway among the Mescaleros. Migeon thereupon challenged their Reverend Mr. Harper vigorously; the rivalry grew bitter, spread into the largely Protestant agency, and spilled into the political arena throughout the countryside when Migeon became involved in the 'Tularosa Ditch War.' Believing the Anglos in general and Senator Fall in particular were trying to deprive the Indians and Mexicans of water, he stirred passions throughout the countryside. The brew boiled over with the murder of Migeon's friend and helper Ralph Connell in June 1914, shot from his horse while driving a herd of cattle to Mescalero. The murderer then threatened to kill Migeon next.

Father Ferdinand arrived in Tularosa to inherit the mess. With the help of Father William Ketcham, Director of the Catholic Indian Bureau (BCIM) in Washington, Ferdinand began to soothe passions and smooth relations. Ketcham had earlier talked with Fall, who, he wrote, "spoke very highly of Father Migeon but contended that he was very unwise in stirring up the Mexicans in regard to the water question in Tularosa. He said that Father Migeon is really responsible for the death of Connell" and feared for the priest's safety "if he continues in this litigation."[22]

When Father Albert arrived in 1916, unaware of the contretemps, he saw his tiny church and the not-much-larger Dutch Reformed structure sitting on their respective hills like bookends propping the agency community in the glen between. Christianity of either persuasion was still tentative among the Mescaleros, he could see. But the ground was fertile, Al Braun was afire and feisty, and the expanse of rugged terrain was an invigorating challenge.

As he learned the trails and the topography he expanded his range of travel. "I have begun to read mass at Whitetail," he wrote in November 1917. "It is my intention to have mass there [every] week. . . ."[23]

Whitetail Spring nestled below Sierra Blanca fifteen miles northeast of Mescalero on the map, considerably farther on winding trails. Here a group of Chiricahuas and Lipans, when released from Fort Sill, had settled with a few Mescaleros, among them two of Eric's companions from the Carlisle school, Victor Dolan and Clarence Enjady. Here lived many who had fought in the Indian wars, or whose fathers had. Here was Kae-e-te-na who had fought alongside Nana and Victorio, remained incorrigible, and once tried to kill Lieutenant Britten Davis. After eighteen months at Alcatraz he had been pardoned, and became a scout. Here were Kayita and Martine, scouts who had led Lieutenant Gatewood through the Sierra Madres to Geronimo's camp to discuss surrender, only to be betrayed and sent with the renegades into captivity. "His son, Kent Kayita," Father Al stated, "was my interpreter at Mescalero" along with Eric Tortilla. "Martine . . . was one of the peaceful ones. He was like old man Kayita—he acted as go-between among the Apaches who went on the warpath with the army.[24]

Here also was the famous warrior Naiche, son of Cochise, grandson of

Mangas Coloradas and a chief in his own right, the real leader of Geronimo's Chiricahuas. "Naiche was a warrior. After being a POW he became very religious—became chief of my lay workers."[25] Naiche had fought a fierce fight, suffered an inevitable defeat, settled eventually and peacefully with the Mescaleros, and became a stable member of the tribal community.

"Geronimo," the padre believed, "had a reason to go on the warpath, a feeling of revenge because his sister had been killed" by a duplicitous White Eyes. Until then, "Geronimo was not so much a warrior as an advisor. He was considered the prudent and wise man among the Indians. He knew when to attack and when not to. There were others more warlike than he was."[26]

There too was Daklugie who, though he never lost his intense hatred for the White Eyes, often attended mass—partly, he said, "because of my love and respect for Father Albert. Much of his teachings were . . . just what we had believed long before the coming of the Black Robes."[27]

The 'Fort Sill' Indians, having so recently arrived at Mescalero, had still vividly fresh recollections: their stories impacted strongly on the padre. "The only reports on the Apache," he often said, "were written by white men"—racketeers, he called them, who followed the army—"evil reports from an unfair side."[28]

Night after night around their campfires they told him their stories. "When they were taking the Indians to Fort Sill"—he told it as they told him—"one of them jumped out the window and escaped. He hid in the shrubbery. They didn't see him. He made his way back to Arizona and went into the mountains between Sonora and Chihuahua. He got lonely and came back to pick up an Indian woman for a wife. He went to Rinconada where the Indian women were out picking *piñones*. He had two stolen horses and . . . a gun. . . . When the women were picking up the piñon nuts he rushed out and grabbed an Indian woman and took off with her. They had six children.

"When he thought he was going to die he decided to take his family back to the reservation. . . . He would die in the mountains. Near Hot Springs one of the horses played out. He killed a cowboy and took his horse. Other cowboys followed and killed him." The mother got the rest of her family to the reservation, where, Father Al reported, "one of the children died of fright at seeing all the people."[29]

Among the younger bucks, closer to his own age, were some of the warriors' sons. Roman Chiquita, son of Chief Roman, was among this group. Asa Daklugie was the son of the notoriously cruel warrior Juh; Daklugie's wife Ramona and her brother Eugene were children of Chief Chihuahua. Here was Geronimo's son Robert, who had attended the Carlisle school, and with whom the padre often talked football in the evenings.

Father Al divided each week between his life on the trail and the needs of his parishioners in the Mescalero settlement—Indian, Hispanic, or Anglo. From his Spartan quarters he maintained correspondence with his fellow clergy, reported regularly to his Father Provincial, his immediate superior Father Ferdinand, and Bishop Schuler in El Paso.

Close by Father Al's quarters lived George and Lucy Dorame and their children. "My parents took Father Albert under their wing," recalled their daughter Mary. "My mother did his laundry and the church laundry and kept the church up. My dad was a policeman on the reservation, and also a maintenance man for Father Albert. . . . He was just like family."[30] The whole settlement seemed like a family. George Dorame and his brother were 'Uncle George' and 'Uncle Frank' to all the children in the community. Their father—'Old Man Dorame' Father Al called him—had been a Yaqui Indian who had somehow landed in Mescalero.

Father Al remained close to the Millers. Blasa seemed like everyone's grandmother. "She was considered a midwife of the tribe. Assisted at the birthings down by the stream. They'd build a little lean-to of branches and she'd go down there and deliver the babies."[31] She took care of any church business that arose while Father Al was riding the trails. She made sure his saddlebags contained, in addition to his mass vessels and vestments, food and other necessities.

Blasa's husband, Captain Sam, served as agency manager of the Mescaleros' farming projects and helped them in many other ways, often policing when too raucous a *tiswin* party threatened the peace of the reservation, though always with wry humor and often with an unseeing eye. The Mescaleros respected him so highly "they wanted to bring him into the tribe as an honorary member, to have all privileges. It went all the way up to Washington," Dick Mackey remembers. "We have the records. But some politician, who didn't even know what was going on, said 'there's no way. He's a white person there on the reservation.' What's interesting is the document the Indians submitted. The signatures of the Indians were just little lines. I guess the writing wasn't to the level expected [in Washington]."[32]

The Millers' daughter Katherine had a musical bent. She learned to play the piano and organ, by ear or from one of the agency wives, and from the time she was twelve years old played for the services in the church. Those who knew her still comment also on her lovely singing voice.

The Mackeys were another long-time Mescalero family. Patrick Mackey, an Irishman who had migrated from Dublin, joined the westward movement (possibly with the army), landed at the agency, married a Mescaleran named Roquita, and stayed. Their son Charles (Al Braun's friend) was, his son Dick attested, "a rascal. He liked to have a good time and so did Father Albert. They used to get together. My dad worked in the boiler room at Mescalero—he was kind of the head plumber. They were just young guys. They'd play cards, have a little wine. Father Albert was that way—he'd go to dances and be the life of the party. He was really a tremendous human being."[33]

Father Albert and Charles crossed often below the border to Juárez. "They'd go down on the train and have a great time. There was some lady on the train one time who really took a shine to Father Albert [who of necessity always removed his collar when crossing into revolutionary Mexico] and she wanted him to meet her that night. He said that oh, he had a terrible headache and just couldn't! They went down there many times and always had a great time."[34]

For all his love of fun, Father Albert was dead serious when it came to his religion, his duty, and his people. He abhorred idleness—"the agent of the Devil" he called it. Though his ultimate mission focused on their souls, he worked always to improve the earthly conditions of these very poor people, ever conscious of what he called his 'worldly motive.' It was his instinct to care for the whole man—the material as well as the soul within—an instinct that would develop throughout his life into a deeply reasoned philosophy.

The padre was soon saying masses all over the reservation. He seemed never to tire. Work energized him. His innate joie de vivre was widened and deepened by his growing joy in having become a Franciscan priest. His enormous exuberance, like a running brook, had found a channel toward that great river of militant faith into which he could merge his own small strength.

"He would say the Gospel and then Eric Tortilla would interpret in Apache," Virginia Shanta Klinekole remembered. "Father picked up some

Apache, but he wasn't a fluent speaker. I might also say that some of our people taught him the not-so-pleasant Apache words, too. He learned them all. He would converse with the Spanish people too. He spoke Spanish and English and some Apache."[35] (He also spoke French and German; but, he told his niece, "he thought in Latin, because that covers everything."[36])

As he went to the people, so they began to come to him—to mass in Mescalero, or to his tiny quarters where "he always had a pot of pinto beans boiling. When anybody came to see him he shared from that pot of beans."[37]

He was in Tularosa frequently to work or consult with Father Ferdinand. There in the largely Hispanic village he made many friends, foremost among them the Baldonado family—'Don Juan,' his wife Virginia, and their children. Often they came up the hill for mass in Mescalero; their sons often served as altar boys. For the rest of the padre's life he would cherish the Baldonados as his second family.

He reached out to everyone, Catholic or not, on the reservation and off. He soon made friends with Senator Albert Fall and his gracious wife Emma and was often a guest in their home. He was likely suspicious of Fall initially because of the senator's bill (introduced in 1912 and again in 1916) for making the Mescalero reservation into a national park—a bill the Indians and the padre opposed vehemently. But the bill went nowhere, and Al Braun seems instinctively to have liked the tall, courteous southerner in boots and black Stetson. Doubtless the two argued the issue hotly, both being men of strong opinions and quick to voice them. Neither changed the other's mind; but both were innate gentlemen, able to differ in viewpoint and remain good friends.

The padre seems quickly to have made friends with virtually everyone in the immediate countryside. In the village of La Luz he met William Ashton Hawkins, a former law partner of Fall's, later attorney for the Rock Island and Southern Railways in New Mexico, and a prominent figure in the state's legal and political circles, during territorial days and into the hard-fought-for statehood. As a partner of Charles B. Eddy (for whom he handled all the legal work) he was, among other ventures, instrumental in founding the town of Alamogordo, in bringing the El Paso and Northeastern Railroad through the Tularosa basin, and in the formation of Otero County. Fall and Hawkins, neither of them Catholics, became staunch supporters of Al Braun and of his many efforts among the Mescaleros.

In a letter written years later, Father Albert tells a poignant love story:

In August 1916 I met Robert Geronimo, soon we became close friends. Robert was conceived at Alabama. His mother go[t] permission to leave prison camp and go to Mescalero, so that her child might be born there. Later Robert often visited his father at Fort Sill. He attended the school at Chilaco and later at Carlisle. For a short time he was at a seminary in New England, but was never ordained.

Ester Rodriguez was a Lipan Apache . . . [from] Coahuila, Mexico. In 1903 Supdt. James A. Carroll authorized Father Migeon to escort the Lipan Apaches from Mexico to Mescalero, New Mexico. . . .[38] The Apaches at Mescalero wanted more Apaches on their reservation to remove the necessity of marrying close relatives. Many of the Lipan Apaches had tuberculosis, among them Ester Rodriguez. Dr. Calaway, the agency doctor, took much interest in his patients. He arrested the progress of Ester's illness. To safeguard her against rain snow and cold weather and also to see that she ate nourishing food Dr. Calaway had Ester appointed an assistant to the girls' matron. She had a private room in the girls' dormitory and three times each day she ate wholesome food.

In 1916 Robert fell in love with Ester and Ester with Robert. They wanted to marry. Ester was only 16 years and needed the consent of her parents to get a marriage license. Dr. Calaway was disturbed when he heard that Robert and Ester were about to get married. He called on Ester's parents and advised them not to sign their consent. Doc told the parent[s] their daughter would become pregnant . . . and in her physical condition could not carry a child and would revert to active T.B.—with the birth of the first child Ester would die.

Robert and Ester were very unhappy. Robert came to me and asked me to change the minds of Ester's parents. First I spoke with Dr. Calaway. He told me what he did and why he did it. I said: Doctor, some people, especially Indians, would rather be dead than not have what they want. Doctor, a good friend, said: Father, from here on you handle the case. I spoke with Ester. "Why are you unhappy." She said, the Doctor has interfered with our marriage. I said: "Ester, Doctor is your good friend; he has done much for you. He knows, soon after you are married you will become pregnant. . . . [W]ith the birth of the first child, you will die.

This beautiful young girl looked at me and said: Father if I can give Robert one child, I will be happy to die. The parents then consented to the marriage. In Jan or Feb of 1917 they were married. Ester gave Robert 5 children and never did die of T.B. When Ester died, Robert married her sister, Juanita, so the 5 children would have an aunt as a stepmother. . . .

P.S. Robert and Ester's first daughter was named "Liberty"; she was born during a [World War I] Liberty Loan Drive. . . .[39]

As Christmas 1916 approached Father Al began to stash gifts for his Mescaleros. (He considered all Indians on the reservation—Chiricahuas, Lipans, or any other tribesmen—'his Mescaleros.') He had received the usual mission boxes of used clothes and, never bashful about soliciting money for his people, he extracted donations from friends in California and elsewhere with which to buy fruit, candy, and toys for all the children and gifts for all adults, Catholic or non, on the reservation. The Millers, the Mackeys, the Dorames, and the Shantas all helped him prepare.

As Christmas week approached the Apaches began to gather, by wagon or astride, and tepees began to stipple the valley. Christmas, like all celebrations, was a time for feasting, and the families prepared for the great tribal barbeque. By Christmas Eve the entire canyon was glutted with tepees, wagons, and horses, and the canyon echoed with shouts of adults and the gleeful cries of playing children.

The church was far too small for such a gathering. No matter: the skies were wide, the hillside broad, and great bonfires warmed flesh and soul as Father Albert intoned the midnight mass. Those who knew the songs sang, accompanied by guitars and led by Katherine Miller and a small choir. Then followed the timeless drums and kirtled dancers, and all looked to the same God, call Him Christ or Ussen. Catholic and non-Catholic were one at the midnight celebration and at the gifts and the feast on Christmas Day as the aroma of roasting meat rolled through the valley.

Perhaps the time for a larger church was closer than Fathers Al and Ferdinand had thought. The dream that would drive Al Braun for the next quarter century apparently began to gestate in the icy December of 1916.

✛✛✛

It was a dream that would have to wait. For 1917 brought crisis and climax—in Europe, in America, and in Mescalero, New Mexico. In the mind and soul of Albert Braun, OFM. Since the outbreak of war in Europe in 1914 he had watched with the rest of America as his country steered its path toward collision. American ships (many carrying supplies to the Allies) became increasingly vulnerable to German submarines; Americans traveling on Allied passenger ships were likewise endangered. The climax came with the torpedoing of the British liner *Lusitania* in May 1915. Nearly 1,200 civilians—128 of them Americans—died. American outrage elicited a German quasi pledge a year later to cease attacking American ships—but with strings attached.

Ignoring the provisos, Americans continued to ship food and munitions to Britain, whose navy in turn blockaded German ports. To break the blockade, Germany announced on 31 January 1917 the immediate resumption of unrestricted submarine warfare. U-boats would sink on sight, without warning, all ships in the war zone. Britannia might rule the waves, but the U-boats commanded the depths.

Four days later Wilson broke diplomatic relations with Germany.

In Europe the western Allied armies were mired in blood, mud, and misery in the trenches of France. On the eastern front Russia tossed rudderless in a sea of anarchy, the weak Nicholas II at the helm, isolated by a mad monk and a corrupt court. Rebellion among disaffected Russian soldiers and starving masses swelled like a tidal wave. Riots bred and spread. The Duma and the army forced the Czar's abdication, and on 16 March the Romanov dynasty fell. The crumbling of their Russian partner set off alarms for the Allies, and for an America sympathetic to the Allies.

In Mescalero, New Mexico, Father Al followed these events closely as (weather allowing) the postman brought mail, newspapers, and his own observations from Tularosa. Already incensed over reports of German spies and saboteurs in America, the padre was doubtless infuriated with the rest of the country when headlines screamed of the bizarre Zimmerman cable, sent in January from the German foreign secretary to his minister in Mexico, intercepted, decoded, and released to the press on 1 March. In the event of war with the United States, Zimmerman instructed, the minister was to work for a German-Mexican alliance, through which Mexico would regain her 'lost' territories of Texas, Arizona, and New Mexico.

New Mexico? The padre doubtless boiled at this arrogance. He followed events closely. Father Ambrose came to visit and they talked long. In the evenings with his young Apaches the talk grew less about football and more about war.

On that same pivotal 16 March when Czarist Russia fell, U-boats sank four unarmed American ships. On 2 April Wilson asked for a declaration of war. On the fourth the Senate voted aye; the House followed at 3 a.m. on the sixth.

Father Albert rose at dawn that 6 April to an America at war. It was Good Friday. Reflecting on the Crucifixion, and on the certain deaths of many American boys, and after the deep prayer with which he faced all significant decisions, Father Albert Braun knew where his duty lay. The Germany of 1917 was the inheritor of the Prussian militarism of Bismarck's *kulturkampf* from which his father had fled. The America of 1917 was the America in whose haven John Braun had reared his family.

Before the sun had set Father Albert had conducted solemnly intense Good Friday services, prepared for the Easter mass, and written a long and deeply committed letter. American forces would be injured and dying in France, he wrote the Reverend Father Provincial Hugolinus Storff. They would need spiritual help; the army would need chaplains. He, Albert Braun, must serve God and his country at the front. With the Father Provincial's permission he would volunteer at once.[40]

Having mailed the letter, and expecting to report soon for duty, he announced his decision to Father Ferdinand and to Bishop Schuler, tended his mission in Mescalero, and awaited his pending permission. Then—

"In answer, I got a dirty letter from father provincial, Hugolinus Storff. 'I always knew you were an adventurer. Never again do I want to hear army from you. What a shame for a Franciscan to even think of leaving the poor Indians, so that he can enjoy the wild life of the army.'"[41]

What inner wrestling Al Braun went through is unknown. Being a young buck, a man of action, and one who always leaped to the challenge, he doubtless chafed when ordered to sit out a war on the sidelines. Having resolved in prayer where his duty lay, he obviously believed it the command of God, which exceeded that of Hugolinus Storff. But Hugolinus was the boss, and obedience was a solemn Franciscan vow. Like Saint Francis, Al Braun must continue to hoe his own garden.

✠ ✠ ✠

Spring looked toward summer. Church attendance was swelling, along with the buds on the apple trees and the tiny swellings on the piñons. Father's bean plants were sprouting. The Mescaleros were happily preparing for the puberty ceremonies, and their young priest anticipated the occasion as much as they. These were rites of solemn passage and joyful feasting, deeply symbolic, the great celebration of life and of the womanhood that perpetuated life. The puberty rituals were the bedrock of Apache tradition.

Then like distant drums came warning signals that threatened to destroy this most sacred of rites. Ussen might be in his heaven, but all was not right in his world.

The first overt signal came from the agency. It was the government's position, and also that of the Dutch Reformed Church, the agent told Father Al, that the pagan ceremony must be banned. This was only one more step in the long-time campaign to Christianize and 'civilize' the Apaches. In this proposed crackdown, the agent continued, they would need the cooperation of the Catholic Church and its mission priest. Would Father Albert stand firm with them and deny the sacraments to all participating in the heathen rites?

Father Albert was noncommittal: he would have to consult his superiors.

In fact he already knew his immediate superior's views. Father Ferdinand had recently instructed him to forbid the Catholic girls to participate in the ceremonies. But the padre could not see the rites as pagan. Nor did he wish to see the tribal culture erode step by step from outside meddling until the Apaches would, as a people, cease to be. Unlike the meddlers, he had observed the Apache ways through close association, from which came his profound respect for their traditions; he understood the deeply spiritual meanings of the ceremonies as explained by Eric Tortilla.

When an Apache girl reaches puberty she is ready to enter womanhood, through the rites conducted each summer. As she had been formed physically in her mother's womb, so must she pass through the spiritual womb to receive her soul and become a woman. The four-day rite signifies this womb-time.

Each movement is symbolic, and follows the instructions of White-

Painted-Woman, the Apache virgin mother. It is in essence a preparation for the sacred duties of marriage and motherhood, for which Ussen had created each female child—as Father Albert's creator had made woman His instrument in the perpetuation of life. Father Al, whose adoration of the Blessed Virgin extended to a great respect for all women, determined that this beautiful rite must not be taken from the Mescaleros. The problem was that Father Ferdinand, his close friend and superior, had already stated his opposition.

Insignificant! The padre would go to the top. He would invite Bishop Schuler to the July ceremony, have Eric explain the meanings as the rites progressed, and let the bishop understand the significance, feel the spirit, and take in the beauty for himself.

Preparations accelerated. The girls' grandmothers, who traditionally made the elaborate buckskin dresses, had been working—some for years—on the robes, which Father Al described as "beautiful and ornate, . . . covered with beaded Indian designs, all of them significant, expressing a deep mystery of life, procreation."[42]

The time grew close, and the young men began clearing the feast ground, erecting the brush shelters where enormous quantities of food would be stored, cooked, and served, and digging the fire pits for roasting the meat. Though the ceremonies were deeply solemn, the occasion was joyous for the entire tribe and was celebrated accordingly. The young men prepared to cut the trees, strip the bark, and amass the foliage for the ceremonial tepee. In each task the girls-to-be-women took part, in anticipation of their coming matronly duties.

Father Albert smiled and kept his own counsel. He too had prepared.

The smoky pungency of roasting meat hung over the canyon long before dawn on the first day of the celebration. The rising sun soon dimmed the campfires and began to burn through the morning chill as the Jesuit bishop and the Franciscan priest walked to the feasting grounds. Anthony Schuler was an earthy man, close to the humankind he served, a man of humor, tolerance, and perception. A man whose instincts Father Albert trusted. As expected, he fell into the activities heartily. As arranged, Eric instructed him, and, knowing the meaning, the bishop understood the ceremony as an act of piety, far from the grotesque pagan screamings so often described by the uninitiated.

The priests watched the large ceremonial tepee go up. To the accompaniment of deer hoof rattles and chants, which is to say of prayer, the first four poles, having already been cut, stripped, and blessed, were erected, each pointing in a cardinal direction. The other eight poles followed and the frame was formed. Green tufts were left at the tips to filter the evil spirits from entering the interior. The tepee was then covered with hides and branches and protected by screens of brush and branch in a horseshoe shape, opening to the east to face the generative rising sun. Within, the men were digging the fire pit in its center, around which the sacred rites would be performed.

The padres visited and feasted with the crowd awaiting the maidens. In proper time the girls entered, solemnly, each newly bathed, anointed, and dressed in her ceremonial garments, her amole-washed hair hanging free. Each was accompanied by her *yadeche*, usually an elder kinswoman, somewhat analogous to the Christian godmother, who had been entrusted with the maiden's care, instruction, and guidance through the ceremony. Outside the tepee's opening, each girl and her *yadeche* activated fire with firesticks, chanting traditional prayers, after which the *yadeche* carried firebrands to light the flame within.

The two fathers saw the medicine man bless the girls with sacred cattail pollen on their foreheads, whereby each symbolically became White-Painted-Woman, and with her power the maiden in turn blessed the medicine men and the line of relatives and friends, each with the golden pollen, which "is the fertilizer. Red signifies the bloodstreams of life."[43] They heard the strange shrill cries of the *yadeches* whenever the Creator or the Mountain Spirits were named; and as evening darkened the canyon they watched the men build the great bonfire in the center of the grounds to give light and keep away the evil spirits. They heard the chants of the medicine men inside the tepee, and the deer hoof rattles, and they knew the maidens were beginning their women's dances around the fire pits. Each dance was a prayer. "Any Indian knows the meaning," the padre wrote. "Any Indian knows heat, warmth, brings new life; plants don't sprout through frozen ground."[44]

Into the arena came the male dancers in separate groups. Kirtled and moccasined, crowned with their great forked headdresses and holding symbolic objects, they danced about the enormous central fire, to pull the evil spirits from the tepee and lead them into the darkness after each dance.

On the climactic fourth night the maidens danced until, with the sunrise, they were ready for the dawn run. With pollen the medicine men drew a symbolic 'devil's pit,' the maidens' mothers bridged it with rawhide, and the *yadeches* covered that with buckskins, on which the medicine men drew a sun symbol and pollen footprints pointing toward the east.

The maidens emerged from the tepee carrying their medicine baskets filled with sacred objects. Each, led by a medicine man with an eagle's feather, then crossed the bridge from childhood into womanhood, following the pollen footsteps to the east. "To the south and north," the padre continued, "the entire tribe lines up in front of the girls, forming a runway to the east. Everybody is silent and in solemn expectation. As the first rays of the sun break over the horizon, the ceremonial girls . . . dash toward the life-giving sun, and thus forcefully express their eagerness for the new life."[45]

They ran a short way, left their baskets, and ran back. The symbolic bridge had been removed, the tepee torn down. Only the four cardinal poles had been left standing. The maidens could never return to childhood.

Four times they ran; each time the baskets had been moved closer to the sun. On the fourth the poles were dropped. Throughout the ceremony they had heard the medicine men chant the tale of creation, and of their own part as women in Ussen's plan for the proliferation of life. Each maiden had entered the ceremony chaste, and on this day each was a woman: she had received from Ussen the great gift of procreation.

"Every Indian, seeing the beautiful ceremony, understands and is filled with awe and respect for the sacred mystery of generation. Every Indian knows the primary purpose of marriage is to have children. These simple people," the padre concluded sternly—and doubtless expressed the same sentiment to the bishop—"put us to shame . . . . They can teach us the sacredness of the natural law, God's law . . . [with] their religious respect for motherhood."[46]

"What a beautiful belief," said Father Al, "to honor a maiden because she is going to be a mother."[47]

At Sunday's mass Bishop Schuler gave his blessing to the rites, approved Catholic girls' participation, and sanctioned the ancient tradition.

That ended the matter. The agency was defanged and Ferdinand silenced, if not sweepingly convinced. The rite remained to him "a weird spectacle, a mysterious religious dance, a remnant of paganism . . ." that took him "back to the time when the Indians were still wild and the dark hills resounded with their songs and yells and the whites, who heard the echoes, whispered that the Apaches were dancing and that new trouble was brewing."

Nonetheless, scholar that he was, he wrote an objective, nonjudgmental description of this "sight that can never be forgotten."[48]

Mescalero-Apache Crown Dancers. Courtesy of SJAM.

The frame is erected for the maidens' sacred tepee, preparatory to the puberty rites. Courtesy of MUA.

At some time in 1917 Father Al acquired an automobile, likely a gift from his father. (By all accounts the padre was a terrible but enthusiastic driver.) Though of little use on the reservation, his 'machine' facilitated access to Tularosa, Alamogordo, and El Paso—forays he seized on gleefully.

That fall Clarence and Isabel Enjady, though non-Catholics, asked that their firstborn son be baptized into the Church, along with Isabel and her sister. At about the same time Bishop Schuler was preparing for the dedication of the newly completed Saint Patrick's Cathedral in El Paso and believed, with the tribe such a part of the area's history, that it would be fitting for a Mescalero to be the first to be baptized there.

So it was that Father Albert arranged to drive the Enjadys to El Paso in his 'machine.' Upon returning he wrote his provincial.

> I went in the machine and took four Indians with me. Marion Sims also went in his machine and took his wife and niece, so there were seven Indians at the dedication. One, . . . a baby fourteen months old was baptized in the cathedral by the Bishop. He received the names Anthony Patrick in honor of the Bishop and the cathedral's patron . . . .
>
> The dedication services greatly impressed the Indians. They didn't think there were as many American Catholics in the whole U.S. as attended the dedication because the protestants here had told them that only Mexicans are Catholic. . . .

He ended the letter with typical Al Braun insouciance. "Father, what are you going to buy me for Xmas? Get me a casing for the back wheel of the auto. I need one very badly . . . . How am I for a faithful mendicant?"[49]

Increasingly the Mescaleros came to Father Albert to ask advice or share a confidence, a joke, a cup of coffee or a bowl of the *frijoles* always bubbling on the tiny rectory woodstove. Often they brought him a haunch of venison or a leg of mutton, which he knew Lucy Dorame or Blasa Miller would be happy to cook.

Some came to talk about the war. Congress had passed a conscription law in May, and on 5 June some nine-and-a-half million men across America registered. Indians were exempted from the draft, and many felt hurt. But they could still volunteer. Their country was at war and they were the sons of warriors. What did the padre think?

He seems not have told them he too had tried to enlist. But he encouraged and blessed them. Some took him up the steep trails onto Sierra Blanca to discuss these deep thoughts on the slopes where the mountain spirits lived. It was a tribute worthy of the man who had enlisted the bishop and secured his endorsement of their sacred Puberty Ceremony. The Mescaleros had learned they could trust Al Braun.

Christmas came, and the new year, and it was 1918. Some of the Mescaleros had gone to war, and so had the padre's friend Charlie Mackey. Al Braun never dwelled on disappointment, but he obviously still believed his provincial wrong. He knew he could best serve his God and his country at the front, and he chafed at the restraint. Of his Franciscan vows, obedience seems to have come hardest to Albert Braun. No penance could have been as harsh: his country was at war, his friends were with the rest of America's men on the playing field, and he was warming a bench on the sidelines.

Father Al with unidentified Apache men and two maidens dressed for the puberty ceremonial. Courtesy of MUA.

III

THE ADVENTURER

"C'est la guerre, soldier.*"*

Lieutenant Albert Braun, Chaplain, U.S. Army, World War I. Courtesy of SJAM.

7: OVER THERE

Father Al followed the war news as it made its sporadic way with the mail from Tularosa. He doubtless exulted (perhaps with a trace of envy) when the first small contingent of the American Expeditionary Force landed in France on 26 June 1917, from which one battalion marched into Paris amid cheering throngs, and on America's Independence Day laid a wreath on the hero's tomb. "Lafayette, we are here!"[1]

He read, too, less exultantly, of the German advance. The Americans could do nothing of significance until their troops arrived in numbers, and that would take months. Parisian spirits may have soared as the doughboys arrived, but French morale at the front was dangerously low. Their armies were bled dry by enormous casualties, pounded by the unceasing thunder of artillery and bursting shells, and exhausted by the endless hell of wet trenches, barbed wire, and the stench of death. The Allied ranks could not stand alone, Pershing advised the War Office and requested a million men by spring.

America began frantically to assemble, train, and equip such an army, to build a navy capable of transporting men, munitions, and rations across the Atlantic, and to boost production of matériel to transport. Time was essential, the race was on to 'make the world safe for democracy,' and Al Braun was not a part of it.

He read of disaster after disaster as the newspapers arrived throughout the troubled autumn of 1917. Following a devastating defeat at Caporetto in October, the Italian army collapsed materially and morally before the sweeping Austro-German advance. British and French troops, already spread thinly, were rushed to stabilize the broken army. The Italians rallied, but a crisis had been narrowly averted.

A British attempt to break the German position above Ypres slogged and bogged in mud and torrential rains that turned to November sleet, and failed miserably. The British had lost nearly a quarter million men. The Hun seemed invincible.

A ray of hope pierced the Allied gloom when, just as the Ypres debacle ended, British tanks smashed the German lines at Cambrai, only to fade when the Germans retook the position ten days later. Tank warfare had made its debut, and would prove a worthy Allied weapon in months to come, but few at the time recognized its significance.

In November Lenin's Bolsheviks toppled the unstable Kerensky government that had followed the Czarist downfall, and on 3 March 1918 made a separate peace with Germany at Brest-Litovsk. With Russia out of the war Ludendorff redeployed, reinforced, and soon had his massive German forces rolling by rail to the western front to deliver, he boasted, the *coup de main.*

The German war machine was not as invulnerable as it seemed. The Allies had lost Russia; but the Central Powers were losing Turkey. Beset in the Holy Land by Allenby's British forces on one front and Lawrence's Arabian tribesmen on the other, the Turkish armies were in retreat and the empire folding. Crippling privations weakened German resolve at home; and mutinies in the shipyards and in the army itself further sapped German strength.

But the men on the streets of London, or New York, or Tularosa, New Mexico, unaware of Teutonic woes, saw only the hulking might of the beast, reinforced on the western front. Would the million Yanks get there in time? The generals wondered too. Ludendorff vowed to crash to a quick victory before they could arrive.

Father Al tended his flock, watched for the mail truck to come bumping up the road, and discussed the war news with his friends. He saw a number of his Mescaleros off to war, blessing each as he left. Among them was the newly married Robert Geronimo. He learned that Augustine too had tried to enlist and been denied permission.

By early 1918 the British and the Americans had considerably reduced the U-boat menace and American soldiers were sailing in swelling numbers for France. *The Yanks are coming, the Yanks are coming . . .*

But without Al Braun.

As America raced to the rescue, Germany launched the first of three tremendous offensives on 21 March. On or about the same day a letter arrived for Father Al. Nearly a year had passed since Father Hugolinus had chastened him as a wild adventurer. Meanwhile, "this same Provincial was reprimanded by the Apostolic Delegate for having no Franciscans in his Province to serve the men fighting for their country." The padre's grin must have widened as he read. "The Provincial was ordered to send four at once. I received a sweet letter asking if I were still interested."[2]

He replied immediately.

> Very sincere thanks for having granted my request.
> . . . I will . . . work to have everything in order for the one
> who is to take my place. One thing I wished to impress
> upon [you] . . . is the fact that I did not make my request
> out of a desire to get away from here. I love these Indians
> and am happy. . . . I longed to be where so very many stand
> in dire need of a priest. . . . You have my promise, if I am
> made an Army chaplain I will do all in my power to be a
> good Franciscan, be an honor to the Province and bring
> souls to God.[3]

Upon posting the letter he headed for El Paso, reported to Fort Bliss for his physical, and returned to Mescalero to finish current projects and ready affairs for his replacement, who he learned happily would be Father Ambrose—his old buddy Willy Trabert. On 27 May he departed Mescalero, reported on 1 June to Fort Zachary Taylor, Kentucky, for chaplains' school, and graduated one month later.[4]

We'll be over, we're coming over . . .

In Europe Ludendorff's hard-hitting army had penetrated Allied lines, though even as Father Al had left Mescalero an American counterattack recaptured Cantigny.

Albert Braun, First Lieutenant, 0134329, awaited his sailing orders. By this time American Marines had stopped the enemy in bloody Belleau Wood and American soldiers had halted them at Château-Thierry. On the fifteenth American and French troops saved Paris and routed the Germans in the critical second Battle of the Marne. The tide was beginning to turn.

Pershing now had his million men, more were coming, and Lieutenant Albert Braun would be among them. On 12 August he sailed from Hoboken, New Jersey, for France. As his father had fled Europe to escape Prussian militarism, he now sailed to confront it.

. . . and we won't be back 'till it's over over there. . . .

**Lieutenant Albert Braun with his parents shortly before sailing for France, 1918.
Courtesy of Dorothy Brown Bumgarner.**

Six days earlier the Allied counteroffensive, largely because of Yankee reinforcement, had reached the Aisne River. What the American doughboy lacked in military efficiency he overcame in spirit. The seventeen-mile advance had cost the Americans over 50,000 casualties, but they had reversed the direction of the enemy and of the war. The effect on morale was as significant as the military gain. A British-French victory at Amiens on 8 August, though costly, deepened German gloom—'The Black Day' Ludendorff called it. But the Germans were far from defeated.

On 10 August the United States First Army was ready to stage the initial all-American offensive.[5] Its mission: to take out the Saint-Mihiel salient. This deadly triangular bulge threatened Verdun, guarding all access from the south via roadway, rail line, and the Meuse River. Behind its base lay the fortress city of Metz, the railway center of Conflans, and the Briey iron mines, all vital to the Germans.

The salient, and the timetable given Pershing to eliminate it, presented a tough challenge. He must first assemble his newly authorized army—most of them green troops—and equip them, with more hindrance than cooperation from the British and French, from whom he must borrow artillery, tanks, and aircraft. The logistics were daunting. Men, munitions, and supplies must be transported in enormous numbers in minimal time. They must build their own roads, lay railway track, and bridge the Aisne just to position for the assault. They would face a densely fortified enemy grimly determined to hold their turf with heavy artillery, trenches, artillery-proof steel-and-concrete shelters, and miles of barbed-wire entanglements.

Once Pershing had deployed, Foch changed the plans: instead of pushing on to Metz, the mines, and the railroad complex as Pershing had envisioned—a thrust, he insisted, that could end the war quickly—he must now stop at the Hindenburg Line, turn his entire army back, and reassemble it for the assault on the Argonne forest, all no later than 25 September.

Within twenty-three days he must organize, deploy, and launch two offensives in areas forty miles apart. To stage this gargantuan production Pershing needed an all-star cast. He had one, though few would get top billing until a later war. Chief of Staff General Hugh A. Drum and Operations Officer Colonel George C. Marshall transferred and deployed over half a million men, with weapons and equipment, to the Saint-Mihiel frontier; and they largely planned the gigantic redeployment for the Argonne offensive, all secretly and at night to keep the Germans expecting an assault on Metz. Pershing had a great I Corps commander in Major General Hunter Liggett. He had a genius of artillery in Major General Charles Summerall, and another in Lieutenant Colonel Joseph Stilwell. He had Brigadier General Douglas MacArthur, who had already made a name with the 42nd 'Rainbow' Division. He had Captain George S. Patton, Jr., a former cavalryman, who became the genius of the new tank warfare. And he had Colonel Billy Mitchell, later called the father of modern air warfare, who managed to scrounge (largely from the British and the French) 800 fighter planes and 650 bombers and get them in the air for the assault on Saint-Mihiel. These were men of imagination, daring, and innovation, men whose unorthodox methods dumbfounded the enemy—and Foch as well. On the battlefields of Saint-Mihiel and the Meuse-Argonne these future titans of World War II were cutting their teeth.[6]

Tactical surprise was essential; the victory must be swift and decisive. The Germans, expecting a single-front attack, planned to pull back to a rear-guard defensive position on the Woëvre Plain and there engulf and slaughter Pershing's army. Masking their movement with heavy artillery fire and choking clouds of gas, they began withdrawing on the tenth.

They were too late. Following a three-hour American artillery barrage, Pershing hit on the twelfth, as the nearly 1,500 planes of Billy Mitchell's patchwork air force roared above, the fighters knocking enemy craft from the air, the bombers decimating German supply, rail, and artillery installations. The withdrawing enemy, trying to reverse its direction, was trapped and in retreat by the third day. By the next—16 September—the salient had been eliminated. The Americans had achieved their surprise, won their decisive victory, and met their timetable. They had taken 15,000 prisoners, regained two hundred square miles of territory, removed the threat to Verdun, and taken out the salient and its defensive positions forward of Metz. The cost: 7,000 casualties. With luck, pluck, and Yankee ingenuity, they must now reconcentrate for the formidable Meuse-Argonne offensive. They had ten days.

Assigned to the Sixth Infantry, Fifth Division, Lieutenant Albert Braun reported to Colonel H. J. Hunt, commander of the Sixth, just behind the Saint-Mihiel attack, in time for the mop-up operations. Mined fields and booby traps still threatened. Cratered roads were largely impassable. Abandoned villages were dead masses of rubble.

Father Al fell in quickly with the chaplains, working around the clock. Prisoners in the thousands must be transported, the wounded cared for physically and spiritually, the dead buried. The stench of death hung everywhere. On 23 September Father Albert wrote on Red Cross stationery to Hugolinus Storff:

> It is about a week now since I have been attached to the Sixth Infantry. I reached the regiment as it was returning from the drive. Till now I could not write you, there being so much to do. The chaplains had to check up on all the personal effects of both German and American dead, which takes up much time.
>
> . . . .
>
> Tell the next man you send to bring . . . as little as possible. We bring too much. After the first few weeks we throw one half away and not much later we lose the other half.

At present except for a few things that I stored away, all I have is on my back. Have lost bedding, clothing, and all. I will have to get blankets and many other things and lose them on the next move.

. . . .

You need not worry about us being good over here. There is no chance to be worldly here along the firing line. . . . We get no leaves and there is nothing here but evacuated towns with a few aged men & women and some youngsters. . . .

. . . .

Am perfectly happy and like the work here, but when all is over I want to get back to Mescalero.[7]

The redeployment for the Argonne offensive was a tactical marvel. The three roads over which the massive army and tons of equipment must pass were pitted with craters, mired with deep mud, and in many places had to be rebuilt. Speed and secrecy were essential. The lines moved at night, blacked out, while an elaborate maneuver of deceptive information via the wireless, designed to be intercepted and decoded, along with planted maps, convinced the Germans the next target was Metz. The wonder is, it worked. As the enemy massed to defend Metz, the American doughboys deployed for the great battle of the Great War.

Three days after Braun wrote his letter the big push began. *"Tout le monde a la bataille!"* Foch had cried with Gallic flourish—"Everyone to battle!"—and in a great pincers movement British, Belgian, and French units rallied in the north and east to strike for the Hindenburg Line, while Pershing's army regrouped to push up the German-infested Argonne Forest, arguably the strongest enemy position on the entire western front.

A central ridge runs the forest's north-south length. The American First Army would push up the Aire Valley on the right side of the ridge, paralleled by the French Fourth Army on the left. They would meet at Grandpré on the northern edge of the heavily wooded Argonne and together push to Mézières and Sedan, the pulsing terminals of enemy communication, the railheads for all east-west tracks that supplied the Germans along the entire western front.

The Americans faced a grim enemy. Savagely determined to yield no foothold and give no quarter, the Germans had entrenched in layers of earthworks bristling with machine-gun nests, miles of barbed wire, heavy artillery, and cement pillboxes that gave onto a network of tunnels through which snipers could emerge and disappear.

The terrain was as hostile as the enemy. Densely tangled foliage and chasm-cut rock formed natural barriers. From the cliffs, crests, and chasms of the central ridge on one hand and the heights above the Meuse on the other the enemy rained devastating artillery and machine-gun fire. It was terrain the Germans knew and turf well suited to a defensive battle. They had every trail covered, every mound, every ravine, and the men who manned them were battle-hardened veterans.

The doughboys, and many of their officers, were by contrast green troops, hastily trained, unseasoned to combat. On unknown ground they were to breach what the British and French had for four years believed unbreachable. The Americans thought otherwise. Their troops were buoyant, vigorous, cocky, full of high humor, and primed to fight; they would prove stubbornly resilient. Their collective attitude was probably the doughboys' most potent weapon, for it was something the militant Prussian mind was never able to comprehend, then or in a later war.

At 5:30 a.m., 26 September, following a three-hour artillery bombardment and covered by an armada of Allied planes, the infantrymen began to surge into the Argonne. Somewhere between the first and second days they crossed an intangible chasm from the old known world into a strange, eerie inferno, as if they had submerged into the underworld. Still, their spirits were high, even heightened, by a sense of crusade.

The euphoria soon wore off. The Argonne was a nightmare. No ray of sunlight penetrated the dense overhead foliage, moisture dripped eternally, and every declivity swirled with mist, concealing God knew what horrors. The mists often eddied with the unnatural greens or yellows of the chlorine, phosgene, or mustard gasses that, alone or in combination, drowned, asphyxiated, or blistered the lungs of those caught without their masks or compelled by tear gas to remove them. Chaplain Braun suffered his foul dose in the Argonne—mustard gas probably, for it seared his lungs—though he mentioned it only in passing, some years later.[8]

Groups became lost in the tangled wilderness and had to find their units by will, instinct, or luck. Rolling stock—trucks, guns, caissons—dead-ended at impassable ravines, and hunting a way around them ran into more ravines.

Units outran their supplies. Messages failed to get through. Mud, mosquitoes, and lice were unheroic miseries. Barbed wire and booby traps greeted every small advance. Artillery shells and machine-gun fire were a constant, amplified frequently by strafing fire from low-flying German planes.

The battle for the Argonne—the largest American action in World War I, and one of the bloodiest—put the Yankee spirit to the sternest test. Green but gritty, soldiers by necessity, the Yanks slogged along with a grin, a gripe, or a grimace through the cold rain and heavy fire and detonating shells with that devil-may-care stubbornness that freedom begets. Such is the spirit that causes empires to fall.

Young Chaplain Braun embodied that spirit. Discomfort seems throughout his life to have meant little to him. He had a joke for every setback, though his humor masked a deeply serious nature. He damned the death-raining fire along with the next man, but always with a jaunty *"C'est la guerre,* soldier!" The most impassable barrier was *Insignificant!*

Although assigned to Hodges' Second Battalion, he made the rounds to all the units, to anyone in need of a confession, a cigarette, or a cheery word, to the wounded who needed comforting, last rites, or burial. The men loved the chaplain with the deep belly laugh and the wide-mouthed grin that stretched up to his ears; the officers relied on him. Where there was action there was Braun.

As green as the rest, the padre often wandered where he shouldn't. On more than one occasion his orderly, a young kid from heartland USA named Chris Papakaikus, pulled him back when he headed unknowingly toward the German lines.

During October a cold rain fell, then turned to sleet, and the men slogged on through the ever-churning mud, slowly, hampered by sustained shelling, fighting bitterly for each small gain. Father Al began to notice a young man, a kid really, who seemed always to be following him, though he never spoke and seemed to need nothing. With sick and wounded men to care for, the padre paid him scant attention.

Men became despondent. Supplies grew scarce at the front, communications fouled up, and there seemed no end. Many (with some justification) blamed their own command for the screw-ups. Believing troop morale an important responsibility of chaplains, Braun consistently lifted spirits with faith and humor.

By the second week in October the Sixth Infantry, in a wooded area between the heights of Romagne and Cunel, was preparing for an all-out assault on a sector called the *Kriemhilde Stellung*, widely believed the most formidable bastion on the Hindenburg Line.[9] The Second Battalion, to which Braun was nominally attached, was assigned as a support unit. The Third was slated for the initial attack, and the soldier-priest knew where he would be needed. So did the Third's commander, Major John Leonard.

It seems not to have occurred to the padre to report to his Second Battalion commander. He spent much of the night of 12 October hearing confessions, giving absolutions, sharing a joke or a smoke with a sleepless man, snatching what rest he could. At first light on 13 October Chaplain Albert Braun, soldier-sans-arms, went 'over the top' with the first wave.

Up a steep hill they clawed, gained the crest, and started down. Then the Germans opened up. "October 13, 1918," Braun recorded. "On that day I was wounded."[10] As usual, he is maddeningly terse, though a few details come to light in small stories he later liked to recount of his lighter moments. Like many combat veterans, he seldom spoke of war's darker side. He often related one incident:

Inching along on his stomach through the mud, he became aware of the young soldier he had noticed shadowing him before.

Could he help him?

No, Father: he only wanted protection.

Protection? Bullets were whining in counterpoint with the jackhammer staccato of machine guns, grenades were exploding, artillery pounding, men screaming, men dying. *Protection?*

Well, the chaplain was a man of the cloth—couldn't get hurt. So— just by staying close to him—

At that moment, as the padre told it, the shrapnel with Al Braun's name on it hit his right ear and traveled along his jawbone. The blood spurted, the kid's mouth fell open, and he took off running. The chaplain never saw him again.

Seeing the padre wounded, several officers during the day ordered him back to the aid station. No way, he snapped: this was where men were being wounded and killed. This was where a chaplain was needed. Ignoring his own wound (*Insignificant!*), he stayed on the battlefield all day and all night, carrying men through flying bullets and crashing shells to whatever shelter he could find, tending the wounded, administering last rites, anointing the dying. Even the medics were ordered out of the inferno. Al Braun stayed.

At battle's end the Germans were pulling back. The Americans held the field, but at a terrible cost. In the first hours of that single assault Braun's unit had suffered 55% casualties—some eight hundred men.

At some time the next day he saw to his own wound, which proved superficial. His jawbone was not broken and only an ear tip was missing. More serious, he learned at the aid station, was what might happen when he encountered his Second Battalion commander. Hodges, they said, had repeatedly wired headquarters asking, "Where's my chaplain?" His chaplain grinned: it would not be his first reprimand.

Hodges found him later that day. Braun stood straight, awaiting the chewing out he deserved. His commander said nothing for a moment, then glanced with a cocked eyebrow at his subordinate's bandaged head. "How in hell," he drawled, "did the Boche get a bullet back where you were?"[11]

Al Braun and Courtney Hodges became lifelong friends.

For his wound Lieutenant Braun received the Purple Heart. "These are the accidents," he reportedly quipped on receiving the decoration, "that happen when a rear-echelon clerk gets that close to the front line."[12] For valor on the battlefield he was awarded the Silver Star.

> Chaplain Albert W. Braun, 6th Infantry. . . . Displayed exceptional devotion to duty on October 14th [Braun logged it the 13th], 1918, near Romange [sic], France, after being wounded by fragment of shell, he remained on duty in the field throughout the day, supervising the burying of the dead, caring for the wounded and administering extreme unction. On ensuing days he took charge of all burying parties and carried on this work although constantly subjected to intermittent shell fire, exhibiting great bravery and utter disregard of personal danger.
>
> By Command of Major General [Hanson] Ely
> C. A. Trott,
> Chief of Staff[13]

The padre was also recommended for the Distinguished Service Cross. One widely told story has it that a stateside adjutant, safe at his desk, refused him the medal, saying he'd never seen a chaplain worthy of any medal. The padre's version differs somewhat. "My Colonel recommended me for a D.S.C.," he confirmed, but "our General is very strict so I did not get one. However, I am proud of the recommendation."[14]

The *Kriemhilde Stellung* was in American hands by 1 November. There followed a brief respite. The padre buried heartbreaking numbers in that field below Romagne (later to become the largest American military cemetery in France, with 14,200 graves), identifying those he could, commending the souls of all to God, and later surveying the endless rows of wooden crosses on which hung the empty helmets of those who had so recently been men.

Pershing turned command of the First Army over to Major General Hunter Liggett to direct the still heavily opposed Argonne offensive, thereby freeing himself to create a Second Army to absorb the incoming tides of American soldiery.[15] Liggett regrouped, brought order to the faulty supply system, mended broken communication lines, rebuilt roads, and redirected the assault. Morale improved.

On 1 November the push recommenced, now veering toward Sedan and its vital railroads just beyond the Meuse. The already famous 'Rainbow' Division led the final push, to be rallied at a near-disastrous point by another of Pershing's stars, 'Wild Bill' Donovan, later to become famous as head of the OSS in World War II.

Father Albert crossed ruined battlefields and combat-leveled villages inhabited by ghosts; he visited half-ruined churches wherein rows of injured men lay, wounded men in wounded churches. Sometimes a confused oldster would emerge warily from a doorway, or an orphaned child, its belly swollen from starvation, and the padre knew then a further horror of war.

Miraculously, some churches remained, heavily sandbagged, their stained glass windows shattered, sightless like men blinded in combat. Some of those walls had stood a thousand years and still stood, pitted but proud, and Al Braun's thoughts, never far from Mescalero, New Mexico, turned often to the church he envisioned rearing like these ancient testaments to faith. Gothic and Romanesque, medieval and Renaissance—often he stopped to marvel and to dream.

So, he noticed, did a fellow chaplain, and the priests began to talk. His new companion had studied architecture, and from him Father Albert learned much of form, intent, and method, and it fueled his dream. He thought of his Mescaleros, those at home and those serving their country, boys whose fathers had fought the Yankees to protect their land, and who now fought alongside them for the same land; and on the battlefields of

France he vowed again to honor these noble people with a church that would "light their lives forever."

Along the entire frontier the Germans were falling back. Behind the scenes the politicians maneuvered. In Supreme Allied Headquarters, Clemenceau—whose obsessive hatred of Wilson, of Wilson's Fourteen Points ("The Lord God only has ten") and by extension Wilson's AEF commander—attacked Pershing's every move, until Foch furiously ordered him to quit meddling with the military.

The German High Command was in like turmoil. Ludendorff, violently opposing Wilson's terms, clashed with Prince Max von Baden, Chancellor since 4 October, who (unknown to the general) had cabled Wilson on the fifth requesting an armistice, and was secretly negotiating toward that end.

In Washington the President informed neither his Allies nor his own officials of this proposal that could have stopped the fighting immediately. He chose rather to negotiate secretly—notably to secure Germany's agreement to his Fourteen Points, which he obsessively insisted must be the terms of surrender and basis for the ensuing treaty—and which both sides adamantly opposed. Only Prince Max agreed. Though neither the President nor the Chancellor had the authority to speak for his own government or its allies, each assured the other he had.

On 26 October, forced by Prince Max, the Kaiser relieved Ludendorff of his command. The general, swiftly and in mufti, fled to Sweden. The Kaiser, despite pressure, clung to his rule. The Central Powers had been falling one by one—Bulgaria on 29 September, Turkey on 30 October; now, with Austria-Hungary's truce on 3 November, Germany stood alone. Her armies were crumbling, her navy disintegrating as seamen erupted in massive mutiny. A dozen cities boiled with uprisings. Mob-rousing Bolsheviks brewed bedlam in Berlin. Throughout the country people neared starvation. Germany teetered on the brink of anarchy.

The soldiers on the front lines knew nothing of these things. While politicians maneuvered the guns roared and the troops buried more comrades. It is history's axiom that the men on any front know less about the war they are fighting than do those directing their fates. Perhaps it is as well.

Still the padre buried the dead, young soldiers snuffed out like candles. He collected dog tags and recorded their data, to notify their next of kin, when possible, though so many were beyond identification. As he often retold it later, he thought how sad it was to bury a country's soldier, a mother's son, in an unknown grave in 'some corner of a foreign field.' Still envisioning the church he would build, he resolved it would be a monument for these unmarked dead, these 'soldiers known to God.'

The bloody offensive continued. The Germans fought savagely in last-ditch desperation. French, British, and Belgian troops pushed east in every sector and united with the Americans, all converging on German lines. "November 2, 1918," recorded Father Albert. "Crossed the Meuse River."[16]

Gaining the high bluffs beyond the banks, the Americans looked over Sedan and trained their artillery on the railroads. Below, the Meuse was alive with troop-laden rafts en route to battle, pitching and tossing amid hurtling German shells and the geysers they made as they crashed into the water; and as the artillery found its targets the flotsam of splintered rafts and shattered bodies littered the roiling water.

Wilson and Prince Max continued to negotiate, the President still excluding everyone—even his commanding general—from the covert transaction, while men died daily in the forests of the Argonne, and the Meuse ran red with blood.

But Germany—rudderless, alone, and anarchic, her people verging on starvation, her troops drained—could stand no longer. "The mighty framework of German Imperial Power," wrote Churchill, "which a few days before had overshadowed the nations, shivered suddenly into a thousand individually disintegrating fragments."[17]

On 8 November the German delegation crossed the lines to meet with Foch at Compiègne. On the ninth the Kaiser abdicated and fled for the Dutch border as a German Republic was proclaimed. Those at Compiègne negotiated their terms and set the time for the armistice at the symbolic eleventh hour of the eleventh day of the eleventh month.

The men at the front heard rumors and waited and prayed.

"November 11, 1918," Braun penned. "Was at Ramonville [near Cunel] when war ended." Nothing at all of his thoughts or his emotions or his actions, or of those of the men around him as the bugles sounded and the guns fell silent, as a great universal silence hit the exhausted armies like a blast of noiseless thunder. In a dense mist the troops huddled in the sleet-mixed rain; they heard the water dripping from the bare limbs of the denuded trees, and it was the only sound they heard. Many—Allies and Germans alike—collapsed in the mud: they just wanted to sleep.

The cities of the world awoke to learn in their various time zones the Great War was over. There was relief and thanksgiving in the Fatherland among the people: defeat hurt less than hunger for the masses, and food might soon arrive. Elsewhere there was jubilation—the cheers, the parades, the dancing in the streets, the small flags waving from every hand, the bells pealing. In time, as the reality sank in, the troops too would celebrate, and think in the bittersweet moments of comrades who would not know the hard-fought end or return to the houses for which they had fought.

It would remain for the diplomats at Versailles to frame the covenant and define the peace. But the war to end all wars was over: yesterday was dead and tomorrow yet unborn, and in that first strange silence the men on the lines stood mute.

View of the main street at Cunel, Meuse, in the sector in which Father Al found himself at war's end. The Germans had used this church as a motion picture theater before destroying it on their retreat. U.S. Signal Corps picture taken 25 October 1918, soon after the Americans entered the village. Reproduced at the National Archives, Washington, No. 157907. Courtesy of Lt. Col. Michael Lauer.

8: THE IMPOSSIBLE DREAM

The battlefields were silent; the padre laid his last fallen soldier to rest; and a new age dawned. The venerable Houses of Romanov and Habsburg, and that of the upstart Hohenzollern, had crumbled. The Ottoman and Austrian Empires had shattered like glass into a handful of autonomous states. Leninist Russia was hardening into a Soviet monster. And a young German corporal named Adolph Hitler, temporarily blinded in battle by his own country's gas and more permanently by his own hatred, was swearing vengeance. The 'Big Four' were marshalling their priorities to glare at each other at Versailles—the cynical Clemenceau, the devious Lloyd George, the cultured but often absent Orlando, and the self-righteous Wilson (who, Clemenceau growled, "talks like God and acts like Lloyd George"). And nearly ten million young men lay dead.

Americans at home, though deeply troubled over the influenza sweeping the nation, shared a vast relief that the war was over. The world was safe for democracy (or presumably would be when the wizards at Versailles got through remodeling it) and the boys were coming home. Within a month of the armistice America began to demobilize: what need for an army after this war had ended all wars?

Lieutenant Albert Braun would not be among those mustering out immediately. Colonel Hunt had taken command from the German officers on 1 December and the Sixth Infantry Division had entered Trier, which was, the padre wrote,

> the most historical town in Germany, like a capital city, in that part of the Roman Empire. What Rome is to the Catholics of the world, Trier is to the Catholics of Germany, Holland, Belgium, Luxembourg, and northern France. Because of the Catholic prominence, the prudent General Pershing assigned the occupation of Trier to Colonel H. J. Hunt, a recent convert to Catholicism.
>
> After instructing the 6th Infantry on the policy of the

army of occupation, Colonel Hunt sent for Chaplain A. W. Braun. . . . "Where does the Bishop of Trier live?" My answer: "I don't know any more about that than you do." The Colonel said: "Find out!" When I did the Colonel's chauffeur drove us to the rectory of the Bishop. . . . The doors . . . had metal clappers instead of doorbells. The Colonel clapped long and hard on the door.

A tall hostile-looking German came to the door. I said in German: "The Colonel wants to speak with the Bishop." After a short hesitation, the hostile German let us in, but told us to stay at the entrance. In a few minutes the Bishop, another tall hostile-looking German, appeared. . . . Colonel H. J. Hunt immediately crossed the hall, knelt, and kissed the ring on the Bishop's finger.

The Bishop, with tears in his eyes, said: How good God is to us to send such a man to occupy Trier. Then the Bishop invited Col. Hunt to attend the Bishop's Mass at 9 o'clock on Sundays in the Cathedral . . . [and] invited me to accompany the Colonel. To accommodate us the Bishop had two kneelers and two chairs placed near the altar. How surprised the German people were to see the American colonel at mass! From that time on, the German people and the German army near Trier became friends, no longer enemies. . . ."[1]

American Sixth Infantry Division, US First Army, marches triumphantly into Trier, 1 December 1918. Courtesy of MUA.

Chaplain Braun had no idea how long they might be in Trier. "My thoughts . . . turn to Mescalero," he wrote his provincial early in December. "I would like to get back there to celebrate Christmas. I don't wish to say that I am dissatisfied with the army, not at all. But . . . this is something passing and soon to come to an end." He had heard that Fathers Ambrose and Ferdinand had been transferred. "I hope Father Ambrose's successor will be tired of Mescalero when I get back so that I can live with my Apaches once again. . . ."[2]

Meanwhile there was much to do. The people had lived too long with war, despair, and hunger. Trier seemed a city of women, children, old people, and ghosts. At first afraid to leave their homes, the people soon found the American doughboys kind, generous, and friendly. They found the American chaplain with the big ears and the big grin to have as big a heart—and he spoke German. (He also spoke French; his knowledge of both was a distinct help in Europe.) Braun, Hunt, and the grateful Bishop of Trier worked together to alleviate the suffering that is the wake of war, and to establish and maintain the order necessary for peace.

"The people here are very glad to have us," he continued. "The fact of our presence frees them from agitators and assures them the necessary liberty for the coming elections, in which all are intensely interested. Possibly you have read that there is a vehemently anti-Christian party seeking control of the [German] government." He was doubtless referring to the Bolshevik faction led by Karl Liebknecht and Rosa Luxemburg.

Colonel Hunt relied heavily on his padre: he was efficient and hardworking; he got along with the people and spoke their language. "We are very comfortable here," Braun reported. In addition to chaplain's duties, "I manage an officers' club. This takes up much time," he admitted, "however it is not disagreeable work." He was also given charge of the deeply in debt general mess, for which he did considerable scrounging to augment the thin army rations. He expected some time "to be taken up with [religious] instructions. Just now I have soldiers taking instruction and there [are] good hopes for two officers. . . ."[3]

When the deadly influenza epidemic that swept Europe and America glutted the hospital in Trier, the padre spent days and nights helping care for the stricken. Predictably, he was soon ill himself. Already vulnerable from the battlefield gassing he had endured, he lay bleeding and unconscious for two days, not expected to live. But a dedicated nurse, his own native toughness, and perhaps the dream he cherished pulled him through.

"I just came out of the hospital," he wrote on 12 January. "It settled in my lungs and caused several hemorrhages. I am weak and suffer from pains in the chest, otherwise I am all right. . . . Pray for me. Also pray that I soon get home again. I have every opportunity to enjoy myself and I get along fine with my outfit but now that the war is over I want to get back to normal life."

There were, however, no plans for a quick return. "I suppose it will be a long time. . . . The 6th Infantry will be one of the last to get back because it is a Regular Army organization. There is much talk that we will be sent up into Russia. I certainly do hope we will not be sent there."[4]

His unit was ordered instead—to everyone's pleasure—to the Grand Duchy of Luxembourg, and billeted in the town of Diekirch, about forty miles north of the city. Here too he was given myriad assignments. "I am kept busy with army school work," he wrote in April,

> besides superintending the schools of the Second Battalion of this regiment. I teach geography and the history of France. . . .
>
> Lent has brought a little more work in the religious line. The soldier I was instructing in the Faith at Trier has gotten his discharge. . . . Yesterday another soldier began instructions. . . .
>
> I know I can't get away till June but I have written to Father Ronan . . . at General Headquarters to arrange that I go then. I am not tired of the army but since I cannot stay with it, it is best that I make room for someone who will remain in the army.
>
> In this regiment, there are scores of men who have not been to the sacraments for eight years and more. I am trying to round them up for Easter. . . .[5]

The padre was also put in charge of recreation. The Americans hosted weekly dances to which the townspeople were invited. Having lived under German occupation since 1914, they were grateful for such occasions, as long as the dances were conducted with propriety. For this Father Albert was assigned to the dance committee, a job he enjoyed as much as anyone. He became enormously popular with both soldiers and townspeople because of the life and fun he injected into the parties.

At one of the Thursday dances he met the dignified and gracious Madame Anna Henrion, the matriarch of her family. "Mama Henrion," he later recalled, "invited me to visit the family." There a close friendship grew quickly.[6] "I spent many enjoyable evenings at the Henrion home. Mama had a special French-gift of sociability. . . ." He also spoke glowingly of "daddy, and their two wonderful children, Eugene and Celine," who were then in their very early twenties. "What an attraction they had for many American soldiers," he recalled, "especially for Father Albert!" Celine "had more American officers after her than any other girl in Diekirch. She was even able to charm the tough old Apache Indian—Father Albert."[7]

Celine seemed particularly attracted to one Lieutenant Oliver Sheehy who, the padre remarked, "had only two attractions: 1, Celine . . . , and 2, the Irish Holy Water,"[8] Father Albert's term for any good whiskey, a libation of which he too was fond. Apparently he and Ollie Sheehy enjoyed many a dram together, played cards with Papa Eugene Henrion, and otherwise jointly enjoyed the family's hospitality.

While in Diekirch Lieutenant Braun, young, lively, and with a penchant for being, as he liked to say, "always in trouble," may very likely have felt some of the attraction for the "wild life of the army" Father Hugolinus had envisioned. He refers somewhat cryptically to unnamed temptations, which apparently he could resist more easily because of the greater pleasures to be enjoyed at the Henrion home.

His "guardian angels, Eugene and Celine," he attested, "shielded me from the fallen angel—the Devil. . . . How can I ever repay them and Mama and Papa! The many times I spent in their happy home, I had a foretaste of the great happiness I will enjoy when—and if—I get to Heaven. There is a dangerous Hi-way, between here and Heaven, and many devils are hiding along that Hi-way. They know what an easy 'Prey' they have when Father Albert comes along. He has no armor—virtues—but much weakness— sinful inclinations."[9] To what temptations he refers he makes no mention—a weakness perhaps for over imbibing in the 'Irish holy water'—but in any case his busy schedule could have allowed for few temptations.

And always he carried his dream.

In Diekirch, as earlier in France and Trier, he spent what leisure daytime hours he could garner visiting the churches of Europe—small country churches and soaring cathedrals, in varying degrees of antiquity. He carefully noted details in design, engineering, and patterns. He paid close attention to the medieval structures built before the age of modern machines, wherein they had utilized the same techniques of hand labor on which he would have to rely when he would begin to translate dream into stone. He seems to have found a special fascination in watching the European workers, in talking to them, asking many questions as they burned lime in kilns and mixed mortar to repair their war-torn churches. He noted each step carefully: theirs was a technique he would find useful.

One can visualize the figure of the lone American priest, small against the enormity of soaring Renaissance spire or sturdy Gothic mass, studying all minutely as he contemplated the church that would one day rise amid the hills of Mescalero. One can imagine the impact of these ancient churches whose silent endurance through the ages have begotten thoughts of the unity of God and Man; thoughts of the dead and the living, separated only by one chance bullet or the spot of soil whereon one stood at a moment in time; and thoughts of the living Church that held it all together. One can almost see him walking at length away, his thoughts unspoken, his eyes focused beyond the reality of these stone structures to the one as yet to build.

His orders came in August. He could now look toward his Apaches, and to the church he would build for them, a sacred monument to his comrades with whom he had served, and to those buried on the field of battle. There was also the wrench of parting—of leaving his unit, the men with whom he had shared the grit and grime and perils of war, and with whom he had served in the peace that followed. And he must say goodbye to his dear friends in Diekirch.

Apparently Ollie Sheehy had also received his orders and must soon return to his home in Chicago. He and Celine wanted to marry—no surprise to Father Al or to anyone else who knew them—but Papa Eugene withheld his permission. If after a year they still wanted to marry, he would reconsider. Meanwhile he called Father Al aside: could he, when back in the States, seek out the parish priest in Ollie's neighborhood and find out more about this young man? The padre could, and would, in person if possible—and he had ways of making things possible.

(The story has a happy ending. Soon after arriving stateside he had occasion to be in Chicago, where he located Ollie's parish and called on the priest: did Oliver Sheehy and his family attend his church? Oliver did, the priest answered, though he attended alone, for he had no family. He was a fine young man. But, the priest added, Oliver had moved to another parish; he suggested the padre check there. The second priest gave the same answer: Ollie was a single man, attended church regularly, and was of excellent character.

Father Al, doubtless with a twinkle in his eye, duly reported to Papa Henrion, who then gave his consent and blessing, and wedding bells soon rang. In time the entire family followed the young couple to America.[10] But that lay still in the future.)

The padre sailed for home in late August. "I will never forget," he wrote half a century later, "when I was about to leave Diekirch to return to the U.S. Eugene, Celine, and Father Albert hugged one another and there were tears in their eyes." It was a scene of which he would speak and write often and lovingly in the years to come. "I always thank God that I had the great blessing to be sent to Diekirch after World War I."[11]

It was not the last he would see of his friends.

☩ ☩ ☩

First Lieutenant Albert Braun, 0134329, reported to Father Hugolinus immediately upon receiving his discharge at the Presidio in San Francisco in September 1919. He carried with him a testimonial given him by Bishop Patrick J. Hays, ordinariate in charge of American Catholic chaplains in the armed services, with instructions to present it to his Father Provincial—the same provincial who until ordered otherwise by the same ordinariate, had blocked the young priest from military service. One can imagine the mischievous twinkle Al Braun must have flashed when Hugolinus read it.

> I am happy to say of Father Braun that his work in the United States Army has been eminently successful. He has shown himself a hard worker and one ready to serve even under most trying conditions. Whithersoever he has gone he has made a splendid name for the Church and himself and I am glad to have had him identified with my great responsibility. His spirit of priestly docility and respect for ecclesiastical jurisdiction have always made a profound impression upon myself.
>
> With best wishes, I am
> Sincerely yours in Christ,
> Patrick J. Hays
> Ordinarius Castrensis[12]

IV

THE BUILDER

*"Christ told his apostles to get out among the people,
not sit on their butts and push papers around."*

9: NEW BEGINNINGS

The padre returned to Mescalero with a Purple Heart, a Silver Star, and a golden dream. Armed with copious notes taken while studying old European churches, he was impatient to get started on the great stone church.

God, it seemed, had already begun the process. "A heavy wind," Father Tiburtius Wand had reported in February, "blew our tower and bell off. . . . The church here was built very badly."[1] Father Al agreed. A widening crack ran the length of one wall; the leaking roof turned the dirt floor to mud; the adobes were disintegrating, "and now we have a tumbling-down church. Unless kept from it," the padre asserted, "I intend to start building next April."[2]

He wrote immediately to Father Hugolinus for permission and funding; and through fellow Franciscan Paul Francis in Graymoor, New York, he located an architect well qualified for his needs. He had only to await the green light.

Meanwhile he had his work in Mescalero, the reservation to ride, friendships to renew. He felt special bonds with those who like himself had joined Uncle Sam's army. He swapped war stories with Robert Geronimo and the others who had served, gave thanks for their return, and vowed again to dedicate the church to the veterans. He visited families of Mescaleros who had died during the postwar influenza epidemic—"fully forty," the *Indian Sentinel* reported[3]—and grieved with Albert and Emma Fall who had lost two children.

And there was Charlie Mackey, also returned from war, still chasing a good time and wondering like Al Braun what had come over their country, which in their absence—and sans their permission—had ratified the eighteenth amendment. Prohibition, like a funeral cortege, rolled glumly over America.

Insignificant! "Across the river," the padre wrote, "was Juárez, a good supply house of the forbidden juice of the Maguey plant. The white man in the United States is hard to understand. First he forbids something, then he runs after that which he forbade."[4] Juárez was abloom with sudden popularity, some fine restaurants, and no restrictions on liquor. "During Prohibition I went to El Paso often" to discuss ecclesiastical matters with Bishop Schuler, "and always went to Juarez."[5]

Father Albert, according to everyone who knew him, was a terrible driver. "They'd go to El Paso and Juarez for a little R-and-R," Charlie's son remembers, "and one time they were driving back to Mescalero—there were a lot of dips between Oro Grande and Alamogordo—and they went down one of those and there was a cow. They rammed into it. . . . Father Al didn't even stop. He was always pretty reckless. Relied on his great faith, I guess."[6]

Fun was fun, and no one enjoyed life more than Al Braun. But the vision was always with him. He rode the reservation and said his masses; he married and buried and baptized, energized by the dream, and his plan for action—as soon as his permission came. The dispensation had to come from Father Hugolinus. It must have crossed the padre's mind that this provincial, who seems to have been singularly unimaginative, was not one to sanction any deviation from a rather dull norm, or any project involving change. But so fired was Father Albert with his agenda that he seems to have believed it would be impossible for anyone, including Hugolinus Storff, not to share his enthusiasm. He was therefore incredulous when the letter came:

Permission denied. The old church must suffice.

After a reportedly spectacular outburst of his soon-to-become famous temper, he dug his heels in with his equally famous stubbornness: if the road's blocked, find a detour. And as the founder of his Order had heard the voice at San Damiano—*Francis, mend my church*—so must his disciple have heard it at Mescalero. *Albert, build my church. . . .*

There was, of course, his vow of obedience, and that must be honored. That his order came from God he seems to have had no doubt; and God outranked Hugolinus Storff. Nonetheless, he could not disobey his provincial. Well then, he must change that provincial's mind. Where there's a wile there's a way.

Quietly Father Albert began to fill the cracks of the crumbling little church with blasting powder. He worked at night, with the help of a couple of his Mescalero friends, and went about his usual duties in daylight. When the long gaping crack was stuffed to his satisfaction, he and his collaborators planted one end of an electric wire inside the powder-crammed fissure, ran it a safe distance, and attached the other end to an automobile battery. It was a tactic that appealed to the Apaches' sense of humor and directness—a trick worthy of the wily coyote.

Soon a mysterious explosion blasted the night's deep silence—and the entire length of the church.

He reported the strange affair to his provincial: the church had somehow blown up, the long wall was gone, the roof had collapsed. What must he do? The agency superintendent had condemned the wrecked building, and his poor Indians had no place in which to worship. . . .

He soon had his permission. But—Hugolinus could spare no funds.[7]

Insignificant! The padre had $100 in leftover army pay, a hard head, a pair of work-hardened hands, and a dream. He was full-to-bursting with faith, hope, and energy, and enthusiastic for the challenge. A big man—"big in the *corazon*," Father Lawrence Jagfeld called him[8]—and he thought big thoughts.

Now, with his permission finally secured, he could contact the architect. He had already spent hours tramping the area and had selected a site behind that of the tiny original structure. There his west-facing church could overlook the canyon and draw all eyes upward toward the high-arched roof, the soaring cross-crowned bell tower, and thence to heaven itself. He had found native rock to quarry. He was armed with sketches and maps and a survey of the area. He had applied for and received a conditional title to the land on which it would stand, valid for as long as there were Indians on the reservation and a church to serve them. He had everything he needed to approach the architect except a ticket to Philadelphia.

Insignificant! His good friend Ashton Hawkins, though his office was in El Paso, spent much of his time at his home in La Luz, at which Father Al was a frequent guest. He was also, providentially, the attorney for the Rock Island and Southern Railways in New Mexico. Ashton Hawkins had, moreover, a nature akin to Al Braun's. Bored by the everlasting Civil War stories at his home in Tennessee and lured by those of the wild frontier, young Hawkins had left the South for the West in 1883 with $15, a Civil War pistol, a law degree from Vanderbilt University, and a lust for adventure.

He found plenty. As a $5-a-week news reporter in the tough, brawling mining camps of Silver City, New Mexico, he had seen a garish variety of the gamblers, prostitutes, saloonkeepers, and gunmen that followed the miners, and had witnessed the shootouts that punctuated the scenes. He had ridden with the sheriff's posse chasing outlaws and renegade Apaches as the occasion offered. He was a short-time legal partner and a long-time friend of Albert Fall, and a prominent figure in New Mexico politics. With Charles B. Eddy he had been instrumental in developing southern New Mexico, in founding the settlements that became Carlsbad and Alamogordo, and in bringing in the railroads.[9]

Hawkins was an adventurer, a dreamer who envisioned great things for the New Mexico he loved, and a doer who made them happen. He was stubborn, nonconformist, quick of wit, and drawn to others of like temperament. Though a quarter-century separated the two in age, a friendship between Ashton Hawkins and Albert Braun was a natural. The young priest was often a dinner guest in the sprawling adobe home Hawkins had acquired in La Luz—so named, he told the padre, because the early settlers built an enormous bonfire on nights when there were no approaching dangers from the Indians. When the people of Tularosa saw *la luz*—the light—they knew all was peaceful. When no fire burned they knew the Apaches were raiding and heading their way. Thus the little settlement became known as the place of La Luz.

This and other stories of the wild frontier he told as they settled back after dinner, when Ashton's wife Clara and the children were abed. The two men, each with a big cigar and a tot of brandy, often talked for hours of the past and present of this land they loved. Hawkins was a raconteur, and there was plenty to recount. His home itself had quite a history, had been a scene in the turf wars of '86 in the midst of the Fountain-Lee feuds, and Ashton had known the contenders.

Albert Braun had his own stories to tell, and his own ambitions to share. He wanted a better life on earth for his Mescaleros, wanted to build a productive community that could function effectively in the encroaching white world and still maintain its own strong culture. For this his people needed a center for their spiritual lives and their physical needs—a church community: this was the dream that impelled him. His resolve to build this center, this huge Gothic church, with a hundred dollars and a problematical handful of Apaches, stirred the imagination of Hawkins.

So when the priest appeared in his El Paso office one day inquiring about a pass to Philadelphia to see an architect, Hawkins ordered that Braun was to have passes whenever and wherever he wanted, "because this young man does more for New Mexico than all the politicians put together."[10]

William Stanton too was impressed with the enthusiastic priest who appeared in the offices of the prestigious architectural firm of Folsom and Stanton with a briefcase full of sketches, maps of the terrain, pictures of the proposed site, a geologic survey, and a plan for the impossible.[11] One can imagine the session:

What funding had the father for this gigantic project?

None at all.

Any machinery for building such a structure?

No; but then, neither had the medieval builders.

How could he keep a work force without funds?

The same way the early Spanish friars had for the great southwestern missions: he'd work alone with whatever Indian helpers he could persuade.

Did he really believe he could achieve such a monumental building as he had sketched?

Would he be here if he didn't?

The difficulties would be—

Insignificant!

As the early settlers in La Luz had beamed the light of safety to their neighbors, so this church would beam its light of hope for his Apaches.

Something of that beacon obviously caught the imagination of William Stanton, or maybe it was the fire that burned in Father Albert. The architect was not convinced that such a cathedral-proportioned structure could be built by will alone, barring a miracle—but perhaps this ardent man before him could work a miracle, or cadge one from above. From Father Al's inner fire a small flame seems to have licked at Stanton's imagination, caught, and kindled.

They began to discuss details, to draw sketches, to match ideas. Stanton would need time to research methods and materials of the Middle Ages and do some adapting. But Father Albert wanted to start immediately. How about a rough plan on which he could get started? A detailed blueprint could follow in time.

They decided on the essentials. The church would be built in the traditional cruciform plan; it would measure a hundred thirty-one feet by sixty-four. The walls would rise fifty feet to the eaves and soar twice that to the cross atop the bell tower. They would quarry native sandstone for the walls, hew pine from the surrounding mountains for the ceiling and cross beams. There was a pottery plant at La Luz that made floor and roofing tiles. The church would be entirely of native materials.

Within a few days Stanton handed the preliminary sketches to Father Al, who, once back in Tularosa, showed them to Father Ferdinand for approval. The older priest was delighted. In Philadelphia Stanton began work on the plans—prodded, it seems, by an impatient Al Braun, to whom he replied in a letter of 21 June:

> Kindly relieve yourself of any fears . . . of having provoked me by your being urgent about your new church. I realize you are very ardent . . . and because I am also enthusiastic . . . I have been taking the greatest pains to have them as perfect as possible.
>
> I am glad that the plans . . . came up to your expectations. I was also glad when I received the telegram from Father Ortiz requesting me to prepare the plans in accordance with the original dimensions and realize that you wish to build in the summer weather. . . . I therefore sent you a plan of the main floor . . . with complete dimensions in order that you might stake out the building . . . and start the excavation.

He went on to urge the inclusion of a basement, to "afford a dryer floor and . . . prevent the dampness creeping up under the floor boards." Enclosed were detailed instructions for each procedure involved.[12] He had carefully researched medieval plans and adapted their methods designed for the hand labor on which Father Al would have to rely. "This architect," the padre wrote, "knew the mission was poor; he drew the plans gratis."[13]

Father Al donned overalls and turned to the work ahead. He began to drill test holes for the foundation. He hunted the best stone to quarry. He razed what was left of the first little church and transferred the furnishings— even the red curtain—to the former recreation center, which would serve as an interim church. If any wondered whether these effects had been removed before the 'accidental' explosion, none asked aloud.

A few Mescaleros were ready to help, Robert Geronimo and Naiche among them; Eric would come often from Elk, and Clarence Enjady from Whitetail; and the padre was sure he could inveigle some war veterans to work on this monument for those who had not returned. But however willing, neither he nor any of his prospective workforce knew the first thing about stone masonry, or the fine points of construction—the Apaches had never been builders—and he may have put out feelers for some expert help from the Mission. At any rate, a providential letter from an old friend in Santa Barbara soon arrived.

"I got a letter from Tony Leyva," the padre recounted, "asking if he could come to Mescalero to work for me. I wrote Tony that I had a life-time stone job, but had no money. He wrote that he did not want money. He wanted to get away from Santa Barbara. His wife was dead and his children were grown. He felt too sad living in Santa Barbara. Tony packed his tools and took the train for Tularosa. . . . I met Tony at the depot."[14]

Tony, already sixty-five, would spend the rest of his life in Mescalero, working for only bed and board, his one request being that he be buried in Santa Barbara next to his beloved wife, Rosa. It was a promise the padre made gladly.

Here began what Father Al later called the happiest years of his life. "Tony and I batched together and worked together. Tony was an excellent cook," having signed on for galley duty on a number of sailing expeditions. "He did the cooking on big Feast Days; I was the ordinary cook, and not a good one at that. During the winter months Tony and I quarried the stone; we hauled the stone and sand in the spring months; in the summer and fall we laid the stone. . . . We used lime mortar. . . . [It] did not cost us five cents. . . ."[15]

Antonio Maria Leyva: "Old Tony." Courtesy of SJAM.

Tony was a pro, a perfectionist, an artist who took pride in his work. He had learned his craft from the finest of many stoneworkers at the mission. He was also a gentleman in the truest sense, a man of stalwart character. "In his youth," wrote Father Al, "he was a sailor. He never went to school but speaks a more correct English than the average high school graduate. Antonio was fortunate in having Pablo de la Guerra as his padrino. He spent some time in his boyhood at Pablo's home and there absorbed a courtesy, dignity and fineness of manners that could not have been acquired anywhere except in a Spanish home of the early mission days."[16]

They tramped the hills until they found a hard, granite-like stone that Tony approved for the foundation. Down toward Nogal Canyon near Bent, just beyond the reservation line the outcropping lay, some four miles from the building site. The property belonged to the Bent estate, from which they obtained permission to quarry whatever they needed.

At Bent they also found Braulio and Rafael Diaz, who volunteered to help quarry. The Diaz brothers remained on the job throughout the years of construction, and in time put their sons on the job as well. Braulio worked for a marble quarrier, and later carved an altar from a large block of Italian marble his boss donated.

Quarrying and hauling stone was backbreaking work. They drilled deep holes along a cliffside and filled them with blasting powder, which they detonated with a battery, loosening massive chunks of rock. They hewed and dressed the stone at the quarry, to be hauled later to the building site.

Workers quarrying stone for Saint Joseph's Apache Mission Church, Mescalero,
New Mexico. Courtesy of MUA.

Laying the foundation for the 'Apache Cathedral.' Courtesy of MUA.

Barbershop Break: Eric Tortilla cuts Robert Geronimo's hair as the foundation is laid. Courtesy of SJAM.

The walls of the new church rise as an old Apache lady looks on from her tepee. Courtesy of SJAM.

Simultaneously they began excavating for the foundation. Down they dug, and farther down, with pick and shovel, and still farther, seven feet before they hit hardpan. An old snapshot taken during the early stages of construction shows a tepee in the foreground, the beginnings of the church in the distance. "An old lady 100 years old lives in the tepee in back of the new church," Father Al had scribbled on the picture's reverse. "We give her chili and frijoles and she often sends us venison and wild turkey. According to the Apache tradition another tribe before the Apaches had their main camps on the site of the new church. In excavating we found stone floors, pottery, arrowheads and many other curios. We also found a skeleton."

While the Diaz brothers toiled at the quarry with what help they could get, Father Al pressed the Mescaleros he could count on to work, however sporadically, at the excavation. He and Tony worked alongside both crews as needs dictated. Never idle himself, he grew irritated when anyone else lazed, and was often gruff with those who shirked. Few took offense, however. Their padre's good nature always returned, usually with a joke, once he had made his point; and because he bent his back with theirs, the Mescaleros saw a man no less a man for doing what they saw as menial work.

Tony too grew popular with the Mescaleros. His eighteenth-century ancestor Juan Agustín Leyba had married a mission Indian woman at Santa Barbara and, reported Father Al, "Tony was very proud of his Indian blood he inherited. He used to brag about it to the Apaches at Mescalero. . . . They loved Tony and he loved them."[17]

Drawn to the project by curiosity or friendship, some of Father Albert's many friends from Tularosa came to watch, stayed to work, and returned to help on days off from their regular employment. Among these were Alberto Gonzales and members of the Baldonado family. The Blazers were always willing to help. The frontier ethos was strong in this country, and Father Al had the gift of friendship. He paid what small wages he could and relied on volunteers when he couldn't.

From the beginning and through the years that followed, Almer Blazer's daughter Vida Jette regularly brought food for the work crews. Often after a day of hard work he visited Vi and her husband Paul, who ran the Blazers' store. With them he "always relaxed. . . . They gave me the support I needed."[18] Periodically after Sunday mass the Jettes, their children, and Father Al picnicked at Headsprings or in the White Sands below.[19]

As they quarried the stones they faced the challenge of hauling the monstrosities, many weighing up to 1,500 pounds, four miles up the steep grade to the building site. They contrived a boom with which they hoisted the stone onto a wagon—one per trip was all the wagon could bear and all a team of straining mules could pull. It was muscle-tearing, exhausting work, and slow enough to consume a lifetime, but they had no other equipment—

Until by happy fortune Father Al learned (likely from Bishop Schuler) of a forthcoming sale at Fort Bliss to dispose of some surplus army vehicles. The padre and Tony hurried to El Paso and with some skillful bargaining acquired two heavy flatbed trucks. Neither of these age-wearied rigs would run, but the price was low. They managed—probably with the bishop's help—to get them towed to Mescalero, where they cannibalized parts from both and built a single contraption that functioned, more or less. Father Al drove the hybrid vehicle between quarry and building site, back and forth, and the stone began to pile around the foundation trenches.

They utilized the talents of David Belin, a Chiricahua who had arrived from captivity at Fort Sill in 1913. David, having learned blacksmithing while a prisoner, built a derrick, attached a handmade boom, and rigged a block and tackle to load and unload the stone.

The padre was chronically in need of funds. "Several months ago," he wrote his provincial in May 1920,

> you said you would help me with some money for my new church. Send it now because I need it badly.
>
> I have done everything possible to cut down expenses. I feed the men and pay them less. Do the cooking myself. Have planted a large garden, four acres of corn and eight hundred pounds of spud which will yield 10,000 lbs. That will cut the cost of feeding the men. I also have seven acres of wheat which will bring enough flour to make all the bread. We use teams and for them I have planted 6 acres of oats. That will reduce the cost of teams. My dad is coming to do all the carpenter work gratis. So you see everything has been done to reduce expenses. I have worked very hard to accomplish this and I know you will cooperate with me to meet what expenses I have not been able to avoid.[20]

Drawing from his close observation of European mortar work, Father

Al built adobe kilns close to the site, where they burned their own limestone to provide quick-lime, mixed in water to slake it to a puttylike substance, and added sand to make the mortar for laying the stones. Lime mortar, one of the oldest building materials known to man, is also one of the most durable, he learned, for it gives off moisture and 'marries' to the stone, as opposed to cement, which retains moisture, freezes, and cracks. And, Father Al exulted, it was free!

Close by the building site Father Al built adobe kilns in which they burned limestone for their mortar. Courtesy of MUA.

His old friend Augustine, still teaching at Saint Anthony's, took his summer vacation "to help Father Albert lay the foundations" for what was already becoming known as the 'Apache Cathedral.' "By that time," Augustine later wrote,

> there was a 'Tin Lizzie' available, but I did not know what to do with it. Fr. Albert gave me a quick lesson; but it took me some time to learn that once the motor began to roar with the brake on, the driver had to keep his foot between low and high gear before releasing that brake; only then could he get started with low gear to start and then when well on the way change

to high. No second gear on a TIN LIZZIE.

On two occasions we got stuck on our way through the mountains. The first time it was late at night. . . . As we were on our way home we were suddenly aware of a man standing in the middle of the road waving his hands wildly. . . . His big car had suddenly come to a stop; having no flashlight, he asked us to throw . . . our headlights into the engine of their stalled automobile. We agreed; but when we went back to our little Ford we noticed that our radius rod had come apart to the extent that our two front wheels faced each other. We . . . decided to walk back to Mescalero. That walk was a long one. . . . On the next day we telephoned Father Ferdinand Ortiz at Tularosa. . . . [He] towed our sick Tin Lizzie all the way to Tularosa. . . . Later that day I got hold of some heavy wire to reinforce our radius rod. While I was still on my back under the Ford, Father Albert came out of the house . . . and mumbled to me: 'Ahhh, you're just too careful.' Yet, with my temporary repairs we could at least drive to a neighboring service station, where our sick little Ford was brought to life again. No more trouble with our Tin Lizzie for the rest of the summer.[21]

Father Al conscripted every able-bodied worker within hailing distance for his construction crew, including the busy bishop, who came to visit and stayed to work. It would become a yearly custom. "No one," averred a fellow Franciscan, "ever said no to Father Al."[22]

"Every summer," wrote Father Al, "when it becomes uncomfortably hot in El Paso, Bishop Schuler S.J. [Society of Jesuits] used to move his office to Mescalero [for the summer]." The Apaches "loved Bishop Schuler . . . because he was so friendly."[23] He was also a hard worker.

Through the summer of 1920 they labored and by late fall had completed the foundation. On 20 November they laid the cornerstone. Fathers Hugolinus Storff and Joseph Rhodes journeyed from California to conduct the ceremony. Workers and well wishers from throughout the countryside gathered. Mescaleros from the far reaches of the reservation came, their wagons, horses, and tepees filling the glen. Expressing their support, the Indians laid objects sacred to Ussen to lie beneath the stone—a gesture not unrelated to the padre's espousal of their puberty rites. Symbolically they had brought Ussen into the Jesus church and the church had welcomed him in. Theirs was the significant act that defines the greater verity.

The actual building could now commence. Slowly the walls began to rise. They built their own scaffolding with the help of master carpenter John Braun, who packed his tools and came from California. Not even his own father said no to Father Al.

New beginnings brought new necessities. The Bishop and Augustine had returned to their duty posts at summer's end, leaving a tremendous hole in the workforce. Most of the padre's crew were by choice or necessity only occasional workers. Traces of latent distrust between Hispanics and Apaches still surfaced occasionally. One observer recalls laughing that "the Mexicans will tell you they did the work on the church and the Apaches just hung around; and then you talk to the Apaches who say, boy, they really worked with Father Albert and those Mexicans just came up from Tularosa and mostly just sat around and watched."[24] In truth, both groups worked, diligently and together; no one dared loaf or quarrel around the padre. But the bulk of the work rested on Al Braun and Old Tony; and when the padre was away riding the reservation, otherwise tending his ministerial duties, or working in the fields, Tony manned the ramparts.

Father Al was perpetually short of funds, though he was becoming a sharp financier. The hard limestone they had quarried so laboriously for the foundation was almost impossibly difficult to mine, lacking equipment they could not afford. Following a visit from the Father Provincial who, having seen the project, was doubtless more cognizant of their problems, the padre seized his opportunity in a craftily reasoned letter.

Since you have left here, I carefully figured on the machinery needed for the work on the church. The . . . items are as follows:

1. A Ford truck. . . . In one day, on gas and oil, I [would] spend $2.50. The same . . . work . . . would [cost] $20.00 if done by teams. When the days are longer I will put in a few more hours each day and the saving would be still greater.

2. An endless chain 'Yale combination.' That costs $60 and saves $4 each day. With . . . cable to be stretched along the

wall . . . we can pick up a stone and with speed and little labor move it anywhere.

3. A boom derrick to be used at the quarry. The complete outfit [would] cost $300 [but] we are making everything but the crab [winch], that we cannot make. It costs $120.

The prices I have quoted . . . except for the truck are one third lower than the general price. I get these items from a Catholic firm and they leave me off one third. When I have finished building, all this machinery will be sold and you will get back most of the money. I already have a man who will sell the machinery for me.

He had hoped, he said, for a compressed air stone drill but could not afford it. But then, he continued,

St. Joseph came to our help. As you know all the stone near Mescalero is supposed to be hard lime stone. Despite this general belief a few weeks ago we found a great amount of beautiful light gray sand stone . . . easily and quickly quarried. What we need to do in a week at the lime stone quarry we can now do in one day. . . . Masons claim this is very excellent material.

He had one more request. "When you go to Europe be sure to get me a German Brother who is a stone mason. If possible get me one who can sing. . . ." Apparently Hugolinus was unwilling or unable to send the mass-singing mason: no record shows that any such arrived.

He added a postscript. "The total amount of money I want you to loan me is $825.90. . . . Don't forget the main reason for asking for a Brother and the machine is to enable us to continue work on the church even when we are broke. With hard times coming it won't be long before I can't get money. Still the church must be built."[25]

There were those in the order who from the beginning criticized the size of Braun's 'cathedral' for such a small and scattered tribe. "But you know," mused one wise father in retrospect, "that's Al! He didn't think in small portions. And I think in the long run—I don't know if I'd agree with that 'cathedral' there—but nevertheless, we get too small. We don't have the expansive blessed soul he had. . . . Al was a real character in the Order."[26]

The grand new church was also a bold challenge to the small Protestant church on its opposite hillside, but without the rancor of Migeon and Harper. From his return to Mescalero the padre had been playing a good-natured but serious game with the Reverend Mr. Overman, the Dutch Reformed pastor. The two were, he wrote, "having lots of fun. During the past few months I got seven of his school children" through their parents. "He got all seven back on me. After a short time I got five of the seven back again. In as short a time he will lose two more, not however, the remaining two of the original seven. Those two I suppose are his. . . ."[27]

The game continued as work on the church progressed. "The very sight of the foundation . . . has brought thirty Indians back to the Catholic Church. . . ."[28] He had long argued the importance of a grand church to signify for his people the magnificence of the universal religion. "This church," he emphasized, "will be the largest and most beautiful" modern mission in the Southwest. "It may appear extravagant to those who do not understand the situation here," he conceded, but it was the only way to rid the reservation of the divisiveness of competing religions. "Since we have begun to build on a rather grand scale there is talk among the protestants of closing up. They will have to do that or in a few years maintain a mission with no congregation."[29]

In October he reported another fourteen who had joined his flock, and "twelve more who have asked for instruction."[30]

The walls grew a little taller that summer, and in September 1921 Father Al wrote jubilantly to his provincial. "On [Christ]mas Day we expect to say mass for the first time in the back part of the church." His exhilaration is apparent. The area they would use was but a partially enclosed dirt-floor section behind a low wall; but with its own birth at its first mass Saint Joseph's would celebrate the great Birth and establish a center and a tradition.

"In about six weeks," he continued, "the freezing weather sets in. . . . Then we will have to quit work. During these six weeks we are going to work at high speed. . . ."

It is a short letter; the padre was obviously in a froth to drop his pen and get back to construction. "Can you give me a hundred dollars?" he asks shamelessly and without explanation, then skips to a quick close. "You had better pray much to St. Joseph for his Apache mission at Mescalero. The Protestants are making the dust fly."[31]

That Christmas of 1921 was the first of many like it. The building would remain partially walled and roofless for years, but like the babe in the womb, there was life in the growing church. Already it was a center where each year the Mescaleros, Catholic and non, gathered for a Christmas week that culminated in a midnight mass within the rising walls and a tribal feast on Christmas day.

"He called on a lot of Mescaleros to help," Virginia Klinekole remembered. "Father Albert would get a lot of used clothing donated to him for the Apache people, and he would put it all in one room, and . . . my mother and another lady would go over there and wrap presents weeks at a time." He involved everyone he could. "He was their leader, saying, 'Well, we're going to do this for the Christmas meal—fix this dinner—and everybody would make all the traditional Apache food."[32]

"Everyone that lived was welcome," Mary Dorame Gomez remembered. "My mother and aunt and some other ladies formed a committee and they'd cook. One of Father Al's favorite food was red chile and this white mush—they called it *cha-ka-way*—and he didn't care whether they had anything else, but they had to have that red chile and mush. And of course the ladies would make fry bread and empanadas."[33] The men were busy gathering wood for the Christmas fires. Everyone took part.

These preparations began long before the celebration. Then about a week before Christmas those from the farthest pockets of the reservation would begin to appear. By Christmas Eve the lights from a hundred campfires were playing on the wagons and tepees that nestled among the snow-swaddled slopes. As the hour approached the Apaches began to converge on the rising walls, advancing afoot up the slope in family groups, the adults with romping children around them and babies at breast.

Inside the roofless shell an enormous bonfire gave light and heat, and smoke rose like prayers into the star-stippled black above as Father Al intoned the ancient litany. "All the Apaches were there, sitting around the fire in their blankets for the midnight mass. He had them helping with the gospel, interpreting."[34] Those who had guitars played the hymns, and usually someone trilled a flute.

After the mass came the drums, and the Crown Dancers leaped into the firelight, masked and painted and kirtled, in their great forked headdresses. Here in the newborn Saint Joseph's two ancient traditions met and married.

On Christmas morning around a decorated tree Father Albert gave out the presents—every person got one—and the enormous feast followed: great sides of pit-roasted meat, and beans and chile and fry bread, and the sticky sweet mescal. "And hundreds of pies," Ellyn Bigrope remembers. "And empanadas. All the women cooked."[35] The padre had, through mass, meal, and music, involved virtually everyone in the celebration. "And you know," Virginia Klinekole mused, "when they all help like that it gives them a meaning. They become part of it."[36]

After the feast the ceremonial drums and dancers again performed throughout the afternoon, further enriching the day with their own traditional gift. Behind them rose the low but growing walls, the promise that would become their center, their 'cathedral.' The impossible dream was translating into solid stone, and into it the entire community—those on the reservation and those from the surrounding countryside—were investing their lives. Father Al's dream had become their own.

Slowly the walls of Saint Joseph's rise as funds and weather allow. Courtesy of SJAM.

10: PADRE AT LARGE

Where he got his vigor no one knew, but he seemed to give off sparks and ignite others around him. He must have tired; he must have wondered if time were long enough and he were strong enough to bring it all together. If so, none—possibly excepting Tony—saw it. Alongside the routine demands of his ministry were the tremendous labor of construction and the miles on horseback to reach his far-flung flock. He tackled every challenge with zest, humor, and an occasional nip of 'Irish holy water.' "It got so the Indians were stealing my Scotch," he told Father Blaise Cronin years later. ". . . I dug a hole under my bed so they'd have to go through me to get a drink."[1]

For all his good humor and genial nature, the padre was deeply serious about his work. Although absolutely in accord with Catholic doctrine, his methods were his own and always briskly to the point. He had no patience with lazy priests who expected the people to come to them in their rectories. "Christ told his apostles to get out among the people," he was fond of saying, "not sit on their butts and push papers around."

He lived as he spoke. He planted crops to feed workers and mules, and set out another hundred apple trees. He expected his Apaches to work their fields and tend the orchards—his pastorate was no welfare state— and he worked beside them. Father Al was like no priest the Mescaleros had known before. His concern for his people encompassed not only their spiritual health but every aspect of their daily lives, which he wanted to make happy, comfortable, and productive. He would later call it his "worldly motive," reasoning that man was both spirit and matter, and the priest's duty was to tend both. This would become a dominant theme throughout his life.

This concern extended to all men. He had a particular empathy for tuberculars, possibly stemming from his own respiratory ailments acquired on the battlefields of France. (On his discharge from the army the doctors had warned him he could expect to contract tuberculosis within two years "because of the effect gas had on my bronchial tubes.")[2] From time to time, on learning of a tubercular friar, he insisted the patient be sent to him. "The worst thing in the world," he opined, "is to send them to a san[atorium], where they spit in a cup, . . . hear coughing all the time, . . . and are forced to keep the dread thought in their mind every hour. . . . Ease of mind, lots of sleep, simple wholesome food, sunshine and desert air beats any san and the best Dr."

He recalled one priest who had been sent in 1919 to a sanatorium in Albuquerque. "I persuaded him to come to Mescalero. Told him to 'sleep every day as long as you can, eat eggs, milk, vegetables, honey and don't worry—you are going to die anyhow in time.' In six months he returned to Quincy [Illinois] to teach. Later he became pastor and is still going strong."

He had wired another tubercular priest to "come to Mescalero—take pot luck." The priest came, recovered, and returned to work. "I really," Father Al concluded, "should run a T.B. house for the Province."[3]

At the request of the Military Ordinate he accepted a reserve commission in the army in 1921, was promoted to the rank of captain, and once a year was ordered on active duty in New Mexico for two weeks.[4] It was an added job to an already packed schedule, but the extra time was—*Insignificant!* He was privileged to be serving his country. And should there be another war. . . .

☩ ☩ ☩

After mass on Sundays, if he wasn't picnicking with the Jettes, he often hitched his team to a buggy or cranked up his Ford 'machine' and drove to La Luz for dinner at the Hawkins hacienda or to Three Rivers ranch to visit the Falls when they were home. Either trip offered a spirited conversation with good friends and a long relaxing drive with uninterrupted time to think. Too, he liked to check on Albert Fall, whose heart trouble and chronic respiratory problems plagued the senator increasingly.

Emma, who believed Washington's climate—physical and political—worsened her husband's condition, had for some years begged him to quit the capital and return permanently to New Mexico. He almost had in 1919. Having lost heavily in oil investments in revolutionary Mexico, he owed back taxes on the ranch. Stating he could no longer afford to remain in the Senate, he planned to resign, return, and run the ranch.

But in 1921 President Harding named Fall Secretary of the Interior. The sale of his newspaper, a $100,000 loan from his old friend Edward Doheny, and the sale of a third of his ranch to Harry Sinclair eased his financial problems and allowed him to stay in Washington. (The Doheny loan, secured only by a personal note with the ranch as security, and without legal formalization, would later prove a tragic mistake.)

The cabinet job was a nightmare. From the beginning, hard-line conservationists undermined his policy of developing the country's natural resources until, opposed at every turn, and with his health seriously deteriorating, Fall resigned in March 1923, to Emma's tremendous relief.

But his enemies in Washington had meanwhile attacked him for leasing some naval oil reserves to private interests; and anti-administration Senator Robert LaFollette instigated an investigation. Fall defended his position, certainly to the President's satisfaction: Harding, having relied on Fall's expertise in Mexico, was expected to name him ambassador to that strife-torn country. The appointment was precluded by the President's sudden death in July.

The investigation concluded in October, hearings began, and Fall testified. The disputed reserves had been set aside in 1912 and 1915 for naval use in case of emergency—there had been fears even then of a possible war with Japan—and in 1920 their control was transferred to the Interior Department. On learning that private companies were drilling peripheral wells and thereby draining oil from the reserves, Fall testified, he had leased Teapot Dome in Wyoming and Elk Hills in California to Sinclair's Mammoth and Doheny's Pan American companies respectively. For this the companies paid the government higher-than-usual royalties and contracted to build enormous steel storage tanks to replace the crude-oil reserves with readily accessible refined oil in United States naval ports, chief among them strategic Pearl Harbor in Hawaii.

Fall documented his facts; the committee found no evidence of fraud and the affair was seemingly over. He could at last return to his beloved ranch where his family and friends hoped he could regain his health. None awaiting his return was happier than Al Braun.

✠✠✠

In 1922 two personnel changes in the Santa Barbara province affected the padre. Father Turibius Deaver replaced Hugolinus Storff as provincial; and Father Ferdinand Ortiz was replaced in Tularosa by Father Bonaventure Nava, a Franciscan who had fled the revolution in Mexico. What decisions Turibius might make regarding Mescalero remained to be seen; meanwhile Father Al was assisting the new pastor on certain business matters, as indicated in a letter he wrote soon after Nava's arrival. He seems also to have been honing his talents in the financial arena:

Adjoining the church property in Tularosa, Braun reported, "is a vacant block of land, the only one nearby, which for a long time Father Ferdinand wanted to buy. The owner now has a chance to sell to someone else and will sell if we do not take the property at once." Discussion with the owner yielded terms he found reasonable: $2,100 in three yearly increments, for the entire block. "To keep the opportunity open till I could get word to and from you I asked for an option. She gave us a $25.00 option but only for three weeks. I called some people together and laid the matter before them. They pledged to raise $700.00 annually till the property is paid. The Bishop will loan the first $700.00 to be repaid him after three years. All we need now is your permission, *no money.*"

The railway, he had been told in confidence, planned to move their shops to Tularosa in the very near future. "As soon as that news gets out the property will jump threefold over night. We need this property badly and to get it must act at once. If the deal is okay with you kindly wire 'Go Ahead'. . . . [Y]ou (the province) assumes no obligations. The Bishop assumes them all."[5] It was a deal he knew Turibius could not turn down.

✟ ✟ ✟

One frigid Sunday in December, having shivered through mass, a group outside the church was complaining of the cold when Father Al came by and with his usual heartiness joined the conversation. As Charlie Mackey's son Charles Jr. tells it:

> "Naw, it's not cold," Father boomed. "A strong man could go swimming on a day like this!" Because these men loved him and also loved to tease him, they managed to maneuver him into saying he would, if the agency pool hadn't been drained for the winter . . . "Well," they said, "how about the creek?" "Naw," he said. "Not wide enough." They said, "how about that nice big pool down by the orchard?" . . . "It's frozen over," he said. "Father, we can go down there and bust that ice to smithereens." They had him, they knew it, and he knew it, but being the man he was he agreed. He could have begged off, but he wouldn't.

The news spread quickly and every living soul at the Agency, . . . all of Carriso and Tularosa Canyons, most of Old Lady's Village, Bent and Nogal were all assembled at that pool awaiting their priest on that cold afternoon.

Then someone shouted, "Here he comes!" He had on an old wool cap, his army overcoat and a pair of old boots. He stopped at the near bank of the pool, looked across to the off bank where a group of men were standing holding blankets. He laughed, shed his great coat, kicked off his boots, stood for an instant in a pair of trucks, and dove through the floating ice into the frigid water. They all gasped and he came up scattering ice, shedding water, running as fast as he could toward the blankets, and yelling at the top of his lungs because of the cold and his joy.

They bundled him into the blankets, gave him a nip of brandy, and the people cheered. The men carried him on their shoulders out of the orchard. The people followed. They were happy, proud, in awe. . . . What a great day they all had. What a glorious experience. What a man this priest of theirs was![6]

Such sport endeared him to everyone—Mescaleros and agency personnel, people of the valley, in Tularosa and La Luz and Alamogordo. To the Mescaleros the antic only proved what they already knew: the padre stood discomfort like an Apache—though, as he liked to tell on himself, they "told me I should sleep with an old Apache woman to keep warm."[7]

He approached spiritual matters with the same zest, for his was a religion of joy, his a God of forgiveness, and he infused his joy into reading the Scriptures, delivering a sermon, saying the mass. "He accepted that all humans were sinners, himself included," a friend commented, "and he freely pardoned with the advice to get on with your life."[8] It was a common-sense message the Mescaleros liked. Sitting around their campfires or in the church, even at tribal meetings, he "told the story of Christ's coming and his willingness to die that all humans—which included the Indians . . . could be forgiven their sins. . . . He impressed [upon] them that we all have our dark thoughts," and reminded them of their tribal wars. As a result, the Indians "came to Father Al with their problems and they left feeling they were forgiven their sins and were free to start over."[9]

A few parishioners after mass. Second kneeling on left is Blasa Miller, tribal midwife, Father Al's trusty helper, mother of Katherine Miller Mackey. Kneeling far right is Roquita Mackey, in whose home Father Al took many happy meals. Courtesy of Dick Mackey.

Bishop Schuler, center, flanked by altar boys and parishioners. Courtesy of SJAM.

Attendance at mass grew steadily in the small interim church, or sometimes in the shell of the rising new one. Many years later an ancient Mescalero lady named Fern Kadakzinnie told Arthur Jones of the *National Catholic Reporter* how she came to the church. "'I was six years old when I met Father Albert. Mother and me would come down from the mountains in a wagon and sleep in a shed behind the old church so we would be there for Mass on Sunday. Then we'd go back to the mountains.'"[10]

The padre loved children. He baptized them, taught them their catechism, romped with them, guided them as they grew. He particularly loved the growing family of Juan and Virginia Baldonado in Tularosa, who often brought sons Juan and Pepe to Mescalero to serve as altar boys, and in time two younger ones who would one day, largely because of Father Al, become Fathers Felipe and Leon Baldonado.

He often visited the Diaz family at Bent. Braulio's grandson remembers his mother "telling stories about when she was a kid they used to have wrestling matches with Father Albert and all my aunts used to jump on him—it took all of them to get him down." Braulio's wife Zenaida "had two sisters that went to become nuns. One came back—she didn't make it—but my other aunt did. Father Albert [many years later] celebrated her fiftieth anniversary as a nun at Saint Francis in Tularosa. He was the influence on her becoming a nun."[11]

Work on the church proceeded steadily. They quarried and hewed and laid stone, and each summer saw the walls rise higher. These were sturdy walls, built to last—three feet thick on front and transept walls, two-and-a-half feet along the sides, four feet for the bell tower.

John Braun came from California during the productive months to build scaffolding and frame the spaces where the windows would be, and Bishop Schuler worked too through his summers in Mescalero. A certain urgency propelled Father Al. It was Franciscan policy to rotate personnel, and priests seldom remained in one assignment long. He had initiated the project, set the immense labor in motion. Should he be transferred a successor could probably take over, but—would a new priest grasp the dream?

He must push ahead as fast as possible for as long as his time held out, and push everyone with him. At best Al Braun, never a patient man, grew annoyed when anyone lagged, and expressed himself forcefully. "He could use the English language in more colorful ways than most of us could ever hope to," a nephew recalls. "He never minced his words . . . and you knew without a doubt what he meant."[12]

Adding to the press of time was the perpetual lack of funds. Summer was upon him and the till was empty when he wrote the Bureau of Catholic Indian Missions (BCIM) in March of 1922 to state his case. By quarrying their own stone and burning their own lime, he explained, they paid nothing for material; his professional mason was working for virtually nothing; they were building at very little cost. He needed only enough to keep his five-man crew on the job.

"If I am not able to continue work on the church," he stated flatly, "the mason will go back to California and that would be a great loss. If we can get help, we will not have to stop work. To keep us at work till January 1, 1923, twenty-four hundred dollars will be necessary. At present the mission has two hundred dollars. If you can send one thousand dollars, I will be able to get the remaining twelve hundred from other sources."[13] The plea, published in *The Catholic Sentinel*, apparently got results, for the work continued, that year and the next.

Even small debts loomed large for the padre. Hauling water was slow and cumbersome; but, he suggested to the new provincial, it could easily be piped from the stream. Father Turibius seems to have been more amenable to Father Al's innovations than his predecessor. "On your last visit," Braun wrote in November 1923, "I asked you if you could and would foot the bill for water pipe at Mescalero. In your cheerful way you consented. . . . The pipe came in June and the bill was $72.50. . . . The hardware co. is now asking payment. I know you are never flush with money but can you see your way clear to pay the seventy-two fifty?"[14] Turibius could and did.

Always there was Eric. "When Father Albert wanted to . . . know something about the customs, they would sit for hours discussing things." Eric's son Reggie was not impressed. "My father used to translate Father Al's sermons. And man, that used to bore me!

"He was one of us." During the puberty ceremonies "everybody would move in and out of camp, and he'd come over. He liked our cooking. One time,"—Reggie laughed remembering—"my mom was cooking, and he threw a firecracker in the fire. Boy! She cussed him a blue streak. And he sat there laughing. She was cooking bread on this slate rock. Then bang-bang-bang! She gave him a blue streak in Apache!"[15]

Front view of Saint Joseph's during the 1920s. Courtesy of SJAM.

Chow time for the working crew. Courtesy of MUA.

It was Eric who suggested what became the Outing System. Educating the Apache children was paramount to the padre. The Mescaleros must cope with the encroaching white world but still retain their own culture. To endure as a tribe they must be economically and societally independent, for which they needed education; as armor against the evils and temptations of the modern white world, that education must be acquired in a proper religious environment.

Although church membership was increasing, he believed "the Apache had not yet imbibed a Catholic spirit," and that "true conversion could be achieved only by working through the children, and only through such children as could be trained in a Catholic school. Efforts were made to find room for Apache children at the mission schools. But . . . it [was] impossible to place more than a few. . . ."

Eric had a solution. While attending the Carlisle School, he told the padre, "'I stayed with a family. I did some work for the people. They clothed me, fed me, sent me to school.'" It had worked there: could it not work for the Mescaleros? "'Send some of our children to Catholic families,'" Eric urged. "'Then the children can go to a Catholic school. It would not cost much.'"[16]

One can imagine the big priest, ever quick to catch a vision, listening intently as Eric explained the system, his wide mouth expanding into a grin, his mind exploding into plans. The padre acted quickly, later reporting to his provincial that on 10 September 1921, "I took eight Apache children to Saint Boniface School at Banning [California]. I also took two Apaches to Los Angeles, a boy and a girl. My mother is taking care of the boy. He goes to Our Lady of Loretta parochial school. The girl is staying with Prof[essor] Jung's family and goes to St. Joseph's School. These two children are receiving a splendid Catholic education without any expense to any mission. Monsignor Ketcham paid the transportation of the children," for whom the padre had obtained reduced fares through Ashton Hawkins.

Having acted without permission—the exigencies of time always took precedent over bureaucratic formalities with Father Al—he then detailed the Carlisle system that had inspired his action. "That system," he concluded, ". . . cut the expenses of educating the children. Moreover, the children advanced further in school than those . . . who stayed in an Indian school. Do you not think we could cut our expenses for educating our Catholic children by sending them into good Catholic homes?"[17]

Margaret Shosh and Frank Second were the first Apache children so placed. Frank stayed several years with Father Al's sister Loretta and her husband James McGrath, whose home on the family grounds was close by that of her parents. He did exceptionally well at the school. So did Margaret, living with the Jungs and attending Saint Joseph's—so well that "'Professor Jung sent a boy to [Mother Mary Borgia's] class asking for Margaret's homework in civics. He wanted to show the boys of the eighth grade what an Indian girl can do. She surely puts many a one to shame.'"[18]

The following year Father Al sent five more children for whom Loretta found homes. The numbers continued to grow, and Mrs. McGrath soon found herself the matron in charge of all arriving Indian children. That year Father Al suggested some Papagos be added to the system. Father William Hughes, Director of the BCIM, agreed to pay the children's travel expenses; and Father Bonaventure Oblasser of San Solano Mission near Tucson sent three Papago girls to Loretta in September 1923. Two years later the system again expanded, this time to include Pimas, who "came with a bang when Mrs. McGrath received word to prepare for the arrival of twenty-five girls. . . ."[19]

Loretta worked with Father Emmett R. Lucey, D.D., Director of the Los Angeles Bureau of Catholic Charities, who saw that proper personnel, including a nurse, visited the children regularly, and was himself always available when needed.[20] In time James and Loretta McGrath built a 'Club House' behind their own. Here the children could live until she placed them. Here also the children had monthly meetings, and a Christmas party each year. Loretta's services would continue almost until her death in 1939. Al Braun was not the only dedicated child of the sturdy immigrants from Alsace.

In 1927 Monsignor Hughes expressed his unqualified approval of the outing system. "The children are given the best possible training, namely that of a Catholic home and parochial school. No boarding school . . . can possibly give the same individual attention. The child is taught to save her earnings by opening a bank account. The child's check will not be honored without the countersignature of the field matron." Margaret Shosh, for example, with her earned money "has from time to time bought sheep and entrusted [them] to her relatives who receive the wool for their care, while Margaret gets the increase [in the herd] so that she can now return to her people and have a sufficient income from her flock to live. I know of no other system that trains for and establishes any such economic independence. Five years of the Catholic Outing System convinces me that it is the best of all."[21]

Margaret Shosh, center, in Los Angeles with her 'outing system' mentors, Loretta Brown McGrath and young son on left and Mrs. Jung and her daughter Frances, right. Courtesy of MUA.

From its genesis with two Apache children in 1921, the Outing System had proved instantly successful and amazingly productive. Years later the padre cited three reasons for its continuance.

> First, the Catholic Outing System solves the financial difficulty of the mission schools. Secondly it prepares the Indian to meet the white man on an equality. Thirdly, it accustoms the Indian to the practice of his religion on his own initiative and without being herded to it. . . .
>
> . . . .
>
> The day is not far distant when the Indian must mix with the white man. The natural growth of our country and the work and lure of the city will effect that. Unless the Indian is prepared to compete with the white man, he will go down to ruin. Is the Church doing her duty if she does not adopt the system which best prepares the Indian for the danger he is certain to meet?[22]

✛ ✛ ✛

Soon after Father Al had launched the Outing System he reacted with fury at what he considered a threat, not only to the Indians' education, but to that of all Catholic children. The state of Oregon, he learned, had passed a bill making public school compulsory for all, thereby forcing those from parochial schools into the public system. "I hereby put in my application for Portland," he wrote the provincial Custos fervidly,

> or some other place in Oregon where there is a parochial school. . . . Can hardly keep my seat since the bill passed making it compulsory for all children between 6 and 16 to attend the public school. We must show these people this country is neither Mexico nor France. When the Bishop, the priests, the sisters, and a good number of lay people are in prison for refusal to comply with the law, Oregon will be ready to reconsider it and other states will think twice before following Oregon. You will soon need more Fathers in Oregon that there are at present. Please send me . . . . I love a good fight. [23]

His pleas, though passionate, were fruitless.

✣ ✣ ✣

More disturbing than the Oregon challenge was the bloody maelstrom to the south. Since first arriving in New Mexico on the heels of Pancho Villa's raid, Al Braun had been keenly aware of Mexican turmoil and had followed the news reports of the violent political upheavals below the border. True realization of the revolution's import came from Father Bonaventure Nava's firsthand accounts. Through their growing friendship the padre developed a great sympathy for his persecuted fellow churchmen in Mexico and for the people of that war-torn land.

Since independence in 1821 Mexico had been plagued by external wars and internal convulsions. Inexperience in self-government and radical new political theories stemming from the French Revolution and its aftermath caused in Mexico a series of rebellions, changing regimes, and new constitutions, accompanied by political power grabbing, summary executions, and spreading banditry. Presidents came and went, often violently.

In the midst of the tempest stood the Church, a rock in the wind, and one the evolving secular state must by its very nature suppress. But Mexico had been Catholic for three centuries, and to attack the Church was to attack the deep-moving soul of Mexico. An attempt in 1833-34 to nationalize the Church aroused such violet protests that the 'reformers' proclaimed Roman Catholicism the official state religion—but the dictum itself subordinated the Church to the state. The erosion had begun.

By mid-century the radicals had seized control; and with a steel-eyed Zapotec Indian named Benito Juárez pulling the strings they enacted a series of overtly anticlerical laws. An act forbidding civil and church corporations to own property triggered the wholesale confiscation and forced sale of Church holdings, which included libraries, hospitals, orphanages, and shelters for the poor and elderly. Religious orders were suppressed, church activities closely regulated, and education secularized. The clergy were forbidden to teach, vote, or hold public office. Such oppressive tactics, and a constitution that ignored the landless masses, kindled a flame that engulfed Mexico in three years of bitter civil war, leaving her a land of widespread devastation, bandit-infested countryside, staggering debts, an empty treasury, and a prey to conquest.

France pounced in 1863. Four years later Juárez defeated the imperial troops, executed the luckless puppet Maximilian, and became a national hero. Although forced to suspend the antireligious laws, he refused to rescind them. His successor imbedded them in the constitution, invoked them, and ignited another rebellion.

The nation was teetering on total anarchy when in 1877 General Porfirio Díaz rode triumphantly into the presidency. Mexico was not ready for democracy and Don Porfirio knew it. Only strength and tight control could achieve unity, stability, and a viable economy.

He achieved all three. Courting foreign capital and technology, he vitalized the economy. Companies—chiefly British and American—developed mines and oil fields, built railways and ports, increased farm and industrial production, created jobs, and opened markets. A growing class of *mestizos* emerged.

He centralized, bureaucratized, and tightly controlled the government, the press, and the army. He made allies of erstwhile antagonists. Bandits, given training, salaries, and uniforms, became a constabulary—*rurales* who kept order throughout the countryside they had formerly ravaged. He won over the clergy by largely ignoring the secular laws. The Church recovered much of its property, revived its religious orders, reopened the seminaries, and resumed its work in schools, hospitals, and charities.

Díaz had saved Mexico and with it the Church, but at a price. Mill and mine workers toiled under deplorable conditions, and nine million Indians still labored in peonage; their discontent, stirred by the radicals, seethed beneath the surface. Porfirian Mexico was a police state. And the anticlerical laws, though dormant, remained on the books.

Díaz could not live forever, and the radicals stood panting in the wings. But it was a wealthy landowner's son, seeking justice for the peons, who challenged Don Porfirio. In 1910 Francisco Madero ran and lost in a rigged election, rallied the people to rebel, and torched the fires of revolution. Supporting him in the north, armed bands led by Pascual Orozco and Pancho Villa attacked railroads, disrupted communications, and soon controlled Chihuahua; in the south Emilio Zapata's hard-riding peasants were torching the sugar plantations of Morelos; in Mexico City seething mobs yelled for Díaz to go. By November Madero was president.

But he had loosed a blaze he could not control. Zapata continued to burn haciendas; guerrilla bands continued to pillage; laborers shouted for foreign capitalists to be expelled. Alarmed American investors asked protection, and by 1912 United States troops were massed on the border. The radicals meanwhile gained control of the Mexican congress and on the night of 22 February 1913 murdered Madero.

There followed a violent three-way power struggle between Victoriana Huerta, Venustiana Carranza, and Pancho Villa. After four years of bloody warfare, with the help of Alvaro Obregón's forces six 'red battalions' mustered by labor leader Luis Morones, and the backing of the United States, Carranza won.

The new president seemed friendly toward the Church and Catholics breathed a collective sigh of relief. But Carranza, willing to drop a principle to grab an opportunity, jumped onto the rising radical tide. A stacked convention hammered out the infamous Constitution of 1917, wildly revolutionary, anti-American, and anti-Catholic. Radical social, land, and labor reforms were mandated, and the framework was laid for government expropriation of private property and all natural resources.

The anticlerical laws provoked enormous outrage. Education was again secularized, the Church once more stripped of its property, its activities tightly controlled, its monastic orders prohibited. No cleric could teach, own property, vote, hold office, or engage in any political activity. Only Mexican-born priests were allowed; they must register and their numbers would be limited. The Church, in short, did not legally exist.

Carranza, though reluctant to enforce these decrees on a federal level, was willing to turn his back on seizures, depredation of churches, and persecution of the clergy in the provinces. When, forced by protests at home and abroad, he granted the Church some concessions, the radicals deserted him. Obregón was already mustering his own ranks. Morones backed him; so did Zapata until a Carranzista general assassinated him. In turn the Obregónistas overthrew Carranza, murdered him, and propelled Obregón into the presidency, whereupon he and the powerful Morones began to consolidate power and mold a Marxist state. Even Villa (given an hacienda as sop) withdrew from the scene. Catholics could expect full implementation of the odious decrees.

To boost the economy Obregón levied new taxes and heavier restrictions on foreign oil producers in Mexico, thereby provoking a three-year tussle with British and American oil companies, and their governments. To silence demands for land reform he distributed some token acreage, but only in the form of collective government farms. In the cities Morones gained virtual control over labor. Together they were well on the way toward total socialism.

But the old stumbling block of Catholicism remained. Confronted with slippery foreign relations, oil disputes, a precarious economy, and popular unrest, Obregón feared and avoided direct contact with the Church. Though a number of governors continued to persecute clerics, Obregón was not directly involved. Instead, he hit circuitously through a program of massive propaganda, focusing heavily on the indoctrination of children through socialist texts taught by socialist teachers.

The usual power grab for the presidency erupted as Obregón's term neared its end. Forbidden by law to rerun, he chose as his successor the radical Plutarco Elías Calles, whereupon Adolfo de la Huerta fomented a rebellion, Pancho Villa reentered the scene, and the usual free-for-all ensued. Hired assassins murdered Villa, Obregón defeated Huerta in battle, and Calles won the presidency.

The faithful throughout Mexico braced for the storm. It was December 1924.

✥✥✥

Churchmen everywhere had for some time been following the Mexican drama with apprehension, none more closely than Bishop Schuler, perched on the border, Father Bonaventure Nava who had fled the cauldron, and Father Al, whose welcome to New Mexico had come on the heels of the Villa raid. The tales of that attack were still fresh: of the gutted little town of Columbus, of murder and rape, of the telephone operator manning her switchboard to summon help, clutching her little child amid flying bullets and shattering glass. His interest, sparked already, had since been fanned by 'Boni's' accounts of the turmoil to the south.

Since Father Nava's arrival in Tularosa there had been talk of bringing exiled seminarians into New Mexico to continue their studies for the priesthood, eventually to return to their people and keep the Church alive in Mexico. Both Boni and the bishop believed Tularosa an ideal location. They also—provided the project was approved—thought Father Albert the man to run it: the padre knew how to make things happen; he sympathized deeply with the torn country to the south; he was a champion of Catholic education; and he spoke Spanish.

It would mean balancing his time between Tularosa and Mescalero, but he was healthy and energetic, and he promised—somewhat reluctantly, he wrote later—he would accept the added work and responsibility should the Mexicans come. So far it was only talk, though now with Calles coming to the helm it seemed more urgent. Meanwhile they continued to monitor the upheaval below the border, awaiting whatever might materialize, and continuing the work at hand as 1924 drew to an end.

It had been an eventful year. In January the Mescaleros had lost their good friend Samuel Miller. Father Al attended the Protestant funeral, prayed for Captain Sam's soul, and consoled Blasa and Katherine.

In June Shanta Boy's daughter Ruth bore a baby girl the padre would cherish throughout his life. "Shortly after she was born," the padre wrote, "I baptized her. She was a beautiful Apache baby."[24] He asked Juan Baldonado and his wife Virginia to be her sponsors. Juan agreed, on condition that the baby be named for his wife. The padre readily agreed: he deeply admired 'Mamacita' Baldonado.

Born in Guadalajara, Virginia Baldonado had lost her mother at an early age, whereupon her father placed her in an orphanage to be reared by the nuns. At age eighteen, having to choose between leaving the orphanage and joining the sisters, she opted to leave. She and her father rode a train to Juárez, her daughter relates, then "followed a man on a horse with a flock of sheep or goats, wound up in Alamogordo, and opened a little school to teach kids how to write their names and read." Virginia had been well schooled in the orphanage. "She could sketch, paint a little, and she read very well—she loved to read. She met my father and they were married."[25]

Juan and Virginia Baldonado were the kind of sincere Catholics the padre wanted as the Shanta baby's godparents. On 15 July he drove with them to Three Rivers for the christening. "I was hoping," he wrote Virginia Shanta years later, "you would have been named Alberta for me. But in respect to Juan . . . I gave you the name Virginia."[26]

In that same year the padre's friend Albert Fall, his health steadily deteriorating, had again been beset when the Teapot Dome affair resurfaced with the 1924 presidential election campaign. The Democrats, hoping to discredit the Harding administration, and by extension that of his successor Calvin Coolidge, now running for reelection, had caused the hearings to be reopened in an attempt to link the oil leases to Fall's improved finances. Some smelled, or said they smelled, bribery; and the old attack, revitalized and fueled by a muckraking press, again darkened the lives of the gravely ill Albert Fall and the long-suffering Emma.

Al Braun scanned the blaring headlines each day, refused to believe press or politicians, and stood by his old friend. It was, for the moment, all he could do.

The walls of Saint Joseph's continued to rise, the Outing System to flourish, the church membership to grow. Increasing numbers of Apaches were bringing their children to be baptized, sending them to catechism classes, and coming to their padre for advice, even inviting him to attend their tribal council meetings—a rare and genuine tribute.

But time was closing in. He had worked furiously through the summer of 1924, making the most of each day, and preparing for what he had known since March: Albert Braun had been ordered to take charge as Superior of Saint John's Indian School at Komatke, Arizona. He had been too successful with his educational innovations, had shown too much talent in working financial miracles for Saint Joseph's; and Saint John's needed help in both areas. Where called he must serve.

But the summons was a blow. His church stood but half built, his work at Mescalero still unfinished. Would his momentum and that of his Apaches all be lost? And what about the prospective Mexican seminarians? The vow of obedience sometimes came hard for Al Braun. God's will must be done—but was this God's will or that of his father provincial? "He didn't worry much about all the rules and regulations that had been developed by the Vatican" (or fathers provincial), according to one who knew him well. "'I've always been my own Pope,' he often said. 'I just try to do what I think Christ would do.'"[27] But he had vowed obedience.

So be it: if God willed this padre's work in Mescalero to continue—and Father Albert Braun obviously believed He did—well then, he would return. (And, the padre likely vowed, God's humble friar would do his own part toward effecting his return.) This transfer to Saint John's was quite possibly only a detour. And a detour was, after all—

Insignificant!

Unloading rock from the old truck Father Al and Tony cannibalized from two. This one ran—usually. Courtesy of SJAM.

Father Albert amid weeds and boulders before the entrance to
Saint Joseph's during the 1920s. Courtesy of SJAM.

11: ROADBLOCKS AND DETOURS

The years between Father Albert's departure from Mescalero and his return seem like a time enclosed in parentheses. This is not to say these years lacked relevance or slowed his immense energy, or that he ceased being "always in trouble"; they were simply an interruption in the pursuit of his overall goal, a divertissement.

His orders to report to Saint John's in Arizona had come in mid-March 1924, effective as of April. Parish records, however, show that he remained active in Mescalero all summer, and that among other duties he performed a number of baptisms—one being that of little Virginia Shanta on 15 July.[1] A letter to his provincial, dated a week earlier, indicates he had not left Mescalero except for a brief visit to his parents, and that while in California he had talked with Father Turibius. He apparently gained an extension (probably until closer to the start of school), for which he thanked his superior for "the efforts you make to enter into the plans of your subjects," adding that though he had little interest in the work at Saint John's, "you are my Provincial, and I fully realize what that means."

In leaving Mescalero he was leaving the Apaches he loved and the church for which he had dreamed so long and worked so hard. Neither Father Bonaventure in Tularosa nor his own replacement in Mescalero—Father Agustín Pozos, exiled like Father 'Boni' from Mexico—could or would pursue its completion as he had hoped to do. Nor could Tony do it alone. Hence, "Tony is going with me to St. Johns."[2]

Franciscans in Arizona had been working since 1896 among the Pima Indians. In 1908 Saint John's Mission was officially established, and a school was soon attached for the Pima children. Though Father Albert's assignment as superior for the school was not one he relished, he tackled it with his usual energy and wrote in October that he was planning "a retreat for the children . . . between X-mas and New Years." But, ever maneuvering for a return to Mescalero, he advised Father Turibius of letters recently received from Bishop Schuler and Father Bonaventure "reminding me of the promise I made two years ago to remain in Tulie [Tularosa] should the Mexicans come. I made that promise, reluctantly . . . [with] the understanding the Mexicans would move their seminary to Tularosa. I would like to go back and work on Fr. Bona to persuade his [Mexican] Provincial to do as he is supposed to do. . . ." But, he added impatiently, "if they can't make up their minds to do something"—they had been talking about it two years—"then I want to be free to hand in my application for China. . . ."[3]

He seems to have clashed almost immediately with other missioners at Saint John's. He was perhaps too innovative, probably too vigorous, too impatient to get things done, and certainly too stubborn when crossed. He was too strict a disciplinarian with the students—and, one suspects, with some of the friars.

He had never given up the old romantic notion of a China post, though the pull of Mescalero was more immediate. In any case, he wanted to leave Saint John's, and toward that end he continued to turn his persuasive powers on Father Turibius. "I believe," he wrote artfully, "you can conveniently make changes now. Fr. Gerard is tired of being alone. . . . I am certain he will be much better for these poor missionaries around here. . . . I am not criticizing the[m]. . . . They are fine, holy, self-sacrificing, zealous missionaries. Only I don't agree with their methods. . . . Fr. Gerard would do much better. Do have mercy on these poor missionaries."[4]

It would be inaccurate to assert he was unhappy at Saint John's, for in whatever geography or situation Al Braun carried his happiness with him. But Mescalero always tugged. He missed his many friends there; and he yearned to complete his 'Apache cathedral.' And after that—China still called. With his keen perception of history and of the tides that move it, he believed the Far East would be the stage of the future, and China's need for Christian strength would therefore be acute. In short, he craved an arena of action.

That he was misplaced at Saint John's there is no doubt; and given his stubborn nature and quick temper, it was no surprise to anyone when the rupture came. But his transfer was not, as he had hoped, to Mescalero. "Was canned by Father Turibius," he summarized later, "for being too tough on some girls, Pima Indians, who were insulting to the nuns. To know what it means to be under a tough boss, I was sent to San Luis Rey, Fr. Alban Schwartz, boss." Then he added—one can almost see the mischief twinkling in the priestly eye—"We became dear friends."[5]

He received his notice in November, before he had served his first school term. "I am really sorry I grieved you," he wrote Father Turibius. "There was never any malice . . . in spite of the many faults I have." He looked forward to San Luis Rey, he assured his provincial meekly, "where the opportunities for self correction are always better.

"[N]ow I am about to leave St. John's I feel the pang of parting. I feel attached to all here. . . . At times feeling ran high . . . but at no time was there any lasting bad feeling. . . . As soon as I get my orders I will move on."[6]

Old Mission San Luis Rey, part of the chain begun by Father Junípero Serra, was founded by Father Fermin Lasuen in 1798 and named for the sainted Louis IX of France, who went on Crusade in the thirteenth century. United States military forces occupied the mission during the Mexican War. In 1893 it became a study house for friars. In 1912 the mission was transferred to Sacred Heart Province to serve Franciscan friars expelled from Mexico, though it remained under the superiors from Saint Louis, who built the adjacent boarding school for Indian girls.[7]

San Luis Rey remained a haven for Franciscans fleeing Mexico, although it had been closed as a novitiate until reopened as such on 8 December 1924, when the newly arrived Father Albert was named Guardian.[8] From the Mexican friars the padre heard firsthand accounts of persecutions; with them he felt the dark agony of Mexico; and when Calles became president he continued to watch closely as the tremors swelled. It would affect his own life profoundly.

✠ ✠ ✠

Churchmen were well advised to fear Calles. Notoriously ruthless as governor of Sonora, he had set his army on any who challenged his authority, be they striking miners or Yaqui Indians resisting his claims on their ages-old tribal lands. He had encouraged the desecration of Roman Catholic churches and the persecution of the clergy in Sonora, while advocating a schismatic church that, with all ties to Rome severed, would give full obedience to the government. Toward this end he had banished priests from Sonora, to be replaced by a new non-celibate clergy.

Now as president he could impose his will throughout Mexico. Obregón had paved the way. The radicals were in firm control, their enemies largely exiled, assassinated, or politically impotent. Calles continued negotiations with the United States and the foreign oil companies;[9] he stimulated economic nationalism, revamped the banking system, and ignored land reform except as a political tool.

Toward the end of his presidency, to guarantee his continuing behind-the-throne power, he established the all-powerful National Revolutionary Party through which he chose each successive president and controlled national politics through voter fraud, a stacked court system, and brute force. As Calles controlled government through the party, Morones controlled through the unions. Both hated the Church and together effectively silenced Catholics and all other dissenting groups. Calles, as president or through the puppets he chose to succeed him, would control Mexico until 1935.

But the Church still commanded the loyalty of the masses. Calles believed like Obregón in the power of secular education; and to undermine the Church's hold on millions of the devout, he was determined to win the rising generation through socialist indoctrination in the schools and massive propaganda for the general populace. He encouraged the spread of Freemasonry, long a significant anti-Catholic force in Mexico. Increasing numbers of Freemasons began filling government positions, and soon virtually ran the Ministry of Education.

But education, propaganda, and Protestant inroads took time, and Calles was a man in a hurry. Knowing Catholicism was deeply imbedded, he opted to sanction the Church—but with its body severed from the Roman head, and a clergy subservient to the state. His would be the overt attack Obregón had avoided. He had the enthusiastic backing of Morones who through the unions began inciting labor to bomb and desecrate churches, hoist the red flag of revolution over them, and murder their priests.

The spark that ignited the fire occurred on the Friday evening of 21 February 1925 when over a hundred men seized La Soledad, a church in a poor section of Mexico City, and installed a schismatic priest pledged to disavow Rome and embrace the state. So was born the Mexican Apostolic Church.

On Sunday a thousand parishioners descended on La Soledad and attacked. Mounted police drove them off, Calles refused to return the building, and the schismatics seized several more churches. Through Mexico alarmed Catholics began mobilizing to guard their churches; by mid-May they had formed the National League for the Defense of Religion, popularly called La Liga. Calles condemned it and ordered immediate and rigorous implementation of all anticlerical laws throughout Mexico. Thereby some hundred government-rallied men attacked San Marcos Church in Aguascalientes. The ensuing battle raged into the night with heavy casualties, concluding when some four hundred Catholics were rounded up, summarily condemned, and driven from the country.

In July militant Catholics mustered in Guadalajara to oppose attacks on several of their churches. Blood flowed, arrests followed, the governor closed the seminaries, and tension grew. Some weeks later, when priests in Tabasco refused to take wives, they were deported.

Throughout Mexico the battle had been joined.

✟✟✟

Father Al closely monitored the escalating violence to the south. Deeply sympathetic with his Mexican brothers, he stood ready to help them should the New Mexican novitiate materialize. Meanwhile, as guardian of novitiates at San Luis Rey, he could be of immediate use in the crisis, there being nine Mexican novices and two lay brothers in his charge who, on completing their novitiates in July, would return to Mexico to rejoin their beleaguered fellow friars. On their departure novices from Santa Barbara Province would enter.

San Luis Rey proved a happier assignment than Saint John's. Having been firmly lectured for his previous offenses, the padre pledged his provincial he would heed his advice, and further reassured him that "Father Guardian [Alban Schwartz] and I have had no disagreement" over the boarding school attached to the mission, run by the Sisters of the Precious Blood. Unwilling to provoke Father Alban, he progressed warily. "So far," he reported, "I have not done much to help the children and under the circumstances it is difficult to do more. I am certain it would stir up a fuss and be the cause of unpleasantness. . . ."[10] He was diligently trying to become a model Franciscan.

Within a week of dispatching his letter of good intent, a new challenge arose, one that pitted him against the Commissioner of Indian Affairs, one Charles H. Burke. Al Braun always relished a good fight—and particularly against such bureaucratic officials as this one proved to be. Commissioner Burke, his mind tightly corseted in Victorian self-righteousness, regarded all Indians as "half-animals" and directed his single-minded fervor toward the eradication of their beliefs, traditions, and cultural identity. To wipe out their "pagan" religion he had proclaimed, among other mandates, a "General Church Service," which the Indian children were required by law to attend.

The edict stirred a brouhaha at Mescalero, of which Al Braun was quickly apprised. "The Catholic Indians of Mescalero," he later reported, "refused to take part in the 'General Indian Service.'" In letters to Bishop Schuler and Father Novatus Benzing, Custos of Santa Barbara Province, they charged that the beliefs and practices of their own faith had been excluded from the mandated service, concluding that "'this General Church Service is just another religion. We forbid our children to attend.' . . . All the Catholic Indians signed a protest against . . . the Government . . . [forcing] Indian children to attend 'General Service.' Bishop Schuler backed the Mescaleros. The papers went to the Apostolic Delegate . . . who backed the Indians. . . ."[11]

On orders from the provincial Custos, Father Albert traveled to Mescalero, arrived on 29 December 1924, surveyed the situation, and promptly wrote Commissioner Burke:

> We, the undersigned, sincere members of the Roman Catholic Church, devoted to her teachings and sacred ceremonies from which we get our inspiration and consolation for our daily life, consider the religious expression of the general assembly as . . . unauthorized and presumptuous. . . .
>
> Because unauthorized and unguided agencies teaching religion . . . can so easily lead into error, we most vehemently protest to have our children forced to attend the general assembly as long as there is any religious feature connected therewith. . . .
>
> We know the general assembly . . . has been introduced [in Mescalero], not by Mr. Young, the local superintendent, nor by Mr. Cooper, the local Principle, but by command of the Indian Department. . . . Both Mr. Young and Mr. Cooper . . . have acted as honest gentlemen . . . but are powerless to make any changes, because [they are] acting under orders. . . .
>
> We consider the General Assembly in its present form a menace, and insist on the right of our children not to attend.
>
> . . .

Beneath the padre's signature were the names of over half a hundred protesting Mescaleros.[12]

On returning to San Luis Rey, Father Al, on Bishop Schuler's suggestion, sent Burke another letter, enclosed further objections, and renewed the request, which by this time had hardened into a demand, with the added threat of court action.[13] Simultaneously he wrote the Right Reverend Monsignor William Hughes, Director of BCIM, who had initially signed onto the edict, that the

> Mescalero Apaches are convinced that the general assembly is absolutely wrong, and they look to the Bishop and the Catholic Indian Bureau to have it abolished. Should you fail it would be a grave scandal to the Mescaleros and they would lose all confidence in the Bureau. . . .
>
> Should the Commissioner refuse to grant the Catholic Mescaleros their request, . . . the Bishop wishes the case brought to court. . . . Bishop Schuler and Father Novatus have authorized me to handle this matter for them because of my influence with the Mescalero Indians, and because of my friendship with Mr. Young. . . .[14]

The Monsignor took exception to the padre's letter. "Permit me," he wrote stiffly, "as your commanding officer, to call you down. Col. Hunt told me he called you down when he ordered you back from the lines [in 1918], but that it did no good." The Monsignor's reason for his pique: "You did not send the protest through channels." He could do nothing, he stated unctuously, without consulting "the three prelates of this board . . ." and so on and on, and assuring Father Albert at great and legalistic length of regulations designed to safeguard against any religious proselytizing in the General Church Service.[15]

This rebuke did no more good than had Colonel Hunt's in the Argonne. Al Braun was at best annoyed with bureaucratic nonsense. One can imagine his bushy eyebrows rising in disbelief at the letter, and then pulling together into battle formation. "Monsignor Hughes is mistaken," he penned at the bottom of the letter, "about not going through channels. I sent the protest through the Catholic Indian Bureau and according to instructions from Bp. Schuler mailed a copy . . . to the Legal Dept. of the N.C.W.C. [National Catholic Welfare Conference] asking the Dept. to cooperate with Msgr. Hughes. . . ."[16]

He then wrote to Hughes directly, answering the Monsignor's glib assurances of safeguards, which "sound well enough on paper . . . [but] guard nothing. Monsignor, there is no use to sacrifice what we hold priceless for the cheap thing of being obliging to the Government, and thus avoid a manly fight.

"It took us years to give the Apaches of Mescalero a right mind and conscience in regard to indulging in mixed religions, and nothing in the world can induce me to corrupt them. . . ."[17] Al Braun too could wield a sharp stiletto.

"The Indians, the Bishop of El Paso & the Apostolic Delegate won out," he reported. "The General Service was dropped all over the United States."[18] When Schuler and Novatus needed a fighter they had picked the right man. And there was no one for whom Al Braun would rather fight than for his beloved Mescaleros.

Back at San Luis Rey he and his superior, Father Lawrence Mutter, got along famously and worked together productively. Having a like mind with which to discuss problems lightened his administrative duties, which tended to be routinely dull. His crustiness comes through in his reports to his provincial:

One lay brother, he writes, "has in his head that he wants to be a priest. . . . You know whether it is allowed for a Brother in the novitiate to leave and study for the priesthood. . . . I know nothing about these matters. . . ."[19] Of a meddlesome friar planning a vacation in Santa Barbara, he requests that Turibius keep him "north for a few months. . . . Give him some work that will keep him away from the school here for a while . . .; then he could return and someone else would be doing the odd jobs . . . that give him the opportunity to get to the school so frequently. . . ."[20] One older friar, he complains, "is continually nagging" certain newer brothers, and "must be removed if we are to keep any of the young Brothers."[21]

The mission was chronically shorthanded. Especially critical was the lack of Spanish-speaking priests to serve the Mexican population. "Both Fr. Luke and Fr. Philemon are doing their best, but they don't know the language, and their efforts are almost for nothing." To alleviate the situation, Father Al suggested an exchange of priests each Sunday between the mission in San Diego, which would send a Spanish-speaking priest to say masses for the Mexican communicants, and San Luis Rey, which would respond in kind for San Diego. Fathers Marciano (from San Diego), Luke, and

Philemon would rotate to serve the two missions and outlying communities, an arrangement the padre believed would be beneficial to all concerned. He enclosed a tentative schedule. "If you approve this plan," he added, "we ask that you authorize us to buy a Ford car on the installment plan. It is not possible to do the work without means of transportation."[22]

Either Turibius nixed the plan or it proved unfeasible in practice, for Fathers Al and Lawrence continued to press their case. "[W]e . . . hope you will . . . send us Father Victor [Bucher]," the padre wrote a couple of months after sending his proposed exchange plan. "[W]e still have the Mexicans of Oceanside, Carlsbad, Vista and Fallbrook and there is no one to look after them. Father Victor has put in much time studying Spanish this last year. He will be able to do justice to the Mexicans."[23]

Transportation to the communities remained a prime necessity. Whether they got the Ford they wanted is not recorded, but at some time a Buick seems to have materialized, and some time after that he wrote guilelessly to his provincial that "Mr. Montgomery, a lawyer in Los Angeles, has offered us a locomobile, 5 years old. . . . I told him to send the car. I forgot to ask your permission. Was not trying to put anything over on you. If you now say we should not take it, that would be O.K. The sun rises and sets just the same. . . ." A long discourse followed on the relative merits of the two cars, the theme being that Father Al preferred the Locomobile which, though high-priced originally, had depreciated with age. "The car uses more gas than a Buick but Mr. Kilty figured that it would take 20 years to save on the difference . . . , enough money to buy a $1000.00 Buick. If we want a Buick we must have the money now. But," he ingeniously caps his argument, "if instead of buying the Buick we put the price of the Buick on interest, that interest will more than pay the difference in gas. We don't want 4 cars here. If you think we should keep the locomobile [we] will dispose of the Buick. Won't get much," he adds. "Would rather give it to one of the Indian missions. Possibly some mission has a car worse than the Buick. I know Mescalero has."[24]

They kept the Locomobile.

In addition to his other duties, the padre was responsible for the spiritual care of the *asistencia* at Pala and the small peripheral communities of Pauma, Rincon, and Temecula, which the Locomobile made more easily accessible. Father Brendan Mitchell later recalled serving his novitiate at San Luis Rey under Father Al in 1925–26: "Frequently on Saturday nights after midnight office Al would take off in a rambling old eight-passenger Locomobile. . . . He drove twenty or thirty miles into the hills where he served as pastor for another cluster of Indians. . . . At Pala Mission and neighboring villages Al was at home with the people he loved—the poor and ill-treated."[25]

From the beginning of his tenure at San Luis Rey, Father Al had been concerned with Pala, the hub of the cluster, whose little mission church, built in 1818 as an auxiliary chapel, or *asistencia*, lacked certain amenities, for which, he reported, the ever-faithful Tony was "making a granite altar. . . . Before we finish it may cost about $175.00. Is that O.K.? Tony wants to have the new altar up for the feast June 13," a month away, for which the padre trusted his provincial "would not object if I ordered [the remaining materials] immediately." He also opined that the tabernacle needed a safe "because of visitors coming into the church" when he was away. "Pala," he assured Turibius, "has more than enough money to cover these expenses."[26] He continued to spend a lot of time at the little mission.

He constantly juggled his many duties, one of which was his commitment as a reserve officer in the United States Army to serve two weeks each year on active duty in or near New Mexico, for which he used his vacation time. Writing from one such tour of duty at Camp Logan in El Paso, he advised Father Turibius he would "leave Friday midnight . . . , reach Tularosa 3:15 a.m. . . . Will get to Mescalero about 5 a.m. [possibly in conjunction with the general assembly controversy, then still awaiting resolution]. The camp doesn't close till Sunday but I arranged with Fr. Vincent to send a telegram saying that it is absolutely necessary that I get back. Leaving a little ahead of time does not affect my pay."[27] He always applied his army pay to whatever building fund he was at the time raising. The small chicanery by which he left camp early seems not to have troubled his conscience in the least. It was, after all, *Insignificant!*

Back at San Luis Rey he resumed his duties. His methods, and his gusto in the role, are best described by Father Brendan Mitchell:

> Al's style was tough and tender, no nonsense but usually with a warm laugh. What he felt had to be done he met head on. He decided one evening to rid the Old Mission of a

pesty infiltration of large owls by firing at them on the fly from the church tower and roof from his old army 45. Another time he went into the ancient church attic to test the rickety ceiling. One hammer blow smashed a hole in it so he decided to finish the job without further ado, knocking the whole structure down. It left a huge mess of rotten wood and a century of owl and bat guano dumped over the church floor and pews for the novices to spend the next three days cleaning up the wreckage. After an episode like that Al always threw a party for the gang. He could bawl you out Army style for making a fool of yourself and half an hour later crack your ribs laughing at his funny stories.

To us novices Al was the Guardian, an "older man" (by the record I note he was 37). He put us to work casting concrete pipes for the new irrigation system or hauling in hay, with time out for immense sandwiches and fresh milk at ten in the morning. At midnight he was waiting for us with the Novice Master in the friars' choir for chanting Matins and Lauds followed by a short, usually sleepy, meditation. If one were late . . . he could expect to kneel on the floor in front of the others, arms raised in "cross prayer", for five or ten minutes. In the morning Fr. Al's cheerful greeting to last night's laggard might be a smiling, 'Come on, frater, it wasn't all that bad.'

Christmas time that year [1925] was full of merriment and it wasn't all the novel liturgy. This was the year of the big flood. The modest San Luis Rey river overflowed the valley, washed out a couple of bridges and closed the road to Oceanside, our one supply depot. At the Mission, electricity for lights and pumping water went out, the plumbing stopped and even the cow barn was awash. The old Army man decided that novices fetching buckets for toilet service were ideally matched. Shortages and short cuts dissolved the novitiate routine. There might have been midnight choir by candlelight. But at the end there was a grand *spielabend* with a couple of bottles of wine thrown in for kids raised during prohibition days. Everybody celebrated the deluge like Noah and his family the day they left the ark.[28]

Deeply concerned as always with education, Father Albert worked constantly to improve the schools at Pala and the other tiny communities in his purview, but seemed always to be pushing against a mountain. Throughout the province the Order struggled desperately to keep the mission schools open without the funds to do so. Al Braun's success with the Mescalero Outing System had spurred some movement in a similar direction among the Arizona Indians, but available homes for the children were limited in number and could only relieve a fraction of the expense.

The Franciscans could not support the schools alone, Braun expostulated: why weren't the bishops in every diocese containing a school doing their part? "There is no thought of making real Catholics out of Indians without Catholic school," he asserted, and since the Order could not and the bishops would not support them, the Order must therefore abandon the mission schools. "This may at first seem rash," he conceded, but "we must take a bold step to wake up the Bishops who can and should do something. . . ."[29]

Always an enthusiastic builder, he found San Luis Rey's badly needed repairs grist for his mill. Following the creation of the Mexican Republic in 1821 and its subsequent secularization of church property, all the missions had fallen into decay. After the American Civil War the church regained possession, and the Franciscans returned in 1892. Restoration of the missions began, though slowly and sporadically. But with the arrival of Al Braun and the ever-faithful Tony at San Luis, an explosion of renovating and rebuilding enlivened the old mission. During his nearly three-year stay he and Tony completed the main quadrangle of mission buildings, installed electricity, restored the choir loft, and overhauled the kitchen. They renovated the original court and built a museum. When Father Alban Schwartz recruited the padre to help with an athletic program at the mission school, Braun organized a basketball team and, with Tony and two German lay brothers, Benedict Schlokum and Salesius Kraft, built a tennis court and a swimming pool, for which they utilized borrowed equipment and salvaged materials from the reconstruction project at the mission.

In August 1925 Father Al advised Turibius that he was going to Santa Barbara "to consult regarding the best means to strengthen the tower of the old mission here which has four bad and dangerous cracks according to Tony. Tony is going along."[30] Whatever proposals they made seem not to have convinced the superiors, for little or nothing was done.

The danger continued to worry Father Al.

Nearly a year passed. Then, during the night of 22 July 1926, the tower collapsed. It happened in the wee hours when no one was in or near the structure, and no one was injured.

Al Braun immediately attacked the crisis. Work should start at once, he wrote his provincial, "because of danger to school children and tourists."[31] He assessed the damage, estimated the cost of renovation, and requested Turibius to "please send Br[other] Sales immediately so that we can build protection against the rains."[32]

The friar he requested was the same Brother Salesius who had impressed the padre while working on the swimming pool, and Al wanted him back. Like the padre, he was a veteran of the Great War, though he had fought on the opposite side as a German artilleryman. Sales had entered the Franciscan Order before the war, left to fight for the Fatherland, and afterward completed his novitiate at Holy Cross Province in Saxony. He was then sent to Saint Elizabeth's in California's Santa Barbara Province to help train German speaking friars in America. A big, robust man, he was hard working, dedicated, and a master builder.

His strength and expertise proved of enormous value at San Luis Rey in what became a complete rebuilding of the tower; it was finally completed and blessed on 8 May 1927. Father Al and Old Tony had, moreover, made a staunch friend: they would see more of the big German friar.

☩☩☩

In the same month that the tower collapsed at San Luis Rey, so did the hopes of the faithful in Mexico. On 2 July 1926 Calles delivered the killing blow to peace via an edict—the infamous Calles Law—by which the Church in Mexico must yield or perish. In California, the collapse of the tower just nine days before the edict was to go into effect seemed to some an omen.

The climax had been building since January. Calles had replaced his moderate minister of the interior with the fire-breathing Colonel A. Tejeda, whose new regulations began closing in on the clergy.

On 4 February the jingoist newspaper *Universal* quoted Archbishop José Mora y del Rio as reaffirming his earlier refusal to recognize the anticlerical articles of the constitution, and declaring he would fight their enforcement. Calles went into a crimson rage, ordered all Catholic schools, seminaries, and convents closed, expelled all foreign priests and nuns (some two hundred), and enjoined all governors to limit the numbers of clergy in their respective states.

Passions flamed, blood flowed, the bishops pondered what to do, and Rome sought compromise by sending another apostolic delegate in March. A straw in the gale, he was gone by May, but, having assessed the situation, resigned his mission and advised the bishops to fight back. Accordingly, they formed an episcopal committee: but should they fight actively or passively?

Calles threw down the gauntlet with his July decree. The Calles Law tightened the anticlerical provisions of the penal code, specifying penalties for infractions and enabling their implementation. Particularly alarming was the emphasis on compulsory registration of all clerics, which the episcopate correctly saw as a trap: those who registered would kneel to governmental control; those who refused would become outlaws. In either case the government could replace them with schismatics.

The bishops bade the priests not to register and appealed the decree. Rome negotiated for a modus vivendi. Tejeda and Calles refused to move. The deadline—31 July—loomed closer.

Still the episcopate pondered: to negotiate with Calles or call his bluff? While they debated, throngs protesting the decree were rising throughout Mexico. Emboldened by the popular swell, the bishops made their decision. In a collective pastoral letter of the 26th, they ordered that, though the churches would remain open and guarded, all public worship would be suspended from the day the Calles Law was implemented. They had called the dictator's bluff.

But Calles was not bluffing. The "decisive battle" was at hand, he proclaimed; and Tejeda chortled. "'We have got the clergy by the throat and will do anything to strangle it.'"[33]

The deadline came and went. But neither Calles nor the bishops had gauged the explosiveness of long-suppressed passions, or the depth of desolation that descended on a spiritual people cut off from the very springs of their spiritual existence.

It started in the villages—Jalisco, Colima, Guanajuato, Coahuila, Michoacán—and it spread. Men, women, entire families were soon rising to defend with their lives the faith that gave those lives meaning. With their backs to the wall they arose, their cry, *¡Viva Cristo Rey!* Long live Christ the King!

On 31 July 1926 a dark age descended on Mexico. For three years no church bell would summon the faithful and, though the bishops had not ordered that the sacraments be suspended, persecution grew so brutal as to effectively curtail such rites. The escalating violence would leave 90,000 combatants and countless nonparticipants dead in its wake. The slave-ship of state had crashed against the cliffs of faith and, trapped in the collision, the long-beset masses rebelled.

Cristeros they were called—people for Christ—and their war the *Cristiada*. They fought for land and for freedom from tyranny and for their human rights. Above all they fought for their faith. The attack on that was the igniting spark and the flame that kept them fighting against gigantic odds. *¡Viva Cristo Rey!*

✞✞✞

Al Braun kept his close ties with Mescalero throughout his years away. His dream lay yet unfinished, half stone, half vision. Even as he neared completion of the tower at San Luis Rey, he wrote his provincial. "I am still sitting here, while my heart is out on the mission at Mescalero."[34]

And as the fire swept through Mexico he was in constant contact with Father Bonaventure. Still arguing for the proposed seminary to be established in the Tularosa-Mescalero area, 'Boni' and Bishop Schuler ardently wanted Father Albert to return, help push their plan, and set it up. The exiled Mexican seminarians' need was more urgent now than ever. This would entail the padre's leaving the Santa Barbara Province temporarily and working under the Mexican Province of San Pedro y San Pablo in Michoacán, in whose hands the Tularosa and Mescalero churches would be placed. Bonaventure wanted to discuss the plan with Father Al, who in turn wrote Turibius.

> Am enclosing a letter from Fr. Bonaventure. Can you get him a pass immediately so that he can come to the coast.
>
> . . .
>
> What do you think of the plans. I am satisfied here but if you will give permission I will resign [from the Santa Barbara Province] and go to work with him. We understand each other. Father Bonaventure is capable but he needs someone to encourage him in times of opposition. That has been my

ambition for a long time, to help the Mexican friar[s]. . . . I am waiting for your answer in this matter. If you can spare someone it will be a great act of charity toward our confreres in Mexico to send help.[35]

Turibius consented, began pulling the necessary strings, and by early 1927 plans were beginning to crystallize. "My dear Father Provincial," Braun wrote in March,

> I can't find words to express my appreciation for the effort you are making to enable me to get back to New Mexico. The greater the persecution in Mexico against the church, the stronger my desire to be with Father Bonaventure to help him build up apostolic Franciscans who will go back to that country and with the same weapons used by the apostles, struggle to preserve our holy faith for the people and overcome the enemies. My greatest ambition is to obtain from God the blessing among the number sent into Mexico and told to stay there. This seems to me a wonderful opportunity for any poor sinful man to find an easy way to heaven.[36]

Father Albert's feet would soon follow his heart back to the homeland of the mountain gods.

12: RETURN TO THE MOUNTAIN GODS

He returned in July.

He was home again—for Mescalero had become his home. He was working once more with Father Bonaventure—'Boni' he called him—and Bishop Schuler. He embraced his old friends and all their children, three years older now, and some new ones too. Virginia Shanta, whom he had baptized shortly before he had left for Saint John's, had just turned three. Katherine Miller and Charlie Mackey—man and wife now—took him under their wings at their little home near the church. He was again baptizing the babies Blasa helped into the world. He rode the reservation and the word preceded him as he rode. "Father Albert is coming! Father Albert is coming!" These were his people, his family.

There on the hill stood the walls of Saint Joseph's in half-built promise, waiting like an abandoned child. The summer of 1927 was already half spent, but the promise was renewed, and by the next spring the church would resume its thrust toward heaven, a beacon of light for his Apaches. He was back to his mission and his people, and Tony would soon follow, once he had finished certain repairs at San Luis Rey—where, the house chronicle notes, he "plastered the outside of both church and mission."[1]

Father Al too had details to address before he could resume building. First were the tedious but necessary chores of raising funds and securing a patent for the land on which Saint Joseph's stood. Both necessitated trips east.

Fund raising was always a challenge. Some, who from the first had been critical of the size and grandeur of 'that cathedral Al Braun was building in the wilds of New Mexico,' were chary of contributing: wouldn't a smaller, simpler structure suffice? But the padre had dug in his heels. This church, he averred, "will become the greatest center of tradition among the Apache. . . . There is in a strong church building a valuable psychological effect," and he cited as example "the greatest of all Indian missionaries, the old Spanish padres. The impressive strength of the church begets the strength of faith. . . . But St. Joseph's will not only be large and strong," he stressed. "It will be full of grace and beauty. Why not? It costs but little more. . . . St. Joseph's will be a monument to the artistic ability of . . . Mr. Stanton, who drew the plans for us and charged us nothing for them. . . ."[2]

Nor was Saint Joseph's the padre's only project. Added to the enormity of building the great stone church came now the happy, frantic preparations for the long-discussed seminary and novitiate for the exiled Mexican Franciscans, finally coming to fruition. Father Al was to orchestrate the venture—"a diplomatic way of being canned," he quipped, failing to mention his own maneuvering for the transfer.[3]

The seminarians would be coming principally from the province of San Pedro y San Pablo in Michoacán—among the strongest hives of rebellion in Mexico and consequently among the hardest hit by the Calles persecution—to which Mescalero and Tularosa had been lent, along with Father Al, for as long as they would serve the exiles. In addition to his own provincial and Bishop Schuler, the padre would now also be working with the Mexican provincial, Father Domingo Resendiz, who had already spent some time in El Paso and Mescalero.

"He decided," Father Al reported in September, "to place [the] novitiate at Mescalero and philosophy and theology up the valley 8 miles north of El Paso" on forty-nine acres already under cultivation and irrigation, "wonderful land and easy terms. . . . Am going to Washington the 26th of this month to get the title to the ten acres at Mescalero [and] do some collecting.[4] Fr. Provincial [Resendiz] wants to invest first novices Feb 1st 1928. It is necessary to start building at once [for which he hoped he could borrow Brother Sales] and likewise to get money at once. Fr. Bonaventure likewise is going collecting. . . ."[5]

He headed east, reporting first from Philadelphia that he had "spent several days in Washington last week" pursuing an unconditional title for the specified land, for which "an act of Congress is necessary. If one of the Senators from New Mexico backs the request it will go through with no difficulty. . . . Will call on one of the Senators. . . ." His quest went through with ease.[6]

In Philadelphia, the padre continued, William Stanton "is drawing plans for the home of [the novices]. Have spent every day with him since coming here. . . ."[7]

Raising money, he found, was far more difficult than securing land titles or architectural plans. Throughout the years prior to World War II the padre would be plagued increasingly with the struggle for funds: America was already steering toward the crash that would trigger the Great Depression. "Private collecting at churches is banned in the East," he reported. ". . . The only way to get help is through established church agencies. . . . Tomorrow I am going to Baltimore to see Archbishop Curley. . . . Everywhere the objection to helping Mexicans is that it will be wasted money because they will pull out in a year or two."[8]

After two days in New York, he wrote, "Feel as if I am at the bottom of the grand canyon. New York is a giant, is interesting and a whole lot more can be said about it, but it would drive me crazy. . . . If the Mexican friars are going to depend upon begging trips to build their novitiate and the houses for philosophy and theology it will be a long time before those houses are built. . . ."[9]

Turibius sent encouragement and a letter of recommendation, which "reached here just when I needed it." As always, Father Al was impatient of hierarchical channels and of what he termed their 'propaganda.' "In the East, collecting is hit on the head by the Archbishops and Bishops. Everything must go through organized agencies. . . . It is only a question of time when the Propaganda will control everything. . . . The Hierarchy does not want anyone else to have a hand in the pie. . . ."[10]

By mid-November he was back in New Mexico. "Had all I wanted of both traveling and begging." A number of groups had shown interest, he reported, but had no funds at that time. "We must have land. Building can go ahead as money comes. . . . [W]e must get $1940.00 before Jan 1st" for the acreage north of El Paso. "If nothing else can be done we must borrow that amount. . . ." If each of the five American provinces would pay one fifth, he suggested, it would burden no one. "For the love of God and the salvation of souls in Mexico . . . I beg you to propose this matter at the next meeting of the Provincials. . . . The 48 acres along the river and under irrigation, today cannot be bought for the price we are paying. . . . Besides the 48 acres we are getting [another] 650 acres, much of it along the concrete highway, for $3000.00. . . . We are tak[ing] it because of the very bright outlook. In ten years its increased value will pay for the building of a very good house of philosophy and theology. Till that time any kind of a house must answer the present need. By Feb. 1st we must have a place."[11]

From the first he was frustrated by the vacillation of Mexican Provincial Father Domingo Resendiz, who, he wrote late in November, "says because we did not . . . get enough money to have a basement in the house of novitiate by Feb he . . . [has] decided to postpone the investment [of the novices] till 1929. . . . We could very easily make a very comfortable novitiate in the barn, eight good rooms and a little chapel. We intend to build on, a long shed for kitchen, store room, refectory and schola. The novices would be entirely . . . undisturbed. . . . I have already bought . . . stoves, bed blankets, large hotel range . . . , everything. It is the same old story of always backing down." However, he added craftily, Resendiz "did not say I should not go ahead with the work. I know they will never move unless forced. . . . I think we should go ahead and equip the barn and then tell Father Provincial everything is ready. He will have no excuse and the entire blame will rest with him." And, he reminded Turibius, "Don't forget about Bro. Sales!" Or Tony: "I need him badly."[12]

The struggle for funds never ceased. "Today," he wrote on 1 December, "the first payment on the land north of El Paso is due. We are short $1420.00. Herman Andreas, who is handling the deal for us is holding [it] up . . . for a few days in the hope we can get the balance. . . . Can you loan us $1420.00 for 90 days. . . . Time is pressing."[13]

Turibius too was pressed and unable to help. The padre was not surprised, and wrote cheerfully that "Herman Andreas . . . will find some way of helping us out. . . . The main thing is to have a big stock of confidence in God."[14]

Al Braun's strategy for forcing the hand of the Mexican provincial worked. In mid-December he reported that Resendiz had agreed "that since all the household equipment . . . is already at Mescalero, he will open the novitiate in March. I am greatly pleased . . . that he has chosen March . . . [when the] worst of winter is over . . . and it will not be so hard on the novices. They are not accustomed to a severe winter. . . ." Some had in fact already arrived and were "suffering from the intense cold." While in El Paso buying for their winter necessities he had run into a Mr. Maloney who "hopes to get me a 3 ton G.M.C. truck, one which has been run less than a thousand miles. Mr. Maloney will put on new rubber and make a present of two extras. The truck cost its owner $3,500.00 and I am supposed to get it for $500.00. . . .

"It will be splendid if Bro. Salesius comes shortly after Xmas," he added. There was less hurry for Tony, for building on Saint Joseph's could not begin until spring. There seems to have been some question about Tony's health. At sixty-one he was not as robust as when they had begun the church, and his eyes may also have been showing signs of the blindness that would eventually overtake him. "It is not so much for the work . . . that I want Tony," Braun insisted, "as for the knowledge he has. . . . Without Tony I am taking big chances that a larger building will be faultily constructed. . . ."

As for the El Paso land, "Mr. Andreas advanced the money to make first payment. . . . He said he will be patient as long as I don't lie down on the job. . . ."[15]

January 1928 dawned clear and bright, and Father Al was exuberant. Work was progressing on schedule for the novices' investment. Several exiled friars had arrived to help with the work; and, he wrote Turibius, he was "happy to hear that Bro. Salesius is about to start. All I need him for is to quickly put up the make-shift novitiate and make a few most necessary table cupboards etc. . . . He should be ready to return to the coast by March. Will try to persuade my dad to stay over and do other jobs that are not so pressing. . . ."

He still needed stonemasons for the work on the church, but reported that the "Mexican Brothers are learning fast to quarry and cut. This big beautiful church will be the strongest inducement for the Mexican Friars to 'stay put' at Mescalero. They love a big church. . . . This week I am getting a truck [presumably the one Mr. Maloney had mentioned] . . . to begin hauling. . . . I am about broke. . . ."[16]

Brother Sales arrived in mid-January. "He is now at work on our 'novitiate,'" Al wrote his provincial. ". . . He said if the weather is good enough he will finish in eight weeks." Could he keep him that long? he asked. Worried about fire in the barn-turned-novitiate, he and Sales "decided to make all partitions and ceiling of metal lathe and plaster," which added an additional $387.50. "This may seem a small amount but it is terrible for me [and] must be paid within 60 days." Could Turibius help? "I have my hands more than full paying for the property and paying off debts that had to be made to equip the novitiate. . . . Do try and get me some help somewhere because I am up against it. . . ."[17]

In February the padre received a press bulletin, copies of which he sent to over one hundred Catholic publications in hope of engendering some financial aid. The article described the Calles persecution, called for

American Catholics to help save the Church in Mexico, lauded Father Albert for his single-handed undertaking, and enumerated his difficulties. "There is at present," the plea concluded, "no more deserving cause in America than the one to which Fr. Albert's superiors have assigned him."[18] The appeal was undoubtedly responsible for some of the subsequent donations.

The candidates soon arrived. The original eight had expanded to sixteen and then to twenty-one, to be invested on 19 March. Two others never came. "Father Junipero de la Vega," Father Al wrote, "was to be our first guardian. On Feb[ruary] 6th he and Bro[ther] Humilde were executed. The padre was a saint. . . . The other . . . was caught while distributing Catholic literature and shot. The memory of these two holy martyrs should be a great blessing to the Friars at Mescalero."[19]

A group of exiled novices from warm southern Mexico shiver in unaccustomed snow outside their remodeled barn-turned-home in Mescalero. Courtesy of SJAM.

In April the padre was notified that orders from Rome had named him Commissary General and Syndic for all exiled Mexican Franciscans in the United States, somewhat enlarging his scope but mainly making official what he was already doing. According to his reckoning, forty-four exiles eventually arrived. In addition to their housing and clothing, they had to be fed. Father Al enlarged his garden and put the friars to work on it, that the community might have fresh vegetables for the summer and food to can for the winter. His sister Loretta came nearly every year for the canning, and volunteers from the community joined to help. Al himself pitched in. "Have not much time to write," he penned hastily in one letter. "Am busy making sauerkraut for the year."[20]

Newly invested novices pose formally before the half-built Saint Joseph's. Father Al sits second from right on first row, beside the centered novice master. Courtesy of MUA.

Fortunately Braun had maintained his reserve status in the army, which entitled him to buy food at the Fort Bliss commissary near El Paso at cheaper than commercial prices. "He would go down and buy all that food for the friars," Elisa Baldonado recalled. "Slabs of bacon, a hundred pounds of beans, potatoes. One clerk said, 'Father, you really buy a lot of food.' And he said, 'Well, I have a lot of children!' They were always kidding him."[21]

By May the novitiate was in full swing. "Next week," the padre wrote the new Father Provincial Novatus Benzing, "Fr. Magister begins midnight choir. I mentioned to him the cold of winter. He answered 'we have a limitless supply of wood and good stoves and will enjoy the warmth the more when it is cold outside.' The Magister means business and intends to have everything as prescribed."[22]

As work in the novitiate progressed so did that on the church. Spring brought the padre's father to help with the carpentering; Loretta made a working visit; Tony arrived, "and is happy. He is working on the fountain," a copy of that at Old Mission Santa Barbara.

"Tony at one time," he added, "was in the Gov[ernment] services. He had an honorable discharge . . . and therefore is entitled to a pension. . . . We should be able to get that for Tony with little difficulty. . . . Will write to Adjt. General of the War Dept for Tony's discharge and then take up the case with the pension Bureau."[23] Dealing with the bureaucracy proved slower than the padre anticipated; he would needle and prod for six years before he could write in 1934 that he "finally got Tony's pension for him. He is to get $20 per month for the balance of his life. . . ."[24]

He also worried over his dear friend 'Don' Juan Baldonado who "lost his school bus job, having bid too high, and now has no way to support his family. I put in a word for him with Herman Baca, who is [Senator] Bronson Cutting's main man in politics. He said he would see that Juan got something to do down this way. It would be a loss to this part of the country should Juan be forced to move away."[25] Baca's word proved good and Juan stayed.

✝✝✝

Al Braun, deeply patriotic and proud of his combat service, enjoyed active membership in the American Legion. He had founded Post 48 in Mescalero as an adjunct to Post 40 in Tularosa; and in the spring of 1928 he was elected Department Chaplain at the Legion's state convention. After Brother Sales arrived, Al often took him to Legion meetings. A combat veteran was a combat veteran, and Sales had served his country, albeit in the German army. *Insignificant!* The other veterans welcomed him, good-naturedly chaffed him about 'choosing the wrong side,' and he as good-naturedly responded.

Sales was invaluable to Al Braun. He had completed the novices' house, was fascinated with the 'Apache cathedral,' and at the padre's behest he asked and received permission to stay and work on the great stone church.

Then tragedy struck.

It happened early on the rainy morning of 11 July 1928, before Al or any of the workers had arrived on the site. Though he had been warned against working alone with the immense stones, the big burly friar, confident of his own strength, thought to unload the quarried blocks, and in lifting one slipped on the trailer's wet metal bed.

Father Al found him beneath the boulder, roared for help, and with those who ran to the site lifted off the stone and rushed him to the hospital in Alamogordo.

The padre tells it best: "Last month this mission suffered a great loss in the death of Brother Salesius Kraft," he wrote Monsignor Hughes in August.

> The Santa Barbara Province Loan[ed] him to me for 5 weeks. I kept him for six months and he was negotiati[ng] his permanent transfer to this place. The Province seemed willing to let Brother stay here because of our great need. Brother Salesius was one of the most valuable Brothers of the Province. . . . His value to me and this mission was his intelligence, his ability to manage affairs and to work. Often he worked till midnight and even to 3 A.M. and was out again at five A.M. While working on the church Brother fell and a stone fell on his stomach. This happened on July 11. July 13th he died and we buried him on the 14th in the Indian cemetery of Mescalero. The Indians considered him a saint and look upon his grave as a holy spot. The entire reservation was shocked at the death of Brother. . . . When I told Brother he must die he said quit your kidding, no such luck. Then he said smiling thank God, I have wanted to die in the harness. In spite of intense suffering Brother joked when conscious till the end. The nurse gave him an enema a few hours before his death. This aroused Brother to consciousness; he smiled at the nurse and said what's the use to bother, that's dead already. The nurse still speaks to everyone of Brother's game spirit. The last night of life Brother became wild for a few hours. I was lying on a [cot] next to him and a Mexican Brother was up watching. The Mexican Brother was helpless in Brother Salesius' powerful grip. All I had to say was Sales be quiet. He would smile and lie back. The old German army discipline showed itself even in death and in spite of the ravings of a tortured body. . . .

"I am sorry," the padre appended, "I can't write up this death as it occurred. It is the most remarkable and impressive death I have witnessed. An iron man of giant's strength and great character dying in excru[tiat]ing pain but with utter contempt for death. . . ."

He hoped Brother Sales would "intercede for us in heaven. We need lot[s] of help now that he is gone." He enclosed a picture of his friend, with the request that the Monsignor please return it. "It is the only one I have."[26]

By the will of the Mescaleros, Brother Salesius Kraft, OFM, was buried in the tribal cemetery—an unprecedented honor. Father Albert officiated the mass and burial of his friend whose loss he felt keenly, and for which he seems to have believed himself in part responsible. It was a weight he would carry throughout his life.

Brother Salesius Kraft, OFM, at Mescalero shortly before his tragic death in 1928. Courtesy of MUA.

✦✦✦

Work continued and so did the need for funds. Every donation was treasured. A check for $166.33 arrived "in good time," he wrote, "as I now have two masons, one stonecutter, a quarry man, a blacksmith and four helpers. . . . My own dear father and a Franciscan Brother are carpenters, I am truck driver. . . . [W]e can go ahead for awhile on the funds I have.

. . . If we have no money next year we will be compelled to go ahead with only Old Tony and the [Mexican] brothers. We have twenty acres in truck garden. I am calling on all the saints to bless the garden. We intend to put the profits in the church building. If you want our votes in the heavenly balloting, now is the time to come to the aid of us dirt farmers. . . ."[27]

Added to other urgencies, the little makeshift chapel in Mescalero needed repairs. "Until St. Joseph's Church is completed, I shall be reluctant to spend a cent on anything else," the padre wrote in the spring of 1929. "But I must do something to save the hall which is serving us now as a church for my Mescalero Apache. The . . . steps are worn through. The roof leaks everywhere, some of the floor must be replaced, and sills and woodwork need paint. I can not make these repairs for less than two hundred and fifty dollars."[28] His plea was one of many that regularly ran in the *Indian Sentinel* and the Marquette *Calumet* from the many Franciscan missions appealing to parishes throughout the country. Presumably his call was answered, for the repairs were made.

✛✛✛

Early in 1929 Father Albert received a check for $2,000—not for the church or the Mexican friars, but for a chapel. It had come through the Marquette League from two ladies, with the stipulation that it be used for a chapel on an Indian reservation for those too far from a mission to worship in a church. It was to be named for Saints Patrick and Bridget, to honor their parents.[29]

He knew instantly where it should go. The Three Rivers area was too far from Mescalero for its people to attend mass there regularly. It was, moreover, a sizeable community. In addition to the extended Shanta clan and their workers, the colony comprised many employees of the Fall ranch and some from the little village of Three Rivers. Father Al regularly said mass for these people in a convenient clearing or, in harsh weather, in Shanta Boy's home—the Shantas were among the few Mescaleros who lived in a house— though it was small for the numbers who attended. A chapel would be truly Godsent.

But would Shanta Boy give permission? He was strong willed, often intractable. He had reportedly participated in attacks on stagecoaches between El Paso and Mesilla in his younger days, when travelers were fair game. There had also been some killings at one time at Three Rivers for, some said, attempted rustling of Shanta Boy's horses—a legitimate provocation. Only a drunken fracas, with no harm intended, said others. Whatever happened, Shanta Boy had spent some time in Fort Leavenworth prison, until he and his friends (one of whom apparently included Roman Chiquita) escaped, eluded pursuit, and eventually made their way back to the reservation.[30] Shanta Boy could be difficult, but he was Father Albert's friend. The padre headed for Three Rivers.[31]

As the much-repeated story goes, Shanta Boy listened. He deliberated. Finally he asked: what would the chapel be called?

Remembering the stipulation, Father Albert began: Saint Patrick—

No good. Ugly name. There would be no Saint Patrick on Shanta Boy's land.

Well, then—Father Al's face doubtless creased into the craggy smile as always when he was bargaining—and he switched to the Spanish version. How about—San Patricio?

San Patricio. A long silence. *San Patricio.* . . . Finally a nod. Okay: the padre could build San Patricio on Shanta Boy's land.[32]

They began to plan. Could they finish before winter set in? Could they build it on the allotted sum? The donors had specified that it be built of stone and have stained-glass windows. This would be a challenge.

But Shanta Boy would help and so, he promised, would his sons. The Shantas had horses and a wagon to haul stones from a nearby creek. Father Al spread the word and volunteers from the surrounding areas pitched in. Old Tony, too, would do his part. During the nearly three-month construction, both he and the padre had a lot of commuting to do, though separately, so that one could be at Mescalero at all times.

Virginia Shanta was still quite small when they built the chapel, but she remembered the bustle well through the years. "All helped each other. Hispanics, Apaches—they were all together building that chapel. My grandfather—he had a herd of goats, and I guess he provided the feeding of the people as they were building. I remember the female members of my family preparing the meals. The neighbors all came. They were there bringing food—chile or beans or tortillas or whatever—and my grandfather provided the meat. They all had open fires and they cooked. And they would eat together and then go back to work again. Daylight to dark. It was a unified effort."[33]

As the word spread through the countryside, and even beyond, people gave what they could. From a parish in faraway Saint Louis came an altar and windows. Someone donated a potbellied stove. Others helped with benches, candlesticks, statuary. What he had to purchase the padre bought cheaply from supportive merchants in Tularosa and Alamogordo.

They finished and dedicated the chapel in time for a Christmas mass. It had cost exactly $1,980. With all items carefully itemized, Father Albert mailed his report to the Marquette League. With it he enclosed the unspent twenty dollars.[34]

The little chapel would serve the community for many years. After the death of Shanta Boy and then of his daughter Ruth, the ranch passed to Virginia, who looked after the chapel and, Elisa Baldonado remembered, "would have a mass each feast day of Saint Patrick's, and have relatives and friends come, and she'd have a big feast for everybody."[35] And on occasion Father Al, with some fellow clergy from El Paso, would find it a quiet place for a retreat.

The chapel Father Al built at Three Rivers, completed in 1929 in time for a Christmas mass. Sierra Blanca towers in the background. Courtesy of SJAM.

✝ ✝ ✝

During that busy fall of 1929 Father Al was asked to testify at the sensational trial of his old friend Albert Fall. He gladly agreed. Although Fall had earlier been cleared of any wrongdoing, the Teapot Dome matter had resurfaced in 1926, fueled by political enemies and the sensationalist press. Fall and Doheny had been acquitted on a separate conspiracy allegation, and further charges against Fall were dropped.

But determined to find a scapegoat from the Harding administration, the politicos struck again in 1929, harping on the $100,000 loan Doheny had made Fall in 1921. A flock of outraged New Mexicans traveled to Washington to testify as character witnesses, among them such notables as former territorial governor George Curry, the controversial Oliver Lee, Episcopal Reverend Hunter Lewis, and Judge J. W. Lawson from Alamogordo. Those in Father Al's entourage included Robert Geronimo, who reportedly appeared in full Apache regalia; former Doña Ana county sheriff Felipe 'Mike' Lucero, wearing his badge (though it is said he was persuaded to leave his six-shooter behind); rancher Gene Baird, booted and Stetsoned; and Father Albert, in clerical collar, with fire in his eye.

Of more note than their trappings was the fact that they were there at all. Everyone in the delegation remembered Fall's proposals for making the Mescalero reservation into a national park, and all had opposed it—none more vehemently than Robert Geronimo who, all agreed later, was among the strongest witnesses in Fall's favor. That these men came to defend him is in itself a testimony to their belief in his integrity.

The surrounding populace largely shared this belief. Fall's former law partner Ashton Hawkins, to whom he had gone for advice, believed him innocent, and provably so. The 'little people' he had consistently represented, oftener than not without pay, stood solidly behind him— Mexican Americans whom he had helped establish property rights in the legal confusion following the treaty of Guadalupe-Hidalgo, and small farmers and ranchers he had defended against the large incoming cattle companies.[36] Even some former enemies—and he had made many as an outspoken lawyer on a brawling frontier—seem to have believed him wrongly attacked. In short, one stated, "Nobody around here believes Judge Fall ever did anything wrong. They know him too well. . . . Fall built up this country."[37] Even as late as 1947 Thomas Fortune Ryan, who had bought Fall's ranch, was still warning, "You'd better not say anything against Fall around here or you're liable to get shot."[38]

But Washington's political climate was far removed from the frontier ethos of New Mexico.

The trial played out like a Greek drama, with Fall cast as the tragic hero: the inexorable movement toward doom, the hubris for which the gods punish mortals, the fatal flaw, or mistake, that leads to downfall—except that no *deus ex machina* appeared to save Albert Bacon Fall.

Suffering from tuberculosis, bronchial pneumonia, crippling arthritis, and a bad heart, he was escorted onstage by his doctor and a nurse and helped into a cushioned Morris chair. His wife and two daughters sat tensely in the courtroom. When on the second day he began to spit blood, the court was recessed for three days, after which, over his doctor's protests, Fall returned. Too weak to testify for himself, this once vigorous, fiery frontier lawyer was dependent on his attorney and his witnesses.

His lawyer documented the facts. Doheny testified—not for the first time—that the alleged bribe was a bona fide loan from an old friend, secured by a personal note on the ranch, unconnected in any way to oil leases. Father Albert, like the other New Mexicans, asserted Fall's honesty in clear and unqualified western candor.

The judge gave what many considered prejudicial instructions to the jury, whose solemn members, after twenty-four hours' deliberation, filed in like the classic Greek chorus. The crowd in the courtroom sat tense, rigid.

The foreman spoke: Guilty, with recommendation of clemency.

Fall fell back in shock. Emma rushed to him. His lawyer fainted. The crowd erupted. "This is not the verdict of the jury," a furious Doheny proclaimed, "but of the court."[39]

Father Albert was stunned. The entire trial was, he maintained throughout his life, "a cruel, cruel crime."[40] Ashton Hawkins believed it a perversion of law. Writer Eugene Manlove Rhodes planned a book in which the final chapter would mount the defense his old friend had been unable to give himself. These sentiments were echoed throughout New Mexico by those who knew Albert Fall and who stuck with him the rest of his broken life. He was part of the passing frontier, and of them all.

The supreme irony hit in 1930 when Edward Doheny was acquitted of having given the 'bribe' that Fall had been convicted of having received.

In July 1931, after his appeal was rejected and pardon denied, Albert Fall was sentenced to a $100,000 fine and a year in prison. Because of his health, and through the intervention of Senator Bronson Cutting, he was allowed to serve in high, dry Santa Fe. He actually served only nine months, most of that time in the prison hospital.

Father Al visited him often. During one visit, the padre recounted, "he told me, 'Father, I came from the South and I was a Baptist; but I got here with the Mexican people. . . . And I studied the Catholic religion, and I thought . . . , I ought to be a Catholic, and now I'm imprisoned here and I want to be a Catholic. Will you take me into the Church?'

"'Right now,' I said, and I grabbed some water and baptized him."[41]

✞✞✞

On Mondays the padre drove to El Paso to buy supplies, confer with Bishop Schuler, and transact whatever business affairs arose. At some time during this period he met Father Dave Kirgan, newly appointed pastor of the cathedral parish, and with whom Father Al stayed in the rectory while in El Paso. Kirgan was, Braun wrote Novatus, "a man after your own heart; he is straight, he is honest; he is a hard worker and he knows how to cut down the debt. The Bishop is more than delighted with Fr. Kirgan. [He] works at least eighteen hours a day. . . ."[42] He was, moreover, young and high spirited, an Irishman with a sense of fun matching that of Al Braun.

An enthusiastic friendship grew from shared work and occasional sorties to Juárez—minus clerical garb, which was banned in the Mexico of Plutarcho Calles—for dinner and a round of 'Irish holy water.' Prohibition still reigned north of the border, and Juárez blossomed with good whiskey, choice wines, and fine dining.

Juárez also had its seamy side that drew the curious and the less refined to its well-known bordellos. On one occasion the padre entertained several visitors from the East with dinner at one of the better restaurants, followed by a tour of the city—the open-air market where one bought good cheeses, the store that sold elegant clothing and fine perfumes, and the magnificent cathedral standing empty and unused under Mexico's communist rule.

But what about the famous red-light district, asked one of the guests: they wanted to see that too—just a quick walk through out of curiosity. Al Braun, always the good host, led them down a side street known locally as 'Gunnery Alley' to a large block of houses. Then—it was a story he later loved to tell on himself—a female voice hailed him from above.

"Father Albert!"

His guests looked at him with strange expressions.

She called again. "Father Albert! Hi!" From a balcony leaned a pert young girl, waving cheerily.

He recognized one of his Mescaleros, called her by name, and waved back. His friends looked at one another with even stranger expressions. "What in the world are you doing here?" he called.

"Making some moneys!"

He must have sighed. The Mescaleros placed a high value on chastity, and so did her Catholic teaching. He suggested she return home where she belonged, doubtless wondered with wry humor how many people had heard her boisterous greeting, and walked on, followed by his amused friends.[43]

A letter written years later refers to a fine frolic the Fathers Al and Dave enjoyed in Juárez with a lay friend, to whom Father Al wrote on Saint Patrick's Day 1949. "I know this will reach you too late to do any good but I will put it this way. I hope you did not put in any phone calls at two in the morning to Mrs. Gilday after the Saint Patrick's Day Celebration. I was just writing to Fr. Kirgan a letter which reminded me of the long ago when we were much younger and much more mischievous than we are now. . . . In spite of the passing years, I know the Irish blood in your veins will rejuvenate you at least for this one day of the year." It was addressed to the Honorable Paul Gilday, United States House of Representatives.[44]

Such frivolities were, however, rare. In describing Dave Kirgan's eighteen-hour workday, Al Braun may have indulged in a bit of hyperbole, but not much. As the cathedral rector, and one on whom the bishop relied increasingly, Kirgan's schedule allowed for little relaxation; and the padre at Mescalero had a barn to transform into a novitiate, a tribe of Apaches looking to him for spiritual and material care, a proposed seminary to build, and a large church to complete.

Always he was haunted by money problems. America had been moving toward financial disaster steadily throughout the high-living twenties, though few heeded the warning signs. The Franciscans hadn't: their focus was spiritual at any time, and their worldly sights during this era were trained largely on the threat to the Mexican Church. The effects of the crash when it hit in October 1929 were not immediately felt in New Mexico, certainly not among the Hispanics and Apaches in the Mescalero-Tularosa area, who were largely self-sustaining, dependent on their own herds, orchards, and vegetable plots, and who asked for little more.

It hit Father Albert harder. The mission always had to depend upon the province, the Marquette League, the 'Bureau' (of Catholic Indian Missions, or BCIM), church charities, mass stipends, and whatever the padre could raise on his 'begging trips.' These funds, at best never plentiful, fell off dramatically as the Depression deepened and spread, and at a time when he must feed, fund, and house the influx from Mexico. Remodeling the barn at Mescalero was relatively inexpensive and had been completed before the crash; but the heavier demand of paying for the land they had acquired and of building a permanent seminary in El Paso fell heavily on the shoulders of Al Braun throughout the Great Depression. Obtaining loans became increasingly difficult, repaying them an incessant nightmare. "I am broke," he wrote in the spring of 1931. "I cannot pay it. There is no opportunity to sell the land at present even at a considerable loss. The depression hit El Paso late but it is certainly there now. . . . I am at a loss what to do."[45]

Throughout the '30s letter after letter intoned the refrain:

"I can't make a loan [in El Paso] . . . for the Mexican Franciscans because I cannot get anyone to endorse the loan," he wrote in 1931. "Even if I could . . . it would be more advisable to get it elsewhere because rates of interest are high in these parts.

"In New York," he added, "90 day loan[s] are being made at 2% and even at that low rate the banks are having difficulty to get people to borrow. . . . Some money must be gotten quickly because the semi annual interest falls due July 1st."[46] That was in May.

In October he reported that "Central Verein . . . gave me $200.00, then loaned me $400.00 at 6% interest. Just sent them a check for $309.00. Will send the [rest] Nov. 1st. Had to draw on mission fund to make the payment.

"Feel fortunate that I have any money at all. When the El Paso Bank failed a month ago, the Bishop and most parishes in the diocese lost money. . . . I have our small amounts in the State National. But there is no more reason for the El Paso National to go broke than there would be for the State National."[47]

"Have been waiting to hear from Fr. Joachim [Grant]," he wrote a week later. "I must have some money by Dec. 1st. . . ."[48] But Joachim, he learned, could get no money before January. "On Dec. 15, 1931 I must have $1011.34. Must pay a note of $765.87 . . . and $245.47 interest. . . . On

Jan 1st must pay more interest on other notes," and another $402.18 that "is long past due. . . ."[49]

The padre tried a last-ditch measure. "Entertaining no hope at all I went into the State National Bank of El Paso and asked for $1010.95 for 30 Day[s]. In a few minutes I had the money. . . . Never so surprised. . . ." But "another note for $1000.00 and interest are due Jan 11th. . . . Let me come to San Francisco to see . . . [frequent lender] Mr. Reichlin. Maybe he will . . . stretch a point. . . ."[50]

His struggles to keep afloat continued well into the next year. "How in the world," he wrote his provincial, after receiving a pay-or-be-sued note in October 1932, "can I continue to make these payments."[51]

January 1933 found him on another 'begging trip' reporting from Saint Paul that he had solicited over $200 for the Mescalero church, plus some stipends for the Mexican property near El Paso.[52] He was not so lucky in New York. "Was to collect at Msgr. Petri's parish but that week two banks failed and all the parishioners lost their savings. . . ."[53]

The thirties were for Father Albert 'the best of times, the worst of times.' Struggling constantly to carry the burden of the Mexican friars and the rigors of the Great Depression drained his strength and brought him often to near despair. Yet throughout his life he looked back on these as "the happiest years of my life." He had the bedrock of Mescalero and his Apaches. He had Old Tony. And though often frustrated with the fluctuations and delaying tactics of Resendiz, he believed passionately in the Mexicans' cause and was deeply happy to be working in their behalf.

And above him reared his church—too slowly, too intermittently for his impatient taste, but there it was, a little taller each year, aspiring to heaven stone by stone. In summers the air resounded with the heavy clank of metal on stone, the calls of the workers one to another, the grinding of the labored old truck as it strained up the slope. He knew Saint Joseph's would be long in building; but he never doubted he would finish it. The mission was his anchor, his Apaches and their church the polestar that gave him direction. And there were always his cherished friends, those nearby and those who came to visit.

There were the Henrions, who had opened their home to him in Luxembourg: now he opened his to them. Celine and Ollie had moved to Chicago, and her parents, having lost everything after the war, soon followed.

Father Al had kept in close contact with the family, had visited them in Chicago, and when Eugene (now married and a father) lost his job early in the Depression and moved to Iowa, the padre invited the old couple to Mescalero. "They are delighted," he reported, "and want to come at once. . . . Would like to have these people with me because they were so good to me . . . in Luxembourg; their home was my home."[54]

Where to house them posed a small problem but solved a larger one. From time to time various people inhabited the living quarters abutting the hall that served as meeting place and dining room for large gatherings. In return they cooked and helped with work around the mission. Bishop Schuler had for some time been after the padre to move a certain family off the property because "they take so many things that belong to the mission."[55] Father Al had hesitated to do so. The eminent arrival of the Henrions gave him the excuse he needed without alienating his friends.

He requested Novatus to write him a letter intended for the current occupant's benefit—even worded it for him: "An old couple are coming to Mescalero," it should read. "They can cook, clean house, and work for the Spanish Fathers who are coming. . . . [They] can live in the room[s] on the west side of the hall. The Fathers can use the two rooms on the east side. . . . If anybody is living in those two rooms tell them to move immediately. . . ."[56]

Mama Henrion, he advised, "is a good cook and is economic. At present I can't afford to buy good food" because of the current occupants' large family for which he had to provide. "For three months I have had trouble with my stomach. The Doctor said it is because of the food I get. . . . So many Fathers visit Mescalero I must have a good cook, but . . . I can't buy all the food for a large family."[57] The ensuing letter from Novatus solved the problem.

The Henrions arrived in October 1931. "What a difference!" the padre relayed. "The house is clean as can be, meals cooked well. Both are busy all day long. . . . [Papa Henrion] is handy at everything. . . . Wish we had a cow. . . . [Mama Henrion] says if we have milk she can cook so many dishes and can make all the butter we need. Can you tell me where to beg $50.00 for a cow? I am broke."[58]

For the rest of his life the padre remembered with nostalgia the Henrions' time in Mescalero. "Every weekend I entertained army officers and their wives at Mescalero," he wrote Eugene many years later. "Your dear Mama did much of the entertaining. Always, with a charming smile, she served my army guests a high-ball or two. Mescalero became a popular weekend resort for the army officers at Fort Bliss, Texas."[59]

The Henrions stayed at Mescalero until 1934, during which Celine and Ollie visited several times. The padre had his Luxembourg family again: it was the best of times.

Father Sixtus Brambilla was another ever-welcome guest. He came intermittently from Boston, whenever his chronic tuberculosis flared and he needed the mission's nourishing food and New Mexico's high dry air. Shortly after the Henrions' arrival he came intending to stay for three months, said masses when and where needed, and had been enjoying Mama Henrion's cooking when, early in December, his provincial recalled him. Father Al was "sorry to see him go. He is a fine man. Expect him back again because he is not at all well."[60] The padre was right. Within a few months he reported Father Sixtus ill again. "I expect him here with me for at least a few months. . . . I am glad he's coming. He is good company."[61]

Father Al also enjoyed the presence of a young priest the bishop and Father Dave had sent him "for a few months to straighten out. He is really a fine priest and very gifted," though inclined to drink too much. "Glad to have him; we have been doing lots of hard work since he came; he is very handy."[62]

Loretta came every summer, pitched in to help, and usually returned with several Apache girls to place for the Outing System. The program's already proven value had with the Depression taken on increasing significance. "The government," Father Al detailed for his provincial, "has loaned four of the Apache girls working in Los Angeles $600.00 each . . . [for agricultural improvements]. I persuaded the Indian officer to make this loan without interest. Each [girl] . . . has a ranch. This year we are planting 1000 cherry trees on each ranch . . . and we have all the land between the trees planted in grain and corn. I am looking after these places."[63] Additionally, all the Apache youth sent money from their modest wages to their families each month. "In these hard times," the padre noted, "that makes Los Angeles very popular with the parents."[64]

Bishop Schuler moved his office to Mescalero in the summers to escape the El Paso heat. He occupied a small house near Father Al's quarters. "There was a swing on the porch" that Mary Dorame and her friends enjoyed. "He'd come out and we'd visit with him. Every summer we'd look forward to him coming."[65] The bishop too relished these summers. "He is in love with the place," Father Al noted. He too was happy when Schuler came: he was a good friend—and good help on the walls of Saint Joseph's.

Each autumn found the padre hosting visitors for the annual turkey hunt. "Can't you come on a visit next week," he urged Novatus soon after the Henrions and Sixtus arrived. "Turkey season opens and . . . [Mama Henrion] is just waiting for the turkey to make us a fine turkey dinner. All the fathers from the cathedral are coming up. Fr. Dave says he will bring the appetizer"—Kirgan could buy 'Irish holy water' cheaply in Juárez. Other than anticipating the hunt, he added, they were "very busy cutting and baling hay and hauling in wood before the snow comes."[66]

"I hear the Father provincial of the Italian Fathers enjoys hunting a great deal," he wrote Novatus the following October. "Give him my invitation to spend some time in Mescalero. This year the turkey and deer are exceptionally plentiful."[67] Another year he apologized to Novatus for not having written, "but due to the hunting season and many visitors I have not been able. . . . Fr. Kirgan came up Sunday and just left . . . with 5 wild turkeys. He says his trip was a success."[68]

Hunting season always resounded with the roar of Father Albert's voice as he hailed arriving visitors and his hearty laugh as he greeted them with *abrazos*. These were times of high hilarity and, in the years of the Henrions, of aromas from Mama's kitchen.

Conclusion of a successful turkey hunt, early 1930s. On the left are Papa and Mama Henrion, turkeys in hand. Courtesy of Eugene Henrion III.

Although Father Al was the essence of warmth and conviviality for those he loved and of compassion for those in need, he had little patience with liars or spongers. When a former worker complained to Father Novatus regarding pay he alleged the padre owed him, Al advised his provincial to "tell him that I paid some of his bill[s] at four places as he requested. . . . Pedro stole from our store room at least as much as I still owe him. He appeals on behalf of his wife and children. That is trickery because when here he would take his wages and spend them on drink, letting his wife and children go hungry. Had Pedro not left the job without a word to me I would have paid him at once. Now he can wait till I am ready."[69]

Neither hunts nor hard times deterred him from his purpose. However slow the work or frustrating the delays, he pushed forward, commandeering the help of everyone within range—Mescaleros, neighbors, visitors. Fathers John Smith and Dave Kirgan from El Paso, the bishop, his own father, and whatever Mexican friars he could snag: no one escaped. One of the latter proved particularly willing and talented when Father Al could get him. "Brother Olivario is helping me for a few weeks," he reported, adding (doubtless with a chuckle), "Poor old lazy Bro. Sebastian does not like that."[70] There seems always to have been a tug-of-war for the better workers between the fathers at Michoacán and Santa Barbara. "I do hope," Novatus answered when apprised of the recall of several to Mexico, "it will be Bro. Sebastian that will be sent to Mexico, and not Bro. Olivario. That Father [Alphonso] Sanchez [in Mexico] is still up to old tricks to outwit others, especially S[anta] B[arbara] Prov[ince]. And he imagines that we don't know how he has no use for us!!! Oh boy, he is mistaken."[71]

And always at the padre's side was Old Tony. "What a man and what a loyal friend," Al Braun later reminisced. "He had all that makes for greatness in a man."[72]. Although too old for heavy labor, and gradually losing his sight, Tony oversaw work on the church and otherwise spent his days carving his cherished stone fountain.

"Tony is working hard and is contented," the padre reported in September 1932.[73] He wrote again in October. "Tony is happy to see the church go ahead. If we have a little luck we can finish the stone work next summer."[74] He was, then and later, over-optimistic. The end stretched longer than he imagined; but always the light was there beckoning.

Tony's increasing frailty made the old man dread the hard mountain winters. "Tony is very restless," the padre wrote in 1932 as the cold weather settled in, "and does not want to stay longer than Xmas. He says it is getting too cold. I will let him go to Los Angeles [to be] with his relations. He said he will be ready to come back in four month[s] and work here again. He is certainly a sailor."[75]

By any conventional logic, the worsening Depression, coupled with the burdens of building a seminary and novitiate for incoming Mexican exiles, should have halted the construction of Saint Joseph's indefinitely. Al Braun thought otherwise: ramparts could be breached, blockades run, obstacles overcome. He would continue to build.

He did, somehow. The walls of Saint Joseph's rose intermittently as funds and weather allowed, as solid as the truth they affirmed. Despite the constant weight of his financial burdens and the billows of despair they occasioned, the padre, like a buoy, always topped the waves. Exuberance was his natural state; his was the joy of faith and friends, and he saw always his church, born of weightless dream and common stone, becoming the greater entity. Depression, however cruel, was but a thing of time, which in the infinite scheme became *Insignificant!*

How, many wondered, was he building on such a scale—or even at all—in such a poor mission? "We have strong arms," he answered, "and strong backs . . . and have dedicated our arms and backs and lives to this task." Without naming Tony he illustrated his point. "So far one stone mason has laid all the stone. He is an old man, the father of seventeen children. . . . Since the death of his wife in 1920, the old workman has been with me as a kind of oblate, offering himself to God. He asks no wages. . . ."[76]

The padre's will and that of the community kept construction going. He put the Mexican friars to work. They fired lime and mixed mortar, and in so investing themselves became part of the 'Apache cathedral.' So did Katherine Mackey and Lucy Dorame, the Shanta women, Eric Tortilla's wife Bertha, and Vida Jette, who cooked food for the workers and hauled it to the site. So did the families who farmed or ran herds on or off the reservation and furnished vegetables and meat, while Father Al and the friars worked the mission's own gardens. Apaches chopped wood to fire the kilns; merchants in Tularosa and Alamogordo sold lumber and hardware with generous discounts and long-term credit. Racial friction present in other areas was not a factor in the Mescalero-Tularosa communities despite past battles. Saint Joseph's was their common mission and Father Al their common priest.

Still, as Depression dragged on, funds dried like drought-struck desert springs, and so did money to pay the construction workers. John Braun came when he could and the faithful Tony remained, though age and infirmity limited his capacity. Then, as if need manufactured its own miracles, one came unheralded up the hill one day in the person of José Mesa.

He was a construction worker, out of work. He had with him his grown sons—husky, hungry, and unhired. They would work without salary, asking only food and a place to sleep. It was a heaven-sent deal for all: the bargain was sealed with a handshake.

The women of Mescalero and Tularosa held bazaars and suppers and *jamaicas* to raise money for the church. During the July puberty ceremonies they set up stands and sold food and wares. Marquita Hill always accompanied her mother, who "sold fruit and gave the money to the church. My dad would come with a truckload of watermelons . . . and sell them very cheap. . . . Every night they would dance around the fire. . . . We used to sit and watch. . . . They had games going on all day. Indians came from all over with their bracelets and their turquoise—different tribes, in their costumes. To me that was the best part of the year."[77]

And they were the happiest years for Al Braun. Always highlighting the bright spots of the Depression, he exulted when "Jouett Elliott, daughter of [Albert] Fall got me $50.00 from Sinclair for the church," adding optimistically that although "the amount is not much" it put him "in touch with a person who has lots of money." Despite the hard times of the thirties, his enthusiasm kept him going, even when the note of realism crept in. "I could get a thousand out of El Paso because I have many friends there and everybody knows about the church." But, he added, he did not want to collect there "because of the heavy debt the Bishop has."[78]

Each small gift meant another small boon. In addition to Jouett's gift, "the ladies here gave a box supper which cleared $66.25. God bless them."[79]

The seasons came and went in their steady progression, and with each Christmas the walls of Saint Joseph's reached higher. How long the Depression would last no one knew, but whatever man measured in years would pass. The seasons rolled eternally, the cycle continued, and Christmas always came.

Each year the wagons rolled in, the tepees stippled the hills, the smell of a hundred campfires sweetened the air, and expectations rose like the smoke they sent to heaven. Inside the sturdy walls the people sat blanket-wrapped around the great fire at midnight mass, the padre intoned the ancient words, and once again the kirtled dancers leaped into the firelight to send their own prayers into the starry depth; and the people therein, enfolded by roofless walls and the spirit that kept those walls rising, were one.

13: THE MEXICAN ADVENTURE

When Father Albert had returned to Mescalero in July 1927, the rebellion below the border was reaching a climax. What had started in the villages had spread. After a round of executions early that year, bishops urged priests to seek safety. Large numbers of fathers fled their parishes, to leave the country entirely or repair to the cities where, dressed as ordinary citizens, they were largely unnoticed. Many, living sheltered in the homes of wealthy Catholics, ministered privately to their hosts, some of whom—even some military officers or government officials—were also closet Catholics.

A few priests joined the Cristeros. Another intrepid handful remained with their flocks, laboring through days and nights to serve their own and neighboring parishes, always covertly, fleeing or hiding when military detachments approached. Over ninety were brutally executed.[1]

Rome opposed the rebellion, believing it counterproductive to negotiation. The Mexican bishops were divided. The majority, obedient to Rome, fostered passive resistance: they would neither register nor become schismatic, and would risk "if necessary, their martyrdom."[2] As violence spread and persecutions intensified, some concluded that negotiation and compromise would not save the Church, and became more militant.

Among the latter were Archbishop Francisco Orozco y Jimenez of Guadalajara and Bishops Manrique y Zarate of Huejutla and Gonzales y Valencia of Durango, who were by 1927 openly praising the rebels. The fiery Orozco was repeatedly banished or forced to flee, and as frequently returned to his see and remained in close contact with the Cristeros. Manrique, when chastised by Rome, refused to recant, was removed from his diocese, and openly supported the Cristeros. Gonzales in a pastoral letter of 11 February 1927 encouraged the insurgents to "be tranquil in your conscience and receive our blessing."[3]

Such free-speaking bishops were a minority; most refused to support the rebellion. The Cristeros, pledging their lives and blood for their faith, felt deserted by such passive bishops and by the priests whose mass exodus from the villages had left a dark abyss in their lives. Still they persisted: their loyalty was neither to priests nor prelates, but to their faith. Their uprising set off three years of warfare in their pursuit of salvation—for themselves, their families, and for all Mexico.

There was little organization at first. Villagers mobilized in small guerrilla bands. They had no military training; but they could ride and they could shoot. Crucially short of ammunition and lacking any national coordination, they struck suddenly, galloped off, and regrouped for the next foray.

Army detachments struck back at the villages, looting, raping, burning, stealing the horses, massacring the innocent, summarily executing any priests or suspected combatants they found. Such actions intensified the Cristeros' zeal; their ranks expanded, and by midsummer 1927 twenty thousand in guerrilla groups, armed with captured weapons, roamed at large and struck at will.[4]

General Amaro, Minister of War, began to muster militias, thereby doubling the strength of many units. He tripled his troops in Jalisco, intending to decimate that hotbed of Cristeros abetted by Archbishop Orozco, and thereby break the back of the rebellion.

The Cristeros were in desperate straits.

But desperation often begets its own salvation, and in seeking finds. Jalisco found General Enrique Gorostieta, a former Díaz officer and a brilliant tactician. Scorning the revolutionary government and its brutal corrupt army, and admiring the cause and courage of the Cristeros, he agreed to take command in Jalisco. It was July 1927, just as Father Albert Braun was taking charge of the Mexican project in Mescalero.

Gorostieta was an artilleryman without artillery, but he saw what a soldier with faith and fervor could do with a machete, a captured rifle, a fast horse, and dedication to a cause. He embraced guerrilla tactics until he could organize his growing ranks into a proper army. Outnumbered, outgunned, and confined to small-scale operations, his forces nonetheless commanded all Jalisco except the city of Guadalajara by year's end, were pushing into neighboring states, and had Amaro calling for more reinforcements. By October 1928 Gorostieta commanded the entire Cristero army. He called it the Army of National Liberation.

✝✝✝

North of the border Father Albert and Bishop Schuler grew great with plans. Having secured the land near El Paso for the permanent house of theology and philosophy, they were eager to begin construction. But as syndic for the exiled friars, the padre was responsible for their legal and financial affairs, and, wary of the Mexican friars' ambivalence, he urged Father Turibius to "get a written agreement . . . that the land belongs to the [Santa Barbara] Province in case the houses are not erected and kept on the property." They would then "have valuable property and through investment would pay a big dividend. . . ."[5]

In Mescalero the remodeled barn was cozy enough for the first novices, who on arriving had been sandaled, habited, and invested. In Philadelphia William Stanton finished the plans for the permanent seminary and for an impressive house of novitiate, around which Father Albert envisioned well-landscaped grounds, to be crowned by the great stone church.

Bishop Schuler too was a man of vision and like Braun saw the El Paso acreage as a valuable investment. Together they looked toward an El Paso-Mescalero axis as a center for Catholic education. Along with the friary at Mescalero and the completion of Saint Joseph's (for which the bishop pledged a thousand dollars from his diocese) they were by 1930 planning a day school for the Apache children, to be staffed by nuns from a teaching order. Together the stocky Jesuit bishop and the rangy Franciscan padre were enthusiastically devising a future Eden in the desert, even as Depression darkened the land.

"Just bought a farm of 148.84 acres adjoining the reservation," Father Al wrote in May. "Traded for a house in Tularosa. The Bishop wants to have some income for the mission at Mescalero. He wants me to plant 1000 apple trees on the ranch. After the trees are ten years old the average annual income from a thousand apple trees is $3500.00. We have a man to take care of the trees. The land cost us about $700.00. Development of springs . . . will require a few hundred more dollars. It will take another $500.00 to buy and plant the trees. The bishop is footing all the bills. He is very enthusiastic. . . . After ten years the ranch will be worth $15,000. . . ."[6]

Novatus was skeptical. ". . . Bishop Schuler is quite enterprising," he observed. "But I can't help thinking of the fizzle of St. John's Mission Ranch. That orchard is not going to pay!"[7]

Apparently Novatus was not alone in his doubts over the grandiose schemes; and many of the Schuler-Braun plans died aborning—a fate that through the padre's life would befall many of his ideas. Father Al sought the expansive; his superiors (Schuler excepted) leaned more to the practical.

He represented the daring, they the status quo. Often through hardheaded persistence he won; this time he lost. The American provinces did not assume the bill and the title for the El Paso land as he had hoped; the Mexican friars could not or would not meet their financial obligations; and Father Al, refusing to default, was left with the ever-recurring payments throughout the Depression.

✝ ✝ ✝

Meanwhile, a storm had blown from Mexico into Tularosa in 1928 in the person of Father Agustín Pozos who, replacing the beloved Father Bonaventure, quickly began generating complaints from his parishioners. He was always gadding about the countryside, they alleged, in a car they and the provincial had furnished him. As syndic, and at the request of Father Novatus, Braun addressed the issue with the roving Agustín.

". . . I see you believe what the people is complaining against me," Pozos replied. ". . . I do not waste money in running the car. . . . If any man down here is complaining, kindly tell him that it is not their business to complain. . . . Besides if you continue to give credit to the evil talking of them then please tell my Superior to take me away from here. . . . I do not like any complain at all. . . ."[8]

Father Al pursued the matter. "In 10 Days," he advised Novatus, "Fr. Agustín traveled 568 miles in his new car. I called his attention to the scandal he was giving. He blew up about it but it does him no good. . . ."[9]

Even the children disliked Pozos. Marquita Hill dreaded his weekly catechism classes. "Father Agustín says, 'I don't want you kids coming here in socks. You wear long stockings.' Ooh, how we hated those long thick stockings. And we hated to go to confession to him. All us girls were scared to death of him. We used to walk on tiptoe by him. He would look us up and down and scold us and scold, like we were bad children. He was something else."[10]

Agustín had also acquired the convenient habit of pocketing the funds intended to be dispensed by the syndic as needed for Tularosa. A furious Father Novatus fired no-nonsense instructions to Braun. "The parish supports its pastor AND pays a salary which . . . is the exclusive property . . . of the order. Kindly bring this home to Fr. Agustín, and make him fork out."[11]

The complaints continued. "Father Giran," reported Braun, "is forever complaining about Fr. Agustín being in Alamogordo" so much and undermining him in his own parish. "I don't think Father Agustín cares at all whether or not he tells you the truth. Since your letter I called him on the phone on several days of the same week. Each time Brother said Fr. Agustín was in Alamogordo."[12]

Agustín, however, was responsible only to Father Domingo Resendiz, without whose orders nothing could be done about the recalcitrant priest. Meanwhile Al Braun was the middleman.

The parishioners wanted Father Bonaventure back. "All the people around here like him very much," wrote one Tularosan. "The people around here is willing to help him work or give him some money if he stays here ever."[13] A similar letter to Father Domingo brought no results. Pozos would remain in Tularosa until 1937, when the parish and Mescalero were returned to the Santa Barbara province.

He was not the only Mexican friar who tried the padre's patience. One he described as "useless to the Order. His doctors have told me [his] physical ailments . . . are mostly imaginary and . . . a result of inertia."[14] Another was "lazy and dirty; won't earn his salt unless driven to it by the lash."[15] But such as these came and went; Agustín remained for everyone a constant irritant.

✞✞✞

The local squabbles were mere sparks from the inferno to the south—distracting but—*insignificant!* Below the border Mexico blazed. Knowing complete victory was impossible, Gorostieta fought a war of attrition, to inflict enough damage and show enough persistence to bring Calles to terms. Toward that end he issued a manifesto enumerating the aims for which they fought—a return to the Constitution of 1857 minus the anticlerical provisions, equitable land reform, and laws based on Mexico's traditions and the people's will. The Cristero army—the people's army—would be Mexico's National Guard, not to dominate but to protect. Mexico's motto would be "God, Country, and Liberty."

Calles, pressed by Gorostieta's victories and an election turmoil in 1928, had to rethink his position. Barred by law from reelection but scheming to ensure his own continuing power through an alternating diarchy, he backed Obregón. But Obregón was murdered ten days after winning election. Calles marshaled his one-party state and assumed the title *jefe máximo*—supreme commander—whereby he would choose and control a series of puppet presidents. From then on the field was his.

That done, federal forces then launched the great midwinter offensive of 1928–1929. But by May the Cristeros, by then numbering 50,000, defeated Amaro's army with a massive counteroffensive. Calles sent emissaries to Gorostieta to seek negotiations.

Through United States Ambassador Dwight Morrow, church and state forged a modus vivendi. Predictably it proved a stalemate: though Calles agreed to mitigate the anticlerical laws, they remained in the Constitution. The peace was but words on paper, and the words were those of Calles. Still, it seemed better than none. Priests cautiously returned to their parishes. Public worship recommenced. The Cristeros were ordered to lay down their arms.

But ninety thousand combatants lay dead, and uncounted thousands of nonparticipants. The Cristeros felt betrayed by the leaders of the Church they had fought to preserve. Gorostieta, who had warned the bishops to beware, "told a friend, on the day of his death, which had occurred in strange conditions, some days before the peace: 'They are selling us out, Manuelito, they are selling us out.'"[16]

There began almost immediately the rounding up and mass murdering of Cristero leaders. Many fled, principally to the United States. A period of mutual church-state back-scratching followed, while religious oppression continued in many states. By 1931 the truce had broken and the government recommenced brutal persecution. Churches were again closed, socialist education stifled Catholic teaching, the faithful fought back, and sporadic guerrilla warfare resumed. President Ortiz Rubio tried to calm the waters, but Calles forced his resignation in September 1932 and the fanatic agenda continued.

✞✞✞

In Mescalero Father Al grew testy over Father Domingo's constant mind-changing which, compounded by the squabbles among the Mexican provinces, greatly complicated the plans for both the seminary and the nuns' school. Despite the confusion the padre and the bishop proceeded, buoyant and undeterred.

"The Bishop expects to have sisters at Mescalero . . . next September," Braun reported in the spring of 1931. ". . . He has $1500.00 to start the school. We won't have any building expenses. The school will be in the hall."[17] His long-dreamed-of schoolhouse (plans for which Stanton had drawn in 1923) would have to wait. And, he wrote in May, he had "high hopes of getting sisters from Mother Katherine [Drexel, of the Sisters of Notre Dame in Milwaukee] to open a day school in September. The Bishop . . . will remodel the old novitiate for the sisters. . . ."[18]

The school did not materialize in the fall. With the rupture in the Mexican truce, more seminarians were expected momentarily, making the quarters unavailable for the sisters. Father Al learned of this situation in August via orders from Rome forwarded by Novatus, who observed that "it knocks the bottom out of the plan to turn your bunks over to the sisters. . . ."[19]

Though postponed, the plan was not dropped. Cardinal Dougherty had signed on to the project, his interest sparked by the somewhat enigmatic reasoning that "a part of Geronimo's band is there." Through Mother Katherine he directed Braun to "get an estimate of the cost of a house and furnishings for the sisters and put in a request for that amount. He will see to it that we get it."[20]

Father Al acted quickly. "Monday I am going to El Paso to get Mr. Frost [a prominent architect] . . . and bring him to Mescalero . . . to decide where to build the sisters' house and also where to put a monastery. . . . The barn is all right for a year or two but will never do for a permanent monastery.

"I am writing Father José Ramon Zulaica [the Visitor General] urging him to come to Mescalero so that I can find out what the plans are. My idea would be to put theology and possibly also philosophy in Tularosa and the novitiate at Mescalero. We should send to Spain for Brothers who are skilled mechanics—a carpenter—a plumber—a cook and a tailor. . . . With the[ir] help . . . it won't cost so much to build a monastery. . . ."[21]

Two weeks later the padre reported that Mother Katherine's sisters "have definitely accepted Mescalero and will open the school next September. The Provincial will send four sisters and more if I need them. . . . The Bishop already has plans drawn for a sisters' house. . . . Bishop will get the money. Will start on the house soon." Schuler, despite the plunging economy, still had hopes of obtaining financing.[22]

The school did not open in 1932, nor in the next two years, but a letter of 1935 indicates plans were still in the making.[23] The school never opened. The ever-escalating Mexican situation prevented the sisters' use of the old quarters, and the projected money for new ones never materialized. It was one of the many bubbles that burst in the thirties.

Father Albert had constantly to contend with provincial quarrels among the Mexican Franciscans, with their reluctance to help pay for the land they had acquired, and with their inertia toward building the seminary to which they had committed. Most of these seem to have stemmed from Fathers Domingo Resendiz and Alphonso Sanchez.

Resendiz obviously felt no financial responsibility for the seminary property. Despite government abuses, the Church in Mexico drew considerable covert support from the wealthy Catholics in the cities, and help from the Knights of Columbus and the Marquette League in the United States. Resendiz, Father Al reported early in 1931, claimed to have no money, but also no debts. "The entire sum to be paid on the seminary property is . . . not a staggering debt even for a poor province. Will you please . . . urge the Mexican Province to . . . complete the payments on the property. . . . Any province can do that much," he added.[24]

The padre's letter, Novatus wrote, "came at the most opportune time." He had seen Visitor General Zulaica, who assured him that "the Province of Michoacán will pay the balance due on the El Paso property,"—though, he added, Zulaica had not said when.[25]

Father Al was skeptical. "My mind does not rest easy," he answered. The gap between Zulaica's promise and Domingo's delivery was wide: the padre had heard rumors that Resendiz was talking of selling the property. "That," he fulminated, would "be a disgrace . . . after having promised our benefactors that the Mexican friars certainly would build a seminary."[26]

As the due date for the first thousand-dollar payment approached, Novatus appealed to Resendiz. That gentleman, however, preferred that Braun make a loan for him above the border—"a poor prospect," Novatus called it: who would make a loan to the Franciscans of Mexico? And, he added, "he wants the same to be done with the other $18,000."[27]

Novatus secured the loans, but had to guarantee payments, which Resendiz consistently failed to honor. Letter after letter repeated the dreary refrain: Resendiz defaulted, Novatus sent what he could, and Father Al went East on one begging trip after another. Together he and Novatus paid what they could, got extensions or refinanced the loans when they could not, and somehow hung onto the property.

The padre was having his own financial problems as banks continued to fail. The railroad, mining, and oil industries were laying off workers and slashing wages, and a third of New Mexico's population was on relief. Prolonged drought and constant wind ushered in the 'dust bowl' days. Despite their self-sufficiency, Father Al feared for his Apaches. "This will be a hard year for the Mescalero Indians," he predicted in 1931. "I notice wool has dropped to 12¢. Last year they got 24¢ and a few years ago 45¢."[28] The first group of seminarians had completed their novitiate and gone, but with the continued religious persecution in Mexico no one was ever sure when to expect new groups.

"Tried to get some financial help from Father Domingo, but had no success," Father Al wrote in September. "[I]t is necessary to hold the land near El Paso. People in Mexico with experience look for another explosion as soon as Calles dies."[29]

Al Braun's Mexican challenge extended far beyond his financial battles. Provincial quarrels brewed in the south, crossed the border, and caught him in the crossfire, leaving Mescalero and Tularosa wondering to whom they belonged. Father Novatus, hosting much of the Mexican exiles' overflow in San Francisco, was drawn into the fray, along with a sizeable contingent of Spanish Franciscans who had also given help and haven to their besieged Mexican brothers. They were added to the mix when it was decided for some reason to transfer Mescalero and Tularosa from the Michoacán province to that of San Evangelio, where the Spaniards seem to have been more influential. Resendiz had agreed and signed the requisite documents, but neither he nor Zulaica informed Father Al of the transfer, leaving him to learn via the grapevine. Resendiz meanwhile was having second thoughts—obviously, Novatus opined, because he "does not want the Province of San Evangelio [to] have any share in the El Paso property."[30]

That was in March 1931. Not until August did he notify Father Al of the change that would become effective as of January 1932. "Am pleased with the transfer," the padre wrote. "So is Bishop Schuler." Resendiz had asked him to meet the ship on which the Spanish clerics were to arrive, "but didn't say which one it would be. . . . Fr. Agustín Pozos," he added, "got tired of his Ford and bought a new Chevrolet" with permission of Resendiz. "The Spaniards can pay for it."[31]

The padre entrained for New York. On the twenty-ninth two Valentian friars arrived, with attendant confusion. Despite written orders for Tularosa they insisted on going to San Francisco. And, the padre reported to Novatus, more were coming—Spanish priests and Mexican seminarians who had been studying in Spain—but no one knew when. Resendiz believed them on their way, but no roster of passengers listed them. "If I could feel sure

[they] . . . would do as told, I would let the Brothers here send them but they do what they want unless made to do otherwise. . . . The two Spanish fathers here have made all kinds of excuses why they should go to San Francisco."[32]

Novatus was irate. ". . . I would much rather that the contingent would go to Mescalero. But without a word from those confounded men in Mexico the whole transaction is most disgusting. . . . [S]omeday they are going to get some plain talk from me. . . . If only they would have enough ass-sense to let a fellow know what to do about the Fathers they called from Spain. . . ." Meanwhile the first two priests were en route to California, where they would await twelve of the Mexican students. "If these gents have to go back to Mescalero it will be up to them how to get there. . . . So far, so bad."[33]

In New York Father Al watched for the missing personnel. Resendiz "hopes they get here sometime in September. I will wait until Wednesday. . . ." He was still waiting to learn "what the province wants to do with Tularosa and Mescalero. . . . It took two letters and one telegram to get any information out of Fr. Resendiz. . . ."[34]

Having left money for the missing clerics' fares, he wrote three days later that he was leaving "on the next train on which a pass is good."[35]

Novatus found one ray of sunshine: "No doubt Fr. Agustín will be moving to Mexico after [it is] officially known that Tularosa belongs to the San Evangelio Province."[36] It proved only wishful thinking, as the padre soon informed Novatus. "Fr. Domingo wrote Fr. Agustín that he had only loaned Mescalero and Tularosa to . . . San Evangelio. Fr. Agustín is green with jealousy because it looks as if . . . San Evangelio might make some headway. . . . There is no love between the Provinces."[37]

Further confusion arose when it was learned the awaited contingent was to debark in Vera Cruz, although their passages west were scheduled from New York. "I can't imagine any people harder to deal with than the Mexicans," Braun asserted. "Certainly am glad the Province of San Evangelio will be mostly Spanish. . . ."[38]

Resendiz, still pulling strings in Mexico, continued to hedge on the seminary, and was apparently influencing Father Zulaica. "I think something is going on behind the scenes," the padre confided to Novatus. "Probably Fr. Resendiz has his hand in it . . . [to judge] from letters that he has been writing to Fr. Agustín. The Michoacán Province will never do anything here and still they are too jealous to let the others in.

"If anything worthwhile is ever to be done with Mescalero and Tularosa it will be done by the Province of Evangelio through the Spanish Fathers. Please write Father General and urge him to make the plans stick of having novitiate, philosophy and theology for the Province of San Evangelio at Mescalero and Tularosa."[39]

Such a possibility apparently roused Resendiz to sway Zulaica, who, the padre reported, "seems to think the Michoacán Province wants & needs Tularosa and Mescalero. Neither is the case. . . . [T]hey hate us both . . . for the very puerile reason that the people once said they wish they had the Franciscans from California back again."[40]

Finally in December word came that the Mexican seminarians expected in September had arrived in New York, where "they stayed long enough to go to mass and then returned to the boat and sailed for Mexico. I am now sorry," the padre added, "that I didn't go to meet them. They can't fool me about not being able to get in the country. . . . The whole thing is this: they wanted to go to Mexico and they succeeded. They are all tricky and always get what they want in their own way. I have experienced their deceit and cunning for four and a half years."[41]

As 1931 neared its end Father Albert had personal decisions to make. He had been lent to the Mexicans for five years, which would soon be up. "I am uncertain what to do," he confided to Novatus. Should he renew his commitment or return to his own province of Santa Barbara?[42] By April he was nearing a decision. "Considering everything I think I should stay with the Mexicans for a while yet. Should I leave, I am afraid the Mexican Friars would try to give up everything. . . . I think as long as I am with them I can hold them to their obligations." Most importantly, he was committed to his beloved Apaches. He could not leave them; to stay he would have to remain with the Mexicans as long as they kept Mescalero.[43]

Novatus agreed. The padre's time with the Mexicans was extended another three years.

Father Gabriel Soto at San Evangelio was, in contrast to Domingo Resendiz, interested in getting things done, a man with whom the padre believed he could easily work. But even Soto seemed not to understand the necessity for making payments. With remittances due on two large notes plus interest and taxes weighing on his shoulders, Father Al exploded to Novatus that Soto must be made to understand. "Unless we face these payments when they come due the property will never be paid."[44]

Novatus must have made some impression on Soto, who immediately sent a check for $52.50. Though but a token, the padre was grateful. "It is such a surprise to be getting a check from the Mexicans instead of passing [checks] out to pay some bill for the Mexicans."[45] Al Braun still had to scrounge for the bulk of the payment.

On receiving a threat of foreclosure on another note, the padre sent a copy to Soto and another to Novatus, with a terse note. "I have no money. . . . What would you advise me to do?"[46] Novatus had little advice: his own situation was desperate. He was hard pressed to keep the province solvent.[47]

Father Al had but one recourse. "I am going to El Paso and try to borrow money to cover back taxes and interest. . . . Will borrow for 90 days . . . in the hope that I can meet the note after [a trip] . . . east." There he hoped "to get stipends to pay all interest and back taxes."[48] That measure was a foreshadowing of many to come; the cycle with minor variations continued.

By the end of 1932, still unable to learn what if any decisions had been made regarding Tularosa and Mescalero, Father Albert began increasingly to believe the mission, the exiles, and the Tularosa parish would all be better off if transferred back to American administration—preferably to Santa Barbara. "The Mexican friars are not fitted to take care of this mission," even under Spanish control, he concluded.[49]

Novatus agreed. If the church were ever to be finished, or a permanent novitiate built, an American province would have to be in charge. As to Tularosa, "an American community is certainly most desirable. . . . Why not transfer both?"[50]

But which American province? Who under present economic conditions could shoulder the burden? The Father Provincial of Cincinnati, who had earlier approached Father Al saying his province would like to take over the Mescalero mission,[51] renewed his request in February 1933, again via the padre, but with the proviso that Santa Barbara would in return take from his province certain missions in Utah and Arizona that were becoming burdensome. "Why," Father Al wrote Novatus bluntly, "don't you take back Mescalero and forget about the territory. It will be much better to have Mescalero than to be forced to take the Cincinnati places. . . ."[52]

But Santa Barbara's definitors were unwilling to assume responsibility during the worsening Depression, and the Mescalero mission, like an unwanted puppy, sat hoping for a home.

✠✠✠

Father Albert's battle on behalf of the Mexican Church did not stop at the border. Three times during the early thirties he and Dave Kirgan journeyed deep into tortured Mexico, traveling incognito: priests, if recognized as such, were executed. It was a danger the two seem to have enjoyed immensely. Father Al, seemingly a simple businessman, was to 'purchase' certain Franciscan properties to save them from government seizure. He seems also to have carried money and messages, probably from exiled Bishop Manrique y Zarate, and possibly through Archbishop Orozco. Of what we know beyond this, much is conjectural and details are few.

The Mexican trips are among the most intriguing facets of Al Braun's lively career—to the historian a fascinating invitation into a maze with many dead ends. That he had underground connections we know; who they were or what exchanges took place we do not.

The lack of information is understandable. Mexico's radical government systematically destroyed or locked away records regarding the Church and the abuses thereof; Church officials did the same to protect their own people from government retribution; and Father Albert, when he spoke of the trips at all, divulged nothing of any substance, obviously to protect his contacts in Mexico. *Veni, vidi, vici.* Period.

This much we know:

A bishop—evidently Manrique—requested Rome to save certain Church properties from confiscation by effecting a transfer of titles to and through an individual seemingly unconnected to the Church. As syndic, Father Al learned of the request, possibly from Manrique himself, volunteered for the job, and was commissioned to go, with a companion for security. He chose Dave Kirgan for the adventure.

His characteristically brief summation for the Provincial records tells little. "Made three trips to Mexico City during the persecution to take over property of Mexican Friars and some nuns. Became a Mexican citizen in 1928." (The date was actually 1931. The summary was written many years later, from time-misted memory.) After giving the routes, the narrative continues. "Was an employee of Momsen, Dunnigan and Ryan Hardware Co. on these trips so as not to be suspected of being a priest. . . . I had a good time three times a week at the Mexican Army Club in Mexico City. Met some splendid men among the Mexican officers" (who would have had their heads had they known who they were). He and Kirgan obviously enjoyed a few rounds of Mexican 'holy water' with their new friends. They may also have gleaned some interesting information.

He and Father Dave had prepared carefully, dressing as vacationing businessmen, even purchasing cheap 'gold' wedding rings. Their ostensible employers, under whose cover they traveled, were friends with whom they traded in El Paso.

There is confusion over the time frame for these sojourns. Dorothy Emerson, Braun's sole biographer until now, gives no dates, but posits the first trip at several months after the summary execution of the beloved 'Father Pro.' If correct, this would place that trip early in 1928, the execution having occurred on 23 November 1927. On his second trip, Emerson alleges, Father Al witnessed the attempted assassination of President Elect Pascual Ortiz Rubio as he rode in his inaugural procession on 5 February 1930. Emerson, however, cites no sources, documents no material, for any of these trips; and her book, which contains factual errors throughout, cannot be considered a reliable source.[53] There is no mention of either incident in Father Al's extant records or correspondence, though his omissions could be deliberate.

Documentation does exist for the trip of 1931. But was it the second or the third? If we accept the first two as having occurred in 1928 and 1930, it would be the third. But according to Father Al's memory, the route of the second trip was via New Orleans and Vera Cruz—which is verifiably the route he followed in 1931. The sequence of the routes, however, was noted many years after the events and from his understandably hazy memory.

It is relatively safe, then, to posit 1928, 1930, and 1931 as correct. All were perilous years for any clerics, doubly hazardous for alien priests in mufti.

Another tantalizing question arises concerning Father Al's connection with Archbishop Orozco. Orozco had, as noted, walked the risky path of passive opposition while covertly giving aid and comfort to the Cristeros, and he remained a thorn in Mexican federal sides. During negotiations leading to the truce of 1929 he and several other oppositionist bishops were distinctly personae non gratae, and were asked by bishops working toward the agreements to stay out of the country during the talks. Under a guarantee of safe conduct Orozco went to El Paso where, according to local tradition, Father Albert met and drove him to Mescalero. He was a man to whom Al

Braun could relate, having constantly followed the dictates of conscience over those of hierarchical orders. What they may have discussed—if they did indeed meet—no one knows.

The padre also seems to have had some contacts in Juárez, a logical junction for exchanges relative to the trips into the interior. Marquita Hill Boetto remembers one occasion when he came through Tularosa with Charlie and Katherine Mackey en route to the border town for some obviously urgent reason. "He took his collar off—priests weren't allowed on the streets in Juárez—and he said 'I have to go.' I don't know what for—I was too young to think about it. But I do know a priest was killed there right in the street."[54]

We learn of the trips in bits and pieces—many from the mouths of children who as adults remembered the fascination of listening to the stories they gathered around him to hear. The padre's life was filled with enough action to give him exciting tales to tell, and the Mexican tales were high on their lists. He stuck to anecdotes, never citing names, dates, locations, or any details that might, if repeated, incriminate anyone involved.

His business was mainly in Mexico City where to inventory property and transfer titles he had to deal with government authorities. His passport showed his service and rank in the United States Army, but omitted his status as chaplain—he had seen to that. As an American captain he had access to the Mexican officers' club, and spent a great deal of time with the officers, especially one captain, nephew Mike Brown recalls. "They became great friends—I guess as part of his cover Father Al was using his position in the army. This captain took a liking to him—such a good liking that he set Father Albert up with a woman. Father Al got around that with his 'wedding' ring. 'No, no' he said, he already had a woman. One was enough!"[55]

They had been warned, he told Elisa Baldonado and her siblings, that "when you sit, don't put your hands on your knees because that would let them know you're a priest. And they had to be very careful and not write anything down while they were down there."

For the most part they were careful, although in one incident they took a terrible chance. Elisa relished that story. "He and Father Kirgan wanted to say mass in a cathedral down there. They had to buy off a guard to let them get in and to stand watch outside." They must have paid well, for they completed the ceremony without incident.[56]

Another time, as Mike Brown tells it, "he was trying to seek out the

Bishop of Mexico City to report to him. The bishop was incognito. Father Albert finally found him—he was working on a building, laying bricks, so the authorities wouldn't know he was a bishop. When Father Albert asked if he was the bishop, he asked, 'Who are you and why do you want to know?' After he explained the bishop admitted yes, he was the bishop. So Father Albert gets down on his knees and kisses his hand. Well, he said the bishop about dropped dead right there. He said, 'go away and come back later and quit doing that or you'll get us both killed!'"[57]

Assuming our dates are correct, the first trip was made during the intense fighting between Gorostieta's Cristeros and the federal troops, and the second during tense negotiations for the uneasy truce. In 1931, when persecution again became rampant and church property was once more endangered, Fathers Al and Dave made the third, and documented, trip.

Not daring to be seen twice by some alert border guard who might wonder about these repeated trips, they never crossed into Mexico twice through the same port of entry. One route—Father Al says the first—was via Laredo; another took them through Chihuahua. In 1931 they sailed.

"Just got my passport for Mexico," the padre wrote Novatus on 12 January. "We are going by way of New Orleans and expect a pass on an oil tanker to Vera Cruz" courtesy of a friend with Standard Oil. "Father Provincial is going to meet us in Vera Cruz. Expect to leave next Sunday night. Am going to stop a day at San Antonio to visit a Major I had during the war." He was glad Father Kirgan was going. "He is good company and the rest will do him good."[58]

The padre wrote one letter—surprisingly and rashly—while in Mexico. Kirgan, he noted, had had a hard time getting away. "Bishop Schuler only let him go to try to collect $10,500.00 the Mexican Bishops owe to Bishop Schuler. No luck so far. . . . Bishop Díaz," he penned in the margin, "got cramps when Fr. Kirgan mentioned the debt."[59]

Though Father Al rarely mentioned his trips to interviewers, he gave journalist Kenny Joel (well after the event) the story of a scare while on the tanker on which they were two of nineteen passengers. As they neared Vera Cruz, a "swarthy character" who had watched them suspiciously throughout the voyage took them aside and questioned their identity. Father Al claimed to be a Greek teacher, at which the stranger eyed the padre's stone-roughened hands and sneered that he was no academic. He and his companion were hiding something, he said, and it was his business "to keep people like you out of Mexico." He turned away at some interruption and did not approach them again. Later they wondered if he might have been an ally warning them to be careful.[60]

Otherwise, Braun wrote Novatus, "We enjoyed the trip by boat. It cost $37.50. That has the train beat by a long shot. The bar opened as soon as we got out of the river. Drinks were reasonable. Here [in Mexico] they are cheap, 5 star cognac $3.50 per bottle and Vermouth $1.10 per quart. We keep supplied and don't feel we are spending money. Wish I could bring you a few bottles. . . ."

He could not get away for another one to two weeks. "The visitation is on. . . . Father Resendiz says he will not be in office again. The Spaniard element is strong against him. The Province of San Evangelio will have its own superior."

And, he reported, "Our dear friend Mr. Calles is slowly dying. He has lost several fingers and soon will have a leg amputated. Doctors say he cannot live long. The Friars . . . seem to think the future is full of promise. Laymen who have been in the country a long time and who know how things run expect another explosion when Calles goes." But Calles did not die. Father Al's informers were overly optimistic.

"Yesterday I became a Mexican citizen," he continued. "That was necessary before taking over the property for Fr. Resendiz and Mother Humilde."

They planned to return by plane, which "is 10 pesos cheaper than by train and . . . much quicker."[61] For some reason the plan was aborted and they returned by slow train through Chihuahua and Sonora.

"Enjoyed the trip but after we started to move north I was anxious to be home again," he wrote on his return. Already he was brimming with new plans. "If the provinces in the States would . . . publish a monthly magazine in Mexico, the rehabilitation of the Order in Mexico would be financed and then the Provinces in the States could dictate to the Friars of Mexico how to behave. . . ." And he knew just the right father to edit it. Still bubbling with ideas, he added that "People down here . . . said they would send us more students than we can accommodate . . . if we open a college in the States. . . ."[62]

Neither of the padre's suggestions bore fruit.

The Mexican journeys make an intriguing, if brief, tale of two padres, their roles as undercover men a fascinating divertissement. Spurred by the call to action, they charged galloping on their mission of danger, disguise, and daring, priests in the armor of businessmen, to tilt perhaps at windmills—or to save a nation's faith. They obviously relished every cloak-sans-dagger moment.

Hugolinus Storff, who had once labeled Al Braun an adventurer, might not have been, in retrospect, so very far from wrong.

✣✣✣

As the Mexican Franciscans labored covertly to keep their religion alive in radical Mexico, those above the border toiled for the seminary forbidden to their southern brothers, that young priests could be trained in successive numbers for that country so desperately crying for spiritual help.

And always over Father Albert loomed Saint Joseph's—the dream he had vowed on the battle-torn fields of France to realize for his Apaches.

Both had to be paid for. The deepening Depression was a cold stone weight on the padre's shoulders. By 1933 the situation had become desperate. "Please . . . ," he begged Novatus in September, "try to make Fr. Prov[incial] Gabriel Soto pay the $2000.00. . . . Action must be taken quickly. . . ."[63] Meanwhile he appealed again. ". . . If they have not the money on hand let them borrow . . . at once."[64] Meanwhile he must, as a man in desert drought, find another headspring.

Salvation came from a surprising direction. In June 1933 Father Albert joined the Civilian Conservation Corps.

The CCC, one of the few New Deal anti-Depression measures that proved of any real value, revived many during the thirties. Under the aegis of the United States Army, the Corps enrolled thousands of young men without jobs or prospects, provided training and discipline, gave them useful work, engendered patriotism, and prevented them from turning to crime, habitual inertia, or the subversive doctrines of Communism and Fascism.

On 31 March 1933 the President had signed the bill federalizing what many states had already implemented on their own levels—programs that would create jobs and use that labor to conserve, restore, and develop endangered natural resources, and preserve regional history and culture. Under Chief-of-Staff General Douglas MacArthur mobilization got underway, camps began to spring up, and the CCC was born. By June sixteen camps were operating in New Mexico, with more to follow.[65]

Quarters in the camps were spartan but clean; food was simple but nourishing; uniforms were army issue. Work and discipline were demanding but rewarding in self-respect. Pay was modest, but adequate enough for the young men to send some home to hungry families. Each day began with a flag-raising ceremony and ended with a retreat and retiring the colors. Pride and patriotism were the hallmarks of the CCC, and with them an emphasis on moral character and religious values.

Homesick boys needed chaplains, and the CCC particularly favored chaplains with military experience. Father Albert Braun saw a chaplain's salary as a means to pay debts, feed and house his exiled seminarians, and finish his church, while simultaneously serving his country. Having kept in touch with officers with whom he had served in France, and through his active status in the Reserve, he was among the first to be contacted. Was he available?

He was.

It seemed an ideal solution until his orders came in June assigning him to Colorado. "I expected duty in New Mexico," he wrote Novatus, "and thus be at my mission much of the time." A young Franciscan priest from New York was replacing him until he could wangle a transfer to home ground. Meanwhile, he admitted, he found duty in Colorado "enticing. I am suppose[d] to leave Wednesday with a brand new Plym[outh] and a good driver. . . . I have 750 miles of the most beautiful country in the U.S. and plenty of time for good trout fishing. . . . What more could a man ask for. However, I want to be near my mission . . . to keep my eye on the work for the church. Therefore I have the Governor, the two Senators and the Dept. Commander of the Legion in N.M. pulling wires. . . . I expect the transfer in a week or two."[66]

He got it. His new assignment covered the whole state, he wrote in July, but "three of the camps are near Mescalero so I get down there almost every two weeks for one day." He used those days fully. "We have practically all the stone quarried and cut. Want to start placing the stones in the wall Sept 1st, so as to have all the stone work finished before freezing weather. Can you send me Bro. Benedict [Schlokum] to supervise the job . . . [and] put on the roof. . . ."[67]

In September he pled again. "I can't supervise the job and earn the money at the same time. . . . Can Bro Benedict be here by Sept 15th. . . ." The priest from New York "is a flop. He says he knows everything but he is one of the dumb Irish with a big mouth. All kinds of bad luck have hit the mission since he is in charge. The other day we lost our fine jersey cow. If I didn't need the money so bad I would resign from the army. Be sure to send Bro Benedict. . . ."[68]

But Benedict was "head over heels at work in California. Why not indefinitely postpone work on the church?" Novatus asked. "When times have improved, people will be liberal again. . . ."[69]

Father Al could not and would not stop work on the church. It doubtless seemed to some—maybe even to the sympathetic Novatus—that he had become obsessed. Perhaps he had. But he knew what he must do. *Albert, build my church. . . .*

One option remained. He was having second thoughts about the CCC, he wrote Novatus. "I am reluctant to give up the opportunity to earn money in these hard times, still . . . I think I should get out." He had sent the New Yorker to the farm and there was no priest at the mission. Having rented out the property on a sharecropper basis, he must oversee the harvest to ensure the mission got its share. And he needed to finish the church wall before freezing weather. "The Indians have raised $100.00. I have $300 [with which] we probably can do the work. The scaffolding is beginning to rot. If I wait another year may have to buy much lumber. . . . Tony is getting very old and so is José Mesa, my two main men. Can't afford to lose them. They understand the job; both have worked from the beginning." Further, the army no longer paid mileage for his extensive driving. Finally, "[a]ll the regular army officers . . . are being replaced by reserve officers. They are neither army men nor civilians. . . . We will probably draw our reserve personnel from Texas and they will have all the Texas bigotry."

He enclosed a sample letter for Novatus to send the commanding general at Fort Bliss, "on your own official stationery and in your own forceful clear style," and suggested that he stress the padre's duties with the Mexican friars. "All this," he added puckishly, "is for effect."[70]

Novatus wrote accordingly, and as of 30 September 1933 Chaplain Braun was relieved of active duty to return to Mescalero for some comparatively stress-free time.[71] Although there was still a $4500 outstanding mortgage against the El Paso property, the Franciscans' lawyer reported, "the owners of the notes have agreed to extend the same over a period of five years."[72]

Still, it had to be paid; and when in March the CCC signaled they needed Chaplain Braun again, Chaplain Braun found he needed the CCC salary if he was ever to clear his debts and finish his church. "Chaplain Arnold wants me back in the army for 8 months," he wrote, "to take care of the C.C.C. camps in and around Santa Fe. I would like to go. . . . Because of the necessity of meeting notes and paying interest on the Mexican property near El Paso I got Mescalero in a hole. . . . With my army pay last summer I paid more than $400.00 on my debt; besides I kept work going on the church from June till Nov. 26. If I could go back for 8 months I would be able to pay off the balance of the debt and finish the church—stone work & roof—However I need someone to take my place. . . ." He could get the New York priest back, but "he is like a child with money and he can beat Friar Tuck drinking wine. With him here I am sure I would be deeper in debt after the 8 months. Have you anyone you can spare . . .? I want a man who knows the value of a dollar and who does not love his drink too much."[73]

Novatus had no one available.

By May he had still not heard "whether I am to go into the army again. If I do then Father [John] Smith will say mass at Mescalero for me. Hope I am called . . . so that I can pay off my debts. With the few dollars I get it is hard to keep things going."[74]

"Would you please," Novatus shot back, "forget about returning into military service? I hope they won't take you back."[75]

But Al Braun's hard head won. As of 11 June 1934 Chaplain Braun was once again on active duty—not in Santa Fe as he expected, but in Arizona where, he wrote from his headquarters camp in Globe, he was expected "to make my home for the next five months."[76] After that his duty would end; his original eight months had been reduced.

By late July he had arranged a transfer to Santa Fe. "When not on the road I live here at the Cathedral with the Franciscans. . . . Most of the time I am on the road.

"Since on this job I have paid out interest and old debts $496.50. By the time I get out Nov. 11th I hope to have every debt of the mission paid. The reason the mission got so deeply in debt is because often I had to use mission fund[s] to pay note and interest on the property of the Franciscan Fathers of [El Paso] Texas."[77]

Through the Franciscans in Santa Fe he met José Ortiz y Pino, became close friends with Don José and his family, and often took the patriarch's oldest daughter Concha on his trips to the area camps. It was a memory Concha would cherish. "Father Albert would pick me up in his little Ford, and I would sing at the different camps. . . . It was such fun with Father Albert. . . . He would say mass first at Los Alamos, and [then] the other camps, and I would sing hymns in Spanish. Then after mass we'd all get together and sing Spanish songs, like *La Cucaracha* and *Las Manānitas*. . . . Sometimes we even danced around the fire. . . . Father Albert would encourage us—he was clapping and yelling, trying to sing. He was . . . so real, so human—and so spiritual. . . . We ate at the camps. The boys made beans, they brought out hot breads, and meats they had barbecued. We had a feast and then we all danced, and sang, and sang. Came back to Santa Fe and then took off for another camp."[78]

Don José was a *patrón* from a long line of aristocratic Spanish ancestors, a devout Catholic, and a favorite with the Franciscan friars. Her father "knew how hard it was to be a priest," Concha continued, "and how little they had materially. . . . He saw that they had warm sheepskin coats. He presented Father Albert with one. And my mother—she adored Father Albert. . . .

"There was something about him that was so real—so kind, so understanding. Even if he said 'don't do that,' you understood why." One morning, having eaten breakfast before mass, she believed she should not take communion. "The priests had told us, 'if you have swallowed anything—even a safety pin—I can't give you communion.' I told that to Father Albert, and he laughed and laughed, and leaned his head down on the driving wheel saying, 'I can't believe anyone that crazy!' So he explained it had nothing to do with today's customs. 'These rules are very old,' he said, 'from when people couldn't get food always, so when they did they ate too much, and they'd be so full when they got to church . . . they'd go to sleep at communion.' So he said, 'I don't want you to swallow safety pins—but you go to communion.'"[79]

At some time in late June or early July of that busy summer of 1934 Fathers Al and Dave made another trip to Mexico at the request of Father Gabriel Soto. He had sent the $2000 Father Al had earlier requested and, sincerely trying to pay his further debts, now urged the padre to see a wealthy widow in Mexico City who he believed might contribute toward the El Paso seminary. Somehow Al Braun found the time to go, apparently on a quick leave from the CCC. The trip was successful, he reported in July: The lady had promised to pay for the seminary.[80]

At the time they made the trip anti-Church violence was rampant. Priests were fleeing in massive numbers, and a power struggle was erupting between Calles and General Lázaro Cárdenas. But the feisty wayfaring friars, now seasoned veterans of the underground, kept low profiles and traveled without incident.

In November, having completed his military assignment, he told the Pino family goodbye, exacted their promise to visit him on the reservation, and returned to Mescalero in time for the Christmas season. He had fulfilled all obligations to the CCC and greatly reduced his debts; he anticipated no more trips into Mexico; and his duties for the seminary were significantly eased with Father Soto at the helm. He could now settle to some uninterrupted time at the mission. And with spring he could resume building and look at last toward completing his Apache mission.

14: APACHE CATHEDRAL

Back at the mission life resumed its rhythm, though among the Apaches that rhythm was showing changes. The New Deal had come to Mescalero, with dubious results. In 1933 Roosevelt had appointed John Collier Indian Commissioner. A small man with big ideas, Collier preached his belief in the beauty of Indian culture and the necessity for its preservation—but under the tutelage of the white man's government and in accordance with the white man's ways.

The Mescaleros replied that their culture was doing very nicely, thank you, without supervision. It was Father Albert, not John Collier, who had defended their puberty ceremony, and by extension their other traditions. He knew more about them and their beliefs and their needs than John Collier or the New Dealers ever would. It was Father Albert, not John Collier, who worked with the tribal council during the woes of Depression and sat with them when invited. He was one of them. They had, moreover, an ingrained distrust of government.

But when Collier introduced the Indian Reorganization Act in 1934 (apparently while the padre was on duty in Santa Fe), he persuaded them this act was really in their favor. By becoming federal corporations, tribes could borrow money for economic development. True, the government would thereby control tribal elections, laws, and grazing regulations; but the plan was not mandatory. The tribes could accept or reject it. Most of the tribes in New Mexico rejected it. The Navajos turned it down flatly, only to find they were forced to obey its regulations anyhow, by which they lost most of their sheep and their way of life.

The Mescaleros accepted the plan, believing it a genuine effort to help them. In many ways it did, if conversion to a white man's world was an improvement. Father Albert had always worked toward educating them to cope with that world, but—and herein lay the difference—on their own terms and within their own traditions. Now the Indian boarding schools were to be closed, supplanted by day schools, and integrated into the public school system. The Mescalero high-school students, except for those Father

Al could send to Catholic schools, began riding school buses to Tularosa. The government began to supervise their herds and resettle families on land away from the center at Mescalero, away from their church on which they had worked so loyally. From that center they had roamed the hills and made their camps. Now they were being made sedentary, each family with its herd and a permanent house.

But the Mescaleros preferred their tepees, and continued to erect them away from the house. Nor did they like the cook stoves inside the houses. Open fires in open air were much better. The stoves went largely ignored.

Bureaucracy had invaded the reservation. It gained momentum after the arrival of a new superintendent in 1935, the iron-fisted E. R. McCray who, once he led the Indians to the bubbling fountain of government benevolence, could not understand why they refused to drink.

Paul Ortega, even as a child, could have told him. Paul rode the school bus to and from the agency's primary day school at Mescalero. His parents, like others, were often not at home when the bus left them in the evenings. "So the bus would take the children to the next place— an aunt or an uncle, or somebody at the next stop—and you stay there till your mother came and got you. They were not worried about us. We ate, we slept there if we needed to. The whole community took care of each other—until they started putting those houses there. They'd take the guys—from Whitetail, from Elk, from Carrizo—and put them all next to each other. They don't know how to help each other because they are not related. That's when we started having our problems."[1]

They would be better off with his changes, McCray kept insisting. They were not so sure.

Neither, apparently, was Father Albert. Force had never been his way nor bureaucracy his means. A few grumbling comments straggle through his letters, ridiculing Collier's ideas. Beyond that he seems largely to have kept out of the affair: the government would implement its program in any event. McCray continued to build houses, the Mescaleros continued to live in their tepees, and Father Albert continued, like Saint Francis, to hoe his own garden and build his Apache cathedral. The Church would serve them far better than a reservation full of empty houses. Saint Joseph's had already become their catalyst, their unifying principle.

Building always stopped during the winter. "Today we are having our first heavy snow of the season," the padre wrote late in November, soon after returning from Santa Fe. "The sight of snow usually makes Tony want to go to California but he has not said anything so far. He is busy working on a beautiful baptismal font. Hope I can finish the church this coming spring."[2]

By December Tony had saved $165 from his pension, with which he ordered a tombstone for his wife. He was, Father Al reported, "very contented this year and says nothing about going home." From Juárez, Father Kirgan "keeps Tony well supplied so that he can take a little 'schluck' every day. He says that makes him feel fine."[3] He had never known the aging Tony "to be more contented. His daily prayer is that he lives to see the church blessed this summer."[4]

Father Al had been home scarcely a month before the army was after him for another six-month stint with the CCC. This time he declined. "Would like to make the money, but have been away from the mission long enough. . . ." He had, moreover, with the help of Fathers Kirgan and Smith, gotten out appeals for mass stipends, which were coming in well, and he had received invitations to collect in the East for his church. He would go soon. "Want to finish the church this summer."

Too, the El Paso seminary seemed to be coming toward some action. Father Domingo, he continued, was sending. Father [Bonaventure] Nava to begin building. "He expects to get help from the large number of tertiaries of El Paso and Juárez. . . . Father Kirgan likes Father Nava because he is energetic and a good builder. He . . . will cooperate with Father Nava in every way. . . ."[5]

He ushered 1935 in buoyantly with three ambitious goals, for which he vowed to "use every push I have. 1st, build the seminary; 2nd open a sisters' day school for the Indians at Mescalero; 3rd put the roof on the church."[6]

He was still working energetically for the Mexican friars—more happily now with Father Gabriel Soto. Believing Americans must more fully understand the plight of the Mexican Church, he suggested a lecture tour for Father Alphonso Martinez, who had made his novitiate in Mescalero, studied German, and could reach the German Catholics in America. If Soto agreed, he wrote Novatus, "I have good hopes of getting the Knights of Columbus to pay his expenses and give him a salary" for the project. It would, moreover, be "a good opportunity to publicize the seminary and may bring in some much needed money."

He had also contacted his "good old compadre of war days Father Veith of Baltimore [who] had organized . . . a society for the defense of the Church in Mexico. I wrote him the fight is on and is a bitter one and that we as Catholic neighbors have our part to play in it."[7]

"Father Kirgan and I were in an auto accident," the padre wrote in June. "He was forced off the road by another car. Both of us were thrown from Fr. Kirgan's car. I was knocked out for about two hours but not hurt seriously. Father Kirgan . . . hurt his spine. It may take eighteen months . . . before he is in good condition again. In the meantime Fr. Smith is running the cathedral parish. . . . Tomorrow I expect to drive Fr. Kirgan's car to El Paso."[8] In the mountainous country four miles east of Mescalero the car had, as related in the *El Paso Times*, "shot over the edge of a cliff and overturned." Kirgan was taken by ambulance to El Paso "after he failed to respond to treatment at Mescalero." He would "remain in bed for three months while the compressed fracture of the spine heals sufficiently to allow him to move about," after which he must wear a brace "and guard his movements carefully." The occupants of the other car, unaware of the accident, had driven on.[9]

It was late August before Father Al could report that "Fr. Kirgan got his braces and is now out of bed. He is a good sufferer."[10]

Father Soto still awaited Father Nava's arrival to begin building on the ranch north of El Paso. Apparently Resendiz had again changed his mind. But Soto, jarred by escalating persecution in Mexico, could wait no longer. Mexico still seethed. In the ongoing fight for power, Cárdenas ousted the hated Calles; but he was as obsessively anticlerical as Calles, 1935 boded little hope for churchmen, and the need for the seminary was urgent.

"Here is a little news," Father Al wrote Novatus in June. "Fr. Soto was here the first of this week. Because . . . he has 7 theologians who must be sent to Spain if he has no house up in El Paso, he looked around. . . . Out by Loretta Academy . . . there is an immense mansion, which was lost by the owner when the First National Bank failed. The Reserve Bank now holds the property and wants to sell. The house when built cost $500,000.00. The Provincial may be able to buy it for $20,000. The terms are very easy. In case he gets the place he will keep theology there and build a monastery for novitiates & philosophy at the ranch. This new house is well equipped. It has a beautiful ball room which will make a beautiful chapel. It has a $15,000 pipe organ. There are several large rooms that can be used for class rooms, also a large dining room and an excellent kitchen. All material in the building is of the highest quality."[11] The mansion would solve many problems, if Soto could swing the deal.

Meanwhile work on the church progressed through the spring and summer of 1935. All Mescalero enjoyed the activity, especially the children. One very small boy, the blacksmith's son, was constantly in the arena, despite orders to stay away. "Father Al would take me by the hand and lead me back home," he recalled, "forever telling me it was dangerous." But danger means little to tots, and James Cissny always came back.[12]

The Mackey boys were also attracted to the site. Dick was fascinated with the kilns, where "they were making lime for the mortar. My mother did a lot of cooking for Father Al and the workers, so we'd end up playing and running around in the mud. They had a barn and some horses—to pull the wagons and pull rocks and whatever—and they had this big place where they had a lot of logs—to burn for the melt—and that white stuff was everywhere. I remember an old truck out there and those winches and cables."[13]

The construction site was a magnet for small boys. One of the Mackey children stands before the rear of Saint Joseph's, ca. 1931. Courtesy of SJAM.

The nuns came in summer, usually in pairs, and stayed for two weeks to conduct catechism classes for the children. Ellyn Bigrope looked forward to their visits, when she and her friends could leave the government school and walk to the mission for the lessons, the ball games the nuns played with them, and the songs they sang.[14]

In that busy summer Soto managed a down payment that secured the mansion. Though for the moment it added to Father Al's responsibilities, he was exuberant. The students would soon arrive, he wrote in September. "There are no beds, blankets, etc. Father Soto expects me to get together a few hundred dollars to help . . . because he turned in all the money he has as a down payment. . . ."[15] It meant another begging trip, but it meant progress.

The padre's many begging trips had begun to bear fruit. He was "surprised at the interest all over the country in the . . . Church in Mexico," he had written in January. Stipends had been coming in since, along with many encouraging letters.[16] Each, however small, was welcome. In April, amid the ever-worsening Depression, Monsignor Hughes had been forced to discontinue the mission's monthly $25 stipend from the Bureau, leaving "not one cent of support outside the meager collection."[17]

Conditions bordered on desperate when in August the CCC again requested his services. Father Al was ready to listen, especially when given reason to believe he could be assigned to camps close to Mescalero. If so, he wrote Novatus, "I would like to get back into the army because it would give me an income and still not take me away from the mission. If I can get these camps, I would say an early mass on Sundays at the camps, say mass at Mescalero at 10 o'clock and a third mass at Bent at 11:00. . . ."[18] Meanwhile he would wait and see what transpired, and work furiously on the church before construction stopped for the winter.

Then, in all the exertion, Father Gabriel suddenly collapsed. He was "still in El Paso . . . in Hotel Dieu and was a very sick man," Father Al reported some days later as Soto was recovering. "There is a lot of trouble to get money to buy the house. . . . Fr. Soto is getting together $10,000.00 from Old Mexico. He is going to sell most of the ranch for $10,000.00. Has Mr. Reichlin that amount to lend at 5%. . . . Fr. Soto is not selling all the ranch. He is keeping enough for the novitiate. P.S.," he added, "Fr. Soto will give a mortgage on the house."[19]

Another worry nagged at the padre. His three-year extension with the Mexican province would soon end. As long as the mission remained within Mexican jurisdiction he must either renew his extension or leave Mescalero—and abandon his unfinished church. "I have no intention to drop everything and run," he had written Novatus in March. "As tired as I am of this job I will stick with it if necessary."[20] But by summer his combined burdens were taking their toll. "I am very tired of being alone here," he wrote again. "However," he asserted, "if by December 1st I see that it would injure the Franciscan and Mexican cause I would wait a while . . ." before terminating the extension.[21]

He still hoped the mission would be returned to American jurisdiction. The conventuals in nearby Carlsbad wanted it, he had reported in June,[22] though he still wished the Santa Barbara province would take it back. Novatus seems to have appealed again to the definitors, who finally agreed to do so on condition they could also acquire the deed to San Xavier Mission in Arizona. On learning this in November, the padre promptly wrote the Bureau toward that end. Obtaining the deed, however, would prove a bureaucratic tangle he did not anticipate.[23]

That same month Braun reported happily that the "Sacred Heart Province [in New York] loaned the Mexican Friars $2000.00 for five years without interest . . . [and would] supply their seminary with two stipends per day. I am trying to get ten per day. That will supply the seminary."[24]

Soto could now proceed. In January he arrived in Mescalero and announced that "in March he will send 7 philosophers to the seminary" to join the theologians already there. "In March two professors from Rome will be here and one from Louvain."[25] About the same time the padre wrote that "three priests and two brothers are coming from Mexico today. They will start to chant offices tomorrow."[26] Whether they were for the seminary or the novitiate he did not say; in either case things were moving along.

By month's end Soto had "paid all that is owed on the ranch except what he still owes Mr. Reichlin. Thank God for that. I wish he were young enough to be Prov[incial] for a long time. He is the only one who gets things done. Zulaica will be here in a few days. I'll bet he will be jealous to see how well established Fr. Soto's Friars are."[27]

By this time the padre was back with the CCC, having assumed duties early in December. "Best wishes for a merry Xmas," he wrote. "Got what I wanted, headquarters in El Paso and the camps near Mescalero."[28] He was now in for the long haul.

The winter of 1935–36 was harsh, and on its back rode widespread illness. Father John, he wrote, "has been in bed several days with the flu. He got very sick at Mescalero last Sunday. I was there with him. I took the mass at one camp and one at Bent. Tony has been sick with the flu for several weeks. He is in the [agency] hospital. For a while I thought he would die. He still is very weak but has a good appetite and is recovering."[29]

The padre's ideal assignment with the CCC lasted scarcely a month before he found his territory expanded widely. In addition to his posts in the El Paso-Alamogordo area, his circuit now stretched east and south to the Pecos Valley camps near Roswell and Carlsbad, into west Texas, and south along the Rio Grande. "Am on the road so much that I find little time to write," he reported in January. "A few weeks ago we had a very heavy snow. I was out in it making the camp. Ran into a man's car, broke his wheel, fender, axle and that of my car. An old lady riding in the other car had a rib broken. It will cost me about $150.00 by the time I pay for both cars, hospital bill & Dr. bill. I guess God wants me to stay broke.

"It looks as if the CCC will pass out of the hands of the army by July 1st," he continued, "and be handled by the Dept. of the Interior. The politicians want it that way. At present they have nothing to say over the C.C.C. . . .

"What do you want me to do with my [CCC] Christmas bonus?" he asked in conclusion. "Can I use it on the church? . . ." In the margin Father Novatus penned a large "Yes!"[30]

Always innovative, the padre immediately began to devise ways to make the most of the money. "I have a good scheme about my bonus. Will you let me use it on the church if I can get people to match it dollar for dollar. . . . I am going to try to have it matched in two ways—locally and then through either the Marquette League or the *Indian Sentinel.* . . ."[31]

He evidently got permission and had some success, for by March building had recommenced. "We are burning lime. After that we will quarry, cut & haul stone till July or August. By that time we should have enough to finish the job. Then we will put the stone in the walls. I can't do it myself. . . . Can't you let Bro Benedict come here for 5 or 6 weeks vacation to get out of the heat of Arizona. In that time we could finish the walls. . . ."[32]

Meanwhile he was busy with the CCC. For the nearer camps he reconstructed the format he had found so successful out of Santa Fe with Concha, but on a larger scale. Instead of one singer, he took with him a choir of girls "to entice the C.C. boys to attend mass. It really did increase the attendance."[33] They called themselves the 'Big Five'—four from the Tularosa parish plus Ethel Mackey, musically gifted like her mother, and having an unusually rich and lovely voice. Katherine often followed with the mission's little portable organ.[34]

The group included Don Juan Baldonado's daughters Elisa and Teresa. The padre "had that little choir going from camp to camp," Elisa remembered. "There was one camp between Alamogordo and Oro Grande, way to the south. All Polish boys from Pennsylvania, and we thought they were so handsome. . . . We'd sing at that mass and later we'd drive to High Rolls and sing again for another mass. He'd pick us up at three in the morning. Those cars had governors on them and it took forever to get where we were going. . . . We got to eat breakfast in the mess hall. That was a big treat. We'd get home late. It's probably just as well the cars wouldn't go very fast [with] . . . Father's driving."[35]

One of Father Al's happiest memories in later life, and a story he often told, was of the romance that blossomed between Elisa and a young CCC officer named Ray Dawson. Ray was an Irish farm boy from Iowa, sent as an educational advisor for the area, and stationed in a camp near Tularosa. He volunteered to help the chaplain and rode with him from camp to camp rounding up the Catholic boys, serving at the altar, helping wherever needed.

At first Ray sat in the front seat with the chaplain. "It was not long," the padre noted, "before Ray . . . began to sit in the back seat . . . , and was holding the hand and heart of one of the Big Five girls. . . . I thought," he added with dry mischief, "they were praying the rosary together."[36]

Ray and Elisa would be married in 1942—not by Father Albert, who would by then be halfway around the world in another war, but by Elisa's brother, Father Felipe Baldonado who through Father Al's influence had pursued the priesthood and been ordained.

Father Al with Elisa and Teresa Baldonado, members of the "Big Five" choir. Courtesy of SJAM.

When possible Father Al made quick trips to California to make a retreat, visit family, transact business, or confer with Father Novatus (who, to the padre's delight, had been reelected to a third term as provincial). Often he combined several objectives in one trip, as when he, along with Fathers Dave and John from El Paso planned a retreat together at Santa Barbara. "Father Tibs [Tibertius Wand] has a window for the front of my church," he apprised Novatus; while there he would try to pick it up.[37]

To wish the padre Godspeed on his jaunts to the coast, Kirgan tried always to send with him a bottle of 'Irish holy water.' Novatus too looked forward to Brother Dave's beneficence. "When you come," he once reminded Al, "I hope you will be able to keep up Father Kirgan's 'tradition.'"[38] Dave (often with Father John Smith) nearly always managed to be at the depot when Al passed through El Paso, with a bottle for Novatus if the padre saw him. "Not having seen you," Braun wrote Novatus after one run, "I gave it to my dad and had some with him."[39]

When possible he visited with his family, usually unannounced and unexpected, but always welcome. "He was a real character," niece Dorothy Brown found him. "We always had family parties when he came. He'd just drop in and say 'here I am.' He'd bring a bag full of laundry and my mother would wash all his cassocks."[40]

Dorothy's parents met him on one occasion at the Los Angeles bus station—for once he had called ahead. The driver began unloading the baggage, throwing the bags roughly onto the concrete—too roughly for the bottle of Scotch Father Dave had tucked inside Father Al's carryall. The whole house reeked when Clara carried the whiskey-soaked cassocks to the laundry room.[41]

If he had business with the Franciscans in Santa Fe, he tried to time it for Fiesta. Held annually, the celebration dates from 1712, when it was established to commemorate de Vargas's reconquest in 1692, following the great Pueblo revolt twelve years earlier. From a simple mass and procession honoring the Franciscans martyred during the rebellion it had grown to the three-day festivity so beloved by all New Mexicans. The solemn procession to the Cross of the Martyrs, the parading of La Conquistadora—Our Lady of the Conquest—it was the sort of celebration Father Albert loved—religious in concept, full of gaiety and the joy of life.

When there he always visited Don José's family and took Concha and her sister to the festivities. "The three of us would go with Father in the morning to mass. Then we'd eat at the booths, and I danced with all my boy friends. My sister did too. Father clapped. My dad always gave him quite a bit of money, to be sure we were all fed."

Sometimes Concha was allowed to return to Mescalero with Father Al. "It was so nice . . . because I never had been around Apaches. . . . They would sit for hours on a *banco* against the wall." One Mescalero girl, called One Eye, loved to tease Concha. "I have a big nose, and that's what she called me—Big Nose. I'd go to mass there with all those beautiful Indians. And I remember—after the ceremony they clapped. I asked Father why, and he said 'because they liked my sermon.'"[42]

The spring thaws of 1936, welcome after the hard winter, along with Father Al's salary from the CCC, spurred furious activity at the building site. By December, the padre predicted, "we will have the roof on the church. . . . I have some men cutting stone. Aug. 15 Mr. Kirgan is coming out from N.Y. to supervise. . . . He is a retired contractor. He built one of the tunnels under the Hudson River."[43] He had met Mr. Kirgan when the family had come to El Paso shortly after Dave's accident. It proved a fortuitous meeting, resulting in a firm friendship and a productive association.

Although they failed to roof the church in time, that did not prevent Father Al's marrying Cecil Russell to Marie DuPuy, daughter of Sylvester DuPuy who had given Bud Braun his first job. The couple journeyed to be wed there, even in its roofless state.

The warming weather failed to bring the cure they had expected for Tony. Father Al had written just days before Tony was stricken that he had never seen him so contented. He later reminisced about "the joy that filled the heart of our Old Tony while he was carving that fountain, . . . [during which] he relived his life at Santa Barbara. From the time he was a boy, he looked at that model in front of the Old Mission. . . ."[44] Tony's fountain, like the original, would have three bowls; on each would be carved one symbol—an anchor for hope, a cross for faith, and a heart for charity, with rosebuds between the bowls. The third bowl was never finished. Tony had dreamed also of carving the Stations of the Cross after he had finished the font. Increasing blindness and his sudden and final illness prevented both.

"I put him in the Government hospital at Mescalero. He stayed there six months till his death. When he realized he would soon die, he asked me to bury him next to his wife. . . . After his death I took his body to Santa Barbara."[45]

Tony's death left an aching hole. The padre's old friend had worked with him on the church for sixteen years. "Without . . . Tony I never would have been able to build the church at Mescalero," he wrote.[46] "'Tony and I batched together and worked together . . . ," Joel quotes. "'We cooked together, prayed together, ate together. When I had to ride the range or work elsewhere . . . , Tony kept the building going up.'"[47]

Antonio Maria Leyva—"Old Tony"—beside the fountain he was carving, ca. 1935. Tony died in 1936 before he could complete his work. Courtesy of MUA.

With hot weather the Mexican seminarians came from El Paso and, along with Bishop Schuler, "always spent the summers here. They sang a high mass every Sunday and their splendid choir filled the big [still roofless] church with vacationists from [nearby] Ruidoso. They also [went] among the Indians [to] teach catechism. . . ."[48] They too were fair game when the padre was commandeering workers.

With Mr. Kirgan's expertise work progressed rapidly. "In two days," Father Al wrote late in September, "we will have all the stone work finished . .

. except the last part of the tower which can wait. The carpenters are working on the trusses. Will have the roof on in a month or six weeks."[49]

Roofing the church was the long-awaited point of triumph, emotionally and physically. Roland Hazard, owner of La Luz Pottery Works, furnished the tiles at less than cost. Lacking actual roofing tiles, they used terra cotta water pipes split lengthwise and alternated, convex and concave sides overlapping, which proved both workable and beautiful.

That roof, high and steep, gave the padre a close call. While laying tile he slipped and, with nothing to grasp, was sliding rapidly toward the edge, as those below stood frozen in horror. At the critical moment he caught onto something, some sort of projection that held him dangling long enough for him to grab another knob or overhang and pull himself up.[50] To those below, still in shock, Father Al only waved and laughed. *Insignificant!*

Saint Joseph's viewed from the northeast, newly roofed, ca. late 1936 or early 1937. The tower remained to be completed. Courtesy of SJAM.

Such feats of daring made him doubly heroic to the children, who already adored him. Marquita Hill often spent the night in Mescalero with the Dorames and went to mass on Sundays in the little interim church. "It was the ricketiest little thing. You had to kneel on the floor. And I'd look up at him during mass and think, 'this priest is so wonderful—he must be something like the Pope.'"[51]

He always found time for the children—"God's gift to marriage," he called them—baptizing them as they came, guiding them as they grew. Dick Mackey and his siblings "kind of grew up under him." None of the boys escaped acolyte duty; the padre saw to that. "He had some missions, at High Rolls and around, and he used to haul us with him to serve at mass. Oh, we were little angelic altar boys!"

Outside the church the padre played and joked with them. "He could say something to us and we'd kind of get back. But he tolerated no nonsense. He was tough on us—used to straighten us up—but we loved him for it." At any gathering "he had us all working. He'd get everybody out and they'd have to work. He didn't know what lazy was."[52]

For Mary Dorame "there was never a dull moment around Father. He could really holler. But nobody got offended—that was his way. That was Father Albert." As the girls grew and learned he put them to work teaching the younger children their catechism after school. "I was just growing up, but he had me teaching catechism in that little makeshift church."[53] To Father Al it was a good way to reinforce the girls' own learning.

The Baldonado boys and Albert Gonzales, members of the Tularosa parish, often served as altar boys at Mescalero. On these occasions their entire families bumped up the hill for mass. The boys enjoyed their importance in serving, the girls got to sing with the choir, and everyone had a high time visiting after mass—especially the children: Father Al always had time for them.

The winter of 1936-37 was relatively uneventful, though busy. Work on the church slowed in cold weather but his chaplain's duties kept him on the road. "Am writing this," he penned in February, "on a bed in one of the camps 30 miles south of Roswell. Tough job!"[54] Three weeks later, "Am way down in the Big Bend country 340 miles from El Paso. . . . It is nice and warm here. . . . Am glad to thaw out. Have had a cold for four weeks. If it is not gone the second week of March when I am in Hot Springs I am going to take the mud baths."[55]

Chaplain Braun rests briefly at one of the many CCC camps he served throughout his wide territory. Courtesy of SJAM.

He was paying his debts as quickly as possible, "because after July 1st may lose my army job. . . ." He had cut a three-thousand-dollar debt almost in half. "If I can get a few hundred from the outside I will have that paid."[56]

April found him "on detached duty to attend the national convention of army chaplains at Chicago. I get 21 hours credits for going and I need the credits. . . . I don't get much time to write. Am very busy making the camps, working at Mescalero Sat. and Sun. and working on a correspondence course to make 200 hours credits for the Army before July 1st."[57]

Meanwhile Father Al was still trying to get Mescalero returned to American jurisdiction. Santa Barbara had still made no headway toward regaining the mission. The legal tangle involving their proviso for gaining San Xavier had dead-ended. Cincinnati had lost interest in Mescalero, and the Mexican friars were now looking at it as a headquarters post in the United States. "It would be a great disappointment," the padre had written Novatus in February, "if the Santa Barbara Prov. does not take Tularosa and Mescalero. . . . Do the Mexicans really want [them]? Some years ago they told me they did not. . . . Why should they want them now? They have the seminary as a place of refuge."[58]

Again Novatus appealed to the definitors, and in April the padre learned sub rosa that "the two places are going back to the [Santa Barbara] Province in the summer and that Father Ferdinand is returning to Tularosa."[59] It did not happen quite that quickly, but by year's end the Santa Barbara Province had again acquired Mescalero and Tularosa.

Even in Mexico church bells were beginning to ring once more. Lázaro Cárdenas, though still as violently radical as Calles had ever been, was also a pragmatist who saw that strife must end; and when churches began cautiously to reopen in some states by 1937 he took no steps to close them, though it would be another year before he would begin openly to allow the churches to resume the functions he knew the government could not stop.[60]

The El Paso seminary continued to operate for the Mexican students, and Al Braun still helped out when he was needed. But the padre, freed from the terrible financial burden, could now function wholly within his old province.

He had never had patience with the lackadaisical philosophy of *mañana,* and had expressed his testiness frequently. But despite his frustrations he had maintained his deep sympathy with the Mexicans' plight and his firm commitment to help them. "They do many things that are provoking," he had written back in 1931, "but we must overlook that in order to help them; they need our help."[61] Through the difficult years he had given that help, despite daunting financial odds and exhaustive physical demands. He had stayed the course.

And that was not *Insignificant!*

✟✟✟

Construction at Mescalero continued apace. "Intend to rebuild the arch in front of the church," he wrote in June. "At present the men are putting in the mullions. The one that is finished looks fine." Further, he believed he was on his last duty with the CCC. "According to latest orders from the War Dept. no reserve officers can have more than two years. . . . Will be very glad to get out. Since according to Collier's wishes the Indians are so scattered and since the Dutch Reformed minister & helpers are so very active, the Catholic mission here will suffer unless the missionary is on the job all the time." However, he added, "This [CCC] district now has so many camps that the Commanding Officer won't want me to leave."[62]

He was correct: the army still needed him. Orders or no, chaplains were always scarce and few could match Al Braun in dedication and physical endurance.

Changes were also occurring in the Santa Barbara province. Novatus had suffered ill health for some time and, the padre learned, would soon be replaced by Father Ildephonse Moser. Through their long association Father Al had grown increasingly fond of Novatus and would miss working with him, though they would continue to correspond.

Before Novatus left the padre made one last request. "I want a healthy, zealous, sensible Father sent to Mescalero to help hold and improve the Mescalero Apaches we now have in the church and win over what we have not. I realize with the little time I have to devote to the work of this mission, little by little the church will lose out. Send me a man who can learn the language. . . . The Protestant mission . . . is sending extra workers into the field. . . . I will lose out unless I get help. . . . It would be a sad thing if I finished the church and in the meantime lost the congregation."[63]

He was, moreover, expecting another group of Mexican clerics from El Paso whom he would have to feed for the summer. When no help came he sent another plea. "Enclosed reports are the best I can do. You can see I don't keep a detailed account of money received and spent. You can also see that the Indians are not receiving as much instruction as they should. I would like to do all these things but can't make it. I need someone to help me. . . ." One can sense his frustration and impatience in the large bold scrawl that rushes across the page.[64]

He soon got additional help from Tularosa when Father Dennis Mahoney was added there, and whose willing help he truly appreciated and commended. Fathers Dave and John from El Paso were also happy to help when his pace grew too demanding.

Returning on 1 December 1937 from a hurried trip to the coast, the padre immediately "started to make the camps. This," he wrote two weeks later, "is my first day of rest since. Will start out again this P.M. and keep going until Dec. 23. Will be back here for confessions & the Xmas celebration. The Army is good to me. I am allowed to be at the mission when necessary."[65] Despite his grueling schedule he kept things moving at Mescalero. He spent every possible hour on the job, and Mr. Kirgan returned faithfully every summer to help. He and Father Dave so endeared themselves to the Mescaleros that one family adopted the surname Kirgan.[66]

But the padre's father no longer came. John Braun had grown increasingly ill for several years; now, Father Al wrote in July 1938, he had been in the hospital "for some time. . . . [T]he Dr. says he can't last much longer. My mother asked me to come home. May I go?"[67]

John Braun died soon after seeing his son. His life had run a full course with all sails billowing, from his youthful flight from Alsace through the founding and rearing of his solidly American family on the Golden Coast.

Still Chaplain Braun continued with the CCC. Where needed he would serve: the extra load was—*Insignificant!* But serving mission and military taxed his strength and, along with breathing problems resulting from wartime gas inhalation, made him susceptible to respiratory ailments. "Was in bed with the flu from Friday to yesterday," he wrote in February 1939. "In two hours must leave for camp." Illness too was—*Insignificant!* He was already projecting plans for spring, when he would take "3 weeks from the army to finish the [church] tower. Already bought the floor tile but didn't pay for it. My credit is good till Jan 1st 1940." Besides extending his credit, Hazard had given him the same discount for floor tiles he had given for the roof; and "old man Momsen promised to pay half the floor tile bill."[68] (This was the same Momsen of the El Paso hardware company who had given Al and Dave their cover as 'employees' during their Mexican forays.) Tom Beavers, a retired army captain and owner of the Tularosa Tile and Lumber Company, let his old World War friend have the necessary lumber at an incredibly low price.[69] Braulio Diaz, who for several years had been carving an altar from a large marble block his boss had donated from his quarry east of Alamogordo, was working double-time to finish it. And the ladies continued to hold bazaars and enchilada suppers to fatten Saint Joseph's thin coffers.

The Apache cathedral had truly become a community effort. From the surrounding earth it rose like a beacon tower of native materials, furnished by native businessmen, built by native labor, fed by native families.

Father Al could now project realistically. "By July 4th hope to have tower completed; all floor tile in; windows boarded up" until funds for glass could be found. "As far as I can see now the dedication will be July 4th. I probably will be in debt some but it won't be bad. . . ."[70]

During this frenetic activity Father Al kept in close contact with Novatus, now ill and growing weaker, still keenly interested in the 'cathedral' and continuing to work with the definitorium. In answer to letters Novatus had written from Saint Boniface showing him depressed, the padre urged him to "go to one of the monasteries where life is more congenial," suggested Santa Barbara, and assured Novatus he always remembered him in his masses.[71]

Novatus made light of his infirmities; but news from others painted a far more critical condition. Al was sorry to learn how serious his old friend's condition was, he answered an informant in June.[72] His letter is written in the hand of Father Felipe Baldonado, while using some time off to help at Mescalero—another native son returned to add his heart and hand for the final push.

Saint Joseph's still lacked windows, light fixtures, and a few other amenities, which would have to wait, as always, for more funds. But basically the construction was in its last phase.

The church was dedicated on 4 July 1939 to the padre's fellow combat veterans of World War I who had not returned. The dream conjured on the fields of France was a reality. It had taken its toll in 'blood, sweat, toil, and tears,' leavened with a healthy dose of hardheaded determination. But there it stood, as strong and as rugged as its builder—"not as good as Stanton and Tony and Salesius wanted it,'" the padre admitted. "'But I wanted to see it dedicated.'"[73]

Nearly nine hundred people crowded the church and grounds— soldiery from Fort Bliss, men and officers from the CCC camps, clergy from all over the country, friends and neighbors from the vicinity. Bishop Schuler was celebrant, assisted by Father Sixtus Brambilla as presbyter. Twenty-some Saint Anthony's Seminarians came from El Paso to sing the mass. Father Arthur Liebrenz from Tularosa preached the sermon, which Mescalero tribesman Kent Kayita translated into the Apache tongue. His text: "How awesome is this place! This is none other than the House of God: this is the gate of heaven."

The Mescaleros marched in procession in full tribal regalia. Two warriors stood as sentries at the door, facing the altar throughout the ceremony. After the mass the Apaches concluded the dedication with ceremonial dances outside the church.[74]

Brother Salesius, who had sacrificed his life in the building, was gone. So was Old Tony, who had labored so long and prayed to live for the dedication. Absent also was William Stanton, who had translated the dream into the blueprint and detailed each step. He had, as late as 1933, sent drawings for the altars, with an apology for not having done them sooner: the Depression had hit him also. But his mind and talents still focused across the continent to the church on the hill in Mescalero, New Mexico,[75] though William Stanton never saw the mission.

Father Albert, in one of life's cruel ironies, was himself glaringly absent. He had been called suddenly, a few days earlier, to the bedside of his dying sister. As Saint Joseph's was being dedicated, Father Albert was preparing to officiate Loretta's High Requiem Mass in Los Angeles. Father Augustine Hobrecht—Gus of the 'three A's'—was with him to deliver the sermon. At Mescalero Bishop Schuler said the dedication mass in Loretta's honor.

Bishop Anthony J. Schuler dedicates Saint Joseph's on 4 July 1939, amid the still-remaining construction rubble. Courtesy of MUA.

Father Sixtus stayed on in Mescalero until the padre returned to offer him "a marble communion rail and some stations of the cross that are appropriate for the church in Mescalero," fine ones from a recently demolished church. He had secured them from Bishop Cushing, assuring him the church was lofty enough to accommodate their very large size. The padre had only to come to Boston to see if he wanted them.

He did. He had twenty-eight days of leave coming from the army, Father Al wrote in September, that he must use before 30 November or lose. He could visit Sixtus, secure the stations, and return via Flint, Michigan, to pick up a car. "The one we have is on its last legs. I will save about $130.00 by driving one back. We can get $400.00 for the car we have. The new Cheve will cost $770. . . . Hope I can collect the $370 from some one."[76]

In Boston he was delighted with the stations, had a fine visit with Sixtus, and acquired his 'Cheve' on the way home. On 6 November he reported that "the beautiful station[s] . . . arrived. They weigh 1900 lbs. Fr. Sixtus . . . has been a great benefactor to this mission."[77]

They had arrived in time to be installed by Christmas. Midnight mass 1939 in the newly dedicated church was a contrast to the early days of bonfires and Crown Dancers in the roofless shell, but as jubilant: what was once the joy of the journey was now the triumph of arrival. Though still without lighting, heat, and windows, the interior was lit by candles and faith, the congregation warmed by love and heavy clothing. Their Savior was born, and so was their church.

Father Albert worried about his mother. "Expect to go home to see my sick and old mother Dec. 30. Will be back here Jan 2nd." And with his usual propensity for utilizing valuable time for double duty he added, "Hope to see the Rose Bowl Game."[78] But a few days after Christmas his mother broke her hip "when a streetcar in which she was riding stopped suddenly." She would be in the hospital another three months, her cash was depleted, his brother had paid what he could, and "if it meets with your approval," he wrote Father Ildephonse, "I will send him my [CCC] check for Jan[uary] hoping that someday I will get it back from the [street]car company. . . ."[79]

Father Al's CCC salary had tided him over many times through debt, Depression, and the demands of the mission and the Mexican friars.

Now it had put him "in a bad way . . . [with] orders from Headquarters to buy the new uniform which is prescribed for our [new] civilian status with the C.C.C. Being broke I had to order the uniform C.O.D. . . . Have you any . . . fund from which you can draw $50. . . . The uniform will be here in 10 days."[80]

Early in 1940 the army presented the padre with another problem. The car they had furnished had 140,000 miles and "with six other cars was condemned. No funds are available to buy other cars. The seven of us who lost our . . . transportation must use our own cars or lose our job[s]. . . . The mission is too much in debt to quit just now." He could not use the mission car he had bought en route from Boston "because Father Dennis needs it. . . . I am forced to buy a new car. . . . Will you please persuade the province to pay . . . [$295] for St. Joseph's mission. I can't afford to make payments on two cars. . . ."[81]

The year 1940 would be pivotal, for Father Al and for the world. Priests were seldom allowed to stay as long on any assignment as the padre had already been at Mescalero, and he knew with Saint Joseph's largely finished his time was limited. If he must leave he hoped to go where he could best serve. Affairs in Mexico were greatly improved; his church was finished; where next?

That China still beckoned is evidenced in a letter he had written six years earlier, when he believed he would finish the church rapidly and would be transferred. "For years I have wanted to go to China. . . . I believe that in years to come the center of human activity will move to the Orient and therefore that it is very necessary for the church to build up in that part. It is the reason that I want to go. . . ."[82] Now, in 1940 and with the prospect of imminent transfer, Father Albert still saw a star in the East.

The world itself stood on a pivot, and Al Braun watched and waited along with the rest of America as the drama unfolded. With his eye always on the Orient he had watched as a saber-rattling Japan renounced the Five-Power Naval Limitations Treaty and began to build a tremendous navy toward creating what they called the East Asia Co-Prosperity Sphere—translate: Asia for the Japanese. He had monitored the bloody Japanese invasion of China—the violent Oriental upheaval he had long foreseen and feared. He had watched as Japan's militarists drew ever closer to the totalitarian powers in Europe.

He watched Europe, which was and would continue to be official Washington's prime focus. He watched Hitler force the *anschluss* on Austria and snorted in disgust as Britain and France at Munich spinelessly allowed Germany to seize the Sudetenland and then to gobble up the rest of Czechoslovakia. "So far," Father Al wrote Novatus on the heels of the Czech crisis, "Hitler seems to be doing as he planned. I have no sympathy for the *democracies*. [Emphasis his.] They had from 1914 till 1933 to do something to straighten out affairs in Europe. Then they could have dealt with the 3rd Reich. . . . Now they are willing to do something if only Hitler will be reasonable. . . ."[83]

Meanwhile he continued to serve with the CCC through many miles and many masses, and he touched the souls of uncounted young men. It was said throughout the camps that when Father Albert came the attendance swelled above that of any other chaplain. For years after he received letters from his former CCC boys.

"It's been 42 years ago when I knew you," one wrote, "and attended Catholic services at CCC camp . . . although I could not take Holy Communion, because I was a Presbyterian. Now I'm happy to say I'm a Catholic, married to a Catholic girl, have two children. . . ." He enclosed a picture of himself and Father Al taken at camp. "The rest of my life I'm going to keep a little donation . . . going to the church you so dearly loved. . . . You were an inspiration to me 40 years ago and you are still an inspiration to me today."[84]

The padre had become a CCC chaplain to pay his debts, help the Mexican friars, and build his church. Once enlisted, he had with his usual enthusiasm dived into his commitment as he had once dived with gusto into an icy pond in the Mescaleros' mountains, and he swam the length as then, dismissing the hours and miles and the tax on his strength with a sweep of his arm and a mighty roar: *Insignificant!*

Some were aware of the cost to him, and knew also of his love for the church he was so determined to finish. Colonel Sam Carouthers did, and sometimes sent boys from the CCC camps to work at the building site. The colonel, Father Al wrote Novatus in 1939, "is asking all the CCC boys of this N.M. District to kick in 25¢ for the church at Mescalero. There are 8000 boys in the N.M. district. It looks like I am having a little luck. The Colonel is a Protestant from Tennessee. A fine man."[85]

✝✝✝

The world marched into catastrophe. Hitler's storm troops invaded Poland on 1 September 1939. France and Britain, having betrayed Czechoslovakia at Munich, now honored their pledges and declared war on Germany. Hitler's army swept through Denmark; Norway fell; and by spring 1940 *blitzkrieg* was rolling through the Lowlands and into a doomed and defeated France. Britain would soon stand alone.

But the defeatist Chamberlain was no longer Prime Minister: Winston Churchill now led the country. Strong and stubborn, that doughty warrior pledged grimly—and it seemed to many he was Britain embodied—"We shall never surrender," and so stirred the nation that the little boats of England, over eight hundred of them—fishing boats and pleasure craft and shrimpers and tugs—set forth churning sturdily, back and forth across the Channel through smoke and fire and dive-bombing Luftwaffe planes to rescue the stranded soldiers—330,000 of them—to write Dunkirk into the annals of courage.

Here was a defiance to strike chords in the heart of Albert Braun, OFM, combat veteran, Captain, United States Army Reserve. Isolationists might protest America's growing involvement, but Chaplain Braun was not among them. Europe was falling country by country, China was burning, and—especially ominous to the padre, who had long believed the Orient to be the focus of the future—Japan was expanding militantly throughout the Pacific. Civilization itself was facing destruction, America was drawing closer to the conflict each day, and Al Braun was a soldier.

The Chaplain might see the Orient yet.

Father Al hoes his bean patch below the church with its newly completed tower, probably summer of 1939 or 1940. Courtesy of SJAM.

V

GOD'S WARRIOR

*Being an optimist kept me alive when we were naked,
sleeping in the mud, and living on two spoons of rice
a day. . . . I learned more in prison camp than
I ever learned in the novitiate.*

Chaplain Albert Braun, OFM, Major, United States Army, World War II. Courtesy of SJAM.

15: RECALL TO DUTY

The windows of Saint Joseph's would remain boarded far longer than Father Al imagined. It was 1940 and the fires of war roared beyond both of America's horizons. Before the year was out Padre Albert Braun, OFM, was once more in uniform, now Captain Braun, 0134329, United States Army.

He was still serving the CCC when his orders came to report for active duty. Monsignor William Arnold, Army Chief of Chaplains—his old friend Bill Arnold who had recruited him repeatedly for CCC duty—needed him in the coming crisis. He would report for duty at Fort Sam Houston on 11 October 1940.

He cannot have been very surprised. He had monitored America's steady approach to war through a series of neutrality acts, each less neutral than its predecessor, capped in 1939 by the decidedly pro-Allies 'cash-and-carry' plan for selling war matériel. With the rest of America he had watched as the aggressor nations enriched themselves of other countries' soil. Having taken his share of Poland, Stalin proceeded to invade and conquer Finland and then annexed the Baltic countries. The German juggernaut subdued Denmark and Norway, then rolled through the Low Countries and into France while Italy hit from behind. The President pledged aid to the Allies and promised a nervous America, "Your boys are not going to be sent into any foreign war."

A belligerently expansionist Japan, aiming at ultimate dominance of the Far East, had been fighting in Manchuria and China since 1931; when France and the Netherlands fell, their orphaned Asian colonies were loot on which the Japanese militarists were ready to pounce. The Nazi-controlled Vichy government in France quickly bowed to demands for North Indochina, and Japanese troops flooded into the vacuum.

Washington responded with a large loan to China, embargoes on scrap metal for Japan, and warnings against any move on the Dutch East Indies. This deterred the Japanese for the moment, though acquisition of that oil-rubber-and-tin-rich archipelago remained a priority awaiting an opportune moment.

But Roosevelt's focus was on Europe. "The Battle of France is over," Churchill declared stolidly. "The Battle of Britain is about to begin." And as the bombs began to batter London and U-boats prowled the waters with intensified attacks, he pledged to the waiting world, "We shall not flag or fail. . . ."

On 3 September 1940 Roosevelt proclaimed by executive order the gift to Britain of fifty overage destroyers in return for ninety-nine-year leases for American bases on British territories in the Atlantic, stretching from Newfoundland into the Caribbean. Two weeks later Congress enacted America's first peacetime draft—but was it really peacetime? many asked edgily. On the twenty-seventh another bombshell exploded on the democracies: Japan had joined the Axis.

Washington replied with another loan to China, more economic sanctions against Japan, and an increase in war production, with Roosevelt repeating his mantra "again and again and again: your boys are not going to be sent to any foreign war"—but now he was adding, "—unless we are attacked." It was election year.

Father Albert was hurriedly making his own preparations. Debts must be settled insofar as possible. Taxes on the mission's ranch must be paid. Many small details on the new church must be finished. He had business affairs to attend in El Paso, among which one was primary: he must have his lawyer transfer the property he had 'bought' in Mexico back to the Mexican Franciscans should anything happen to him. He had also to make final arrangements for the seminarians; Father Gabriel Soto, with whom he had so happily worked, had died in January. He must bid Bishop Schuler and Fathers Dave and John goodbye—and, it can be assumed, enjoy a farewell feast in Juárez.

He had also to arrange for the transition of the Mescalero mission into the hands of Father Dennis Mahoney, who had for some time helped out in Mescalero from his assignment in Tularosa.

The padre squeezed in a quick trip to Los Angeles to see his mother. While there he met niece Dorothy's fiancé, Jess Bumgarner. Father Al was playing poker at his brother Ray's house when Jess dropped in. Dorothy introduced him, explaining a little hesitantly that Jess was not a Catholic. The padre grinned and shrugged. "Come join the game," he invited Jess. "I'd just as soon take your money as anyone else's."

"He did, too," Jess remembered. "He was a sharp player."[1]

At that gathering Father Al promised to take a leave and officiate their spring wedding. It would be the high point of the celebration, Dorothy declared. None could foresee that Chaplain Braun would sail for overseas duty just one week before the wedding.

Last and hardest were his goodbyes to his Mescaleros, among whom he had lived and worked, baptized their babies and watched them grow, with a few interruptions, for nearly a quarter century. It was hard for them too to send their beloved priest off to what seemed to be an ever-nearing war for America.

On 11 October 1940 the man of the cloth once again donned the uniform of the soldier. Five days later the young men of America formed lines in every courthouse across the country to register for the draft: conscription had begun. Captain Braun, Chaplain, Second Division, Fort Sam Houston, San Antonio, Texas, along with his fellow officers prepared for the influx soon to come. "All the key officers," he found to his delight, "were friends from World War I."[2]

A note of homesickness crept into his first letter to his provincial after reporting for duty. "Have been here three days; it seems like three months though I have been busy. Am very lonely; will have to become accustomed to this. What amuses me is . . . that some people think I enjoy this type of life. . . . [T]he fact that I don't complain much is often misconstrued. I hope the day will come . . . to enjoy the solace of religious life.

"This is a very busy place," he continued. "My predecessor Chaplain O'Neill tells me the average [number of] Catholic patients in the two military hospitals are 150 and because of sick calls must consider myself on duty day and nite seven days of the week. On Sundays there are three masses—one by an outsider—and two by the post chaplains, two sermons and two catechism classes for army children. Twice each week instructions for converts and Holy Hour every Thursday. The personnel of this post is 15,000; about a fourth the number are Catholics.

"San Antonio is a great place for retired men of the army. For that reason funerals are frequent. I have one tomorrow. . . ."[3]

The padre was still a captain—had been since 1921, all rank in the military having been frozen during the Depression. Rank, however, was *Insignificant!* to the padre who, even had it mattered, was too busy to think about it.

Fort Sam, though an old post and well run, was subject to the growing pains of rapid mass mobilization and to the resultant shortages. "As soon as I got here," he wrote his provincial, "I could see a car is indispensable. No Gov. car is available. Tularosa has two cars, Fr. Dennis one and Fr. Francis [Redmon] one. For that reason I phoned asking . . . to use the Cheve at Mescalero. It seems a shame that I should be forced to buy a car when there is one available at Mescalero, especially since all the money I can save goes to Mescalero. If Fr. Dennis turns the Cheve over to Fr. Smith he will bring it to me. Will you wire Fr. Dennis to do that? . . . I must have a car. . . ."[4]

He got the 'Cheve.'

To Elisa Baldonado he wrote nostalgically of the CCC days and the 'beautiful songs' they had sung. "This noisy, unmusical jazz and swing that I hear on every radio . . . here in bachelors' quarters . . . drives me crazy. . . ."

But, he added, "The religious spirit of the soldiers and officers at this post is excellent. I never saw anything like it in the army. . . . Some of the nurses and officers' wives go to mass & communion every day. There is a good crowd that attends Holy Hour every Thursday. We lack a choir; two nurses with good voices [are] all we have."[5]

From his lonely rock amidst the tempest of the burgeoning post the padre reached out to his old mentor Father Felix Raab, under whom he had studied philosophy during his novitiate, and with whom he had enjoyed an affectionate friendship since. Please, he enjoined his provincial, thank Father Felix "for answering his phone so promptly. I enjoyed to hear his voice."[6]

✝✝✝

Still pledging "your boys are not going to be sent to any foreign war (unless we are attacked)," Roosevelt was reelected in November. Three days later he promised half of all war matériel produced in the United States to Britain, proclaimed in December that America must become the "arsenal of democracy," and in January presented to Congress what became Lend-Lease in March—in effect an unofficial declaration of war.

On 24 January 1941 Admiral James O. Richardson warned from Hawaii of a possible attack on Pearl Harbor and cited deficiencies in American defenses.[7] Three days later United States Ambassador to Japan Joseph C. Grew cabled a similar warning from Tokyo.[8] Roosevelt, engrossed in the Lend-Lease bill, ignored the warnings.

That same month top United States and British naval and military planners began coordinating their plans for an overall 'global strategy' for the war in which it was becoming increasingly evident America would sooner or later become an official belligerent. The outcome was a secret treaty, signed on 27 March, whereby the United States pledged to give top priority to the defeat of Germany and to fight only a holding action in the Pacific *even if the United States was attacked by Japan.* Thus was born the "Get Hitler First" strategy.

In Tokyo the militarists were making their own dark plans.

✠ ✠ ✠

Those working at home to mobilize America knew nothing of strategic decisions. They had their own snafus to correct. Among other problems attending the frenzied buildup of the armed forces, as draftees began flooding into the old established forts, was a lack of chaplains. "The Second Division is fast being filled up to full strength," the padre wrote Father Dennis in March. Of the replacements, "About 80% are Catholic. . . . Only one out of every six . . . is able to go to mass on Sunday. A few get to town." An army bishop was due to visit soon. "I have invited him to say mass at the Post Chapel so that he can see conditions for himself. The army has asked officially for a Catholic chaplain for the hospital and for two more . . . for the Second Division. They are not available."[9]

That same month a radiogram from General Arnold requested Braun to "send the names of four chaplains who would go to the Philippine Islands without families." There were already those who feared attack in the Far East. Father Al promptly called a meeting, after which Father Herman C. Baumann, who had arrived with a Pittsburgh contingent, put it to his superior. "Three of us will go," he announced, "if you will."[10]

The padre had already requested duty in Europe. But young Bud Braun had never walked away from a challenge. Neither, it seems, could the middle-aged Captain Braun.

They sailed on 25 April. He had driven the old 'Cheve' to the coast, detouring to Mescalero for a last goodbye there. Mary Dorame saw the old car coming up the hill. "We weren't expecting him and he drove up. He had his uniform on. When we saw him coming we all just ran. 'Father Albert's coming!'"[11]

From his childhood Dick Mackey kept "a memory of him coming to the house. It was early evening, and I see him in a green uniform—I can see that in my mind—and he came to say goodbye. It was traditional to receive a blessing; so he knelt down in front of my grandmother Blasa and she gave him a benediction."[12]

From there he drove to Los Angeles for a hurried goodbye to his family. Driving on to San Francisco he enjoyed the company of his old friend Father Ambrose, nee Willie Trabert. The 'Cheve' would cross to Manila by transport.

Aboard the USS *George Washington* were crammed three thousand enlisted men and twelve hundred officers, among them six Catholic chaplains, their tour of duty ostensibly for two years. Those who could elbow to the rails saw San Francisco grow smaller, watched until the Golden Gate and the Golden Coast melted into mist, then turned back to check out the ship. She had been one of the luxury President Liners, newly chartered as troop transports, their once elegant lounges now lined with double-deck military cots.

The padre and Father Baumann had mustered General Arnold's chaplains quickly. Three from Fort Sam received their orders almost immediately—Baumann, Braun, and a Father Stober—and three from other posts joined them—Fathers Matt Zerfuss, Tom Scecina, and John Wilson. Of the six only three would come home.

Although the padre seems at first to have been skeptical of Baumann, he soon found the younger priest a solid soldier, a dedicated priest, and a trusted friend. He would find him more so in the months ahead. Father Al shared a stateroom in transit with Protestant Chaplain John K. Borneman, during which, Borneman later wrote, "we became very good friends."[13]

Three thousand miles from American shores they saw the islands begin to appear, mistily at first, deepening to green as they rose from the Philippine Sea; and then the *Washington* was approaching Luzon, steaming into Manila Bay past the rock that was Corregidor, toward the gleaming white city. The bay churned with vessels—liners, merchantmen, and naval craft, tugs and dugout canoes and fishing boats, inter-island steamers and spray-throwing speedboats. They docked at Pier 7, welcomed by a military band from Fort McKinley.

After the salty sea breezes, the heat and humidity of the island closed on them like a smothering blanket. From their military shuttle en route to their quarters they saw Manila flash by. They would explore the city later. More immediately the arriving officers were expected to attend a reception that evening at the posh Army and Navy Club on palm-lined Dewey Boulevard.

It was a lavish affair, a wining-dining-dancing occasion to welcome the new officers and on a more sober note to wish bon voyage to the large number of military and navy wives who with their children were, on War Department orders, returning to the States immediately on the *Washington*. Those in the know were growing edgy about the Philippines.

On hand to greet the guests were the gracious commander of the Philippine Department, Major General George Grunert, and the not-so-gracious commander of the Asiatic Fleet, Admiral Thomas Hart, who made no effort to hide his disdain for anything or anyone relating to the Army. Hart especially disliked Major General Douglas MacArthur, now serving as Military Advisor to the Philippine Army, who with his wife and aides arrived late and with his imposing presence eclipsed the stiff little admiral.[14] Though of small import, the moment was a foretaste of sterner, farther-reaching clashes to come between the two. Such a stagy bit of battling egos in the lavish social hub of Manila must have amused the padre.

He was assigned to the 45th Infantry Division at Fort William McKinley, just south of Manila, along with Fathers Stober and Scecina, with whom he shared quarters. He found it "pleasant for all of us," though they had to furnish their lodging from their own pockets.

The padre was quickly appointed Sixth Sector Chaplain.[15] There was little time to explore the island, though in small intervals of leisure Manila proved a kaleidoscope of color and movement, its wide boulevards and modern buildings a contrast to the old walled section, the Intramuros, with its ancient Spanish churches. The whole world seemed to meet in the teeming port city, pulsing with brightly attired Filipinas, old ladies with betel-reddened teeth, turbaned Moros, and costumed Orientals. Vendors hawked their wares in a dozen jargons. The streets were jammed with heavy carts drawn by carabao, GI Jeeps, and wildly honking Pambusco buses that emitted sweetish exhaust fumes from the sugar-cane fuel.

He had not yet called on the friars in Manila, he reported to his new provincial, Father Martin Knauff, in June. "They are not liked because they own so much property. If they were wise they would get rid of it . . . before they lose it."[16]

"We are in our second month here," he wrote Father Felix. "It seems we are going to have to spend 36 of them in the Islands. I do my best not to think about it. I have always tried to like the place I have to be. . . .

"I well remember all the sentimental songs and movies . . . about the tropics and the South Sea Islands. All I can say is 'bologna.' Mexico has it all over these countries in romantic atmosphere. . . .

"The Philippines," he continued, "are a great mission country. The enemy of the Church here is . . . ignorance in religious matters. . . . These people are intelligent but 95 percent of them have received no instruction whatever. This is the statement of the Archbishop of Manila. There are not enough priests. . . ."

That he felt cut off from the fraternity of his province is apparent. "Let me hear from you occasionally," he prompted his old friend. "I get lonesome over here."[17] But melancholy was fleeting for Al Braun, no more than a ghost that dissolved like mist in the morning sun.

Accustomed to the high dry air at Mescalero, he found the humid heat oppressive, he wrote Father Martin, though he was "gradually becoming adjusted. In many respects adjustments are necessary. Don't think I will ever become adjusted to tropical climates." But he was not alone in adapting to the islands. "Fr. Baumann spent a day with us. He is now getting used to it here. In the beginning he thought he would lose his mind."

He had hardly settled into a routine, he continued, when his unit was sent on maneuvers. "Was glad to have the opportunity to see some of the country. It rained day and night . . . the whole time we were out. Even in this climate one gets chilled by the rain. Before going to a wet bed I took a good glass of mass wine."

Worse, however, than the rain was the treatment he found being given nine German priests from the Society of the Divine Word. "I felt sorry for one of the old priests. He has given forty years of his life to the natives. Still they are ungrateful enough to taunt him and call him a Nazi. Poor fellow, he should get a great reward in heaven. He is not getting the reward of natural kindness here."

On returning to Fort McKinley he had learned that the "Air Corps has already received notice they must stay here three years. The same order is about to come out for the rest of us. . . ."[18]

The tropics provided yet another surprise. The mildew had ruined his vestments, he wrote Father Martin in September. "I ordered five sets of chasubles from the Good Shepherd Sisters. The poor things need the money." He too was short, "because every month I pay on Mescalero's debt and some of my salary is withheld because the army does not have all my records here." Could the province lend him fifty stipends? With that and "what I can spare of my salary I will be able to pay the good sisters."[19]

As always, the padre felt the old tug of China. "When this fuss is all over," he had written his provincial earlier, "I would like to visit our missions in China. They are not a great distance from here. If you can grant that permission, will you . . . , [or] get it for me from the General."[20] He wrote again in September. "I understand you headed this way as far as Honolulu. Why not make a trip to your missions in China? If you do be sure to let me know."[21] None of his attempts got Father Al to China. The 'fuss' was far from over.

The padre's assignment was unlike any he had yet encountered. The 45th Infantry to which he was assigned was part of the Philippine Division, comprising Americans and an elite group in training, the Philippine Scouts, all under the command of Lieutenant General Jonathan M. Wainwright— tall, angular, and immensely popular. Father Al liked 'Skinny' Wainright immediately, and it was mutual; the general would later always refer to Al Braun as 'his' chaplain.

They were part of an overall effort to train a Philippine army preparatory to the islands' independence. The United States, in the course of the Spanish-American War, had freed the Philippines from Spain in 1898, subsequently helped them subdue Emilio Aguinaldo's insurgents, and gave them territorial status until they could be made ready for self-government and self-defense. With the Tydings-McDuffie Act of 1934, the United States had voluntarily granted independence to the Philippines, scheduled to take effect on 4 July 1946 after a ten-year transitional period during which American bases and personnel would remain to oversee, advise, aid, and protect the emergent nation.

Within a year the Philippines had a constitution and an interim government, and in late 1935 elected Manuel Quezon President of the Commonwealth. He in turn asked his old friend Douglas MacArthur (then Chief of Staff in Washington) to help him build Philippine defenses and train a Philippine army in the face of the growing Japanese threat. With Roosevelt's concurrence, MacArthur retired from active duty, accepted the role of Military Advisor to Quezon, and began immediately to mobilize, train, and organize a Philippine army. He was still engaged in this capacity when Captain Braun reported for Philippine duty.

With the large number of Filipinos attached to the 45th, Father Albert found himself in the kind of work he liked: his duty took him among the people. "Time," he wrote Father Felix in September, "passes quickly. There is a lot to do and with the mobilization of the Philippine army the work will double. Our position here is different from that of most chaplains due to the fact that the Philippine soldier marries and has a very large family. We are responsible for the religious care of these families. That gives us some interesting mission work among very fine people. We have over 1200 children in the public grade school here at Ft. McKinley. We teach catechism in the public school. On Sundays we have our own Sunday school classes and first communion classes in the barrios attached to Ft. McKinley. Every Saturday nite I teach church history from 7:30-8:30—it is usually 9:30 or 10 before the class is over. High school boys & girls, college boys and girls and a few in the university—also some soldiers attend this class. There is nothing dull about this life."

The Jesuits from New York, he continued, "are here in large numbers . . . doing great work in . . . education. The University of San[to] Tomas has an enrollment of more than six thousand. . . . Here women are as eager for an education as men. San[to] Tomas caters to that and has coeducation.

"The educated Filipina is a high class person. Culture & refinement ooze out of her. Our women have a lot to learn from the Filipina. Till now higher education, generally speaking, has not destroyed the mother instinct." He believed "there is too much [secular] schooling in the Islands. Too many of the young . . . develop tastes and desires that can never be satisfied; that creates discontent. It will be a regrettable thing, to see the beautiful contentment which now exists, pass away from these people."

He had by this time met many fellow clerics, some of whom had been in the islands for extended periods. He found it "surprising how satisfied the American priests and sisters are over here. One never hears a desire expressed for a trip to the States. I take my hat off to them; it shows a fine spirit. After all, this is the Orient and different to the ways of life to which we are accustomed. . . ."[22]

On 16 September a letter arrived from Virginia Baldonado advising him that her sons Juan and Pepe had sailed on the USS *President Pierce* on 30 August. Their destination was top secret; but rumors flew like gnats, and their guns and trucks all had 'Manila PI' stamped in large white letters.

Father Al was at the dock when the *Pierce* arrived. When no troops filed off he went aboard to see why. An overnight quarantine had been ordered. *Insignificant!* He was looking for the Baldonado boys, he told the captain, and when they reported, wondering what sort of trouble they were in, he greeted them heartily, waved aside the quarantine, told the captain he was taking them to his quarters for dinner, and promised to have them back by midnight.

Few said no to Father Al, and the captain was not one of them. But how, he wondered, had Braun known when and where the *Pierce* would land?

Easy, boomed the chaplain: he knew when they sailed. Newspapers and simple logic were all it took. So much for top-secret intelligence.

His erstwhile altar boys had the ride of a lifetime. Even Jap bombers, Pepe swore later, didn't scare him as much as Father Al's driving. One got used to being bombed; the padre's driving was a terrifying experience. Manila's left-lane driving was unsettling at best; on top of that, Father Al wove at top speed in and out of the heavy traffic, to which he paid little attention—he was too engrossed with looking at his back-seat passengers while he laughed and talked. But it was a warm reunion over Scotch highballs and thick steaks, and one all three would remember with nostalgia in the months ahead.[23]

On the *Pierce*, the padre wrote, were "at least 100 New Mexico boys I knew. Many . . . used to be in the C.C.C. They went to Clark Field about 50 miles from here."[24] These were the first of two battalions from the New Mexico National Guard. Having been federalized in January, the former cavalry regiment was now the soon-to-be-legendary 200th Coast Artillery, Anti-Aircraft. Congress had lengthened the terms of enlistment and relaxed the restrictions on overseas assignments. The rest of the regiment would follow on the USS *President Coolidge.* Many of them Father Albert already knew; he would soon know the rest.

Among other old friends he met at Fort Stotsenberg (adjacent to Clark Field) was, he wrote Elisa Baldonado, "Sam Carouthers who used to command the Tularosa [CCC] camp. . . . He was always good to us. It was Sam who sent all those boys from the camp to work on the church at Mescalero."[25]

He sent Father Felix a list of books he needed constantly for his work and asked for an additional list of recommended reading. "At present I borrow them when I [can] . . . but that is like a mechanic borrowing his tools." He needed complete sets of moral and dogmatic theology, canon law, church history, apologetics, exegetics, "and the Bible, new and old testaments. . . . Should we go into action," he added, which was beginning to seem likely, "I can store these books with the Quartermaster. . . ." It was September 1941, and he closed with what would prove prophetic words. "Dark clouds are gathering; what we have seen so far will be considered 'a calm' in comparison with the storm that will break. God help us! I wonder if Fr. Provincial ever warns his men to prepare themselves for the great test that is in store for them."[26]

✝ ✝ ✝

War would smite the islands sooner than those who were there imagined. Events had burst like machine-gun fire throughout the summer, though German actions were more widely publicized, and most American eyes, like those of their president, were primarily watching the Atlantic.

Naval war had begun on 21 May when a U-boat sank the American merchantman *Robin Moor* off the coast of Brazil. No lives were lost, but Germany's message was clear: America's Lend-Lease policy was far from neutral; her ships were fair game.

In August Roosevelt and Churchill, meeting secretly off Newfoundland, jointly issued the Atlantic Charter. It contained little of significance; but the act of a technically neutral power joining with a belligerent to call for the "final destruction of the Nazi tyranny" was unprecedented, and seemed to many another giant step toward a war the President professed to be avoiding. Even Churchill found it "astonishing."[27]

The President, by executive agreement with Denmark and Britain, then sent protective American forces to Greenland and Iceland and ordered American convoys to escort Lend-Lease shipping as far as Iceland. On 4 September a U-boat fired torpedoes at the American destroyer *Greer*, which had been trailing the sub and broadcasting its position to British patrols. The torpedoes missed; but Roosevelt broadcast sensationally that American ships would henceforth "shoot on sight" German and Italian ships.

On 22 June Hitler startled the world by turning on his erstwhile ally with a massive invasion of Russia. Roosevelt immediately extended Lend-Lease to Stalin, and Americans found themselves lying with strange bedfellows.

Japan, deficient in oil, rubber, and metal, had long been eyeing the Dutch East Indies. The Netherlands government-in-exile in London, however, refused to cede Dutch territories. The Japanese must either abandon their expansionist goals or seize the colonies and face certain war with Britain and the Netherlands, and probable war with the United States.

The militarists chose the latter, protected their rear by negotiating a five-year neutrality pact with Russia in April, launched a massive conscription to enlarge their army, and recalled all Japanese ships from the Atlantic. On 2 July they began planning for simultaneous attacks on Malaya, Hong Kong, Singapore, Guam, Wake, Pearl Harbor, and the Philippines.

On 24 July Japanese troops landed in South Indonesia and began to establish air and naval bases, thereby cutting off all avenues into China except the Burma Road. To keep that one access open, American planes began to augment the China Air Force. All Japanese assets in the United States were frozen; Britain and the exiled Netherlands governments quickly followed suit.

Meanwhile a deadly struggle raged inside Japan between the extreme militarists, led by War Minister Yosuki Matsuoka and General Hideki ('The Razor') Tojo against the moderates, led by Prince Fumimaro Konoye who, believing the militarists' policy suicidal and seeking to avoid war, quietly sent unofficial envoys to Washington with a draft understanding offering generous concessions to be used as a basis for negotiations between Secretary of State Cordell Hull and the newly appointed Japanese Ambassador Admiral Kichisaburo Nomura, due to arrive in April.

Hull was suspicious.

On 16 July Konoye forced Matsuoka from the cabinet and sought a personal meeting with the American president. Time was critical: the Supreme War Council had given Konoye until 10 October to break the diplomatic deadlock. After that, if he failed, they would prepare for war. It was a last desperate attempt. Nomura delivered the invitation on 28 August, on Roosevelt's return from the Atlantic Conference.

Ambassador Joseph Grew urged the President to accept. British Ambassador Sir Robert Craigie believed it "a superb opportunity to avoid war."[28] Major General Charles Willoughby, Chief of Intelligence in the Far East, added his appeal.[29] Chief of Staff George C. Marshall and Chief of Naval Operations Harold Stark believed the proposed meetings would at least buy the four months they needed to arm the Philippines.

The deadline approached and passed. Hull and Roosevelt refused to talk. On 16 October Konoye's government fell. Two days later the free world shuddered: Tojo now led the nation.

Still Roosevelt focused on the Atlantic. As naval confrontations escalated, Congress, at the President's request, voted that merchant vessels would now sail armed, wherever they wished and carrying whatever they chose. The President, committed to "the final destruction of the Nazi tyranny," was openly inviting attack. But Hitler had failed to subdue England; he was fighting a far more difficult war in Russia than he expected; and he was in no position to take on the United States. Der Führer declined the invitation.

Tojo was not so reluctant. The weakly defended Philippines were a major obstacle to Japanese expansion and must be eliminated. With the Japanese occupation of South Indochina, whereby they largely surrounded the Philippines, America responded by incorporating the Philippine army into the United States services and creating an overall command, USAFFE (United States Army Force in the Far East). MacArthur was recalled to active duty, promoted to Lieutenant General, and given the command.

Time was running out. The Japanese top-secret 'Purple' code had been broken and, through a miraculous decrypting machine dubbed 'Magic,' intercepted messages were streaming daily into Washington. Though MacArthur was told nothing of the intercepts, he knew war was imminent and he understood the weaknesses in Philippine defense more acutely than anyone else alive. Despite the urgency, the President had decreed as late as January 1941 there would be no naval reinforcement of the islands.[30] The European theater and the needs of Britain and Russia were still given priority over those of MacArthur.

The general began furiously reorganizing, mobilizing Filipino reservists, building defenses. He reworked the obsolete war plans into a comprehensive defense of the entire archipelago, not merely to repel an invasion but to defeat it. He needed men, matériel, and an air force. On 1 October he sent his plan to Marshall, who began sending reinforcements as they became available, though the Joint Board did not send official approval until 21 November.

✜ ✜ ✜

In the upheaval of reorganization Chaplain Braun was transferred in late September to the 92nd Coast Artillery at Fort Mills on Corregidor, the great rock fortress that, with three smaller islands, guarded the entrance to Manila Bay.[31] Of key strategic importance, the three-and-a-half-mile-long Corregidor, the heart of Harbor Defenses, pulsed with purpose under the quietly efficient command of General George F. Moore.

Father Al was one of two—later three—Catholic chaplains on Corregidor. The second, happily for both, was Father Herman Baumann, with whom he would share quarters. Here also the padre found his friend John Borneman, his erstwhile roommate on the *Washington*. Braun and Baumann assessed the island and divided it between them. The north side of the Rock faced the Bataan peninsula just two miles off its shore; the south side looked toward the province of Cavite. "The 92 C[oast] A[rtillery] was spread out at many locations, each with a nest of batteries," Braun recalled. "I took all the installations on [the south] side and Father Baumann on the side facing Bataan." Their assignment also included the outlying island defenses and extended up Bataan's west coast to Fort Wint on Subic Bay and a nearby detached shore unit, all of which they visited weekly.[32]

Meanwhile, the chaplains had their own logistical concerns. "Grapes do not grow in the Philippine Islands," Father Al tersely informed his provincial. "All mass wine must be shipped in. Since the recent war scare there has been a general scramble for mass wine. We would be out of luck if shipping to the Islands should be cut off. I am responsible for the Catholic end of the chaplains' work at Fort Mills; therefore I must see to it that we have enough mass wine on hand to say mass even if we are cut off from the outside world for a year." Would Father Martin please have the Concannon Vineyard send him "two 15 gallon kegs of tokay mass wine" from San Francisco?

That he understood the gravity of their position is clear in his next paragraph. "The situation out this way is not any too good. I want to be prepared for any eventuality. Therefore the next time I go to Manila I will go to the Philippine Trust Co. and make out a statement in the proper manner so that you can draw what money I have in the bank in the case of my death."

He would do the same, he continued, "in regard to the St. Joseph's Mission account with the State National Bank El Paso Texas." He carefully detailed his financial situation at Mescalero lest he leave any problem unresolved for another to inherit. He would socratically pay his cock to Aesclepius. "Till March I won't have more than a few dollars at the end of each month with the Philippine Trust Co. because it will take till then before the debts of St. Joseph's mission have been liquidated, and the debts I have made since coming on active duty with the army—car, uniforms, . . . living expenses—have been paid."[33]

"The sands are running fast," Ambassador Grew wired Hull on 3 November. War could erupt "with dangerous and dramatic suddenness."[34] Military intelligence, monitoring Japanese ship and air movements and utilizing intercepts, knew something big was in motion. They knew too that Tojo had opined that "war with the US would best begin in December or February."[35]

The day after Grew's warning, Konoye's moderates, still seeking to avoid war, pushed through two alternate proposals to submit to Hull, and quietly slipped Saburo Kurusu out of the country to join Ambassador Nomura in Washington in a last-minute attempt to reach a modus vivendi. "It is absolutely necessary," Tojo warned Nomura, "this agreement be completed by the twenty-fifth of this month." After that, he added, "things are automatically going to happen."[36]

Hull read the intercept. It was détente, he knew, or war. But he had already decided: Japan must be given an ultimatum. Not yet, Marshall and Stark continued to plead: give them the four months needed to reinforce the Philippines. Secretary of War Henry Stimson added his own pleas for three months to build an air force of B-17s—the great 'Flying Fortresses'—in the Philippines. On the eleventh Secretary of the Navy Frank Knox added his own warning of "grim possibilities in the Pacific." Neither the Army nor the Navy was yet in place for a Pacific war. If nothing else, a modus vivendi could buy the time they needed.

Japanese invading forces were sailing to their launching points. Lieutenant General Masaharu Homma established his command post in Formosa and awaited orders to strike. His target: the Philippines.

Kurusu arrived in Washington on the fifteenth; three days later he and Nomura presented the first of their two proposals. Hull and Roosevelt (who already knew the contents of both through intercepts) rejected it. On the twentieth the Japanese diplomats presented the second, containing unprecedented concessions. Hull gave no immediate reply. Tokyo extended the deadline to the twenty-ninth.

But Hull was already penning his own modus vivendi.

✢✢✢

Across the world from the sparring diplomats Father Al was writing letters, one of which to Elisa Baldonado gives a good description of his life on Corregidor. The preceding week, he wrote, he had been driven "from Manila to Subic Bay 144 kilometers. Beautiful country, rice, sugar cane and mountains. The natives were harvesting the rice. Their methods are primitive. The rice is threshed by the tread of the carabao then the grain is separated from the chaff by throwing into the wind. I said mass for an outpost in one place (we can't tell where they are); had almost 100% attendance; then went by boat to another outpost on an island; there were about 400 at that mass. The ship did not arrive to take me back to Corregidor so I took a boat to a naval base and got a ride in a big naval bomber to Cavite; took a taxi back to Manila, then a boat . . . to Corregidor. . . .

"This week I went to two other [island] outposts. . . . Fortunately I love water and . . . boats."

Again he spoke of the scarcity of priests. "There is so much to do it seems hopeless. We are opening large catechism classes to prepare as many as possible for 1st Com[munion] for Xmas. After I got here I took over the stockade. . . . The first Sunday there were 41 at mass. I noticed a few of the prisoners could play instruments. I invited them to play at mass. Now we have a large orchestra and sometimes I feel like jigging but the music draws the crowd. Last Sunday I had more than 400. . . .

"Sunday I am having field mass. The choir I had at Ft. McKinley is coming to sing the mass. There are seven girls and 12 soldiers. Most of the soldiers are fathers of the girls. The choir is happy to be able to make the trip. . . ."

Having seen Elisa's brothers Juan and Pepe, he reported that Juan was slated, along with others over enlisted age, to return soon to the States. "I don't think Pepe will like it to be left here alone."[37] He need not have worried: the ship never sailed. The padre's letter was written only three weeks before the Japanese attack.

A week after writing Elisa, Chaplain Braun wrote to Father Felix. His mass wine had not arrived. "Am becoming anxious because of the situation over here. For a long time I did not think that war would spread to the Orient. At present the situation looks very black. . . . I would be in a bad situation if we did not get mass wine."

He was also concerned for the safety of the missionaries in China, ironically overlooking his own danger in the islands. "When Father Walter leaves California for China will you let me know when to expect his ship in Manila. I want to see him. If he and his missionaries are forced to leave China why not stay in the Philippines? It would be safe here and it would not be far from their mission field. . . . I am sure the Archbishop of Manila would give them a good place to stay and work."

He had yet to attend to his financial affairs, but asked Felix to "tell Father Provincial as soon as I can find some time to spend in Manila I will arrange with the Philippine Trust Co. so that Father Provincial can draw the balance of my account should anything happen to me. The Archbishop of Manila owns the Philippine Trust Co. It is the greatest banking institution in the Philippine Islands. The church over here," he added, "is both very poor and very rich. It will have its troubles. The Province of Pampanga is strongly communistic. In that province the church owns plantations. The rice planters get from 20 to 50 centavos per day. . . . I dread to think of when the day of reckoning comes. Ninety five percent of these people are catholic; in spite of their calm appearance they are excitable and I am afraid under certain leadership they can easily be led to bloody violence. . . ."[38]

Never one to brood, however, the padre enjoyed life on Corregidor. He later wrote that he "had a great time till war came." He seems to have played badminton, as indicated in the list of articles destroyed in war, in which he includes "2 Badminton rackets" purchased in October 1941. He enjoyed visiting with the gun crews, sitting in on a poker game in their batteries, or sharing a cigarette, a joke, or a funny story.

But he was also a realist who saw the brewing storm. "I hope it will not be many years before I can pass back that way," he continued, but "I never allow myself to think about going home. It is a dangerous thing for me to do, even for a moment, . . . because all around me there are so many yearning to get back. We are supposed to keep up morale."[39]

He would keep up the morale of many men before the ordeal was over, in more ways than he could have imagined in those closing days of 1941.

✙✙✙

In Washington the President and Hull weighed the situation. That they would reject the final Japanese offer they had already decided; Hull would issue his own demands, which they knew Japan would not accept. One uncertainty remained. They knew the Japanese would move south; just where they would attack was the question. The Philippines, a block in the Imperial path, seemed likely. British and Dutch possessions were an inevitability, and Roosevelt had secretly promised America's declaration of war if these possessions were attacked. But he had also promised the American people he would send no American boys to battle "unless we are attacked." Therein lay the uncertainty. Would Japan be so foolhardy as to make the move that would trigger the declaration to which he was bound?

The President called a White House meeting on 25 November. An attack was likely, he told a tense Cabinet, perhaps as early as the coming Monday. "The question," Stimson recorded in his diary that evening, "was how we should maneuver them into the position of firing the first shot without allowing too much danger to ourselves."[40] On that same day Army Intelligence notified Stimson that a large Japanese fleet carrying five divisions had been sighted off Formosa.[41]

The following day, 26 November, Hull delivered his ultimatum: Japan must withdraw all troops from China and Indochina and disavow the Axis pact. Nomura paled and sat abruptly.

Meanwhile Admiral Stark and Brigadier General Leonard Gerow (standing in for Marshall) had drafted their own memorandum for the President's consideration, designed to avert war or postpone it until the Philippines could be defended.[42]

They were too late. The President and the Secretary had set their course.

So had Tojo. Having on the twenty-ninth secured promises from Germany and Italy of their backing when Japan struck, he summarily rejected Konoye's frantic pleas for peace and set the final movements in place. Nomura and Kurusu were left entirely in the dark and instructed to continue negotiations.

✠✠✠

General Moore ordered all units on Corregidor on war alert. Father Albert doubtless checked again in Manila on his mass wine, and from there, time allowing, may have visited his New Mexico boys at Fort Stotsenberg and Clark Field, where they had been on twenty-four-hour alert since the twenty-third, their guns set up around the base and under complete blackout. Some had reported strange fires burning along a runway and wondered why. Those in the searchlight batteries had reported unidentified aircraft flying over.

Tension mounted through the islands. Some feared fifth-column activity: many Germans lived in Manila. Others clung to the hope that because of the Philippines' commonwealth status the Japanese might pass over them when hostilities began. Those in the know knew better.

More personnel kept landing on the Rock. By the end of November over six thousand men and nurses were jammed onto Corregidor and the tiny surrounding islets. The gun crews were by then living at the twenty-three batteries, training constantly and intensively, checking their fifty-six guns, digging foxholes, and sandbagging around the emplacements.

Father Albert's letter of 21 November to Father Felix was the last of which we have knowledge before the siege of Corregidor. Knowing the situation as he did (chaplains were present at briefings) and being the assiduous letter writer he was, he doubtless scribbled some hasty words to friends and family. If so, they seem to have disappeared. Some may still be packed away in attics; others may have missed the last boat out. His actions from this point until war's end are traced from his later memories, from sparse military records, and from the recollections of those with whom he served.

✝ ✝ ✝

Streams of intercepts flooded into Washington through 'Magic.' The now-famous "Climb Mount Niitaka" was received and decrypted on 1 December. This was the signal the commanders of the striking forces awaited. Zero hour was set for 8 December Tokyo time—the seventh in the States. It could still be canceled should Washington ease toward a compromise.

On the third American Intelligence intercepted instructions to Nomura to burn all codes except the one needed for the last section of a fourteen-part message. That afternoon Japanese personnel were seen burning papers behind their embassy.

A message that night reported alien planes again over the islands; and American reconnaissance planes had spotted a large Japanese convoy moving south.

On the fourth the naval station at Cheltenham, Maryland, received the "East Winds Rain" war message for which they had been watching since 28 November. It was quickly relayed to the President.

On the sixth Roosevelt appealed in a final quixotic gesture to Emperor Hirohito for peace—a bit of stagecraft he knew would have no effect, except on the American public. That afternoon the first thirteen-part section of the long 'pilot message' to Nomura was intercepted. That night the President read the decrypt and turned to Harry Hopkins.

"This means war," he said.

In the Philippines warnings and instructions had been almost daily fare at Army and Navy headquarters. Negotiations were going badly, the Fleet Commanders were told; "a surprise aggressive movement in any direction" could be possible, "including an attack on the Philippines or Guam."[43]

"Hostile action possible at any moment," Marshall radioed MacArthur. "If hostilities cannot, repeat cannot, be avoided the United States desires that *Japan commit the first overt act. . . .*"[44]

On the sixth (Philippine time) Braun and Baumann made their final preparations for war. "Father Bauman and I should get a special medal of recognition," the padre later asserted, "as the greatest influence for good morale among the Catholic Chaplains in the U.S. Army and Navy in Philippine Islands.

"Three days before Pearl Harbor, we read . . . that Germans sunk a British ship with 10,000 cases of Scotch destined for Manila. Next day we bought a supply of Bourbon, Scotch, Gin, Rye, Rum, etc. which would last for two years, our tour of duty in the Philippine Islands. Two days later came Pearl Harbor." The value of this foresight was proven later, he added. "During the siege of Bataan we kept all the chaplains, plus Skinny Wainwright, in good health and spirits."[45]

Tension was almost palpable during those last days of waiting, but Al Braun was never one to brood over the present or dread the inevitable. He was, in the interim, enjoying Corregidor. He found it a tropical Eden, ablaze with bougainvillea and hibiscus and orchids among tangles of green foliage and graceful palms. The sea breezes tempered the oppressive heat he had experienced on Luzon, and his lifelong ability to enjoy life is evident. "At this time of year," he wrote Felix in that last peacetime letter, "the climate of the Philippines can't be beat. . . . In a protected part of the surf we do a lot of swimming. It is dangerous to swim outside the net because the China Sea is infested with dangerous sharks and barracudas."[46]

There were far more deadly predators than sharks and barracudas prowling the China Sea; and in that first week of December they were moving massively toward their prey.

16: COMBAT PADRE

While Chaplains Braun and Baumann were prudently buying booze against a possible war-caused shortage, MacArthur, having just met with Hart and British Vice-Admiral Sir Thomas ('Tom Thumb') Phillips, was assessing air defenses with Major General Lewis Brereton, Commander of Far Eastern Air Forces (FEAF).

The Philippines were far from war-ready, although Marshall, trying to offset Washington's calamitous delay, was sending reinforcements as fast as possible. A seven-ship convoy, led by the cruiser *Pensacola*, was already steaming toward Manila laden with men, planes, artillery, and ammunition; and, Marshall radioed MacArthur on the seventh, he could expect "every possible assistance within our power."[1] The convoy was eight days out of Manila.

Only hours away, hidden from American surveillance planes by heavy fog, Japanese assault boats were churning south toward Luzon.

That Sunday of 7 December—the sixth in the States—was for the Americans, despite the tension, almost studiedly relaxed. At Fort Stotsenberg Father Al's New Mexico boys staged a polo game that afternoon. Crews on duty talked idly at their gun posts. In Manila air crews from the 27th Bombardment Group were giving a gala welcoming bash for Brereton at the Manila Hotel. It stretched into the early hours.

On Corregidor the chaplains spent a busy Sunday saying masses at the gun batteries, whose crews they found somewhat bored with what most believed only another precautionary alert. Some idly watched a States-bound liner steam past the Rock.

The chaplains were also preparing for Monday's celebration of the Feast of the Immaculate Conception, a day of obligation and a Philippine national holiday. Processions and an early mass would begin the day of feasting and frolic. Having always loved fiesta time in Santa Fe, Father Al doubtless anticipated this holiday as happily.

The gods of war poised on the brink.

Chaplain Albert Braun was fifty-two years old, already something of a legend. He had been a frontier priest nearly a quarter century. He had been wounded on the battlefields of France in 1918. Four times he had daringly penetrated revolutionary Mexico incognito. He had weathered the Great Depression, during which he had driven thousands of miles to minister to the boys in the CCC camps, supported exiled Mexican clerics, and built a church of such size and beauty it became known as the 'Apache cathedral.' He was about to meet his greatest challenge.

"AIR RAID PEARL HARBOR. THIS IS NO DRILL."

It was 0230 in Manila when the naval operators intercepted the message. Within minutes Admiral Hart had it relayed to all ships. He failed to alert MacArthur, who learned it from a commercial broadcast half an hour later. All units were ordered into position.

Few knew it in these early hours, except for those ordered to report. The big event throughout the predominately Catholic Philippines was the holiday. Bells were pealing, processions winding toward the churches.

Lieutenant Madeline Ullom, US Army Nurse Corps, soon to become a close friend of Father Al's, attended mass before reporting for duty at Sternberg Hospital in Manila. After the service the priest quietly informed his congregation that Pearl Harbor had been attacked. He left the obvious unsaid: the Philippines would be next.

Lieutenant Ullom sped to Sternberg.

Brereton, expecting an attack soon after daylight, was at USAFFE headquarters by 0500, frantically requesting authority to bomb Japanese air and naval centers on Formosa before they hit first. Prepare but wait, he was told.

As the morning ripened every radio on Luzon seemed to be tuned to KMZH in Manila, from which Don Bell's rapid-fire reports blared as news came in, though many, knowing Bell's predilection for the sensational, discounted much of it. Hearing they were under attack, the men at Clark Field looked to the peaceful skies and laughed. So did the New Mexicans, deployed around Clark's periphery. But one, trying to call his battery captain, found the wires dead.

Early reports of enemy aircraft approaching Lingayen Gulf sent several pursuit squads to intercept the attack. But the Japanese bombers veered east, decimated the little barrio of Tuguegarao, hit Camp John Hay at Baguio, and headed back north.[2]

Brereton, still without authorization to bomb Formosa, but determined to protect his seventeen Flying Fortresses, ordered them aloft. All morning they circled Mount Aryat.

Washington officialdom was stunned. They had expected an attack—but at Pearl Harbor? "My god," Secretary of Navy Frank Knox, exclaimed. "This can't be happening! This must mean the Philippines!" None had seriously believed it could be elsewhere. Roosevelt had dismissed repeated warnings regarding Pearl Harbor, and none had believed Japan capable of multiple strikes. But as the day advanced, reports rolled in: Kota Bahru, Singora, Singapore, Guam, Hong Kong, Wake. Only the Philippines had not been hit.

They would have been had not heavy fog rolled over Formosa. There 108 Mitsubishi bombers awaited takeoff, their pilots praying to the gods of Holy Nippon for the fog to rise before the now-warned Americans from Luzon would hit them.

Brereton, finally authorized, was preparing to do just that. The bombers had landed for briefing and loading. But the fog on Formosa had lifted, and even as the planes at Clark readied for action, the Mitsubishis were streaking south.

Noon approached. The bombers were loading, the pursuit planes refueling. Reports of high-flying aircraft, presumably heading for Clark Field, began flooding into Interceptor Command. Pursuit squadrons from Iba and Nielson Fields took off for intercept. Teletype and radio warnings were beamed to Clark.

Clark Field never got them.[3]

Corregidor braced for action. On the high western head called 'Topside' the post headquarters pulsed with activity; the barracks teemed with incoming troops. Below on 'Middleside' the electric plant generated power for all installations. Farther eastward at the Rock's lowest and narrowest point, inter-island boats disgorged men and materials on 'Bottomside's' three docks.

Just beyond towered Malinta Hill, a formidable barrier against invasion. Through its interior ran a huge tunnel, an engineering marvel from which branched a maze of laterals, all walled, floored, and arched with reinforced concrete, soon to house a hospital and all Philippine defense headquarters in bombproof safety beneath four hundred feet of rock. Beyond Malinta tapered the island's tail, which housed the Naval Radio Intercept Station and a small airstrip euphemistically called Kindley Field. A trolley serviced all the island's important points.

Twenty-three gun emplacements dotted the island, all heavily sandbagged, their ammunition pits stocked, their crews well drilled. The guns were ancient, but they were large and powerful, and the men who manned them were ready for action.

Soon after sunup Navy launches docked at Bottomside with their first prisoners of war—thirty-some Japanese 'fishermen' whose unusual interest in Corregidor and frequent prowling within the three-mile limit had for some time aroused American suspicions. So had their boats, equipped with spotting telescopes and other sophisticated apparatus. Boats and crew were now in custody. The 'fishermen' now found themselves guests of the island that had so provoked their curiosity, complete with an inside view of the post stockade.

Beyond that Corregidor was quiet. A few planes patrolled the bay until recalled to Luzon. Shortly thereafter three enemy bombers appeared just off the south shore. Two batteries fired. The planes were beyond their range, but the crews enjoyed the action.

The chaplains went about their usual duties as the tension of waiting thickened the air. Father Albert's hearty laugh and earthy humor had long since made him a favorite among men of all faiths. He was a combat veteran; he knew what war was; he spoke their language. More than one face lit as the tall chaplain with the wide grin approached.

✠✠✠

The Japanese pilots neared Luzon. Half their forces peeled off and headed for Iba. The rest streaked south.

At Clark Field the B-17s, now pregnant with bombs, were lined in proper precision, the crews awaiting takeoff orders. The P-40s had refueled. Their pilots were bolting a quick meal in mess hall or cockpit. In the field the lunch trucks were making their rounds to the antiaircraft batteries. Some looked up to watch the planes bearing from beyond the horizons, two formations of twin-engine bombers, high and beautiful. Many, believing them the aircraft Washington had promised, cheered. "Here comes the Navy!"

Then the bombs began to fall. Explosions rocked the field. The shriek of the air-raid siren then joined the battle. It seemed to many like an afterthought.

It was 12:35.[4]

Erupting from mess halls, men raced for planes or battle stations. In the field the New Mexico artillerymen were manning their obsolescent guns, scouring the corrosion off the antiquated shells, leftovers from World War I. Most proved to be duds, and those that did explode were unable to reach the bombers, which flew just beyond their range. A few men, in the excitement of first blood, began happily firing pistols or their 1903 Springfield rifles.[5]

The well-planned attack, executed with cold precision, targeted operational buildings. The communications center was knocked out. So were planes in line on the runways, some as they taxied for takeoff.

Behind the bombers came the Zeros diving, strafing, riddling hangars, barracks, motor pools, and the grounded aircraft. Gas tanks and fuel caches ignited; the flames spread to the thick-growing cogon grass. The antiaircraft guns could reach these low-diving strafers and, despite antiquated weapons and corroded ammunition, they downed five Zeros that day. Half a dozen elderly B-35s, arriving from Del Carmen field, got two more; but, outmoded and outmatched by the faster, more maneuverable Zeros, there was little they could do.[6]

As fires spread the roar of flames added to the din. Hundreds of explosions shook Clark and Fort Stotsenberg. Men dashed through smoke, heat, flying shrapnel, and the hail of strafer bullets to rescue the wounded, to pull the helpless from burning buildings and doomed planes. Many rescuers became themselves victims.

As Clark writhed so did Iba. Hit simultaneously and in like manner, Iba and the nipa huts of the little barrio that abutted it were demolished. With Iba also went the control tower, the only operable radar shack on Luzon, and the hapless crews within.

The din of battle abruptly became the silence of the void. Late-bursting explosions still detonated at Clark and Stotsenberg, and the wails of fire trucks and ambulances continued through the night. The terrified neighs of wounded horses echoed the agonies of numberless men; and some thought of the polo game, a day and a lifetime ago, when men and horses were still in the prime of vigor and the innocence of peace. Burning debris still flew through the smoke-blackened air, and beneath its pall were scattered the bodies, or pieces of bodies, that had been men an hour since.

Cleanup crews went into action repairing communications lines and cratered runways, salvaging parts or equipment from twisted planes and skeletal buildings. Rescue crews searched through the carnage. Men sought missing buddies, burial crews prepared for their grisly tasks, and those who yesterday had spurned foxholes now dug furiously. Doctors, nurses, and chaplains worked through the night.

✠ ✠ ✠

The day of infamy had ended; the day of reckoning began. As reports began to stream in by bits and pieces, a grim picture emerged: all Southeast Asia was in flames.

By the end of that first day the Japanese had secured beachheads at Kota Bahru in British Malaya. They had taken Singora, were spilling into Thailand, advancing south toward Singapore. The most powerful battleships in the Pacific, the British *Repulse* and *Prince of Wales,* were streaming north to challenge the enemy's troopships.

Singapore and Hong Kong were Britain's key defenses in Southeast Asia. Air attacks had already destroyed Hong Kong's airfield and its planes. If these great fortresses fell the way would lie open to the Dutch East Indies, and their oil, tin, and rubber so vital to Japan.

Guam and Wake were under air attack. Washington's failure to reinforce these remote island outposts glared redly accusing.

The Japanese had achieved their immediate aims with incredible success. Their most formidable enemy, the United States, had suffered shattering blows. The Pacific Fleet—their single largest deterrent—lay mangled in Pearl Harbor. So were the bulk of army and navy planes at their Hawaiian bases. The cost in American lives, still being counted, had already mounted to over two thousand.

The Philippines lay open for invasion. Their air defense—FEAF— had effectively ceased to be. Most of Clark Field's P-40s were destroyed and all but three B-17s. Although two squadrons of bombers were intact on Mindanao, they were powerless without pursuit cover. With the loss of Iba's radar, the early warning system was gone. If Guam and Wake fell—which in their near-defenseless state they almost certainly would—the Philippines' line of communication to America would be severed. The nearest Pacific base would be at Midway—and Midway was 4,500 miles from Manila.

Still (except for the defeatist Hart) those in the islands were confidant. Their country would not let them down. The *Pensacola* convoy would arrive any day, and Marshall had promised MacArthur "every possible assistance." Help was on its way.

Washington recoiled. No one had believed Japan capable of such massive and widespread assault. Now, after one day of war, America must believe the unbelievable, comprehend the incomprehensible, and plan a course of action.

The President's hope of Japan's firing the first shot had been overwhelmingly realized. But the gods of war had scorned his condition that it be "without too much damage to ourselves": that boon they gave to the enemy. Japan had lost only twenty-nine planes and five midget submarines at Pearl Harbor, and seven Zeros over Luzon.

The Japanese followed their initial strikes with intensity, precision, and staggering gains. Guam fell on 10 December. On that same day the enemy sighted and sank the *Prince of Wales* and the *Repulse*—the greatest threats to the Japanese armada afloat—and with them three destroyers. After heroic resistance Wake, learning that its promised help had been recalled, surrendered on the twenty-third. Hong Kong fell on Christmas Day.

The invasion of Luzon was about to begin. With FEAF all but eliminated the way was clear. On the tenth, as Guam collapsed and the British ships went down, Japanese forces landed on the beaches of Aparri and Vigan preparatory to the main invasion, while Manila and its nearby defense installations reeled under an air barrage that left Cavite Naval Base a blazing ruins.

That night Admiral Hart decided to send the bulk of his remaining ships to the Dutch East Indies. MacArthur furiously objected, reminding the admiral of orders to defend the Philippines "as long as that defense continues." Hart was unmoved. He had already dispatched Task Force Five; the rest of his fleet would follow.

On the thirteenth MacArthur learned the *Pensacola* convoy had been rerouted to Brisbane, hence to continue as soon as possible to Philippine relief. Another stormy session with Hart followed. The defenses of all Southeast Asia depended on the Philippines. The admiral must, the general charged, keep the sea lanes open and provide escort for the convoy. The main invasion was coming. He must hold the enemy at the beaches, and to do so he needed naval cooperation.

Hart refused to commit ships for defense or for escort. MacArthur sent a desperate appeal to Marshal.

The main invasion of Luzon began on the twenty-third with massive Japanese landings at Lingayen Gulf in the north and at Legaspi in the south, from which to mount a giant pincers movement on Manila. Wainwright's inadequately reinforced Fil-American forces, unable to repel the enemy at the beaches, withdrew to the Agno River. MacArthur, as planned, began to remove his headquarters, along with those of President Quezon and of United States High Commissioner Francis B. Sayre, to Corregidor, declared a strategic retreat to Bataan in effect, and ordered Brereton to Australia, from which he could operate more forcibly.

Bataan and Corregidor now held the key to Philippine defense. The Rock denied the enemy use of the bay, without which Manila was of no strategic value; and Bataan was a natural fortress that MacArthur could hold until reinforcements arrived.

What no one in the Philippines knew was that there would be no reinforcements. The President, obsessively pursuing his 'get Hitler first' policy, was writing the islands off. Even Churchill, arriving in Washington for a conference, was startled to learn that the President, despite American devastation in the Pacific, had no intention of shifting his priorities. On Christmas Eve, as the troops began rolling toward Bataan, their President was casually offering Churchill a present of the *Pensacola* convoy and its cargo, specifically marked for Philippine relief. Only after the Joint Chiefs exploded and a furious Henry Stimson threatened to resign as Secretary of War did Roosevelt back down.[7]

Marshall at once insisted on, and won consent for, naval support of Philippine defense. Colonel Dwight Eisenhower, at Marshall's request, provided a detailed plan for a supply line from Australia, for which Hart was enjoined to make ships available.

MacArthur was elated. Help was on the way.

✛✛✛

The men on the Rock watched the parade of Hart's navy sailing away, and of nearly a hundred merchant vessels. If some felt they were being abandoned, few said so. Though air-raid sirens blared intermittently, no enemy planes appeared, except for one lone group of Mitsubishis returning from a raid on Manila. The artillerymen seized the chance, shot one down, and cheered lustily. Christmas approached, and still the skies were silent. But the island pulsed with urgency as Corregidor readied for the mass invasion of Manila's top brass. The Rock was about to become the nerve center of Pacific defense, and the seat of Philippine government.

As crews on the docks unloaded boatloads of supplies from Manila, men at the gun pits were tunneling storage pits for ammunition and shoring up positions. Over the island men dug foxholes, laid barbed wire along the beaches, filled sandbags, built tank traps. Chaplains Braun and Baumann were always ready to wield a pick or shovel or to help heave sandbags. They were also preparing for Christmas Eve mass.

Malinta tunnel was being readied for occupation. The station hospital was moved from Middleside into its lateral within and sectioned into wards, surgery, mess hall, and nurses' quarters. Rear Admiral Francis Rockwell, replacing Hart to command what remained of the Asiatic fleet,[8] had already set up his headquarters in the Navy lateral. With the destruction of Cavite, the radio facilities in Malinta provided their only direct contact with the United States. Additionally, a Navy radio intercept capable of picking up and decoding Japanese messages had been installed in a tunnel at Monkey Point at the island's eastern end. Data so gathered would prove invaluable.

The population of the two-square-mile island was swelling into an anthill of civilian refugees and military personnel—nurses, headquarters staff, troops, ordnance, engineers, survivors from Cavite, and the Fourth Marines.

On the afternoon of 24 December President Manuel Quezon, with his family and entourage, arrived on the inter-island steamer *Mayan,* along with Commissioner Sayre and his retinue. A few hours later MacArthur, with family and key personnel, stepped ashore from the *Don Esteban.*

Supplies continued to arrive into the night. It had been "[o]ne hectic day," the quartermaster officer logged at 2:30 AM. "MacArthur and his whole dam staff [had arrived]. I never in my life have ever seen such disorder and excitement, officers and men swarming about like ants. . . . Barges and barges of supplies and equipment." Unloading and dumping had been "one hell of a job. Dogtired, good nite."[9]

That night Father Albert said mass, though where is unclear. As senior Catholic chaplain, and in lieu of Quezon's personal priest, who seems not yet to have arrived, he may have officiated for the military personnel and Filipinos, among them the Quezon family, in the tunnel. If so, the padre would have said mass for his gun crews earlier.

On Christmas Day a boatload of nurses arrived from Manila and began organizing the tunnel's hospital wing. In another lateral Quezon's headquarters for the Philippine government were being set up. Above-ground personnel, still furiously readying for attack, watched as Hart's last forces steamed out, heard the explosions from Cavite, saw the smoke and flames billowing where the giant oil barrels had been torched ahead of the approaching enemy.

Hart left for Borneo via submarine the next day, to establish headquarters for the defense of the Malay Barrier and the Dutch East Indies. Believing the Japanese unbeatable, he refused, despite orders, to supply a single ship for Philippine defense.[10] MacArthur, vainly hoping to save Manila from destruction, declared it an open city; and a host of prominent civilians alit on the Rock fleeing Homma's fast-closing 14th Army. From Rockwell's radio came the news that Hong Kong had fallen.

The bombardment of Corregidor began on the twenty-ninth. The Marines had arrived after an all-night transfer, and were preparing to deploy when it began. Their concrete quarters were among the first hit by the 550-pound bombs hurtling from above as if hell and heaven had exchanged places. USAFFE headquarters on Topside was a prime target. Men erupted after the first hit, fled on the General's orders to the bombproof telephone exchange during a lull.

In the midst of the raid a dozen nurses, the last to leave Sternberg Hospital, docked at the north pier, Madeline Ullom among them. Rousted out at two AM, she grabbed a few belongings, jumped with the rest into an ambulance that dodged bomb craters as it raced to the dock, ran for the little inter-island steamer *Mactan*. Minutes after they pushed off a bomb hit the pier behind them. The *Mactan* hid in shadows until dawn, when a minesweeper escorted it through the mined waters and dozens of sunken ships. Amid falling bombs and strafing planes, the little steamer managed to get through. On Corregidor a truckload of soldiers slowed, pulled the nurses aboard, and roared through the falling bombs to Malinta's west entrance. The hospital lateral was already filling with wounded. The nurses went to work immediately.[11]

The great guns of Corregidor roared continuously. The 60th Coast Artillery brought down a number of bombers—thirteen by their count; the machine-gunners sent four low-flying dive bombers into the bay.

MacArthur stayed in the open throughout the raid. So did Chaplains Braun, Baumann, and Borneman, hurrying where needed, tossing in a joke or two while assisting a comrade or helping shore a revetment. Braun, Borneman reported, "said Mass constantly under the most trying conditions, . . . a brave man in every respect."[12]

For over two hours bombers pounded the Rock in three assaults of alternating army and navy craft. They left barracks, warehouses, and the newly vacated station hospital at Middleside in smoking ruins. Several small craft were hit; two planes were destroyed. Flames billowed from Kindley Field and smaller fires burned throughout the island. The post exchange, officers' and enlisted men's clubs, the Topside movie house, and a number of homes (MacArthur's included) were badly damaged or destroyed. The electric trolley tracks were smashed in dozens of places, the entire island cratered, USAFFE headquarters wrecked. Eighty men were wounded, twenty dead.

Not a gun battery remained, the enemy reported, nor a military installation. Tokyo, omitting any mention of downed planes, boasted that the island's defenses were annihilated and that for all purposes Corregidor was no more.

The Japanese had much to learn about the defenders. Crews on the Rock had gone immediately into action filling craters, fighting fires, digging more tunnels, repairing telephone lines, water pipes, and the electrical system. (Malinta had been thrown into darkness; throughout the raid the medical staff in the hospital lateral had treated the wounded by flashlight.) Damage to the rails was too extensive for repair, except for a limited area at Bottomside. Remarkably the nerve centers survived. Two guns had suffered minimal damage but were quickly back in operation. The vital water tanks, the pumps, and the indispensable power plant were still intact, the radio installation was safe in Malinta, and the interceptor at Monkey Point untouched.

Tokyo had grossly exaggerated the destruction. Corregidor was alive, in working order, and ready for the next attack.

None came for the next three days, during which the defenders took advantage of the interlude, shoring their defenses, attending official matters, and welcoming in an uncertain new year.

The day after the raid USAFFE headquarters moved into Malinta. That afternoon Manuel Quezon was inaugurated for his second term as President of the Philippine Commonwealth. Father Albert was chosen to give the invocation, an honor the padre wore humbly. The ceremony was simple, sans pomp or pageantry, profound in significance, strangely dignified. Beneath a draped tarpaulin from which hung the United States and Commonwealth flags, stood a makeshift dais, hastily hammered together, and on it sat MacArthur, every bit the general, beside the shrunken president in his wheelchair, his face and frame so emaciated it seemed as if all remaining life had drained into his blazing eyes.

The audience sat in chairs dragged from the mess hall. Into the clearing, in true military tradition, marched the 92nd Coast Artillery Band—Philippine Scouts, full of spunk and spirit, but sadly without music: their instruments had been shattered by Japanese bombs. From the wheezy little hand organ Virginia Bewly (herself an evacuee whose father had stayed in Manila to face the enemy) coaxed the strains of "Hail to the Chief."

Speeches were short, determined, moving. Quezon and Vice President Sergio Osmeña were sworn in, after which the president, his voice high-pitched from tuberculosis and passion and punctuated with labored coughing, spoke of "human liberty and justice" for which "we are sacrificing our lives and all that we possess." MacArthur spoke slowly, moist-eyed, soft-voiced, of "this new nation" and its "bed of birth" amid the "thunder of death and destruction."

No one present could have been more aware of the significance of the strange little ceremony than Chaplain Albert Braun. Of his personal relationship with Quezon we know little. The big unassuming chaplain was likely amused at the autocratic little president—the padre always found humor in the trappings of prestige—but he would also have seen the nobility in the face of disease and impending death; he could recognize courage and understand dedication. Above all he would have perceived the historicity of this solemn ceremony at the crossroads of human annals, and all of this came through in the strong steady voice as he invoked God's blessing on the cause of freedom, the beset country, and its valiant president.

It seemed an answer from heaven when Quezon read a message he had recently received from the American president. In flowing Rooseveltian prose the Commander in Chief pledged that Philippine freedom "will be redeemed and their independence . . . protected," for which he solemnly promised "the entire resources in men and materials of the United States."[13]

Tears welled in many eyes as both national anthems swelled from the little organ. Help was indeed on the way. Roosevelt had himself sent his word—

But, as it turned out, little else.

A determinedly merry party in the tunnel welcomed in the war-torn New Year. Again the little organ came to life and those clustered around it sang and laughed and defied the future. The padre always loved and livened a party, and likely attended this one, unless he was spreading good cheer to the gun crews at their batteries. It is certain he was sharing a drink and a joke with his fellow soldiers, in tunnel or in field.

It was nearing sunset on 2 January when the Japanese began to pour into Manila. They commandeered schools, hotels, government buildings. They closed banks, newspapers, restaurants. They confined British and American civilians to their homes and warned Filipinos against hostility toward the conquerors on pain of death.

But with the fall of Manila the Philippines had not crumbled as Japanese Lieutenant General Masaharu Homma had predicted; and the city was strategically useless without access to the bay. "They might have the bottle," MacArthur pronounced, "but I have the cork!" And he meant to keep it. His army, still intact, was streaming undeterred into Bataan.

That same day the Japanese resumed the bombardment of Corregidor. Nurses Madeline Ullom and Ann Mealor had climbed, as they often did, to the top of Malinta Hill, "and we'd look out to the China Sea to see if the [American] fleet had come in. They never came. But we believed they [would]—all the time. This one morning—it was about ten o'clock—we heard the planes coming in. There they were—nine and nine and nine—and we said, 'Oh, aren't they wonderful? The Americans can do anything!' And then the bombs started to come down."[14]

The following day, 3 January, the massive assault continued. From Topside Father Albert saw the command post at Rock Point take a direct hit. He raced to the scene. Bodies sprawled amid the dust-choked wreckage.

Other men, dead and living, lay buried in the rubble of collapsed concrete. He quickly took charge, organized a stunned crew, and with them began to dig.

Finding one man still alive but pinned beneath the leg of a dead artilleryman and, knowing the leg must be removed before the wounded could be pulled out, he jumped into his vehicle and tore for Malinta, dodging strafers all the way. At the hospital he borrowed a surgical saw, raced back through flying bullets and falling bombs and, in his own terse words, "sawed off the leg of the dead soldier so that the living soldier could be evacuated."

He was not yet through. "When we thought we had rescued all the living we still heard a moaning. Following the sound we dug deeper till we reached the buried soldier. We had cleared the debris to his waist when it seemed he was dying from shock. Just then I spied Father Baumann and [yelled], 'Herman give me that bottle of whiskey in the trunk of your car.' Father Baumann and I had more whiskey than anyone on Corregidor," thanks to their pre-war foresight. (It was not, he added in postscript, for their personal use, "but for such emergencies as that at Rocky Point. In the military, when the chaplain is down to earth, he is close to the men and can be of service to them.")

Without an immediate stimulant, he knew, "this soldier will be dead in a few minutes. . . . Father Baumann got the whiskey for me. I pour[ed] a good slug down the man's throat. In a short time the color came back and he revived. We got him loose from the debris and took him to the hospital. The next day he died."[15] Borneman, working alongside, reported that "[t]wo men were rescued . . . but two others we could not dig out."[16]

For his actions this day Father Al would receive his second Silver Star. "Despite grave danger from exploding ammunition," the citation reads, Chaplain Braun "courageously directed and personally assisted in the swift extinguishing of numerous fires in the vicinity. . . . Through his heroic actions at great risk to his life, Chaplain Braun upheld the finest traditions of the Corps of Chaplains."

The bombardment lasted five days, leaving buildings smashed to rubble, the dock damaged, several water tanks destroyed. Fire had consumed warehouses and an oil tank. Craters gaped everywhere. But the bombproof power plant still operated. Telephone lines had been hit every day, restored every night. The artillery crews repaired their guns after each raid and kept them firing. Medical personnel and chaplains worked around the clock.

Morale remained high. The big guns were still intact, military installations operable, and Malinta impregnable.

During Corregidor's bombardment the army on Luzon had been retreating onto the Bataan peninsula for which the Fil-American forces of Wainwright and Major General George M. Parker fought delaying actions. Like a great centipede they crawled, a column of rolling stock—trucks and ambulances, guns and huge prime movers, ox-drawn carts and yellow Pambusco buses, and on the edges of the roiling dust trudged Filipino families fleeing with the army. Bombed and strafed as they went, they rolled tenaciously toward Bataan, burning bridges behind them. On the night of 5-6 January the last of the troops passed onto the peninsula, as Wainwright made the final withdrawal across the Culo River. The last bridge blew at 0200.

Too late Homma learned that what he had thought a panic-driven rout had been a brilliantly planned and executed withdrawal into a strong defensive position. Now, with the Fil-American forces intact on Bataan, he must marshal his forces to defeat MacArthur's entrenched army. It was 6 January. His deadline for conquering the entire Philippine archipelago was 7 February. He had lost a significant number of planes over Corregidor for minimal military results. The bombardment ceased; the invasion of Bataan was about to begin.

Those on the peninsula dug in and those on the Rock waited and all were confident. He could hold Bataan forever, MacArthur had said. And help was on the way: the President had said so.

MacArthur would later call the Battle of Bataan one of the world's decisive battles. Those who fought it called themselves the 'battling bastards.' Homma, butting his head repeatedly against these truculent Yanks, doubtless used other epithets.

The battle began on 9 January at 1500 hours as massive Japanese artillery opened on the Fil-American forward defense, the Abucay line. Parker's artillery answered in kind. On the tenth Homma demanded MacArthur's surrender. The Americans laughed derisively: they'd just begun to fight.

By logical reasoning Homma's attempt to force a quick surrender was not unrealistic. MacArthur's army was undermanned, underequipped, and underfed. The combined forces of Parker and Wainwright had shrunk by 13,000 men (mainly through desertions of untrained Philippine reservists). Of the theoretical 80,000 Fil-American troops, only 27,000 were trained soldiers. The two 'hospitals' behind the lines consisted of cots laid out on the ground. The troops were short of ammunition, of medical and surgical supplies, of clothing and shelter halves and mosquito netting. Their weapons were obsolescent, their vehicles too few, their gasoline supply too small. The 'Bataan Air Force' comprised seven battered P-40s. Above all was the acute lack of food. Rations were cut to half, and then to quarters.

But morale was high. They had gained the strongest defensive position on Luzon, had destroyed 184 bridges behind them, and sustained fewer casualties than the enemy. Two lines of defense stretched thinly coast to coast. Stakes and barbed wire and mines lay in the enemy's path. Foxholes and gun emplacements were camouflaged with branches and grass and rice straw.

The peninsula was a natural fortress of mountains, ravines, and tangled growth, through which wound mysterious paths known only to the dark children of the jungle. It was a well chosen bulwark, and MacArthur knew the terrain. They could hold Bataan until help came. And help was on the way.

✞✞✞

The *Pensacola* convoy reached Brisbane on 22 December; more were to follow. On 4 January MacArthur radioed Marshall a plan for running the blockade in submarines. Again Marshall ordered Hart to assist. Again the admiral declined. Grimly determined, Marshall's operatives flushed a few ancient vessels from the Australian coasts, and the men who manned them spit at logistics and dared the dark seas where enemy predators prowled. A few pushed through—enough to spark hope. Enough to prove heartbreakingly that a properly mounted operation could have broken the blockade.[17]

But the gods in Washington, pledged to 'get Hitler first,' had cast the die. Such an operation, the War Plans Division proclaimed, was unjustified.

No one told MacArthur.

✞✞✞

Soon after the battle began Father Al had a visitor. He was an old friend from New Mexico, Captain Frederick B. Howden, formerly the Episcopal minister in Roswell, now chaplain of New Mexico's 200th and 515th Coast Artilleries. His regiment was heavily Catholic, he told the padre, and would feel safer with a Catholic chaplain. Would Father Al be willing to cross to Bataan occasionally to serve their needs?

Of course he would. The two got quick authorization "that I spend one week each month on Bataan with [the New Mexicans]. I knew most of the men. . . ."[18] Regularly thereafter he chugged across to Bataan on a small courier boat, thence to the bivouac areas where the men protected two small airstrips to defend the seven P-40s that still flew and await the promised hundreds to come.

Visiting Bataan seemed almost like coming home to the padre. He was again with his boys. Pepe and Juan Baldonado and Alberto Gonzales, his erstwhile altar boys, now assisted him in the jungles of Bataan. Once again he sat around their campfires to shoot the breeze or join in a lively chorus of "El Rancho Grande," a lonely cowboy ballad, or a fervent "God Bless America." Those nights were not unlike those he remembered in the Mescaleros' camps, even to the throbbing drums the Indians in the regiment beat, though the chants were different now: *Better scram Tojo, better scram Tojo.* . . .

His services on Bataan were not confined to the New Mexicans. Some of Borneman's men were on Bataan and needed a Catholic priest, for which the padre "very kindly consented to take on this extra work," Borneman wrote, "and made frequent trips across . . . until Bataan fell."[19] Father Al also served men in Captain (later Colonel) William ('Wild Bill') Masello's unit, and any others he ran into in need of a Catholic chaplain. He traveled from group to group rallying the exhausted, cheering the discouraged. Men of all faiths welcomed this priest who seemed to know no fear; many attended his masses regularly.

"A very strong character," Masello—himself a strong character—called the padre. "Never asked for anything and even refused a tent." Dedicated, lean, and hard, he described the padre, "my idea of an Army chaplain. Because of his appearance and ease of movement . . . we called him the 'Indian fighter.'" But, Masello added, "not to his face."[20]

In the frantic activity the padre managed one quick note to his provincial, to go out on one of the few boats that occasionally eluded the Japanese blockade. "Don't know when I can get a few lines out to you again. Did not get the mass wine. Luckily we could buy some (not much) $6.00 per gallon from a pious Spanish Catholic."[21]

The initial Japanese attack on the east side failed overwhelmingly as Fil-American troops closed in, leaving two-thirds of Homma's infantry dead or disabled. Homma reinforced his positions; MacArthur redeployed his thin lines. Three times the enemy assaulted the line; three times the defenders hurled them back. But night attacks and heavy air bombardments chained MacArthur's forces to round-the-clock duty; sleeplessness, malaria, and quarter-rations took their toll; and a Fil-American counterattack failed. On the west side the Japanese broke through a section of the Abucay line and began to infiltrate Wainwright's positions.

The line began to crack.

The troops fought desperately. With outmoded weapons they faced the Japanese artillery, air bombardments, and flank attacks. They were hungry, exhausted, malaria-beset. They had lost thirty-five percent of their entire force, MacArthur reported.[22] On the twenty-third they began to fall back. By the twenty-sixth they were entrenched along the Orion-Bagac line, their rear defense.

On that day Homma, pressured by Tokyo to end the campaign quickly, launched the first of five landings on the west coast that began the three-week Battle of the Points. Wainwright augmented his thin forces with a makeshift infantry of planeless airmen, shipless soldiers, Marines, and two batteries of New Mexico artillerymen, and was on the beach himself at their head to oppose the landings. At Agoloma Point the American artillery fired on the strafers until they ran out of ammunition. The landing forces, meeting heavy fire, began to barricade themselves in caves along the cliffside. At this the Americans, carrying fifty-pound boxes of dynamite, were lowered on ropes, lit the fuzes and hurled, then jerked the ropes to be hauled up seconds before the charges detonated.

Torpedo boats and artillery attacked another large flotilla at Quinuaun Point,[23] and from Cabcaben the six remaining P-40s, with fragmentation bombs lashed onto improvised bomb racks, struggled aloft, dropped their loads, and returned for more. The beset barges began to sink, the rest to turn back.

By 7 February Wainwright had pinned the Japanese at Silaiim Point and driven back an attempted rescue mission. As the Fil-Americans broke through, the beach erupted with Japanese plunging from the cliffs into the ocean. Corpses littered the sand. On the twelfth a last Japanese counterattack failed and within a few days the exhausted troops had cleared the area.

Wainwright's warriors, at the cost of approximately seven hundred dead and wounded, had destroyed two entire battalions of Japanese infantry.

While the amphibious troops stabbed the coast, Japanese infantry pierced a gap and set up two deadly cells behind Wainwright's lines. As the Fil-Americans fought to cut them off, a third salient, trying to unite with the upper pocket, threatened Wainwright's flank. Against this, Major General Albert Jones on 4 February launched a three-week offensive known as the Battle of the Pockets.

As the Japanese penetrated American lines, dusky Igorot warriors were penetrating theirs. Transported to the front in army trucks, the small dark natives crept through the night, lobbed primitive spears and modern grenades, then glided silently to rupture another Nipponese line, and returned to the trucks dangling ears or parading heads on poles.

By mid-February Fil-American forces had wiped out the last of the cells. The Japanese 20th Infantry had been virtually annihilated. Bataan was safe, for the moment.

The Japanese were not beaten, but Homma was on the defensive. His 14th Army was effectually destroyed, his deadline for taking the Philippines had passed, and he was forced to lose face further by requesting more reinforcements. And therein lies the final answer to Bataan: Homma got help; MacArthur got promises.

He had repeatedly pled for the resources with which to fight a war. When on 13 January Quezon charged America with abandonment and Roosevelt with broken promises, the general relayed the message to Washington, received new assurances, and relayed the President's promise to the gaunt troops: "Help is on the way . . . hundreds of planes and thousands of troops. . . ."

But none had arrived when on 8 February President Roosevelt broadcast that thousands of planes were being sent to Europe. The infuriated Quezon told MacArthur he would request immediate freedom, disband his army, and neutralize the Commonwealth. Again MacArthur relayed the message to Roosevelt and added one of his own, hoping to jolt the administration into action. Again the President lulled Quezon with placebic pledges; but to MacArthur he alluded to last-ditch resistance. The significance was not lost on the general.

✣✣✣

As the armies battled on the west side, bombs were falling on the airstrips, and Japanese infantry hurled their strength against Parker's troops on the east. Three times they were beaten back. The hillside 'hospitals' were glutted with the wounded, lying in rows upon the ground. The shortage of medical supplies grew critical. The men grew hungrier.

As the fighting intensified Father Al's trips to Bataan grew more frequent. As in his first war, he went where he was needed. Like Wainwright, for whom his respect mounted daily, he went where the bullets were flying, always quick with a prayer, a bandage, a joke. Men of all faiths greeted this big man with the hearty laugh as his Jeep came bumping into camp. He gave them the lift they needed. Man for man they were outfighting the enemy and they knew it. But they were running out of fuel and ammunition and food. And three more of their trusty P-40s had gone down.

Singapore fell on 15 February. They heard it on their short-wave radios; and a week later they tuned in to a presidential 'fireside chat,' as hungry for hope as for food. Roosevelt stressed the vast distances of the Pacific, the difficulties of sending a fleet through Japanese waters. He spoke of the great demands on American production—yet he was sending thousands of planes to Britain and Russia, the men crowded around the radios knew. MacArthur's men, the President continued, were "gaining eternal glory"— but he also spoke of ground that must be yielded and sacrifices that must be made, and the gaunt and ragged men in the jungles of Bataan knew whom he meant. The Philippines were being abandoned.

They kept fighting. When another Japanese flotilla appeared in Subic Bay the four remaining P-40s headed into action again with their makeshift bomb contraptions, and by day's end had sunk both large transports and several smaller ones. But they paid the price: one lone plane was left.

About this time, the padre recalled, "we all started calling ourselves the BBB—Battling Bastards of Bataan." Journalist Frank Hewlett had penned the lines, and the men began to chant.

We're the battling bastards of Bataan;
No mama, no papa, no Uncle Sam;
No aunts, no uncles, no cousins, no nieces.
No pills or planes or artillery pieces,
And nobody gives a damn.
Nobody gives a damn.

On 5 March, despite valiant Allied stands on land and sea, Java, the last bastion of the Indies, fell. The Japanese conquest of the Southwest Pacific was complete; they now looked toward Australia. Within this vast sweep of empire only the twin nests of Bataan and Corregidor still stood in the Japanese path. The BBBs kept fighting.

Father Al kept crossing to his beset men; they called him their honorary chaplain. Diving strafers and flying bullets seemed to this warrior without a weapon—*Insignificant!* He too was a 'battling bastard.'

He was on Corregidor when MacArthur left. On the day of his 'fireside chat' Roosevelt ordered the general to Australia, naming him Supreme Allied Commander of the Southwest Pacific. Earlier MacArthur had refused Marshall's overtures to go. Now it was a presidential command. He left on 11 March, leaving Wainwright in command of the Philippines.

Father Al had seen little of MacArthur—the imperious general had small contact with subordinates—but the padre admired his determination under duress, his military brilliance, and his utter professionalism; and he staunchly defended his general during the war and long after. (At a gathering years later a man began criticizing MacArthur loudly and at length, until Father Al had had enough. MacArthur, he snapped, was not only a great general, but also "a great man . . . a real, great man," and turned away.)[24]

But it was to the earthy, front-line Wainwright that the padre warmed. 'Skinny' was Braun's kind of general, and Braun was the general's kind of chaplain. Where the battle was, they were, sticking always with the troops and for the same reason. They inspired courage; they kept up morale. Throughout his life Wainwright would speak of Al Braun as "my chaplain."

They also enjoyed a nip of good Scotch whiskey together on occasion. The supply Braun and Baumann had bought on the eve of war served well, for a wounded private or a heavily burdened general. "During the siege of Bataan," the padre reminisced years later, "we kept all the chaplains, plus Skinny Wainwright, in good health and spirits." Al Braun saw himself chiefly as a morale booster, "a job," Father Louis Vitale wrote on Father Al's death, "he succeeded at with faith, charm, and a lot of booze."[25]

"I came through," MacArthur radioed from Australia on 18 March, "and I shall return." It was a promise, a beacon, a rallying cry for some. The only man who could work the miracle they needed had gotten out to work it. To others, unaware of his early refusals to leave or of Roosevelt's ultimatum, he was the general who ran away. Most saw it as the final proof that Washington had written off the Philippines. That opinion seemed confirmed when, on the same day the message came through, Quezon also left Corregidor, to rejoin MacArthur eventually in Australia.

At some time in March—Father Al was never sure of the date—he learned he had been recommended for promotion to Lieutenant Colonel. It was a commendation he appreciated, but found, given the circumstances, rather irrelevant. He had more pressing concerns.

The big Japanese push was about to begin.

On the day MacArthur arrived in Australia and Quezon left Corregidor, Japanese planes dropped beribboned beer cans behind the lines, containing Homma's ultimatum to Wainwright. "Accept honorable defeat," he warned, or suffer the terrible losses in the mass offensive he would launch had Wainwright not surrendered by noon of the twenty-second.

It was not empty bombast. Front-line attacks increased, patrols from both armies skirmished more frequently, snipers clustered more thickly in the trees. Alternating pilots from the lone P-40 reported a massive buildup behind Japanese lines. Increased air attacks concentrated on the artillery of the old 200th with rarely a letup. Men crawled from one foxhole only to dive for another. Fires ignited continually.

Homma's massive artillery bombardment began on the twenty-second; and on 1 April, reinforced with troops, weapons, and bombers from the Singapore campaign, opened the heaviest barrage yet. The whole peninsula seemed to rock with the roar of artillery and diving planes. Starved, weak, and facing annihilation, the troops determined to sell every inch dearly.

Their chaplains served them well—Fathers Braun and Baumann when they could get across, and their regimental Chaplain Howden, who daily at each battery said a rosary with the Catholics and a service for the Protestants. One soldier set up an altar at his gun section when Father Al appeared in the middle of battle. After a necessarily short mass he turned to the padre. "Father, I sure feel sorry for those poor devils at the front." The padre looked at him a moment. "Son," he said softly, "you are the front line."[26] Another, a Protestant who always attended Father Al's masses, remembered how, during a service, the Japanese opened up with a massive artillery barrage. "Everyone jumped into a foxhole—except the padre, who kept on calmly saying mass."[27]

Through bombs and bullets and flying debris, amid fires and explosions, as hope faded but courage clung he moved among them, heard their confessions, led a rosary, said a mass, his altar an ammunition box. "You use so few words," he said. "There are so many men you don't have time to preach a sermon." Always later, when asked about life on the front, he insisted he enjoyed it: he was proud to serve these men who "showed their heroism and love of their country." And about his own devotion to duty? "I loved my country," he answered simply. "The men on the front lines are in danger of being killed. . . . You're glad to make any sacrifice."[28]

Easter fell that year on 5 April. Fathers Braun and Baumann said masses on Corregidor and the smaller islands, drafting whom they could to sing or serve at the altar. Then, as they prepared to cross to Bataan, their orders were abruptly canceled: the final Japanese offensive had begun.

It had started on 3 April—Good Friday—with a five-hour barrage that pounded the defenses to rubble, while incendiaries ignited cogon and bamboo thickets and Zeros strafed the exhausted troops. The infantry lines began to break as men fled south trying to get to Corregidor. On Easter morning the assault on strategic Mount Samat began; by dark the enemy controlled it. The Fil-Americans had lost two divisions. A counterattack on the sixth failed, and by dusk only a short line stood between the enemy and the bay. Hospital 1 was twice bombed and its wounded evacuated to Hospital 2 amid falling bombs and exploding shells. Men kept streaming past. The end was nearing.

The old 200th, now reunited as a brigade, was the only unit on Bataan still intact as the end came. Ordered to form the last thin line of defense against the enemy whose tanks they knew would roll with dawn, the ragged little band climbed the ridge overlooking Cabcaben airstrip and, with nothing but small arms to fight tanks, prepared to die. It was as well the padre did not know the impending fate of his boys.

But General Edward King, commanding on Bataan, knew, and refused to sacrifice this gallant little band for a cause already lost. On the morning of 9 April he was driven to meet the Japanese generals, his flag of surrender a dirty white tee shirt nailed to a pole. He did not inform Wainwright: he would take all responsibility.

Father Al knew only that a terrible battle raged across the narrow strait, and he agonized to be with his old friends who must need him now. Then, as the ninth dawned, the thunder of battle ceased, and from across the water there issued the deadly quiet of foreboding.

Bataan had fallen.

"We from Corregidor . . . watched the tragedy," the padre wrote. "It seemed the whole of Bataan Peninsula was ablaze, and being blown up. Then we saw [probably through an antiaircraft range finder] that long line of prisoners forming to make [what was later called] the Death March."[29]

One can only conjecture what images flashed through the chaplain's mind in the hours that followed, what conflicts wrenched his soul, what questions he asked, knowing no answer would come. Cut off from the world, he wrote few letters; he kept no journal; and even in later years he spoke or wrote sketchily of his wartime thoughts. He had to have wondered what was happening to his boys on Bataan. Certainly he prayed for them.

Nor did he know of the oral order of the fanatic Colonel Masanobu Tsuji to "kill all prisoners and those offering to surrender." Although some officers refused to carry out the savage order, many did, resulting in the deaths of an estimated seven-to-ten thousand men on the March alone.[30]

Ever the realist, Al Braun would have quickly assessed the status of Corregidor, knowing the Rock would be next, and immediately. He understood the significance of Bataan's higher ground from which Japanese artillery would quickly command a formidable offensive position.

He had not long to wait.

On the twelfth Homma's artillery opened fire from Bataan, and, augmented on the eighteenth with the arrival of ten 240-mm. guns, continued for twenty-four days. The attacks intensified daily and with deadly accuracy, guided by balloon observers.

Battery Geary had seriously incapacitated the Japanese Seventh Tank Regiment on the first day. But, as on Bataan, obsolete equipment, lack of air cover, and failure to receive reinforcements loomed darkly.

The tunnel was a stinking hellhole of dust, heat, and flies, worsened by an agglomeration of safety seekers those on the outside sneeringly called 'tunnel rats.' The hospital laterals filled, expanded into more laterals, and filled again with the constant stream of wounded. Braun and Baumann "only went in when called. We stayed outside with the men."[31]

He was called frequently to the hospital lateral to attend the wounded and dying. He worked often beside surgical nurses Ullom and Mealor. "He would come and give last rites," Ullom remembered. "They'd die in a few minutes—so many of them did. It was awful—so hot and no air conditioning."

On 26 April a shell hit the main entrance to Malinta, killing fourteen and wounding seventy. The medical teams, and Father Al, worked all night. "There was a lot of loose gravel and stuff," Ullom remembered. "And dust— we had to take pieces of gauze and soak them and put them over the patients' mouths, so they wouldn't breathe in all that dust. After they died—Father Albert was always so good. They wrapped each body in a blanket . . . and took them to the entrance of the tunnel, and then afterwards Father Braun went out and blessed the area—gave all the prayers. It was five o'clock in the morning before we got through."[32]

As the bombardment continued, and later when Japanese landings meant hand-to-hand fighting, Ullom saw Father Al appear more often in surgery, bearing the wounded from the field in the absence of litter bearers, "and when we'd get through operating—he was big and strong . . . and he'd go over and pick up these patients from the operating table and carry them out to the corridor. That's when he'd do the blessings on them. We had some that survived—maybe one in ten. I'll never forget him carrying them out and then performing the last rites on them."[33] She often stood at his side during these solemnities, when her duties allowed.

The padre's respect for the nurses was enormous. In these young women, confined in the stinking, stifling tunnel, working almost beyond endurance, he saw a quiet, steely, almost uncanny strength. When the generator failed, as it often did, they and the doctors worked by flashlight. To accommodate the floods of wounded, the beds became double-deckers and then triple-deckers. The blinking red ceiling lights that warned of incoming attacks, soon followed by the thuds of bombs and shells hitting above became so routine they paid small attention beyond preparing for each new influx of wounded men.

Madeline and Ann stayed ready. "Our beds were in another lateral, so when we got finished operating, I used to just take a blanket and put it on the operating table, or on the floor, and go to sleep, and then if we got a lot of casualties in—they didn't have time to run around and find you—there we were. We didn't think anything about time. Time was just immaterial."

Like his chaplain, Wainwright liked to mingle with his men, and took time each day to do so. It was all he could do. He knew the intense barrage foreran the invasion of Corregidor, and he knew he had nothing to stop the successive waves that would soon hit the beaches. The once-formidable guns of Corregidor, though they died fighting, were being silenced one by one.

The chaplains worked incredible hours. Following a dawn mass in the officers' mess where they used a table for an altar and the communicants knelt on bare concrete,[34] they fought fires, aided the wounded, filled sandbags, shored up revetments, and lifted sagging morale. A colonel who had believed chaplains a waste of government money watched Father Baumann as things got really tough. "If I ever get home," he vowed to the padre, "I intend to recommend Father Baumann for the highest decoration I can get for him."[35]

The outlying islands too were besieged. On 21 March during intense fire a shell penetrated a concrete tunnel roof, killing twenty-eight men and wounding forty-six.[36] Father Al volunteered immediately for the rescue team—"an extremely dangerous mission," Borneman reported, "because of the long trip by water," over twenty miles, under fire from Cavite. Somehow they made it. The padre considered his own actions *Insignificant!* He was only doing his job.

The barrage continued. Shells from Cavite and Bataan pounded the Rock, bombs rained from the skies in raid after raid. By the end of April six batteries comprising ten guns had been destroyed by almost constant fire from a hundred artillery guns and over eighty hours of aerial bombardment.[37] On the twenty-ninth—the Emperor's birthday—the assault reached a terrible crescendo. By nightfall Corregidor lay pulverized, a smoking, dust-palled heap of rubble, lit by raging fires, reverberating with explosions.

That night two battered navy PBY seaplanes slipped through the blockade, landed offshore, unloaded quinine and artillery fuses and, still covered by night, departed quickly. They carried a few evacuees—certain older officers Wainwright believed physically unable to sustain the captivity that lay ahead, and thirty nurses, chosen for similar reasons—age, illness, wounds, or those deemed likely to break under duress.[38]

April gave way to May and hope to resignation. Beach defenses were a shambles, the pitifully small pittance the seaplanes had brought were a mockery of the promised reinforcements, and the main power plant on which all Corregidor depended was repeatedly damaged, constantly mended, and straining to operate. Without power the guns could not be raised or lowered, the searchlights could not function, Malinta would be without fresh air or light, and the water pumps could no longer operate. It was dry season and the reservoirs were dangerously low. Water was already rationed to one canteen daily per man. By the end of May, Moore estimated, Corregidor would be out of water and power.

The barrage continued, intensified on May first, again on the second. An explosion that rocked the whole island marked the demise of Battery Geary, with all its guns, on the north shore where the invasion would begin.

"SITUATION HERE IS FAST BECOMING DESPERATE," Wainwright cabled MacArthur. The few guns still operative were without height-finders, directors, or communications. Men continually repaired telephone lines while under fire. Beach defenses were underequipped and, excepting the Fourth Marines, the only men with combat infantry experience were some overage veterans from World War I and those few ill and exhausted men who had made it from Bataan.

That night the submarine *Spearfish* slipped through the blockade to evacuate a few additional aged or ailing officers and a dozen nurses—twenty-five in all. A small craft carried them the four miles to the vessel waiting just beyond the mined waters. She surfaced long enough for the passengers to board quickly and quietly. The *Spearfish* also took on last letters home and a few important documents: Wainwright sent a list of all service personnel still alive on the Rock, the final financial and military records, and a list of promotions.

The last evacuee had just boarded when the clouds parted, revealing the dark hull in the moonlight, clearly silhouetted for Japanese patrols to sight against the fires and explosions on Corregidor. Closely tailed by Japanese patrol boats in the mined waters, the *Spearfish* dove quickly from sight.

Among the letters aboard was one from Al Braun. With Corregidor's fate closing in and death or capture looming, he had one pressing matter to which he must attend. He addressed an envelope to his old friend Bishop Schuler, penned what might be his last correspondence, and enclosed a check drawn on his stateside account. The good bishop had lent him the money to finish the roof on Saint Joseph's. This would pay his last debt in full and honor the faith in which it had been given—sent via a submarine winding deeply through mined waters, pursued by enemy craft. There were at this time four Japanese destroyers and a mine layer patrolling just off Corregidor.

It would be the first time since pre-Depression days Father Albert had been out of debt—if the *Spearfish* made it through.[39]

Nurses Ullom and Mealor remained on the Rock. Mealor, though on the list slated for evacuation, had refused to go "'as long as there's a patient in the hospital'"—a "truly great act of heroism," Wainwright wrote. "She knew as well as I that she was signing her captivity warrant."[40]

Ullom felt the same as Mealor. Asked later if she would have gone had she been on the list, she said no: she came to take care of the troops. They would soon be overwhelmed with casualties.

With the departure of the *Spearfish* the troops on the Rock had lost the last tenuous contact with home. They had little time to think about it. The bombardments of the fourth and fifth virtually wiped out the beach defenses. Of the seacoast artillery only three 155-mm. guns could still fire. By day's end on 5 May the telephone lines were a mass of tangled threads; all orders must now be sent on foot under heavy fire. The power plant was on its last gasp, Moore reported, and the pumps and pipes were beyond repair. Corregidor had at most four days' supply of water. It was now a matter of hours. Corregidor writhed in its death throes.

The Japanese massed for invasion. Wainwright's intrepid agent in Manila reported the Japanese of the Fourth Division were practicing landing maneuvers and had thousands of bamboo scaling ladders, obviously intended for Corregidor's cliffs. Shortly after dark on the fifth, sound locators began picking up telltale movements off Bataan. Soon troops manning their battle stations on the tail of the Rock sighted approaching landing barges.

Intense artillery fire opened against the north shore at eight o'clock, continued for three hours, then suddenly ceased. It was in his quarters, Wainwright wrote, "at 11:15 P.M. on that night of May 5, 1942, that I got the word that had to come. . . . 'The Japs are landing. . . .'"[41]

The padre had been among the men almost continuously since the evacuees had left. He had probably said mass in the tunnel this day, but preferred always to be in the field, and contributed greatly to the high morale that still held among these men who knew the end was near. Then, whether by instinct or summons, he knew where he was most needed and when: he reported to the hospital as the casualties began to arrive in numbers.

The men on the beaches still fought furiously. Contrary currents separated the Japanese landing forces, swept them to shore east of where they had planned. The Fourth Marines were waiting for them; two 75-mm. guns still operated, and a supposedly silenced mortar from Battery Way opened up. In minutes the water off North Point was a maelstrom of Japanese bodies and sinking barges.

But numbers told. Despite tremendous losses in men, landing craft, and ammunition, the Japanese made a beachhead, landed tanks and artillery. Headed toward Malinta, they seized Battery Denver and established a line. They directed artillery fire at the tunnel's west entrance and awaited the second, larger wave that soon followed.

In a desperate dawn attack the Americans, after bloody fighting to regain the position, were overcome by tanks, machine guns, and fresh combat infantry. The forts in the bay fell one by one, until only Fort Drum still fired.

Defeat was inevitable, thousands of lives the price.

Malinta was in turmoil, a den of despair. Several hundred men died trying to defend the east tunnel. Inside, fat green horseflies swarmed in the airless heat; the stench of old sweat and overflowing latrines and of dead and dying bodies hung heavily throughout. On the hospital lateral's floors lay the wounded, waiting to be treated. Father Al never stopped lifting them, carrying them into surgery and out again, perhaps to live, more probably to die; and they kept coming and coming, over a thousand that day, walking if they could, or crawling, because there were no more corpsmen left to bear them on litters.

In the tumult of torment that was Malinta none was more tormented than Wainwright. Gaunt, exhausted, his face a map of agony, he paced the tunnel, his mind, he recounted, "reeling with the task of trying to find ways and means of averting the inevitable." Casualties were mounting, men dying. His troops could hold out perhaps another day. In the end, "it was the terror that is vested in a tank that was the deciding factor. I thought of the havoc that even one of these could wreak if it nosed into the tunnel, where lay our hapless wounded and their brave nurses."[42]

By midmorning he had made his decision. They would cease firing at noon. He ordered General Beebe to relay this to the enemy. It was then 10:15. "There is a limit to human endurance," he radioed his commander-in-chief, "and that limit has long been past. . . ."[43] It was 6 May 1942.

Corregidor's last rites began. In the tunnel men frantically destroyed records, codes, equipment, and money. Outside, obeying orders, men began demolishing the larger weapons, naval and military stores, and equipment. They heard the last "Taps" float over the desolated Rock. They watched the Stars and Stripes slide down the flagpole, and they saw her burn as the white flag ascended. It was high noon. Those who had not wept before wept now.

The chaplain stoically pursued his sad duties through the chaos: there were many to whom he must minister, many to bury before the captors arrived. He never stopped carrying the dying for last rites, the dead for burial. Toward that day's end Madeline Ullom came out with some wounded. "There was Wainwright, sitting outside the tunnel watching the casualties, and Father Braun giving last rites to the soldiers. It was the last time I saw him."[44]

The guns of Corregidor are silent now. Some still lie in quiet ruins. Courtesy of Marcello B. Gerez, photographer, Philippine Department of Tourism.

17: SKY PILOT IN HELL

Bataan and Corregidor had held out longer than any believed possible, waiting for help that never came. Sick and starved, ill equipped and outnumbered, they had cost the enemy dearly in men and time. Those on Bataan had decimated the Japanese Fourteenth Army and caused Homma to requisition forces needed elsewhere; those on Corregidor had smashed the Fourth Division on which Japan had relied for offensives in New Guinea and the Solomons. They had denied Homma the use of Manila Bay. They had intercepted messages and provided valuable intelligence. They had slowed the Japanese advance in the Pacific by six months, protected Australia from invasion, and enabled MacArthur to mount the offensive that would win eventual victory in the Pacific. Theirs had been a decisive battle in the history of the world.

The men who had fought them had no comprehension of the significance of their epic stand, nor were they at the moment particularly interested. They only knew they had done their damnedest. As the Rising Sun ascended the flagpole, "tough old soldiers who had not cried since babyhood sat on the ground and wept bitterly. Our way of life was wiped out," the padre recited. "We took on a hard life that none of us knew. Discipline, routine, work details, food, health, all took on a new look—an Oriental look."[1] Facts must be faced, "but it was a disaster; one couldn't help from feeling terrible. . . ."[2]

But his was ever the philosophy of hope. With strength and faith they would endure, knowing their country would some day come. He knew too that that day was behind a horizon lost in the mist of battles yet to be fought. The present realities were stark and demanding and immediate.

He knew the chaplains must lead. It was their toughest call yet. "We priests at no time had been prepared for what we now faced. We . . . were on the spot. We . . . sought guidance from one another, did the best we could. We . . . needed something to reorient us, . . . to meet as priests this new hard kind of life. We decided on a retreat."[3] But how? They must first assess the situation and attend to immediate needs.

The medical personnel remained in Malinta with some eight hundred sick and wounded. The senior officers were also in the tunnel, detained for interrogation, except for Wainwright, who was sent to Manila and forced to broadcast his surrender. All remaining personnel were herded into the 92nd Garage area, a ten-acre block of concrete on Bottomside, formerly a motor pool for the 92nd Coast Artillery. To break morale among the prisoners, the Japanese severed all unit cohesion by separating men from their comrades and their officers, mixing over sixteen thousand men into jumbled, confused hundred-man groups—defeated, despairing, demoralized.[4]

Bodies lay everywhere. The captors quickly forced the Americans to gather and cremate the Japanese dead. The American and Filipino bodies were left untouched. American officers, despite the pleas of the senior Protestant chaplain, dared not ask permission to bury their dead. The knew the consequences: the hospital mess officer, Captain Burton C. Thompson, had already been executed for refusing to take food away from the patients and medical staff for the Japanese officers.

Father Albert took charge. Going over the heads of his superiors— not for the first time in his life—he found an English-speaking Japanese soldier to interpret and with him approached an enemy officer who seemed to be in charge. His comrades were aghast: didn't he know he was risking his head?

Insignificant!

Apparently his persuasive charm worked. "I got permission," he later wrote in his usual brief style, "to bury the dead. In the tropics decomposition sets in very soon. Some of the bodies were in such condition that they came apart when handled. The stench was so bad that men on the detail vomited. The worst cases we burned, then buried the bones."[5]

Burial was a hasty, shallow matter in rock and without adequate tools. Chaplains were not allowed to compile rosters of the dead. They performed what rites they could, commended the spirits to God and eternity, and moved on, prodded by guards shrieking for more "Speedo!" until they had completed their grisly duty.

Rumors bred like flies in the dung heap of 92nd Garage. Facing the machine guns trained on them from the peripheral hills, many expected to be obliterated en masse at any moment. After a few days of pure bedlam the chaplains and other officers managed to restore some order, and the men settled into primitive existence. The sun seared like the fires of hell on the shadeless concrete. Two riddled hangers, once used for seaplanes, afforded the only shelter in the area. Filipinos who had arrived earlier had taken one; the first five hundred officers to arrive seized the other. The remaining thousands made makeshift shelters from blankets, pieces of tin, remains of shelter halves—anything that could provide a spot of shade. Supply Officer Cyrus Crews found and opened a cistern, from which long lines of parched men could fill their canteens. Eventually the Japanese issued rice enough for two scanty meals a day.

"Filth was beyond description," Father Al found. "Dysentery, malaria, yellow jaundice took over."[6] The only latrine facilities were open-air slit trenches that quickly began to overflow. Armies of flies swarmed everywhere, crawling into men's eyes, noses, mouths. In the steaming air hung the stench of human feces and decaying bodies.

The Japanese pressed their captives into work crews to clean up the island and to salvage any usable weaponry, ammunition, or machinery. In Malinta large caches of food, water, and medicine were discovered in a lateral when the thin layer of concrete across the entrance was broken through. Seeing five shiploads of food loaded onto Japanese vessels did not improve the morale of men who had suffered near-starvation while holding off the enemy with every ounce of their dwindling strength. Al Braun was always slow to condemn; yet thinking of Bataan's starving defenders—men who kept firing when they were so weak they could barely stand—he found the enormous food caches on Corregidor hard to condone.

"But," reasoned Baumann, "who to put the blame on for the poor logistics is hard to say. When you know you are not going to get any more supplies you no doubt get miserly with what you have. . . ."[7]

Braun and Baumann, trying to raise morale, found their most difficult challenge yet. In addition to the physical hell, the disoriented men were slowly absorbing the numbing fact of captivity, facing a black void of horror and humiliation that could stretch on for months, for years, or forever. They had only God and His chaplains on whom to rely.

For the chaplains the need for a retreat grew more pressing. But how? "Circumstances difficult," the padre recorded later. "We worked on details. Each chaplain gave conferences. Early morning, [while] still dark, another late at night. . . . We listened eagerly . . . learned it the hard way—all the best lessons in the history of man have been learned under great suffering. The subjects were: . . . need of men (Catholic and non-Catholic) for sound guidance, especially by example. . . ; our commission to all men . . .; care for body and soul. Faith, Hope, Charity. . . . Value of prayer. . . . Esprit de corps. . . . Never made a better retreat; never made a better confession."[8]

Braun and Baumann, having managed to cling to their mass kits, were allowed to say mass in Malinta's entrance and in the hospital. Though forbidden to hold services for the thousands penned in the garage area, they did so covertly and at great risk.

On 23 May, after nearly three weeks of hunger, horseflies, sun, stink, and sewage, the men were herded in groups to the docks, ferried to Manila Harbor, dumped, and forced to wade shore with whatever effects they had managed to hang onto. There they were forced to march—soaked, ragged, stumbling, and humiliated before the onlooking Filipinos—down Dewey Boulevard and then circuitously to Bilibid prison. The large wheel-shaped stone-and-concrete dungeon built in 1865 by the Spanish seemed a haven after the 92nd Garage. For all its forbidding grimness, scanty food, and concrete floors on which they had to sleep, it was cool, relatively clean (or seemed so after their late sty), and it afforded the luxury of toilets and cold showers.

The chaplains remained on Corregidor with the sick and wounded until June, then made brief stops at Bilibid and the Jesuit university in Manila, to the newly established camp called Cabanatuan. That camp was, the padre said simply, "hell on earth."[9]

Cabanatuan, situated on a wide plain about ninety miles north of Manila, comprised three former Philippine training camps, all having deteriorated considerably. All prisoners were eventually moved to Camp 1, along with the thousands of emaciated wretches from Bataan who had somehow survived what was later known as the Death March, to be penned in a hell-hole called O'Donnell, which proved so untenable that even the Japanese admitted the impossibility of remaining and began moving the prisoners to Cabanatuan early in June. It was not much better.[10]

Soon glutted with some nine thousand men, most of them wracked with dysentery, Cabanatuan soon became an incubus of contagion, spread by overflowing latrines and millions of flies, abetted by malnutrition and brutality. In addition to the diseases that swept the camp, they had to endure the harsh rules imposed by the sadistic camp commander, Lieutenant Colonel Shigeji Mori. Their every act was stringently regulated—when and how much water they could drink, when they could visit the latrine. They must assemble twice daily for roll call. They must never go within two meters of the inside fence. (Three soon ringed the camp.) They must salute or bow to all Japanese soldiers. Most chilling of all was Mori's division of all POWs into ten-man squads: if one escaped or tried to, the other nine would all face the death penalty with the perpetrator.

It was in this state that Father Al found 'his boys' from Bataan when he arrived.

When barred from any religious activity, the padre resorted to covert means—leading a rosary behind a chicken coop, or saying a mass in a latrine, behind a barracks, or in a wooded copse on a work detail while the guard was otherwise occupied. On one such clandestine operation soon after he arrived, he came on one of his altar boys from Tularosa, Alberto Gonzales. The word had been quietly passed around that a priest would hold a service if possible at a certain time and place, and Alberto had made his way to the tryst. "And there was Father Albert saying mass," after which "the first thing he said to me was 'How's your brother?'"[11] Theirs was among the first of happy reunions with his old friends.

Tom Foy remembered him saying mass behind a barracks "where the Japs couldn't find us. Al Suttman and I and some others served as altar boys."[12] Suttman remembered masses in the fields. "He'd hear our confessions—knelt right down by his knee. Of course, as a POW you couldn't sin much."[13]

Such furtive operations were difficult and risky. When apprehended, the padre took the beating, shrugged his large shoulders, and resumed his clandestine rites.

It was from 'his boys' that he learned of the Death March. "Men were covered in their own filth," one related. "Eyes were blank, and we were walking zombies. We had seen men drown in human excrement; bodies laid open by bayonets; heads cracked by blows from gun butts. The days and nights became progressively more nightmarish. Our brains, bodies, and souls were numb, and we were no longer human."[14]

He learned of beheadings; of men crazed with thirst, shot or bayoneted for trying to get a canteen of water from the artesian wells flowing along the way; of men pushed into latrine pits and held under until they died. He learned of many who fell by the roadside, around whom the guards gathered to torture before they killed. He learned of men gone mad on the March. He learned of the filth, starvation, disease, and continuing brutality his friends had endured at Camp O'Donnell, and he vowed to do all within his strength to alleviate such suffering in this camp.

Dysentery and malaria were the biggest killers at Cabanatuan, the contagion of the first brought from O'Donnell and spread by the blankets of flies, the second carried by the mosquitoes that bred in whining droves in the stagnant water that collected during the beginning rainy season. A primitive hospital comprised a number of erstwhile barracks; but without medical or surgical equipment, soap or cleaning supplies, they quickly became pestholes. Doctors and medics slipped on the feces-covered floors trying to tend their patients. There was little the doctors could do, and some gave up trying. Others worked ungodly hours, and these Father Al vowed to help.

The camp was divided into three sections, that of the Japanese in the middle, through which all must pass to reach the hospital area, which Mori declared "out of bounds to rest of camp. They can't come over here," Dr. Calvin Jackson recorded, "and we can't go over there, unless Nips give permission."[15] Somehow the padre wangled access, if only to dispense a kind word here, a cigarette there, a little hoarded food when possible, or a few canteens of water gained after a long wait in line.

He was forbidden to go near the cemetery, where constant processions of men on burial details carried dead comrades on shutters of woven *sawali*, to dump them into mass graves, perhaps to whisper a hurried prayer. Neither rites nor chaplains were allowed.[16] Half a hundred men had died by the end of June; July took another seven hundred sixty-eight.[17]

The doctors repeatedly pled for medicine, beds, surgical equipment, disinfectant, soap; Mori as repeatedly refused. Father Albert began surreptitiously to seek contacts with the outside, for the hospital and for the rest of the camp, which fared little better. "They promised us 750 grams of rice per day per man," he wrote, an amount on which the doctors predicted they would all be dead in a year. "We actually received 400 grams of rice a day, and except for a little fruit we could swipe and a cup of water daily, that's all we got." Despite predictions, "48% survived. A lot depends on a man's will to live."[18]

In time an elaborate underground system would evolve wherein agents on both sides of the fence smuggled food, medicine, and other badly needed supplies into the camp. But that was still in the offing when Father Al arrived. Working on his own he met and began covertly working with the courageous Father Buddenbroch. Described as "a tall, white-haired, rosy-cheeked padre, wearing the sweeping, brimmed black hat with round crown and black cassock of his order,"[19] Buddenbroch had lived in and worked out of Christ the King cloister in Manila for almost a quarter century. Because he was a German citizen, and hence a supposed Japanese ally, Mori sometimes allowed him to enter the camp, and even on occasion to bring specified gifts—musical instruments for the band the prisoners were organizing, sometimes a little food and tobacco. What Mori did not know was that the amiable priest had enormous pockets sewn into his overlarge cassock, laden with contraband articles—medicine for the doctors, mass wine and wafers for the chaplains (Catholic and Protestant), mail, and money.

In addition to Buddenbroch, Father Al seems to have made covert contacts from among the Philippine civilians and priests in the nearby barrio, who did what they could to pass on messages and smuggle in necessities. They would soon prove invaluable.

The padre had not been long at Cabanatuan when diphtheria struck. Within days it was epidemic. Despite warehouses full of antitoxin, Mori rejected the doctors' pleas. When the Bishop of Manila brought in a large supply, Mori sent it back. Always resourceful, Father Al went in the night to the fence, got word through somehow, which in turn was relayed to Buddenbroch. Priests began combing Manila for serum.

Then Father Al was himself stricken.

Men in the diphtheria ward watched their friends die, each wondering when he would be next. Despite the padre's own illness, one patient observed, he said mass daily, "and the Jap guard would pause and then go on by."[20]

Among the desperately ill Father Albert found Captain Gerald Greeman, of the old 200th, close to death. About that time the doctors walked into the ward with a timely supply of smuggled-in antitoxin. Buddenbroch's priests had come through. There was not enough for everyone, Greeman attested, "so we drew straws. I was paired with the padre, and he won. But he said, 'Give it to Gerald.' I would have died except for him."[21] Greeman recovered. So, miraculously, did Father Al, who quickly resumed his smuggling activities.

"He thought of us first," Tom Foy remembered. "He constantly gave up his food for others he believed needed it more. I don't know how he was able to find medicine. . . . I learned later he had a connection with some priests in a barrio outside camp—they'd send medicine in to him. If the Japs had found out he'd have been shot immediately." Nor, he added, did the padre care what a man's faith was. "Catholic, Baptist, Methodist, Presbyterian—the men were all the same to Father Braun. And he saved a lot of lives."[22]

Foy's was one. Someone had sneaked some jalapeño peppers in from work detail, which Foy and some friends mixed into their rice. It proved too much for Foy's weakened stomach. "Pretty soon I grew dizzy and suddenly started bleeding from the mouth. The boys took me to the sick area's gate, and when Father Braun came along he saw me bleeding. He ran for a doctor, and came up with the last morphine in the camp," after which Foy passed out. The Japanese threw him into 'Zero Ward,' reserved for the dying. A friend who worked in the Japanese kitchen was alerted (apparently by Father Al) and began smuggling in soup he stole each night. Foy recovered.

The largest undertaking at Cabanatuan was a three-thousand-acre farm, for which several thousand starving POWs drew what they called 'Farmer Jones detail.' They cleared ten-feet-high cobra-infested cogon grass with knives; they attacked giant termite hills taller than a man; they hauled water and human fertilizer in ten-gallon cans; they tilled clay soil with pick and hoe. No one dared lag. As one recorded in his well hidden diary, "they beat men unconscious, then kick and beat him some more. They work men inhumanely. Had six of us carrying heavy boards from the old farm to the new. Our muscles knotted and we staggered, and two men collapsed. Our shoulders were so bruised and cut, we could hardly get back."[23]

The resultant produce, they were told, would feed the POWs. In reality they got nothing from it except what they could steal, which was hazardous though not impossible. They risked, and reaped, many a beating to fill a canteen with beans or to stuff pigweed beneath their hats. When one reached for a piece of okra through the fence, "a Nip guard shot him twice, and as he lay dying, crying for help, drove away any who sought to succor him."[24]

Morale plunged. Many gave up, willed themselves to die. Father Al did what he could to cheer the cheerless, always made himself be happy, no matter how tough the going. "You're whipped," he insisted, "when you start feeling sad."

The padre worked in the fields alongside the men, even when still weak from his bout with diphtheria. He constantly covered for men caught stealing food, or men too weak to produce their quotas, and took many a beating for them. The tougher the going, the more jokes he found to tell.

He made friends of all faiths. One with whom he spent many hours talking was a tall Kiowa-Comanche from Oklahoma named Bruce Klinekole. They met through the Baldonado brothers, with whom Bruce had made the Death March, and later in prison camp persuaded the non-Catholic Indian to come with them to Father Al's sub-rosa masses behind the barracks.

The Baldonados decided Klinekole would make a good husband for Virginia Shanta if any of them ever got home. They began talking about her beauty, her firm character, her many virtues. Father Al joined in their praise, and they spent many hours talking in the night about many things, Virginia Shanta among them. Bruce Klinekole fell in love.

One night, as he and the padre talked privately and softly, he confided his intentions. He was going to live through this, he said. Sooner or later, he agreed with Father Al, the Yanks and tanks would come. And when that happened, he vowed, he was coming to Mescalero and marry Virginia Shanta.[25]

Bruce would come home: he had someone to come home to. One can imagine Father Al's craggy face creasing into broad smiles in the dark. Even in a Japanese prison camp the padre was matchmaking.

✠✠✠

Early in October a large group, Chaplains Braun and Baumann among them, were told they were to leave Cabanatuan. One detail had already shipped out for Manchuria and Japan, where the Japanese, to ease their serious shortage of manpower, would augment their war industry with the forced labor of the prisoners.[26] Braun's group was destined for the southern Philippine island of Mindanao.

John Borneman was sorry to lose his fellow chaplain. "During the critical period . . . as prisoners of the Japanese Father Braun went about giving the men hope, comfort, and easing their pain. He gave them good advice and in general contributed greatly to their peace of mind. . . . In every way Father Braun is a priest of whom your order may well be proud. He is most faithful, humble, a hard worker and keenly interested in the welfare of the men. . . . [H]is morale was always high but he faced reality and facts as they presented themselves to us."[27] Borneman was not the only man at Cabanatuan who hated to see the padre leave.

After several alerts and many rumors, close to a thousand men, mostly ill but ambulatory, were assembled at two in the morning, given a small portion of watery rice porridge, and marched fifteen miles in pounding rain to board a train to Manila. There they walked from the depot to the docks. "Manila dead as we marched to ship," Doctor Calvin Jackson recorded in his carefully secreted diary. "Shops locked or boarded up. . . . Filipinos lined streets. We got lots of winks and saw tears in women's eyes."[28] At Pier 7 they were forced into the steamy hold of the *Erie Maru,* a one-time American freighter. They sailed at noon the next day. It was 28 October 1942.

As on the other 'hell ships,' the latrine facilities for the vomiting, dysentery-plagued men consisted of buckets raised and lowered on ropes, their contents dumped overboard. Heat mounted in the almost airless hold, and with it the stench. Even so, those on the *Erie* fared better than their comrades on other ships. The food was adequate, the crew less abusive. The doctors and chaplains were allowed to bring the sickest cases onto the deck where they could breathe fresh sea air. But for those in the crowded, stinking hold the ten-day voyage was one of pure horror. Two men died en route.

Except when needed on deck the doctors and chaplains stayed below with their men, to minister as best they could to bodies and souls. They led men in prayer and song throughout the long sweltering hours of filth and darkness. Father Al's good friend Chaplain Ted Howden, who had enlisted his aid on Bataan, was aboard, ill with dysentery and the starvation-induced pellagra that would soon claim his life. Braun and Baumann bathed, fed, and otherwise cared for him during the voyage.

While docked briefly at Cebu to unload supplies they saw many wrecked and burned ships. More signs of Allied activity appeared as they neared their destination. Off Mindanao, hugging the shoreline, "Nips shot off antiaircraft guns a few times. . . . Nips told us we were in dangerous waters."[29]

On 7 November they docked at Lasang, twenty-five miles up the bay from Davao. No tears were shed at leaving the *Erie Maru.* After spending several hours in a treeless, sun-broiled clearing, all who could walk began the final fifteen-mile trek to Davao Penal Colony—Dapecol for short. Howden gathered enough strength to make the walk, "but was immediately sent to the hospital. . . . [H]e had gone the end of his rope. . . ."[30] At some time after two in the morning the long line of POWs staggered into their new camp and fell exhausted.

With morning they began to settle into large wooden barracks, take their bearings, and meet, mingle, and exchange news with the eleven hundred Americans captured in the southern islands after Corregidor fell. Most were from Malaybalay in northern Mindanao who had arrived shortly before. These men, thus far well fed and well treated, and having experienced relatively little combat, were shocked on seeing the gaunt, ragged survivors of Bataan and Corregidor. The newcomers were just as astounded to see the healthy specimens who greeted them.

If the group from Malaybalay expected Dapecol to be another easy berth, the Japanese camp commander, Major Kazuo Maeda, immediately disillusioned them. "You not here to lazy," he informed the assembled men. This was a work camp, originally built as a prison where convicts worked in the surrounding rice paddies and vegetable fields, or in related trades. Most of the convicts had been relocated; the hard labor would now fall to the POWs.

Annoyed at finding so many of the new group too weak to work, grumbling that he had asked for workers, not skeletons, Maeda ordered an increase in rations until they were fit for the labor he expected. Meanwhile anyone who could walk must go to work immediately. Details were dispatched to work the fields, chop wood, dig ditches, or repair roads. Some worked on the pig or chicken farms or drove carabao for plowing. One group went to Davao city to work in a hemp mill. "Our very sick cases," to Jackson's horror, "were ones marked 'light duty.' Nips had them outside fence digging details in hot sun and working in the sawmill."[31] The most grueling duty, and one few escaped, was in the backbreaking toil in the rice paddies.

It rained almost daily, sometimes a quick shower, often intense and prolonged downpours. Men sweated in boiling steam or shivered in wind-laced torrents. Rain-collecting hollows and water-filled paddies bred mosquitoes by millions, and men not already malaria-ridden soon were.

Food was for a time adequate if uninspiring; but even with increased rations they were always hungry. There was never enough. Some few, among them Chaplains Braun, Baumann, and Howden (even in his illness) often did without, giving their shares to others. Braun, with his inborn toughness, survived. So did Baumann. Howden, ill before the journey, did not. From the time he contracted dysentery at Cabanatuan, he "began to go down," wrote John J. Morrett, Howden's close friend and fellow Episcopalian, though he "continued to work holding services each Sunday, going to the cemetery almost everyday. . . . [T]he trip down [to Mindanao] was most difficult. . . . It was just too much for him and the long march at the end . . . was difficult."[32] Howden seems to have been in the hospital more than out from then on. Father Al did what he could for his friend until, on 11 December 1942, Howden died. "I diagnosed him with pellagra," Jackson recorded.[33]

Two services marked the Americans' first Christmas Eve in captivity. Maeda allowed an Episcopal service at midnight and a Catholic mass an hour later. Many attended both, grateful to again be allowed to worship. Another boon was granted on 29 January as long-awaited Red Cross boxes were distributed—food and toiletries, and for the doctors badly needed medical supplies.[34] They came none too soon. Many felt that except for family and friends most of America had forgotten them. Morale soared: the 'battling bastards' were not forgotten. Somebody did give a damn.

But to counter the boxes, Maeda sharply cut rations; and when the Red Cross supplies were gone he refused to restore their former food allowance. Morale plummeted. Even these scant rations would be cut again on several occasions.

Optimism was inborn in Father Al. "Take what you get in life and like it," he always stressed, and would later assert that "being an optimist kept me alive when we were naked, sleeping in the mud and living on two spoons of rice a day."[35] But the ever-innovative chaplain spiked his optimism with large doses of gumption. There was indeed manna from heaven, he asserted; it was growing right outside the fence—papayas, bananas, avocados, and acres of fields rich with rice and vegetables. With a little ingenuity, a little bit of luck. . . .

Getting outside the fence compound was easy. Daily details fanned in all directions, and he routinely headed thirty-man groups. Getting back inside past the guards was harder. *Insignificant!* He devised ways of getting through these shakedowns and trained his crews in such fine arts. "We had no clothes except sandals, a loincloth, and a Chinese-style hat," he wrote his Provincial later. "We made our own hats and I told my men to make mine with big crowns to hide stolen food in." Loincloths could be artfully draped to conceal contraband. He quickly learned which guards could be distracted, and he had an incredible ability to diffuse tension at critical moments with suspicious guards. When he failed he took the blame and the beating.

He became so adept at stealing food the men began calling him 'Al Capone,' which made him grin: it was an accolade. "Fortunately," he explained, he had lived on the Mescalero reservation, where "the Apaches taught me how to steal and not get caught."[36]

On one detail, as Father Baumann remembered it, the padre psyched out the Japanese sergeant in charge and decided he looked "like a decent Joe." Father Al worked his crew hard a day or so and then approached him: if he wanted the boys to keep working that well, they needed food. Could he—the chaplain—and three men go into the forest and pick some coconuts?

No, no! They would attack the guard and escape—and he—the sergeant—would be blamed.

Father Al proposed a bargain: if anyone tried to escape, he promised, "you can cut off my head!"

It seemed fair enough to the sergeant. Okay: three men, with Braun's head at stake.

The padre ran back to his crew. Would anyone like to see a Catholic priest's head on a platter? A few grinned. "Okay, you Texas Baptists," he whooped. "Here's your chance!"

They got their coconuts; the padre kept his head.[37]

On another detail, he wrote his provincial years later, "I worked hard for two weeks, [until] the Jap guards no longer watched me. Then I stole some wild bananas." He kept this racket going throughout his time at Dapecol, "and kept myself and many friends alive." 'Al Capone' earned his nickname.

"One priest," he continued, "—a chaplain—told me: 'Father, don't you realize it is a sin to steal!' I answered him, 'Yes it is a sin to steal, but it is a great[er] sin to kill. You keep on killing because you won't steal bananas. . . . Then in a few years from now, we will see who goes deepest into Hell, Father Albert Braun OFM for stealing or you, my dear friend, for killing because you would not steal some bananas to keep friends alive.'

"My dear Father provincial," he ended his letter, "you solve that problem!"[38]

"I am sure," his provincial answered, "you will win and have a high place in heaven for your craftiness in obtaining bananas."[39]

Although the Japanese at Dapecol tolerated church services, religious duties were considered extracurricular, and chaplains could not miss any work details. Father Albert therefore said mass at three-thirty each morning to allow time for other chaplains to conduct their services before work, which began at six.[40] Other ministerial obligations had to wait until after work details.

There was always the problem of procuring mass wine and wafers. In this he was aided by a Filipina named Lulu Reyes. About six months after arriving in Mindanao he was handed a package. "My dear Chaplains," the attached note began. "Thru the kindness of Mr. Abe we are sending you some rosaries, medals, novenas and a few cakes of soap.

"If you need any religious articles please let Mr. Abe know and the Chaplain's Aid Association will try its very best to help you. . . ." Who Mr. Abe was is unclear, but he was obviously someone to whom the chaplains had some access, directly or through channels.

Father Albert kept the message and later appended a note. ". . . Lulu is a great heroine. After the surrender of Corregidor with her mother she went to the Hq of the Com. Gen. of the Japanese armies in the P.I. and asked permission to carry on her duties. At great inconvenience and many risks she kept us supplied with what was necessary for religious services. . . ."[41]

At roll call on the evening of 4 April 1943 a ten-man group was reported missing. They had gone out on detail that morning and failed to return.

It was not a total surprise to Father Albert. For some time whispers had made their quiet rounds. One chaplain, Father Richard Carberry, had spoken with the padre relative to plans in progress among the now-missing group. If given a chance to escape, Carberry had asked the padre, would he take it? He had, like others, dreamed of such a chance, Braun answered. But no longer: his work here was important. He said his daily masses; his men depended on him; he had comforted many in need of spiritual guidance, hope, and the laughs 'Al Capone' could give them. Most significant was what the camp would suffer because of any escape. Even should Maeda not invoke the ten-man rule, the rest of the camp would suffer harsh recriminations. He could not be party to any such escape.

Carberry, swayed by this reasoning, refused at the last minute to go.

Much later, on learning that Carberry had died on a hell ship, the padre suffered the guilt of his own advice, a weight made heavier when he learned that the escapees had gotten safely away.[42]

At the time, however, Father Al's judgment proved wise. American Camp Commander Colonel Kenneth S. Olsen, the barracks officers, and men in whose squadrons any of the missing men had belonged were taken to Japanese headquarters for questioning and later confined "to meditate."

"Our whole barracks was locked in a compound for thirty days on one ration a day, to await the execution order," Captain Russell Hutchison recalled. "We couldn't even speak to each other. Each morning we were taken out, wondering if we were going to be shot." They were not, but they came close.

Maeda, who had never stressed the ten-man death rule overmuch, had, unknown to the Americans, flown to Manila to intercede. "Then," Hutchison continued, "came the big morning of our audience. We were scared—had been for thirty days. They always executed for escapes. Troops with their guns stood on either side of the road, and a group of sedans rolled up. Our little old hunchbacked interpreter got out of a car and passed down the word: Maeda had stayed the execution."[43]

Meanwhile, as those pent in the compound awaited their fate, Japanese patrols searched for days, though men reported to Dr. Jackson that "Japs will not get off trail as they are afraid."[44] Their fear was well founded. Two days after the escape a guard was shot and killed, apparently by guerrillas who forever stalked the jungle. Guards grew more surly. Men were clubbed, kicked, beaten for small lapses or none. Work hours grew longer, labor harder. The POWs were ordered to show penitence: they could no longer laugh or sing or converse in groups. Church services were limited to one weekly, without sermons or masses.

This presented a challenge Father Albert could not refuse. As at Cabanatuan, he resumed covert operations. Behind a barracks, in forest or field, wherever he could smuggle his scarred and dented mass kit, he defied his captors. Years later men still recalled their padre, barefoot, his habit a g-string and a large-crowned straw hat, offering the host as solemnly and as eloquently as if he were elaborately robed and in a fine cathedral. Apparently Lulu Reyes still managed somehow to slip mass wine into the barbed-wire prison.

Father Brendan Mitchell, some years after the war, recounted a story the padre had told of sitting "among a group of starving buddies in the dirt and stifling heat. His only vestment . . . a sort of loin cloth. Among them they had a crust of bread, and Al had secreted a couple of capsules smuggled through . . . Filipino natives, I believe, containing a few precious drops of wine. That bleak day Mass was celebrated at the edge of hell."[45]

Hard labor and slashed rations began to exact their toll on bodies already ravaged by malaria, dysentery, and pellagra. The starving men watched as the food their toil had produced was loaded onto trucks and hauled away. When American officers begged Maeda to increase rations, he answered angrily that he had none, even as papayas, bananas, and avocados ripened and rotted just outside the fence. Then in August he cut the rice ration again.[46]

Smuggling food into camp became more necessary than ever. It also became more difficult and more dangerous. Guards on detail were more watchful, shakedowns at the gate more frequent, and punishment more severe. Well, then, shrugged the padre, they must take more care not to be caught. That was a challenge worthy of 'Al Capone.'

G-strings, if lined and lapped, held a surprising amount of purloined produce. So did the ponchos they made from scraps of tarpaulin, ostensibly for rainwear. The crowns in their barracks-woven hats grew taller. Fruits and vines from the jungle, produce from the fields, eggs from the chicken farm—all were quickly grabbed, eaten on the spot, or furtively stowed. They noted which guards were less attentive or more easily distracted. The padre in his genial way grew masterly at sidetracking the guards, and when their attention was diverted his speed at snatching the coveted morsel was worthy of Houdini. When short of mass wine he found the guards' cache and lifted the loot. He dug through the supply-room wall and found rice. He had always enjoyed life, he wrote later, "even as a POW. My main fun then was stealing. . . . It was only by stealing some food that one could remain alive."[47] In the fine arts of thievery and trickery 'Al Capone' excelled. The need was greater than the sin. On details the thieves ate what they could not hide and smuggled what they could for friends too weak to work or for doctors to give their patients. They saved many lives.

Still, it was touch and go, and the rugged padre wasted to a six-foot skeleton. Like so many others, he was struck with beriberi, apparently in the spring of 1943.[48] Resulting from vitamin deficiency, beriberi damages the nerves severely and causes an extreme pain in grossly swollen feet and legs, often likened to electric shock. Walking is, if possible at all, excruciating.

After a stay in the prison hospital, the hardheaded Braun, refusing to give in, returned—though painfully—to his duties, still laughing, still making others laugh. Sometimes he started a song, and it lightened the load, especially in the rice paddies where, often toiling from four in the morning until nine at night, they plowed, planted, and harvested in water. "We threw it in huge baskets hung from bamboo poles with a man at each end," one prisoner recounted. "It was all we could do to pick the thing up—carry it knee-deep in water to the little railroad, then push the cars uphill. I often wondered how we'd make it."[49] Sometimes mild-to-medium earthquakes roiled the water in the paddies, threw it crazily against the dykes, the palm trees swayed dizzily, and it seemed to some symbolic of the whole warring world.

One rainy night, as the men, weak, ill, discouraged, strained miserably at pulling the rice train, a voice rose. "While the storm clouds gather . . ." someone sang, and others joined in. "'God bless America!' We were all singing, and the Japs were scared—thought we were going to take off and do something. But—there wasn't any place to go."[50]

Father Albert never forgot the Christmas of 1943. As the holiday approached the men faced another Yuletide far from home and wondered how many others they might spend in captivity. Late in October two more Americans and a Filipino had killed a guard on detail and escaped, and rations had again been cut. The long anticipated Red Cross supplies, they learned, would not arrive.

They made the best of it. One group staged a variety show of skits and music that cheered the homesick men; and apparently Father Baumann, covertly or otherwise, said a mass. It is easy to see head chaplain Braun's hand in arranging the event.

There were of course no crèche, no tree, no gifts—except for one. It was a small booklet, made of whatever tattered pieces of paper the prisoners could scrounge, tied together with a scrap of cord. On the cover, sketched in pencil, was a wooden altar with a bamboo rail and a small plaque marked "Sacred Heart Church." Beneath was lettered "Peace on Earth to all Good Will."

Inscribed within to "Major Albert William Braun, O.F.M., Chaplain," the text followed. ". . . As a fellow prisoner, you have carried your share of the load; as a soldier, you have been a guide and an example; and as a priest, you have aided us immeasurably in living in conformity with God's laws.

"We thank you, in these troublous times of untold physical suffering and mental anguish, that the Christ Child permits us . . . the inspirational consolation of your presence." Dated "Christmas Day 1943."

Nearly three hundred signatures filled the pages for their chaplain who, as later summarized, "had taken beatings for them, who had made up excuses to keep them from being penalized, and who had given up his own food so that they could eat."[51] He kept and cherished the ragged little gift throughout his years.

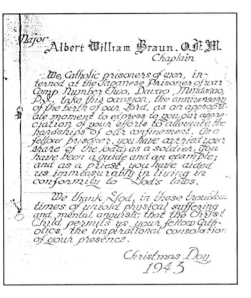

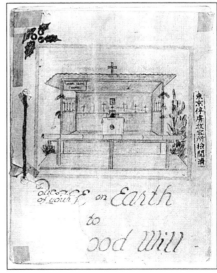

Booklet given Father Albert in Mindanao prison camp.
Courtesy of Archives, Old Mission Santa Barbara (SBA).

The prisoners were heartbreakingly happy when the Red Cross packages arrived in the spring, to be doled out sparingly and eaten bit by bit, that they might last as long as possible.

It was well they held some back. On 27 March another eight men escaped, leaving five guards dead. Recrimination was hard and swift. As patrols fanned out in wide search, many details were canceled, which drastically cut chances for smuggling. The guards grew more watchful and more vengeful. Rations were cut again.

But with each cut in rations, with each increase in cruelty, the prisoners knew the Allies had won another battle. Air activity heightened. Rumors filtered in from Filipinos via prisoners on truck-driving detail. Each time their captors boasted of winning another battle, the Americans noted it was closer than the last: the Allies were obviously pushing the enemy back, an observation further emphasized by Japanese preparations for attack. The Americans were put to work clearing banana trees for a field of fire—against guerrillas? Or Allied landings?[52] By late summer they were digging revetments and foxholes; by the following spring a detail returning from Lasang reported a runway being built there.[53] Small signs of increasing guerrilla activity cheered the men—packages of Lucky Strike cigarettes, small caches of food, sometimes a scribbled note on the edges of the fields in which they worked, a dead guard. Native drums—the 'bamboo telegraph'—rolled mysterious messages through the nights, and they knew the unseen unsurrendered were about their dark work. The guards grew increasingly edgy.

Rumors were rife and men fed on them: there was always the chance one might be true. Many were in fact true, their source the most closely guarded and most dangerous secret on the island of Mindanao. If the advancing American forces neared the area, Maeda had told Colonel Olsen, all POWs would be executed. To keep the camp intact and save the men when the Yanks came, Olsen had to know ahead. He found his answer in Russell Hutchison.

'Hutch' was a captain in New Mexico's old 200th, and adept at electronics. He believed he could build a radio, he told Olsen, if he could steal parts. Olsen immediately assigned him to the machine shop. There he began to steal—a filament here, a tube there, wire, tapes, resistors from junked radios, telephones, electrical discards. With the help of trusted—and expert—friends he smuggled the parts into camp. There he assembled the tiny set in a piece of hollowed-out mahogany four inches long and half that wide. It looked like any other scrap of wood.

Finally he began to operate, setting up in the watch shop run by Colonel Arden Boellner. "We had to keep it secret," Hutch stressed. "Clyde Ely, Charlie Brown, Boellner, and Jack Day—an Air Corps instrument man—worked with me. The guards inspected on the hour," at the same time the news for which they listened came through. "It took them fifty-five seconds from the gate to Boellner's shop. Charlie sat on a bench facing the guard shed, and Clyde sat on another halfway down.

"When the gate opened, Charlie crossed his legs by Barracks 1, which was Clyde's signal to come from behind Barracks 4, walk past our building toward the latrine, and knock on our window. On that knock, Jack and I dismantled the set. He'd leave with the wood and coil. I'd slip Clyde the radio, wrapped in an old piece of shelter tent. I fitted the tube and head set into an old sewing kit.

"Clyde sat in one latrine and Charlie in the other, holding the radio and sewing kit between their legs, to drop if the Japs came. After the guards left, they'd bury the parts under the barracks, and I'd go and brief Olsen on the news." Olsen relayed what was important to certain officers, who let bits and pieces leak as rumors. It was the only safe way to do it.

"The object of the radio was to know ahead and keep the camp intact, to save everyone when they came. We weren't risking our necks every night just to give out news. . . . My radio was a regenerative set, which sends out a signal. You can tell in a minute if there's one anywhere, and you can locate it. . . . The shakedown lasted two days."[54] It was incredibly dangerous. The *kempetai* (secret police) were constantly searching for radios as perpetrators of possible sabotage, subversion, or communication with Allied forces.

How much Father Al knew of the operation is uncertain. Names were never mentioned. As head chaplain he was certainly among those on whom Olsen relied to keep the camp intact when the time came. The padre knew Hutchison, Ely, Brown, and Boellner. What knowledge he had of the radio was probably peripheral; but he would soon be drawn into the ring.

☦ ☦ ☦

Bits of filtered-down news, telltale clues, and tension among the Japanese all gave the Americans hope: the Yanks were coming! Their captors too marked the progress as MacArthur and Nimitz leapfrogged up the Pacific. As American forces continued to advance, the Japanese, acting on orders regarding prisoners—*that none, under any circumstances, should be recovered*—began to move the POWs north, beginning with the southern islands.

Early on the morning of 6 June 1944 the first and largest contingent of Americans on Mindanao "were stripped of clothes, except shorts, searched, and put in truck[s], standing, blindfolded, and tied together, no shoes." At Tibunko the 1,239 Americans were herded into the filthy hold of an old freighter, "so crowded most of us had to stand."[55] Once more the weary men faced a passage by sea, this time on the hell ship *Yashu Maru*.

They missed the biggest news yet: even as they boarded, the Allies were landing on the Normandy beaches. Hutch's radio was stowed among the ratty baggage in a separate hold, sealed in Red Cross corned beef cans, packed so carefully no one could detect they had been tampered with. The tube, too large for the corned beef cans, fit into an innocent looking cocoa tin. Hutch had dropped an okra pod into the side pocket of his old musette bag that held the precious cargo, so he could identify it in the dark. "Thank God," he said later, "I did."

They sweltered in Davao Harbor for nearly a week before the *Yashu* sailed, to anchor briefly but eventfully in Zamboanga harbor on the fourteenth. There two men, in separate escapes, jumped ship and swam narrowly but successfully to shore, eventually to join guerrillas.[56] In retribution, rations aboard were cut, the nearly thirteen hundred men shoved and beaten into two already crowded holds, and the hatches boarded down.

Debarking at Cebu on the seventeenth, they were herded into a fenced compound in the old San Pedro prison. A tin shed accommodated a few; the rest remained outside. Wrecked ships in the harbor and the bomb-cratered city attested to recent Yank activity, marked by darting eyes and poorly suppressed smiles among the POWs.

That joy was tempered for Olsen and Hutchison when a detail sent to unload the *Yashu*, having been alerted to locate Hutch's bag, failed to find it among the piles on the wharf. By the time the prisoners were rushed to board a second ship four days later, Hutch was frantic.

"I dropped into the hold, onto all this ratty baggage. Just a tiny light came through the cracks over the hatch, and I was feeling among hundreds of bags for one okra pod. It was just luck I found it—

"And the cans had been twisted open!

"But looters wanted food, I guess, and they'd left the parts." How to repack them? "Some of the men had some Red Cross soap, which Olsen scrounged, and for two days I squatted in that hold under a little crack of light, in 120° heat, carving out those damned bars of soap! Then I spent another five days packing the pieces inside, and I stuffed the shavings back and reformed the bars. I had only one source of liquid to stick them together—I urinated on the blooming things!"

The choke was too large for the soap, but Dr. Calvin Jackson had a pill bottle. "I don't know what the hell it is," he grinned, "but I'll take it."

Unaware of the frenzied activity of Hutch and Olsen, the rest of the POWs were elated: the hasty boarding and hurried sailing signaled an impending attack. They knew then that American troops were getting close.

The ship, known only as *824*, Jackson noted, was sizeable, "but we are in two small holds. . . . Only air through hatch. Dirty, dirty! . . . We can only get out of hold to go to latrine. . . . 600 in a hold, so there is no lying down. . . ."[57]

They docked at Manila on 25 June and walked to Bilibid, where mail from home cheered many. Fathers Braun and Baumann each received packages from their families. Though they had been stored for some time, Baumann found it "exciting getting a package from home. . . . [T]here were worms in the packages—but we didn't mind." On opening his, Father Al "found vermin has sucked all the sugar out of the chocolate." No matter: they scraped off the vermin and enjoyed a feast.[58]

One more hurdle loomed for Hutchison and his abettors, each of whom carried one of the critical bars of soap. Inspection at Bilibid was cursory, but, as Hutch recounted, the guards at Cabanatuan closely inspected Day's cocoa can . . . Ely's soap . . . Brown's soap . . . and handed each one back. But the doctors had to pour their pills onto a blanket. Jackson scratched a hasty hole and buried Hutch's choke before the inspectors got to him. Two guards lingered, and he had to march on. He carefully noted the spot.

That night, under cover of heavy rain, the doctor crawled through mud and darkness, groped until he located the contraband, and crawled back in. Hutch had his choke by morning.

The once-teeming Cabanatuan to which Father Albert returned seemed a ghost camp. To prevent any POWs from being retaken by the oncoming American forces, the Japanese had launched mass evacuations.

Hell ships, armed and unmarked, their holds crammed with hapless human cargo, steamed to Manchuria and Japan, where the prisoners were forced into slave labor for Japanese war industries. The factories, the steel mills, the smelters and mines and shipyards were manned by the POWs, and the war-bound ships were loaded by Allied stevedores. His group would soon go as well, Father Al knew; Cabanatuan was only a stopover.

Meanwhile he would serve what was left of his own group from Mindanao—five hundred had been left at Bilibid for a hasty trek north—and the few prisoners remaining at Cabanatuan who were too sick to leave plus a skeleton crew to look after them and keep the camp open. One overwhelming fact drew the padre's immediate attention: the men in Cabanatuan were starving. Rations consisted of a dab of rice, a few wild greens, and some watery soup per serving.

Nor was any food or medicine filtering in through the underground. In May 1944, about a month before Father Al arrived, the Japanese, having uncovered the network, had seized and tortured the ringleaders inside the camp, interrogated, beaten, and executed civilian intermediaries outside it, and thrown the operatives into Santiago prison. They tortured Father Buddenbroch until he died.

'Al Capone' and his Dapecol gang, put to work immediately on the farm, resumed their old pilfering habits. The padre always welcomed a game of wits—and the sick were better fed.

The Japanese had relaxed their ban on religious services and the padres set up an altar in a building near the Japanese headquarters dubbed the 'chapel.' "We still had our Mass kits with us," Baumann wrote, "which we carried at all times. Pretty badly beaten up vessels and vestments, but I am sure the Good Lord was pleased with our efforts."[59] Agapito 'Gap' Silva, one of Father Al's New Mexicans, carved a cross from a sapling for the altar.[60]

They had not been long at Cabanatuan when Hutch approached Father Al. On arriving he had learned of another clandestine radio, a battery-operated set enclosed in a mess kit, built, oddly, by another Hutchison. For safety's sake the two Hutchisons never met. Through a go-between it was agreed that the other—Homer Hutchison—would continue to operate his, and Russell would stand by for emergency.

That emergency had arrived, he told Father Al one afternoon. But he needed a power source; the prisoners' quarters had no electricity. Could he use the outlet for the small red light over the altar?

"Russell," the padre said, "you can use my altar any time you want. But," he added with a wink and a twinkle, "if any Japs come by, you'd better be praying like hell!"[61]

As at Davao, the news filtered down as rumors, as corroborated by Jackson's diary: On 24 July: "Rumor: Tojo has resigned." (Fact: Tojo had resigned, six days earlier.) "Rumor: Three attempts to assassinate Hitler." (Fact: Assassination attempts were made on 11, 16, and 20 July—the last only four days before the 'rumor.') On 12 August: "Rumor: Roosevelt, Nimitz, and Gen. MacArthur had a conference in Hawaii." (Fact: The three had met at Pearl Harbor 27–28 July.)[62] And so it went: the Allies were winning, the Yanks were coming, and morale was soaring at Cabanatuan.

As American forces pushed closer to the Philippines the Japanese grew edgier. By mid-August the prisoners were digging foxholes, and it was rumored they would soon be shipped out, away from MacArthur's oncoming path. On the fifteenth, Jackson recorded, "we had a physical inspection of the detail. Lt. John Lamey and Chap. Albert Braun, friends and all agreeable. We were not told where we were going."[63]

They cleared the altar, disposed of the little red light, and destroyed Hutch's tiny listening set. It had served its purpose. On the seventeenth they walked to the nearby town to entrain for Manila. En route they "met several Nip troops going toward Balear with machine guns and portable mortars."[64]

Braun was the only chaplain on the five-hundred-man detail until Baumann arrived on the twenty-first with a second group. Both were happy they would still be together. On the twenty-fifth they boarded the *Noto Maru.*

Theirs was a nine-day cruise through hell. Over a thousand men were loaded into the hold. The guards closed the hatch. "Within five minutes," one recounted, "all hell broke loose. They finally opened one hatch and let us bring out about a hundred who had passed out. You sat between a guy's legs and opened yours for the guy in front of you. We used wooden tubs [for latrines], and those in the back had to struggle fifty or sixty feet—half with dysentery. I think about seventy died."[65]

When the *Noto,* fully armed and carrying depth charges, shook with a terrible blast, some thought the ship had blown up. "But it was a dud. The hatch was open, for once, and everybody started up the ladder. But [the guards] ran three or four machine guns in and started to fire. That quieted people down. They fired depth charges and told us it was an American sub and they'd sunk it. But if there was a battle anywhere they always said they'd won it, so we didn't believe them."[66]

"No room to lie down," Jackson noted, "can only sit. It's very hot. . . . Many passed out from heat. Though I was allowed to bring heat prostrations and lay them on deck. . . . Nips are very nervous. They will allow only one to come on deck to latrine at a time."[67]

At Subic Bay they joined a convoy of "26 ships, freighters and fighting vessels. I was not supposed to look around. Around supper time the Bay became fogged in, and I feel we are in a very frightening place."[68] In the night "we took off sometime and the sea is rough. Many seasick. . . . Men are noisy and unruly. . . . Odor is terrible. . . . Many have diarrhea and heat exhaustion. . . ."[69]

On 2 September Father Albert became so ill that Jackson brought him up on deck. "He says he's sick all over. . . . A grand guy, all wool and a yard wide."[70] By the next morning the padre wanted to return to his men in the hold. "I said 'no' you are staying here and if a Nip questions you, you put your hand over your heart and say 'kaze' . . . . I think 'kaze' means heart in Nip lingo."[71]

Two days later they docked. It was 5 September 1944, Father Al's fifty-fifth birthday, when he set foot in Japan and entrained for Tokyo. Some were sent north. Braun and Baumann, still together, went to Omori.

✟✟✟

They arrived on the tenth. Camp Omori, on a dredged-up island in Tokyo Bay, was the center for all the camps in the Tokyo industrial complex and headquarters for Colonel Kaname Sakaba, district commander of all POW camps in the area. Omori's population numbered about four hundred Allied POWs, all of whom, men and officers, policed the camp, carrying 'benjo buckets' of human waste, with which they fertilized the small fields; those too weak for heavy work cooked or sewed and performed menial tasks; the great number worked as stevedores, loading and unloading ships in the harbor and stealing what food they could while so doing.

Discipline was ironclad, punishment swift and merciless, inflicted for any reason or none at the discretion of Sakaba's henchman, Sergeant Watanabe. Known as 'the Beast,' Watanabe peered through a peephole in the frosted-glass window of his office—the POWs called it 'the cage'— before which all, when passing, were required to halt and salute, on pain of Watanabe's short-fused wrath. He passionately hated officers and vented his rages on them with bloody beatings and inhuman punishments. "A vicious and cruel man," Father Albert testified after the war, who "caused the prisoners at Camp Omori untold suffering. . . ."[72]

The padre, having grown up in California, had had Japanese friends, had no prejudice against the Japanese and, to best protect his men, could usually get along with his captors. The Beast, who directly supervised the prisoners, was the great exception. Watanabe was endowed with what Dr. Albert Weinstein believed "one of the basic characteristics of the Japanese: their emotional instability . . . [and] hair-trigger, unpredictable response; rattlesnake with the power to mutilate and kill."[73] If a salute was not given as rapidly as he wished, or a worker was too slow, if a facial expression displeased him, if he perceived or imagined a 'bad attitude,' he flew into a murderous rage.

There were some very decent Japanese officers at Omori, but they were powerless. When an American officer protested to one, "he pointed out that this animal [Watanabe] received direct permission from Colonel Sacaba [sic] to punish prisoners as he saw fit."[74]

Prior to Father Al's arrival at Omori a papal delegate, Monsignor Paul Marella, had visited POW camps in the area to check conditions. He reported their treatment extremely fair, the prisoners having been ordered "not to create any impression . . . except one that would be most favorable to the Japanese," Braun stated in his postwar affidavit.

Neither Marella nor his representative visited Omori while he was there, Braun testified. "It is evident that he could not know the condition of the prisoners of that camp during that time. Many of the prisoners . . . asked why I . . . did not make an effort to contact Archbishop Marella and thereby obtain better conditions for us. After consulting with some of the more prudent prisoners, it was decided that any effort to have someone intercede for us would only bring added hardships . . . , so we refrained."

Regarding conditions at Omori, Father Al testified, "The prisoners received about 400 grams of rice a day until the rice played out," and was replaced by "400 grams of cori, which is a grain similar to milo maize, chicken feed, that is all it is. Aside from that we usually received a very liquid form of soup. There was always a deficiency of medicines; however, the prisoners did receive some medical care and two doctors who were prisoners of war in that camp aided the Japanese doctor in administering to the patients. . . ."

For recreation, he continued, "possibly four times in the year, the prisoners put on a show that they themselves organized. The English . . . prisoners . . . had a band and we were permitted to listen. . . . We had some holidays when all the prisoners were at rest . . . , Thanksgiving, Christmas, New Year's, Easter, and the Emperor's birthday. . . ."

After the tropics, Japan's frigid climate and virtually heatless buildings seemed doubly harsh. They were always hungry and always cold. The barracks, icy and vermin-ridden, were probably "the same the Japanese soldiers lived in. The harshness of the prisoner's lives," he asserted, was less from the physical conditions than from "the innate cruelty of individuals who boastfully said that their policy is the rule by power. And following that policy, without justification, they beat and tortured the prisoners."[75]

The priests had somehow managed to acquire and smuggle in a bottle of mass wine. (They had started with two, but a Japanese officer had confiscated one.) This they offered in drops to make it last for God only knew how many more masses. They heard confessions, advised as best they could, and prayed for Yanks and tanks—soon. "When they were not doing physical labor or being beaten," Weinstein remembered, "they held mass for Catholics and heavily attended non-sectarian services for the rest of us."[76]

Father Al gave religious instruction and baptism to all who asked. Among these was naval officer 'Max' Wilson, as attested in a letter of gratitude written years later. He and his wife had just placed their son in a seminary, he wrote, with "profound wonderment when I ponder over the chain of events leading up to that day. . . . We know you pray for us, and have a lot of influence with the Boss, because we are so blessed."[77] Instruction was given at odd moments in latrine or work duty. How many other converts for which Father Al was responsible is unknown: priests dared not keep records.

There were no hidden radios at Omori, but news did filter in. Those working at the docks, utilizing what they had learned of the language, overheard bits and pieces of conversation among Japanese civilians, many of whom were sick of the war. An English version of the Tokyo *Times* made its concealed way into camp, to be analyzed and passed around. The 'news' was largely propaganda—the Japanese won every battle, trivialized every setback—and they themselves scoffed at the exaggeration of the press.

Saipan and Tinian fell to the Americans in July, Guam in August; on 20 October MacArthur waded ashore on Leyte, and the reconquest of the Philippines was underway. The POWs were largely unaware of these details, but each battle the Japanese 'won' was closer than the last. Nor did the POWs need a radio to tell them the war was turning when bombs began to fall on Tokyo in November, and kept coming. December was punctuated by the undulating wail of air-raid sirens, the roar of bombers, and the crash of detonations. The damage was small—precision bombing was as yet impossible from the heights at which they flew—but the psychological impact was enormous. The Japanese were appalled that the war had reached their homeland, and the POWs knew their long-held faith was coming to fruition. Uncle Sam was storming the walls. And the walls were crumbling.

Christmas approached and the padres prepared for midnight mass. Their captors had authorized it; but one large problem loomed, in the form of Watanabe.

"Only one Mass was permitted on a Sunday," Baumann recorded, "and that by Father Braun . . . because Watanabe thought that I was a bad priest—not good like Japanese priests. . . . Watanabe in searching my miserable few possessions . . . found a deck of playing cards my good mother had sent . . . through the Red Cross. A few days later he found me playing cribbage—and decided I was no good. . . . Also Watanabe accused me of thinking evil of him. (How true.)"[78]

"I just have to say a Christmas mass," Baumann told Father Al. But with the Beast—

Insignificant! He would get him to the altar, the padre promised. With the craft of a born outlaw, Father Al braved the wrath of Watanabe who, as he told it, "for some unknown reason wanted to have a big Christmas." Playing on the Japanese obsession with ceremony and with staging a good show, he promised a magnificent production, with "a solemn mass, for which we'll have to have two priests, like we have in the States."

Ah so! Watanabe was pleased.

The two priests practiced every movement, every bit of timing, and added some Japanese flourishes.

Christmas Eve approached.

But the United States Army Air Corps chose that night for a bombing raid. Midnight Mass was delayed until Christmas morning. Their church was a sizeable bathhouse, their altar a small table. The ceremony began and, wrote Baumann, "we said Mass side by side. Fortunately we . . . knew each other well and had served each other [mass] many, many times. So when

Albert spoke, I spoke, when he bowed, I bowed, when he extended his arms, I did the same. It must be obvious we got away with it, because we are both alive today. Watanabe was present and smacking his lips at how nice it was. (I still get sick when I think of what would have happened had he discovered the deception.) But we both set up our chalices etc. We were just side by side. You could call it the Synchronized Masses. . . ." Someone played the violin Watanabe had procured, "and Patty Ward, a Scottish boy sang the Ave Maria. He was terrific. He was good enough to keep Watanabe from catching on to what we were doing. One thing I can tell you is that there were a lot of anxious POWs that Christmas."[79]

"Twenty years before Vatican II we concelebrated," Father Al commented. Max Wilson made his first communion that morning. Father Al had baptized him the day before, secretly and quickly, while other POWs staged a fight that drew the guards' attention.[80]

Even the Beast was pleased with the show, and in a rare moment of amiability said to the padre, "I give you something nice." It was a jar of peanut butter.

Watanabe's good humor was short lived. A day or so later he exploded into one of his sadistic rages. Father Al, hurrying past the 'cage,' had neglected to stop and salute. Through his peephole the Beast was watching.

There followed what the padre later said was the bitterest night of his life—Braun's Last Stand, he called it. In the middle of the floodlit prison yard he was forced to stand at rigid attention, barefoot and clothed only in a g-string and sleeveless shirt in the freezing wind. For three hours he willed himself to stand, until the Beast appeared, a long, steel-tipped bamboo pole in his hand, hatred in his eye. Back and forth he strutted, stopping before his captive, making practice thrusts with his weapon.

Knowing what was coming, the padre breathed a silent prayer to Saint Joseph that the planes might come, now, "and blast this damn place off the face of the earth."

Suddenly the Beast gathered his momentum, raced toward the padre, aiming his lance at the jugular. A second before impact Braun swerved. Watanabe fell sprawling, screaming in fury. Gasps of fear swelled from the POWs gathered around.

At that moment Saint Joseph answered in the voice of the air-raid siren and the roar of Uncle Sam's bombers.[81]

Watanabe was seen nowhere the next day. He had lost face. The camp held its collective breath, awaiting the worst. But Saint Joseph had not finished. On New Year's Day 1945 the prisoners found Watanabe gone. His transfer probably saved Father Al's life; it certainly eased everyone else's. The men at Omori were rid of the Beast.

Although Colonel Sakaba remained in charge, the men believed Watanabe's successor was sent by God. Sergeant Ogori, Father Al testified, "was a very fine and high-type man. . . . He was assisted by Mr. Cano, who had been a tea and coffee merchant at Yokohama, and . . . much like Sergeant Ogori . . . treated the prisoners with great consideration and the only thing he had to watch out for was that Colonel Sakaba did not catch him being . . . kind to the prisoners. . . ."[82]

Events in the Pacific were moving rapidly. By mid-January MacArthur's forces had landed on Luzon at Lingayen Gulf; by month's end Eichelburger's Eighth Army was ashore in the Zimbales Mountains and the race was on for Manila. The Americans entered the city on 3 February and began liberating Bilibid Prison and the surrounding camps. During February United States forces retook Corregidor and the Marines landed on Iwo Jima.

The Yanks were coming. When?

March came and Father Bauman went, transferred to the POW hospital at nearby Shinagawa. Father Al missed him; they had endured three years of war together.

More planes were coming over now; 150 hit Tokyo on the fourth, and on the fateful night of 9-10 March another 334, sweeping low this time, releasing napalm-filled incendiaries. They destroyed a quarter of the city in the most destructive single bombing of the war.[83] From Omori they watched the city burn. The next night the bombers hit Nagoya, and followed with massive raids on Osaka, Kobe, and Yokohama. From Omori the men saw a red glow in the eastern distance; it was, a guard told them, another city burning. Conventional raids had proved ineffective. Only the complete destruction of Japanese war production, it was obvious, could shorten the war and end it without the invasion that would prove far more costly in American and Japanese lives.[84]

In the course of the attacks some American pilots were downed, taken prisoner, and given especially brutal treatment. "In time," Father Al testified, "these prisoners were brought to our camp and assigned to a special barracks, apart from the rest of the camp. Among this group were many Catholics. They requested Mr. Cano, in the spring of . . . 1945 to permit them to go to Confession and to attend Mass and Holy Communion. Mr. Cano stated that he was unable to grant them their favor because the Colonel had ordered that they should have no contact with the rest of the prisoners, but he said he would do what he could for them at great risk to himself, namely that he would sneak the Catholic Chaplain, who was myself, into their barracks at a time when one of his close friends was on guard. . . . He sneaked me into the barracks of these aviators, gave us time to hear Confessions and to say Mass and then quickly got me out again."[85]

✟✟✟

Japan prepared for invasion. By the end of March Iwo Jima, steppingstone from the Mariannas to Tokyo, had after terrible fighting fallen to the Americans, who from there began regularly to hit Tokyo. After Germany's surrender on 8 May America turned full attention to the Pacific war. Okinawa fell in June and on 4 July MacArthur announced the Philippine campaign completed. Four days later a thousand planes pounded Tokyo.

As the noose tightened and Japan's perimeter bastions crumbled, internal defenses intensified. The coasts and mountains bristled with fortifications. Caves behind the beaches were filled with tons of food and ammunition. To augment the over two million ground troops, the government was arming four million army and navy employees and a militia of some 28 million men and women—a total of 32 million, all pledged to fight to the end. Civilians sharpened bamboo spears with which to greet descending paratroopers.

In July, Father Al testified, a number of young Japanese were brought to Omori where Sakaba briefed them: they were to be scattered among the prison camps to be at hand when the Americans invaded Japan. "Several of these men were very friendly to the prisoners and after the last lecture one . . . told us prisoners that when the end comes . . . the gates of all prison camps will be left open, but that we should not leave the gate but rather should remove some boards in the middle of the fence and take to the hills through the openings we made. The reason . . . was the final instruction Colonel Sakaba had given . . . [that] the gates would be open for the prisoners to escape . . . , and then as they leave the camp the guards will . . . shoot them down. . . ."[86]

With this warning the POWs made their plans and awaited the invasion.

It never came. Instead:

Hiroshima: 6 August.

Strange tales crept into Camp Omori. Something had happened, something enormous and terrifying, but no one knew what. The guards were on edge. Air-raid sirens wailed intermittently. Two days later they learned that Russia had finally declared war on Japan.

Nagasaki: 9 August.

The guards grew more jittery. Whatever was happening, the men agreed, the Allies were winning, the war was winding down—it couldn't be much longer—and they would again see that Golden Gate, from which they had sailed an eternity ago. . . .

Then it was 15 August. The prisoners at Omori were herded into the prison yard to listen to a blaring radio. They had no idea why, nor did they know that in every camp, town, and village throughout Japan, soldiers, civilians, and POWs were also congregating to listen.

The Emperor, for the first time in history, was speaking directly to his people. Nor did they know that young militarists had staged a fierce palace revolution in an attempt to prevent his action.

The prisoners understood little of what he said, but someone thought he heard *senso owari*—'the war is over.' They learned soon enough, very likely through Sergeant Ogori, and the news rolled like a tidal wave throughout Omori, throughout Japan, throughout the world.

Almost immediately, Colonel Sakaba, having unleashed the beatings on the hapless men and having planned to gun them down as they fled the opened gates, complained officially to the American camp commander: someone, he railed, had fouled his boots, urinating in one, defecating in the other.[87] The commander doubtless felt Sakaba was lucky; it was nowhere nearly what he deserved.

Until they could be evacuated, all ex-prisoners were ordered to remain in their camps, where over-flying army and navy aircraft began dropping food, clothing, and medicine for them. At Omori Father Albert was put in charge of distributing the supplies.

Negotiations for the surrender seemed to crawl for the long-imprisoned men who wanted only to get out and get home. At length Commander Harold Stassen's task force came steaming into Tokyo Bay.

"Hundreds," writes Dawes, "climbed onto the pilings of the wharf in jubilation. . . ."[88]

Al Braun watched from Omori. Whatever his reactions at that defining moment were between himself and his God. His emotions, like those of all others standing on the long-sought threshold of freedom, were too deep, too complex to be quickly untangled. The four-year ordeal had drawn deeply on his great reserves of courage, strength, and faith; but he had gained in turn a new awareness of man's nobility, had found his journey through hell a harsh but strangely soul-enriching school whose lessons would for the rest of his life guide his path and broaden his vision. "I learned more in prison camp," he declared years later, "than I ever did in the novitiate."

On the twenty-ninth of August 1945 Major Albert Braun, Chaplain, United States Army, stepped aboard the hospital ship *Benevolence* a free man.

18: SENTIMENTAL JOURNEY

Armistice (now Veterans') Day, 11 November, fell on a Sunday in 1945. The Apaches, after four years of waiting for their padre to return, had learned he was alive, free, and on his way: Father Marcian Bucher, then mission priest, had spread the word. For a week the canyon had been stippled with wagons and tepees as the tribe gathered.

They had followed the news throughout the war, hoping for word of their braves and their padre. Lacking radios, many had trekked from outlying areas into Mescalero to listen to those at rectory or agency, and walked home through the night. "We had no flashlights," Ellyn Bigrope recalled, "and there were snakes. But we knew how to take care of ourselves—look down and make noise."[1]

Virginia Shanta was among those waiting that Sunday morning. "As I was going up that hill I heard his voice—and it just—it moved me—that strong voice he had—talking to my people."[2]

She and her people were not the only ones so stirred. For Father Al it was the true moment of homecoming, the moment he had awaited since 1940. All roads—all dreams—led to Mescalero. He had come home to his people.

✞✞✞

Two months had passed from the moment he stepped onto the *Benevolence*—not an unpleasant time, despite his eagerness to reach his New Mexico mountains. It was a time of reunions with old comrades about whose fate he had wondered, a time for memories of those who would never see homes and families again. It was a time of transition—from war to peace, from captivity to freedom, from loss to victory. It took adjustment. Freedom was too new to be quickly digested. Like food after long starvation, it must be assimilated a little at a time. Meeting with one's fellow soldiers was the first stage of healing.

On the *Benevolence* they were sprayed with DDT, deloused, shown to hot showers, given fresh clothes and clean bunks—and food. The six-foot priest who had weighed nearly two hundred pounds at war's beginning was now a hundred-and-fifteen-pound skeleton. "On the 29th," he wrote friends in El Paso on 3 September, "the navy dramatically dashed up in boats alongside P.O.W. camp Omori, Tokyo, and released us from the Japs. Some thrill. It is all over now. . . ." They were still in Tokyo harbor, but "they say we are about to start for home." He sent happy hellos to various friends and told them to "have one on me."[3]

Between ships on Okinawa his grand reunions began. Gutted from battle, blackened by fire, much of it yet to be cleared of land mines, stippled with rows of new-made crosses, the island was now the site for tears and *abrazos* as those long separated came together. Here he was reunited with Herman Baumann, with whom he had served through battle and captivity almost to the last. Home seemed nearer when Father Dennis Mahoney, who had taken his place at Mescalero when he left for the army and was now serving with the 69th Field Hospital, appeared to greet him. From Dennis he learned that Father Provincial Martin Knauff had died in office two years earlier and had been replaced by Father Gregory Wooler. "This is a late date," he wrote Wooler from Manila on 9 September, "to be writing to you 'congratulations.' Hope it will not be long before I can shake your hand. It was a great surprise," he continued, "to run into Father Dennis. . . . We had a good time together." Mahoney had also procured some good stateside bourbon and left a bottle for Braun and Baumann to enjoy. They did, until someone stole it from its evidently too obvious cache. 'Al Capone' was slipping.

"Tell Father Felipe," he continued, "that I saw Juan [Baldonado] at Okinawa." Then sadly, "Very few of the priests captured out here are alive. I doubt if 30% of the prisoners taken in the Philippines are alive." He was not too far off. Fewer than half the prisoners survived, and many died soon after returning. They had been starved and abused too long.

There was much more to tell his provincial, but it would have to wait. "Am writing this on the sole of a wooden shoe. Too much noise and confusion."[4]

He was still in Manila, he wrote Father Gregory on the fourteenth, "but expect to be on way soon," and hoped to arrive with other chaplains "in time to be present at the consecration of Chaplain Arnold in New York." In Manila he and Juan Baldonado were soon joined by Pepe. The three had a grand celebration and prepared for a grander one in Tularosa.

"Padre," he added almost apologetically, "I don't have any breviaries, nor do I have a habit. Can I be provided these two items when I reach San Francisco?"[5]

He landed in Honolulu on the twentieth, "thirty-eight hours after we left Manila. Thank God we have our feet on U.S. soil." Bands greeted them wherever they went, all playing "Sentimental Journey" over and over. Here he learned he was one of eighty heroes of Bataan and Corregidor chosen from all ranks and services to form a ceremonial detail to be flown to San Francisco to represent their comrades. "We are a group . . . called Ramps [Recovered Allied Military Personnel]. We represent all P.O.W.s from the Phil[ippines released] in Japan. The country is telling us thanks in a grand style. Will [soon] leave here for Hamilton Field. . . . The Gov. is having our folks meet us. . . . There is some program of welcome in S[an] F[rancisco]. . . . We appreciate this great welcome but all of us will be glad when it is over. . . ."[6]

On 25 September, nearly a month after their dramatic rescue, they flew over the Golden Gate, circled the city, landed at Hamilton Field, and stepped onto the tarmac in the USA. Father Al walked again on native ground, enfolded his mother in his arms. Awaiting him also were his brother Ray and Clara, joyful at his return, appalled at the gauntness writ large and deep upon his face, in dark wells beneath eyes that had seen too much and comprehended more. After a tickertape parade through cheering crowds and a banquet at the Saint Francis Hotel he and his weary comrades finally headed for Letterman General Hospital and a badly needed rest.

But idleness was never his lifestyle. After a quick trip to Los Angeles to see his family—the hospital personnel were cooperative about absences—he boarded a train east to arrive in time for Chaplain Arnold's consecration. That his mind was churning in fast rhythm with the clack of the wheels is evident in a letter penned to his provincial en route. There were matters to clear, work to be done. His army pay had accrued, of which he knew "not a cent belongs to me, but to the Holy Father." Accordingly, "Enclosed is a check for $4,000. Have some money in National Bank of Ft. Sam Houston. . . . As soon as I can get settled will . . . send it to you. . . . Was not able to begin to save anything until June 1941. When I left Mescalero . . . I took all debts with me. It took some time to pay them." As the enemy closed on the Rock, "I sent out post-dated checks on the last submarine that left Corregidor on May 3. Did not want to die owing debts. Still owe 100 pesos ($50.00) to the Philippine Trust Co. Tried to pay that when in Manila but the bank is not yet open for business."[7]

En route to New York he stopped in Oskaloosa, Iowa, for a quick visit to Celine and Oliver Sheehy and Mama Henrion, now widowed: Papa had died shortly before the padre had shipped overseas.

On the East Coast he visited his old friend Father Sixtus. He called also on the heads of two provinces, to whom, as he reported to Father Gregory, he stressed "the necessity of salvaging what is left of the historical records of the Franciscan mission activity in Mexico. . . . Photostatic copies . . . should be made and sent to the States for safe keeping. Then those documents should be translated into all modern languages so that people might know something of the glorious history of the Order in Mexico. . . . Many of those documents have been destroyed during the revolution."

He then turned to the Philippines. "Most of the friars there . . . are living in centuries past. Today [the Philippine Order] is like an old man quietly dying. It would be a great thing . . . if some American province could take over what is left." American friars, he opined, could "replace the losses suffered during the war. . . . In time you would have native Priests, Brothers and Sisters." Finally, it "would certainly be a splendid thing for the Fathers in China" to have "a place in Manila . . . to rest and recuperate."

Both provincials, he reported to Father Gregory, were interested. "Maybe you can . . . have the matter . . . considered by the American Provincials. . . . Now is the time."

He had met Father Baumann in Boston, he added. Together they were calling upon "the next of kin of a few close friends who . . . will not return. This task is taking longer than I expected." Having further business in Washington, "I may have to ask for a ten-day extension of sick leave."[8] He had been, after processing at Letterman, released to Beaumont General Hospital in El Paso.

Preparing to leave Boston he found himself reduced to a few coins. It was a Sunday and, unable to cash a $500 check from the army, he repaired to a Catholic center hoping to borrow enough to tide him over. To his surprise it was Bishop Richard Cushing who admitted him. He had met the bishop briefly during the Depression while on a 'begging trip,' and it had been Cushing who had given the Stations of the Cross to Saint Joseph's. But there his acquaintance stopped. Now he explained his predicament. The bishop listened, smiled, pulled a wad of bills from a desk drawer, and thrust them on Father Al who, expecting far less, proffered his check.

Cushing shook his head. "Keep it, Father," he said, obviously amused. "You're the first priest I ever met who was broke." This was the real beginning of a long friendship.[9]

The padre got his requested extension from Beaumont, a generous one that allowed him, after quick visits to Washington and the West Coast, time for the one thing he wished most and of which he had so long dreamed: he could now, for a time at least, return to Mescalero. His people awaited him. And there was work to be done.

✝✝✝

He came home on the tenth, just in time for mass on the eleventh, when his voice came so strongly to Virginia Shanta as she climbed the hill. At that nostalgic mass, which Father Marcian Bucher graciously turned over to him, Father Al dedicated Saint Joseph's, on which he had labored so long, to all the veterans of both World Wars who, buried on foreign fields or resting in the ocean's depths, would not return.

The following Sunday, 18 November, Father Al officiated a Solemn Mass of Thanksgiving "because of those," he wrote, "who came through the war alive." Of seventy-five Apaches who had served their country in World War II, seventy-four had returned. The church was festive with bunting and a large American flag. The padre was fittingly assisted by a priest from Saint Anthony's Seminary in El Paso, of which Father Al had been such a vital part, and by the chaplain of the military hospital at Fort Stanton, Father Jules Molini, an old friend. His acolytes were five returned veterans. A small choir of seminarians from Saint Anthony's sang, and Father Marcian served as master of ceremonies. The church overflowed as people streamed from all corners of the reservation and from the surrounding countryside. The tribe welcomed their old padre and their veterans with a huge feast and ceremonial dancing. Only one had not returned: Bernard Dolan, killed in action in Europe. For him Father Al said a solemn requiem mass the following day.

Home again, November 1945. Courtesy of SJAM.

The community welcomes home its area soldiers with a banquet at Alameda Park, Alamogordo. The girls serving behind the veterans are from Alamogordo High School. Courtesy of Prof. Pete Eidenbach and Mary Serna.

The padre with ex-POW comrades Juan Jr. and Pepe Baldonado, far left and right, and Bruce Klinekole, center, with Father Al. Courtesy of SJAM.

The padre was home. He could hunt again with Eric and Robert; he could visit with Shanta Boy and his family. Here too were the Mackeys and the Millers and the Blazers, the Diaz family down the canyon, and those he had left in Tularosa. Elisa Baldonado and Ray Dawson, who had courted while riding with him to the CCC camps, had, he learned, been married in 1942 by her brother, Father Felipe. He learned also of Albert Fall's death, and of Emma's. His old friend Bishop Schuler had retired after long and productive service and been replaced by Bishop Sidney Metzger. Dave Kirgan too had left the cathedral, but had his own parish in Las Cruces, a little closer to Mescalero than he had been in El Paso. Dave and the new bishop, it seems, were generally at cross purposes—"can't see anything the same way," Father Al wrote. "However, he is able to hold his own and the Bishop pretty well leaves him alone."[10]

Awaiting him too were Charlie and Katherine Mackey and their children, five years older than when he saw them last. Among the items he had brought home—one that caught the children's eyes—was his mess kit. "It had dents in it," Dick remembered, "and a cross in the middle, and some names scratched in it. . . . It was, you know, something from his experiences. I was fascinated with it. To a curious little boy it was impressive." The padre gave it to the children.

They loved to listen to his war stories. He was their hero. He never minced words when recounting the atrocities. They listened bug-eyed to his story of Watanabe. "But then"—Dick could hardly believe it—"he'd say, 'You know, I never hated the Japs. I never did.' All the rest of us were saying, 'Jeez, they—' and he'd say, 'They were doing what they thought they had to do.'" It gave a real meaning to loving one's fellow men.[11]

"Have been enjoying a rest here," he reported to his provincial. "Went hunting several times. I need exercise badly. Father Marcian's company is restful. I am enjoying it here.[12]

Once he had rested, he plunged into a brief but intense flurry of activity; it could not be otherwise with Father Albert. He had always been short on patience, especially with sloth or negligence, and he returned from war a little shorter of fuse, a little testier. Though he retained his natural good humor, his occasional explosions could be memorable. One was of particular moment:

Two weeks before he was to report to Beaumont, while going through his desk and files, he discovered a colony of mice nesting in the drawers among the shreds of church registers, financial records, and legal documents. Worse, his perspectives for the completed mission were mounds of filthy shreds. Proposed additions to the church and grounds—a choir loft, a small stone chapel, an *acequia* flowing from the creek, a pond and fountain, a retaining wall, a statue of Saint Joseph, two carved angels to flank the buttresses on either side of the door—all his tattered plans now housed migrations of mice.

Further, he had left specific instructions for a drainage system to protect the church from excess moisture, for pentagon stone steps at the entrance, and a fountain to be completed during his absence. Nothing, he found, had been done.

Then, like a blow in the solar plexus, was the discovery of damage to the roofing tiles of his beloved church. Four years of war and captivity, death and disease, filth and starvation, and of brutality so long endured, came crowding to the surface. Four years of suppressing the temper he dared not show at risk of his and his comrades' survival gathered to a head. Had none in his absence cared to preserve what he and Old Tony and the crew had labored twenty years to build? What Brother Sales had died for? What so many had built their lives into?

As they still tell it at Mescalero, the padre erupted. Who had let mice take over the office? Who had neglected to finish the project as directed? Who had let his work gather dust?

Those nearby looked at each other, at the sky, the ground, the church tower. No one knew.

What had happened to the roof?

'The pigeons . . . they roost, you know, they poop, all over the floor and the altar and the pews. . . .'

What happened to the roof?

'Father Tom—just trying to get the pigeons. . . .' Father Thomas Aquinas Zeigan, passion exceeding prudence, it seemed, had called the state police.

The police? For a few birds?

'Well, yes. To shoot the birds. . . .'

Inside the church?

'Inside, outside. . . .'

A long moment of dense silence. Then—*le déluge.*

An explosion worthy of Vesuvius.

For several days the Apaches found it advisable to melt silently into the mountains. It was as well Father Tom had gone, replaced by Marcian three months before the padre's return. "They shot forty tiles off the roof and the tower," the padre wrote in April. It would cost $300 to replace them."[13]

Once his fury was spent—and it had by all accounts been a spectacular eruption—Father Albert, always the pragmatist, waved it aside with a roared *Insignificant!* and looked ahead. The war was over, he was home—or would be once he was discharged from Beaumont—and he was ready for the challenge.

Meanwhile he looked forward to visitors; even while at Beaumont he planned to wangle permission to come and go between the various medical tests the army scheduled for all returning POWs. His provincial, among other guests, was expected. "Let me know," he wrote Father Gregory, "when you will pass through El Paso. . . . I might be able to meet you and drive up with you. Would like to be at Mescalero with you."

He also expected one Louis Knecht, who had spent some time with him at the mission. "He went in the army when I did in 1940 and is just now getting back. He took part in seven battles and rose from a private to the grade of captain. I want to be in Mescalero with him a day or two." Meanwhile, he ended, he was making the most of Mescalero until he had to report to Beaumont. "Have enjoyed myself here. Fr. Marcian is easy to live with. He and I drove to Roswell today to see the Friars there."[14]

Father Marcian returned the same feeling. In a posthumous testimonial in a pastoral review, he spoke among other accolades of the padre as "a generous, caring and holy son of St. Francis," a man whom he "always looked up to . . . and tried to learn from," a "true model for the many priests that his life touched," and "a gift of God to us, his Franciscan brothers [who] were privileged to . . . work with him." He was particularly interested in Father Al's recollections of his POW days. "Al had more stories, all true . . . [and] he could tell them with gusto." The POWs, he had told Father Marcian, were of two classes: "Those from good homes and disciplined upbringing and those who were self-willed and spoiled. Most of the former group returned from captivity, the latter did not."[15]

He reported to Beaumont on 6 December, mainly as a formality. Like all ex-POWs he had to undergo examinations and medical evaluation prior to discharge from duty. He was not, however, confined to the premises. He had always hated hospitals and elected to stay with his confreres in the institution he had been such a part of establishing. "Have been staying at St. Anthony's Seminary," he wrote his provincial, "and have enjoyed it. . . . They have made wonderful progress since the days of 1928 when they had their novitiate at the barn at Mescalero."

Father Marcian, scheduled for transfer to San Marcos Indian Reservation, was ready to turn Mescalero over to Father Al on his discharge from Beaumont. But the projected thirty-day hospital stint was proving typical of the 'hurry-up-and-wait' tradition of the military, and the padre grew testy. "Have been trying to find out when I can expect to be free from the army. The medicos . . . are a good natured easy going group. . . . The only answer I can get out of them is: 'why worry you will draw a salary so long as you are in our hands.' I know I will not be free before Jan. 1st. Any time you want to make your changes in the Indian Mission field, just go ahead. . . . I can always get off weekends to say mass at Mescalero. . . ."[16]

On 20 December the Father Provincial received a disquieting telegram from Father Francis Redmon in Tularosa. "Albert has pneumonia Beaumont Hospital El Paso." Within a few days, however, a letter from Father Al eased his mind. Either Francis was misinformed or the padre threw off his illness with his usual *Insignificant!* before Redmon learned of it. "Spent last Thursday night [the date of the telegram] with Father Kirgan at Las Cruces. He is an old friend of mine and I am desirous to [talk with] him because of the Mexican Franciscans in Las Cruces. The [seminary's department of] philosophy has been moved from Saint Anthony's in El Paso to Las Cruces. The Bishop in permitting the Mexican Friars to locate in Las Cruces put very harsh terms for them to sign. Father Kirgan has been kind to them and gives them much work which means some income. That neutralizes the harshness of the Bishop." Meanwhile, "Father Marcian is very busy getting ready for Xmas. He is certainly an excellent priest, very popular and easy to live with."[17]

The new year saw him still at Beaumont. "I thought I would be able to start for home tonight," he wrote on the fourth, "but the army is always able to kill a few extra days. I go before the board today but it will be Tuesday nite [the eighth] before I can leave. I'll be back in Mescalero for the mass of Sunday Jan. 19."

He was also being pulled from another direction, he added. An army comrade, General Cheves, had apparently been urging the erstwhile chaplain to return to military duty. From Army Service Command 24 in Korea he had followed with a Christmas card on which he had scribbled another plea. "Padre," he begged, "come back."

But he could not serve God and mammon; Mescalero came first in his heart, and like a blooded race horse he was pawing and snorting at the starting gate. "Have been looking around for a good army truck that does not cost much so I can go to work soon." Additionally, "the Mexican Friars want me to buy cheap for a lab. for physics and chemistry. The army and the navy [have] a great supply of such equipment. Maybe one of your returned chaplains can buy lab. equipment on the coast. . . ."[18]

Friends in El Paso were also awaiting Father Al's release, among them some of his old friends from the 200th. One, Louis Mendoza, "saw Father Braun when he was being released . . . and I took him home with me. Within an hour I had 25-30 ex-POWs in my house, each insisting that he personally should take care of Father Albert."[19]

But Father Albert had been taken care of long enough. Despite his gaunt appearance, he was afire to get back in the saddle. After a quick trip to California to make a retreat and see his ill and aging mother, he left Los Angeles on the eighteenth. "Will be at Mescalero tomorrow," he wrote joyfully en route. "Father Marcian can leave for San Carlos any time next week. . . . I left this morning so as to be with him a few days so that he can show me what is to be shown. Enjoyed my vacation but am anxious to get to work."[20]

There was indeed work, a lot of work to be done on his great stone church. The windows, boarded when he left, must be opened and completed. A number of people had sent donations for frames and stained glass. Saint Joseph's still lacked heating, lighting, and a drainage system, and the bullet-scarred roofing tiles must be replaced. And he had to fulfill a duty to Brother Sales. Intending to pay respects at the friar's grave, he had been unable to find it, so long untended and overgrown. He enlisted the help of Victor Dolan and Eric Tortilla, who located the grave and helped him rebury Brother Salesius just outside the entrance of Saint Joseph.

Before he could settle to the rhythm of work at Mescalero another military duty called, this one concerning a friend who had died on a Japanese hell ship. Captain Joseph R. Radosevich, of the old 200th, had just before the surrender written a will in the form of a letter, which he entrusted to Father Albert. The padre had somehow gotten it to the States, probably on that last submarine out of Corregidor. In January a letter from attorney Herman Atkins requested Father Al's presence in Gallup, New Mexico, for the probate. "This officer and I were close friends," the padre wrote. The will as written would not hold up under state law, though Atkins believed that "because of the war and conditions under which it was made" it would be accepted if Father Al, the only witness, would testify.[21] He did, and the will was declared valid.

Shortly after Christmas the very popular Father Marcian—'Butch,' Father Al called him—had left Mescalero, and the padre had to turn down Dave Kirgan's invitation to drive with him to Florida to pick up his father: too many duties called.[22]

After a quick trip to Los Angeles, where he was called to bury his sister

Mary's husband, another matter was brought to his attention. Before leaving for the army Father Al had carefully made sure—or thought he had—that the titles for all the church property he had 'bought' in Mexico were turned back to the Church. Somehow one convent had been omitted. He hastily had the oversight rectified. The sisters, he was told, had prayed earnestly throughout the war for his safe return. "Mother Humilde," he always added chuckling, "was afraid she'd lose her convent. Those prayers were probably what brought me home."

He still had to go to Fort Sam Houston for his final physical before he could be discharged, he wrote his provincial. "Don't know how long I will be in San Antonio. My records show that I still have trouble with my left leg because of beri-beri. That may hold me up a little while—maybe two weeks. . . . I can't take holy hour because of my leg," he admitted, "and I must sit down when I teach catechism. When I have two masses I am bothered during the second one." He could probably get a pension, he added, "if I went after it, but I don't think it is a good thing for us Friars to be too interested in pensions."

Having acknowledged his physical limitations, reluctantly and only as a matter of record, he swept them aside with his usual optimism. "As soon as I get back from San Antonio will start work on the church."[23]

Prior to retiring he requested the promotion that his commanding officer had recommended in March 1942. The recommendation, he wrote, "was not acted upon because of existing military conditions at Bataan and Corregidor and since the army informed prisoners of war that those recommendations would be accepted as an actual promotion, I therefore request that I be reinstated in my rank of Lt. Colonel."[24] As of 25 April 1946 the promotion came through.[25]

He reported to Fort Sam that same month. Exactly what the doctors told him is unclear; that his legs were still troubling him is evident. That he made little of it, sought no disability compensation and wanted only to get back to the mission is consistent with his nature. He was relieved from active duty as of 26 August 1946, when his terminal leave was concluded.[26]

Back in Mescalero he pitched into work with a vigor born of joy. If his legs pained him—well, so did those of Father Junípero who despite his painful infirmity had trekked dauntlessly to and through California, building missions as he went. Working on Saint Joseph's Al Braun was afire with plans, so that when the guardian of Saint Anthony's came from El Paso to ask if his friars could come to Mescalero for the summer as they had done each year before the padre had gone to war, he was exuberantly receptive. But, he reported, "after saying yes to Fr. Guardian, I remembered that Fr. Francis has a great dislike for the Friars from Michoacán Province. I don't think he will interfere up here but for safety['s] sake I am asking your permission."[27]

Father Francis, from the time he had become parish priest at Tularosa in 1940, had clashed with the padre. He resented the Mexican friars and Father Al's espousal of the seminary in El Paso, carried the grudge against him personally—even against the Mescalero mission itself—and had dragged Father Dennis Mahoney into the dispute.[28]

Al Braun was soft of heart. He was also hard of head, he was home now, and he was fueled with plans. "I sent Fr. Provincial of Michoacán Province all the literature our Province put out on the Brothers. The Mexican Friars need a training school. . . . An ideal place for their school would be Mescalero. Would you or the Province object to turning this place back to the Mexican Friars? I may be able to persuade them to establish a school for their Brothers here." But, he warned, "Don't let this out. If Father Francis hears about it he will do everything in his power to prevent the Mexicans from coming here. With their one school in El Paso and one at Las Cruces this is an ideal place for them."[29]

Nor did it take him long to rekindle the old crusade for a Catholic day school at Mescalero. The plan, though defeated earlier by the limitations of the Depression, had not died in the padre's hard skull.

Work at the mission progressed happily throughout the summer. A stream of visitors livened the activity—army comrades (among them Madeline Ullom), Franciscan confreres, family, friends—"so many," he wrote, "that so far I have not found the time to write Fr. Felix. . . . I have held him in esteem and affection for more than forty years." Felix was preparing for his fifty-year jubilee; the padre would like to have attended, but was sadly unable to go.[30]

The busy padre put everyone to work—tribesmen, friars, army brass, anyone coming up the hill. None escaped, even the children. On one family visit his grandnephew Ray recalls "hoeing weeds in the garden close by the church."

But Father Al also took the children fishing. "He and my grandfather cut some poles and we went fishing down at the creek bottom. . . . I remember going on a hike with Father Al and my grandfather, up the side of a mountain. . . . We spent several days and had quite a time."[31]

Among his many visitors was Herman Baumann who, he wrote early in July, "just left for home. . . . When he left he gave me a check for $150.00 toward a memorial window for the Catholic chaplains who died during the war."

The Apaches made their own gifts—"three houses," he reported, "one a kitchen" which he "moved from Nogal Cañon to Mescalero"; the others went to Carrizo and Elk, to use as places to stay while in those areas, and as temporary chapels. All, he reported, were in good shape. These were doubtless among those government-built structures the Apaches had shunned for themselves and were happy to let Father Al have.

In the flurry of summer's activities the padre "did not send a report for the chapter. Have been away from the run of things so long that I overlook some things that should be remembered."[32] He regretted the omission but, disapproving as always of priests who "sit on their butts pushing papers around," he was obviously not overly concerned.

By mid-August he was again pushing for a day school. "There are 25 Apache children of Mescalero going to St. John's Indian School. Last March the sisters of St. Catherine's agreed to take the children from Mescalero," but the Mother Superior later wrote "that the school was filled and she could not take the children." He had managed to place them with Father Regis at Saint John's in Arizona, paying with funds from his own mission, but made the point that "a day school at Mescalero would solve the problem permanently."

Father Kehoe from the cathedral in El Paso, he continued, having spent several days at Mescalero, was also enthusiastic about a day school, and "is all powerful with the Bishop." Moreover, the agency superintendent, Mr. Crow, "who has been wonderful to me came over yesterday to object to so many children leaving the reservation. He said it will cut down Gov.

appropriations. . . . I told him . . . it is too late now because all arrangements have been made . . . [but that] next year I would take only children of High School age . . . [because] we probably would have a Catholic Day School at Mescalero. He smiled and said I am with you."[33]

Meanwhile another trip to California was in the offing. "I was elected," he wrote in August, "by the New Mexico Department Convention of the American Legion, as a delegate to the national convention to be held in San Francisco the last of September and the beginning of Oct. Is it okay if I go provided I have someone to take my place at Mescalero?" A niece in Los Angeles wanted him to officiate her wedding on 28 September, "and Louis Knecht . . . also wants to get married about that same time. He wants me to do the job."[34]

Church and religious affairs necessitated some of his trips, at which times he always tried to garner a quick run to Los Angeles and family, including, he liked to say, "all the in-laws and outlaws." His niece Dorothy and her husband Jess Bumgarner were often the recipients of these impromptu visits. "We'd get a phone call in the middle of the night: 'I'm here at the bus station, come get me.' Or 'I'm flying into LAX, come pick me up.' Then BANG went the receiver. Oh man, we'd have to call him back: 'What's your flight number?'

"'I don't know. I arrive at nine tonight.' Then we'd have to go find out what airline he was on."[35]

Father Al's trips to the coast, hurried as they had to be, were always an occasion for family celebrations. The families had now burgeoned into a new and ever-expanding generation, and all within the radius of possibility gathered when Father Al visited. Grandnephew Ray Brown, living with his grandparents Ray and Clara, remembered Father Albert coming "frequently. We used to have large family gatherings. We would get these big tables out of the basement. We'd pull all the boards and saw horses that held them up and the chairs and benches and set them up," outdoors if the weather was friendly. When forced indoors, "my grandmother would put canvas on the floor so the kids wouldn't spill food on her carpet, and she'd bring in turkey and chickens and ham. . . . It was just wonderful. Thirty or forty people would come. The kids would all run around and play. . . .

"Father Albert used to love to have the children gather around. He used to tell us stories. I was amazed at this guy who'd been so many places and known so many people. He could speak I don't know how many languages. I never knew another priest who could put the fear of God in me so thoroughly as he could. And yet—he could have such a good time with the children. He was so loving."[36]

The adults had as much fun as the children, when they could pry him loose from them. "Loads of fun," niece Dorothy remembered. "So happy-go-lucky—and yet so serious when it came to religion." To Jess, "he just had something about him that made people feel happy"[37]—except for his terrible driving, which was the family horror.

He loved to gather the children in his old car and they loved to go. Their parents were always relieved when they returned from a jaunt with Father Al. The Bumgarners held their collective breaths on picnic outings with the padre at the wheel. Ascending a steep winding mountain road, with his eyes on them more often than on the road as he recounted a funny story was not their idea of a relaxed Sunday outing.

On one occasion Cecil and Marie Russell, having hosted their padre for a merry evening, heard an ominous thud immediately after he left. They rushed out. Was he safe? Oh, yes. But their fencepost, lamps, and a good-sized section of the fence were a crumpled mess. He was, everyone who knew him agreed, a better sky pilot than earthbound motorist.

He seemed to know everyone. The Bumgarners and friends were at a little Mexican restaurant one evening, "sitting there talking, and the bar tender was listening to us. 'Are you talking about Father Albert Braun?' he asked. We were—and he said, 'I know him. I was in the army with him.'"[38]

With autumn came harvest in Mescalero. "Am harvesting beans," he wrote hurriedly in October. "Had a pleasant visit from Frs. Marcian & Eddie. They came with St. John's big truck to get a load of our delicious apples. Father (Colonel) Duffy was here and left me a qt. of Old Forester and Haig & Haig 5 Stars for Christmas. We anticipated and sampled both bottles. . . ."[39] The padre reaped more than beans and apples.

The following week he was apprised that he had been awarded the Legion of Merit "for meritorious service from December 1941 to May

1942."[40] His former commanding officer, Colonel Octave DeCarre, had informed him back in January that he was recommending medals for Braun and other officers, praising him for his "wonderful work with the 92nd," and requesting information and names of any enlisted men the chaplain knew should receive medals.[41] Father Al supplied what he could but told his old commander to forget about medals for him. DeCarre nonetheless recommended the padre for a Distinguished Service Cross, a Bronze Star (with V), and a Silver Star.[42]

Now in October he was notified of another honor. "The Commanding General, Fourth Army, Fort Sam Houston, Texas [General Wainwright], has been directed to present the Legion of Merit to you with suitable ceremony. Your wishes relative to the date and presentation should be communicated to that officer."[43]

He knew as he read where the ceremony must be held. His Mescaleros had already honored him with a plaque of their own: "God's Warrior" it read, and in the center of the large disk rode an armed Apache warrior astride a charging steed. Where else but here among his Apaches could his ceremony mean so much? He must share it with them.

God's Warrior. Father Albert speaks to his people. On the church wall hang the plaque and title bestowed on him by the Mescalero Apache tribe. Courtesy of SJAM.

On a crisp bright day in late November the canyon began to fill. Apache tents and wagons already clustered throughout the glen. Cars and pickups climbed from the desert; army vans from El Paso arrived early with the brass bands of the 62nd and 247th Army Ground Forces and a platoon of troops. Major General John L. Homer, Commander at Fort Bliss, arrived with his staff, along with a long line of colonels and a bevy of officers' wives.

The grounds swarmed with visitors. An estimated 1,500 people—Apaches, military personnel, and neighbors—milled happily, children and dogs ran about, the bands played, and the aroma of roasting meat permeated the canyon. For days the tribe had been preparing a feast for the huge crowd. Father Al cheerily greeted everyone, though his *abrazos* were left-handed: while working on the church the day before he had slipped from some scaffolding and broken his right arm.

Early in the afternoon the military personnel assembled before the church and General Homer, delegated by Wainwright, whose duties prevented his presence, pinned the Legion of Merit on the hero-priest of Corregidor. Though not, under the circumstance, required to salute, Father Al stubbornly refused to let a broken arm (*Insignificant!*) prevent him from performing with strict military propriety. Slipping his arm from the sling, he stood stiffly at attention, snapped a crisp salute, and held it for the duration of the national anthem, disdaining Apache-like to show pain. At the conclusion of the presentation a tribal member presented an Apache headdress to General Homer, who accepted it on behalf of Wainwright.[44]

The padre felt deeply honored to receive this citation to hang with his others. In characteristic fashion he always placed them too high above eye level to be easily seen—"lest I should get a swelled head," he always explained.

FATHER AL RECEIVES THE LEGION OF MERIT AT MESCALERO, NOVEMBER 1945.

Chaplain Albert Braun stands at head of formation with Major General John L. Homer, Commander at Fort Bliss, Texas, representing General Wainwright. (top and bottom) Courtesy of SJAM.

Concluding the ceremony, Fred Pellman, on behalf of the Mescalero Apache tribe, presents a war bonnet to General Homer, who accepts it for General Wainwright. Courtesy of SJAM.

Father Al with Mescalero friends after the ceremony. Courtesy of SJAM.

His final project for 1946 was to enhance Saint Joseph's tower with a carillon. Lacking a church bell, he had priced electronic tower systems, which ranged from $325 to $1,000 plus installation. He preferred the latter. "The beautiful melodies will mean so much to the Indians. Will you give permission?" He proposed to pay for the system from monies forthcoming from the army.[45] Father Gregory authorized the purchase.

By early December he had the heating system installed, "except for the stoves. This week we expect to have the electric carillons installed. The men are now installing the steel window frames and the translucent glass; they hope to have this job done by Christmas. . . ."[46]

Another event during this period would live happily in his memory throughout the years. Among his visitors was Bruce Klinekole, who arrived from his native Oklahoma as he had so vowed in prison camp, to meet and—he hoped—to marry Virginia Shanta. She was all he expected, and he returned often over the next year to pursue his courtship.

But Virginia was a Catholic. Bruce was not, and she insisted she must marry a Catholic.

He consulted the padre. Soon Father Al was giving Bruce religious instruction, baptized him in time, and then, Virginia recounts, "he allowed us to set a date. We married in Saint Joseph's mission—Father Albert married us there. We didn't have a big wedding.

"Bruce was in and out of Oklahoma before we were married, but of course we stayed here in Mescalero afterward. He was a ranch lover—he loved horses and cattle. That's my love too. We rode horseback together, he and I, we herded cattle together, we had our children and ranched together. And my husband was very insistent that our four children were all baptized."

Recounting this years later, after Bruce's death, Virginia told with choked voice and wet cheeks how proud and grateful she was to know that long before they met, "I gave an inspiration to him, through that prison time, you know, to come home from the war."[47]

As 1947 approached a sense of urgency seems to have propelled the padre. His legs were growing progressively worse and much work remained. He might shrug off his increasing disability as *Insignificant!*, but Al Braun was a realist. And the reality was that he must finish his work at Mescalero while he still could.

It was during this necessity that his cherished mother died, and he hastened to coast and family. Father Gregory officiated the funeral. "I appreciated more than I can tell you," the padre wrote his provincial after returning in January, "that you came from San Francisco . . . to say the Mass for my mother." Again he alluded to the urgency of time, his race against it, and the projects he wished to complete. Topping his list of priorities was his old crusade for the day school.

> I talked with Mother Edna over the phone. She is now visiting the various schools taught by her Sisters among the Indians of the Southwest. She plans to visit Mescalero. . . . She has halfway committed herself to send teachers to . . . Mescalero. . . . I hope she can . . . send three Sisters next summer. . . . I will turn over the quarters I now occupy to the Sisters and will move to the other side of the Hall. There is considerable work to be done there to make these quarters habitable. . . . Mr. Mills has drawn complete plans. . . . He . . . estimates the cost of everything to be $2,000.00. I already have $1,600.00 on hand for that project. The other $400.00 will come from somewhere, perhaps from you.
>
> There are some things I am very desirous to accomplish in the near future. First, to put the windows in the Church, and the heating system and possibly, to grade the ground surrounding, and put up the fountain. Second, to have the Sisters established at Mescalero, . . . and thirdly, to have another Father at Mescalero, one who is young and zealous and interested in the Indians and who has a heart for them. After these things are accomplished, I won't mind leaving Mescalero. I have been away from all regular life in a religious community for so many years. . . .

Until then he wanted to stay at Mescalero. Switching to present concerns, he again alluded to the hostility of Father Francis in Tularosa.

> I am aware . . . that our next door neighbor has no use for Indians. He either does not realize the value of the immortal Soul, or does not think that Indians have one.

The Bishop himself told me that [Father Francis] . . . would destroy the Mission at Mescalero if it were in his power. Another year should make the Mission safe from any outside interference.[48]

Having laid out his blueprint in that revealing letter, he went back to work. Even when hit by a cyclone in February—an almost unheard-of phenomenon at Mescalero—he mentioned it only in passing and more as nuisance than adversity. Although "it blew $300 worth of glass out of the new church, . . . we hope to have all the glass back by the end of the week." In contrast, "at Alamogordo Air Base the damage was three hundred thousand."

Of more moment, "Mr. Mills is drawing up . . . plans for a house alongside the stone church," rather than adding onto the hall which "is too far from the church in winter."[49]

By early April he was nearing completion of the most critical repairs to the existing structure, and he wrote on the eighth.

> Either this week or next we will win[d] up the work on the church for awhile. All bills are paid except the enclosed [for the heater]. Can the province take care of that one for me? The windows are in. The screens are up to protect the windows. The floors are in the tower. The tiles which Fr. Tom had shot off the tower & roof have been replaced. Leaks have been sealed. The heating system has been installed, electricity has been install[ed]. The whole church & baptistery & sacristy are wired. Lamp[s] (big ones) made to order are installed. We have the beautiful chimes. . . . I wish you could see the church now. The people are proud of it. Last Sunday (Easter) it was packed. . . ."[50]

Still perking with enthusiasm for the proposed residence adjacent to the church, he mailed the completed plans to his provincial on the sixteenth. "The location is magnificent," he exulted.

> All the five bedrooms face the warm south and have a commanding view of the beautiful meadow and stream below and also of the towering mountain to the south of the mission.

We are always crowded here through the year, for that reason the 5 bedrooms. Last summer we frequently had as high as 14 staying here, for that reason the screened porch. There will be an attractive secluded patio between the residence and the church. An arched veranda goes from the rear of house to sacristy. There will be glass in each arch of the veranda which glass can be raised to shut out inclement weather.

Mr. Prestridge, owner of the saw mill at Alamogordo and State Highway Commissioner, wired the District Engineer to meet him at Mescalero Saturday to see about putting in the road around the location for the new house and to grade around the church. It is a big project and would cost the mission five thousand dollars. If the state does not do the job, Mr. Prestridge said he would do it.[51]

But despite his enthusiasm, strain and exhaustion were taking their toll. "If I can finish the work this week I will go to vets' hospital next week, but not with the intention of staying there as a patient—I hate hospitals. Just want to see what their plans are." Meanwhile, he asked, "Can I drive to the coast with Fr. Louergrau [who had been visiting] from Pittsburgh. I am tired and want to rest."[52]

He and his friend left after mass on the twentieth for a week and returned "safe but tired from the trip. . . .

"The Bishop and Fr. Kehoe were here last nite. The Bishop is pleased with the church and is amazed at the amount of propaganda carried on against the church. He expected to find [it] . . . in ruins." Apparently Father Francis was still sowing dissent.

Still afire with plans, Father Al hoped for approval "at your next meeting. We need the room. . . . This place must have a Sisters' school. Because of the cut in appropriations many Gov. school[s] are going to be closed or consolidated. The Indians are looking to the mission schools to take care of the situation. If we don't take a hand . . . the whole thing will fall into the hands of the Protestants. . . ."[53]

Many Mescaleros believed the incursions of the Protestant missionaries were causing a rupture in the tribe. "It used to be there was no division," medicine man Paul Ortega remembered. Tribe and church prayed together for the rains and the crops as the seasons necessitated.

Certain time of the year they have a get-together—a mass, you know, and the Apache dancers. There was no division . . . [until] the Protestants—the Dutch Reformed, the Holy Rollers, the Mormons—they all came. . . . Then . . . they're separated somehow, they're not relatives no more. So there is a brother not going to his brother's funeral, because he's going to another church. All kinds of separation going on. The Catholics say 'you can't participate in the Dutch Reformed across the road, you are committing a sin.' The same things the Dutch Reformed are saying—'you no longer belong to us. We won't like you no more because you are over there with the Catholics doing all the things they do.' I've seen it happen, in my lifetime. . . .[54]

Father Al too saw this division and, determined to prevent further separation, reiterated his belief that a Catholic day school for all the Mescalero children would go far toward reuniting the tribe.

That the padre's exhaustion grew more acute is evidenced in his uncharacteristic pessimism in a letter he wrote in July while attending an American Legion convention on the Coast.

General Hodges, an admiral, and some big shot from the air corps spoke. They sounded very doubtful whether [we] can save ourselves when the Russians attack. Russia has the largest airfield in the world within six minutes from Alaska. This year Russia is manufacturing one hundred thousand planes—mostly heavy long distance bombers. We are manufacturing 1800. Russia can land a large army not far from our northern border and will meet with little effective opposition. The outlook is discouraging. Apparently history is about to repeat itself. The barbarians from the north are about to wipe out another Roman Empire and the World will go through another Dark Age.[55]

There was doubtless another factor in his blue mood. His days at

Mescalero were, he knew, numbered. The padre faced increasing pain and weakness in his legs. The aftermath was setting in from the distress he had suffered as a Japanese POW and the diseases he had incurred—diphtheria, malaria, dengue fever, pellagra, and beriberi, plus the avitaminosis resulting from four years of starvation. He recognized his growing physical limitations, knew his usefulness at the mission was declining and his time with his Mescaleros would soon end. It was a hard truth to accept: he loved them.

One option remained. By extending his active military duty he could receive medical attention while still serving usefully as a chaplain. "The army," he reported from the convention, "will put me on duty as soon as I get the necessary permission from the Order and the military ordinate."[56] Meanwhile he would work as long as possible.

Back in Mescalero on the eleventh he found letters awaiting him. Mr. Prestridge informed him "that the War Assets Administration had Hammond Organs which he could obtain and thought it a very nice gesture if [he] donated such an organ to the church," and had put the process in motion. "After he buys the organ," Father Al wrote with some return of the old enthusiasm, it would be time to build the organ loft. But more immediately, the Sisters coming to teach summer catechism classes "will be here Wed[nesday]."[57]

There was also a letter from his old friend and military boss Bill Arnold. "It will seem like old times to have you back in the service and goodness knows, there is room for you and your zealous spirit in the poor, old army which is getting batted around by Congress and most everybody else. I am overjoyed to know you are really able to do duty for I had a fear that the medicos would find you incapacitated."[58]

Only a few details of military red tape remained before Father Al would be recalled. Arnold was expediting these rapidly—too rapidly for the padre, it appears. "I need a trunk, a suitcase and a hand bag," he wrote his Provincial hastily. "Maybe these items, in fairly good shape, are in the attics of some of the monasteries around the bay. I begrudge spending the money for them, because I want to leave as much money in the bank for Father Marcian when he takes over. The bags I have are very old and shabby. One cannot report at an Army Post with shabby equipment." And for Father Marcian: "Tell Butch . . . to have a good time while he can."[59]

Two days later he wrote frantically. "This morning I got telegraphic orders to report for duty July 31st at Brooke General Hospital, Army Medical Center, Fort Sam Houston, Texas.

"There are many things I want to tell Father Marcian. Can he reach Mescalero by July 26? The Sisters have the summer course in religion going full force. 66 children are attending. At present I am bringing them in and taking them home after classes. It will be necessary to have someone do that after I leave. I don't know if it is prudent to trust anyone else but the Father with that job."

Moreover, he added, "There are no quarters available at Fort Sam Houston. I will have to live off the post. Brooke General Hospital is the largest the army has. There will be sick calls at all times also at nite. It will be necessary for me to have a car. If I can get a Cheve will the Province pay for it? . . . I think I can get a Cheve from a friend. . . ."[60] Father Al could still finagle a deal.

The army, whose wheels traditionally grind slowly, caught Al Braun—and Butch Marcian—by surprise. Bill Arnold had indeed expedited the process. "As soon as you okayed me for the Military Ordinate," the padre advised Father Gregory, "that office sent the endorsement on to the War Department which in turn immediately issued orders. . . . There is nothing to do but report when ordered, so I will have to leave Mescalero the beginning of next week." But Marcian, he had just learned, could not arrive until mid-August. "I am terribly upset over it because the place needs a priest with summer school on and the Sisters here. I will have the Mexican Friars send someone for next Sunday." He blamed only himself. "Maybe," he admitted ruefully, "I should not have started the summer school, but I always tried to act as if I were going to be here forever. Then too I wanted the Sisters to come here and get acquainted with these Indians. They are wonderful and deserving of a Sisters' school. . . . Will try to hire some dependable person to bring the children to and from school every day till Fr. Marcian gets here. As far as I am responsible I am sorry for this mixup. Am not too happy anyhow and this disturbs me a lot."[61]

On the last Sunday in July Father Albert Braun said his final mass as pastor of Saint Joseph's. A few last-minute preparations, a day of sad goodbyes, and the big priest who always had a pot of beans on his stove for any who came to his door was gone from the people and the place he loved best in all the world—the place, he told them, he would like to return in death, had even picked the spot he wanted beneath a certain oak tree.

So departed the last of the frontier priests, and one of the most extraordinary. He had defended the traditions of his adopted people against those who would destroy them. He had embraced their culture and, building the magnificent church of which he knew they were worthy, had built their souls into it—and brought within its folds over sixty percent of the tribe. It was an incredible melding of beliefs.

He had not done all he wanted, and many of the plans he left for his successors never materialized. The sisters' day school for the Mescalero children never came, nor that for the Mexican friars. The five-bedroom residence with its patio and portals was never built; neither fountain nor choir loft materialized, nor the statue and carved angels. Whether his visions would have solidified into substance had he stayed—*¿quién sabe?* Perhaps his dreams were too grandiose, too impractical, too vast for one small mission. Or perhaps those of his fraters were too small.

But in climbing for the heavens he had reached a mountaintop. Against all obstacles he had built the great church he had so long envisioned, and he had built many lives into it. Now it stood, for fallen heroes a monument, and for his chosen people a center that would 'light their lives forever.' The rest was—*Insignificant!*

And there were other mountains to climb.

19: OPERATION SANDSTONE

He arrived at Fort Sam on 1 August, a Friday, reported for duty the next morning. "Signed in; got my quarters; bought about $150.00 summer uniforms etc, got my bags from S[outhern] P[acific] Depot, was given three masses for tomorrow and put on sick call for the week. There are about 1800 patients. Till Monday I am using Chaplain Barnabas C. McAlarney's O.F.M. quarters. At present he is back in N.Y. on leave. I raided his ice-box and made myself a high-ball. He being a good Friar will be glad I found what he has and used it."

He was still fretting about his abrupt departure from Mescalero, but glad Father Marcian was replacing him. "The people are more than happy that he is coming back, and so am I."[1] He was concerned also over discord arising from Father Francis, who seems to have been making more waves at Tularosa. "Am enclosing a letter from Father Leon [Baldinado]," he wrote his provincial, "to show you what you already know—what a bastard old Frank is. I never paid any attention to him but it is a shame a young priest has to run up against so much malice in a fellow priest."[2]

Large of heart but lean of purse, the padre had, true to form, left Mescalero owing money for some of his renovations. He would pay these through extra mass intentions which he requested from the province. "However," he stipulated, "don't mark me down for any Gregorians or Novenas." Assigned as senior chaplain for post hospitals, including Brooke General, he found "a tremendous amount of work to do in the many hospitals here. I am not lazy but this is too much. . . ."[3]

"There is one financial matter I still have to bother about," he wrote Father Gregory. "A car is indispensable. I walk my legs tired every day and get far behind in work. Just can't get transportation from the army. . . . Want a Ford Cheve or Plym. I have my bid in everywhere. . . . Will the Province stand for it. I hate to borrow money. I will never get out of debt."[4]

A few days later he reported that the "Chief of Police in Alamogordo is getting a new Chevie. He is letting me have it. It is already on hand. . . . It has a radio license and insurance. The whole thing as is cost $1800.00

Can you send me at once that amount of money." He added ruefully, "Can't pay you back more than $50.00 per month because I already have so many obligations."[5]

It had been a depressing month, but his depression went deeper than the personal. His concern over the postwar world had not lightened. His deep fears of communism were intensified by growing evidence of red agents and subversives in high-level posts in Washington, at a time when America was demobilizing at an alarming rate: when Father Al reported at Fort Sam, Congress had cut the total manpower of the armed forces to a million and a half, with more cuts coming. Communist forces were advancing in China; and the Russian menace was escalating in Europe. "There is nothing to stop the Russians if they make up their mind to move," he wrote in mid-August. "It appears the complete destruction and disappearance of Western Civilization is not far off. You have a big task to prepare your men for what is coming. God alone knows how many of us will be able to stand up under the ordeal."[6] His apprehension is easy to understand: he had known the savagery of the aggressor.

Still depressed—this time over his debts—he wrote a week later, "I can see I am going to have a hard time financially. My senior chaplain, an Episcopalian, my present boss who is very good to me wants me to join him in throwing a party once a month for the doctors and nurses. It is an excellent way to get a lot of cooperation in handling the sick calls but I am sure it will cost about $50.00 a month. Have been in the dumps since coming here. There is plenty of work and people have been kind to me but I just can't get interested. This is no way to be but I can't help it. If it were not for the money I wouldn't stay on this job at all. Maybe time will change this attitude."

He was doubtless suffering from normal postwar depression. Still, he kept busy and was by nature happy. "Next week," he wrote in the same letter, "I have a number of weddings and Friday we have a big picnic for Gen Wainwright who ends his army career Aug 31st."[7] Too, the padre was himself scheduled for a great honor.

"This morning," he wrote the day after the picnic, "General Wainwright decorated me with a Silver Star. He goes out of the army Aug. 31. It is the last he will pin."[8] Wainwright had insisted on presenting the medal to 'his chaplain' personally. It was a simple ceremony, held indoors, a quiet, very personal moment between the two old warhorses—an emotional moment doubly charged by their friendship, their shared wartime memories, the honor itself, and the beloved general's impending retirement.

"I guess Skinny felt he had to give me something," the padre quipped afterward. "I gave him the last drink from my bottle before he surrendered." He passed it off with a grin and a twinkle; but the twinkle, one suspects, was brightened by a tear.

General Jonathan Wainwright presents Chaplain Albert Braun with the Silver Star. "I guess Skinny felt he had to give me something. . . ." Photo source: US Signal Corps.

By contrast the general's retirement ceremony was, Father Al wrote, "imposing." An estimated ten thousand spectators attended, three thousand troops marched in review, and thirty planes thundered over.

"For an old soldier to say it is a pleasure to take his last review is . . . a far cry from the truth," Wainwright declared in his farewell speech.

Military men, he said, were "lovers of peace" who guarded that peace with strength—a theme he had long repeated and would continue to repeat until his death. He praised the young soldiers "in whose hands the destinies of the army and the nation will rest," and ended with a simple "Thank you, goodbye, and God bless all of you."

"When band played and the crowd sang Ol Lang' S.," the padre observed, "there were not many dry eyes."[9] Certainly not Father Al's: he and Skinny had shared a war.

The padre's somber mood hung on, though he assured his provincial, "I always adjust myself in time. It is somewhat harder this time than ever before. It was very hard to leave Mescalero."[10]

His depression lingered. "I don't like this job any more than when I first came," he wrote in mid-October. "Have made a lot of friends here, more than I care to. Never have liked hospital work. I think if I do this job well my boss might help me get another job after I am here a year. In that way most of these army people are good sports. They reward good will. We will see what the next year brings. I am very pessimistic about the future . . . because of the obligations I have." But, he added, "My boss Chaplain Kenney (an Episcopalian) . . . is a fine man."[11]

Kenney was sensitive to Father Al's enervation, or susceptible to his persuasiveness. The padre was far from well, in need of lighter duty and more tranquil surroundings in which to regain physical and emotional momentum. In November he received orders for what most considered choice duty: Hawaii, paradise of the Pacific. "I would have preferred . . . foreign duty in Japan or Europe," he wrote an army friend later. "I am more interested in international affairs than in scenic beauty and a lovely climate."[12]

Assigned to the 1220th Provisional Engineer Battalion, he found life at Fort Shafter dull, pleasant, uneventful, and of short duration. His tasks were light—probably too light for his taste—so that when his chance came for a special temporary duty assignment on a lonely atoll called Eniwetok, he doubtless jumped at it, likely even lobbied for it. Al Braun was about to embark on an assignment of far more international import than he would have found in Europe or Japan.

✝✝✝

The plane taxied, lifted, gained altitude. Hickam Field fell behind as they banked and headed southwest, and then there was nothing but scudding clouds and the blue Pacific, over two thousand miles of it stretching ahead to the naval base at Kwajalein, and from there another three hundred to Eniwetok. It was early January 1948, and Chaplain Albert Braun, Major, USARPAC (United States Army Pacific), 0134329, was en route to the most top-secret American project of its kind, something called 'Operation Sandstone.'

He with others had been briefed in the nature of the operation, though only in general terms. It would be a nuclear bomb test, strictly scientific, exclusively American, and of utmost secrecy. That United States-Soviet relations were reaching a crisis he was well aware, and that these tests were crucial to maintain the American lead in arms superiority he doubtless intuited. What Stalin had gained at Yalta he was consolidating. Always acutely interested in the Far East, Father Al had noted with alarm the Russian-spurred spread of communism in the Orient, and America's virtual abandonment of Chiang Kai-shek to an advancing Red army. As during the war, Washington's focus was on Europe.

By the time preparations were beginning for Operation Sandstone, the ravenous Russian bear had already devoured much of eastern Europe, established puppet governments in country after country, enclosed them behind the Iron Curtain, and incited ferment elsewhere. Communist parties were thriving in France and Italy. Communist forces, supplied by Russian satellites Yugoslavia and Albania, fomented civil war in Greece; and Russia pressured economically prostrate Turkey for control of the Dardanelles and ports on the Black Sea. Britain had aided Greece and Turkey until, in February 1947, she could no longer bear that financial burden.

"It must be our policy," the President declared, "to support free people who are resisting subjugation by armed minorities or by outside pressure." Congress agreed, the 'Truman Doctrine' was actuated, and with American economic and military assistance, Greece and Turkey were enabled to preserve their territorial integrity.

In June the policy was amplified in the proffered 'Marshall Plan' to extend help to countries throughout economically stricken Europe. Stalin angrily countered the 'imperialist scheme' by forbidding any Soviet satellite to accept the proposed help, intimidated nominally independent Czechoslovakia and Finland against so doing, and organized the nine-nation Cominform.

War with the USSR loomed distinctly possible, even probable.

How soon Russia would develop an atomic bomb was the vital question; that Russian scientists were not idle was a certainty. The Atomic Energy Commission (AEC) had notified the President in April that the A-bomb stockpile was insufficient to protect American security: the arsenal must be enlarged and the pace of production accelerated. America must maintain thermonuclear superiority. To that end scientists were envisioning a bomb to be detonated by a fusion of deuterium and tritium, isotopes of hydrogen, as contrasted by the earlier fissionable explosions. If successful, such bombs would be lighter, and theoretically have an explosive force much greater than those at Hiroshima and Nagasaki.

The hypothesis itself, and each stage of development, would require elaborate testing, for which the AEC chose Eniwetok as best meeting the requirements. Situated in the extreme northwest quadrant of the Marshall Islands, it was remote enough for safety and secrecy; the lagoon, twenty-three miles in diameter, offered anchorage for a fleet of large ships; the prevailing currents and winds were favorable; and of the forty islets that formed the atoll, enough were of a size adequate for the shot towers and elaborate instrumentation necessary for the three test shots scheduled for Sandstone.

Preparations moved rapidly in the States—in the laboratories producing the nuclear material; in the AEC and related agencies; in the armed forces, upon which the logistics for the enormous and distant project devolved; and among the scientists at the nuclear facility at Los Alamos, New Mexico, who would be responsible for technical oversight, for preparing the test weapons and later for analyzing the results.

Activity on Eniwetok was as vigorous. By November 1947 the 140 native inhabitants of the atoll had been evacuated and the first building crews were at work. By the time the padre arrived in January with the army contingent, temporary quarters were in place and the atoll was teeming with civilian construction crews, navy transportation teams, and army engineers. The emerald waters of the once-quiet lagoon churned with cargo ships and small craft as those ashore threw up tent camps, temporary housing, latrines, and mess halls, while others cleared and leveled the islet of Engebi on which the first test dubbed, 'X-RAY,' would be made. Construction then began on the 200-foot steel tower atop an asphalt disk whose diameter equaled the length of two football fields, as well as surrounding reinforced concrete buildings to house electronic measuring equipment and a central command post. All would soon be connected by miles of submarine cable. Similar setups would quickly follow on islets Aomon and Runit for the ensuing tests, coded as 'Yoke' and 'Zebra.' An old airfield that had briefly served American forces in 1944 had to be overhauled, and all structures completed in a ten-week time frame, before the scientists and top brass would arrive in mid-March.[13]

Having set up a chapel, Father Al's duties were those routine to any priest—confessions, daily masses, special observances, counseling if needed. There were no families; and had any serious illness or accident occurred, the stricken would have been flown to the naval base at Kwajalein. He found the project intensely interesting, even without knowing the scientific particulars; and though he was but a spectator, he obviously quickened to the urgency of time, the importance of the operation, and the anticipation of the tests. And as always he would have enjoyed the camaraderie of the crews.

The sense of crisis increased with the news of the Stalinist coup in Czechoslovakia. Soviet troops occupied Prague, overturned the democratic government, murdered beloved President Jan Masaryk (reporting it suicide), established communist rule, and began to scrutinize Berlin.

Postwar Germany had been divided into four zones of occupation. So also had Berlin, deep in the heart of the Soviet zone, with the proviso that the western Allies have rights of access to their sectors. To help Germany and thereby all Europe recover, the British and Americans had in February combined their zones into a single economic and political unit. (The French would soon follow.) Russian objections grew louder, nastier; and on 5 March General Lucius Clay, the American commander in Germany, warned that Soviet attitudes were hardening and that war could come "with drastic suddenness." The Defense Department prepared for war. The Joint Chiefs began devising emergency war plans, and a war scare energized all Washington. Britain, France, and the Benelux countries, with American backing, signed the defense treaty that would grow into NATO.

The men on Eniwetok had already noted Soviet interest in their operations. In late February a Russian ship began skulking about twenty miles offshore, and on 3 March Navy planes sighted at least one submarine, "complete with snorkel," AEC director David Lilienthal logged, "whatever that is. . . ."[14] For everyone on the atoll the Russian ships underscored the crucial nature of their mission.

On 16 March four United States ships left their convoy and quietly churned into the lagoon carrying top Sandstone brass, a bevy of scientists, technicians, test equipment and, in one ship, laboratories. From the converted seaplane tender *Albemarle* crews began unloading test equipment and elaborate instruments onto the northern island Engebi, site for the first test, where technicians commenced the processes of installment. From the command ship *Mount McKinley,* anchored off the southernmost isle of Eniwetok, General John E. Hull, Commander of Joint Task Force 7, began inspections of the facilities; aboard the seaplane tender *Curtis,* test director Navy Captain James S. Russell and scientific director Darol K. Froman set up their headquarters; and scientists aboard the *Bairoko* and the *Albemarle* plunged into their own spheres of work.

A submarine alert on the night of the seventeenth heightened awareness considerably, but failed to disrupt the rhythm of intense preparation.

Meanwhile the world's eyes focused on Germany. The Soviets had begun to obstruct rail and road traffic through the Russian zone to Berlin. Tension neared a breaking point. The Joint Chiefs met in Washington. Could the armed forces deliver any atomic weapons? they asked General Kenneth Nichols, commander of the Armed Forces Special Weapons Project. They could not, Nichols answered: the qualified assembly teams were all at Eniwetok.[15]

Those crews too were tense. All knew the possibility of a sneak attack on the ships in the lagoon, which could not only scuttle the tests but wipe out the only weapons-assembly crews America had. As war kindled, America's need for advanced weaponry was crucial. Was fusion feasible? If so, would the detonation be too great, and the islands be blown to a mass of rapidly submerging rubble? Would the weapon detonate at all? The answer was terse: it had to.

April 14. Countdown. Task Force heading south, away from Engebi, to the control point at Parry islet. Final checks at firing site, and a test run with a dummy weapon to confirm firing procedure. Firing crew checking circuits, reporting hourly by radio to Parry all night.

April 15. Predawn. Last of personnel speeding south from test site. Weather report favorable. Minus one hour. Timing signal starting blast-measurement equipment. From his southern position, the padre stood watching eight B-17s, piloted by remote control, rising one by one from

Eniwetok islet, beginning to circle the tower at different levels to pick up radioactive samples.

Minus 15 minutes. Sequence timer activated for firing.

Minus 2 minutes. "Adjust protective goggles or turn from site zero." Al Braun donning his goggles, facing Engebi. Intense silence.

Detonation. A red ball of incredible brilliance. An enveloping cloud. An enormity like the creation of the universe, or its end. . . .

The fireball, they learned later, was seen as far as Kwajalein, three hundred miles away.

The padre saw the helicopters rise, then drop technicians swathed in protective clothing, saw the landing craft speeding for Engebi, headed to collect the telling samples by remote-control devices. He saw the pilotless planes return and land, carrying samples to be quickly transferred to C-54s already revved for fast relay flights to Albuquerque, while the radioisotopes were still active, to be analyzed at Los Alamos.[16]

It was an experience Al Braun would never forget or ever discuss. Of the scientific details he was ignorant—would not have understood the rarified levels of nuclear physics even if privy to such information. But as an astute observer of history, he placed the tests in the context of world events, was well aware of the significance of Operation Sandstone, grateful for his chance to witness the drama, and in his own humble way to be a part of it.

Though the full analysis from Los Alamos would take weeks, the scientists were confident the first test was highly successful. Implosion of fused materials was feasible; its yield of 37 kilotons was, according to Hewett and Duncan, "equivalent to 37,000 tons of TNT, compared with about 20,000 tons for the Nagasaki weapon."[17] Several days later via a press release in Hawaii the world learned, without fanfare or elaboration, only what the Soviets would have deduced anyhow, that a nuclear weapon had been successfully detonated in the Marshall Islands.

Activity was now directed toward modifying details for the next two tests, to follow at two-week intervals. Father Albert would certainly have shared the brief respite of exhilaration and relief following the initial test, would have joined merrily in a few toasts. After that, while the various crews prepared for the succeeding shots, he would have had little to do beyond his usual pastoral duties. So within a few days of X-RAY, hating idleness, he applied through the Chaplain School at Carlisle Barracks, Pennsylvania, for an extension course, completed it in due time, and received twenty hours Army credit in Military Government.[18]

The final test was completed on 15 May. Once the planes carrying the precious data disappeared beyond the watery horizon, the crews began to dismantle, lade, close down the site, and prepare to leave Eniwetok. The scientists were elated. They had demonstrated that the theory of fusion weapons—or H-bomb—was valid, that composite bombs of fission and fusion worked, producing large yields from small quantities of fissionable material.[19] It meant, in practical terms that even a layman could understand, that more bombs could be produced from less material, that they would be lighter, more powerful, and more efficient. America could now increase its dangerously low stockpile to meet the developing crisis.

More tests would follow, with increasingly powerful results; and in the hydrogen bomb that grew from Sandstone, America gained and maintained the thermonuclear superiority that, through its deterrent power, defined the consequent course of history, to spare the world from its own insanity, until President Reagan could ultimately, triumphantly, demand, "Mr. Gorbachev, tear down that wall!"

But that was for the future.

Father Albert Braun, OFM, knew only that something very big, very important had happened, something vital for his country and for all free countries battling to beat back the barbaric horde from ravishing the civilized world. And that this humble friar had bagged a front-row seat on the fifty-yard line.

✞✞✞

Scarcely had the padre returned to Hawaii than his notorious driving caught up with him. "Dear Sir," the letter read. "A report . . . indicates that you were recently cautioned by one of our police officers relative to a violation of the Traffic Code . . ." and so on, signed by Honolulu's Chief of Police.[20]

He would in the future, the Chaplain replied, do his best "to observe all traffic regulations. . . ."[21] It was an easy promise to keep, inasmuch as he had no car to drive until August. The incident that had elicited the warning had demolished the entire left side of his treasured 'Cheve.'[22]

A letter from Celine Sheehy arrived in July telling the padre of the recent death of her mother. He replied immediately, writing nostalgically of Mama Henrion's time at Mescalero. "Will say a mass for her," he promised.[23]

The padre's remaining time in the army can be quickly condensed.

His largely uneventful year in Hawaii, after the drama of Sandstone, seems to have dragged for the action-oriented friar. "It is a lot like after the first World War," he complained in August. "There has been a letdown . . . and it is hard to get things moving as they should be in the Army. . . .

"We are expecting the Chief out here for the dedication of the grand chapel of the new Tripler Hospital," which chapel, he added drolly, "does not exist. . . ."[24]

He watched the international situation closely—often agonizingly, sometimes triumphantly, as when Truman replied to Russia's blockage of Berlin by ordering on 28 June the massive airlift of supplies to the Allied people in the isolated city.

When the President announced in September that Russia had detonated an atomic bomb, the padre could be grimly confident from what he had seen and heard at Eniwetok that the United States was still ahead and would remain so—if the politicos in Washington would keep the faith and follow through on what the scientists had so brilliantly begun. He feared the bureaucrats' increasing head-in-the-sands policy—especially in the Far East, where Mao's Communist forces were swelling alarmingly, backed by Russian might.

Reporting on "what appear to be reliable facts" from a lecture in October "on Russia's manpower, Russia's equipment and Russia's ability to produce . . . I would not hesitate to place an even bet that Russia today can whip the free people. The thing that makes me feel so bad is . . . that it is our own fault that we are in such a sad plight. . . . It is a strange fact about human beings," he reflected, "how they are governed by fads, even those men who are supposed to be practical and intelligent. Someone has created the fad to soft pedal a grave and imminent danger in which not only our nation but all nations who strive to live as free people should live. This attitude works to the advantage of the Communist[s] . . . and makes us more and more vulnerable. I . . . am greatly worried and can see nothing but great danger ahead for us."[25]

Meanwhile he followed the election campaigns in the States throughout the fall, particularly that of his friend Pat Hurley, running in New Mexico on the Republican ticket against Democrat Clinton Anderson.[26] Through their mutual friend Archbishop Edwin Byrnes in Santa Fe, he kept abreast of the race. "I am sorry that I am not in Mescalero and . . . able to invite [Hurley] in for some real stew," he wrote the archbishop, "that thus he might be invigorated enough to carry on his strenuous campaign. Give the General my best wishes. . . ."[27]

The race was close, Byrnes replied. "It is hard to know who is going to win. The General thinks a lot of you. It's too bad that you are not in Mescalero now to help him."[28]

As the election neared the padre grew testy when his absentee ballot failed to come. "It has become embarrassing," he began in his third appeal, "to continue putting in requests for an absentee ballot . . . so that I might be able to fulfill my obligations as a citizen of New Mexico and the United States and cast my vote."[29]

"Long ago," he fulminated to Jack Roak, "you should have learned not to place any confidence in . . . anyone who holds a political job." He enclosed a copy of his third request. "If this one is not acted upon, I will send a copy of this letter and all others to the Republican headquarters at Albuquerque and request that they send a delegation to the Secretary of State to find out why. . . . So if you do not want to see your Secretary of State humiliated see to it that he sends the absentee ballot *muy prompto.*"[30]

Presumably he received his ballot. Of where he stood on the presidential race there is no mention; but he was definitely chagrined at Hurley's defeat—although politics were, after all, *Insignificant!*

In September he had requested a ten-day detached service order back on the mainland to make his annual retreat, to be followed by a short leave of absence to attend to family business regarding his mother's estate.[31] The matter had dragged out and become unnecessarily complicated, the family wanted to replace the lawyer they believed incompetent, and Father Al wanted to transfer title of his share to the Province.[32]

His request was granted, but finding military transportation was difficult. "[S]ince the Berlin affair there are so few planes out here that one must wait a week or two to get a ride. . . . [A]ll army families have been ordered out of Europe. Some of the transports have been ordered from the Pacific to the Atlantic to help move the forty thousand army dependents out. . . ."[33]

On 28 October he was notified of space on an army transport leaving on 5 November. "If it is okay . . . I think I will make my retreat at Malibu," he wrote his provincial. "I have two tickets to the N.D.U.S.C. game. . . . In fact I have asked Father Phil to buy tickets for the games in L.A. Nov 14, 21, and 28."[34] Father Al was, as always, adept at spicing his obligations with a dash of pleasure.

Looking toward retirement and acting on the recommendation of his superior, Chaplain Kirtley, he requested restoration in rank of Lieutenant Colonel, his rank prior to discharge. Not having served in grade long enough for terminal promotion, he had retired a major, at which rank he was still serving.[35]

"Chaplain Braun is the best Chaplain I have ever known," wrote Kirtley in his recommendation. "I served under him for three years, 1937-1940, while on duty with the Civilian Conservation Corps, and have carefully followed his career since that time. He was a chaplain in World War I and has been a reserve chaplain ever since. He served in the Philippine Islands at the beginning of World War II and was taken a prisoner of war by the Japanese and held by them for three and one-half (3½) years. Chaplain Braun meets every requirement for serving in the capacity of a lieutenant colonel in the Chaplain Corps and his record will substantiate this opinion. . . ."[36]

He received his promotion the following April. "Thanks to you and Colonel Poch for promotion," he wrote the Chief of Chaplains. "I was as proud of that silver leaf as any general was of his first star."[37]

He still chafed at the easy life in Hawaii. "I am sorry I am not in Europe with you," he wrote Paul Maddox, Chief of Chaplains in Europe. With the Berlin airlift and the Russian problem it is easy to picture the padre agitating to be where the action was. "I requested that but . . . I was not permitted to accept foreign duty in Germany or Japan. I don't see the logic . . . to give me foreign duty where I am now and not to give it elsewhere for the reason of age," though he did grudgingly concede that Hawaii "is beautiful country and I have a good boss. . . ."[38]

The Sandstone adventure and the pleasant duty in Hawaii with colleagues he liked, along with his natural resilience, seem to have pulled him from his postwar depression. A touch of the old fire blazed in an Easter greeting to his provincial in April. "Best wishes for the blessing of Easter. Couldn't buy a religious Easter card at the P.X. . . . I refused to buy a secular Easter card. Wrote the P.X. officer a letter complaining that he is neglecting his customers who still believe that Christ rose from the grave on Easter."[39]

The padre was still far from recovery and sought one last checkup before he retired. "As a result of deficient food while a prisoner of the Japanese Army," he wrote Chaplain Martin Poch, "I have suffered from beri beri in both legs since 1943. I am not seeking retirement on physical disability," he stressed. "I am not incapacitated. I am restricted in activities and suffer because of the beri beri. So far nothing has been done to improve my physical condition. . . . Maybe nothing can be done. I want to find out. I never want to enter a Veterans' Administration Hospital; therefore, I am seeking this last opportunity for a physical check in an Army hospital."[40]

After that he wanted to travel during his terminal leave, and—above all—to return to his Apaches. He had been indulging in such plans for months. The previous August he had written someone named 'Joe,' obviously an old friend, that he would like to meet him in Mescalero, where "I think I will get a lot of use out of my car traveling around the country before I turn in to Fr. Provincial. I will at least wear out the tires. It would be nice if you, Chaplain Kirtley, and myself could visit those old spots. I would be glad to take you to Juarez again. As far as I can remember, that was the last time I saw you, when you were on your way to spend one year in the regular army. I remember you learned how to make a Tequila Daisy. You never told me if that was the means you used to rise so rapidly in the Army."[41]

That he still nursed an ember of hope to be reassigned to Mescalero is apparent in a few wistful words with which he ends a letter to Archbishop Cushing. "Soon I will be 60, and then I can again return to my mission and enjoy some of the fruits of my years of service. According to present pension laws, my status as Reserve Officer will be pensioned. That will help a lot where I hope to be."[42]

He was still planning travels in April 1949. "I have thought of going to Mexico," he confided to another friend, "and just wander all over the country . . . for the purpose of picking up my Spanish again. I enjoy Mexico. . . . I have also thought of going to the Philippines for a few months and then up to Japan but with the situation as it is in China, I doubt the wisdom of that trip."[43] He had followed the Chinese tragedy closely as Chiang's forces, effectively deserted by the West, grew weaker. Mao's Chinese Communists, powerfully backed up by the Russian bear, were, even as he wrote, massing to cross the Yangtze and begin the inexorable push that would drive Chiang to Formosa and transform Nationalist China into Red China.

The padre then began considering a trip to Germany, "if it is okay with my bosses," he wrote Paul Maddox, "for visiting around over Europe and of seeing and hearing what people are . . . thinking. I have a good friend in Munich who has invited me to stay with him."[44] That friend was Captain Jack Roak, now in Munich with the Central Intelligence Corps.

In June Father Al returned to the States, reported to 6th Army Headquarters at Camp Stoneman, Presidio of San Francisco, "to spend my last few months in the Army," he wrote a friend in the Pentagon. "I like it here a lot. . . . [T]his beautiful big-hearted city has always had something that fascinated me. I am happy to be here." He had found a last service he could render his fellow ex-POWs, he continued, "Many of whom have done nothing to put in a claim for a dollar a day" for each day they had been prisoners of war. "Some few have placed their claim in the hands of sharks who will get 20% of that anguish money." Would his friend send him an application form immediately? "All the P.O.Ws here will appreciate your help."[45]

As of 5 October 1949, Lieutenant Colonel Albert Braun was retired from active duty for the final time. He had served "approximately 14 years active duty, 16 years inactive duty."[46] They were thirty years on which he would always look back with nostalgia, packed as they were with pride in his country and love for the many friends with whom he had served.

Among these was Naval Chaplain (Admiral) Dewitt C. Ramsey, "the son of an army officer. In 1888 he was born at Whipple Creek Barracks, Arizona, while his father was . . . fighting the Apaches. Possibly the solemn grandeur of the southwest and the uncertainty of life in that place, in those days, had an ennobling influence on the soul of this great childlike man." Sending his provincial a copy of an address the admiral had made, he felt sure it "would be gratifying for you to know in the top brackets of the service, we have some excellent men."[47]

Admiral Ramsey's words had struck deep chords in the padre, could have been uttered by him, and certainly applied to him. Chaplains, Ramsey averred, were "the custodians and guardians of that most precious ingredient of life—the soul. The degree of success you [chaplains] attain . . . is measurable directly in the spirit and morale of those under your charge. Thus in a real sense, the efficiency of our services is dependent on you and . . . the security of our nation is in considerable measure based on our ability to carry out our obligations. . . . It truly can be said that you are vital elements in the survival of American civilization."[48]

Having so served his God, his country, and his fellow men, the padre could with truth report his 'mission accomplished.' He would ever after refer to himself with pride and humility as 'just a soldier.'

Just a soldier.

"Just a Soldier." Courtesy of SBA.

VI

OLD SOLDIER

Do you really want a church?
You bring me bricks and we'll build a church together.

20: NEW DIRECTIONS

The year 1949 ended auspiciously for the padre. He was home, soldiering behind him for good; his old buddy from seminary days, Augustine Hobrecht—'Gus' of the 'three A's'—had been elected provincial; and his province needed Al Braun. He waived the military physical evaluation he had requested, scrapped his dreams of travel, and declared himself ready and eager for whatever duty called. "I only prayed I wouldn't be sent to a hot climate—I'd suffered enough heat in the Philippines—or to a place of sickness and death, at least for awhile—I'd seen so much of that. So where did they send me?" He always told it with a wry grin. "To hot Phoenix—and a hospital!"[1]

Saint Joseph's Hospital, founded by the Sisters of Mercy, depended for chaplains on Saint Mary's Parish, to which Father Albert was assigned. It was a post he could admirably fill and, his superiors believed, one not too physically demanding on the far-from-well padre. It also, being the largest hospital in Phoenix, would keep him busy enough to suit this priest who hated idleness. In this latter assumption they were correct: he was on call day and night.

The psychological effects, however, were something his superiors, having known nothing of war and captivity, had not considered. The suffering and death that constantly surrounded him in the hospital had to have been erosive, though he reported to Father 'Gus' only that he liked the people, the parish, and the hospital,[2] and immersed himself in work with his usual zest. "He saw everyone in the hospital," noted Sister Roqueta Lazzio, a nursing nun with whom he worked, "regardless of their religion. Father was very ecumenical." As he strode down the hall everyone brightened. "He always gave you his blessing. You never had to ask."[3]

Still he could not cut his ties to Mescalero and the valley below. Plans for a hospital in Alamogordo had him writing to Father Gus in November for help in securing sisters from a nursing order to manage it.[4] Then there was the matter of an automobile for the mission at Mescalero, which followed two weeks later. His old 'Cheve' was too beaten up for any real use, he wrote, but he had offered it to Father Marcian to use for its trade-in value on a new one they badly needed. The hitch was that the Province wanted its $650 equity back. Then suddenly—as was usual with Father Al's car deals—"an opportunity came up to get a new car [in return] for the Mescalero car and the one I had. The dealer . . . advised [us] to grab the opportunity because the market for used cars is rapidly deteriorating." There had been no time to consult his provincial, and the padre had urged Father Marcian "to act while there was yet time." Could the Province persuade the Franciscan Missionary Union to pay the equity? . . . He belatedly hoped "this whole transaction receives your blessing."[5]

Presumably Mescalero got the car; whether the province recovered its equity remains the x-factor.

In March another matter intruded on his busy schedule at the hospital. The long delayed transfer of the padre's share of his mother's property (to be ceded to the province) was still unsettled. "My dad and I have always spelled our name 'Braun'; the rest of the family 'Brown.' I must prove . . . that Albert Braun and Albert Brown are the same person. . . . in the presence of a county assessor of California before the last Wednesday in May."[6] This necessitated another quick trip to the coast.

A happier diversion soon came with the arrival in Phoenix of his old friend Father Ferdinand Ortiz.[7] It had been thirty-four years since the slender ascetic priest had driven the newly ordained Al Braun up the mountain to his first mission with the Apaches he had grown to love so dearly. Ferdinand had through the years become known and loved throughout the Franciscan world. The Vatican had sent him to Mexico during its troubled years, where he was eventually elected a provincial.[8] Now he was returning to the Santa Barbara province which, Augustine wrote happily, "can certainly use him to good advantage."[9]

By June, on learning of a leak in the roof of his 'Apache cathedral,' he was in a froth to show the workman at Mescalero how to fix it. "Fr. Marcian," he wrote, "is a fine man but he is the most helpless man I have ever known when it comes to keeping a place shipshape."[10]

Since first arriving in Phoenix Father Al's legs had been growing increasingly painful, for which Gus had encouraged him to seek medical attention.[11] Having waived his earlier request for an army evaluation, the padre now renewed it "for reevaluation because of physical disability that I believe was present prior to separation."[12] His old friend Paul Gilday, now a United States Representative, added his own plea on behalf of the padre.[13] The Adjutant General curtly denied the requests: the routine examination on his retirement showed only "a neurological defect . . . not severe enough to render the officer unfit for duty."[14] The padre shrugged. *Insignificant!*

But the legs continued to worsen. By May 1950 he realized something must be done, made the necessary inquiries, and wrote Father Gus that on the "tenth of June I expect to go to veterans' hospital either at Van Nuys or Long Beach. They are going to kill sensation in nerves of right & left leg. I should be okay for 3 years. Is it okay to go? V.A. pays my way."[15]

Augustine sent his permission with "an extra prayer that the operation will be successful. Perhaps," he added, "they will up your pension" despite its having been set, though that was of less importance than Al's "recovery to the extent of further usefulness in the Apostolate."[16]

Father Al too was looking toward extending his usefulness. The work at the hospital was proving far more wearing than he and his superiors had anticipated. Moreover, he believed himself a far more effective missioner out among the people than one stuck in a routine hospital chaplaincy. In simple fact, the padre was very tired, physically and emotionally. War, captivity, and his almost immediate return to work were taking their toll. A complete change of venue would, he believed, benefit his long-term effectiveness as a Franciscan priest.

As usual, he had a plan. "According to the G.I. Bill of Rights I can go to school for four years," he wrote Gus late in May; the government would pay tuition and expenses. He must, however, utilize the privilege by 25 July 1951 or lose it. "I want to go to the University of Mexico City . . ." he proposed, "to perfect my knowledge and use of the Spanish language and also to study Mexican Colonial History, and the folk-lore of Mexico. I am interested in the Mexicans, and will be pleased to work among them anywhere in the Province after I return. . . ."[17]

More than one provincial could have attested to the often unorthodox ideas that flourished so verdantly in Father Al's brain. Gus must have smiled: he had known Al Braun for many years. He did not brush the idea aside, but suggested further discussion, "to be sure . . . your plan is feasible." And, obviously sensing a real if unstated weariness in his old buddy, he added that he was relieving him from his hospital work. Father Al would remain in Phoenix at the parish to try teaching in Saint Mary's High School. "I do not know just how this will suit you or how it will work," Gus admitted, but it was at least a change.[18] The padre was free of the hospital; the Mexican plan, though shelved, was not dead; and he anticipated a cure for his legs, after which he had the summer to prepare for teaching subjects he loved—history and civics.

He entered the veterans' hospital as scheduled in June, but returned promptly to Phoenix: the head neurologist, he reported, advised against the proposed treatment as at best "temporary and often [with] bad results. . . . He said the nerve shrank because of starvation and never had gone back to normal. . . . There is only one lasting remedy—sever that nerve in each leg. It is a simple operation and effects a complete permanent cure. It won't be necessary to stay in a hospital even for a day or two. Will have that done in Aug. . . . Didn't stay in L.A. because they are so short of help here at St. Mary's." Nor, he added, would he be able to join Gus for the celebration to which they had looked forward—2 July would mark the thirty-fifth anniversary of their ordination.

On his return he found Juan and Pepe Baldonado in Phoenix with Father Phil, and drove with them to Saint John's for the day "to visit Brother Fritz. We had a grand time. After a glass of wine Fritz sang all the Spanish religious songs he knew; the Baldonados joined him in the singing."[19]

Fritz—Brother Frederich Zeller—had been part of Saint Mary's for years, most recently as sacristan and bell ringer. He had helped raze the original adobe church in 1902 and remained through the construction of the basement and during the building of the superstructure. Years later, during World War II, Fritz had given his most treasured possession to the war effort—a discarded cracked bell he had saved "for sentimental reasons." But with America fighting for freedom's survival, Fritz had given his bell "'to be used to make bullets . . . against our enemies—the enemies of world freedom and humanity.'" The American Legion displayed the bell outside the *Phoenix Gazette's* offices to help stimulate a drive for salvageable material for the war effort. Beneath it a sign read, "I've praised the Lord, now I go to make ammunition."[20]

They would return, Father Al continued, "to celebrate Fritz's birthday June 27 at St. John's. Then the guardian will bring him back to St. Mary's. Fritz is already homesick." It was a malady to which the padre could relate.

In the same letter, still pressing his case for attending the University of Mexico City, he reminded Gus that "unless we are already in school by July 25, 1951 we lose our G.I. rights."[21] It was a wasted plea: Saint Mary's could not spare him that long. Apparently he underwent the surgery in August and returned quickly to Phoenix. Though any letters he may have written are missing, the pain seems to have been alleviated and he was again able to resume his duties with the old galloping stride.

The work was challenging. Phoenix was growing rapidly in the restless postwar world; so was the Catholic community, and Saint Mary's was keeping pace with expanding social and cultural programs—television presentations for the elderly and incapacitated, food banks for the poor, parish publications, extended counseling and instructional agendas. Father Victor Bucher, pastor since 1947, had instituted a number of ambitious building projects, and spurred an increasing awareness of social activism, both of which drew Father Al's attention. He saw growing slum sections in the expanding city, noted desperate poverty among the many migrant workers in the outlying fields, and watched for his chance. Meanwhile friars were few, the workload overwhelming, and school would soon begin. But challenge had always energized Al Braun.

As an older priest, he sometimes had younger ones to counsel. One in particular he mentioned, a priest who had erred in some way and become unnaturally withdrawn. "I was worried about his defeatist complex and his persecution complex," the padre reported. "I tried to help him by inviting him out to work so that he would get physically tired and get away from morose introspection." Having heard some of the young priest's sermons, he pronounced him "sound in his ideas of the Christian life; therefore I think he will be unhappy away and will soon return to his Province. Show him the error of what he did but receive him with fatherly kindness, otherwise he will be hopelessly crushed."[22]

At Saint Mary's the padre met another young priest, Father Blaise Cronin, who was to become his very close friend for the rest of his life. Blaise, having taught physics and chemistry at Saint Mary's since 1944, doubtless oriented the padre in his new teaching duties. Finding his old friend and altar boy Father Phil Baldonado on the faculty was another stroke of luck. And to ice his cake, he found the Mackeys had moved to Phoenix.

The Mackey boys attended Saint Mary's where, Dick remembered, Father Al "couldn't stand for the guys to be with their hands in their pockets.

He didn't go for that at all. It would be so cold and we'd all be out in the yard waiting for the bell to ring, with our hands in our pockets, and Father would come round the corner and everybody would yell 'Here he comes!' And he'd straighten us up. He'd say 'quit your whining, this is the way it is.' He was tough on us—but we loved him for it." He never used a paddle: he never had to. The 'God squad,' they called him—but not to his face.[23]

He also coached the baseball team. One afternoon Father Blaise spotted a group of students pointing to the schoolhouse roof. Following their gaze, he saw—to his horror but not much to his surprise—Father Albert, his habit hiked to his calves, his sandals flopping as he strode about on the steeply inclined tiles.

What did he think he was doing? Blaise called.

The padre waved back, scooped up a baseball, aimed it at Blaise, and grinned. Another followed and another. Errant balls had been collecting in the roof gutters for years.[24]

He attacked teaching with his usual gusto. On Sundays he said mass at the nearby Cottonwood community. He also helped at Saint Theresa's, where he became so popular the church often overflowed and he had to say mass in the courtyard.[25]

Still he was restless; a few extra masses were not enough. However much he enjoyed teaching, he was a missioner, one who believed in being among the people, not one now 'sitting at a desk pushing papers around.'

It came to a head in January 1951, halfway through his first year at school, and it came via Korea. He had followed that turmoil closely since June, when communist North Korea invaded the free southern republic. The old soldier was elated when 'give-'em-hell Harry' galvanized the United Nations to respond (in the absence of the boycotting Russian delegate), ordered American forces into action, and appointed MacArthur overall commander of the largely American force. The padre doubtless agonized as they met defeat after defeat, exulted when the general's Inchon landing turned the tide and pushed the enemy north with the goal of reuniting the divided country under democratic government. Then through the autumn the padre's hopes began to fade, along with his opinion of Truman who, even as MacArthur's forces pushed on unstopped, began to waver in the face of Soviet intransigence and Red China's threats.

By late October Allied forces had reached Korea's northern border on the Yalu River and MacArthur was projecting victory by Christmas. A month later Chinese troops poured massively across the border, drove the Allies back across the 38th parallel, and captured Seoul. MacArthur prepared for a major counterattack, to begin by bombing bridges over the Yalu and Chinese supply bases beyond, and blockading the Chinese coasts.

But Truman said no. There would be no bombing of China's 'privileged sanctuary,' no invasion beyond the Yalu.

The President and the general had taken their opposite stands. The one, fearing a general Asiatic conflagration, took the course of limited war. His focus was still on Europe. The other refused to stomach appeasement in the face of evil, believing the focus of future history would be decided in Asia.

The priest, believing the President had hamstrung the general, had had enough of appeasing communism. "God alone knows what the year has in store for us," he fulminated to Gus. "If we will only wise up and rearm Japan and Germany, throw in with Spain & Turkey and forget about France we can rid the world of the worst scourge since the days of Attila."

But lip service was not enough for Father Al. "I understand," he continued, "one of the purposes of your meeting next week is to designate Fathers for the services. I hereby submit my application. Ordinarily," he conceded, "those over 60 are not taken but before this mess is cleaned up the U.S. will be glad to get even the very old & the very young. Some of my friends in the army are trying to have the age limit waived in my case. I enjoy teaching at St Mary's but in times like this every citizen should offer his services to his country." Moreover, he added, "if I went in it would set a good example to our boys around here. Most of them feel they have been sold down the river. And," he added, "they are not far wrong."[26]

The answer came quickly. Gus had put it before the Definitorium. "[Y]our offer to return to active duty in the Army was considered but the final decision was unanimous: You have done your share and also you are now filling a spot of great importance to the province."[27]

It took more than one simple *no* to stop the padre. While observing the most difficult vow of obedience, he could still offer an alternative, and within two months had found one, as evidenced in a letter from Father Victor Bucher, pastor of Saint Mary's, to Bishop Daniel Gercke in Tucson.[28] Both the bishop and General Alex Tuthill of the Arizona National Guard had requested a Franciscan chaplain for the Guard; and Victor, knowing the padre's disappointment at being denied active duty in the army, had—likely at Father Al's instigation—phoned the Provincial. Knowing Al's penchant for persistence, Father Gus probably considered limited duty in the state Guard the easiest way to let the hardheaded Braun have his way, and gave permission.

Father Albert, Victor assured the bishop, "is very willing to serve in this capacity." The principal of Saint Mary's High School, Father Ronald Culloty was, he conceded, younger, but had already been recalled to active service in June. Despite the army's age limit, Victor believed, "this should not be an obstacle for such limited service. . . . And doubtless General Tuthill will appreciate the valued experience of Father Albert. . . ."[29]

Father Albert, however, had his own opinion of Victor's idea of 'limited duty.' "Should I be accepted as chaplain of the Arizona National Guard," he wrote General Tuthill, "it would be with this understanding: that I do the full duty . . . at all times. By that I mean: if the Arizona National Guard were to be federalized and ordered to the zone of combat, I would expect and desire to go along. . . . I am still in excellent physical condition and am able to do hard work and to endure physical hardships."[30]

The general, the provincial, the bishop, or all three apparently objected to the padre's insistence on full duty, and the matter ended abruptly following the padre's letter.

Father Culloty was meanwhile preparing to report for duty in June. He had sent his uniform to the cleaners, having first removed his insignia. On replacing it, he could not remember whether the stem of the major's gold leaf went up or down and, according to the popular story, asked Father Al. "In the army," Braun reportedly answered, his deadpan belied by a twinkle, "when a man was old enough to wear a maple leaf, it always hung down."[31]

Meanwhile in Korea, though the Allies had rallied, recaptured Seoul, and recrossed the thirty-eighth parallel, Truman abandoned the reunification policy and announced he would negotiate for reestablishment of the original temporary boundary at the thirty-eighth as permanent. A passionate debate erupted in Congress. MacArthur sent House Minority Leader Joseph Martin his own appraisal. On 6 April Martin released the letter to the press, and Father Al, along with the bulk of other Americans, agreed with the general: "There is no substitute for victory."

On the eleventh Truman relieved MacArthur of his command.

Outcries burst from across America. The halls of Congress rang in bitter argument. Father Albert wired Arizona Senator Ernest McFarland stating his own strong convictions, and on receiving the senator's pacifist reply, fired back. He could no longer wear his country's uniform, but he could still fight. His letter is worthy of note in its entirety, for it reveals the essence of Father Albert Braun:

> Your announced policy: "To keep the United States out of World War Three" would be sound if war were the most tragic thing in human life. Countless Russians, Czechs, Hungarians, Germans and Chinese know an infinitely greater tragedy: slavery, starvation, imprisonment, torture, and death. These people long in vain for the opportunity to war against their human oppressors. We Americans, Democrats and Republicans, know the horrors of war but prefer them to the indignity of Communist slavery. This Truman-MacArthur episode is not one of personalities; it is one of policies toward a philosophy of life. The American people, and that includes Arizona Democrats, instantly and vigorously rose up in defense of the man in the Orient who has so valiantly defended us against the Communists. It is not because of MacArthur but because of what he stands for that we are with him to the end.
>
> Dear Senator, I am not writing rashly. I was in World War I and saw the destruction of life and property in that war. In the past war I was at Corregidor and then a prisoner for three years and four months. The last year of the war I was in Tokyo. That destruction of so much property and that loss of so many lives is a small evil when compared to the sufferings of those who are [so] unfortunate as to be inhumanely oppressed by Communist rule. Therefore, "My policy is to keep U.S. out of world War Three" falls flat and has little meaning. I am here in Arizona among the people who entrusted you with your great responsibility and I know what they are thinking. They want no appeasement of the Communists, even if that means war.[32]

✞✞✞

Father Al still pursued his quest for knowledge. Denied his year of study in Mexico and still trying to exercise his privileges granted in the GI Bill, he requested permission to attend a six-weeks summer course at the University of Southern California that included South American history and Russian history "with special attention to the Asiatic and Far Eastern phases of its revolution. . . ."

The Father Guardian at Saint Mary's and Father Ronald, who would not report for duty until June, had given their permissions, but to attend a secular university he needed permission from Rome: would Provincial Custos Father David Temple (who had succeeded Father Gus as provincial) please apply for that? "Many of our graduates go to secular Universities," he argued. "How can we advise them against the dangers of secular universities if we have never attended a secular university?" Finally, "I am sixty-two years old, and hardly will be harmfully influenced."[33]

He matriculated in July.[34]

✝✝✝

By the end of his first year of teaching his restlessness was abating. He had come into teaching needing more, hence the thwarted desire for school in Mexico, and the vain plea for military service. But during the year he had been drawn into a project that, though only a part-time field of endeavor, had by the end of his second semester, become a full-time passion. His old friend Father 'Phil' Baldonado, had opened a door.

That door back into the mission field was a small but growing group with which Father Phil had worked since its inception, a lay apostolate called the Workers of the Sacred Heart. The seed had been planted by a former Maryknoll seminarian from Utica, New York, named Peter Karl who, having left the seminary because of ill health, arrived in Phoenix for a visit in March of 1948. There, Father Al learned, "he borrowed a car to visit the labor camps" of thousands of migrant workers in the area. Mexican field hands had for years found seasonal work above the border in reasonable numbers. The incoming volume swelled dramatically during World War II when, to alleviate resultant manpower shortages, federal agencies promoted legal entrance under the *bracero* program. By 1948 the need for workers had declined but the migrant population had not. Appalled by their material and spiritual neglect, Peter Karl met with a young singles Catholic group. "The priests don't have the time to take care of the farm workers," he told them. [I]t is up to the lay people."[35] In the group were two young women, Jeanne de Lue and Mary Grupp who, impressed with his message, recruited others to meet with him. From that meeting, Jeanne later recalled, "our lives would be changed forever."[36]

The migrants, Karl told them, lived in hovels, without medical care, often without adequate food and clothing. Parents labored in the fields daylight to dark, seven days a week. Many of their children had never been baptized; all were growing up without any religious instruction. Priests and nuns in Phoenix were too few to reach the peripheral migrant colonies. Would these young people volunteer a couple of hours a week?

They would. In the then rigidly segregated society of Phoenix, and a parish that had persistently ignored the Mexican workers, they would go to a migrant colony and teach catechism one night a week. They contacted Father John Forest McMorran, OFM, pastor at Saint Mark's parish, which had been established two years before in a mainly Mexican area of southwest Phoenix, where he worked with the poor. He agreed to lead the little group.

Within two weeks they had the first classes underway in an open field of a settlement called Santa Rosa, about eight miles northwest of downtown Phoenix. "It was the beginning," wrote Jeanne de Lue, "of what was to become . . . one of the foremost apostolates in the Southwest."[37] She recounts the early months:

"During that summer about forty children attended classes every Monday evening. Some . . . sat where they could swing their bare feet over an irrigation ditch; one group perched on a woodpile; others stretched out in the tall grass. Gradually they memorized prayers and learned about Adam and Eve, and Jesus. . . . After classes there were games. . . . Occasionally there was a . . . short moving picture or a party. A prominent young Phoenix attorney [William Mahoney] organized athletic events. It was a good summer. . . .

"As fall approached, early-evening darkness precluded teaching in the open field. Providentially, a warm-hearted Phoenician donated several picnic benches to [what would become] the center. Electricity was relayed from a nearby house, and a bright outdoor classroom evolved."

Meanwhile two more centers were being organized in other sections of Phoenix. Little by little the group of instructors increased until, guided by Father John, they formed what became the Workers of the Sacred Heart and "struggled through the first winter—with no funds and no official standing. . . . God seemed to be with them, however, for whenever things looked dreariest, an unexpected donation . . . turned up. . . ."

On the morning of 12 December 1948 Father Ernest Wilson of

Saint Mary's Church celebrated Santa Rosa's first mass, in the cleanly swept dirt yard outside the little adobe shack of the Hernandez family. It was, fittingly, the feast day of Our Lady of Guadalupe, for whom the women of the community erected a shrine. They set up benches and folding chairs; and from the front wall of the house they hung a large sheet festooned with tinsel rope as a backdrop for the small wooden altar brought over from Saint Mary's. Eleven children received their First Holy Communion, after which the women served them a communion breakfast, and the solemnity of the mass gave way to an air of fiesta. The day marked a true milestone for the migrant community.[38]

The Workers' two hours a week expanded to fill most of their spare time, enveloping not only their lives, but those of the surrounding community in collecting food, clothing, and basic necessities for the destitute migrants.

Father Phil, in addition to his teaching duties, worked tirelessly with the group, "visiting the people, hearing confessions, saying outdoor mass, administering Holy Communions, holding a prayer service at a night vigil for a small child who had died. . . . He taught a private Spanish class for the Workers. . . . Eleanor Waskow, M.D., a Lutheran doctor who volunteered with the group, used to bring her german shepherd, Prince, to our class. I don't know if he learned anything, but he was very attentive.

"Father Phil had a warm relationship with the Santa Rosans." Jeanne recalled the day when "someone told him Grandma Vidales wanted to go to confession. He found her out back in her little dirt yard soaking her feet in a galvanized bucket, and he promptly administered the Sacrament."[39]

Father John guided, advised, coordinated activities, conducted services, and largely held the group together. In the spring of 1949, with Bishop Gercke's permission, he was able to buy a large lot and abutting field in Santa Rosa at a very low price, for which the community pledged to pay $15 a month. They now had a center. The surrounding community fenced the property, hooked into electricity and water, and "Santa Rosa Center was born. A surplus army tent . . . offered protection in winter and, with the sides rolled up, shade from the hot sun in summer. Often five or six classes, a total of sixty to seventy children, were held simultaneously. . . .

"A large portrait of Our Lady of Guadalupe was brought from Hermosilla . . . for which the men . . . erected a beautiful shrine. . . . The men also built a large desert-stone barbecue and laid a . . . cement dance floor. Then came a small open pavilion . . . [to house] a portable altar for mass, or musicians for a Saturday night dance. They took pride in their Center, planting, weeding, and painting, tending it with care. . . .

"Family life at Santa Rosa revolved around the Center, where Masses and First Communions, May Devotions, Cinco de Mayo and Dieciseis de Septiembre fiestas, Christmas parties, movies and athletic teams offered respite from the poverty and backbreaking field work."

To meet expenses the Workers held a *tardeada* at the Center. The entire community pitched in. That all might wear Mexican dress, the women went into "a frenzy of sewing. The men were soon busy building a food center and booths for games. Small children practiced Mexican folk dances. A band and Mexican entertainers were lined up. Food was ordered from a downtown wholesaler. Costumed children were taken to sell tickets after Masses at several Phoenix parishes. St. Francis Xavier parish lent tables and benches which the men hauled in borrowed pickup trucks. . . ."[40]

The *tardeada* was a great success, which meant immediate financial relief for the Center. More importantly, it had drawn the community together. In throwing themselves into the effort, the migrants and the surrounding communities had made the Center theirs. More than a place, it was a communion of souls: the Church had come to the people.

It had not always done so. The pastor at the neighboring parish had initially ignored the migrant colony. Mary Grupp and Jeanne de Lue, seeking a church in which an indoor First Communion could be held, were spurned by that priest. But they found the Jesuits at nearby Saint Francis Xavier "good neighbors" who "went all out in welcoming the children and their families with a truly beautiful Mass followed by a communion breakfast served by the Altar Society."[41] The Jesuits forthwith became involved in the Santa Rosa effort.

The Church was going to the people: it was a practice fundamental to Father Albert, a mission for which he was made, a group to which he was inevitably drawn—an assignment he would like. Father Phil, having watched his old mentor from the first day of school, could see his restlessness, and having known him since the Mescalero years, knew where his passions lay. Al Braun was a shepherd without a flock, a soldier without an army, a missioner without a mission. He needed more to do. The old fire was trying to rekindle; it only needed a little stoking. The superiors in the Order, believing the war hero and ex-POW needed rest, had given him lighter duty. Father Phil disagreed: Padre Alberto had to be in the front lines. The old war horse needed a challenge. No one knew it better than Felipe Baldonado: the Workers and Father Al were made for each other.

An opening came during the first semester of school, when Father John was transferred to California. The Workers needed another chaplain and, on Father Phil's recommendation, requested Father Al. The bishop appointed him immediately. It was only a part-time job, utilizing after-school hours, weekends, and school holidays, but the padre had found his cure. And the Workers had found their chaplain.

From the first day they loved this down-to-earth priest. "He didn't go around blessing people," Jeanne noted. "He gave hearty hugs—*abrazos*—and firm handshakes. He was not a holy-holy. Full of life, he loved working with his flock. He didn't worry much about all the rules and regulations that had been developed by the Vatican. 'I've always been my own Pope,' he'd say. He took his orders from God."[42]

Centers took root at other migrant colonies, and as the demand for services grew, so did the need for more workers. Why not lower the age limit for membership, suggested Father Al, to include carefully selected juniors and seniors from Saint Mary's high schools and from the Jesuits' Brophy Prep and Xavier High? Why not indeed? The membership swelled.

Despite his ongoing attempts to serve in the military during the Korean war, the padre continued full speed in his teaching and chaplain's duties, and by school's end in June 1951 he was wholly immersed in the work of the apostolate. When Father Phil was transferred to San Juan Bautista Retreat Center in California, the resultant increase in Father Al's work load was grist for his happily grinding mill. He heard confessions, said masses, baptized babies, prepared children for First Communions. He helped with fund raisers and fiestas and sports teams for the migrants; in addition to Santa Rosa he was soon ministering to the Yaqui Indian settlement near Scottsdale and to several barrios farther south. He drove himself and the Workers hard and demanded the best from everyone. "He was," one Worker said, "our severest critic and our greatest admirer. We would have been lost without him."[43]

One afternoon at Santa Rosa Center the padre met young county attorney Bill Mahoney. A former track star at Notre Dame, Mahoney had volunteered his time and talents to organizing athletic events and coaching the migrant youths. The priest and the lawyer liked each other immediately.

"'Oh my lord,'" Mahoney told his wife that evening, "'there's this great new Franciscan in town! A real Franciscan,' he called him, 'tough and strong and simple. He looks at everything the way I do.'"[44] Mahoney was ex-Navy, had like the padre served in the Pacific during World War II, and later worked as prosecutor before the War Crimes Tribunal.

Theirs became a long friendship—"sent from heaven," Father always swore later. "Soul mates," Alice Mahoney said. "They were both individuals—strong, strong characters who told it the way it was."[45] The brown-robed priest was soon a common sight in the Mahoneys' orange grove, picking crates of oranges for the migrants, usually with a crew he had rounded up and a borrowed pickup truck.

In June Father Phil returned to Santa Rosa during his annual vacation to stage a five-day mission in Spanish. Father Al and the Workers had readied everything in the outdoor pavilion. The migrants flocked to the Center each evening during the mission, along with Spanish-speaking Catholics from throughout Phoenix. Sermons, rosaries, hymns—all were in Spanish. Father George Dunne, a Jesuit from Saint Francis Xavier, trained a choir of Santa Rosa women for the event—a choir that in time became permanent.

For the closing benediction on Saturday night they borrowed from a local parish a monstrance containing the Host, which Father Dunne, escorted by candle bearer and bell ringer, carried through the kneeling worshippers to the altar and Father Phil.[46] After the concluding Sunday morning mass, Father Phil flew back to San Juan Bautista and his busy schedule there.

Children dressed for First Communion at Santa Rosa. Courtesy of Jeanne de Lue Marsteller.

Phoenix Radio Station KIFN, which broadcast in Spanish to a potential 65,000 listeners, had carried segments of Father Phil's mission. When the priest responsible for the weekly program "La Hora Catolica" was suddenly transferred, station manager Frank Redfield, remembering the zeal of the Workers at the mission, turned to them with an SOS. Father Al was away at that time in California pursuing his six-weeks' university course, and Jeanne de Lue received Redfield's frantic call. Would she take Sunday's program?

It was already Friday evening, she had no radio experience, and the program must be all in Spanish. "But I did say yes. . . . I remember hauling the Workers' large tape recorder over to the neighboring parish where Father Frank Long (himself half Hispanic) was stationed. We put the first program together."[47]

The station gave the time as a public service as long as its own crew was not responsible for filling the time. "I hate to shut down 'La Hora,'" Redfield told Jeanne, "because the bulk of our listeners are Catholics." As long as the Workers would be responsible, he added, "you have my blessing. Otherwise, we'll have to cancel it."[48]

In no way would they cancel it, said Father Al on his return. Jeanne would be responsible, he mandated, and he drew others in to help. The Jesuits were especially helpful. Father Dunne wrote a play for La Hora, "The Battle of Lepanto," based on the legend that, as the naval battle of 1571 against the Turks raged in the Corinthian Gulf, the Christians on land recited the rosary all day, thereby in part effecting the final victory. Translated into Spanish, the Workers produced it on 7 October, the date of the famous battle. Other programs played recordings of masses. Father Frank Long taught a Spanish hymn, "O Madre Mia," line by line, and then led the singing, in which he invited the audience to join.[49] Help came also in the person of Father Phil's younger brother, Father Leon Baldonado, who was teaching at Saint Mary's. Father Al had earlier drafted him into service in the field; now he put him to work with La Hora.

Then suddenly they were all without the tireless help of Jeanne, whom serious illness had forced to return to her parents' home in Boston. The padre was doing double duty, and so was young Leon. "The Hora Catolica is still going," the padre wrote Jeanne, "but Fr. Leon wants to give up his part which means we would have to close down. That would be a calamity. . . . Fr. Leon says with all his other work he can't do justice to the job. . . . I had a talk with him and got him to promise to go on for awhile. I want to get a hundred or more recordings and keep them [to use when necessary]. . . . We must keep La Hora Catolica going. . . . This is real missionary work."[50]

A second letter soon followed. The program was doing well, after a big benefit dance for its support, and "Father Leon is in much better spirits."[51] Goaded by Father Al and with the help of the station crew, the Jesuits, and Mary Grupp, they kept the program on the air.

Father Albert, nearing sixty-three and by now a living legend, set a demanding pace that kept everyone around him panting to keep up. He had added to his work load a Yaqui settlement, which was, he wrote Jeanne, "doing okay. We now have the church packed with children. On Dec 9th we are going to put on a big celebration in honor of Our Lady of Guadalupe. Saturday nite we will put the small statue of Our Lady on an altar in front of the church and burn candles in front of [it] all nite. Sunday before mass we will carry the statue in procession through the entire village. Girl[s] dressed in white will carry the statue; will get . . . 12 of the old drunks to walk beside the statue as guards of honor. Twelve of the Mexican nurses from St Joe's are going along to sing Spanish hymns. I'll bet the entire village turns out. . . ." How like Al Braun to include 'the old drunks' as guards of honor. How like him to see their need, pull them into the solemn rite, allow them the dignity of God's chosen.

After the early mass with the Yaquis, he added, he would say mass at Santa Rosa. "I can be there by 11 a.m. Will try to take the nurses along."

The letter, written on Thanksgiving day, gives an idea of his galloping gait. "Went to the eight o'clock solemn high mass and had the 9 o'clock mass at St. Mary's. . . . It is now almost one o'clock, time for an appetizer and the turkey dinner. Want to get this letter started before I get down to. . . ." Here he was interrupted. "(The bell just rang for 'haustus'—refreshments. Will have one on Jeanne.)" Much later he resumed writing. "Didn't get back . . . till seven o'clock. Spent most of the afternoon . . . visiting some polio patients at Memorial Hospital and the Children's Hospital. We have some of our school children in both places."[52]

As 1952 and Saint Mary's second semester began, Father Al knew he must work full time in the mission field. He had in his roving duties come onto the large sprawling stretch in southwest Phoenix, part of Saint

Mark's parish where Father John had labored before his transfer. The mostly Mexican population existed in hovels, without sewage, gas, electricity, or running water. He was appalled.

He was not the first to note the conditions in these barrios. Father Emmett McLoughlin had done yeoman's work during the Depression and war years, describing the area as "permeated with the odors of a fertilizer plant, an iron foundry, a thousand open privies, and the city sewage-disposal plant," the houses "built with tin cans, cardboard boxes, and wooden crates," where infant mortality was so rife, hunger so universal, filth so rampant, and crime so unchecked that government officials had labeled it "the worst slum area in the United States." Lacking support from the city and at odds with the Order for his often unorthodox methods, Father Emmett had left the priesthood in 1948.[53]

Father John too had tackled the odds while serving with the Workers during his short time in Phoenix. With his transfer conditions remained hopeless, and the lone priest at Saint Mark's could not alone minister to the roughly 8,000 destitute people in the barrio in addition to his regular duties. It was a desperate situation needing a full-time priest. It beckoned Al Braun.

He requested a transfer to Saint Mark's, to work full time. He should be relieved of his teaching duties, he stipulated, but wished to remain chaplain for the Workers of the Sacred Heart.

His superiors may have had qualms sending him into such heavy duty. The aging padre had never fully recovered from the ordeals of war and Japanese prisons. They knew also that wherever they assigned him he would turn it into something much heavier. Pushing 'light duty' on Father Al was the wrong medicine for a hardheaded priest heavily allergic to idleness. And few said no to Al Braun.

At the end of the school year, Gus agreed, the padre would go to Saint Mark's, full time. He would take the church to the people.

The work before him would have overwhelmed many a younger priest. But Al Braun's energy sprang from a deep well of something profounder than that of the body. He was poised to launch what would become one of the great Franciscan missions in an order known for great missions.

21: BRICK BY BRICK

Since walking off his first job on Sylvester Dupuy's farm Bud Braun had sought many challenges, fought many battles, wrought many changes, and welcomed each new venture. Now, striding into the barrios of south Phoenix, he wound among dirt lanes, first through the better section of modest adobe homes—dirt floored, heated by wood-burning stoves, watered from their own shallow wells, flanked by outhouses. He continued into a worsening scene of gang-prowled, drug-and-crime-infested warrens where hopeless-faced adults and hungry children existed in tumbledown shacks. There was in the entire unpaved area no electricity, no running water, no sewage disposal. He saw before him a gargantuan challenge. But Al Braun, his fellow friars knew, "flourished under difficulties."[1]

The core of the largely Mexican area, stretching roughly from Washington Street south to the Salt River, was the Golden Gate community, born like Santa Rosa of migrant workers. Coming into the valley early in the twentieth century, they soon found other barrios forming on their peripheries—Cuatro Milpas, Green Valley, El Campito. In time they merged. Squeezed and surrounded by the growing city, and backed against the encroaching airport, they were isolated and largely neglected by the Church.[2]

They felt that neglect keenly. Many had attended Saint Mary's faithfully until, on completion of the upper sanctuary in 1914, they found themselves relegated to the basement. This segregation, the friars insisted, was to enable the Mexican congregation to hear sermons in Spanish, and was in keeping with a long tradition of ethnic churches that reflected their respective cultures. The Hispanic membership nonetheless perceived it as discriminatory and began to press for a church of their own. This became a reality in 1928 in the Immaculate Heart of Mary Church, served by the Claretian fathers.[3]

Wanting services nearer their homes, however, a group began in 1938 to raise money through annual fund-raising bazaars, or *jamaicas*, hoping to build at least a small chapel.[4] In time they acquired a former Saint Vincent de Paul store and converted it into the tiny Sacred Heart Chapel—La Capilla del Sagrado Corazon—in whose cramped adobe quarters masses were held sporadically. Still they yearned for a real church.

In 1947 the Reverend Daniel Gercke, Bishop of Tucson (which then included Phoenix) transferred jurisdiction over the barrios from the Claretians to the Franciscans. The community thereby became part of Saint Mark's, itself a relatively new parish, housed in an erstwhile barracks building. But in October 1951 the parish acquired a new rectory north of the railroad tracks, in a largely Anglo community; again the people of the barrios began to look toward a church of their own. Among their leaders were the Ávila and Arvizu families.

Providentially a sympathetic neighbor named Victor Staneger donated a lot at Seventeenth and Sherman streets. Here an open-air *ramada*—hastily built, dirt-floored and brush-roofed—would serve as a church of sorts for the next several years. Services were still irregular as short-term priests came and left before they could forge any bonds with their parishioners. When Father Albert Braun arrived in June of 1952 the community had grown wary of itinerant Anglo priests, and though cautiously hoping for the best, they were ready to shrug him off as just another of the same Franciscan cloth.

They had yet to see Father Al in action.

On arriving at Saint Mark's the padre moved into the new rectory. "He was always happy," Jeanne de Lue noted, "to continue living in a Franciscan house . . . , to have a dog and an old car, and to be working among the poor Mexicans where the need was so great." Many years later she "could still visualize his little room with his few belongings and work paraphernalia. . . . It was far from shipshape; he needed more space, but that was immaterial to him. Most days he was out on foot . . . mingling with the people. He disliked the days when he had to take his turn in St. Mark's office."[5]

He soon requested, and received, permission to work exclusively in the poor section south of the railway tracks. He began to rattle into the barrio in a battered old car Father Tom Schneider lent him from Saint Mark's, parked, and with his mongrel dog began making that day's dusty rounds, house to house, person to person. By heritage most were Catholic, though many had fallen along the trail. Marriages needed to be validated, babies were unbaptized, children had no catechetic instruction. Few attended mass. The padre took notes, listened to problems, assessed needs, and made friends. This priest, the families began to realize, seemed actually interested. Wariness gave way to cautious optimism.

He reported to the bishop: some eight thousand souls peopled his beat, all needing material and spiritual help. Those who still professed the faith were divided in loyalty between their old parish at Immaculate Heart and the new one at Saint Mark's. He must unify the community and he outlined plans for doing so. Bishop Gercke promptly appointed Father Al pastor of the entire Mexican area, a territory stretching south from the Southern Pacific tracks to the Salt River and east from the expanding airport to embrace the migrant communities, by then known collectively as Corazon.

To impress Bishop Gercke with past diocesan neglect of the migrants, the padre took him on a driving tour through miles of acreage surrounding the barrios, pointing out the hundreds of laborers in the scorching fields. Father Al described the conversation later:

"Are many of them Catholics?" asked the bishop.

"They're all Catholics," the padre answered.

"They go to mass every Sunday?"

"They never go to mass."

"How can you say they're Catholics if they never go to mass?"

"Listen," said Father Al, "a man's first obligation is to provide food and shelter for his family. These men work in the fields daylight to dark seven days a week, and earn barely enough to survive."[6]

The rest of the conversation went unrecorded; but Father Albert seems to have made the bishop graphically aware of his people's needs and his proposed program for bringing the Church to them. By whatever means, Bishop Gercke became increasingly heedful of the problems, and would remain among the padre's most solid and enthusiastic supporters.

✝✝✝

Always focused on what he called his 'worldly motive,' the padre determined to better life for his people. Soon after his conversation with the bishop he attended a Phoenix city council meeting. Mincing no words he described conditions in the barrios; he castigated the city fathers for their shameful neglect of their poorest; thwacking the podium, he demanded the basic amenities of civilization for his people: we *will* have street lighting, he asserted, and electricity in the homes; we *will* pave the streets; we *will* have a sewer system.

A few councilors squirmed.

But one listened closely, as if he were recording in his mind the priest's every word, his eyes noting every gesture. After the meeting he approached Father Albert. He wanted to know more. He would work with the padre to get these things done, he pledged, and he extended his hand.

"My name is Barry Goldwater," he said.

They discovered they were both combat veterans and attended the same American Legion post. Both were men of strong convictions and both spoke them freely. They became fast friends. In that fall of 1952 Goldwater was elected to the United States Senate; but he kept his ties to the city and his promises to the padre. Progress came slowly, but little by little the improvements began to materialize—water, sewage disposal, pavement, electricity. When the city lagged the council could count on seeing Father Albert again. "He'd go right in there and start pounding. And," Tony Valenzuela remembered, "he left almost always with whatever he wanted."[7]

"I have come to serve," he announced at his first mass in the little adobe *capilla*. It was 10 August 1952. Those attending were few; he would soon rectify that. As he had ridden the Mescaleros' mountains astride, he now stumped the barrios afoot. As he had brought the Church to his Apaches, he now took it to his Chicanos. He regularized marriages, baptized babies, counseled the troubled, found food for the hungry, clothing for the threadbare. Still chaplain to the Workers, he directed their duties, organized the catechism classes, and in his area alone kept sixty-five Workers and four nuns teaching. He said masses, planned or impromptu, beneath a tree, in an open space, wherever a few could gather.

"That was his key," Father Finian McGinn believed. "He was out meeting and being with the people . . . every place he went—shared a meal, spent a night."[8] The congregation at the tiny *capilla* began to swell and then to overflow. He began to say mass in the old barracks that had temporarily housed Saint Mark's, now moved to the barrio and converted into a second, slightly larger chapel. When that proved too small for his growing flock, he rebuilt the old brush-covered *ramada*, which offered no protection against rain. "Later," Valenzuela recalled, "he took time to put a roof on it—but he didn't need a roof. He didn't need anything."[9]

Father Al says mass in the roofless *ramada*. Courtesy of *The Way of St. Francis*.

A letter he wrote in December reveals the deep concern that threads through the padre's years of correspondence. Ever the optimist, he always brightened the darkness with his quick humor; still the darkness was there, beyond the near horizon, the evil that must ever be fought. He was fighting it in the south Phoenix barrios. But, he wrote his provincial passionately, evil must be fought in farther fields so long closed, where "missionaries are free to go again. . . . The Philippines are a natural for us Friars. . . . Japan is another great field . . . ," and South America, where efforts to crush the faith must make "every red blood[ed] Friar . . . want to get into that fight. . . ."[10]

He too must be nearer the fray. Although he enjoyed the company of the friars at Saint Mark's, he knew he must live closer to the people. He must build a rectory in the heart of the barrios. He argued also that to preserve continuity his mission must be long term, uninterrupted by transfer until he accomplished his far-range goals. He requested another priest to help with what he envisioned as a massive building campaign: a rectory was only the first step.

He soon had his priest. "I don't know how to thank you," he wrote Father Provincial David Temple in January 1953, "for assigning Father Reynold [Coriell] to the work among the Mexicans of Corazon. He is so sincere, so zealous, so simple. There are many good priests but not many quite like Fr. Reynold. . . .

"Today," he continued, "we bought the lot on 16th Place & Tonto where our residence will be built. . . . Fr. Victor [Bucher, pastor at Saint Mary's and Father Al's immediate superior] would like to see the house abuilding in a few weeks and . . . us living in it by Easter. You know Father Victor's DRIVE. I think we will get much labor-help from the people."[11]

He was right. The people had learned to trust their padre, were ready to commit themselves and the modest funds they accumulated through their *jamaicas* toward his efforts.

He and Reynold were not in the projected rectory as soon as they and Father Victor had hoped. Money and permissions had to be obtained and coordinated, plans to be drawn. The padre, now aided by Reynold, continued making his rounds, performing his clerical duties, updating the census for his fluctuating population, and saying mass in the *ramada*. By this time he was working closely with long-time barrio residents and committed parishioners Pete Ávila and Abe Arvizu. He had met Paul Guerin, a contractor who quickly became a close friend with whom he would work from initial planning through final execution of the ambitious project.

Father Victor's backing was of immense value. His drive matched that of the padre; each seemed to strike sparks of energy and enthusiasm from the other. Father Al kept in close contact with Victor and his confreres at Saint Mary's, tending to ecclesiastical business, and enjoying an occasional game of vigorously competitive pinochle. Through this camaraderie he became concerned about Victor's health. Doctor Huger, he wrote Father David in

March, "told us unless Father slows down we will find him dead in bed. Dr. urged Father V. to slow down and so did Fr. Guardian. Apparently neither have had much success. Doctor Huger thinks it is up to Father provincial to do something about it before it is too late. . . ."[12]

Father Al might also have given a thought to his own health, which he mentioned seldom and only in passing. Like Victor, he kept on going. Refusing to slow down, he walked everywhere, through rain and sun, sandals flapping, brown habit grayed with dust or splotched with mud, his lined face creased with a grin. He said evening masses for those who must work every day—"the latest mass on Sunday evenings in the city," Father Finian noted. "So many people would go to Father Albert's mass—and not just the Chicanos."[13]

Response from the people was enormous. By May, to meet the needs of his growing herd, he was requesting another priest—specifically, one Father Marcos Cabrera, "the kind of Friar the place needs—he is zealous, he is willing to work hard and does not ask . . . to spend a lot of money. . . ." He could, moreover, deliver a sermon in Spanish. "I realize," he continued, "that my usefulness may come to an end at any time,"—a rare admission, and testimony to his declining physical condition, for which he needed someone already there "to take over without a hitch when I leave off. This sudden quitting of one man . . . and beginning of another works great harm. . . . These Mexican people . . . say in thirty years whenever they were lucky enough to have a Father among them he did not stay long enough to . . . get acquainted. . . ." Moreover, the padre added vehemently, he needed Father Marcos full time, not divided between him and Father Thomas at Saint Mark's, "and no make believe or I am not interested."

To point his need he cited figures. "Next Sunday one hundred and fourteen children will make their First Holy Communion at Corazon Chapel thanks to the splendid work of the four Sisters and the boys and girls of St. Mary's High School." But, he added, in a field of over 7,000, it should be far more, and would be but for the years of ecclesiastical neglect in the barrios. "Who fell down on the job?"[14]

To this and a second letter like it,[15] his provincial replied affirmatively. "With such sentiments uppermost in your mind the work at Saint Mark's is going to progress a long way, even beyond the substantial beginning which you have made. . . . [W]hat you have done has been an example to us all of how we should get out and tackle the work which lies beyond our doorsteps. . . ." He hinted that the young Father Marcos would soon be his, primarily if not exclusively.[16]

"Keep very good care of Fr. Marcos," Father David instructed once the assignment was definite. "He is young and willing and zealous but needs someone with good judgment who will keep him on an even keel. You will be just the one."[17]

"We must bring the Church to the people!" How often Padre Alberto said it; how often he was overwhelmed by their desperately grateful response as he worked among them. Thousands hungered for the solace of their native religion, and there were too few priests tough enough and dedicated enough to meet the challenge—or fluent enough in the Spanish language. The padre thanked God for Fathers Reynold and Marcos; but he and they were only three among thousands. They must have more friars in the field.

Why not send a few theologians, he suggested to Father David in May, "to one of the Franciscan seminaries in Mexico . . . so they can learn the language well and also the Mexican ways. . . . They might have a tough time in a Mexican Franciscan seminary," he conceded. "That too will be good training. The sooner we get and like hard times the better for us and our work."[18]

He wrote too of the "threatening storm in Mexico," where radical ideas were again spreading. "According to the Jesuits . . . the communists have strong organizations in the northern border towns . . . especially in El Paso. Many of the[ir] recruits . . . are Mexicans who have abandoned their Catholic Faith. . . ."[19]

He was delighted to learn a month later that his provincial was planning a pilgrimage to the shrines of Our Lady of Guadalupe and Zapopan where, he wrote, "you will see with your own eyes the deep faith of countless Mexicans and you will feel keenly the tragedy of the loss of that great faith by many Mexicans in the U.S. . . . because they are without priests to be among them." Phoenix, he added, "is an example and we bear our share of the guilt. . . . There are ten thousand . . . Mexicans in our area," of whom he cited shocking statistics. Of the three thousand he and his crew had visited, only one in forty attended mass regularly; two-thirds of their marriages were outside the Church; many adults had never partaken of Holy Communion; and so he continued, piling figures upon figures.

"I am giving you this picture," he added sternly, "that you might take it with you to the shrine of our much loved Lady of Guadalupe. She will be waiting for you . . . with some wise counsel, not only concerning neglected Mexicans but concerning all neglected people under your jurisdiction."[20]

Among those neglected he found another group. That summer of 1953, while shooting the breeze with a handful of Negroes, he asked, "How come so few of you colored folks are Catholic?"

One old man replied with what Father Al believed "must have been inspired by the Holy Ghost." Maybe, the old man said, "it's because no priest has ever told us why we should be Catholics." Doubtless the padre proceeded on the spot to do just that. The message had stuck with him since: he thought of it every day, he added,[21] and he often repeated it to underscore his perpetual argument: the Church must go to the people.

All the while he was planning his own large work. He would build three neighborhood chapels within walking distances of his scattered populace, and eventually the longed-for church of their own. He already had the lots; but, he assured Father David in September, "We will go ahead slowly so as not to incur much debt."

He was planning for permanence, for a future beyond his own tenure, he added. "I will work here as long and as hard as I can, but I know I am getting old and I know this place and this job needs a much younger man. One who can stay here ten years or more and can plan . . . over that period of time. I have been suggesting to Fr Victor that Fr Reynold is just the man. The Mexicans are attached to him, he knows Spanish, he likes the people, he is dependable and he is capable. . . . These people are the poorest there are in Arizona. . . . Because there is no priest living among them . . . some of the people die without sacraments (two this week) and there is missing that close contact (so necessary) between people and priest."[22]

By mid-November he was requesting, though not expecting, two full-time priests who "have nothing else to do but work among the people [and] live where they work." He also needed "Sisters for catechetical and social work. . . ."[23] Meanwhile, construction must get underway—and quickly. Others were as impatient as he was. Victor was making waves from Saint Mary's; so was Bishop Gercke in Tucson, who, tired of ecclesiastical fiddling while the barrio yearned, made an $8,000 loan to Father Al with terse instructions to "build now."

It was all the padre needed. On 20 January 1954 work started on the rectory, almost simultaneously with work on the first of three chapels, Santa Isabel (later called Saint John's) at Eighteenth and Magnolia Streets. With the help of contractor Paul Guerin, some dedicated parishioners, and his own labor, the work went quickly.

As at Mescalero, Father Al wanted to be on the spot at both sites, and, Pete Ávila recalled, during the construction the padre lived in "a small shack. It had no kitchen so he ate with our family."[24]

By mid-March both rectory and chapel were completed. Santa Isabel had its first mass on the eighteenth, just one day after Fathers Al and Reynold and a newly arrived lay brother had moved into the rectory. The padre objected vociferously to the air conditioning some friends had insisted on installing: why should he gain a comfort his people lacked? Nonetheless, "We are comfortable and happy in our new home . . . and the people are very happy that we are among them. They now enjoy a sense of security in regard to their spiritual care." He was also "happy to have a Brother; he seems to like it here."[25]

But the friar soon left. "He said," Father Al wrote dryly on 5 May, "he became a Brother during the war to get out of military service. He said it was all a big mistake; he is made to be a married man." He and Reynold concluded the "brother had no qualifications whatever for the religious life." They would, however, appreciate another lay friar when Father David had one to spare.[26]

In mid-May they broke ground for the second chapel at Eleventh and Hilton Streets; by late October it was nearing completion. "The people are enthusiastic," the padre wrote. This one "is twice as large [as the first and] will be named Santa Maria Magdalena." Reynold was already using it, "even though the chapel has not yet been blessed. The blessing will be Dec. 12. Can you be there? At S[an]ta M[aria] Mag[dalena] there are already two Sunday Masses and mass every day of the week," all well attended, and "over 200 children in the catechism class. You can easily guess that Father is doing excellent work. . . . If Fr. Reynold can stand me for a few years he will make great progress in many virtues. I spent too many years . . . in military service to be an easy man."[27]

Father David's reply was immediate and ecstatic. "Please continue to encourage Father Reynold. He has walked into very necessary and vital work which will test not only his patience but likewise all of his courage. After all, you and he are trying to make up for the neglect of almost fifty years. It is a mammoth job."[28]

Having said the mass for nearly three years under the *ramada* for "most of the people of Southeast Phoenix . . . in hot weather and cold rain," the padre later recapped, "it was evident Sacred Heart needed a much larger church."[29] With Saint Mary Magdalene nearly completed, both chapels in well attended use, and the *ramada* overflowing, the time had come.

Even as preparations went forward for the church, Father Albert's mind leaped far ahead, beyond his goals for Sagrado Corazon; and on 20 December 1954 he wrote his provincial a proposal startling even for Father Al.

"When Father Custos [Augustine Hobrecht] was here," he began, "he reminded me of the sad condition of the Catholics in the Philippine Islands—one priest to sixty-two thousand Catholics. . . . We are not doing right if we stand by and do nothing. . . . Therefore I am asking you to let me go to the Philippines. . . . I would like to take a Brother—there is one at the Casa who wants to go. I don't know his name; he is young, he was in the P.I. during the war and he talks like a Texan. . . . You may have misgivings because of my age. An old man can get older just as well anywhere in the world and a man can die just as well anywhere in the world."

Nor would Father David have to worry about Corazon with Father Reynold in charge. "By Sep[tember] he will have the help of Sisters of the Most Blessed Sacrament. We are starting their convent in Jan[uary]. If I get permission to go it will be late fall before I can get away. By that time the convent and the new church will be completed."

His incentives, he said, were simple, foremost among them what he called his "worldly motive—a man made of spirit and matter has to have a worldly motive or he is not a man—I love the people and the country." And whatever turmoil might come," he promised, "I will gladly & thankfully stay with the people." In typical Braunesque fashion he ends on a light note. "What I will miss most of all," he adds in postscript, "will be that wonderful community spirit at St. Mary's. . . . I will certainly miss those pinochle games. . . ."[30]

One can only imagine Father David's expression as he read. That he was startled, incredulous, even amused, is safe to guess. That he could not send his aging and unwell confrere on such a mission is a given, though he assured the padre at length that friars would be sent. Above all, the letter moved him profoundly. It was, he declared, "one of the most manly pieces of Franciscan thinking I have every read."[31]

By late January Father Al had the plans for both church and convent, as well as those for the center he proposed to build adjacent to the church. As soon as approved by the bishop's building committee, construction would begin. If approved, he reported, "we should begin work on all three projects in two weeks."[32] Meanwhile they were gathering materials.

The church was to be of adobe, in keeping with Southwestern tradition and economic limitations. The site became a hive of parishioners who in their free hours were making molds for the mud bricks, mixing the adobe, pouring it into the molds to bake in the sun, stacking the adobe bricks. Father Al labored along with the rest. They had stockpiled rows and rows of bricks when an untypically heavy downpour hit suddenly, deluged the barrio, and dissolved a major part of the hard-earned bricks. They quickly decided the church must be built of commercial red brick.

The added expense? *Insignificant!* They sold the remaining adobes and Father Al mounted a campaign for bucks or bricks. "'Do you really want a church?'" Valenzuela heard him ask. "'You bring me bricks and we'll build a church together.' In a couple of weeks they had thousands—bricks all over the place."[33] As the padre later detailed it, a $26 donation bought a thousand bricks, $13 got half that many, and $2.50 furnished a hundred. "We . . . got fifty thousand too many bricks, so we built the Center too."[34]

Parishioners gave happily from their small earnings to be a part of what they had dreamed of so long. Even the children could participate—a single brick cost 26¢—and build their own lives into the church. Nor was Father Albert shy about soliciting heavier funding from affluent citizens, civic organizations, Phoenix politicos, and Catholic organizations. Bishop Gercke gave $1,000; he also came to lay the cornerstone.

Again the people pitched in to work in whatever capacity they could. Abe Arvizu Jr., an electrician, did the wiring; others applied their various skills. The padre and Bill Mahoney inspirited the Saturday work sessions with plenty of cold beer. When on more than one occasion city inspectors appeared with citations for violations of the building code, Father Al shrugged and grinned: let them send him to jail, he said—he'd been in worse prisons during the war than anything Phoenix had. He also leaned on Mahoney to run interference with the city authorities.

"You bring me bricks and we'll build a church together."
Courtesy of SJAM.

Father David sent another lay brother for Al to try out and train. The padre found him "all in all a good religious. . . . I know he has a hard time with his Irish temper. . . . [H]e flew off the handle with me once but only once. I told him Brother every time you lose your temper I am going to get tougher with you so you had better start getting over that right now. . . . Since then . . . he is doing okay. He [doesn't] even turn red as he used to."[35]

The brother was both help and responsibility for Father Al, who was obligated to train and assess him. "Whether or not Brother Danny should make Solemn Profession," Father David wrote, "will depend in large part on your recommendation. . . . I think that he has what he has long needed right now—good, strong, straight Franciscanism."[36] The padre recommended that the feisty friar "be sent to a large community of regular observance"—but not right away: "Brother is transforming the old Corazon chapel into a hall. We will be on that job for about one month."[37]

Apparently Brother Dan stayed on, for in May Father Al recommended him for solemn vows, despite some lapses. He still had his hot temper; but "we all have many faults." Overcoming them often "takes years and years," and Dan had many Franciscan virtues. "The Order," the padre stressed, "is not for angels, but for men."[38]

Construction continued. "Father Albert did a lot of the work himself," Pete Ávila recounted. "He made us work, too. We had to follow his example when he worked so hard."[39]

Sometimes the padre grew testy, especially at meetings, which he considered a waste of time. Jeanne de Lue, now recovered from her illness, was back in Phoenix and, though physically unable to rejoin the demanding routine of the Workers, helped Father Al as her time and strength allowed. She often watched him during such meetings, grew amused at his impatience during long hair-splitting discussions, or when some committee member made an inane suggestion. Though he hid his annoyance, she could always gauge his reactions by watching his sandaled feet: the thinner his patience grew the harder he clenched his toes. "I loved that old man," she said, "though sometimes he could be a real grouch."[40]

He was already looking toward a separate Corazon parish. In a letter of 3 May he reported that he and another priest had, as instructed, toured the area and agreed that "when the Bishop decides to make Sacred Heart a parish" they would "recommend the boundary be . . . R[ailwa]y tracks to River. . . ."[41]

That the padre had met some opposition to his massive building program is suggested in a letter he wrote in September. Lauding the generosity of the Fleischman Foundation for a large contribution to the province, he wished "that all of our Friars had that same great spirit of Franciscan charity. There are some . . . who make little effort to hide their opposition to fields of apostolic effort that bring no financial returns. . . . The importance of money is stressed so often that some of the young Fathers are beginning to wonder who is right, . . . Christ and Saint Francis or the financial geniuses of the Province. . . ."[42]

In October Father David sent the padre a check for $3,000 donated by "an anonymous benefactor . . . for the construction of the church at Corazon. . . ."[43] It was a tremendous boon; so were those parishioners who continued to work alongside the paid crews. For as work on the church progressed, Father Al was bursting with plans for more projects to follow.

Chief among these he envisaged a parochial grammar school and center, for which he needed his provincial's backing. "By Easter," he projected in December, "the church should be ready for use though not completed. . . . In late spring we want to build a small Center with two medium sized rooms for a medical center to be operated by St. Joseph's hospital; a large kitchen and cafeteria . . . for the grade school; one room for a kindergarten . . . ; two rooms for meetings. . . . We will complete this building between late spring and midsummer. By the end of Sept we want to start work on four class rooms (40 children each room) so that by Sept 1957 we can open school with first and second grade. . . . We have reason to hope the Precious Blood sisters will teach. . . ."

Only one discordant note sounded, that from his good friend at St. Mary's. "Fr. Victor has been a great help to us but he is opposed to a parochial school. . . . These people have been so completely secularized by the public schools that our only hope lies in a parochial school. . . . I hope to convert Fr. Victor. I certainly don't want to antagonize him because he has been such a great friend of Sagrado Corazon. I want your backing before I speak to him again on the matter. . . . I know the bishop will back us to the limit but I want moral not financial backing from the Province. It is hard to have to disagree with a good friend."[44]

Meanwhile a host of other duties demanded his attention.

Juvenile crime had been a major problem in Corazon for years, and one Father Al determined to reduce by interception. In this he worked closely with probation officer Tony Valenzuela. "He helped me out a lot of times," Tony affirmed. "He'd say, 'take him and lock him up—then let me have him and I'll take care of him.' So I'd look at the kid and I'd say, 'Well, do you want to go with me or with Father Al?' He'd look at me and then at him. He wasn't quite sure. Finally he'd go with Father Al. But he knew Father Al was very strict.

"He'd take him directly to the kid's home and talk with the kid and his parents. The kid had to come back and report to Father Braun—so the padre was really a probation officer. He had a great impact on people. He dealt with the families—they had to respond to Father Al. And if the kid got a little bit out of line he had to report to Father Al and the parents. 'You're not getting away with anything,' he'd say. Father Al would not play games. He was very calm, very strong, very fair. . . .

"One of them—an attorney now—Father Al was responsible for his going to Saint Mary's High School, and then to Notre Dame." When the time came to go, the boy was hesitant: all he had to carry to the prestigious school was an old cheap suitcase. Notre Dame had taken him for his potential, not his suitcase, Father Al assured him. He must keep his head high and his brain busy and make the most of his opportunity. Young Richard Trujillo did, returned to Phoenix with his degree, and became one of Arizona's outstanding lawyers.

"That's the kind of impact he had," Valenzuela noted, "for a lot of kids. He'd see me coming, knew I was going to pick up somebody, and I'd see him coming down the street—he could hit a long stride. He could walk blocks and blocks. . . . Father Braun was not a priest who believed in spending all his time in the church—he liked to do things for the people of the community. . . . He used to go to all of those chapels on a Sunday—he would walk. They were about a mile apart, maybe a little farther. He'd walk to each one, say a mass there, and take off—people would be waiting for him."[45]

He never hesitated to call on the county attorney when a parishioner was in trouble with the law. "Father Albert was constantly calling Bill," Alice Mahoney recalled. "He'd say, 'So-and-so is in jail—a couple of drinks too many last night. Now listen, Bill, you get the sheriff to let him out. He has a wife and seven kids and he has to get back to work.' And Bill would call the great old sheriff here, and he'd say, 'Cal—' and the sheriff would say, 'Bill, I know—Father Al wants somebody else out of jail.' And he'd cooperate."[46]

Ray Salazar believed Braun was "the greatest man I ever got to know. He used to help everybody. Whenever kids got in trouble he would go to bat for them. . . . He never slowed down. And if he didn't like something he'd let you know, or if he wanted anything done he'd get it done—the way he wanted it."[47]

Living so closely with the people he knew what was going on, often before it happened. He knew the participants and the locales of planned rumbles, arrived ahead of the combatants, met them head on, and forestalled more than one gang fight. He could be as tough as they were. Soon he had them working, and coming to mass. Through his close contacts with the community he exposed and broke up a sizeable drug ring, for which he would later be appointed to the Governor's Narcotic Studies Committee.

On learning that one young delinquent had stolen an expensive clock (by some accounts a camera) he confiscated the loot and, the story goes, secreted it in his Franciscan sleeve, returned to the store and, utilizing his old Al Capone dexterity, slipped it back onto the shelf. The young thief, though saved from jail and a court record, likely decided facing a judge would have been easier than answering to Father Al.

Many such stories were told, retold, and chuckled over. Some are doubtless apocryphal; but juvenile crime in Corazon dropped significantly after the coming of Father Albert Braun. More erstwhile delinquents began attending school, church, and church-sponsored recreation programs; and they learned to work. The padre was compassionate, but he tolerated no nonsense. He cased the bars—especially on Fridays when many got paid—and shamed men into going home to their families, paycheck and human dignity intact. He frowned on government welfare programs, which he believed fostered dependence. He gave hard love, practiced jump-start assistance, and emphasized self-help and personal responsibility. "You have to do it for yourself," he said repeatedly. "No one's going to do it for you."[48]

Father Maurus Kelly never forgot the time a parishioner lay dying in church. "They called in Braun, told him the fellow was drunk—he was lying on the floor, slurred speech and everything—but he was having a heart attack. Al had the reputation of being a bear. If anything touched his people, his claws would come out and he would fight hard. So—the man died, and Al lit into those people who were saying he was drunk. He really laid them out over that."[49]

Though largely Mexican and Catholic, Corazon included other ethnicities, and people of other religions, or none. The padre believed his duty embraced everyone in his territory. He already had seventeen Negroes attending mass, but believed that a drop in the ocean. "We are doing nothing," he reported, "for the Okies and Arkies and Negroes in our area." He proposed an extensive program for these people at once. The more practical Father Victor, however, convinced him to "wait a year until we get some of the building out of the way."[50] But once the projected parochial school was open, he vowed, "I plan to spend most of my time working with the many colored people down here and Father Reynold would like to do the same with the Okies and Arkies." Too many priests, he fulminated, "act as if they have only Catholics as their responsibility."[51]

Father Albert had the gift of friendship. He made friends and kept them, valued them, stayed in touch. Through his provincial he always sent greetings to his beloved old professor, by now the very aged Father Felix. On learning that Father Ferdinand was dying, he drove to Tucson with Charlie and Katherine Mackey, arriving sadly too late; his old friend had died a few hours before.

He officiated the marriage rites for numerous nieces and nephews, and in turn for their children and those of his friends, among them the Mackey children. Dick even gave him a chance for some matchmaking—something he always enjoyed. Appearing at the rectory one day, Dick confided he was seriously contemplating marriage. But Sue was not a Catholic: what should he do?

"Marry her!" answered the padre.

When the time came to plan the wedding, the couple was told that no priest would officiate nor would any church host a mixed marriage. Again they consulted the padre.

Father Al had never had patience with hierarchical hair-splitting. "He didn't care that I was not a Catholic," Sue reflected. "He said 'no problem' and married us at Saint Gregory's."[52] He also ignored traditional prohibitions, and "gave them the nuptial blessing," recounted Father Blaise Cronin, who officiated beside the padre. "They had everything the Church could give them."[53]

In time Sue joined the Church. Father Al had made another convert.

On another occasion a friend of Alice Mahoney came to see him. She had divorced an unfaithful husband, wanted to remarry, and feared doing so. "'Well,' he said, 'you and God can settle that.' He said, 'You are innocent—don't worry about it. Trust God and you'll do the right thing. Some of those old cardinals don't know what they're talking about. Don't let them ruin your life.'"[54]

Dinner with his friends, when he could take a rare night off, were special occasions. On one occasion Father Al had invited the Mackeys to dinner at the rectory. "We were going to have steaks," Sue remembered, "but he forgot to get the steaks out—they were frozen solid. So he just threw them on the floor to break them apart, picking them up and throwing them down again and again. It was so funny. That's what made him so great to be with—he was so much fun."[55]

Through the years he had kept in touch with friends exiled during Mexico's revolutionary days. In January 1956 Al made a hasty trip to El Paso to meet with one, Father Raymundo Garcia, now a Mexican provincial. They were good friends, he advised Father David. "He [had] made his novitiate at Mescalero." Work was progressing on the Corazon church; he was already holding services, as he had done in the roofless Saint Joseph's in Mescalero, and was looking toward completion in the spring. Hence the trip to El Paso:

"I want Fr. Raymundo to get me a married man from Mexico who is a good organist and choir director. Through Senator Goldwater we will get this man a passport to the U.S. When he gets here we will see that he is well employed. For those two favors he will live in this area, twice a week practice with the choir, and take care of the organ and choir on Sundays & feast days. . . ."[56] Raymundo was happy to send such a man.

Always among his dearest friends was Dave Kirgan. On returning from El Paso the padre stopped overnight with the friars in Las Cruces. "Fr. Kirgan," he recounted, "drove me to Mescalero. Had a happy visit with many Indians." While there he and Dave "took a look at the church." Unable to resist needling his provincial over Saint Joseph's necessities, he reported on his return to Phoenix that "Father Sylvester said some years ago he got an estimate" on some badly needed repairs. "He said it would cost twenty-two thousand dollars. That is ridiculous. It should not cost five hundred dollars." Temple took the hint: repairs on Saint Joseph's were quickly on his agenda.

"The trip wore me out," the padre admitted, but he wanted to get back in Corazon "to see the trusses put in place on the church."[57]

"Keep pushing," Father Provincial replied, ". . . but do not over exert yourself, because after all you are pretty well out of the newly ordained class."[58] It was a wasted injunction. Al Braun was propelled by the urgency of advancing age and ebbing strength, a church, center, and school to finish, his yearly census to take, and the ever ongoing needs of his people.

By mid-March he was able to write that they had virtually finished the church, "except for altar, pews and a few other accessories. . . . Thank God we don't have a cent of debt. . . ."[59]

He had reached a milestone where he could take a few days off, and with Dave Kirgan. "After ten years of not infrequent disagreements with his Bishop," the padre wrote, Kirgan had "asked for [and received] a six-months vacation since he had not taken one in ten years. . . . Fr. Dave has been spending a week with me each month [and doubtless working on the church]. . . . He knows I will be honest with him. Many of his friends thought he was on the way out of . . . functioning as a priest in the church. They don't know Fr. Dave. He would never turn traitor. During the weeks he spent at Corazon we had many long talks. He is going back to Las Cruces and I think he will always bow before the will of his Bishop."

Having finished with explanations, Braun got to the point: "Father Dave wants me to go with him to Hermosilla, Mexico leaving Easter Monday . . . and will return two days later."[60] In Hermosilla they doubtless reminisced about their hair-raising sorties into revolutionary Mexico, and certainly toasted the old days with a few rounds of 'Irish holy water.'

It was the last trip they would make together. The following year Dave Kirgan visited briefly at the Corazon rectory en route to the coast, planned to stop on his way home but, feeling ill, went straight back to Las Cruces. Within a few days he was rushed to Hotel Dieu Hospital in El Paso where he lingered, unable to speak, for several years. Father Al visited his old friend regularly, told him funny stories, recounted the adventures they had shared, until Kirgan's death. The padre missed him terribly.

✝ ✝ ✝

Meanwhile, he was not long back from Hermosilla when in May an outbreak of vandalism at Saint John's Indian School at nearby Komatke, coupled with infighting at the mission, demanded his attention. The end of the school year approached, a summer-school program loomed, and a group of young Indians had been drinking and destroying mission property. Saint John's was on the padre's beat; he tackled it in his usual head-on manner.

It was clear, he reported, "that a partial housecleaning is necessary. . . . Keep the cook, the laundress, Myra the secretary and the maintenance man. The rest [of the lay personnel] should go." One woman, chronically at cross purposes with most of the staff, had butted into and exacerbated a quarrel between the coach and the priest in charge of the school. It was the sort of tiff with which Father Albert had little patience. "Irene is a big bluff," he pronounced, and certainly was not going to intimidate him. Further, a "feud between the Sister and Irene has reached the bitter stage. . . . Deep down," he added puckishly, "I am mean enough to kind of enjoy it. Nuns have a way of making their enemies wish they were somewhere else."[61]

He was more concerned over the vandalism. "Last summer," he advised Father Provincial, "much mission property was damaged by the young Indians at Komatke. Moreover, the day before graduation they brought wine onto the school grounds. Some of the . . . students got drunk." An armed guard was necessary, for which he would ask Bill Mahoney to "tell the sheriff's office to send me a prudent and fearless man authorized to carry a shot gun loaded with rock salt to protect the place," and he would tell Irene, "at the request of 3 Fathers, that it is up to her to keep discipline among those Indian children who are staying over for the [summer] program. Last year there was drunkenness and promiscuity."[62]

He next hired a night watchman, despite which the vandals still had the personnel in an uproar. "Last night," the padre wrote a few days later, "Frs Camillus, Walter and most of the Sisters were up all night. This is a lot of nonsense." The night watchman needed backup help. The tribal police had no jurisdiction over patented church property; the county sheriff had none on the reservation—or thought not until Mahoney advised him otherwise "and told him to give St. John's full protection."[63] This seems to have quelled the young braves.

Muzzling Irene was another matter, for which Father Al's patience was wearing thin. She had taken over publicity for a fund-raising raffle, antagonizing her contacts; the padre removed her from that activity.[64] To curb excessive "running around in cars," he directed Camillus to "take in all the keys"; Irene demanded "a car at her disposal." The padre said no. "If there is less running around more of the real work will be done. . . . Her departure," he advised, "is long overdue."[65]

Amid other problems at the mission, an elderly friar was stricken with lung congestion, for which Father Al sent him to Saint Joseph's and Dr. Huger; it was good for the brother, he opined, to go to the hospital every six months. "Twice a year is not too often to get a bath."[66]

To cap the situation, on the last week of school "Sister Modesta, the superior, tells me that excellent cook is beginning to hit the bottle. I hope he lasts until Friday."[67]

As always, Father Al looked beyond the immediate problems to see the whole picture: what was wrong at Saint John's was symptomatic of the overall field. "What the entire Indian missions need is control and it is a sad thing there has been none since . . . Father Novatus."[68] There was too much "traveling over the country outside the assigned mission field. . . . For more than twenty years the missionaries have been given the opportunity to put their house in order and have failed to do so." The solution, the padre and Father Victor advised, was for the provincial to take charge himself, appoint a representative to visit each mission regularly and demand accountability. "I don't know of a better place to loaf than the Indian missions," he asserted, "if one is not controlled and does not have zeal."[69]

☩☩☩

As Saint John's boiled with disorder that June of 1956, Corazon radiated with the joy of unity. On the twenty-third they celebrated Corpus Cristi Day with the first of what would become a beloved yearly tradition. Outside certain houses the families had erected altars. Bedecked with flowers and icons the poor little dwellings stood proudly affirming their faith. "Do you remember our procession?" Father Al asked Jeanne years later. "The whole Mexican population joined the procession . . . to the altars scattered over the area, singing as they marched. How they loved the great occasion!"[70]

Awaiting the procession of the barrio's first celebration of Corpus Cristi Day, 23 June 1956. Courtesy of Jeanne de Lue Marsteller.

The increasing tempo of work, confusion at Saint John's, final preparations for the dedication of Sacred Heart Church, and Phoenix heat seem to have taken their toll on Father Al, nearing sixty-seven years and never having fully recovered from the ravages of war and captivity. Though he seldom mentioned his ailments, intermittent attacks of the dengue (he spelled it 'dingy') fever had plagued him since his return to the States. In a letter to his provincial written during the trouble at Saint John's he described being "so sick I was not worth a thing, . . . aching all over, chills and dysentery. . . ."[71]

During the summer the heightening activities seem also to have overpowered Father Reynold, though by August the padre could report that ". . . Reynold is okay now," though he was "still under observance by Dr. Huger. Fr. is not strong. We say three masses and preach three sermons besides confessions etc etc every Sunday. I think the three masses are too much for Fr. Reynold. Like so many holy men he lacks prudence. . . . Father Reynold needs someone to hold him in check."[72]

On a festive 14 October Sacred Heart Church—*La Iglesia de Sagrado Corazon*—was dedicated. Father Provincial David Temple came to sing the Solemn High Mass at noon, Bishop Gercke preached the sermon, a host of Franciscan and diocesan clergy attended, and the people of Corazon filled their new church for which they had waited so long and worked so faithfully.

There remained another chapel to be built for the people of Campito, farthest from the Center. Scarcely a month had passed before Father Al was breaking ground for Santa Rita. He finished it in April. One of the first celebrations he officiated in the little chapel, along with Father William Ferrell from Saint Francis Xavier, was the wedding of his dear friend and long-time faithful worker Jeanne de Lue, henceforth Jeanne Marsteller.

He would soon complete, close by the church, a center for meetings, recreation, and social affairs. The church, with its Center and three chapels—each with its own catechetical hall—radiating out from the core, was now the beating heart of the community, the catalyst that transformed the several barrios into one stable community.

"It was more than a church," one parishioner said, "it was a family. The good times we had building it. . . . We grew together, we loved together, and we prayed together. We were a family."[73]

22: MISSION ACCOMPLISHED

One roadblock remained: he must build that school. For months, even before the church was completed, he had begun agitating to start; but he had no permission from the province. Father Victor still opposed the project, and time was passing. *Insignificant!* He would find a detour.

He had earlier turned to the bishop. There were bricks left from the church, he explained, enough for a parochial school; he would keep costs low; and the children would be rescued from the secular influences of public schools.[1]

But Father Victor had also written to the bishop. Gercke showed both letters to a trusted clergyman. "When the Bishop asked me my opinion," that father recalled later, "I suggested that with Albert's faith he should be permitted to go ahead." Gercke agreed: he would give his permission, and a thousand dollars "'to encourage Albert.'"[2]

On receiving the bishop's check and a letter instructing him to begin building "immediately after Easter," the padre wrote his provincial. It was mid-March 1956. "Do I have your permission to start work April 9th? If you say okay, I'll go to Father Victor. He has been our consistent staunch friend. I want to win him over. . . ."[3]

Father Provincial and the Definitorium (of which Father Victor was a member) were still hesitant over "the size of the project, the expense involved, the maintenance and other hard realities. . . ." Father David would, however, discuss it with the padre soon. "Your desire to make real Catholics of your people and to use the school as the means of accomplishing this I realize very well since the whole temper of the age and the country . . . makes this need clear. May God prosper your good endeavors!"[4] God—and the definitors, he seemed to imply. It was not the clear-cut sanction for which the padre had hoped, but neither was it a veto.

A telephone call from Father David followed. Whatever was said elicited a spirited letter. "When I argue," Father Al wrote in response, "it is because I am interested in causes," and he proceeded to plead his case. "Every missionary is aware of the need of money to run a mission." He acknowledged that the province had had to adopt "sound business methods," though he added, "maybe overstressing of the importance of *money* in God's work. . . . [A]ll the ugly monsters of today and the past are the direct result of the interest of priests, bishops, & popes in money." Saint Francis had saved the Church from such corruption, he continued; his model was still the Order's ideal. "Therefore with the prudence and the spirit of sacrifice we should go ahead with our mission . . . not worrying too much what it will cost."

Having established his thesis, he moved for the coup. The emphases are his, in heavy underlining: "The shrewd devil . . . *is attempting* and *is making us* secular. . . . That the devil's greatest opponent is the Catholic school system is evident from the *world* wide efforts to crush the Catholic schools. How any church authority can stand in the way of establishing a Catholic school . . . is a mystery of the power of the devil. . . ."[5]

Late in April he was still awaiting provincial consent. "I can't go before the Board of Supervisors for permission to build to our property line till I have the plans for the school," he reminded Father David. "However I had Bill Mahoney . . . look over the situation. He . . . will see to it that we get the necessary okay. . . ."

Meanwhile, he continued, the Bishop was paying $5,000 "to buy out the Baptist missionary. . . . She has two lots and a house adjoining the property where we plan to build the school. This Baptist missionary is a good lady. . . . Several years ago she had more than a hundred children in her Sunday school classes. . . . Little by little she lost all the children and now is convinced the baptist cause in this part of Phoenix is hopeless.

"The Bishop," he added, "seems to get great delight out of buying out his opposition."[6]

Summer came, and fall, and still he waited. Final affirmation had to come from the Definitorium, and Victor's opposition had necessitated prolonged discussion. But Father Provincial's nod-and-wink sufferance had provided the detour Father Al sought. With that, the bishop's encouragement, Mahoney's legal help, and his own stubbornness the padre, working closely with Paul Guerin, went forward: Father Provincial had not said no.

Always he must make his annual retreats, which he greatly enjoyed, and on which he commented freely. Of his most recent he wrote in February 1957 that he thought it "a mistake for us older Friars to make a retreat with the clerics. We . . . are so much more hardened and need a swift spiritual kick in the pants. . . . We need the tough stuff of our Lord. . . ." On a note of amusement he described one participating friar as "so kind, so conservative, so exact—so cold." Another was "a spark plug. I always suspected he slept with one eye open." Of his own inability to bottle the bubbles of laughter "shared by all men since Creation," he mused, "there must be something so funny in the Divine Nature; that must be why God made risibility a distinctive mark of man whom He created after his own image and likeness."

His joviality at the retreat continued into the trip home, when he and two others "stopped at San Turibio for *spielabend* with Father Tibs [Tibertius Wand]. We heard he had a leakage of one of the vessels from the heart and knowing that he like all men must die—soon—we wanted to have a brotherly jovial evening of fraternal charity added . . . to [help him] meet his Maker. Fr Tibs, and we too, enjoyed the *spielabend*. . . ."

But even in the midst of frivolity, his mind was always on work, and on its necessities—in this case his usual need for manpower. "All the foregone," he admitted, "was to put you in a generous mood. While having that spielabend . . . I saw an opportunity to give one good man by the common name of FIDO [Father Fidelis Kuban] an opportunity to get a 'job' that would be a challenge for his ability. . . . This good Friar is doing so much less than he could do. . . . I now make this suggestion:

"We now have eight thousand baptized Catholics in our area, besides the 13 thousand Okies, Arkies, and Negroes (for whom we must give an account to God). . . . You can come to our assistance by sending us Father Fidelis. He can be a great missionary by taking over [the new chapel at] Campito. . . . Those people have been neglected a long time. . . . We know that many are asking you for priests. The fact that Father Fidelis speaks Spanish so fluently should favor our request."[7]

The padre did not get Fidelis immediately, but he would continue to ask.

Through the spring of 1957 he concentrated on the building project. "Our first stage of the parochial school [presumably the foundation and framework] is about completed," he reported in April. "I think I can pay the bills and then be flat broke." They would have "a good kitchen . . . a cafeteria for 700 children . . . four classrooms for our preschool [and] first graders . . . a clinic; two rooms for heating . . . a spacious veranda and patio for teen-age affairs. . . . The start is a good one. Let's hope we can carry on through the eighth grade as years go by. For all that must be done," he added, "we need another man who won't mind being worked hard."[8]

Fido was still unavailable, but the province was sending Father Elias Galvez, though not until late August—too late for the annual census, Father Al wrote the custos in Father David's absence. "Each year," he explained, "we are forced to use the summer months to take a census . . . to plan our catechetical work for the year," because of the large turnover. "The priest in charge must take the census or it will be of little value to him. In spite of the extreme heat we do this job every summer. That accounts more than any other work, for what success we have." He needed Elias to cover his own designated area. "Neither Father Reynold nor I can do more than what we are doing. Every day is crowded with work. Sunday we both hear many confessions, say three masses and preach four sermons. This summer [to cover another priest's absence] Father Reynold and I will have the many sick calls from Memorial Hospital and County Hospital. . . . If there is any way to jar Father Elias loose and send him here *now* you will be putting the work of this place in order and on a sound basis."[9]

The custos was sympathetic; he would send Elias as soon as possible. He did so in early August. At the same time the padre learned happily that he could expect additional help, which meant four friars would be living in the tiny rectory. He called Paul Guerin about "adding two more rooms without disfiguring the house" and as cheaply as possible, got a quote, and began the addition.

"The walls are completed & in a few days the rooms will be ready to be occupied. I took it for granted I had to build right away and overlooked the fact that I should have gotten permission," he admitted.[10] For Father Albert the necessities of the moment outweighed bureaucratic protocol. *Insignificant!* The custos promptly sent the permission for the fait accompli.[11]

That busy summer Father Ambrose died after a lengthy illness. The padre learned too late to make arrangements to attend the funeral. "I know the family is disappointed and hurt," he wrote. "Our families were very close; since we were three years old we played and fought together. Father Ambrose is responsible that I am a Franciscan and a priest. I certainly would have been at the funeral if I had been able to provide for Corazon while away. . . ."[12]

In October he acquired Father 'Tibs' (who seems to have recovered sufficiently from his heart problems) in time to help with a *jamaica* on the twenty-seventh from which they hoped "to make $1200. In five years we will have all our debts paid—13 lots, church, school, house, sisters' house—Santa Isabel & Santa Maria Magdalena will have their debts paid in five years. Santa Rita came later; that chapel under Fr. Elias has seven years to go." He also learned he would soon have 'Fido' to work among the *braceros*.[13]

By the spring of 1958 work was proceeding in well ordered, if often breakneck pace. "Most of us," Father David wrote the padre in April, "feel that you are holding the Corazon situation together and that while all the other friars are doing a certain part, your leadership is the thing that is putting the effort over."[14]

How Father Albert kept up with his demanding schedule no one knew. Spurred by the success of the October *jamaica* and their ever-recurring needs, he and his parishioners held another in April, for which he had to forego a meeting in San Antonio and send Reynold in his place with Fido.[15] These frequent *jamaicas* were exercises in self-help: besides providing funds they brought the community together in common effort. So did the fiestas for which he often imported musical entertainment from Mexico—preferably mariachi bands.

He oversaw the Saint Vincent de Paul's Society of Corazon, which stocked used clothing and food donated by more affluent parishes, to sell cheaply to the needy; and when food reserves ran low he bought on credit from Fong's Market[16]—doubtless at discount.

Al Braun had long since severed official connections with the army, but his ties to the men with whom he had served in battle and imprisonment remained strong and enduring. At the annual American Ex-Prisoners of War convention in 1957 the members had elected him their national chaplain. It was a real honor his old comrades-in-arms had accorded him, though because of his busy schedule he had been reluctant to assume the responsibility. "These honorary positions often prove inconvenient and expensive," he wrote his provincial, but on Father Victor's insistence he had accepted. The convention for 1958, he learned, would coincide with his annual retreat, which he had promised Father David to attend. "I had no intention of going [to the convention] he explained, "but Vic said I had an obligation [and] settled it by calling you. . . . I am not happy over the whole affair because

I dislike not carrying out a promise. If I am again appointed as national chaplain I'll turn it down."[17]

He seems to have been trying more to convince himself than his provincial. He clearly loved his old wartime buddies, enjoyed reliving old times with them, and though his functional links with the army were severed, he still felt the pull of the military. The padre attended the convention, obviously enjoyed himself immensely, was reelected—and jovially accepted.

Father Albert with some Bataan veterans, his 'New Mexico boys.' L to R: Calvin Graef, Tom Foy, Juan Baldonado, Father Al, unnamed 'Airman of the Year' (presumably from nearby Holloman Air Force Base) and Jack Rupe. Courtesy of SJAM.

In July Father Albert celebrated his first Jubilee. Half a century had passed since the day in 1908 when the 'three A's' made their first vows on entering the Order and beginning the rugged schooling for the priesthood. Into those fifty years he had packaged marvelously successful apostolates among the Apaches of New Mexico and the barrios of Arizona, forays into revolutionary Mexico, miles of driving among the CCC camps of the Depression era, and combat in two World Wars. He had built churches and chapels; his school would soon be finished; he had converted or reclaimed a multitude of souls; and he was not yet finished.

The friars at Casa de Paz y Bien retreat house at Scottsdale had already begun the celebration on Ascension Thursday in May with a gathering for the padre, "since many of us will not be on the scene" for the actual mass, wrote Father Conrade Wear on the invitations. "All the Arizona Friars are being invited to this clam-bake," he penned on Father David's: he hoped the Father Provincial could come.

Father Albert said his anniversary mass on 26 July at Sacred Heart. From all reaches of Corazon and all corners of Phoenix the people came for the standing-room-only celebration. Father David came from the coast and officiated after the mass as Father Albert renewed his vows. His friends and parishioners presented him with a donation of $1,917, which, he reported, he could use on the school.[18]

Father David apparently suggested a well-earned month's vacation, but the padre refused. "If I took a month off [I] would be unhappy while away. However on August 25 after my masses I would like to drive with the Dawsons to Santa Barbara." He had remained close to Ray and Elisa Dawson through the years since the old CCC days when they had held hands in the back seat while the padre drove. They lived now in Albuquerque. "The Dawsons named their first son after me. He is going to the seminary at Santa Barbara. I think two other boys . . . are going with them." They would also take one from Phoenix whom the padre had recommended and was sponsoring.[19]

"So many things are happening," he wrote early in August, "it is hard to keep up. Fr. Victor wants me to go to Parker with him for a day. Then Father Augustine is having his [Jubilee] celebration Aug. 28. Since I will be in California that week, if it is all right with you I'll go to San Juan for the great event. I'll fly back here . . . [in time for] Sat[urday] Conf[essions]. . . . In September we are putting on a campaign for bricks for the school."[20]

Back in Phoenix after that sojourn he complained of the lack of a priest for the Catholics at the county hospital. "I have been urging this for six years. The spiritual care . . . at the county hospital is deplorable. . . ." The only solution, he lectured his boss, was for the Province to assume responsibility. Having dismissed the foreseeable objections (*Insignificant!*), he followed with what probably did not surprise his provincial. "I am now asking you to assign me as Chaplain at Maricopa Co[unty] Hospital." By the time the always lengthy arrangements could be made, "we will have our school built and this place should have a younger man."[21]

So, Father David doubtless opined, should the hospital, though he dared not communicate such a sentiment to the crusty old padre. "I know that you would do a terrific job at it," he replied diplomatically. "You are also doing a great job where you are." He would take the matter of a hospital chaplain to the Definitorium, "and do what we can."[22]

In the autumn he lost Father Reynold to Saint Turibius Church in Los Angeles. It was a blow, having relied on this close friend and hard worker so long; but with Elias, Tibs, and Fido he would carry on.

Father Al never let go his ties with Mescalero: these were his people. Too, he had enjoyed the company of Father Hubert Mounier, mission priest there since 1953. The padre's lifelong interest in the Orient was doubtless whetted by Father Hubert's thirteen years as a missionary in China, including four years during World War II when the Japanese had impounded him. Four years after he was freed, Mounier had been forced to leave China as the communists drove in.

But despite his keen interest in Father Mounier's experiences and his love for Mescalero, the padre had always been careful never to intrude on another priest's mission. His trips to the reservation were therefore infrequent and of short duration. "[I]t is not good," he opined, "to return too often to a place where one has been assigned before."[23]

Still he kept up with old friends and current affairs at Mescalero, largely through correspondence with the Klinekoles. On learning of Virginia's election in 1958 as President of the Tribal Council (the first woman ever to hold that position), he had written her with congratulations and counsel.

It was Virginia who called him late on the night of 24 March 1959 to tell him of Father Hubert's sudden death. He had been killed that afternoon while working in the orchard when the tractor he was driving overturned and crushed him beneath it.[24]

Despite his own shock, Father Albert thought first of the impact on his Mescaleros. "The Indians admired and respected Fr. Hubert because of his simplicity and friendliness," he wrote Father David immediately. He hoped his provincial could "find a hardworking, zealous and saintly Father to take Father Hubert's place among the Apaches of Mescalero. Those Indians are going through a spiritual crisis and are in need of more than an ordinary spiritual Father. I have great attachment to those people and will never cease to pray for them."[25]

Father Hubert Mounier, OFM, and Eric Tortilla. Photo courtesy of MUA.

During the summer, as work progressed to ready the school for its September opening, Father Albert was still negotiating for a teaching staff. No arrangements had been concluded with the teaching order for which he had hoped; and without money to hire instructors he turned to his trusty friend, Bishop—now Cardinal—Richard Cushing in Boston. Cushing had instigated a program through which newly graduated Catholic college students could volunteer for a year's mission work. Through this program Father Al was able to initially staff his school: one group, rather than going as they had planned to China, opted for Sacred Heart School.

On 13 August, with the school virtually completed and knowing his 'Boston girls' would soon arrive, Father Albert wrote two letters.

"For some time," he advised Bishop Gercke, "I have realized that Sagrado Corazon needs . . . new blood; a younger man should take over. . . . I will stay on during this year and the next. By that time it would be in the best interest of all . . . that a younger man be placed in charge." He wanted "a top-notcher" and recommended Father Reynold. "He has worked successfully here for several years; he is a good religious; he is a tireless worker; he knows the Mexicans and is loved by them and he speaks 'Mexican' better than most Mexicans. He is now in charge of St. Turibius Church in Los Angeles. A year ago when he took over, St. Turibius was on the rocks; today he packs the church at all Masses. . . . I will do my best," he pledged, "to convince Father Provincial and his Councilors. . . ."[26]

In a similar letter to Father David he was a little more personal. "In two years I will be 72. I would like to be free from some of the present responsibilities. The ideal place to prepare for death is a Retreat House. . . . I would expect to hear confessions, give conferences and do whatever other work assigned me."[27]

He directed his final entreaty and long-time goal to the bishop. Before he left he wanted to see Sacred Heart "on a firmer footing. For this purpose I am asking Your Excellency to give Sagrado Corazon the status of *parish* in the Diocese of Tucson." There followed a list of finely argued reasons: the size of the area; the eight thousand Catholics and "others of good will"; the fully equipped buildings; the four priests already assigned; the improving financial condition. "Without the status of a parish," he concluded, "Sagrado Corazon could easily wilt and die and nobody would notice it because it is only a part of St. Mark's."

Were it not for Father Victor, he concluded, "Sagrado Corazon would today have only one Mass on Sundays in a shabby barracks and would be attended only part time with one priest. . . ."[28]

His letters were quickly answered. "You have done a truly apostolic and wonderful piece of work," Father David wrote the padre, "and have reawakened the faith throughout the area where formerly there were only about 60 people who went to Mass on Sunday. Now . . . there are 3000. . . ."[29]

"I shall be delighted," Gercke replied, ". . . to make Sagrado Corazon a parish," and instructed the padre to define and sketch the boundaries.[30] He had meanwhile sent the necessary papers to the Province and had written the authorities.

There remained only the usual slow machinery of ecclesiastical bureaucracy that had always irked the padre. But its enactment was assured.[31]

Sacred Heart School opened in September. The 'Boston girls' had arrived and settled in. "Each gave a year of her life," the padre reminisced, "to help us with the poor Mexicans of South Phoenix. . . . How the Mexicans loved these wonderful Boston girls."[32] To transport the children to and from school, he somehow finagled an old school bus and, lacking funds to pay a driver, drove it himself. Doubtless his friends first shuddered and then prayed for the safety of the children: the years had not improved the padre's driving.

The Mackeys cited a classic example. While stopped at a red light one day, Dick recounted, "we saw a station wagon coming, and it was Father Albert, right through the red light. A day or so later I saw him. 'Father,' I said, 'you've got to be more careful.' He said, 'No way—I was going to Saint Francis Cemetery for a funeral service, and by law I had the right of way. I had my lights on.' He scared the bejesus out of us—because there was no funeral procession—he was the only one."[33] Something always seemed to protect the padre, the bus, and the children.

Through the years the school flourished, was enlarged as enrollment grew and funds became available, and eventually extended through the eighth grade, preparatory for Saint Mary's High School.

On 11 November 1959 a special Veterans' Day celebration in his honor brought Father Al 'home again,' if briefly, to Mescalero. A Solemn High Mass opened the day: once more the padre served his people in the great stone church on which he and his Apaches had labored for twenty years with little but faith.

A sizeable contingent of the Knights of Columbus from the valley attended and presented him with a cash donation, after which the military band from Holloman Air Division (later Holloman Air Force Base) near Alamogordo played for the large crowd until eleven o'clock when the program opened. The service, conducted by American Legion Posts 48 and 108, honored all veterans, the padre in particular. Homer Yahnozha, who had served with him in the Philippines, presented a portrait of Father Al. He was given a Forty-Year Certificate and an American Legion life membership card. Father Solanus Haugh, then pastor at Saint Joseph's, wrote a tribute, which Virginia Klinekole delivered. The Legionnaires served a dinner, and an afternoon of tribal dances completed the day.[34]

"I was more than pleased," the padre wrote on his return to Phoenix, "because of the splendid work done [at Mescalero] by Father Solanus. He is tops. Besides, he knows how to get along with Brother Dan," whom Father Al had once disciplined for his Irish temper. "Brother is doing good work under Father Solanus."[35]

Later that month he received a letter from Father David, apologetic in tone, but directed by the Definitorium, which "feels that it is proper for each house of the Province . . . to send some sort of subsidy to the Provincial Office each month," if only a token. He was well aware of Father Al's financial strain, suggested $50 a month, but "if nothing at all is possible, kindly let me know.

"It has been a source of universal admiration to all of us to see you build up the chapels, the school and other services for the people of your district and we surely are not unmindful of the burden that this has placed upon you and of the manner in which you have had to scrape in order to get together the necessary funds."[36]

Father Al may have sighed at the request; but the years had inured him to money problems, which in the overall scheme of life were, after all—*Insignificant!* His reply was classical Al Braun. "To make the assessment look good," he noted with his enclosed remittance, "I told Father Elias to write out a check for $600. Now we won't have to bother till 1961. We are almost broke," he added, but "thank God no one in this house worries much whether or not we have anything in the bank."

Referring to a meeting scheduled with Father David in December, he was "thankful I bought the round trip ticket before I got your letter." He might, however, have a baptism while there; if so, the parents would pay for the transportation, and he could refund the province. "Pray," he advised, "that the baby is a little premature."

He concludes in his usual jaunty style. "During Advent I am going on the water wagon. Made three exceptions, Dec 4, Dec 8 & Dec 12. That," declared the padre who did enjoy his share of 'Irish holy water,' "makes the penance not too hard."[37]

With the school's opening Father Albert had accomplished his main objectives for Corazon. His building projects were completed, and through time and his personal ministry he had brought the spiritual care that had for so long been neglected. The city had installed the facilities he had demanded for the barrios. He had brought the Church to the people and the people to the church; and in so doing he had forged a community based on human dignity, common cause, self-help, and faith. Much remained to be done, but through his almost constant entreaties Corazon had four priests, and the soon-to-be parish was a pulsing reality he could safely leave to a younger leader.

Until that time he continued his routine. He organized *jamaicas,* he drove his school bus daily, pursued his work with juveniles, created work programs, self-help projects, and youth centers. He continued to oversee the Saint Vincent de Paul Society and La Hora Catolica. He still served as chaplain for the American ex-POWs and as Department Chaplain for the American Legion, and he remained on the Governor's Narcotic Studies Committee. He said his three Sunday masses, officiated weddings and baptisms and last rites and burials, made his door-to-door calls, took his yearly census, made his treks between chapels and church.

But now he walked a little slower, Tony Valenzuela noted. He seldom spoke of the hardships of war or of the infirmities that never went away, "but you could see it—you could see him limping as he walked. . . ."[38]

The padre's legs grew steadily worse. Whether it was the old affliction returning or a new one arising, he had never recovered from the abuses he had suffered in Japanese prison camps. In July 1961 he was forced to spend eleven days in Beaumont General Hospital in El Paso. The nature of his treatment is unclear; but his legs would grow increasingly worse throughout his life. He said little about his pain: Father Junípero too had suffered painful legs and kept on going. So would Father Albert.

✞✞✞

It was clear to his superiors Father Albert needed lighter duty. In the fall he was assigned as Retreat Master at Casa de Paz y Bien, to begin in January 1962. Here was the religious community life he had requested, and at nearby Scottsdale. He could leave Sacred Heart knowing the soon-to-be parish was in good hands, for—also as he had requested—Father Reynold would be in charge.

A number of farewell festivities honored him. Of particular moment was that at Sacred Heart Church, whose parishioners proclaimed Saturday 18 November 1961 'Father Albert's Day.' A Solemn High Mass, followed by the blessings of a bronze plaque, was the tribute of a grateful parish: they were his people; he was their Padre Alberto.

At some time during these final months Father 'Gus' came to visit—Herman Hobrecht, classmate at Saint Anthony's, Augustine of the mischievous 'three A's,' erstwhile Father Provincial, friend through many years. Though not Gus's first visit to Corazon, it was probably the most impressive. "Fr. Albert," Gus wrote in retrospect, "took me on a grand tour from church to church and for many home visits." He stayed at the rectory the padre had built and enlarged. He toured the chapels and the halls adjacent to each. He visited the church from which all the rest radiated, remarked the ornate chandelier and heard the deep-toned bells Father Victor had given—bells that had once graced Saint Mary's. He visited the school, and the house Father Albert and his parishioners had bought and converted into a convent for the Sisters who were by then teaching in Corazon. He visited the outlying farm communities where Father Albert had served with his indomitable Workers of the Sacred Heart.

He saw hope revived for the hopeless, faith for the faithless, the impossible made possible by the stubborn drive of one aging priest. "Literally thousands of those mostly poor Mexicans filled those churches and went to the Sacraments in great numbers," Father Gus marveled. He saw the culmination of an incredible life's work.

"This great apostolate," he summed, "was just short of a miracle."[39]

23: LIGHTER DUTY

A new assignment always energized Father Al, and he tackled this challenge with his usual verve. Duty at Casa de Paz y Bien was considerably lighter than that at Corazon; but idleness was not the padre's way, nor passivity his means. There was no wilderness to brave at the Casa, no tribe to seek out by horseback, no multitudes of forgotten people, no schools or churches to build. But there were hard-working friars in need of renewal, and some not so hard-working who, he believed, could use a "swift spiritual kick in the pants"; the Casa was due for some reorganizing; and it offered the fraternal life for which he had longed. "There is so little community life in many of our houses," he lamented. "The new, young crops of screw-balls consider it a waste of time."[1] Immediately, Father Gus observed, "he set the pace of a good community life, which then was in real need of a leader."[2] His was a more demanding stride than that to which many of his fraters had grown accustomed. In addition to his work at the Casa he was soon teaching a course in the history of religion at the Newman Center in Tempe,[3] and he was still working on the Governor's Narcotic Study Committee.

Always a hard-core realist, he never welcomed new priests with a Pollyanna approach. "When we were newly ordained," Father Finian McGinn recalled, "he gave the retreat to all the priests from the college. It was all based on his life as a military chaplain, as a missionary, and his life as a pastor, and he stressed that it was not going to be easy. It was hard for him and it was going to be hard for us. We were going to have to learn to be strong. He was not one to paint a very easy picture. . . . He'd talk about the difficulties—and you could sit there and listen to him and you realized that he had certainly lived that life. You could see the wrinkles on his face. But when he smiled that wonderful smile you could see him light up. He was a very happy man—and yet he suffered a lot in life. . . . He lived everything he taught, and yet he could still laugh."[4]

That he worked assiduously on the retreats he led is attested by the five thick journals he left behind filled with notes and drafts of finely reasoned lectures. Few are dated; all bear the Braun hallmarks of honest zeal, down-to-earth reality, and crusty humor. He had never hesitated to speak his mind to anyone, from young seminarians to his august superiors. As retreat master he sometimes seems to have relished tweaking a few stately (if figmental) beards, but so genially that, though they squirmed, they could not help grinning with their puckish padre.

✙✙✙

Who needs a retreat? the padre asks. His answer: all men. He recounts his own drastic need when the tenor of his life was shattered by war and surrender, when, looking into a grim uncertainty, the chaplains had to learn to cope. On them rested the spiritual welfare of their men—even their very survival. They found their answer in the covert retreats from which they drew strength from one another and learned how best to take care of their men.[5]

For his topics at the Casa he drew on those qualities he had forged so tenaciously in Japanese prison camps, from which he had sculpted a full, forceful, and fervent priesthood.

Heading his list was *faith*, the unmoving bedrock and animating spirit of the Church. "Without a strong and lively faith," he charges his fraters, "you may wear the habit, you may wear the vestments of the priesthood, but you will never be a true Franciscan, you will never be a zealous priest. . . . An Irish wake is not a sad affair, because the Irish have faith." So had the Spaniards, who for seven hundred years "suffered and fought and died for their faith," which became "the basis of the[ir] national character." He notes the faith of the Apache who sees God's presence in the turkey's tracks, and that which sustained the thousands of fighting men through the bitter years of war and captivity.

Inseparable from faith is *charity*, which "must take in all men . . . or it is not the charity of Christ. In spite of the way we Catholics often think and act"—and one can imagine his sardonic glance, one eyebrow raised— "Christ really did die for all men." He cites Chaplain Howden who, dying of starvation in Japanese prison camp, gave his own meager rations to others. "Protestants," the padre comments, "often give us a splendid example. Prejudice has no room in charity," he stresses. "In the war, as before the throne of God, men of many creeds stood naked in the showers, and we all looked the same—like the dickens. All skin and bones."

He takes to task those priests who argue on moralistic lines that their duty is only to Catholics. "Thank God there were no moralists around in the first years of the Church, or the Church would still be bogged down in Palestine."

True charity, he emphasizes, flows from *love*. He distrusts the godless and demeaning 'charity' of the welfare state, which causes dependence and reduces human dignity. "Charity does not mean being soft": he had not straightened out the young hoods of Corazon or the hoodlums at Saint John's with permissiveness.

His lecture on *obedience* left a lasting impression on Brother Timothy Arthur while attending a retreat with his class just entering the seminary. "In the army," the padre recounted, "they had a curfew, and if the MPs found any GIs out after that, they shot them. And that," he said, "is what is meant by obedience." Father Al often indulged in hyperbole to make a point, but the unknowing young seminarians looked at one another in dismay on hearing the hard-lined old warrior. "We were ready," Brother Tim affirmed, "to pack up and leave then and there."[6]

A constantly recurring theme is the padre's deep *respect for women*, "teachers of the race, capable of great love and great suffering. Every great man had a great mother." Priests must stress the sanctity of marriage, he instructs, which "is not primarily for pleasure but for children. The pleasure is the driving force intended by nature to secure children." It is, he expounds, "the wonderful collaboration of parents, of nature, and of God, whence comes to light a new human being made according to the image and likeness of the Creator." He emphasizes the role of the woman, who bears and rears the child; and in today's world where so many ignore the sanctity of marriage and motherhood, he thanks God "there is still among us that beautiful and heroic creature, the true woman."

To illustrate his theme he turns to the Apache's puberty ceremony, the great celebration for the perpetuation of life, and interprets its profound symbolism. "Every Indian, young and old . . . understands the meaning and is filled with awe and respect for the sacred generation. . . . These simple people put us to shame."

Father Al frequently addresses the subject of *suffering*, "the lot of every man. Tranquilizers and sleeping pills are not the answer." The key is to bear one's burdens willingly, courageously, and cognizant of the value; through Christ's suffering came the Resurrection. . . . By suffering we learn to suffer," and he cites the Apaches' harsh training that their youths might become men. He reflects on his own wartime experience: the young men reared indulgently were those who gave up and died; those who survived had learned to endure pain. Because Church leaders incur special obligations, "our whole training should be like that of the Apaches—a training that will enable us to meet life as we will undoubtedly find it. . . .

"We can expect hard times for the Church in the United States," of whose lapses he is all too conscious. "When the Church ceases to be Christlike, God [has always] come in, in a hard way, to preserve His Church from going wrong." Noting the steady spread of Communism and persecution, he asks, "Are we ready for whatever great trial God has in store for us . . . to correct the widespread godlessness and secularism of our day?"

The churchman, he contends, must therefore eschew that secularism. But the modern world "has a way now to get back at you that it never had before: the radio and television. You find them in all our monasteries and residences," he fulminates, "these two agencies of propaganda for all that is worldly." But the priest must not, on the other hand, withdraw so completely as to give up all pleasures. "Be careful," he warns, "not to confuse the crank with the saint, nor the jovial religious with the worldling."

Among life's greatest pleasures, he affirms, is the fraternity of common cause. "A group working together for high and important purpose are bound together by a strong bond known as *esprit de corps*." He liked to stress this to the young, newly ordained priests. "Anyone familiar with the military can tell a good outfit by its *esprit de corps* and the [consequent] valor of their deeds. We had it among the chaplains," and he cites those who lifted morale in the black holds of the infamous hell ships. "There was no place for rivalries, jealousy, insubordination or hatred between religions or different orders."

Along with conviviality the padre had always enjoyed a nip of 'Irish holy water'—"Drink is God's gift to man"—but he cautioned against its immoderate use, citing "the old army rule that 'a man who drinks on the job is fired.'" Old priests sometimes set bad examples by over-indulgence: "If you find one," he concludes wryly, "tell him about AA."

Addressing the need for *humility*, he evokes the image of Christ on the Cross, of Saint Francis who traded the robes of wealth for the rags of poverty, and "the composer Anton Dvorak" who humbly "laid a wreath before Beethoven."

"*Silence*, the soul of religious life," he notes, "fosters meditation, is a bulwark against distraction and dissipation. "In the Old Testament, when

Balaam's ass talks it is a miracle; in the new [age] when some Friars keep quiet it is a miracle."

Al Braun had no patience with lazy friars. The priest, he declares, is the "key man in the most important job in the world," and cites "the great Father Kino, who labored unceasingly to serve the whole man—his body and his soul." He stresses the *sanctity of manual labor* that gives a man dignity and self-respect; he lauds the "Mexican men [who] day after day walk to work with a lunch pail in hand, real men, faithfully meeting their responsibilities to provide for the family." He expounds on the "great things God has let man accomplish by labor." He talks of Brother Sales, fatally injured in labor's harness, and challenges the priests to do no less, ever reminding them that "idleness is the workshop of the devil."

Nor does he spare those priests who mask their laziness behind excessive piety—though he emphasizes the value of real and *sincere prayer*. He notes the religiosity of the Apache, the saving grace of prayer in battle; he speaks of Lulu Reyes who risked her life to get the necessities for mass to the priests in prison camps; and of how he and Father Bauman risked their own necks contriving to say their dual mass at Camp Omori.

Above all he argues against priests who "sit on their butts and push papers around." He loved to tell the story—always with a grin—of one particular retreat, attended by a prominent bishop. "I'm praying every day," the padre had asserted, "that the Communists will take over this country and blow up all these damned rectories and force the priests out among the people."

The bishop, he always added with a twinkle, had frowned and waggled an admonitory finger at him. *Insignificant:* "I've been in trouble all my life."

☩ ☩ ☩

Within Saint Mark's parish a large housing project had been erected for poor families, many living in the same state of spiritual neglect Father Al had encountered at Corazon. The two parish priests were unable to devote the many hours the project needed. That the padre knew of the situation is certain; that he was growing restless with too little to do at the Casa is probable. Whether he instigated the change of assignment is unclear, but when he was transferred to Saint Mark's in May 1964 he leaped into work at the project, and had enlisted Jeanne Marsteller to help, when his assignment was suddenly terminated.

"Was having a grand time in the housing project," he wrote an unnamed friend, "when I got a telegram ordering [me] to leave for McNary at once." McNary was a small lumber town in the White Mountains where many Apaches from the nearby reservation at Whiteriver worked. When the parish suddenly lost its priest, his superiors clearly saw in the vacancy a less demanding job for the aging and unwell padre, and relief from the Phoenix heat.

He did not leave Saint Mark's without enjoining his superiors passionately to replace him at the project. The two fathers there, he pled, "cannot meet this urgent demand. . . . They are already overburdened. . . ."[7]

"It is beautiful and cool at McNary," he wrote, "7250 ft high. Am stepping out to get acquainted. Visited the hospital this morning. Will visit the jail this afternoon. Within a short time I should know every Catholic in the parish."[8]

That Al Braun would dive into work was inevitable: where there was a church there was a challenge. His immediate intentions were to increase attendance at mass and—to no one's surprise—to enlarge the little Saint Anthony's church to meet the resultant demand. Paul Guerin brought a crew from Phoenix, and by the end of October the padre wrote Jeanne they were "about finished with the addition. . . . It will double the seating capacity," which, he added, "is badly needed. During the summer half the people are outside looking in through the windows & the door. Then just before the collection is taken it begins to rain and the outsiders go home."[9]

"Wish I had a few of the Sacred Heart workers here at McNary," he grumbled in December. "Never met a group of Mexican Catholics who knew less about their religion."[10] Meanwhile he enjoyed the beauty of the autumn colors in the mountains, which he spoke of sharing with some friars visiting from the Casa.[11]

He had other company that fall. Father Phil Baldonado, recently named pastor at Sacred Heart, squeezed time for a quick visit. Charlie and Katherine Mackey came also, with Dick and Sue in tow. "We stayed with him at his little place, and then in the morning he was out in the kitchen fixing beans." All occasions, the padre believed, called for a pot of frijoles. "He didn't clean them," Sue noted. "Just dumped them in the pot with the rocks and mud. 'That's good for you,' he said."[12]

Winter came early in the mountains, and with it Father Al's arthritis grew excruciatingly painful—though it did not stop him from building a snowman with Jeanne's two young sons when they and their mother visited in December. They had arrived to the cacophony of clanging metal. Alighting from the car and rounding the rear corner of the small rectory, they beheld the brown-robed Father Albert, spoon in hand, banging joyously on a skillet. Answering his summons, leaping and yapping happily around him were what seemed like the entire canine population of McNary, anticipating the food he began to toss among them. It was, Jeanne learned, a daily ritual. Saint Francis had been content with his birds; Father Al embraced all dogdom as well.

Winter was taking its toll. His friends noticed it, and his superiors realized the padre must return to a warmer clime. Even he admitted his growing infirmity, and early in January wrote Jeanne that he expected to return to Phoenix as soon as his provincial could find a replacement. "Had a hard time to make the second mass today," he confided. "The old legs can't take it any more."[13]

He was still at McNary when a letter arrived. "It is with grateful appreciation for your outstanding contribution to my administration and the State of Arizona," Paul Fannin wrote, "that I leave the office of Governor." He spoke of the padre's service in battling the drug problem and of his personal pleasure in their working together. For his "diligence, integrity, and faithful service" on the Arizona Narcotics Study Committee, the governor awarded him an enclosed certificate "in tribute and respect to this outstanding citizen who has contributed in a tangible way to the highest ideals of public service."[14]

Father Al's physical pain eased greatly on his return to Phoenix. Assigned to Saint Mary's, he rotated as he was needed between there, the Casa, and Sacred Heart. He had always enjoyed time at Saint Mary's, where so many of his friends resided. During this period his friendship with Father Blaise Cronin deepened. And he particularly enjoyed assisting Father Phil Baldonado at Sacred Heart. Phil had set the parish back on stable ground following a dismaying psychological unraveling of Father Reynold, whom the padre had so confidently left as his successor. Having worked so hard and fervently through the difficult years, Reynold seems, after Father Al left, to have undergone a strange spiritual introversion, which culminated in his smashing the many statues of the saints so lovingly collected in Sacred Heart. They were idols, Reynold had proclaimed; his people must not worship them.

Father Al, having learned of the incident while still at the Casa, had been as shocked as the parishioners, and after a furious explosion spent itself, tried to reason with his old friend. "Is a picture of a family member an idol?" he reportedly asked. No? Then why was a statue any different? But his arguments had been futile and he had left, saddened at Reynold's breakdown, praying for his recovery, and concerned for Sacred Heart.[15] Now he found Father Phil the cure the parishioners needed, and was delighted to help him whenever asked.

✞✞✞

Father Al had reached a significant year: 1965 marked a half-century of his priesthood. Seven years earlier he had celebrated fifty years since joining the Order. Now, fifty years after his ordination in 1915, his Golden Jubilee was upon him.

Three solemn high masses marked the event. The first, at Sacred Heart on the afternoon of 30 May, evoked those years when, brick by brick, the community's dream had become its reality. Herman Baumann came to deliver the jubilee sermon. He spoke of the war years he and Father Al had endured together, of the human will and faith that had triumphed over the miseries of war and prison and forged bonds of brotherhood too strong to break.

The church was packed. Crowding the front rows were veterans. Legionnaires from several posts fired a twenty-one-gun salute on the grounds and hosted the reception that followed, complete with the padre's favorite entertainment, a mariachi band.

On 20 June his second jubilee mass at Saint Joseph's in Los Angeles rekindled earlier memories. His father had helped build this church, had reportedly carved the Stations of the Cross and worked on the altar. Here John William Braun had been christened; 'Bud' Braun had served as altar boy; now Father Albert said his jubilee mass. Father Provincial Terence Cronin preached the sermon. There also was Father Gus, whose own jubilee mass Al had attended in Sacramento a month before. Members of his own large and expanding family packed the pews.

Meanwhile in Phoenix two other celebrations honored Al Braun. Governor Sam Goddard presented the rarely given Arizona Medal of Honor "for his many years of faithful service to the State, the Great Southwest and the Nation."[16]

"Gosh," the padre responded. "If you stay out of jail and hang around as long as I have, they've got to give you something."[17]

Father Al's Jubilee Mass at Saint Joseph's in Los Angeles, the church of his boyhood.
June 1965. Courtesy of Barbara Brown.

Father Al surrounded by members of his prolific family, following his Jubilee Mass in California. Courtesy of Barbara Brown.

On 10 July the parishioners at Sacred Heart and a group of Mexican-American organizations hosted a testimonial dinner for the nearly fêted-out father. Seeming almost embarrassed by the plaudits and ovations, he replied, somewhat curtly, "I only did my duty."

On 15 August the third and last of his jubilee masses—perhaps the most nostalgic—was that held in Mescalero among his beloved Apaches. Over a thousand people attended from all reaches of the reservation and the surrounding countryside. Father Gus flew in to preach the sermon; the padre's old friend Sixtus Brambilla came from Boston. Army friends arrived from Fort Bliss with a delegation and a military band that, during the after-mass barbeque the tribe hosted, played alternately with tribal dances and drums throughout the afternoon.

Virginia Klinekole opened a short afternoon ceremony with a tribute. Eric Tortilla spoke in English and Apache. On behalf of Governor Jack Campbell, George Fitzpatrick, editor of *New Mexico* magazine, presented the padre with a Colonel's Aide-de-Camp commission on the Governor's staff for his years of dedication to the New Mexico Apaches. An army friend from Fort Bliss gave him a bronze plaque to match the one dedicated years earlier to the veterans of World War I and mounted near the entrance to Saint Joseph's—this one inscribed to those of World War II. With a short prayer, Father Al attached it on the other side of the doors.

It was, in a sense, the final act in completing his beloved 'Apache cathedral.'

✣ ✣ ✣

During these years the padre visited his family on the coast more often than he had in the busier times. His walk was slower, his humor crustier, his merriment intact. Niece Dorothy Bumgarner found him "as much fun as ever," his mind and tongue as sharp, his eyes still shooting sparks of mischief. The large and growing family congregated at their various homes, or sometimes at a family ranch near Tehachapi for a barbeque.[18]

His brother Clarence's grandson Mike was one of the new generation who loved Father Albert's visits. "When it came to kids, all the adults could go jump off the bridge. He'd play Yahtzee with us for hours. The adults would get upset because he wouldn't come talk to them."

Mike remembered one afternoon when the padre loaded the children into his ancient 'Cheve' to "take us all to get ice cream. He gets us all into this big old car—five or six of us—and starts driving up and down the streets, and he picks up all the little Mexican kids along the way. He had this car loaded, and tells us, 'If the police see this many kids in the car I'll get a ticket, so we're going to practice. When I say 'duck,' everybody go down.' So we practiced, and pretty soon we were all lying on top of each other, rolling all over and laughing, and he'd say, 'Okay, you can get up.' We were all laughing and he was too.

"We came to an old grocery store run by some ancient Chinese people. They saw all these kids come running—but then they saw Father Albert and it was okay. Everybody got whatever kind of ice cream they wanted—there were at least twenty of us. The old couple were watching to make sure we didn't tear the place apart, and Father Al was just laughing—

"Then going home we had to duck once more."

With his cousins Mike listened gape-jawed as Father Al recounted his adventures—as an undercover man in Mexico, as a combat veteran in two World Wars, as a lone priest living among the Indians—heady stuff for young boys. "But my aunts and uncles were waiting for him at a restaurant. Finally one came over to get him, and he said, 'Oh, I'll be there when I get there. Go ahead, I'm happy here,'" and turned back to the children.[19]

He was as outspoken as ever. On learning one evening at the Bumgarners' home that their adult son Craig was a Democrat, he growled, "I don't even want to hear your confession."[20] When his grand-nephew Ray Brown, having recently graduated from college, accepted a job with the forest service in Logan, Utah, he warned him to "be careful of those Mormons—they'll try to convert you." He continued to caution him in letters, and later at a family reunion. "First thing when we walked in the door," Ray recalled, "he had me come over and sit with him, have a glass of wine, and he wanted to know about 'those damned Mormons,' and he went on and on about them. He could use the English language in more colorful ways than most of us could ever hope to. He never minced his words, said exactly what he thought . . . and you knew without any doubt what he meant."

Ray remembered another piece of fatherly advice. When someone suggested the padre was drinking too much wine one evening, "he said to me, 'You know, there's a way to keep from getting tipsy on occasions like this: keep a couple of hard-boiled eggs in your pocket and every once in a while have one.' And," Ray added, "it does seem to work!"[21]

Al Braun also visited any friends within feasible distance. On learning that Madeline Ullom, still in the Army Nurse Corps, was stationed at Bataan Memorial Hospital in Albuquerque, he made a quick jaunt to see her.[22] He visited Ray and Elisa Dawson. And, always maintaining a soft spot for his 'Pino girls,' he twice visited Concha, now married and living in Albuquerque.

"I sent him an airline ticket," she recalled. While there, "he wanted to go to Santa Fe. We put up a great big lunch and coffee, and a bottle of wine, and drove. We stopped at some of the Indian villages where he had friends, and in Santa Fe, and we were exhausted getting back to Albuquerque. I put him up in a hotel and I ordered breakfast for him. . . . He thought it was so funny that someone would come to the door with coffee and bacon and eggs at six o'clock in the morning. He said he was thinking about going to mass—instead of that he ate bacon and eggs."

While in Albuquerque "he met some of the newspaper people. He particularly enjoyed talking with one editor, who was Jewish, about the differences—and samenesses—of the religions. He didn't care what your religion was. He was just a great, great spirit."[23]

And always, whenever possible, he visited Mescalero. By this time he had become a legend, among the tribe and throughout the Tularosa Basin, and many hailed his coming as if heaven itself had opened. The children had all heard the stories about him and ran ahead as their parents had, yelling the old refrain: "Father Albert's coming! Father Albert's coming!"

✜ ✜ ✜

"My dear Jeanne," he wrote in October 1965 from Saint John's at Komatke. "This is my new home." The humidity caused by extensive irrigation had worsened his arthritis in Phoenix. "St. John's is much drier. I love it here: the desert, the Indians and the school all fascinate me. The community life in this Franciscan house is excellent. Father Solanus [Haugh] is Superior; he ranks among the best."[24] The unruly gangs and internal dissension with which the padre had dealt some years before were gone. Saint John's was now a model mission.

He still drove to help Father Phil at Sacred Heart on weekends, using a car Jeanne and her husband Otto lent him. He seems to have led a fairly routine, though busy, life through the winter, commuting to other Phoenix parishes when needed.

"Just returned from Sacred Heart," he wrote in February, where he "had a requiem mass for Mr. Bennett, the old man who use[d] to live on 16th St. He and his wife . . . were poor, but very generous to Sacred Heart. Each gave a dollar every Sunday and five extra each month—a lot of money for two poor old people. Then, when we started to build the church, they were always buying a hundred bricks. If you hear I've been kicked out of the Diocese you will know it is because of burying dear friends outside their parish. You know me—long ago I learned never to ask too many questions. All these laws interfere so much with charity. I have tried to pay attention to Christ. He told that to the Jews. Most of them loved Him for it; some," he concluded, "killed him for it."[25]

A few days later he helped at St. Mark's. "Held confessions yesterday and two masses this morning." He hoped Jeanne and her sons could make it to the "big annual celebration at St. John's" in March. "Am in no shape to be running around and still I get all kinds of tempting invitations. The Franciscans in Guadalajara asked me to be chaplain of the American

Catholics living in that beautiful city. How I would love to but my Provincial and Dr. Huger say nothing doing. Just got a letter from Fr. Brian asking me to take his place at the Retreat House at San Juan Bautista. . . . I am already obligated to be at Whiteriver in June & first week of July while Fr. Sylvester celebrates his Silver Jubilee in Italy. I should be 50 years younger. Wouldn't I have a time!"[26]

Still he stayed active, and when the need for a priest at Parker became acute he went there, technically on loan from Saint John's. Parker lay on the Arizona side of the Colorado River, west of Komatke across a hundred and fifty miles of cactus desert. His territory was wide, and he often said masses at the barren little settlements of Salome and Aguila. "The Mexicans and Indians," he wrote, "feel no one [in the Church] cares for them, so they are joining other churches." It was the sort of challenge he welcomed. "How I wish I had the Sacred Heart Workers in Parker."

Katherine and Charlie Mackey were there visiting him, he reported, and urged Jeanne and her children to join them. "It is great at Parker, as dry as a dead cow's bones in the desert and from June till Oct as hot as hell. The people: Anglos, Mexicans and Indians—are wonderful." And, Katherine penned below Father Al's signature, "I'm sure Father will like it here—lots of missionary work to do."[27]

He did: work always invigorated Al Braun. Finding many unmarried couples living together, he performed wedding ceremonies en masse, as he had done at Mescalero and Corazon. He envisioned building a parochial school at Parker, for which, he wrote, "the people here are all eager. . . . Our biggest obstacle[s] will be the bishop and the Provincial."[28] Apparently bishop and provincial prevailed, for there is no record of his having built at Parker.

But he could not resist working on the little church, as the Bumgarners discovered when they visited. It was, Jess remembered, "a run-down beat-up thing. And he had more people working for him—they plastered it and built a wall around it. He always had half a dozen guys working around there. He could get work out of anyone."

Attached to the church was his small living area and a utility room where, during one of the Bumgarners' visits, Dorothy and her sister had been doing some laundry and returned to find the ancient washing machine overflowing. "This room opened into the church, right behind the altar. Everything was floating. You think we didn't scramble to get the water out!

Father's room was on the lower level and the rugs were floating. He was at the altar saying mass, and the water was streaming in there. But nothing flapped him." Dorothy and her sister were trying to staunch the flow, "and of course there was this wall he'd built all around—you should have seen our husbands trying to get over it to get the mops."

Through it all the padre continued saying mass.[29]

Some eighty miles east of Parker lies the village of Yarnell, a spot dear to Father Albert because of a chapel, a school, and the story behind both. Bill Wasson, a village youth, had joined the Franciscan Order and was in time ordained in Mexico, where he stayed to serve. When a small homeless boy appeared one evening, Father William took him in for the night; the next day another street child appeared. This was the beginning of what became a large orphanage and elementary school—Nuestros Pequeños Hermanos: Our Little Brothers.

Meanwhile at Yarnell Father William's parents built a chapel in his name. It too grew, and in time became a retreat center. Father William then envisioned a school in the States where youths from the orphanage could learn English and receive a high-school education. The school was built at Yarnell. Lacking money for teachers, he staffed it, as Father Al had done at Corazon, with volunteers.

It was a place that drew the padre. Here he sometimes made retreats; keenly interested in the school, he often visited it; and always he did what he could for the Yarnell project.

Al Braun was never happier than when reuniting with his old combat buddies, sharing a few jokes, a few memories, and a few nips of 'Irish holy water.' One annual affair he always tried to attend was the deer hunt for the veterans of Bataan and Corregidor, hosted by Thomas Fortune Ryan who had bought the erstwhile Albert Fall ranch. Ryan had been with the Sixth Army that had liberated Bilibid prison at war's end, had found many New Mexicans among the men inside the stinking sty and, shocked at their condition and appalled at what they had suffered, vowed to do something special for these men. Annually thereafter he hosted a week-long hunting party at his plush lodge.

One year the news spread that Father Albert was there. Many of the ranchers had known him from his Mescalero days, and Ryan invited them to the feast with which the week climaxed. As told by one veteran, "One group arrived, heard music inside—a Victrola or a piano, I don't remember just what—and a lot of clapping and whistling. A rancher knocked on the door; no one answered, the music continued; he knocked louder, and finally pounded until someone opened the door.

"There was Father Albert, a derby on his head and a cane in his hand, dancing an Irish jig. Like a true vaudeville trouper, he finished the dance before he came over to greet his old friends with a shout and a healthy *abrazo*."[30]

Since first elected, Father Al had remained national chaplain of the American Ex-Prisoners of War and attended the yearly conventions as long as he could. His last was in Spokane in 1966. By 1967 his health prevented any more long-distance traveling. Soon after that year's gathering a letter arrived. "Our dear Father Braun," it began, ". . . Your absence is felt by all present and we sincerely wish you all the blessings the good Lord can bestow upon you.

"With extreme gratitude the organization unanimously voted to present you a life membership. . . ." Signatures of his old comrades followed, three closely packed pages of cherished names.[31]

Deteriorating health continued to plague him. Father Gus, visiting at Parker in August 1966 found him "all alone, but still working hard for those people, who are eager to cooperate with a zealous priest." But the padre, Gus reported, was "not in good health; he looks worn out and really should retire."[32] His legs grew weaker and the illnesses contracted in Japanese prison camps, from which he had never recovered, grew more acute. In September he was forced to return to Phoenix for medical care. He did not stay in the hospital, preferring the community life at Saint Mary's, and admitting that "from time to time I sneak down to Corazon. . . ."[33]

Though he hoped to return to Parker, he was still in Phoenix in February of 1967, apparently continuing medical treatment, though he did motor with the Mackeys to attend Father Bonaventure Nava's funeral at Topowah.[34] By March he was planning a retreat at Holy Cross Retreat House in Mesilla Park, New Mexico; then, after a quick trip to the coast and a stopover in the Parker-Salome area, he would return to Holy Cross indefinitely, for its proximity to William Beaumont Hospital in El Paso, where he could receive medical care.[35]

On his return he advised Bishop of Tucson Francis Green (Bishop

Gercke had died in 1964) that he was being transferred from his diocese to that of El Paso "for physical reasons," and thanked him and his priests for his joy in working among them. "Yesterday I told the people at Salome & that area goodbye. . . . I hope those people can continue to have a mass every Sunday. A week-day mass simply does not fit in a farm area." The padre could not leave the people in the little desert outposts without addressing the bishop on their behalf.

Father Fidelis, he suggested, "is idolized by the people of that area around Salome. How fortunate [they] . . . would be if the Bishop could place Fr. Fidelis in that area," where he could also say mass at Aguila. "How I wish I were younger and could spend the rest of my life in the area. . . ."[36]

Mesilla Park, with its proximity to El Paso, seemed the perfect spot within an easy drive to the hospital, close enough to Mescalero for visits there, time for badly needed rest, and with enough duties to keep at bay the idleness he so dreaded. He seems to have held several retreats there and worked in the area where needed.

"Summer will soon be here," he wrote Jeanne in May, and "the Mackeys will be returning to Tularosa and Mescalero" for the hot months. He hoped Jeanne could come with them, where she and her boys "would enjoy the Apache Puberty Feast. . . . I will be at Mescalero from June 28 till August 4th."[37]

Jeanne was unable to come at that time, however, which, the padre wrote, was "providential" because he would "be there only a few hours. The boss here [at Mesilla] is very likeable but he changes his mind every 15 minutes. Before I left Phoenix he wrote me if I came to Mesilla Park I would be free till Sept.; I could go to Mescalero or anywhere. The other day he called me from Portales, N.M. that he would be back July 4, 5, or 6, that I should take his place at a concelebration of the mass at the cathedral in El Paso. These people don't realize I am almost 78 and crippled with arthritis. I love work but to do the work of a young man I need a boss with miraculous power to enable me to do it. If it gets beyond endurance I may surprise them by turning in at a Vets' Hospital. I know I can do good there even if in a wheel-chair." He would still spend most of July on the reservation relieving Father Justin Moncrief for a month. If Jeanne could come then, "we will make real Apaches out of the boys. . . ."[38]

Though still feisty in spirit, the padre was declining. "All week," he wrote in July, "I have spent at Mesilla Park: high blood pressure, arthritis and a sick stomach. My days of having a good time are over. Soon I may turn in at a Veterans' Hospital. When sick it is difficult to receive proper care in a monastery."

He still worked, however, still performed his duties at Mescalero, and he still drove, as badly as ever. "Last Monday," he confessed to Jeanne (whose car he was still driving), "an Indian rushed to the church at Mescalero and told me to take his wife to the Doctor. The Dr. was not at the hospital so we went to his house. The road was very narrow. No place to turn around. I had to back down the steep hill. The car turned over on its top. We were all pinned under but no one was seriously hurt. The car was badly damaged. The mechanic said it would not pay to repair the damage."[39]

He would not stop driving, however, and seems to have found a vehicle at the mission. "Tomorrow," he wrote in August, "I am going to offer mass for some old folks living ten miles up the river. They never have had mass. Priests are scarce in this part of the country." Soon he was going "to Tularosa for two weeks so the Pastor can get away. I will still spend the two weeks visiting the people. How I miss the car you gave me. I will have Charlie and Katherine Mackey take me around. . . .

"If I get any worse I will be returning to Phoenix in October . . . [and] will go to the Veterans' Hospital." His health seems to have improved, however, for he flew to California to officiate the renewal of brother Ray's and Clara's wedding vows on their fiftieth anniversary[40] and thence to Phoenix to bury a friend at Sacred Heart, where he "saw many of my people. . . . Hugged them all." From there he looked forward to another two weeks in Tularosa. "How I will love those two weeks, taking the parish census. . . ."[41]

It would be his last census. "My boss," he fumed in December to Eugene Henrion, "won't let me drive any more. He says my eyesight is bad and my reaction slow, so I spend my old age trying to find a way to kill time. I should raise so much hell in the house, so that my boss would be happy to have me out on the road. . . ."

But he was still planning trips. "Am going to the National Convention of Ex-Prisoners of War at Plainview, Texas," in the coming summer of 1968, he continued, "then to Poplar Bluff, Mo., to see some friends, then to Oskaloosa" to see Eugene and Celine.[42] He did not attend the convention. Whether he visited his friends is unclear but doubtful, though he wrote Jeanne in mid-July that he "took a plane for Phoenix" from somewhere. "I was in such misery that friends (apparently in Albuquerque) would not permit me to continue the trip. They placed me in the Veterans' Hospital. The doctor found amoebae in my intestines, that caused the bleeding. Have had that since a prisoner. Must return to Albuquerque for treatment July 22. . . . How long that will take I don't know."[43]

On 26 July he was "still at the V.A. Hospital. Why? I don't know. Feel tops, only I find it hard to walk. Will leave here Tuesday July 30 for Alamogordo, Tularosa and Mescalero. Will spend one week there."[44] Even that seemed to tax his strength. "Can't do any more running around," he admitted. "Have been wanting to . . . spend a week or two with my brother and his family" in California. "Wish I could celebrate my birthday with them. Sept. 5th I will be 79."[45]

"A Mescalero Apache visited me the other day," he wrote from Phoenix in August. "She bawled me out for not using some of their good medicine for arthritis. I have sent for some. . . . If I continue going from bad to worse . . . I will soon be in a wheelchair."

But the old warhorse was still in harness. "Tomorrow I leave for Kingman," he wrote in August. "The pastor pulled out and left his people without a priest. . . . I can still say mass but I must hold on to the altar."[46]

Winter found him back in the hospital; when released in January 1969, he returned to Saint Mary's, protesting against "being idle. If they can't keep me busy, I will do what I can to move to San Xavier."[47] But Father Al's days of active duty were nearing the end. His friends—particularly Father Blaise—had long tried to persuade him he had more than fulfilled his mission. For months Al Braun held on mulishly. But for all his stubbornness he was also a realist, and the sands were running fast. In March, following another hospital stay, he turned toward the Sacred Heart Nursing Home in Phoenix.

"My dear Mother Superior," he wrote. "Came home yesterday, thank God! The doctor said 'lay low' for a while. If it is okay . . . I will come to the Little Sisters of the Poor April 7, Monday after Easter." He had lived a simple life and wanted "a plain simple room. . . . I can visit with the old men and women every day. That will keep me busy. I hate idleness. . . .

"I feel obliged," he added, "to let you know, the Xray showed a growth on the bladder. Six days ago the doctor burned the growth. Later he told me it was cancer. . . . I am not at all concerned; then too, I don't believe the doctor. I feel tops, except for the arthritis. . . ."[48]

He told Blaise sometime afterward he had consented to the bladder procedure on condition that he be given no anesthetic: he wanted to watch. "Whether that happened," Blaise remarked years later, "I don't know. But it sounds just like him."[49]

This old soldier had no intention of fading away. He would not be a passive patient. God kept him alive for a reason. Those who knew him could have predicted this crusty old friar would find some ramparts to man.

The role of patient would just be another challenge.

24: IMPATIENT PATIENT

"In the veterans' hospital [I] could never say mass," the padre wrote soon after entering the home, "so I moved to the Little Sisters. Here I say mass every day," albeit sitting in a wheelchair, "because I can't stand nor can I walk."[1] He was soon leading a rosary each evening as well; and before long he had organized two weekly classes in church history.[2] He spent Mondays at Saint Mary's with the friars, taxied by Father Blaise, who always made sure Father Al enjoyed a good nip of 'Irish holy water' before dinner.

For his eightieth birthday the Little Sisters gave him a party and an ornately penned poem one of their number had written. Likening him to Saint Francis, the opus lauded him for his heroism and his service to mankind—a sincere tribute from the hearts of the sisters. They too had fallen under his spell.[3]

He returned their affection, often citing their charity, saintliness, and dedication. But the older love still pulled strongly. "Am trying to find a way to get back to New Mexico," he wrote the Dawsons. "I feel tops, only I can't walk."[4]

Al Braun's greatest fear was of idleness—'the workshop of the devil'—and he would not become mentally or physically lazy. He was still in this world, he would keep busy, and he would enjoy it. "To make sure of an old time Franciscan celebration," he reported to Jeanne (now living in Tucson), he had reminded Blaise that "Oct. 4th is the Feast of St. Francis. Father Sebastion picked me up. . . . We had a good noon day lunch, at 2 p.m. there was a Mexican wedding in church, at 3 p.m. a reception and dance in the basement. I made my way to the basement and had a grand time with Mexican friends from south Phoenix. Came back to the recreation room at 5 p.m. We had a good *haustus*—two highballs, then a steak dinner cooked by Father Juan. At 10 p.m. I returned to the Little Sisters.

"People ask me, how do you manage to keep looking so well at your age—80. I tell them, 'By raising a little hell now and then.'"[5]

Friends visited constantly. Father Blaise was his closest companion, looking in almost daily, bringing him to Saint Mary's on Mondays, often taking him to football games, where people flocked around him. The Mackeys came often, and the Mahoneys, and both couples always brought a libation. "The Sisters didn't much like him to have it," Alice Mahoney remembered, "so Father would tell Bill, 'Put it in my underwear drawer—they won't look there.'"[6]

On a more solemn side, he still worried about the future of Church and country, about which he carried a lively correspondence with the Dawsons, who shared his views. These were the Vietnam years, times of upheaval throughout America, fracturing the country and invading the church as well, which "all over the world is going through a crisis."[7]

Ray agreed, but believed the Church "will endure the present assault from within and without. . . . What we need in the ways of Bishops is tough Army Officer types. . . . [W]e have a doosey over here, . . . parading with the so-called poor marchers one day and swinging golf clubs at the country club the next, and all the time tapping the poor parishes for 7½% of their gross take. He backs the asinine left wing causes and can't be located when he is needed to help. . . . I hope the Bishops meeting in Rome give a vote of confidence to Pope Paul, and I hope he puts the damned dissidents in their proper place. I saw old Shannon making a moratorium speech for peace, and of all places—the [Catholic] College of Santa Fe on TV. I'd have run his butt off the premises."[8]

Invigorated by the spirited response, the crusty old friar replied in quick agreement. Moreover, he added, "I don't see how our Government can last another ten years. . . . What is in store for us only God knows."[9]

But despite the laxness of many churchmen, he noted the countless dedicated friars still tending their flocks. Three such visited him from the Navajo reservation, "a great bunch of Cincinnati Franciscans. . . . You won't find any of the 'New-Breed' priests in that crowd."[10] Recent talk of ordaining women outraged him. "The day they have women hearing confessions," he snorted, "is the day I'll come in with some of the dirtiest stories I can think of. That ought to chase them off."[11]

Father Al quickly found the home too confining: there was work to be done in the surrounding area. Soon the people in south Phoenix grew accustomed to the feisty old padre, occasionally with a cane, more often in his wheelchair, taking a census, gathering the young (or anyone else he could persuade) for catechism classes, urging the youths to join the army ("It'll make a man of you"), and in election years canvassing the area to get out the vote. He soon knew which unions lacked the blessing of marriage, whose babies had not been baptized, whose children not confirmed, and was busy arranging these rites. He started saying a Sunday mass at Saint Francis, a small Jesuit church within Saint Mary's parish, whose young members soon learned that Father Al distributed candy for all who attended. Children began flocking to mass.

His infirmities—and Blaise's orders—increasingly restricted him to the immediate area, however. He regretted being unable to attend the funeral of a friend at Topowah in January 1970, he wrote Jeanne, despite "several invitations. . . . Brother and I were close friends. The day before Brother Robert dropped dead in the kitchen at St. John['s] he came to . . . visit me. Brother Robert was a great Franciscan. . . .

"For the past month I have been sick, at times so sick I could not eat. If my condition does not improve soon I will turn in at the Veterans' Hospital. . . . I have a class in church history tomorrow. I can't turn it down no matter how I feel, but I can make it short."[12]

He was "too impatient to be a good patient," he wrote Dan Bumgarner from the hospital a few days later. "They took 15 Xrays, looking for a tumor on the brain." But, he told the doctor, "'I don't have a brain'. . . . When I get out . . . I hope they let me go back to work."[13]

Always ready to counsel the younger generation, he advised Dan (then studying at the seminary) to "take Spanish on the side, and use every opportunity to speak the language. If you . . . are ordained I hope they will send you among the poor Mexicans of South Phoenix. . . ."[14] And he continued to warn Ray Brown "to be careful of those Mormons" in Utah.[15]

His correspondence, always important to him, grew especially so during these years of his increasingly frequent illnesses. A new friend came into his life in March via the mail, one who became very dear to him. "My dear Mrs. Boyd," he answered posthaste. "It gave me a thrill to get a letter from the grand-daughter of that great Antonio Maria Leyva. He was my dearest and most devoted friend." Five pages followed, describing his life with 'Old Tony.'[16] The correspondence that followed between Barbara Boyd and the padre enriched the lives of both. (In one letter she, married and a mother, aspired to emulate Saint Barbara. He answered wryly that "to imitate your saint would be very difficult. She was not only a virgin but a martyr as well.")[17]

He never forgot a friend or abandoned one with whom he had

disagreed. He continued to write Father Reynold. "Preaching to a confrere does no good," he wrote his provincial. "Just a friendly letter does much good. . . ." And though his old friend had left the priesthood after his breakdown at Corazon, "Reynold will always be my confrere."[18]

When forced to slow his pace, he sat outside for an hour or so in the afternoons ("better than a bottle of pills")[19] or visited with friends. The friars from Saint Mary's—especially Father Blaise—came often. When a problem arose or a decision hung in the balance, the fraters came to consult the elder statesman, to "see what Al thinks."

His hearing was beginning to dull but his wit stayed sharp. "The reason so many people come to me for confession," he often told Blaise, "is they know I can't hear well."[20] His eyes too were weakening, though he still read as widely as his sight permitted, and commented freely. Geronimo, he opined regarding a book Jeanne had sent him, "was a good man," though the padre did not know the son to whom the book referred. "Those Apaches had so many children scattered around the country I couldn't know them all," and Robert, whom he did know, "seldom spoke of his 'Geronimo' relatives."[21] On reading Shirer's *Rise and Fall of the Third Reich*, he confessed to the Dawsons that "I almost changed my name from Braun to Brown so that nobody would know I am a German."[22]

Late in April he rode with some fellow friars "to San Carlos Indian Agency . . . to celebrate the Golden Jubilee of Brother José as a Franciscan. There were," he reported to Jeanne, "25 visiting Franciscans and 7 diocesan priests there. . . . We had a concelebration mass—9 priests—a few drinks . . . , then an excellent dinner. . . . I met some Apaches I had not seen since 1921."

The next day he learned that his sister Mary "had a serious heart attack. My sister is 83. I may have to go to Ojai. . . ."[23] But Blaise and Doctor Huger ruled against the trip, for Mary's illness or for her funeral. Nor, on learning four months later of Augustine's death, could he attend that of his friend of half a century. But, he wrote his provincial, "I know Gus will be waiting for me to join him; we were close friends over a long lifetime. . . ."[24]

But when he learned in November that the province was thinking of giving up the Mescalero mission, he leaped outraged into the fray despite his infirmities. "If you are short of priests," he begged Father Provincial Alan McCoy, "send me to Mescalero. In spite of my age, 81, I am in perfect health, except for arthritis. . . . It would add years to my life. What a spiritual tragedy that would be, if the Catholic Apaches . . . did not have a priest. If the mission were abandoned I would take a leave of absence to take care of those Indians. . . . and may the Blessed Mother Mary guide your thinking. . . ."[25] To what extent this startling letter may have influenced his superiors one can only guess; but, though Father Al was not given the assignment, the province kept Mescalero.

Still fuming, he wrote the Boyds that "Dr. Huger told me I would live to be 100. I still have 19 to go,"[26] and soon after opined that he was "too mean to die."[27]

He prognosticated too soon. "I enjoyed Christmas," he wrote Ray and Elisa early in January 1971, "even though I was in bad physical condition—bleeding from the bowels. I have had that ailment off and on since a prisoner of the Japanese. A few days after Xmas I turned in at St. Joseph's Hospital. A few days ago I returned. . . . Am now back to normal." He planned almost immediately to start his annual census, which "will keep me very busy and will make me very happy."[28]

He continued to teach catechism to the youth in the area and to say mass at Saint Francis, often from his wheelchair. He still led the rosary daily at the Little Sisters and taught classes there, often with self-deprecating honesty. Teaching a series on the Ten Commandments he got as far as "Thou shalt not steal," one friend remembered. Here he stopped. "I can't preach that," he said, and alluded to his 'Al Capone' days while a Japanese prisoner. "I'm the biggest crook there is!"[29]

He soon found himself back in the hospital for an undetermined period—six days according to one letter, three weeks in another—for an equally hazy reason. "Just got out of the hospital," he wrote the Boyds in late January. "Too weak to write."[30] By mid-February he had bounced back to wonder, "What did St. Valentine do to make all the women love him?"[31]

By spring he was able to travel to Santa Barbara, where "Franciscans 70 and older have been called . . . to decide what to do with the old Friars. . . ."[32] His only suggestion, he wrote Virginia Klinekole, was "to give the old men plenty to do. . . . Idleness is hard on old age."[33]

These alternating periods of distress and energy became a pattern for the rest of his life. "I planned to go to California for 2 weeks," he wrote in August, "but the dr. upset my plans. At times my leg bone comes out of the socket and then I fall to the ground." It did not, however, stop him from teaching his classes. "It is hard to be idle."[34]

The padre continued to lobby for a job. "Often I have asked the

Provincial [Father Alan McCoy] to let me work in a parish," he fumed. "I always receive the same answer: 'You have done more than your share of the work, take it easy.' That certainly is not the answer I want."[35]

The sisters, however they tried, could not keep him quietly in the home. There was work to be done, he snapped, with people "as neglected as those were down at Sacred Heart parish," and he argued for a chapel to be built in an outlying section of the parish. "These families are poor. They have one car, the old man works 7 days a week. The mother with many children cannot walk to St. Mary's."[36] He continued to importune Father Blaise: if they didn't give him something to do, he warned, he was going to raise a lot of hell.[37] He probably did.

The padre always began addressing his reams of Christmas greetings in the fall—five to six hundred, he once estimated. "It keeps me broke buying stamps."[38] But, refusing to send a card without a religious theme, he found those Blaise brought him unacceptable. "There are four boxes of Christmas cards," he grumbled to the Boyds. "Not one has any mention of Christ. . . . Am using this letter paper instead. . . ."[39]

Christmas as always brought nostalgia. A greeting for Ray and Elisa (written on the same plain paper, and probably written that same Christmas) cries out in homesick longing. "My God, how I wish I could spend this Christmas at Mescalero, New Mexico with the people I dearly love!"[40]

✝✝✝

In the spring of 1972 Father Albert wrote two letters to the Mother Superior. It was for him a year of decision.

The first addressed his realization that he was drinking too much. He had always enjoyed a convivial quaff with a frater, a friend, or a fellow soldier. But the nursing home held potential danger where enforced idleness and nearly constant pain beset him, while generous friends kept him supplied with the means for relief. Al Braun had never taken the easy way; and, alarmed at what he perceived as a growing dependence, he confronted his dragon face on. "My dear Mother Anthony," he wrote in March:

> After serious reflection, I realize I must take a definite stand on my problem of excessive drinking. I came to this conclusion:

1. Never take a drink when alone.
2. Never take more than one drink when in the company of friends.
3. If I fail to keep these two resolutions, I will report the failure to you. I want you to expel me from this home.

Pray for me! God bless you, my mother.[41]

Realistically he did not target total abstention; there was no need. The padre was no alcoholic and would not become one. He continued to enjoy his 'Irish holy water,' in company and in moderation. It was, he averred, a gift of God. "Look what our dear Lord did at the marriage feast at Cana," he wrote Ray and Elisa. The letter is vintage Braun:

> When the parents of the bride noticed that they were out of wine, she told the servants to fill a big barrel with water. Then she told Mary, the Blessed Mother of Jesus, 'We are out of wine.' Mary called her son Jesus over and had him bless the barrel of water. Then the bride's father came over and tasted the Irish holy water and he exclaimed, 'Where did they get that wonderful wine?' So you see, Mary and her son Jesus were not Prohibitionists. Of course, they and their many friends never drank too much.[42]

Nor, from that time did the padre, who reserved his libations for good times and good friends.

Mother Mary Anthony, however, seems to have believed in the curative powers of a glass of wine for certain afflictions, among them arrhythmia, and saw that her patients so plagued received the needed potion. "I have a glass of burgundy . . . on my desk," the padre wrote the Dawsons after a day in which his heart had pounded ceaselessly. "A glass or two makes the drinker very normal. How I wish I had Ray and Elisa in my room to enjoy being normal with me."[43]

"This home is flooded with many pamphlets on 'Alcoholism,'" he once apprised them. "Every time someone places one of these pamphlets on my desk, I take a 'snort' before reading it. Normal, sound judgment is a valuable possession."[44]

His second letter to the Mother Superior addressed provisions for his burial. That his heart was in Mescalero everyone knew; evidently he had long been weighing his wishes against his conscience. By April he had made his decision.

"For some time," he wrote Mother Mary Anthony,

> I have been thinking of a request I made, namely, 'when I die, I want to be buried at Mescalero, in the Apache cemetery.' That is an unfair and unwise request. Among the friars of Santa Barbara Province it is customary to bury a friar in the cemetery of that place where he dies. What right do I have to make my burial an exception? Then too, consider the difficulties with making the arrangements. This is now my wish, to be buried like any other friar who dies in Phoenix, . . . in the Franciscan plot at the Catholic cemetery of Phoenix, Arizona.[45]

A few days later he mailed a like request to his provincial.[46] He had settled the matter for good, in writing, as his conscience dictated. But a wrenching sentence written not long thereafter shows where his heart still lay. He had never ceased wishing, he admitted to Old Tony's granddaughter, "to be buried at Mescalero with my Apache Indians."[47]

✞✞✞

While the padre was wrestling with important decisions, an exciting project was brewing: Father Albert was to be the subject of a movie. The president of Kachina Productions had come to the home to talk to the padre, and the news had spread to cause quite a stir among the padre's friends. The padre, though appreciative of the honor, was less enthusiastic. He had lived too long and seen too much of real significance—bloody revolution, war, the upheaval of nations, the hungry eyes of forgotten people, the heroism of man—to be overly impressed by a movie; but he would cooperate.

Kachina Productions, based in Tempe, had been founded in November 1971 to film documentaries in and about Arizona and the men who made its history. Father Al's name headed the list. Company president Larry Merchant quickly made friends with the padre, who in turn provided him and his writers with facts, anecdotes, comments, and doubtless a few *copitas* of 'Irish holy water.'

He duly signed a contract—Bill Mahoney drew it up—though he balked at Merchant's suggestion that he appear in the film. He continued to resist until, tired of being importuned, he wrote his provincial in April. "The Kachina people," he reported, "want me to take part in the movie. . . . Till now I said '*no*.' These people keep on insisting. . . . Today I told them I would have to get the permission of my Provincial. Deny or give permission; it is all the same to me. Considering my physical condition, I don't see how I can take much of a part. . . ." He enclosed a copy of the contract, which, among other provisions, stipulated he was to receive a fifty percent royalty. Should this materialize, he wished it used in part "to send poor but talented Mexicans to St. Mary's Hi-School."[48]

If Al Braun thought his disinterested attitude would elicit a negative response from Father Alan McCoy, he was mistaken. The provincial was pleased "that the Kachina people are going ahead with the movie; you surely have a lot to tell. . . . As for you actually taking part in the movie, I give permission provided the doctor thinks it will not be too taxing for you. . . ."[49]

Meanwhile Merchant was gathering data and anecdotes from Father Al's widespread friends. The Dawsons not only shared their memories, but drove to Phoenix to help Father Al compile and organize his input. In Mescalero Virginia Klinekole was collecting material.

Trying to raise funds was the biggest hurdle, Merchant wrote Virginia in October. "With the help of Bill Mahoney . . . we drew up pre-investment agreements for Phoenix people who had indicated their willingness to finance the development phase. . . . Unfortunately, we were unable to raise all the needed funds there. We are short about $4000.00 and I decided to come to California to attempt to raise it. I am now working with the Franciscan Communications Center. . . . We simply must get this project done. . . ."[50]

Still it moved slowly, he wrote a month later. "I've had good meetings with Fr. Emery and Fr. McCoy, who have given me leads for story material but not much in the way of money. . . ." Father Al, he added, requested that his royalties "go to the parish at Mescalero and to the one in South Phoenix. He felt that it was one more thing, perhaps the last, that he could offer in the way of material help to those whom he loved so much."[51]

In California Barbara Boyd was doing her part. "In your city," she wrote Bishop McCarthy of the National Committee on Human Development in Phoenix, "there lives a very great man whose life is slowly ebbing. . . . Surely you know this man, Father Albert Braun, OFM." After describing

Merchant's financial needs, she made her appeal. "Most Rev. McCarthy, . . . this film has to be made. . . . [W]e who know him must share this life with people who do not know him." She hoped the good bishop's agency could contribute.[52]

The agency was "well informed" of the project, "well acquainted with Larry Merchant," and wished him well, she was assured, "but the Diocese of Phoenix does not have funds . . . for the production of motion pictures. . . ."[53]

Merchant was never able to raise the remaining funds; the film that 'had to be made' never materialized; and Father Al's movie career fell by the wayside. It is safe to say the padre was not overly concerned. Except for the money he had hoped to send those he loved—funds he had always considered problematical at best—he seems to have taken small notice. Movies were, after all, *Insignificant!*

While Larry Merchant was negotiating finances Father Albert continued making his rounds. He seems also to have added another class for his residents, this one in religions of the world. "I enjoy preparing for these classes," he wrote, because it entailed "much interesting reading."[54] Taking his census was becoming more difficult. "My legs refused to carry me around," he wrote in July 1972,[55] whereupon he continued in the wheelchair.

But time and toil were exacting their dues. The friars at Saint Mary's hosted a party on 5 September to celebrate his eighty-fourth birthday. "Can't go," he wrote the Dawsons that day. "I am too sick, caused by cancer. I know it won't be many years till we meet in the happy Hunting Ground."[56]

Father Albert was ready to die. "But Heaven doesn't want me and I don't want to go to hell, so I'll stick around awhile longer." And, he might have added, stay happy and keep busy. South Phoenix had not seen the last of the old Franciscan in the wheelchair.

"I can no longer walk," he wrote in September 1973, but with his usual twist of humor said he would love to visit the Henrions, but a visit to Iowa "would be like a trip around the world" in a wheelchair. "Just think of all the traffic tickets I would get!"[57]

A month later, on publication of a biographical sketch of the padre, he was honored along with the author at a book signing at Casa de Paz y Bien. Although confined to his wheelchair, he could still enliven the affair with his typically wry humor, some of which the loyal Jeanne Marsteller, who had driven up from Tucson, caught on tape:

"This must be a very happy day for you," someone says. "Every day's a happy day," he replies chuckling. "I get a little rich wine at mass every morning!"

"God is good to us," he tells another, whose name he has forgotten. "When we get old He destroys our memory so we don't worry about the sins of our youth."

"The young priests today," one complains, "are too lazy to do what you did." He disagrees. "They're not too lazy. I was full of the devil—I had to work hard to keep him out."

Another asks what OFM stands for. Although it had been erroneously labeled in the book being signed, the padre is too polite to correct it: it stands for "Order of Fat Men," he quips, or "Out for Money."[58] And speaking of money, he remarks, "God is good. He knew I couldn't handle money, so He never gave me any."

Would he write something in his Bible? a gentleman asks. Of course: "I'll write 'Read this once in awhile.'"

And to Marshall Townsend, editor of the University of Arizona Press, which had published the book, the irrepressible Al Braun complains, "You left out the best part—all of my love affairs!" To which Townsend, as quick with riposte as the padre, shoots back, "Well, you know, we looked at this and we thought, 'What would we do with another thousand pages!'"[59]

"We lost our dear Mother Mary Anthony," the padre had written in August. "She is now Superior at the old folks' home in Oakland. Our new Superior . . . came to us from Mobile, Alabama. She will soon find out," he commented, "that white old folks are no better than black old folks."[60]

The new superior was less congenial than Mary Anthony—"a real business-like gal," Blaise found her, who "would not smile at you"[61]—though Father Al, with his usual charm, seemed to get along with her, and doubtless coaxed an occasional smile.

"Usually on Saturdays," he reported to his provincial, "we have what is known as 'Happy Hour.' Mother . . . gives us all a little drink of wine. That is the only time some of these little old ladies smile."[62] After a Valentine party he wrote Ruth Jette that she "would be surprised how full of fun some of these old folks are, especially if they get a drink of Irish holy water."[63]

That was not, however, the usual refreshment, he wrote Ray and Elisa. "The Sisters provide music," after which "we are served a soft drink, cookies, and candy. . . . I tell the sister, 'this is Happy Hour, a soft drink does not make anyone happy,' so she gets me a glass of wine. I thank her and say, 'In half an hour I will begin to be happy.'" Levity aside, however, "our food is good and we are provided music and an opportunity to associate with one another. . . . I can't imagine a better place in which to spend the last years of our old age."[64]

"The good Sisters do their best to make life enjoyable for us old folks," he wrote the Dawsons. Still—"In spite of that. . . . I wish I could spend my last years in New Mexico."[65] Later and more specifically, he stipulated "in Mescalero and Tularosa."[66]

His room was large, airy, and filled with pictures of friends; his military decorations and honorary citations were hung as always above eye level. Here too, he wrote Old Tony's granddaughter, "there is a picture of the church on which we worked together so many years."[67] Over that picture was an American flag, small in size, enormous in significance.

Here he entertained his friends who helped fill the times of enforced idleness—the Mackeys, the Mahoneys, and countless more from throughout Phoenix and the countryside. Felipe Baldonado—Father Phil—while chaplain at Saint Joseph's hospital, came often, and after being transferred to California continued to come when he could. Father Kieran McCarty visited from the coast, found the padre still "very active in the apostate," and was impressed by how he "knew all the little children, and got them together for catechism."[68] And from as far as Boston came his old friend Father Sixtus Brambilla.

Father Al always looked forward to visits from Jeanne, who, when he was able, drove him to visit old friends, or took him on the picnics he loved in South Mountain Park.

Ruth and Vi Jette came often; Ray and Elisa drove frequently from Albuquerque to see him; the Bumgarners came from California; and Eugene Henrion journeyed from Iowa on at least one occasion, after which the padre "stayed awake a long time recalling those happy days I spent with the Henrions in Diekirk, Luxembourg."[69]

He was always delighted to see his old army comrades, especially those combat veterans with whom he could relive old memories. They nearly always brought him a fifth of Scotch or good red wine. When Pepe Baldonado visited on one occasion, however, the padre had no 'Irish holy water' on hand. "When I have a supply it never lasts long. Too many friends visit me." Nonetheless, "we had a grand time talking about the good times we had when prisoners of the Japs. We reminded each other that the pessimists all died. That was a great lesson to learn."[70]

Father Al always enjoyed his occasional picnics with Jeanne Marsteller when she was in town. Courtesy of Jeanne de Lue Marsteller.

From time to time Apaches came from Mescalero, Virginia and Bruce Klinekole chief among them. And "what a surprise," he wrote the Dawsons, when Wendell Chino, long-time tribal leader, paid him a visit.[71] He described another visit from two tribal members with whom he "spent an enjoyable afternoon talking about my dear Mescalero Apaches. I told those two Apaches to stay with me a few days. They said 'we don't have the time, because we have to walk back to Mescalero'. . . . I gave them fifty dollars so they could ride the bus. . . . I will bet," he added, "they spent some of that money to buy Apache holy water."[72]

He still dreamed of visiting the Dawsons, advising them to "put in a good supply of frijoles, chile, garlic and . . . many tortillas. . . . When I die,

I am sure some of my darlings from New Mexico will be at the door with a big plate of frijoles, singing those Mexican songs. . . . I don't know why I am not permitted to die," he added. "I do want to . . . again be 'con mis amigos de Nuevo Mexico.'"[73]

He received a letter "from one of the Boston Girls," he wrote Jeanne, "inviting me . . . to a reunion. . . . How I would love to be at that gathering of all those wonderful girls."[74]

Even as he neared his eighty-sixth birthday he was still agitating for work. Though the province had kept the Mescalero mission, it had dropped the church at Tularosa, over Father Al's vociferous disapproval. In 1975 he saw his chance. "I am very, very happy," he wrote his provincial, "that Bishop Metzger of El Paso Diocese has requested that the Franciscans of the Santa Barbara Province take back St. Francis. . . ." What part Father Albert may have played in instigating the bishop's appeal is conjectural; relevant letters are missing, but it is easy to suspect he had added his opinion to the mix. "Am begging all my favorite saints, especially Saint Francis, to move Father Provincial and his Definitorium to comply with Bishop Metzger's request. Then too"—and here he fired his broadside—"I beg you to assign me as an assistant to the pastor of St. Francis Church in Tularosa. The U.S. Army has me classified as totally disabled. . . . To move around, I depend on a wheelchair. However, I offer mass every day sitting in my wheelchair, I hear confessions, and each week I have four classes. It would drive me crazy to be idle."[75] The province did take back Saint Francis; but his superiors did not share the padre's enthusiasm for assigning him there.

July of 1975 marked the padre's Diamond Jubilee—sixty years as a priest—and he was determined to celebrate it in California. He had been planning the trip for over a year. "By that time I will be 85," he had written Eugene Henrion. "People usually speak of 'Sad Old Age.' I must still be young, because I am never sad, just full of mischief, and in a big crowd can always have a great time. Maybe that is the Apache in me."[76]

"My relatives insist that I come to Los Angeles for the event," he wrote the Dawsons. "July 3rd, in spite of my physical condition, I will take the bus to Los Angeles; will take my wheelchair. . . . I will . . . concelebrate the mass with Father Phil. I plan to spend one month with my 89 relatives. What a grand time we will have!"[77]

But Blaise was having none of Father Al's riding any bus. "July 2nd," the padre amended in May, "I will offer mass in this home; I owe that to these good sisters. July 3rd at St. Mary's . . . , July 4th at Sacred Heart Church among my very dear Mexican people. . . . July 5th my boss, Father Blaise, will take me to Los Angeles. . . ."[78]

The trip went as planned. "Many thanks," he wrote his provincial, "to you, Father Marcian, and the other confreres who were at my Diamond Jubilee Mass. . . . I want to compliment Father Luis Baldonado [a younger member of the extended Tularosa clan] for the great work he is doing to keep the faith among the Mexican people. The church was packed . . . at the 10 o'clock mass. . . . The basement was also packed. . . ."[79]

Among those present was his ill, aging, and now-widowered brother Ray, to whom he later wrote how happy he was "that you were allowed" to come. "It was a wonderful sight to see all the children, the in-laws and out-laws of Ray and Clara. . . ."[80]

Apparently the trip was not as enervating as some had feared it would be, for he reported he was "back to normal, working hard so as not to be idle. I am afraid of idleness; that is the reason for so many crooks in our country. . . ."[81]

He had envisioned a stopover in Mescalero on his return trip; whether he made it is conjectural, though Mary Dorame Gomez remembered his coming at some time during his later years "to visit a last time. . . . Here he came to our parish, to our front door, in his wheelchair, and he wasn't helpless."[82]

Father Albert was delighted (presumably along with the other residents) when the beloved Mother Mary Anthony returned in the summer of 1977 to again take charge of the home. Life then resumed its pleasant rhythm and the more relaxed atmosphere they had all enjoyed before. Only one matter still plagued him: despite his earlier selfless decision, he had never completely given up his lingering wish to be buried at Mescalero.

Nor had the tribe who loved him. The council had some years earlier voted that he be buried in the sacred tribal grounds—a signal honor for a white man. "My Apache friends write me," he confided to Ray and Elisa Dawson five years after his renunciatory letter to his provincial, "that I should return to Mescalero and die there so that they can bury me in the Apache cemetery in Mescalero. That is what I would like to do but I have nothing to say about it."[83]

He broached the subject again to Father Blaise as they sat talking one day on the grounds of the home. "Al asked me, 'where shall I be buried? My family is [buried] in L[os] A[ngeles], my Franciscan friends at Santa Barbara, and the Indians want me buried in Mescalero.' I said, 'Al, I can't say where you should be buried. . . .'"[84] But Blaise knew where Al Braun's heart still lay. He did not forget the conversation.

Father Al's condition continued to worsen. By January 1977 the pain in his legs had so intensified, he wrote the Dawsons, that he could no longer dismiss it as "only arthritis" caused from "sleeping all night in the mud as a prisoner of the Jap army."[85] By summer he admitted something must be done. Eight years had passed since the cancerous growth had been removed from his intestine. He had paid little attention to it at the time. Now he suspected the cancer had returned.

"Next Tuesday, August 22nd, I am going to the Veterans' Hospital here in Phoenix for a physical examination," he wrote his provincial. "Cancer is a lifetime ailment. At present it has been very active and painful. Often because of the pain I can sleep only two or three hours during the night. I will not be able to celebrate mass except on Sundays. A friend will take me to St. Francis Church. . . ."[86]

The doctors confirmed what he suspected. The cancer was in the bones of both legs.

"Into the life of each human being . . . an exceptional person is likely to appear. . . . Such . . . in our lifetime has been Father Albert Braun. . . ." It was May 1979, and the Arizona chapter of the Disabled Veterans of America was about to present Father Albert with its Hall of Fame Award.

The old padre heard his life unfold—his labors among the Apaches in Mescalero and the migrant workers of south Phoenix; his valorous combat service in both World Wars, and in the Army Reserve between them; his stubborn determination to build his 'Apache cathedral' as a monument to his fellow soldiers in those wars. ". . . a true friend to many, an inspiration to all, a warrior and a hunter, an apostle and a soldier. . . ."[87]

He seemed a little embarrassed at such passages, a little nostalgic at some; but at hearing himself called "the biggest thief in [prison] camp," he was openly amused. "There were stiff penalties for stealing food," the erstwhile 'Al Capone' acknowledged on accepting the award. "But I've lived with Apaches. I know how to steal and not get caught."[88]

Father Al's eyes could still glint with mischief, but they were focusing poorly and, among other inconveniences, hindering his usually prodigious correspondence, including his Christmas greetings for 1979. For this reason "he is hesitant to write now," Blaise explained after the holiday, but at the padre's request wished "to thank all of you who . . . expressed the beauty and wonder of the Christmas season by your own thoughtfulness and generosity. . . ." The doctor believed it only an allergy, and Blaise felt sure "he will get around to writing again.

"Otherwise," Blaise continued, "he is amazingly well. . . . The twinkle in his eye and his spontaneous laughter are still there. The delight in God's creation is still as always a deep part of him—he loves feeding the birds and typically even wants to pay the nuns for the bread he uses. His mind is clear and memory very good concerning the past. As all of you know he is an amazing person in practically every aspect of human goodness and strength. . . ."[89]

In June 1980 the Little Sisters were forced to raise their rates, and so notified the residents. Father Al believed it should not apply to him because of the many services he performed for the sisters. Talking to him did no good. In the face of his obstinacy Mary Anthony wrote in frustration to Father Provincial Louis Vitale.

"Father, you are probably aware that Fr. Albert's [monthly] pension amounted to $811.49 last year and since then all Veterans have received a substantial increase. We do not know the amount he now receives. From this he gives $50.00 to some man to feed the poor; pays $75.00 a month tuition for two neighborhood children to attend St. Mary's High School; gives a large sum to St. Vincent de Paul Society; . . . other amounts are allocated for other purposes. He gives us $225.00 and some of the small stipends he receives for baptisms and marriages, etc. He does not wish to make any change."[90]

His pension was considerably larger than Mother Mary Anthony knew. Father Blaise, who cashed Father Al's checks for him, recalled that it was "better than eleven hundred dollars" per month. He disposed of the money as the padre directed. A great deal went to Sacred Heart parish, and he doled out smaller amounts according to the padre's whims. ("I need five dollars . . . *in paper money*," one urgently underlined note reads, "so that I can mail each five to a different friend. . . .")[91]

"But he was sharp enough to know that if someone came in who should not get any money," Blaise affirmed, "he'd tell me, 'well, she's going to show up tomorrow—you take the money and don't let me have any of it. . . . Those gals come in here always asking for money.'"[92]

"All of us know," Mother Superior wrote, "what a saintly and unselfish man Fr. Albert is. There is no question of his hoarding any funds at any time. I doubt whether he ever has a penny by the tenth of the month."[93] Blaise could have confirmed that.

By return mail the father provincial was "sorry that Father Albert has not been more attentive" to the matter, believed "that Father feels he is helping there and that makes up the difference," assured her the province would "be responsible for Father's bill beyond what he pays personally," and promised to write the padre.[94]

Mother Mary Anthony thanked the provincial for his help, but believed that "even your suggestions will not make him change. . . . It might be wise," she continued, "to tell you how Father 'helps out.' He says Mass in the sacristy each morning which is fine and he will often accommodate the hour to our needs. . . . However Father performs weddings and baptisms for almost anyone who present themselves. They are mostly Mexican friends of his friends. . . . [H]e will marry anyone who comes along and it is very dubious and most improbable that they have complied with Diocesan and maybe even civil regulations. The Bishop knows about this but feels it would be impossible to stop it while Fr. Albert lives. Father thinks he is doing the people and the Church a great service."[95]

Father Louis had written as promised to Father Al. "There's a bill and [it] must be paid. . . . We [the Province] will have to pay them the difference. . . . Perhaps you are able to give them more from your pension check. . . ."[96]

He seems to have hit a nerve. "Please help me, so that I don't violate my vow of poverty," the padre wrote the Mother Superior ingenuously. "I have too much on hand. I know you can make good use of these few pennies. . . . God asked me to help you. . . ."[97]

His body might weaken, but the old stubbornness surged as strongly as ever, and he refused to concede that he owed what he considered an arbitrary levy. Instead, with courtesy, grace, and doubtless a saintly smile, he presented Mother Mary Anthony with $140.00—but not as a debt. It was a gift.

Father Al's intellect remained as sharp as his stubbornness, though he grew absentminded at times. Once he summoned Blaise: the padre wished to make his confession. Blaise went to hear it as requested. After ordering the younger priest from one side to another and back again, to "get on my good ear," the old friar suddenly looked puzzled. "Why did I call you over here?"

"You said you wanted to make your confession."

Al thought for a minute. Then, "Well, kneel down and go ahead."

"So," Blaise recalled laughing, "I ended up confessing to Al."[98]

As his pain intensified Sister Michael came to his room each evening bearing her rosary and a two-ounce shot of his favorite Scotch whiskey—the first to intone prayers with him, the second to help him sleep. ("Which came first?" Blaise asked once. "The rosary, of course," snapped the padre.)[99]

On 31 August 1980, six days shy of his ninety-first birthday, Father Albert's left leg was amputated just above the knee. "There was," Blaise wrote the padre's close friends, "a very fast decision on the part of the doctor Saturday evening August 30th. . . ." Knowing the padre would never consent, the physician conferred with Blaise, who as guardian must authorize the surgery. All involved—doctors and friars—agreed it must be done.

". . . Tough as you know Father Albert to be, he went through the operation successfully . . . , even better than can be expected for one his age. . . . He should be returning to the Little Sisters of the Poor the week of September 14th. . . ."[100]

The "cancer was moving up the left leg," the padre wrote Father David Temple a year later, and conceded the surgery had saved his life.[101] That, however, was considerably after the fact. At the time he was furious.

The friars had known he would be and were terrified to tell him following the surgery. They even, one confided to Dick Mackey, considered blaming the decision on the provincial, who at his distance would not have to face an irate Father Al.[102] It was, predictably, Blaise who broke the news, and when asked who had given permission, looked his old confrere in the eye.

"I did, Al." That, Blaise said later, was one of the hardest things he had ever had to do.[103]

On 5 September, his ninety-first birthday, as the padre lay recuperating, he was handed a letter from the Most Reverend James S. Rauch, Bishop of Phoenix. Addressing him as "a scholar, pastor, friend of the poor and the oppressed, American patriot, citizen of Mexico, missionary to Apaches," the bishop continued,

> You have experienced enough adventure to fill the lives of several extraordinary men.
> Bound to a wheelchair in recent years . . . , your vivaciousness belied the term 'handicapped person.'
> A phrase too easily ascribed to some, most appropriately belongs to you: you are a living legend. . . .

With the letter was the highly prized and rarely given Bishop's Medal.

The leg seems to have healed well; but by November the doctor became "quite worried about the condition of the other foot," Blaise wrote the padre's friends. "Circulation there was very poor and there was fear he might have to lose the other leg. . . ." The following week "they ran a chemical through the leg and cleaned out the blood. . . . It really did the trick. . . . The doctor said the leg should last as long as Father Al lasts. . . ." He was doing well, "enjoys being outside in his wheel chair, has taken to feeding the birds, but still does not feel up to writing letters. . . ."[104]

Father Al with Father Sixtus Brambilla, OFM, visiting from Boston, 12 November 1982. Source unknown.

Still unable to write as Christmas approached, the padre dictated his message for the sisters to type and mail. "I feel the deep significance of Christmas, as always, at this time of year," the greeting read:

> The event of Christmas has always been to me the happiest and most world shaking event . . . in man's history. God loved us to the extent of being born into our human family and becoming one of us. In the remarkable statement of Saint Paul, God did not cling to His divinity but emptied himself and became one of us. Christmas opened heaven to us once again and we will never feel perfectly at home till we get there. . . ."[105]

Al Braun had indeed, as the bishop attested, become a living legend; in his fading years the honors he had never sought continued to accrue. In March 1981 he was the guest of honor for the twenty-fifth anniversary of Sacred Heart Church, for which he had been the prime mover. Bishop Rauch officiated the high mass; the church and reception hall overflowed with parishioners celebrating with their beloved Padre Alberto.

On his birthday the padre received a memorable greeting, hoping "your special day is filled with warmth and celebration and that you may enjoy much happiness in the year to come." It was signed "Ronald Reagan."[106]

On 10 February 1982 Father Albert wrote a letter to Blaise. Though they visited every day or so, certain matters were of necessity best committed to writing. With his days growing fewer, the padre was putting his house in order. On 5 September, he reminded Blaise, he would be ninety-three years old:

> . . . I know I cannot live much long[er]. Here is what I want you to know:
> When I die I want to be clothed in the Franciscan habit in the coffin.
> I want to be buried in a Catholic cemetery where Franciscans of the Santa Barbara Province are buried.
> The U.S. veterans will want me clothed in my U.S. uniform.
> . . . You can place my military cap on my coffin and

also the chaplain's insignia and my military rank—Lt. Colonel. . . .

When I die you take care of all this. Many thanks.[107]

Nor could he forget Blaise on a special 27 March: "Happy Birthday! One can notice that you are an Irishman, you were born only ten days after the Feast of St. Patrick. . . ."[108]

Despite the mandate that he remain on the Little Sisters' premises, the eternal mischief in him resurged sometimes on his good days, and he took off on his own, determined to continue making his rounds. "He'd get unhappy, want to go out and see the world," niece Dorothy recalled. "He always wanted to go some place. He'd go out, get to a curb, and just go ahead and go off—and fall over. He'd lie there until somebody would come along and pick him up. Then he'd do the same thing again in a few days. Of course everybody knew him. They'd wheel him back—he didn't want to go, but most of them had instructions: they were to ignore his protests. So they'd wheel him back, and I suppose he'd grumble. They'd get him back in his room and he'd say, 'See! They didn't even know I got out!'"[109]

In June 1982 Governor of Arizona Bruce Babbitt conferred the rank of Honorary Colonel on the old soldier;[110] and on 8 October the padre received a second message—a telegram—from the President:

LONG AGO, YOU ANSWERED A CALLING WHICH FEW ARE PRIVILEGED TO HEAR. YOUR LIFE'S WORK HAS BEEN AN INSPIRING EXAMPLE OF ONE MAN'S STEADFAST DEDICATION TO GOD AND TO HIS FELLOW MAN.

FOR THE SOLACE AND COMFORT YOU HAVE BROUGHT TO THE HUMAN SPIRIT, WE ADD OUR PRAYERS OF THANKSGIVING TO THE MANY BEING SAID AT THIS TIME. FOR YOUR INDOMITABLE SPIRIT AND SERVICE TO OUR NATION, I AM PROUD TO EXPRESS MY APPRECIATION.

GOD BLESS YOU.

RONALD REAGAN.[111]

Once more the holidays approached. Laboring doggedly, his once bold handwriting now shaky and thin, he managed to write his own Christmas greetings; but they were not mailed until January. "I hid them," he explained in another dictated message, "and when it got near Christmas I couldn't remember where. . . . The other day . . . I [found] them hidden in my books, so I am sending them a little late."[112] These, written soon after his ninety-third birthday, would be his last.

Father Al continued to say mass in the nursing home almost to the end. His liturgical calendar records his last mass scheduled for 1 March 1983, five days before his death. Whether he fulfilled that last duty is not recorded; but it is certain he did if physically able. He was ill, he was weak, but he was still breathing—and he would never be idle.

25: WARRIOR'S RETURN

He was taken to Good Samaritan Hospital to spend his last few days, where he alternately slept and feebly greeted friends. Dick Mackey talked with him the day before he died. "No matter how much he suffered, or how badly he felt," Mackey noted, "he could always laugh. He never lost his sense of humor."[1]

The sisters at Good Samaritan were in constant attendance, and Blaise was at his side almost around the clock. "Once, when he opened his eyes I asked him, 'Al, are you suffering?' He thought for a moment and then said, 'I don't know how to answer that question.'"

Blaise was with him at the end. A nun came in, whom the old padre apparently confused with Sister Michael and the nightly ritual they had shared so long at the Little Sisters—the rosary, followed by two ounces of good Scotch whiskey. "He said, 'when do we start?' and I told the sister, 'I think he's saying when do we start the rosary?' The sister was smart enough to say, 'Why don't we say the Hail Mary together?' Al had a tremendous respect and reverence for women, and his devotion to the Blessed Virgin Mary . . . was unbelievable."

They began the prayer he had said throughout his life, so many thousands of times. Weakened though he was and nearing the end, "Al said the Hail Mary as strongly as anybody can say it. But when he came to the part in which he said, 'pray for us sinners now and at the hour of our death,'—I knew—I felt—I would say for the first time in my life—the power of those words. . . . You could almost feel the power of heaven engaged as we prayed those words so much a part of Al's life. *Pray for us sinners now and at the hour of our death.*"[2]

Those were the only last words Father Al needed. It was 6 March 1983.

Father Albert had directed that he be buried among the friars in the Catholic cemetery in Phoenix. But he had yearned to lie in Mescalero, and Father Blaise knew this; so did others close to the padre. The Mescaleros wanted him there, and so did their pastor, Father Justin Moncrief, who, bristling at plans to inter the padre elsewhere, had begun making phone calls when Father Al's end seemed near. He called Blaise first, and then the provincial; Father Ricardo Ramirez, Bishop of the recently created Diocese of Las Cruces, made similar calls. All agreed: Father Al should lie finally at Mescalero.

But not in the village cemetery, Father Felipe Baldonado told Blaise. He, Justin, and the Mescaleros themselves believed passionately the old friar should lie in the church he had labored so long to build. Father Provincial Louis Vitale agreed. "It seems appropriate," he wrote, "that he should be buried in the great shrine that so symbolized his life and its commitments. At the request of Bishop Ramirez . . . the Apostolic Delegate granted the special privilege to allow Father Albert to be buried in the sanctuary of the church. St. Joseph's Church in Mescalero," he proclaimed, "will be an ongoing shrine to this giant of a man with the heart of a gentle child."[3]

Newspapers from over the country wrote editorials of stirring tribute as Phoenix bade Father Albert farewell. Crowds thronged to the rosary service on the evening of the eighth and to the funeral mass the following morning. Bishop Rauch spoke, and Father Felipe; so did Dick Mackey, and Sister Michael. And Father Blaise, to whom Father Al was "a great tiller of the soul, a masterpiece of God's creation. I would pay him the compliment that he would pay himself: that he was a simple Franciscan priest. . . . He lived what he was saying—he meant what he said, and he said what he meant." Blaise spoke of the padre's love for his country and for his fellow man, and of his tremendous respect for the priesthood.

With a bit of levity he recalled Father Al's well known fondness for 'Irish holy water,' and for good red wine. "His favorite miracle was performed at Cana. He always believed that because Christ changed the water to wine, wine was something beautiful, and so was whiskey, and that if anybody ever believed in prohibition, they had never heard that story."

He recalled Father Al's often repeated words, 'Heaven doesn't want me, and I don't want to go to hell. . . .' But, Blaise added, "as I followed the casket this morning, it seemed we heard, somehow or other, Al Braun saying, 'They really do want me in heaven. . . .'"[4]

Then the thin blue notes of Taps rose for the old warrior, and a hymn, and the padre's last journey on earth was about to begin, to his beloved Mescalero.

Father Al was going home.

✞✞✞

. . . a friend, a warrior, an Apostle and soldier . . .

Simple words, significant words, like the order of burial service in which they were inscribed. Like the man of which they spoke, eloquent in simplicity.

Father Albert was home. The man and the moment he had longed for met. He had come full circle, to end his earthly journey where his great apostolate had begun. "He was 93 years old," Father Provincial Louis Vitale wrote. "In July he would have celebrated 75 years in the Order, 68 as a priest. His was a full life, a Franciscan life, the life of a godly man."[5]

Get off your butts and out among the people. . . .

And now the people came to him, by the hundreds—Apaches from all reaches of the reservation, and some from other reservations; his many relatives; clerics and laymen from the wide stretches of America, Catholic and non; friends from the military, most prominently his battlefield brothers from Bataan and Corregidor, even a few from World War I, and they were given special seats; neighbors from the countryside; all merged to cram the great stone church and overflow onto the hillside.

In a harmony like that of the padre himself, the rites interwove Catholic liturgy, Apache tradition, and military punctilio, the latter provided by the 833rd Air Division Color Guard. Apache symbols graced the bishop's stole; from the altar cloth hung a drape depicting Apache spirit dancers, the work of Mescalero artist Ignatius Palmer. Palmer's work also included frames for the Stations of the Cross reminiscent of the Crown Dancers' headdresses; and on a wall hung his painting of the Last Supper, echoing da Vinci's classic, but with Apache figures.

Marching in processional were several units of Knights of Columbus. Apache braves bore the casket; honorary pallbearers were the padre's comrades-in-arms, members of families dear to him, and tribal chairman Wendell Chino. Bishop Ricardo Ramirez and Bishop Emeritus Sidney Metzger concelebrated the mass with Chaplain Cordoso from Holloman Air Force Base, Monsignor Madden from El Paso, and Fathers Justin Moncrief and Felipe Baldonado.

Mescalero artist Ignacio Palmer's "Last Supper" adorns the altar of Saint Joseph's Mescalero Apache Mission. Courtesy of SJAM.

Protestants often give us a splendid example. Prejudice has no room in charity: Christ really did die for all men. . . .

The padre's ecumenical philosophy was returned by a group of Mescalero Baptist children who recited the Lord's Prayer in sign language, and echoed in the diversity represented in the congregation.

Eulogies followed, in English and Apache (*Insignificant! I only did my duty*).

Tribal ceremonies honored the priest who had always honored theirs. And as he had brought so many of them into the Church, an Apache honor guard brought his body to its final repose beside the altar of that church, beneath a granite slab. *Apostle to the Mescalero Apache* the inscription reads.[6]

The happiest years of my life were spent in Mescalero, New Mexico. . . .

Happy years and fruitful: he had won an estimated sixty percent of the tribe into the Church while their pastor, and had continued to draw disciples with his genuine love and frequent visits thereafter. "We are grateful," Virginia Klinekole said, "that he was returned to our homeland."

As the casket was lowered into the crypt an Apache stepped from the ranks of the color guard, and over his padre he gently placed a heavy handwoven blanket, "to keep Father warm." There were few dry eyes.[7]

But tears beget smiles, and memories brought still-warm images. Marie Dupuy Russel, who with her husband Cecil had journeyed to the services in Phoenix and then to those in Mescalero, where the padre had officiated their wedding so many years ago, was "sure Father is happy to be buried where he is. After all, his roots were there."[8] Father Provincial Louis Vitale was "certain heaven is a more lively place now that he has arrived."[9] Jeanne Marsteller could still "visualize Father Al driving a school bus in heaven as he did at Sacred Heart. (Dear God!)"[10] Dick Mackey imagined him "probably raising a fuss right now with Saint Peter over something he wants to build or get done in heaven."[11] Others, with variations on the theme, have pictured him among a celestial company—Dave Kirgan most likely, Father Gus and Old Tony, Brother Sales, departed Baldonados and Apaches—sitting after a busy day of heavenly maintenance work, all enjoying a convivial *copita* of 'Irish holy water' as they look to earth and its petty problems—most of which are, the padre must be insisting, *Insignificant!*

Home is the warrior. His soul with his Maker, his body at rest, he lies among his Apaches where his ministry first began—back, most agreed, where he belonged. Those filing from the great stone church felt the chill mountain wind of early March; but spring swelled soon to burst, life was in the piney air, and a warmth breathed in Mescalero. Father Albert had walked their way.

A life, a legend, a legacy.

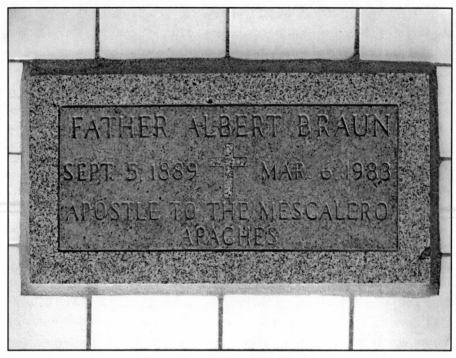

Plaque above Father Albert's tomb.
Courtesy of Brother Peter Boegel, OFM, photographer.

EPILOGUE: THE LEGEND

Bishop Thomas O'Brien proclaimed the padre's ministry the greatest modern apostolate in the Southwest, and equated it in significance to that of the legendary Father Kino's among the Pimas in the seventeenth century.[1] Some compared him with Father Junípero Serra; others to Saint Francis himself.

The comparisons are apt. Like Serra he built where he went despite infirmities and opposition; like Saint Francis he lived among the people and was one with them; he cited Kino often, and labored like that great Jesuit "to serve the whole man—his body and his soul."

But Al Braun's visions were his own, for which he often butted heads with his superiors, and they found his head hard. He was his own pope, he liked to say: he took his orders from the Father, emulated the Son (or tried to), and drew his own incredible energy from the Holy Ghost. His work encompassed many fields, any one of which would have made a successful priesthood; together they made a great one.

He was a frontiersman. With a stout Indian horse and a tough backside he sought out the camped Apaches, matched stories with them around their fires, slept with them on the ground, and found a sermon in a turkey track.

He was a builder—of churches and chapels and schools, and more importantly of lives.

He was a missioner, in its largest sense. He pointed a path to the life eternal while easing and enriching that on earth. He lived in the finest Franciscan tradition, among the people. That, Father Finian McGinn believed, was his key to an apostolate Father Gus called "just short of a miracle."

He was an educator. He founded the Outing System; he taught history, catechism, and character. He secured tuition for poor but promising students; and he built the school at Sacred Heart.

He was a double agent. Journeying into revolutionary Mexico by varying routes, he and Dave Kirgan worked with the Catholic underground, throve on danger, 'Mexican holy water,' and the exuberance of their *faits accomplis.*

He was a soldier—not a hero, he insisted, "just a soldier." He worshiped the Prince of Peace, but he knew peace must be won by battle, and he paid his share twice over. "I loved my country," he said simply.

By his deeds he is known, for the deeds define the man. The *anima* within is more elusive; still it glimmers through, to be caught, to be understood perhaps, if only partially, through a series of images, fast forwarded—the puckish grin and the glint of mischief from beneath the bushy brows, the echo of a laugh, and an oft-repeated line. *I've been in trouble all my life.*

There comes to mind a gangling big-eared boy at Saint Anthony's, uninvited, unwanted, who became a priest quite, it seemed, by accident, through a glob of manure in an overseer's boot, or a bit of divine irony . . .

~ a priest and a few Apaches covertly filling cracks with black powder in the night, a fiery blast lighting a craggy smile as a crumbling church and a provincial's veto are simultaneously gutted . . .

~ a young chaplain going 'over the top' into bloody battle, against orders, refusing to repair to the rear when wounded, tending the mangled and dying under savage fire; and superimposed comes the image of an older chaplain in a later war saying mass in a jungle amidst falling bombs, digging men from collapsed concrete rubble as shells explode and shrapnel hurtles . . .

~ a padre intoning mass by a bonfire's light inside half-built walls, and Spirit Dancers leaping into the firelight as two cultures meld and marry . . .

~ a sky pilot in straw hat and g-string, 'Al Capone' gleefully stealing food for his starving fellow POWs . . .

~ or facing the oncoming lance of Watanabe, unflinching, praying for God to *bomb this damned place off the earth* . . .

~ a humble friar saying mass in open-air *ramadas* to hundreds of faith-starved migrants . . .

~ a merry friar dancing an Irish jig with his fellow veterans in a New Mexico ranch house . . .

~ or conducting 'police drill' with a bevy of children en route for ice cream in his illegally overloaded old 'Cheve' . . .

~ a mulish priest limping, sandals aflap, his dog by his side, raising dust in the barrio and hell in the city council . . .

~ or calmly saying mass as the floodwater from his ancient washing machine pours through the sacristy into his church . . .

~ a hearty host greeting all mankind with a laugh, an *abrazo,* and a pot of beans . . .

From the image rises the legend that grew with every deed to reveal a man of the ages. Sometimes he seems in his simple humility a medieval monk, hunched over his desk in old age writing through the sleepless nights his deepest thoughts to those he loved, and they were many.

Yet the essence of Al Braun is that of the Renaissance man, forever looking beyond the horizon, engrossed in life's earthly journey. As at Eniwetok he witnessed the birth of the future, fascinated by the incredible blast of the world's first hydrogen bomb, he is forever watching history happen and racing to join the action.

The padre was often testy, easily annoyed by petty rules, impatient with red tape. He was no plaster saint: his stubbornness when crossed was formidable, his temper spectacular. He was overly fond of 'Irish holy water'; he drove recklessly; and when bureaucratic impedimenta endangered a project he could be devious. He was both visionary and doer who, Blaise marveled, "lived a life a hundred men couldn't."

His bedrock was faith. From it he drew his strength and courage, his focus, his energy, his obstinacy. It was the wellspring of his ever-bubbling humor, the reason he could laugh at anything—the Great Depression and war and Japanese prison camps, sickness and pain and the growing weakness of his body. He faced reality, bowed to it when he must, outfoxed it when he could, and always looked past it to the city on the hill. He saw the worst in human nature, but kept throughout his life an almost unbelievable innocence, for he saw also, and always, the holy spirit in all mankind.

His life was the legend, and it is epic. Its significance lies in the lives he changed; and therein lies his legacy.

✝✝✝

Soon after Father Al's death groups began to coalesce to perpetuate his memory and his work. Alumni of Saint Mary's High School established scholarships in his name for poor but deserving students; and two large movements in Phoenix attest his import in Arizona.

The first arose to save Sacred Heart. As Phoenix grew the entire Corazon community faced extinction. Bisected by the invading Squaw Peak freeway, squeezed between the industrializing city and the expanding Sky Harbor International Airport, the barrio, seen as an eyesore to be removed and turned into valuable real estate, became the victim of eminent domain. Unable to fight back effectively, some six thousand residents were relocated— bought out at low prices, their homes razed to make way for commercial development.[2]

Only Sacred Heart Church remained—"a tiny little jewel," Alice Mahoney called it, set in weeds and sand[3]—and it too was in line for demolition when the city bought it in 1985 and boarded it up. Those who had lost their homes submissively now rose in fury to save their church. The result was the Braun-Sacred Heart Center, founded to preserve their cultural heritage and promote "the concerns of the late Father Braun through the operation of a museum/cultural center on the premises."[4] The church was to remain intact.

For several years the city answered the pleas of the ex-parishioners by allowing Sagrado Corazon to be unboarded for one annual mass on Christmas, until 1991, when they declared the building unsafe. Heated meetings between city personnel and Abe Arvizu, the people's spokesman, ensued. The impasse was resolved when Arvizu dashed into the city offices minutes before they closed on Christmas Eve with the sundry documents the city manager had set as proviso. "At least for one day," Arvizu declared, "we're going to be together . . . as a family again."[5]

The church was jammed.

Support had been generating meanwhile from other parishes, organizations, businesses, and individuals. American Legion Post 41 lobbied municipal brass until the city council agreed in May 1990 to "explore means of rehabilitating the building at the present location," though a later report found the project impossible "until access and utilities are available, which is not expected for two to four years."[6]

Plans remain on the drawing board as of this writing. Preliminary sketches include several studios, a visitors' center, a cultural arts building, and amphitheater, all surrounding the church. Sacred Heart waits alone, encaged behind chain-link fence while the campaign continues its efforts to preserve the church and to honor the man who built it, brick by brick.

A second movement was more easily resolved. On the grounds of the Arizona State capitol the Wesley Bolin Memorial Plaza commemorates figures of historic import with appropriate markers or statuary. Tony Valenzuela, believing Father Al should be among those so honored, spearheaded such a project with American Legion Post 41. Endorsed by the city council and funded by public donations, Valenzuela's committee in a ten-year period raised the $60,000 needed to commission a statue on the plaza. They unanimously chose Tempe sculptor Carlos Ayala, graduate of the National Institute of Fine Arts in Mexico City, and widely known for his religious art.

Placed at intervals behind the statue are three boulders, each from an arena of significance in the padre's life, all acquired and transported by the Legionnaires. The first stone, quarried at Yarnell, offered little difficulty. For the second, Valenzuela and Ray Salazar drove to Mescalero where, with the help of tribal members, the crew at Saint Joseph's, and a heavy-duty front loader, they affixed the one-ton boulder onto a trailer and began the haul through mountain and desert to Phoenix.

The greatest challenge was a sixteen-ton slab quarried from Mount Pinatubo in the Philippines. Trucked to Clark Air Force Base, then to Subic Bay Naval Base, the monster was then shipped to Oakland courtesy of the United States Navy. With the help of former senator Dennis deConcini and the Arizona National Guard, the great volcanic chunk made the last leg to Phoenix.

On the afternoon of Sunday 4 March 2001 Ayala unveiled the statue and Father Luis Baldonado blessed it.

The memorial, dedicated as "a tribute to all servicemen and women who served with honor in defense of America" and to the warrior priest, called for a patriotic program. The Legionnaires were again prominent, from the presentation of the colors to the final 21-gun salute and Taps for their old chaplain. Apaches from Mescalero, to the cadence of drums and chants, blessed the statue with their own ritual, sprinkling the figure and the stones with the sacred pollen, symbol of life. Mariachi bands played before and after the ceremony—the music on which at all festive occasions Padre Alberto had always insisted.

This statue of Father Albert Braun, OFM, stands in the Wesley Bolin Memorial Plaza, Capitol Grounds, Phoenix, Arizona. Carlos Ayala, sculptor. Courtesy of Tony Valenzuela, Chairman of Father Braun Memorial Committee.

✚ ✚ ✚

While communicants of Sacred Heart were battling urban encroachment in Phoenix, those of Saint Joseph's in Mescalero were combating the weathering of time and the elements, compounded by legions of bats that nested in the rafters. The need for major restoration had become glaringly evident by 1988, when tribe and mission celebrated a century of Catholicism among the Mescaleros. The many visitors attending, among them Vicar Provincial Raymond Bucher of Santa Barbara Province, took note of the rapid deterioration. All agreed something must be done, and without further delay.

Those at the mission had long been aware of the problem and had through the years made what improvements they could. Since the creation of the Diocese of Las Cruces in 1969 the mission had been under its supervision. Although part of the Franciscan Province of Santa Barbara, actual ownership of the property, and responsibility for its maintenance, was lodged in the diocese.

Improvements came slowly. New heated tile flooring had been laid to prevent the tiles from freezing and cracking, and the baptistery converted into a small chapel in 1986, with diocesan blessing and Franciscan funds. Artist Henry Schnautz donated four of his paintings of famous Apaches connected to Mescalero—Cochise, Geronimo, Victorio, and Naiche, which hang on either side of the entrance.[7]

New Stations of the Cross, sent from the Philippines in memory of the courageous chaplain the people there would never forget, replaced the timeworn originals; Bruce Klinekole II framed them with symbolic Apache motifs.

In 1990 the now famous Apache Christ was installed behind the altar. BIK'EGU'INDA'N, it is titled: Giver of Life. Standing atop sacred Sierra Blanca, the Christ, dressed as an Apache holy man, looks to the life-giving sun, a halo wreathing his head, a basket containing sacred items at his moccasined feet. It is the work of Robert Lentz, then of Albuquerque, later a Franciscan friar in Gallup.

But the building itself was in danger. Assaulted by time, southwestern winds, mountain winters, and the freeze-thaw cycles of temperature extremes, the mortar was eroding. "Bats, birds, wind and rain pass easily to the interior through the gaps between the stones," it was reported.[8] Attempts to repair the cracks with concrete had worsened the erosion, causing the stones to crack, from which chunks fell frequently inside the church. Bat guano had to be cleaned from floor, pews, and altar before every service. The roof was badly damaged. The church needed heat: parishioners huddled in blankets during winter services. Major renovation was necessary.

In July 1989 Brothers Peter Boegel and Tom Herbst arrived for some repair work on the Church at Bent and the Three Rivers chapel. Noting the deterioration of Saint Joseph's, they turned to Father Al's "cathedral" with what funds they could gather, to be joined in 1991 by Brother Harry Vasile. Then in 1994 Brother Tom was transferred.

Meanwhile, the diocese, reluctant to invest in what many believed a liability, were talking of condemning the building. Peter and Harry sprang to arms, got a preliminary assessment from a preservation architect, and began fundraising—until Peter was transferred in 1995 to Mission San Miguel in California, whereupon their efforts were aborted and Saint Joseph's was left in limbo.

For nearly two years the faithful at Mescalero watched, waited, and labored to maintain their church and Father Al's tomb within, amid bat guano and falling rock fragments. Resident Sister Juanita Little, OSF, prayed daily for help.

At San Miguel Brother Peter made waves until he secured his return in June 1997. With Harry he reactivated the restoration committee, and contacted Peter Mold, a British expert in restoring old buildings. Mold demonstrated the old process of restoration with lime mortar, for the brothers and Ernesto Martinez of Bar-M Construction Company at La Luz. Within three months Martinez submitted his proposal: estimated cost, $1.2 million. Harry, to enlist workers, activated an on-site training program.

Fund raising began in earnest, within the community and from without. In 1997 the Schola Cantorum, a small choir from Saint Francis Cathedral in Santa Fe, presented in Saint Joseph's a benefit concert of sacred music on the feast day of Saint Francis of Assisi, who had answered the call to "mend my church" seven centuries before. "The choir was humbled," director William Turney reported, "by the Apache Christ inside the church, and by the poignant history of . . . Father Albert Braun. . . . Before we left we were already planning our return."[9] The choir continued to give well attended concerts, eliciting donations from around the countryside in what had become an expanding community effort.

In 2000 former Marine Tommy Spottedbird, a Kiowa from Oklahoma married to a Mescalero, joined the crew; within two years he was job foreman. Described as "a real ecumenical man, . . . a baptized Baptist who . . . works to restore a Catholic church,"[10] this hardworking professional ensures that the renovation progresses steadily and with precision.

In May 2001 Brother Peter recruited Mary Serna as Restoration Administrator—a fancy title, she says, "meaning general factotum." Mary serves as office manager, grant writer, public relations officer, and business overseer, while gathering material for an on-mission museum centered around the life of Father Albert Braun. Saint Joseph's, through her work, has been added to the New Mexico State Register of Cultural Places (11 June 2004), New Mexico List of Most Endangered Places (January 2005), and the National Register of Historical Properties (1 February 2005), making it both a state and national monument.

Several grants have contributed toward the restoration; the principle thrust is coming from private donations, a notably high percentage from military veterans, to whom the patriot-priest dedicated Saint Joseph's. Work proceeds in stages as funds become available. At times, upon some fortunate occurrence, a worker will glance skyward and murmur a soft "thank you, Father Al"; when obstacles rear, Brother Peter sweeps his arm in Braunesque fashion, grins, and snaps a jaunty *Insignificant!* [11]

✟✟✟

Father Albert Braun, OFM: apostle to the Apache, torchbearer in the barrios, chaplain among the embattled, hero among the heroic, friend of man. Despite his many honors he remained a simple friar in brown Franciscan habit, a continuum in a long line of spiritual warriors, the last of the southwestern frontier priests. And like the founder of his Order he hoed his own garden to the end.

In the orchard below Saint Joseph's Father Albert's apple trees still bear their fruit each year.

Father Albert's apple trees still bloom.
Courtesy of Brother Peter Boegel, OFM, photographer.

NOTES

Chapter 1

1. Records show he was born in 1860. If family tradition is correct, he was seventeen when he departed for America; on his next birthday he would have reached the age of conscription in the hated Bismarckian army.
2. Fr. Albert Braun to Fr. Terence Cronin, Custos, 9 August 1957. SBA.
3. Author interview, Jess and Dorothy Bumgarner, 12 September 1999, Lancaster, CA. Letter, Cecil Russell to Bro. Peter Boegel, OFM, February 2001.
4. As quoted by Kenny Joel, "All American Padre," *Friar,* September 1967.
5. Russell, *op. cit.*
6. Fr. Albert Braun, OFM, undated biographical synopsis, written ca. 1967, probably at the request of a superior. Hereafter cited as Braun, bio synopsis.
7. *Ibid.*
8. *Ibid.*

Chapter 2

1. Joel, *op. cit.*
2. Janet Burke, "Fr. Albert: Love with a Little Salt," *Alive,* March 1972.
3. Fr. Augustine Hobrecht, OFM, to Fr. Pacificus Kennedy, OFM, 16 August 1966.
4. Hobrecht to Kennedy, 23 August 1966.
5. Among the most readable accounts of Kino's life and explorations is that of Herbert E. Bolton, *Padre on Horseback,* San Francisco 1932; San Francisco 1936; Chicago 1963.
6. Herbert E. Bolton, *The Spanish Borderlands: A Chronicle of Old Florida and the Southwest* (New Haven: Yale Univ. Press 1921, 1948. Albuquerque: UNM Press), 266–67.
7. Brother Timothy Arthur, OFM, Archivist, *Santa Barbara Fioretti: Stories from the Friary* (Santa Barbara: GEC Research Press, 1992).
8. Louise P. Peck to Barbara Leyva Boyd, 25 April 1953. "Descendants of José Agustín de Leyba," courtesy of Jerry Leyva, 1 April 2003 to author.
9. Braun to Boyd, 11 March 1970.
10. Book of Confirmation, No. 32, 274, attested by Fr. Leverin E. Westhoff, OFM, Old Mission Santa Barbara.
11. Braun, bio synopsis.

12. Maynard J. Geiger, *The Life and Times of Junípero Serra, O.F.M.: The Man Who Never Turned Back, 1713–1784* (Washington, DC, Academy of American Franciscan History, 1959), 19.
13. Hobrecht, 23 August 1966, *op. cit.*
14. Santa Barbara was at this time still part of the Sacred Heart Province, headquartered in St. Louis.
15. Last will of Albert Braun, OFM. SBA.
16. Duplicate letters, Braun to Fr. Prov. Louis Vitale, OFM, 6 February and 3 July 1982.
17. Hobrecht, *op. cit.*, 23 August 1966.
18. Braun to Vitale, 6 February 1982.
19. Braun, bio synopsis. The Sacred Heart of Jesus Province, St. Louis, had received its provincial status in 1879 on the arrival of ninety-nine German priests, twenty-two candidates, and three tertiaries from the Recollect Province of the Holy Cross in Saxony, whose provincial sent them to the Franciscans' American Commissariat to escape the persecution of Bismarck's *kulturkampf*—about the same time as Braun's flight from Alsace and for the same reason. Santa Barbara had been incorporated into the expanding province in 1885 and became a separate province in 1915. Bernard H. Stokes, OFM, *The Franciscan Province of Saint Barbara 1915–1965* (Serra Press, n.d.), 3–4.
20. Joel, *op. cit.*
21. Hobrecht, *op. cit.*, 23 August 1966.
22. Author interview with Dick and Sue Mackey, 5 March 2001, Phoenix.
23. Braun to Vitale, *op. cit.*

Chapter 3

1. Paul Horgan, *Great River: The Rio Grande in North America,* 2 Vol. (NY: Rinehart & Co., 1954), 221. Herbert E. Bolton, *Coronado: Knight of Pueblos and Plains* (Albuquerque: UNM Press, 1949, 1971), 34.
2. Its full name was La Villa Real de la Santa Fé de San Francisco—The Royal City of the Holy Faith of Saint Francis.
3. Horgan 221.
4. *Ibid.* 220–29.
5. *Ibid.* 219.
6. John L. Kessell, *Kiva, Cross, and Crown: The Pecos Indians and New Mexico 1540–1840* (Albuquerque, UNM Press, 1987), 103.
7. Testimony of Fray Nicolas de Freitas, 1961, as related in C. L. Sonnichsen, *The Mescalero Apaches* (Norman: Univ. OK Press, 2 ed.), 44–45.
8. Kessell 180.
9. Horgan 252.
10. López died in prison. Aguilar was pronounced guilty and heavily sentenced. Peñalosa was convicted on 237 counts and received the harshest sentence ever imposed by the Inquisition in the New World, including perpetual banishment from New Spain

and the West Indies. He eventually died in France, still scheming, this time against his own country.

11. Bandelier, F. A. and Fanny R., *Historical Documents Relating to New Mexico, Nueva Viscaya, and Approaches Thereto to 1773,* ed. Charles Wilson Hackett (Washington, DC: The Carnegie Institution, 1923), Vol. 3, 271–72. Also Kessell 212 and Horgan 263.
12. Braun as quoted in Joel *op cit.*

Chapter 4

1. *El Paso Times,* 6 April 1898 as quoted in C. L. Sonnichsen, *Tularosa: Last of the Frontier West* (reprinted from Devin-Adair 1960; Albuquerque: UNM Press 1980), 118.
2. Antonio Serna Candelaria, *The Valley of Peace,* privately printed, n.d. Candelaria is a descendant of original settler José Candelaria.
3. Eve Ball, "Father Braun to Observe Golden Jubilee August 15," *El Paso Times,* 8 August 1965.
4. Braun to Vitale, 6 February and 3 July 1982.
5. Braun, bio synopsis.
6. The names of the twenty-six men who had fought and returned are framed and still hang on the wall of the church.
7. Almer M. Blazer, *Santana: War Chief of the Mescalero Apache,* A. R. Pruit, ed. (Taos, NM: Dog Soldier Press, 1999), 155–57, 284.
8. *Ibid.* 258.
9. Mackey interview.

Chapter 5

1. Report of Brevet Capt. A. W. Bowman, 21 April 1850, *Report of the Secretary of War for 1850,* 250–97. Sonnichsen, *Mescalero Apaches,* 69. James L. Haley, *Apaches: A History and Cultural Portrait* (Norman: Univ. OK Press, 1997), 192. *Santana* 5.
2. E. Steen to Lt. L. McLaws, *Report for the Secretary of War for 1850,* 73. Sonnichsen, *Mescalero Apaches* 67; Haley 186.
3. Soon thereafter Ft. Stanton was founded and named for Captain Stanton.
4. Brig. Gen. John Garland, Report to War Dept., 28 February 1855, *Report for the Sec. Of War, 1855,* 55. Sonnichsen, *Mescalero Apaches,* 88.
5. Col. C. R. S. Canby to Ass't. Adj. Gen. of the Western Department of the Army at St. Louis, 1 December 1861. US War Dept., *The War of the Rebellion: A Compilation of the Official Records of the Union and Confederate Armies,* Series I, Vol. 4, 77, as quoted in William A. Keleher, *Turmoil in New Mexico, 1846–1868.* (Albuquerque: UNM Press, 1982), 156.
6. The Territory of New Mexico included the present states of New Mexico and Arizona. Baylor's short-lived Confederate Territory of Arizona comprised the southern half of both.

7. *War of the Rebellion*, Series I, Vol. I, Pt. 1, 942. Keleher *op. cit.*

8. Averam B. Bender, *A Study of Mescalero Apache Indians, 1846–1880*, prepared for the US Dept. of Justice, 1960. The Expert Testimony Before the Indian Claims Commission (NY: Clearwater Pub. Co. Reprint NY: Garland Pub. Co., 1974), 101–02.

9. Brig. Gen. James H. Carleton to Col. Christopher Carson, 12 October 1862, as quoted in Keleher, *Turmoil*, 286.

10. John C. Cremony, *Life Among the Apaches 1850–1868* (San Francisco: A. Roman & Co., 1868. Reprint Glorieta, NM: Rio Grande Press, 1969), 201.

11. *Ibid.*

12. *Ibid.* 321.

13. It remained to set the boundaries, which took surveyors until 1876 to complete. Meanwhile the reservation had been extended south into the Sacramentos. In 1887 gold was discovered and the boundary again shifted to accommodate the miners, compensating the tribe with the addition of non-gold-bearing land to the east. By then the reservation was largely as it remains today.

Chapter 6

1. Mackey interview, recounted as Braun had told it to him.

2. Author interview with medicine man Paul Ortega, 15 January 2002, Mescalero, NM.

4. Braun, bio synopsis.

5. *Report of the Commissioner of Indian Affairs for 1895*, 217. Report of V. E. Stottler, as quoted in Sonnichsen, *Mescalero Apaches*, 246.

6. Braun, bio synopsis. The Carlisle School, founded in 1879 in a former army barracks in Carlisle, PA, started with one hundred Indian children Capt. Richard H. Pratt brought in from various western tribes. Here they learned the English language, white man's ways, and skills useful for employment in a white man's world, progressing through an eighth-grade level. The children worked for their board on the school's farms or in its shops, and were placed in nearby farming homes during the summer. Used to the freedom of tribal living, most were extremely unhappy. Many contracted tuberculosis; some died. In time conditions improved and Carlisle became the model for other Indian schools.
   Athletics were stressed. In the twentieth century, Jim Thorpe, from the Sac-Fox tribe in Oklahoma, was generally considered the outstanding athlete of his time. Eric Tortilla and the others had known Thorpe at Carlisle.
   The school closed on the advent of World War I when the army again needed the barracks.

6. The agency had moved from Fort Stanton to Blazer's Mill in 1874, where the agent lived in a section of the Blazer home until Major W. H. H. Llewellyn, agent from 1881–1884, built a residence on the reservation near the commissary, about half a mile above the mill. Around this nucleus buildings began to cluster in the expanding agency as the settlement grew.

7. Joel, *op. cit.*

8. Braun, as taped by Jeanne de Lue Marsteller, 28 October 1973, Scottsdale, AZ.

9. *Idem.*

10. Author interview with Mary Dorame Gomez, 20 July 2000, Tularosa, NM.

11. Author interview with Virginia Shanta Klinekole, 3 May 1999, Three Rivers Ranch, Mescalero reservation.

12. As quoted in Sherry Robinson, *Apache Voices: Their Stories of Survival as Told to Eve Ball* (Albuquerque: UNM Press, 2000), 168. See also Eve Ball, with Nora Henn and Lynda A. Sanchez, *Indeh: An Apache Odyssey* (Norman: Univ. OK Press, 1988), 296.

13. Author interview with Reginald Tortilla, son of Eric, 9 October 2001.

14. Author interview with Elisa Baldonado Dawson, 6 October 2002, Albuquerque.

15. Mackey interview.

16. *Ibid.*

17. Sometimes spelled Yusn.

18. Some ethnologists believe this correlation may have stemmed from early Spanish contact and have been grafted onto the primal Apache religion.

19. *Report of the Commissioner of Indian Affairs for 1881,* Report of W. H. H. Llewellyn, 194. Sonnichsen, *Mescalero Apaches,* 233.

20. Billy Charles Patrick Cummings, *Frontier Parish: Recovered Catholic History of Lincoln County, 1860–1884* (Lincoln County, NM: Lincoln County Historical Society Publication No. 4, 1995), 74.

21. Henry Granjon, Bishop of Tucson, *Along the Rio Grande*, 1903 (Albuquerque: UNM Press 1986), 110.

22. Msgr. William Ketcham, Dir. Bureau of Catholic Indian Missions (hereafter cited as BCIM) to Fr. Ferdinand Ortiz, 17 March 1915. BCIM.

23. Braun to Fr. Prov. Hugolinus Storff, 30 November 1917.

24. Braun, as taped by Marsteller, 4 October 1973, Tucson.

25. *Ibid.*

26. *Ibid.* These remarks have been condensed and the order of Fr. Albert's random recollections slightly rearranged for clarity.

27. Asa Daklugie, as quoted in Eve Ball, *Indeh: An Apache Odyssey.*

28. Braun, Marsteller tape, 4 October 1973.

29. *Ibid.*

30. Gomez interview.

31. Mackey interview.

32. *Ibid.*

33. *Ibid.*

34. Mackey interview.

35. Klinekole interview.

36. Author interview with Jess and Dorothy Bumgarner, 12 September 1999, Lancaster, CA.

37. Klinekole interview.

38. It was 1905 when Fr. Migeon brought 37 Lipans from Mexico to Mescalero.

39. Braun to Dr. Martingale, 18 February 1966.

40. Braun to Storff, 6 April 1917.

41. Storff to Braun, as recounted in Braun, bio synopsis.
42. Braun's notes made in later years, used for conducting retreats. Undated. Collection found in his briefcase at Saint Mary's Basilica, Phoenix. Hereafter cited as Braun Retreat Notes.
43. *Ibid.*
44. *Ibid.*
45. *Ibid.*
46. *Ibid.* The ceremony today integrates many details from the Chiricahua puberty rites with those of the Mescaleros, as the groups have themselves intermarried and become one Apache people, known now collectively as 'the Mescaleros.' This integration was doubtless already developing when Fr. Albert arrived.
47. Klinekole interview. Sources for the rites include firsthand observation, interviews with Mescaleros, and a variety of texts. Good accounts can be found in Blazer, *Santana,* and Haley, *Apaches.*
48. Fr. Ferdinand Ortiz, OFM, "The Maidens' Dance: Mescalero Indian Reservation, New Mexico," *The Indian Sentinel,* July 1920.
49. Braun to Storff, 30 November 1917.

Chapter 7

1. This famous pronouncement, attributed to Pershing, was made by Col. Charles E. Stanton, not as part of the ceremony. S. L. A. Marshall, *World War I* (NY: American Heritage Press, 1985), 295.
2. Braun, bio synopsis.
3. Braun to Storff, 23 March 1918.
4. Braun, bio synopsis.
5. Foch did add six French divisions to the nineteen larger American divisions, but all were under Pershing's command. Pershing had from the first insisted the American Expeditionary Force be an independent army under American command, but had been forced to lend units to support Allied forces. Now, with the force of America's role in recent victories and swelling American numbers, Supreme Allied Commander Ferdinand Foch could oppose him no longer.
6. Of those named, only Billy Mitchell did not live to serve in World War II, although his influence was notably present in America's air war. His strong belief in the future of wartime aviation was instrumental in building America's military air power, which he believed would be the decisive weapon in future wars. He also presented a detailed scenario of a possible Japanese attack at Pearl Harbor, which, though few took seriously at the time, proved almost eerily correct in nearly every detail. His vision for military aviation proved likewise prophetic, and the independent United States Air Force for which he had fought became a reality in 1947. Brigadier General William 'Billy' Mitchell died in 1936, too soon to see the 'winged victory' he had envisioned and of which he was so much a part.
7. Braun to Storff, 23 September 1918.
8. Braun to Fr. Prov. Novatus Benzing, OFM, 28 January 1934.

9. Three sectors of the Hindenburg Line lay between the advancing Allied armies and Sedan. The first, *Giselher Stellung,* had fallen after two weeks of desperate fighting. The formidable *Kriemhild Stellung,* to be taken by Father Al's unit, was the second. Beyond that lay the *Freya Stellung,* the last barrier before Sedan.
10. Braun, bio synopsis.
11. Joel, *op. cit.*
12. Fr. Ramon L. Varela, OFM, Chronista of Sacred Heart Parish, Phoenix, to Kennedy, 17 August 1966.
13. 6 March 1919. Records of American Expeditionary Forces: World War I. NARA II, RG 120, Box 16, Entry 1941. LOC: 190/83/26/2. File Folder 5th Div. Gen. Orders, 1919, Case 17, Drawer 3. NA.
14. Braun to Storff, 12 January 1919, Trier, Germany. As to who blocked the award, both versions are based on conjecture; but that Col. Hunt recommended him is certain.
15. They would number over two million before war's end.
16. Fr. Albert's first entry—*Miuse*—is crossed out; the second reads *Muese.* Spelling—even in English—was never his forte.
17. Winston S. Churchill, *The World Crisis: 1911–1918* (NY: Free Press, revised from 1931 ed., 2005), 838.

Chapter 8

1. Braun to Marsteller, 28 November 1973. The paragraphing in this letter is the author's, in the interest of easier reading.
2. Braun to Storff, undated, December 1918. Fr. Ferdinand was still at Tularosa; Fr. Tiburtius Wand had replaced Fr. Ambrose at Mescalero. Archival records, St. Francis de Paolo Church, Tularosa, NM.
3. *Ibid.*
4. Braun to Storff, 12 January 1919.
5. Braun to Storff, 6 April 1919.
6. Tradition has it that Father Al was billeted in the Henrion home, but because the family kept studiously aloof from their military 'guest' he had not seen them before meeting Madame at the dance. A similar assertion is found in an incomplete and often incorrect biographical account of the padre; but its author cites no source, and no documentation can be found. It may be that the padre was so billeted, though Father Al's letters give no such indication and seem to imply otherwise.
7. The above-noted snippets are quoted from letters to Eugene Henrion II, dated 19 May and 21 June 1974, 7 March 1975.
8. Braun to Eugene Henrion II, 21 June 1974.
9. Braun to Henrion II, 2 October 1973.
10. Eugene Henrion III, grandson of the elder Henrions, letter to author, 7 July 2002.
11. Braun to Henrion II, 19 September 1973 and 7 March 1975.
12. Patrick J. Hays, Ordinarius Castrensis, to Very Rev. Hugolinus Storff, OFM, 20 August 1919.

Chapter 9

1. Fr. Tiburtius Wand, OFM, to Ketcham, 29 February 1919. BCIM.
2. Braun to Ketcham, 20 September 1919. BCIM.
3. *The Indian Sentinel,* July 1919.
4. Braun to Mike and Mary Brown, December 1975.
5. *Ibid.*
6. Mackey interview.
7. This is a widely known and often repeated story on the reservation and throughout the countryside, confirmed by those who were there.
8. Fr. Lawrence Jagfeld, OFM, Secretary of the Santa Barbara Province, 21 March 1983, on the death of Fr. Albert.
9. Elizabeth Hawkins Seymour, daughter of William Ashton Hawkins, to author in numerous conversations; Gardiner Hawkins's account of his father as quoted in Beth Gilbert, *Alamogordo: The Territorial Years, 1898–1912* (Albuquerque: Starline Printing Co., 1988), 10ff; William A. Keleher, *The Fabulous Frontier* (UNM Press, 1962).
10. Elizabeth Hawkins Seymour to author.
11. On his graduation from Penn State Univ., William Stanton had won a world tour as a first prize in architecture. (Santa Barbara Provincial Annals for 1939), 16. The early churches of Europe would certainly have inspired the young architect as they had the young chaplain, which may have contributed to his espousal of Fr. Albert's project.
12. Stanton to Braun, 21 June 1920. The basement was never dug, presumably deemed unfeasible, given the shortage of manpower, equipment, and money. In 1923 Stanton also sent plans for a school, which for varied reasons, and to Fr. Al's acute disappointment, never materialized.
13. Braun to Boyd, 11 March 1970.
14. *Ibid.*
15. *Ibid.*
16. Braun, "War Time Chaplain Winning Apache," *The Indian Sentinel,* Winter 1929–30.
17. Braun to Boyd, 11 March 1970.
18. Braun to Vida Blazer Jette, 19 December 1971.
19. This and other information regarding the close association of Fr. Albert and the Jette family were given the author by Sister Nancy Johnson and her mother, Ruth Jette Johnson.
20. Braun to Storff, 22 May 1920.
21. Hobrecht to Kennedy, 23 August 1966.
22. Author interview with Fr. Blaise Cronin, 15 March 1999, Phoenix.
23. Braun to Mike and Mary Brown, 5 September 1981.
24. Author interview with Mike Brown, 23 June 2000, El Paso.
25. Braun to Storff, 8 December 1920.

26. Author interview with Fr. Maurus Kelly, OFM, 14 September 1999, Old Mission Santa Barbara.
27. Braun to Ketcham, 21 December 1919. BCIM.
28. Braun to Ketcham, 12 July 1920. BCIM.
29. Braun to Ketcham, 20 April 1920. BCIM.
30. Braun to Ketcham, 6 October 1920. BCIM.
31. Braun to Storff, 22 September 1921.
32. Klinekole interview.
33. Gomez interview.
34. Klinekole interview.
35. Author interview with Ellyn Bigrope, 1 March 1999, Mescalero, NM.
36. Klinekole interview.

Chapter 10

1. Blaise Cronin interview.
2. Braun to Benzing, 28 January 1934.
3. Braun to Fr. Prov. David Temple, OFM, 14 May 1955.
4. Braun to Vitale, 6 February 1982.
5. Braun to Fr. Prov. Turibius Deaver, OFM, 28 October 1922. A Catholic elementary school was later built on the property.
6. Charles Mackey, Jr. to Boegel, 30 November 1998.
7. Braun to Henrion II, 21 June 1974.
8. Cecil Russell, unpublished memoir, copy sent to author, 20 November 2001.
9. *Ibid.*
10. Arthur Jones, "Grace with the Cross in Las Cruces, N.M.," *National Catholic Reporter*, 10 February 1989.
11. Author interview with Ralph Diaz, 25 June 2002, Mescalero, NM.
12. Ray W. Brown, tape, November 2001.
13. Braun to Ketcham in *Catholic Sentinel*, April 1922.
14. Braun to Deaver, 11 November 1923.
15. Author interview with Reginald Tortilla, 9 October 2001, Mescalero, NM.
16. Braun, "The Catholic Outing System," undated report, ca. 1946.
17. Braun to Storff, 22 September 1921.
18. Msgr. William Hughes, "The Outing System," *The Indian Sentinel*, July 1922.
19. Father Bonaventure Oblasser, OFM, "The Catholic Outing System," unpublished treatise, 1942.
20. Hughes, *op. cit.*
21. Hughes to Fr. Augustine Schwarz, OFM, 26 October 1927.
22. Braun, "The Catholic Outing System."
23. Braun to Rev. Fr. Joseph Rhode, OFM, Custos, Santa Barbara Province, 10 November 1922.
24. Braun to Boyd, 1 August 1970.
25. Dawson interview.

26. Klinekole interview.
27. Marsteller to author, 21 May 2003.

Chapter 11

1. Parish Baptismal Records, Mescalero, Vol. 1, 28.
2. Braun to Deaver, 8 July 1924.
3. Braun to Deaver, 9 October 1924.
4. *Ibid.*
5. Braun bio summary.
6. Braun to Deaver, 22 November 1924.
7. Without documents to show the transfer of San Luis Rey, the mission's status was cloudy when the Province of Santa Barbara was created, and remained so until 1919, when it was ruled part of the new province, although it took until 1922 to become official by decree.
8. House Chronicle I, San Luis Rey, 1890–1949, 13.
9. These negotiations were eventually resolved after the arrival of Dwight Morrow as American ambassador. The companies retained their rights on fields they had developed prior to the 1917 Constitution proclaiming Mexican ownership of subsurface rights. Payments on Mexico's national debt were adjusted in 1925 and again in 1928 after Mexico had twice defaulted (and would again).
10. Braun to Deaver, 22 December 1924.
11. Braun to Terence Cronin, 31 January 1963.
12. Braun to Commissioner of Indian Affairs Charles H. Burke, 4 January 1925.
13. Braun to Burke, 12 January 1925.
14. Braun to Monsignor William Hughes, Director BCIM, 12 January 1925. BCIM.
15. Hughes to Braun, 15 May 1925. BCIM.
16. Braun to Benzing, Custos of Province of Santa Barbara, appended to letter of 15 May 1925, Hughes to Braun, *op. cit.*
17. Braun to Hughes, May 1925. BCIM.
18. Braun to Terence Cronin, 31 January 1963.
19. Braun to Deaver, 15 May 1925.
20. Braun to Deaver, 4 August 1925.
21. Frs. Albert Braun and Lawrence Mutter to Deaver, 5 August 1925.
22. Braun to Deaver, 6 February 1926.
23. Braun to Deaver, 24 April 1926.
24. Braun to Deaver, 15 November 1926.
25. Father Brendan Mitchell, OFM, "The Man Who Never Quit," Santa Barbara: Saint Anthony's Seminary High School, *Westfriars,* April 1983.
26. Braun to Deaver, 15 May 1925.
27. Braun to Deaver, 21 July 1925.
28. Mitchell, *op. cit.*
29. Braun to Deaver, 21 July 1925.
30. Braun to Deaver, 14 August 1926.

31. Braun to Deaver, 23 August 1926.

32. Braun to Deaver, 31 August 1926.

33. As quoted in Jean A. Meyer, *The Cristero Rebellion: The Mexican People between Church and State, 1926–1929*, Richard Southern, tr. (Cambridge Univ. Press 1976), 44.

34. Braun to Deaver, 24 April 1926.

35. Braun to Deaver, 15 November 1926.

36. Braun to Deaver, 1 March 1927.

Chapter 12

1. San Luis Rey House Chronicles I, 14.

2. Braun, "Building as the Old Padres Built," *The Indian Sentinel*, Fall 1927, 14.

3. Braun, bio summary.

4. The land on which Saint Joseph's stood had been reserved for the mission by order of the Secretary of Interior in 1912, but no patent had been issued.

5. Braun to Deaver, 12 September 1927.

6. On 4 March 1928 New Mexico Representative John Morrow wired the padre that, having passed the Senate, HR 10475 had that day also passed the House. On the President's signature Land Patent 1030295 thereby assigned ten acres unconditionally to the BCIM.

7. Braun to Deaver, 13 October 1927.

8. Braun to Deaver, 20 October 1927.

9. *Ibid.*

10. Braun to Deaver, 26 October 1927.

11. Braun to Deaver, 16 November 1927.

12. Braun to Deaver, 30 November 1927.

13. Braun to Deaver, 1 December 1927.

14. Braun to Deaver, 10 December 1927.

15. Braun to Deaver, 17 December 1927.

16. Braun to Deaver, 11 January 1928.

17. Braun to Deaver, 24 January 1928.

18. Press bulletin of the Central Bureau of the Central Verein, Vol. XV, No. 35, February 1928, 22.

19. Braun to newly elected Fr. Prov. Benzing, 3 May 1928.

20. Braun to Benzing 18 November 1935.

21. Dawson interview.

22. Braun to Benzing, 3 May 1928.

23. Braun, undated letter fragment, probably to Benzing, ca. May 1928.

24. Braun to Benzing, 6 May 1934.

25. Braun, undated letter fragment, *op. cit.*

26. Braun to Hughes, 5 August 1928. BCIM.

27. Braun letter dated 2 September 1928, pub. In *Indian Sentinel*, Fall 1928.

28. Braun, letter run in *The Indian Sentinel* and the Marquette *Calumet*, both Spring 1929.

29. These were blood sisters, not nuns as sometimes erroneously reported. Through a misunderstanding their money had been sent to the Papago Indian Reservation in Arizona, to be applied to a badly needed school. On learning this, the outraged ladies demanded it be redirected as per their initial instructions.

30. Ball, *Indeh: An Apache Odyssey*, 296–99.

31. Although the tribe owned the land, the Shanta family held it under tribal law until the clan should die out, at which time it would revert to the tribe. As patriarch, Shanta Boy controlled it, and it was to him Father Albert must apply for permission to build.

Gaining this permission was likely eased by Father Al's having earlier that year secured Shanta Boy's pension for having served as a scout in the US Army in 1886. US Rep. John Morrow to Braun, 7 February 1929.

32. Klinekole interview; Dawson interview; Braun to Boyd, 16 September 1970.

33. Klinekole interview.

34. *Idem*; *Alamogordo Daily News*, 6 May 1990.

35. Dawson interview.

36. Emadair Jones in *Ruidoso News*, 26 November 1987.

37. Albert Burch as quoted in Sonnichsen, *Tularosa*, 267.

38. *Ibid.* 82.

39. David H. Stratton, *Tempest Over Teapot Dome: The Story of Albert B. Fall* (Univ. OK Press, 1998), 327.

40. Braun as taped by Marsteller, 28 October 1973. The padre so firmly believed in his friend's integrity that he wrote (after Fall's appeal for retrial had been rejected), that although "this state is petitioning for a full pardon for A. B. Fall, I advised him to go to jail in protest of his innocence." Braun to Hughes, 8 May 1931.

41. *Idem.*

42. Braun to Benzing, 13 January 1931.

43. This story is well known and often recounted, because it was one he delighted in telling. Like most oft-repeated tales, this one has variations on the theme. This version is as Mike Brown, grandnephew of Father Al, remembers the padre's having recounted it. Author interview, Mike Brown, 23 June 2000, El Paso.

44. Braun to Representative Paul Gilday, 17 March 1949.

45. Braun to Benzing, 13 April 1931.

46. Braun to Benzing, 26 May 1931.

47. Braun to Benzing, 8 October 1931.

48. Braun to Benzing, 16 October 1931.

49. Braun to Benzing, undated, late October 1931.

50. Braun to Benzing, 5 December 1931.

51. Braun to Benzing, 19 October 1932.

52. Braun to Benzing, 10 January 1933.

53. Braun to Benzing, 9 February 1933.

54. Braun to Benzing, 22 September 1931.

55. Braun to Benzing, 18 and 22 September 1931.

56. Braun to Benzing, 22 September 1931.

57. Braun to Benzing, 18 and 22 September 1931.
58. Braun to Benzing, 16 October 1931.
59. Braun to Eugene II and Leota Henrion and Celine Henrion Sheehy, 19 May 1974.
60. Braun to Benzing, 7 December 1931.
61. Braun to Benzing, 7 and 12 September 1932.
62. Braun to Benzing, 8 October 1931.
63. Braun to Benzing, 6 April 1932.
64. Braun to Benzing, 6 November 1932.
65. Gomez interview.
66. Braun to Benzing, 16 October 1931.
67. Braun to Benzing, 19 October 1932.
68. Braun to Benzing, 20 November 1934.
69. Braun to Benzing, 22 September 1931.
70. Braun to Benzing, 19 October 1932.
71. Benzing to Braun, 25 October 1932.
72. Braun to Boyd, 1 August 1970.
73. Braun to Benzing, 7 September 1932.
74. Braun to Benzing, 19 October 1932.
75. Braun to Benzing, 28 November 1932.
76. Braun, "Building as the Old Padres Built," *op. cit.*
77. Author interview with Marquita Hill Boetta, 16 September 2000, El Paso, TX.
78. Braun to Benzing, 12 September 1932.
79. Braun to Benzing, 19 October 1932.

Chapter 13

1. Meyer 74–75.
2. *Ibid.* 43.
3. *Ibid.* 68.
4. *Ibid.* 52.
5. Braun to Deaver, 16 November 1927.
6. Braun to Benzing, 29 May 1930.
7. Benzing to Braun, 7 June 1930.
8. Fr. Agustín Pozos, OFM, to Braun, 27 February 1928.
9. Braun to Benzing, 2 March 1928.
10. Boetta interview.
11. Benzing to Braun, 7 June 1930.
12. Braun to Benzing, 13 January 1931.
13. Sebastián Cháves to Braun, 21 February 1928.
14. Braun to Benzing, 29 May 1930.
15. Braun to Benzing, 19 February 1931.
16. Meyer 58.
17. Braun to Benzing, 14 March 1931.
18. Braun to Benzing, 26 May 1931.

19. Benzing to Braun, 15 August 1931.
20. Braun to Benzing, 4 September 1931.
21. Braun to Benzing, 17 September 1931.
22. Braun to Benzing, 30 September 1931.
23. Braun to Benzing, 25 March 1935.
24. Braun to Benzing, 14 March 1931.
25. Benzing to Braun, 19 March 1931.
26. Braun to Benzing, 12 April 1931.
27. Benzing to Braun, 22 May 1931.
28. Braun to Benzing, 26 May 1931.
29. Braun to Benzing, 5 September 1931.
30. Benzing to Braun, 19 March 1931.
31. Braun to Benzing, 22 August 1931.
32. Braun to Benzing, 29 August 1931.
33. Benzing to Braun, 2 September 1931.
34. Braun to Benzing, 5 September 1931.
35. Braun to Benzing, 8 September 1931.
36. Benzing to Braun, 12 September 1931.
37. Braun to Benzing, 17 September 1931.
38. Braun to Benzing, 24 September 1931.
39. Braun to Benzing, 30 September 1931.
40. Braun to Benzing, 16 October 1931.
41. Braun to Benzing, 7 December 1931.
42. Braun to Benzing, 5 December 1931.
43. Braun to Benzing, 6 April 1932.
44. Braun to Benzing, 12 September 1932.
45. Braun to Benzing, 13 September 1932.
46. Braun to Benzing, 17 November 1932.
47. Benzing to Braun, 26 November 1932.
48. Braun to Benzing, 10 December 1932.
49. Braun to Benzing, 10 December 1932.
50. Benzing to Braun, 21 December 1932.
51. Braun to Benzing, 10 December 1932.
52. Braun to Benzing, 9 February 1933.
53. Dorothy Emerson, *Among the Mescalero Apaches: The Story of Father Albert Braun, O.F.M.* (Univ. AZ Press, 1973).
54. Boetta interview.
55. Mike Brown interview.
56. Dawson interview.
57. Mike Brown interview.
58. Braun to Benzing, 13 January 1931.
59. Braun to Benzing, 31 January 1931.
60. Joel, *op. cit.*
61. Braun to Benzing, 31 January 1931.

62. Braun to Benzing, 19 February 1931.
63. Braun to Benzing, 2 September 1933.
64. Braun to Benzing, January 1934.
65. Richard Melzer, *Coming of Age in the Great Depression: The Civilian Conservation Corps in New Mexico, 1933–1942* (Yucca Tree Press, 2000).
66. Braun to Father Custos Ildephonse Moser, OFM, 19 June 1933.
67. Braun to Benzing, 20 July 1933.
68. Braun to Benzing, 2 September 1933.
69. Benzing to Braun, 6 September 1933.
70. Braun to Benzing, 11 September 1933.
71. Benzing to Commanding General, Fort Bliss, Texas, 14 September 1933; H. C. Holdridge, Major, A.G.D., Adjutant Fort Bliss to Benzing, 26 September 1933.
72. R. F. Momsen of Norcop & Momsen, Attys., El Paso, Texas, to Benzing, 19 January 1934.
73. Braun to Benzing, 13 March 1934.
74. Braun to Benzing, 6 May 1934.
75. Benzing to Braun, 10 May 1934.
76. Braun to Benzing, undated, June 1934.
77. Braun to Benzing, 31 July 1934.
78. Author interview with Concha Ortiz y Pino de Kleven, 8 April 1999, Albuquerque.
79. *Ibid.*
80. Braun to Benzing, 13 July 1934.

Chapter 14

1. Ortega interview.
2. Braun to Benzing, 20 November 1934.
3. Braun to Benzing, 19 December 1934.
4. Braun to Benzing, 3 January 1935.
5. Braun to Benzing, 19 December 1934.
6. Braun to Benzing, 24 January 1935.
7. Braun to Benzing, 3 January 1935.
8. Braun to Benzing, 27 June 1935.
9. *El Paso Times*, 19 June 1935.
10. Braun to Benzing, 30 August 1935.
11. Braun to Benzing, 15 June 1935.
12. James Cissny to author, 3 August 2003.
13. Mackey interview.
14. Bigrope interview.
15. Braun to Benzing, 9 September 1935.
16. Braun to Benzing, 3 January 1935.
17. Braun to Benzing, 26 April 1935.
18. Braun to Benzing, 30 August 1935.
19. Braun to Benzing, 14 September 1935.

20. Braun to Benzing, March 1935.

21. Braun to Benzing, 9 September 1935.

22. Braun to Benzing, 15 June 1935.

23. Braun to Benzing, 18 November 1935; Rev. J. B. Tennely, Dir. BCIM, to Braun, 29 November 1935; Braun to Benzing, 30 June 1936; Tennely to Braun, 14 March 1936. Santa Barbara did not get the San Xavier deed.

24. Braun to Benzing, 1 November 1935.

25. Braun to Benzing, 22 January 1936.

26. Braun to Benzing, undated, probably late autumn 1935.

27. Braun to Benzing, 30 January 1936.

28. Braun to Benzing, undated Christmas card, December 1935.

29. Braun to Benzing, 22 January 1936.

30. Braun to Benzing, 22 January 1936.

31. Braun to Benzing, 30 January 1936.

32. Braun to Benzing, 13 March 1936.

33. Braun to Ray and Elisa Dawson, 17 January 1980.

34. Mackey interview.

35. Dawson interview.

36. Braun to Ray and Elisa Dawson, 17 January 1980.

37. Braun to Benzing, 1 November 1935.

38. Benzing to Braun, 19 December 1931.

39. Braun to Benzing, 24 January 1935.

40. Bumgarner interview.

41. *Ibid.*

42. De Kleven interview.

43. Braun to Benzing, 10 May 1936.

44. Braun to Boyd, 26 August 1970.

45. Braun to Boyd, 11 March 1970.

46. Braun to Boyd, 1 July 1973.

47. Joel, *op. cit.*

48. Braun to Fr. Prov. Gregory Wooler, OFM, 25 March 1946.

49. Braun to Benzing, 21 September 1936.

50. Mackey interview.

51. Boetta interview.

52. Mackey interview.

53. Gomez interview.

54. Braun to Benzing, 3 February 1937.

55. Braun to Benzing, 24 February 1937.

56. Braun to Benzing, 3 February 1937.

57. Braun to Benzing, 13 April 1937.

58. Braun to Benzing, 24 February 1937.

59. Braun to Benzing, 13 April 1937.

60. The radicals finally lost their control in 1940 when President Manuel Camacho made his now famous pronouncement, "I am a believer."

61. Braun to Benzing, 19 February 1931.
62. Braun to Benzing, 4 June 1937.
63. Braun to Benzing, 12 June 1937.
64. Braun to Benzing, 21 June 1937.
65. Braun to Benzing, 13 December 1937.
66. Mary Serna to author.
67. Braun to Moser, 23 July 1938.
68. Braun to Moser, 22 February 1939.
69. Kate McGraw in *El Paso Times*, 8 July 1974.
70. Braun to Benzing, 22 February 1939.
71. Braun to Benzing, 22 March 1939.
72. Braun to Father Victor Bucher, OFM, 26 June 1939.
73. As quoted in Joel, *op. cit.*
74. Provincial Annals, Santa Barbara Province, 1939, p. 17, based on material supplied by Fathers Albert Braun, Arthur Liebrenz, and Dennis Mahoney; dedication program.
75. William Stanton to Braun, 16 December 1933.
76. Braun to Moser, 12 September 1939.
77. Braun to Moser, 6 November 1939.
78. *Ibid.*
79. Braun to Moser, 29 January 1940.
80. Braun to Moser, 6 November 1939.
81. Braun to Father Gerard Brenneke, OFM, 27 February 1940.
82. Braun to Benzing, 31 July 1934.
83. Braun to Benzing, 22 March 1939.
84. Julius 'Joe' Valcik to Braun, 3 May 1982.
85. Braun to Benzing, 22 February 1939.

Chapter 15

1. Bumgarner interview.
2. Braun, bio synopsis.
3. Braun to Moser, 15 October 1940.
4. *Ibid.*
5. Braun to Elisa Baldonado, 28 October 1940.
6. Braun to Moser, 15 October 1940.
7. Mark Skinner Watson, *Prewar Plans and Preparations, United States Army in World War II*, Office of the Chief of Staff: Washington, DC, GPO, 1950, 470.
8. United States Department of State, *Peace and War: United States Foreign Policy 1931–1941*, Vol. II, Document 196, 618–19. Washington, DC: GPO, 1943. Hereafter cited as *Peace and War*. Also *Papers Relating to the Foreign Relations of the United States: Japan 1931–1941*, Vol. II, 133. Washington, DC: GPO, 1943. Hereafter cited as *Foreign Relations*.
9. Braun to Fr. Dennis Mahoney, OFM, 17 March 1941.

10. Braun, bio synopsis.
11. Gomez interview.
12. Mackey interview.
13. John K. Borneman, Chaplain, Lt. Col., to Wooler, 15 August 1945.
14. Eric Morris, *Corregidor: The End of the Line* (NY: Stein & Day, 1981), 11–12.
15. Braun, bio synopsis.
16. Braun to Fr. Prov. Martin Knauff, OFM, 9 June 1941.
17. Braun to Fr. Felix Raab, OFM, 13 June 1941.
18. Braun to Knauff, 9 June 1941.
19. Braun to Knauff, 18 September 1941.
20. Braun to Knauff, 9 June 1941.
21. Braun to Knauff, 18 September 1941.
22. Braun to Raab, 2 September 1941.
23. Author interview with Pepe Baldonado, 1986, Albuquerque.
24. Braun to Knauff, 18 September 1941. The men were actually stationed at Fort Stotsenberg, adjacent to Clark Field, which they were assigned to guard.
25. Braun to Elisa Baldonado, 13 November 1941.
26. Braun to Raab, 2 September 1941.
27. Winston S. Churchill, *The Second World War* (Boston: Houghton Mifflin, 1950, 1951, 1953), Vol. III, *The Grand Alliance* 444.
28. US Congress, Joint Committee on the Investigation of the Pearl Harbor Attack: *Hearings Before the Joint Committee on the Investigation of the Pearl Harbor Attack*, 79th Congress, 2nd Session (Washington, DC: GPO, 1946) Part 12:51.
29. US Congress, Senate Committee on the Judiciary, Internal Security Subcommittee, *Institute of Pacific Relations Hearings*, 82nd Congress (Washington, DC: GPO, 1951) 2:382.
30. Watson 124–25.
31. The islands comprised Caballo, home of Ft. Hughes; El Fraile, the 'concrete battleship' of Ft. Drum; and Carabao, housing Ft. Frank.
32. Braun to Prof. William M. Belote, October 1963.
33. Braun to Knauff, 23 October 1941.
34. *Peace and War*, Vol. II, Doc. 245, 772–75.
35. Watson 503.
36. Samuel Eliot Morison, *The Rising Sun in the Pacific, 1931-April 1941,* Vol. III of series *History of the United States Naval Operations in World War II* (Boston: Little, Brown & Co., 1948), 71. *Pearl Harbor Hearings* 14:1055.
37. Braun to Elisa Baldonado, 13 November 1941.
38. Braun to Raab, 21 November 1941.
39. *Ibid.*
40. Stimson diary, 25 November 1941. *Pearl Harbor Hearings*, 11:5433. See also Stimson's testimony, *Pearl Harbor Hearings*, 11:5421-22.
41. Morison 76.
42. Dated November but drafted before the *modus vivendi* was rejected. Morison 74. Rear Admiral Edwin T. Layton, USN Ret., *And I Was There* (NY: William Morrow,

1985), 210–11.

43. Rad. OPNAV to Cmndrs. Pacific & Asiatic Fleets, 24005, 24 November 1941, in *Pearl Harbor Hearings*, Pt. 14, 1405. Louis Morton, *United States Army in World War II: The War in the Pacific: The Fall of the Philippines* (Office of Chief of Military History, Dept. of Army, Washington, DC: GPO, 1953), 71.

44. Rad. Marshall to MacArthur, 27 November 1941, OCS 18136–118. *Report to the Joint Committee on the Investigation of the Pearl Harbor Attack,* 79th Cong. 2nd Sess., Doc. 244 (Washington, DC, 1946). Morton 71. Emphasis author's.

45. Archival Records, SBA.

46. Braun to Raab, 21 November 1941.

Chapter 16

1. Rad. Marshall to MacArthur, No. 736, 7 December 1941, WPD 4544–20. Morton 146.

2. Baguio, boasting the cool breezes of the Zambales Mountains, was the summer capital. Pres. Manuel Quezon was there at the time. He was unhurt.

3. Why the warnings failed to get through is still a mystery. Theories abound, the most credible being that the airways were jammed to make reception impossible, and the teletype wires cut. The dead telephone lines of the antiaircraft units support the theory of sabotage. (The only call that allegedly got through was made on a civilian line.) But without proof the theory remains inconclusive.

4. The exact time of the attack is disputed, though 1235 seems to fit sequentially with other documented times of the chaotic day.

5. General Wainwright later named the 200th the "first unit in the Philippines . . . to go into action defending our flag in the Pacific." General Jonathan Wainwright, December 1945, Deming, NM. John Pershing Jolly, Adjutant-General New Mexico, *History New Mexico National Guard, 1606–1963* (Pub. New Mexico National Guard, 1964), 36.

6. With Clark's communications center knocked out at the beginning of the raid, the other fields were unaware of the attack until too late to get the planes to the scene. Except for those at Clark, all fighters were in the air patrolling where ordered. An earlier order had assigned the eighteen P-40s at Del Carmen to cover Clark Field, but the message never got through. The six pilots who did arrive had spotted smoke and followed it to the attack.

7. John Toland, *The Rising Sun in the Pacific 1936–1945* (Random House 1970, Bantam ed. 1980) 292–93. William Manchester, *American Caesar: Douglas MacArthur 1880–1964* (Dell. Pub., 1978), 240.

8. Admiral Rockwell had in his command, besides the submarines, only three gunboats, three minesweepers, half a dozen PT boats, a few minor craft, the 4th Marines, and his vital wireless station, all under MacArthur's command.

9. As quoted in Belote 54.

10. In Borneo also Hart hesitated to commit his ships to action, and did so only when forced by the hard-fighting Dutch Vice-Admiral Conrad Helfrich. The success of

the ensuing raid in Macassar Strait—four American destroyers sank three Japanese transports and returned safely—proved the Japanese were not, as Hart contended, unbeatable. See John Toland, *But Not in Shame* (Random House, 1961), 220.

11. Author interview with Madeline Ullom, 6 March 2001, Tucson, Arizona.
12. Chaplain John Borneman to Wooler, 15 August 1945.
13. *New York Times*, 29 December 1941. Manchester 272.
14. Ullom interview.
15. Braun to Belote, 15 October 1963.
16. Borneman, *op cit.*
17. Besides refusing ships for Philippine relief, the obsessively defeatist Hart was protesting a proposed sea battle to stop the Japanese advance to Java, an action Dutch Admiral Helfrich contended was the only way to save that beleaguered island (and hence the Indies). General Sir Archibald Wavell, commander of the combined American-British-Dutch-Australian (ABDA) forces in the Southwest Pacific, agreed with Helfrick. Waves of the brewing storm reached Washington; Hart was recalled in February, officially because of age—he was sixty-four—and poor health; and Helfrich replaced him as commander of the ABDA navy.
18. Braun to Belote, *op. cit.*
19. Borneman, *op. cit.*
20. As quoted by Justin Gleichauf, "The Hero Priest of Corregidor," *VFW* Mag., January 1984. Masello was commander Battery E, 60th CAC, on Corregidor until deployed to Bataan, 31 November 1941.
21. Braun to Knauff, 8 February 1942.
22. Rad. MacArthur to Marshall, 23 January 1942.
23. The torpedo boats were led by Naval Lieutenant John Bulkeley, the indomitable red-bearded hot-blood who would later command PT 41 to evacuate MacArthur from Corregidor to Australia.
24. Braun to unidentified gentleman, taped by Marsteller, 28 October 1973.
25. Vitale, "A Legend in His Time," March 1983.
26. Author interview with Vicente Ojinaga, quoted in Dorothy Cave, *Beyond Courage: One Regiment Against Japan, 1941–1945* (Yucca Tree Press, 1992), 129.
27. Jack H. Aldrich to author.
28. As quoted by Barbara Yost, "Hero Priest Recalls Bad, Good Days," *Phoenix Gazette*, 30 November 1981.
29. Braun, notes for retreat lecture, ca. 1964.
30. John Toland, *The Rising Sun: The Decline and Fall of the Japanese Empire, 1936–1945* (Random House 1970, Bantam Ed., 1980), 336–37. Japanese Colonel Nobuhiko Jimbo, "Dawn of the Philippines," privately published pamphlet, 14; Cave 176.
31. Joel, *op. cit.*
32. Ullom interview.
33. *Ibid.*
34. Nurse Maud Williams, as quoted in Lt. Gen. E. M. Flanagan, Jr., *Corregidor: The Rock Force Assault* (Presidio Press, 1988), 65.
35. Lt. Col. Floyd Mitchell, Adjt. 91st CA, as quoted in Joel, *op. cit.*

36. Morton 487.
37. Flanagan 59–61.
38. Both planes reached Mindanao for a stopover. One continued to Australia; the other was unable to take off. Its pilots and passengers were eventually captured by the Japanese.
39. The *Spearfish* did make it to Australia after a harrowing seventeen-day trip, part of it literally below a Japanese fleet. From Freemantle its passengers and mail traveled by troop train across the continent to Melbourne, thence by ship via New Zealand, rounded the tip of South America, and headed north to New York City, arriving on 2 July 1942, two months after escaping Corregidor.
40. Jonathan Wainwright, *General Wainwright's Story* (Doubleday, 1946; Bantam ed., 1986), 90–91.
41. *Ibid.* 94–95.
42. *Ibid.* 98–99.
43. *Ibid.* 101.
44. Ullom interview.

Chapter 17

1. Braun, retreat notes.
2. Braun to Temple, 24 December 1952.
3. *Ibid.*
4. This includes 1,000 men surrendered at Fort Hughes. Figures according to Belote 186.
5. Braun to Belote, 15 October 1963.
6. Braun, retreat notes.
7. Unsigned note, identified as that of Father Bauman, attached to a typewritten unsigned questionnaire.
8. Braun, retreat notes.
9. *Ibid.*
10. Cabanatuan became the largest POW camp in the Far East.
11. Gleichauf, *op. cit.*
12. Author interview with 2/Lt. Thomas P. Foy, Jr., 12 June 1999, Bayard, NM.
13. Author interview with 2/Lt. Al T. Suttman, 12 June 1999, Silver City, NM.
14. Cpl. Cone J. Munsey, unpub. ms., quoted in Cave, *op. cit.*, 186.
15. Col. Calvin D. Jackson, M.D., *Diary: Kept during World War II, 1941–1945* (Ada, OH: Ohio Northern Univ., 1992), entry 8 June 1942, 56.
16. One chaplain was eventually allowed to accompany burial details late in 1942, after Father Al had been transferred out of Cabanatuan.
17. E. Bartlett Kerr, *Surrender and Survival: The Experience of American POWs in the Pacific 1941–1945* (NY: William Morrow & Co., 1985), 94–95.
18. Joel, *op. cit.*
19. Alfred A. Weinstein, *Barbed Wire Surgeon* (NY: MacMillan Co., 1947), 156.
20. Charles James to author, 22 July 2001, Carlsbad, NM.

21. Author interview with Capt. Gerald Greeman, Deming, NM, quoted in Cave 224–25.
22. Foy interview.
23. 2/Lt. LeMoyne Stiles, unpub. diary, Cave 232–33.
24. 2/Lt. John D. Gamble, unpub. diary found at Cabanatuan after liberation. Copy provided author by John B. Farquhar. Cave 223.
25. Klinekole interview.
26. The Japanese refused to accede to the mandates of the Geneva Convention, asserting they had never signed the accords. Their delegates had attended the Second Hague Conference in 1907 and signed the resultant agreement, by which they were bound to abide by specified conditions of humane treatment for POWs. Japanese delegates attended the Geneva Conference of 1929, which amplified the provisions of the Hague Agreements, and the head of their delegation did sign the convention, although Tokyo did not ratify it. They did, however, pledge in February 1942, through the Swiss government, to adhere to its provisions vis-à-vis POWs. Additionally, regulations issued in 1904 by the Japanese government, and still nominally binding during World War II, listed in detail the specifics for the humane treatment of POWs.
27. Borneman to Wooler, 15 August 1945.
28. Jackson *Diary*, 28 October 1942, 81.
29. *Ibid.*, 4 November 1942, 83.
30. Capt. John J. Morrett to Mrs. Frederick B. Howden, 11 December 1944. Courtesy of Alfred Howden.
31. Jackson *Diary*, 7 December 1942, 88.
32. Morrett, *op. cit.*
33. Jackson *Diary*, 11 December 1942, 89. Allegations that Father Albert received Howden into the Catholic Church shortly before his death stem largely from assertions of Emerson, *op. cit.*, and of Adrian R. Martin, *Brothers from Bataan: POWs, 1941–1945* (Manhattan, Kansas, Sunflower Univ. Press, 1992). Emerson cites no source; Martin quotes from a letter allegedly written by Father John Duffy long after the fact, and unsure even of Howden's name. Both books contain inaccuracies. None of Father Albert's extant reports, letters, or retreat notes make any such assertions. John Morrett, who visited Howden daily until his death, and who seems to have been his closest confidant, says nothing of any deathbed conversion. Of Howden's burial, which Morrett attended, he states the services were conducted by Protestant Chaplain Dawson and Catholic Chaplain LaFleur. Father Al, apparently out on work detail, was not present at Howden's death and burial, which occurred on the same day. In the absence of any records, the matter cannot be proven either way. The weight of the argument seems, however, to point to Morrett's account as the most reliable.
34. While the German-held POWs received almost weekly Red Cross boxes, shipments to Japan were rare events, required strenuous negotiation with the Japanese, and those that did get through were usually rifled before the POWs received them.
35. As quoted in *Alive* magazine, March 1982, 9.

36. Braun to Vitale, 8 July 1982.
37. Fr. Herman Baumann, undated recollection. Father Al also liked to tell this often repeated story.
38. Braun to Vitale, 8 July 1982.
39. Vitale to Braun, 14 July 1982.
40. Military Ordinate in New York to Wooler, 20 November 1944, relaying a report of an unnamed escapee from Dapecol who had made it to Australia.
41. Braun, undated note attached to Lulu Reyes's message.
42. The escapees, with the help of guerrilla groups on Mindanao, were able to get three of their group aboard an Australia-bound submarine. MacArthur, appalled at learning from them of the Death March and the inhuman conditions in Japanese POW camps, had the three flown to Washington, where they gave sworn testimony and a detailed report. Roosevelt ordered these and all reports of atrocities withheld, ostensibly because revelation might endanger the POWs, a rationale many refused to believe when the President finally, and only when threatened with forthcoming British and Australian disclosures, released the news on 27 January 1944.
43. Author interview with Capt. Russell J. Hutchison. Cave 249–50.
44. Jackson *Diary*, 5 April 1943, 106.
45. Mitchell, *op. cit.*
46. Jackson *Diary*, 9 August 1943, 125.
47. Braun to Ray and Elisa Dawson, 31 October 1979.
48. Most Rev. William T. McCarty, C.SS.R., relaying message to Wooler, 28 January 1944. Braun to Hobrecht, 12 April 1949. Braun to Chaplain Martin Poch, Chief of chaplains, 18 April 1949.
49. Author interview with Pfc. Harold A. Knighton. Cave 257.
50. Author interview with 1/Lt. James Walter Donaldson, Deming, NM. Cave 257.
51. Bulletin, American Legion Mescalero Post #48, undated, "Sketch of the Life of Father Albert Braun."
52. Jackson *Diary*, 22 April 1943, 108.
53. *Ibid.*, 20 March 1944, 159.
54. R. Hutchison interview. Cave 278–80.
55. Jackson *Diary*, 6 June 1942, 172.
56. Lt. Col. John H. McGee and 1/Lt. Donald H. Wills.
57. Jackson *Diary*, 21 June 1944, 175.
58. John Baumann, undated statement.
59. *Ibid.*
60. Author interview with Agapito Silva, 12 June 1999, Silver City, NM.
61. R. Hutchison interview. Cave 282.
62. Jackson *Diary*, 183, 185, 186.
63. *Ibid.*, 15 August 1944, 186.
64. *Ibid.*, 18 August 1944, 187.
65. Cpl. Woodrow M. Hutchison to author. Cave 294.
66. Author interview with Pvt. James C. McCormick. Cave 294.
67. Jackson *Diary*, 25 August 1944, 188.

68. *Ibid.*, 27 August 1944, 189.
69. *Ibid.*, 28 and 29 August 1944, 189.
70. *Ibid.*, 2 September 1944, 189.
71. *Ibid.*, 3 September 1944, 190.
22. Braun, affidavit for "Investigation of Incidents between 10 September 1944 and 29 August 1945, Occurring at Prisoner of War Camp Omori, A Suburb of Tokyo, Japan, subscribed and sworn for Summary Court at Fort Shafter, Honolulu, 6 July 1948." Hereafter cited as Braun affidavit.
73. Weinstein 221.
74. *Ibid.*, 246–47.
75. Braun affidavit.
76. Weinstein 246.
77. 'Max' Wilson to Braun, 11 September 1960.
78. Baumann, undated recollection.
79. *Ibid.*
80. Author interview with Bro. Joachim Grant, OFM, 14 September 1999, Old Mission Santa Barbara.
81. Joel, *op. cit.*
82. Braun affidavit.
83. This raid cost an estimated 100,000 lives, wounded another 125,000, and left over 1,000,000 homeless, as contrasted with the A-bombs at Hiroshima, where estimates range from 60,000 to 80,000, and Nagasaki, estimated at between 36,000 to 40,000. Damage and deaths from the incendiary bombings far exceeded those of both A-bombs together. A single incendiary raid on 2 August leveled six Japanese cities.
84. Military planners estimated the invasion of Japan would cost over 1,000,000 American lives, countless millions in Japanese troops and civilians, and would almost certainly guarantee the death of every POW held in Japan, Manchuria, and Korea. In view of the indiscriminate Japanese bombings of civilians in China as early as 1932, it is ironic that the Japanese government protested these American bombings as 'inhuman.'
85. Braun affidavit.
86. *Ibid.*
87. Gavan Dawes, *Prisoners of the Japanese: POWs of World War II in the Pacific* (William Morrow & Co., 1994), 337.
88. *Ibid.*, 342–43.

Chapter 18

1. Bigrope interview.
2. Klinekole interview.
3. Braun to Mr. and Mrs. Jack Roak, 3 September 1945, from Tokyo Bay.
4. Braun to Wooler, 9 September 1945, from Manila.
5. Braun to Wooler, 14 September 1945, from Manila.

6, Braun to Wooler, 22 September 1945, from Bataan.

7. Braun to Wooler, 7 October 1945, from aboard Rock Island Railroad.

8. Braun to Wooler, 18 October 1945.

9. Arthur, *op cit.*, 61.

10. Braun to "Joe," no last name given, apparently a fellow Franciscan, 11 August 1948.

11. Mackey interview.

12. Braun to Wooler, 16 November 1945.

13. Braun to Wooler, 19 April 1946.

14. Braun to Wooler, 28 November 1945.

15. Fr. Marcian Bucher, OFM, "A Priest to All God's Family," *Homiletic and Pastoral Review*, November 1984, 63–64.

16. Braun to Wooler, 22 December 1945.

17. Braun to Wooler, *Ibid.*

18. Braun to Wooler, 4 January 1946.

19. Louis Mendoza, as quoted in Gleichauf, *op. cit.*

20. Braun to Wooler, 18 January 1946.

21. Braun to Wooler, 22 January and 6 February 1946.

22. Braun to Wooler, 22 December 1945 and 6 February 1946.

23. Braun to Wooler, 25 March 1946.

24. Braun to Adj. Gen., Dept. of the Army, undated. The recommendation had been made by Col. Octave DeCarre, 96th CA.

25. Army of US, official notice of promotion, 4 March 1947.

26. Military Record and Report of Separation Certificate of Service.

27. Braun to Wooler, 25 March 1946.

28. Letters, Braun to Redmon, 17 March 1941; Mahoney to Braun, 1 April 1941; Mahoney to Knauff, 15 April 1941; Braun to Knauff, 9 June 1941.

29. Braun to Wooler, 25 March 1946.

30. Braun to Wooler, 20 February, 5 July, 4 August 1946.

31. Ray Brown, tape recording, November 2001-February 2002, Logan, Utah.

32. Braun to Wooler, 5 July 1946.

33. Braun to Wooler, 30 August 1946.

34. Braun to Wooler, 4 August 1946

35. Bumgarner interview.

36. Ray Brown tape.

37. Bumgarner interview.

38. *Ibid.*

39. Braun to Wooler, 25 October 1946.

40. Edward F. Witsell, Maj. Gen., Adj. Gen., to Braun, 21 October 1946.

41. DeCarre to Braun, 21 January 1946.

42. DeCarre to Braun, 24 March 1946.

43. Witsell to Braun, 21 October 1946.

44. *Franciscan Friar*, June 1958. Undated archival document, unsigned. Gleichauf, *op cit.*

45. Braun to Wooler, 25 October 1946.

46. Braun to Wooler, 1 December 1946.
47. Klinekole interview.
48. Braun to Wooler, 8 January 1947.
49. Braun to Wooler, 17 February 1947.
50. Braun to Wooler, 8 April 1947.
51. Braun to Wooler, 17 April 1947.
52. Braun to Wooler, 8 April 1947.
53. Braun to Wooler, 27 April 1947.
54. Ortega interview.
55. Braun to Wooler, 5 July 1947.
56. *Ibid.*
57. M. R. Prestridge to Braun, 8 July 1957; Braun to Wooler, 14 July 1947.
58. Gen. William R. Arnold, D.D., Military Delegate, Military Ordinate, to Braun, 11 July 1947.
59. Braun to Wooler, 16 July 1947.
60. Braun to Wooler, 18 July 1947.
61. Braun to Wooler, 26 July 1947.

Chapter 19

1. Braun to Wooler, 2 August 1947.
2. Braun to Wooler, 12 August 1947.
3. Braun to Fr. Cornelius (no last name given), Prov. Hq., 12 August 1947.
4. Braun to Wooler, 12 August 1947.
5. Braun to Wooler, 17 August 1947.
6. Braun to Wooler, 18 August 1947.
7. Braun to Wooler, 24 August 1947.
8. Braun to Wooler, 25 August 1947.
9. Braun to Wooler, 1 September 1947.
10. *Ibid.*
11. Braun to Wooler, 17 October 1947.
12. Braun to Maj. Gen. John W. Leonard, 29 April 1949.
13. Descriptions and activities at Eniwetok are taken from Richard Hewlett and Francis Duncan, *A History of the United States Atomic Energy Commission*, Vol. II, *Atomic Shield, 1947–1952* (University Post and London Penn State Univ., 1969), 162.
14. Lilienthal, David E., *The Journals of David E. Lilienthal*, Vol. II, *The Atomic Energy Years* (NY: Harper & Row, 1964), entry for 3 March 1948, 301.
15. Maj. Gen. Kenneth Nichols, Cmnd. Armed Forces Special Weapons Project [AFSWP] to Joint Chiefs of Staff, 31 March 1948, as quoted in Richard Rhodes, *Dark Sun: The Making of the Hydrogen Bomb* (Simon & Schuster 1955), 320.
16. Description taken largely from Hewett and Duncan, *op. cit.*, 161–165.
17. *Ibid.*, 164
18. Braun, Application for Extension Courses 50 and 60, 20 April 1948; Endorsement of Approval, Erwin T. May, 22 April 1948; Certificate of Completion, rating

"Satisfactory," John F. Chalker, 22 March 1949.

19. The second test had yielded 49 kilotons, "the largest yet coaxed from any atomic weapon, almost four times that of the Hiroshima bomb." Rhodes, *op. cit.*, 320.
20. William Hoopai, Chief of Police, City and County of Honolulu, to Braun, 28 June 1948.
21. Braun to Hoopai, 30 June 1948.
22. Braun to Aloha Motors Limited, 24 August 1948.
23. Braun to Celine Henrion Sheehy, 9 July 1948.
24. Braun to 'Joe' (apparently a fellow chaplain), 11 August 1948.
25. Braun to Roak, 7 October 1948.
26. Hurley had been Secretary of War under Hoover, and later Ambassador to China.
27. Braun to the Most Reverend Edwin V. Byrne, Archbishop of Santa Fe, 24 August 1948.
28. Byrne to Braun, 27 August 1948.
29. Braun to N.M. Secretary of State, 7 October 1948.
30. Braun to Roak, 7 October 1948.
31. Braun to Cmdg. Gen. US Army Pacific, 8 September 1948.
32. Braun to Wooler, 1 July, 5 July, 4 September, 15 September 1948.
33. Braun to Wooler, 3 October 1948.
34. Braun to Wooler, 28 October 1948.
35. Braun to Cmdg. Gen. USARPAC (US Army Pacific), 17 August 1948.
36. Chaplain Edwin Kirtley (Lt. Col.), USARPAC, To Whom it May Concern, 17 August 1948.
37. Braun to Maj. Gen. Luther D. Miller, Chief of Chaplains, 13 April 1949.
38. Braun to Chaplain Paul J. Maddox (Col.), 4 May 1949.
39. Braun to Wooler, 12 April 1949.
40. Braun to Chaplain Martin Poch (Col.), 18 April 1949.
41. Braun to 'Joe,' 11 August 1948
42. Braun to Most Reverend Richard J. Cushing, Archbishop of Boston, 24 August 1948.
43. Braun to Leonard, 29 April 1949.
44. Braun to Maddox, 4 May 1949.
45. Braun to CWO James McArthur, OCS Plans and Operations, the Pentagon, 29 June 1949. The dollar a day was paid out of Japanese assets frozen before the war, through the War Claims Commission, under legislation introduced by Senator Dennis Chavez of New Mexico. Later an additional $1.50 was added.
46. Braun to Poch, 18 April 1949.
47. Braun to Wooler, 15 October 1948.
48. Admiral Dewitt C. Ramsey, address to Service Chaplains' Association, Territory of Hawaii, 13 October 1948.

Chapter 20

1. Arthur to author, 13 September 1999.

2. Braun to Hobrecht, 13 November 1949.
3. Author interview with Sister Mary Roqueta Lazzio, 4 March 2001, Phoenix.
4. Braun to Hobrecht, 13 November 1949.
5. Braun to Hobrecht, 8 December 1949.
6. Braun to Hobrecht, 7 March 1950.
7. Braun to Hobrecht, 25 May 1950.
8. Author interview with Father Provincial Finian McGinn, OFM, 25 May 1999, Mescalero, NM.
9. Hobrecht to Braun, 27 May 1950.
10. Braun to Hobrecht, 22 June 1950.
11. Hobrecht to Braun, 24 November 1949.
12. Braun to Witsell, 29 November 1949.
13. Gilday to Witsell, 6 January 1950.
14. Witsell to Braun, 26 January 1950.
15. Braun to Hobrecht, 25 May 1950.
16. Hobrecht to Braun, 27 May 1950.
17. Braun to Hobrecht, 29 May 1950.
18. Hobrecht to Braun, 7 June 1950.
19. Braun to Hobrecht, 22 June 1950.
20. *100 Years: The Franciscans and St. Mary's Basilica,* (privately published, Phoenix, n.d., ca. 1996), 22.
21. Braun to Hobrecht, 22 June 1950.
22. Braun to Hobrecht, August 1950.
23. Mackey interview.
24. Blaise Cronin, as recorded on tape at Friar Al's funeral mass, Saint Mary's, Phoenix, 9 March 1983.
25. Mackey interview.
26. Braun to Hobrecht, 2 January 1951.
27. Hobrecht to Braun, 12 January 1951.
28. Phoenix was then in the Diocese of Tucson, not to become a separate diocese until 1969.
29. Victor Bucher to Most Rev. Daniel J. Gercke, Bishop of Tucson, 29 March 1951; Braun to Maj. Gen. Alex M. Tuthill, Adj. Gen. Arizona National Guard, 2 April 1951.
30. Braun to Tuthill, 2 April 1951.
31. Arthur, *op. cit.,* 76.
32. Braun to Hon. Ernest W. McFarland, US Senator, 13 April 1951.
33. Braun to Temple, 14 May 1951.
34. Fr. Alanus McCoy, Prov. Sec. To Rmo. P. Augustino Sepinski, OFM, Ministero Generalis, 22 May 1951; Sepinski, 23 June 1951.
35. Braun, retreat notes.
36. Marsteller to author, 21 May 2003.
37. Marsteller, "Remembering the Workers of the Sacred Hearth, Three Franciscans, and some Jesuits," unpublished memoir, to author, February 2002.

38. Compiled from Marsteller, several undated mss.
39. Marsteller, "Remembering. . . ."
40. Marsteller, undated ms.
41. Marsteller, "Remembering. . . ."
42. Marsteller to author, 21 May 2003.
43. *Arizona Register,* June 1954.
44. Author interview with Alice Mahoney, 5 March 2001, Phoenix.
45. *Ibid.*
46. *Arizona Register,* 14 June 1951; Marsteller, "Remembering. . . ." and "Santa Rosa Center"; Fr. Felipe Baldonado to Jeanne de Lue, 23 May 1951.
47. Marsteller to author, undated letter.
48. As quoted in *The Way of Saint Francis,* November 1953.
49. *Ibid.*
50. Braun to de Lue, 22 November 1951.
51. Braun to de Lue, undated.
52. Braun to de Lue, 22 November 1951.
53. Emmett McLoughlan, *People's Padre: An Autobiography* (Boston: Beacon Press, 1954), 40–41; also quoted in *100 Years. . . .,* 50.

Chapter 21

1. Grant interview.
2. Pete R. Dimas, "Progress and a Mexican American Community's Struggle for Existence: Phoenix's Golden Gate Barrio," Ph.D. dissertation, Arizona State University, 1991, 97–99.
3. *100 Years,* 31–34.
4. Dimas, 114–15.
5. Marsteller, "Remembering. . . ."
6. Braun as quoted by Marsteller, to author.
7. Author review with Tony Valenzuela, 7 January 2001, Mescalero, NM.
8. McGinn interview.
9. Valenzuela interview.
10. Braun to Temple, 24 December 1952.
11. Braun to Temple, 11 January 1953.
12. Braun to Temple, 23 March 1953.
13. McGinn interview.
14. Braun to Temple, 6 May 1953.
15. Braun to Temple, 25 May 1953.
16. Temple to Braun, 31 May 1953.
17. Temple to Braun, 23 June 1953.
18. Braun to Temple, 14 May 1953.
19. Braun to Temple, 25 May 1953.
20. Braun to Temple, 22 June 1953.
21. Temple to Braun, 14 May 1955.

22. Braun to Temple, 27 September 1953.
23. Braun to Temple, 21 November 1953.
24. Pete Ávila as quoted in *Arizona Republic*, 10 March 1983.
25. Braun to Temple, 25 March 1954.
26. Braun to Temple, 5 May 1954.
27. Braun to Temple, 25 October 1954.
28. Temple to Braun, 27 October 1954.
29. Braun to Kennedy, 17 August 1966.
30. Braun to Temple, 20 December 1954.
31. Temple to Braun, 6 January 1955.
32. Braun to Temple, 28 January 1955.
33. Valenzuela interview.
34. Braun to Temple, 7 August 1958.
35. Braun to Temple, 10 January 1955.
36. Temple to Braun, 15 January 1955.
37. Braun to Temple, 28 January 1955.
38. Braun to Temple, 4 May 1955.
39. Pete Ávila as quoted by Richard Lessner, *Arizona Republic*, 10 March 1983.
40. Marsteller to author, 14 April 2004.
41. Braun to Temple, 3 May 1955.
42. Braun to Temple, 30 September 1955.
43. Temple to Braun, 22 October 1955.
44. Braun to Temple, 20 December 1955.
45. Valenzuela interview.
46. Mahoney interview.
47. Author interview with Ray Salazar, 7 January 2001, Mescalero, NM.
48. Author interview with Dimas and Abe Arvisu, Jr., 15 March 1999, Phoenix.
49. Kelly interview.
50. Braun to Temple, 6 January 1956.
51. Braun to Temple, 19 March 1956.
52. Mackey interview.
53. Blaise Cronin interview.
54. Mahoney interview.
55. Mackey interview.
56. Braun to Temple, 20 December 1955.
57. Braun to Temple, 6 January 1956.
58. Temple to Braun, 9 January 1956.
59. Braun to Temple, 15 March 1956.
60. Braun to Temple, 14 March 1956.
61. Braun to Temple, 16 May 1956.
62. Braun to Temple, 18 May 1956.
63. Braun to Temple, 22 May 1956.
64. *Ibid.*
65. Braun to Temple, 5 June 1956.

66. Braun to Temple, 22 May 1956.

67. *Ibid.*

68. Braun to Temple, 5 June 1956.

69. Braun to Temple, 14 June 1956.

70. Braun to Marsteller, 24 June 1973.

71. Braun to Temple, 22 May 1956.

72. Braun to Temple, 9 August 1956.

73. Guadalupe Herrera, as quoted in undated clipping from the *Arizona Republic.*

Chapter 22

1. Braun to Gercke, cited in Dimas 132.

2. Holy Ghost Fathers, Glenwood Springs, CO, to Kennedy. Signer's name withheld at his request.

3. Braun to Temple, 15 March 1956.

4. Temple to Braun, 5 April 1956.

5. Braun to Temple, 7 April 1956. Emphasis Father Albert's.

6. Braun to Temple, 24 April 1956.

7. Braun to Temple, 5 February 1957.

8. Braun to Temple, 2 April 1957.

9. Braun to Terence Cronin, 8 June 1957.

10. Braun to Terence Cronin, 9 August 1957.

11. Terence Cronin to Braun, 12 August 1957.

12. Braun to Terence Cronin, 9 August 1957.

13. Braun to Temple, 16 October 1957.

14. Temple to Braun, 24 April 1958.

15. Braun to Temple, 22 March 1958.

16. Dimas, 133.

17.Braun to Temple, 2 July 1958.

18. Braun to Temple, 31 July 1958.

19. *Ibid.*

20. Braun to Temple, 7 August 1958.

21. Braun to Temple, 10 September 1958.

22. Temple to Braun, 17 September 1958.

23. Braun to Temple, 18 November 1959.

24. "Necrology of the Province of Saint Barbara, Order of Friars Minor," Vol. I, 1967. SBA.

25. Braun to Temple, 25 March 1959.

26. Braun to Gercke, 13 August 1959.

27. Braun to Temple, 13 August 1959.

28. Braun to Gercke, 13 August 1959.

29. Temple to Braun, 18 August 1959.

30. Gercke to Braun, 20 August 1959.

31. On 13 September 1962 Sacred Heart Parish was officially designated.

32. Braun to Marsteller, 29 May 1974.
33. Mackey interview.
34. *Alamogordo Daily News*, 6 November 1959; *Ruidoso News*, 6 November 1959; *El Paso Times*, 8 November 1959; Program, American Legion Post #48; "Tribute to Father Al" written by Fr. Solanus Haugh, OFM, Pastor of Saint Joseph's and delivered by Virginia Klinekole, 11 November 1959; Newsletter, American Legion Post #48, November 1959.
35. Braun to Temple, 18 November 1959.
36. Temple to Braun, 25 November 1959.
37. Braun to Temple, 28 November 1959.
38. Valenzuela interview.
39. Hobrecht to Kennedy, 15 and 23 August 1966.

Chapter 23

1. Braun to Marsteller, 23 August 1966.
2. Hobrecht to Kennedy, 23 August 1966.
3. Provincial Records, Santa Barbara Province.
4. McGinn interview.
5. This and the following excerpts (unless otherwise noted) are taken from Father Albert's notebooks, recovered from his briefcase found in Saint Mary's Basilica in Phoenix and kindly lent the author by Blaise Cronin.
6. Arthur to author, 13 September 1999.
7. Braun, undated letter, presumably to his provincial.
8. Braun to Fuad Ganem, 24 July 1964.
9. Braun to Marsteller, 30 October 1964.
10. Braun to Marsteller, December 1964.
11. Braun to Marsteller, 30 October 1964.
12. Mackey interview.
13. Braun to Marsteller, 1 January 1965.
14. Governor Paul Fannin to Braun, 31 December 1964, with enclosed certificate, 30 December 1964.
15. Marsteller et al. to author.
16. State of Arizona, House of Representatives, 27th Legislature, Second Special Session, House Joint Resolution 1. Passed in House 2 June, in Senate 4 June, signed by the Governor 8 June 1965. Father Ramón L. Varela, OFM, to Kennedy, 17 August 1966.
17. As quoted by Vitale in *The Franciscan* newsletter of Saint Louis Province of the Sacred Heart, 21 March 1983, signed by Sec. Jagfeld.
18. Bumgarner interview.
19. Author interview with Mike Brown, 23 June 2000, El Paso.
20. Bumgarner interview.
21. Ray Brown tape.
22. Ullom interview.

23. De Kleven interview.
24. Braun to Marsteller, 21 October 1965.
25. Braun to Marsteller, 16 February 1966.
26. Braun to Marsteller, 20 February 1966.
27. Braun to Marsteller, 12 March 1966, with appended notes from Katherine and Charles Mackey.
28. Braun to Marsteller, 16 April 1966.
29. Bumgarner interview.
30. Jack Aldrich to author.
31. American Ex-Prisoners of War, Inc. to Braun, 20 July 1967.
32. Hobrecht to Kennedy, 15 and 23 August 1966.
33. Braun to Marsteller, 25 February 1967.
34. *Ibid.*
35. Braun to Marsteller, 20 March 1967.
36. Braun to Bishop Francis Green, undated.
37. Braun to Marsteller, 20 May 1967.
38. Braun to Marsteller, 18 June 1967.
39. Braun to Marsteller, 22 July 1967.
40. Ray Brown tape.
41. Braun to Marsteller, 6 September 1967.
42. Braun to Eugene Henrion III, 26 December 1967.
43. Braun to Marsteller, 16 July 1968.
44. Braun to Marsteller, 26 July 1968.
45. Braun to Marsteller, 18 August 1968.
46. Braun to Marsteller, 23 August 1968.
47. Braun to Marsteller, 9 January 1969.
48. Braun to Mother Mary Anthony, Sacred Heart Nursing Home, Phoenix, 26 March 1969.
49. Blaise Cronin interview.

Chapter 24

1. Braun to Albert Dawson, 6 August 1969.
2. Braun to Dawsons, 14 January 1970.
3. Sister Mary Margaret Walsh, "Poem for Father Albert on His Eightieth Birthday, September 5, 1969: from your Little Sisters and residents," Sacred Heart Nursing Home.
4. Braun to Dawsons, 22 August 1969.
5. Braun to Marsteller, 7 October 1969.
6. Mahoney interview.
7. Braun to Albert Dawson, 6 August 1969.
8. Ray Dawson to Braun, 16 October 1969.
9. Braun to Dawsons, 20 October 1969.
10. Braun to Albert Dawson, 2 April 1970.

11. Braun as quoted by Betty Beard in *Arizona Republic*, 5 August 1996.
12. Braun to Marsteller, 13 January 1970.
13. Braun to Dan Bumgarner, 29 January 1970.
14. Braun to Dan Bumgarner, 28 January 1970.
15. Ray Brown tape.
16. Braun to Boyd, 11 March 1970.
17. Braun to Boyd, 4 December 1970.
18. Braun to Fr. Prov. Alan McCoy, OFM, 28 April 1972.
19. Braun to Albert Dawson, 2 April 1970.
20. Blaise Cronin interview.
21. Braun to Marsteller, 6 August 1970.
22. Braun to Dawsons, 28 May 1970.
23. Braun to Marsteller, 30 April 1970.
24. Braun to McCoy, 8 August 1970.
25. Braun to McCoy, 12 November 1970.
26. Braun to Boyd, 14 November 1970.
27. Braun to Boyd, 4 December 1970.
28. Braun to Albert Dawson, 6 January 1971.
29. As told by someone identified only as 'Donna' to Marsteller, taped 28 October 1973.
30. Braun to Boyd, 18 January 1971.
31. Braun to Boyd, 14 February 1971.
32. Braun to Marsteller, 17 April 1971.
33. Braun to Bruce and Virginia Klinekole, 15 April 1971.
34. Braun to Bumgarners, August 1971.
35. Braun to Marsteller, 5 July 1971.
36. *Ibid.*
37. Blaise Cronin at Braun's funeral mass, Saint Mary's, Phoenix, 9 March 1983. Tape recording, Saint Mary's Basilica.
38. Braun to Eugene and Celine Henrion, 2 October 1973.
39. Braun to Boyd, 15 December 1971.
40. Braun to Dawsons, undated, probably December 1971.
41. Braun to Mother Mary Anthony, 4 March 1972.
42. Braun to Dawsons, 27 June 1980.
43. Braun to Dawsons, 25 May 1972.
44. Braun to Dawsons, 21 September 1974.
45. Braun to Mother Mary Anthony, 23 April 1972.
46. Braun to McCoy, 28 April 1972.
47. Braun to Boyd, 6 August 1972.
48. Braun to McCoy, 28 April 1972.
49. McCoy to Braun, 6 May 1972.
50. Larry Merchant, Pres. Kachina Productions, to Virginia Klinekole, 17 October 1972.
51. Merchant to Klinekole, 14 November 1972.

52. Boyd to Most Rev. Edward McCarthy, National Committee on Human Development, 8 March 1973.
53. Jerry Burns, Dir. Communications, Diocese of Phoenix, to Boyd, 16 March 1973.
54. Braun to Dawsons, 3 April 1973.
55. Braun to Marsteller, 5 July 1972.
56. Braun to Dawsons, 5 September 1972.
57. Braun to Eugene and Celine Henrion, 19 September 1973.
58. The letters OFM stand for Order of Friars Minor, the official name of the Franciscan order.
59. Braun remarks as taped by Marsteller, 28 October 1973.
60. Braun to Dawsons, 16 September 1973.
61. Blaise Cronin interview.
62. Braun to McCoy, 4 October 1974.
63. Braun to Ruth Jette Johnson, 14 February 1976.
64. Braun to Dawsons, 28 May 1977.
65. Braun to Dawsons, 18 June 1972.
66. Braun to Dawsons, 11 January 1977.
67. Braun to Boyd, 6 August 1972.
68. Author interview with Fr. Kieran McCarty, OFM, 13 October 1999, Old Mission Santa Barbara.
69. Braun to Eugene Henrion II, 25 July 1974.
70. Braun to Juan Baldonado, 21 July 1976.
71. Braun to Dawsons, 20 January 1973.
72. Braun to Dawsons, 6 April 1977.
73. Braun to Dawsons, 21 September 1974.
74. Braun to Marsteller, 29 May 1974.
75. Braun to McCoy, 25 June 1975.
76. Braun to Eugene Henrion II, 20 June 1974.
77. Braun to Dawsons, 9 and 23 January 1975.
78. Braun to Dawsons, 6 May 1975.
79. Braun to McCoy, 9 July 1975.
80. Braun to Ray Brown, 30 August 1975.
81. *Ibid.*
82. Gomez interview.
83. Braun to Dawsons, 11 January 1977.
84. Blaise Cronin interview.
85. Braun to Dawsons, 11 January 1977.
86. Braun to Fr. Prov. John Vaughn, OFM, August 1977.
87. Arizona DAV presentation, 3 May 1979.
88. *Phoenix Gazette*, 3 May 1979.
89. Blaise Cronin, undated draft of letter to Father Albert's friends, post-Christmas 1979.
90. Mother Mary Anthony to Vitale, 19 May 1980.
91. Braun to Blaise Cronin, 21 October 1983.

92. Blaise Cronin interview.

93. Mother Mary Anthony to Vitale, 19 May 1980.

94. Vitale to Mother Mary Anthony, 28 May 1980.

95. Mother Mary Anthony to Vitale, 6 June 1980.

96. Vitale to Braun, 28 May 1980.

97. Braun to Mother Mary Anthony, 6 June 1980.

98. Blaise Cronin interview.

99. *Ibid.*

100. Blaise Cronin to friends of Father Al, 11 September 1980.

101. Braun to Temple, 20 November 1981.

102. Mackey interview.

103. Blaise Cronin interview.

104. Blaise Cronin to friends of Fr. Al, 26 November 1980.

105. Braun, Christmas message, 1980.

106. President Ronald Reagan to Braun, 5 September, no year given, probably 1981. SBA.

107. Braun to Blaise Cronin, 10 February 1982.

108. Braun to Blaise Cronin, 27 March 1972.

109. Bumgarner interview.

110. Gov. Bruce Babbitt, Commander-in-Chief Arizona State Militia, to Braun, 2 June 1982.

111. President Ronald Reagan to Braun, 8 October 1982. SBA.

112. Braun, Christmas greetings, 1982.

Chapter 25

1. Dick Mackey, funeral eulogy, 9 March 1983, Phoenix. Tape.

2. Blaise Cronin interview.

3. Vitale, "A Legend in His Time," *op. cit.*

4. Blaise Cronin, at funeral mass, 9 March 1983, Phoenix. Tape.

5. Vitale, *op. cit.*

6. Descriptions of burial ceremony from Gleichauf, *op. cit.*; *VFW Magazine*, January 1944; *Alamogordo Daily News*, 11 March 1983; *El Paso Times*, 12 or 13 March 1983; Order of Service, burial mass.

7. Charles James, Bataan veteran, to author.

8. Marie Dupuy Russell to Blaise Cronin, 21 March 1983.

9. Vitale, *op. cit.*

10. Marsteller to author, undated letter.

11. Dick Mackey to Marsteller, 10 June 2001.

Epilogue

1. Bishop Thomas O'Brien, on the occasion of Pope John Paul II's visit to Saint Mary's Basilica in Phoenix, 14 September 1987.

2. Dimas dissertation.

3. Mahoney interview.

4. Braun-Sacred Heart Center, undated brochure.

5. David Schwartz, in *Arizona Republic*, 25 December 1991.

6. Phoenix City Council Report, Denny R. Maus, Community and Economic Development Director, 28 May 1992.

7. The pictures are not signed. "Henry never seemed to sign his work," his wife wrote. He had, she continued, "lived a very interesting life. He speaks fluent German and Spanish and can translate Latin and French. In 1938–40, Henry lived in Mexico City and was Leon Trotsky's bodyguard," after which he saw combat duty in Europe during World War II. "He became interested in St. Joseph's through author Eve Ball, to whom he sent clothing to be distributed on the reservation." Mrs. Henry Schnautz to Mary Serna, 13 July 2003.

8. Press release, Saint Joseph's Apache Mission, April 1999.

9. Schola Cantorum of Saint Francis Cathedral, Santa Fe, press release, November 1998.

10. Mescalero *Burden Basket*, Vol. 1, Issue 3, May 2003.

EPILOGUE

11. Shortly before this volume want to press, Brother Peter Boegel was transferred to Saint Elizabeth's Friary, Oakland, California, though like Father Al, he continues to visit Mescalero as his schedule allows.

REFERENCE LIST

ABBREVIATIONS:

BCIM: Bureau of Catholic Indian Missions
GPO: Government Printing Office
MUA: Marquette University Archives
NA: National Archives
OFM: Order of Friars Minor (Franciscan Order)
SBA: Archives, Old Mission Santa Barbara
SJAM   Saint Joseph's Apache Mission

ARCHIVAL SOURCES:

Mescalero, New Mexico. SJAM. Records.
Milwaukee, Wisconsin. Marquette University. Raynor Memorial Libraries. Department of Special Collections and University Archives, Marquette University Libraries. Archives, BCIM. Correspondence. Microfilm 1913 through 1947.
San Luis Rey, California. San Luis Rey Mission. House Chronicles 1890–1949. Vol. 1.
Santa Barbara, California. SBA. Archives, OFM Province of Santa Barbara. Provincial Annals. Correspondence. Records.
Tularosa, New Mexico. St. Francis de Paolo. Records.
Washington, DC. NA.

UNPUBLISHED MEMOIRS, MANUSCRIPTS, TAPE RECORDINGS:

Baumann, Father Herbert. Recollections. SBA.
Braun, Father Albert, OFM. Autobiographical synopsis. Undated, ca. 1967. SBA.
_____. "The Catholic Outing System." Undated report, ca. 1946. SBA.
_____. Notes for Retreats. Undated. Saint Mary's Basilica, Phoenix.
Brown, Ray. Tape recording. Memories of Father Albert Braun. Recorded November 2001–February 2002. Logan, Utah.
Cronin, Father Blaise, OFM. Tape recordings:
    Father Blaise Cronin and Father Albert Braun, 11 August 1982. Phoenix.
    Funeral Mass for Father Albert Braun, 9 March 1983. Phoenix.
    Rosary for Father Albert Braun, 8 March 1983. Phoenix.
Dimas, Pete R. "Progress and a Mexican-American Community's Struggle for Existence: Phoenix's Golden Gate Barrio." Ph.D. dissertation, Arizona State University, 1991.

Haugh, Father Solanus, OFM. "Tribute to Father Al." Delivered by Virginia Klinekole 11 November 1959. Recorded in program of Jubilee Service. SBA.

Hobrecht, Father Augustine, OFM. Recollections of Father Albert Braun, OFM, to Father Pacificus Kennedy, OFM, 15 and 23 August 1966. SBA.

Leyva, Jerry. "Descendents of José Augustine de Leyba." Copy in author's collection.

Marsteller, Jeanne de Lue.

"Remembering the Workers of the Sacred Heart, Three Franciscans, and Some Jesuits." February 2002.

"Santa Rosa Center." Undated.

Tape recordings:

Father Albert Braun, OFM, conversation, 4 October 1973, Tucson.

Father Albert Braun, taped at book signing, 28 October 1973, Casa de Paz y Bien, Scottsdale, Arizona.

"Necrology of the Province of Saint Barbara, Order of Friars Minor." Vol. 1. SBA.

Russell, Cecil. Memoir. Undated. Excerpt regarding Father Albert Braun, OFM, sent to author 20 November 2001.

Vitale, Father Provincial Louis, OFM. "A Legend in His Time." Provincial Newsletter, March 1983.

OFFICIAL DOCUMENTS:

Braun, Albert, OFM, Lieutenant Colonel USA. "Affidavit for Investigation of Incidents between 20 September 1944 and 29 August 1945, Occurring at Camp Omori, A Suburb of Tokyo, at Fort Shafter, Honolulu, 6 July 1948 for War Crimes Tribunal."

Records of American Expeditionary Force: World War I. NARA II, RG 120. Box 16. Entry 1241. File Folder 5th Div. Gen. Orders, 1919. Case 17, Drawer 3. NA.

State of Arizona. House of Representatives. 27th Legislature. Second Special Session. House Joint Resolution 1. 8 June 1965.

United States Congress. Joint Committee on the Investigation of the Pearl Harbor Attack. Hearings Before the Joint Committee on the Investigation of the Pearl Harbor Attack. 79th Cong. 2nd Session. Washington, DC: GPO, 1946.

United States Congress. Senate Committee on the Judiciary. Internal Security Subcommittee. Institute of Pacific Relations Hearings. 82nd Cong. 1st Session. 15 Pts. Washington, DC: GPO, 1952.

United States Dept. of State. Papers Relating to the Foreign Relations of the United States. Washington, DC: GPO, 1943.

United States Dept. of State. Peace and War: United States Foreign Policy 1931–1941. Vol. II, Doc. 245. Washington, DC: GPO, 1943.

United States v. Albert B. Fall. Supreme Court of District of Columbia. Criminal Case No. 42304. (October 1929). NA.

War of the Rebellion: A Compilation of the Official Records of the Union and Confederate Armies. Series I. Vol. 4. Washington, DC: GPO.

LETTERS:

Institutional Collections:
  BCIM, 1922–1928.
  MUA.
  SBA. 1915–1983. The bulk of Father Albert's (exclusive of personal letters) is housed here.
Personal Collections.
  Boyd, Barbara Leyva. March 1970–July 1973.
  Dawson, Elisa Baldonado. October 1940–July 1982.
  Henrion, Eugene III. April 1921–January 1976.
  Jette, Vida Blazer and Ruth Jette Johnson. Courtesy of Sister Nancy Johnson. December 1969–October 1976.
  Marsteller, Jeanne de Lue. November 1951–October 1976.
  Morette, John J., Capt. to Mrs. Frederick B. Howden, 11 December 1944. Courtesy of Alfred Howden.
  Stanton, William C. June 1920–December 1933. SBA.

INTERVIEWS:

Arthur, Bro. Timothy, OFM. 13 September 1999. SBA, Santa Barbara, California.
Arvisu, Abe. 15 March 1999. Phoenix.
Bigrope, Ellyn. 1 March 1999. Mescalero, New Mexico.
Boetto, Marquita Hill. 16 September 2000. El Paso, Texas.
Brown, Mike. 23 June 2000. El Paso, Texas.
Bumgarner, Dorothy Brown and Jess. 12 September 1999. Lancaster, California.
Bumgarner, Craig. Telephone conversation. 1999.
Cronin, Father Blaise, OFM. 15 March 1999. Phoenix.
Dawson, Elisa Baldonado. 6 October 2002. Albuquerque.
De Kleven, Concha Ortiz y Pino. April 1999. Albuquerque.
Diaz, Ralph. 25 June 2002. Mescalero, New Mexico.
Dimas, Pete R., 15 March 1999. Phoenix.
Foy, Thomas. 13 June 1999. Bayard, New Mexico.
Gomez, Mary Dorame. 20 July 2000. Tularosa, New Mexico.
Grant, Bro. Joachim, OFM. 14 September 1999. SBA, Santa Barbara, California.
Holley, Father Walter, OFM. 16 March 1999. Phoenix.
Kelly, Father Maurus, OFM. 14 September 1999. SBA, Santa Barbara, California.
Klinekole, Virginia Shanta. 3 May 1999. Three Rivers Ranch, Mescalero Reservation, New Mexico.
Kruse, Patricia Leyba. 29 October 2002. Mescalero, New Mexico.
Lazzio, Sister Mary Roqueta. 4 March 2001. Phoenix.
Lundy, Josephine Brown. 7 June 2001. Mescalero, New Mexico.
Mackey, Richard and Sue. 5 March 2001. Phoenix.
Mahoney, Alice. 5 March 2001. Phoenix.

Marsteller, Jeanne de Lue. 6 March 2001. Tucson.
McCarty, Father Kieran, OFM. 14 September 1999. SBA, Santa Barbara, California.
McGinn, Father Provincial Finian, OFM. 25 May 1999. Mescalero, New Mexico.
Mold, Peter. 19 May 1999. Mescalero, New Mexico.
Ortega, Paul. 15 January 2002. Mescalero, New Mexico.
Salazar, Ray. 7 January 2001. Mescalero, New Mexico.
Silva, Agapito. 12 June 1999. Silver City, New Mexico.
Suttman, Al. 12 June 1999. Silver City, New Mexico.
Tortilla, Reginald. 9 October 2001. Mescalero, New Mexico.
Ullom, Madeline. 6 March 2001. Tucson.
Valenzuela, Marco 'Tony.' 7 January 2001. Mescalero, New Mexico.

SELECTED PUBLISHED MATERIAL:

BOOKS

Arthur, Bro. Timothy, OFM. *Santa Barbara Fioretti: Stories from the Friary.* Santa
    Barbara, California: GEC Research Press, 1992.
Ashton, Paul. *Bataan Diary.* Privately printed, 1984.
Ball, Eve, with Nora Henn and Lynda A. Sánchez. *Indeh: An Apache Odyssey.* University
    of Oklahoma Press, 1988.
_____. *Ruidoso: The Last Frontier.* San Antonio, Texas: The Naylor Co., 1963.
Bandelier, F. A. and Fanny R. *Historical Documents Relating to New Mexico, Nueva
    Viscaya, and Approaches Thereto to 1773.* Edited by Charles William Hackett, Vol. 3.
    Washington, DC: The Carnegie Institution, 1923.
Bannon, John Francis. *The Spanish Borderlands Frontier 1513–1821.* New York: Holt,
    Rinehart and Winston, 1970.
Belote, James H. and William M. *Corregidor: The Stirring Saga of a Mighty Fortress.* New
    York: Harper & Row, 1976.
Bender, Averam B. *A Study of Mescalero Apache Indians, 1846–1880.* Prepared for the
    US Department of Justice, 1960. The Expert Testimony Before the Indian Claims
    Commission. New York: Clearwater Publishing Company. Reprint New York:
    Garland Publishing Company, 1974.
Blazer, Almer N. *Santana: War Chief of the Mescalero Apache.* Edited by A. R. Pruit. Taos,
    New Mexico: Dog Soldier Press, 1999.
Bolton, Herbert E. *Coronado: Knight of Pueblos and Plains.* Albuquerque: University of
    New Mexico Press, 1949, 1971.
_____. *Fray Juan Crespi, Missionary Explorer.* Berkeley, California, 1927.
_____. *Padre on Horseback.* San Francisco, 1932. Reprinted Chicago, 1963.
_____. *Rim of Christendom: A Biography of Eusebio Francisco Kino, Pacific Coast Pioneer.*
    New York: MacMillan, 1936. New York: Russell & Russell, 1960.
_____. *The Spanish Borderlands: A Chronicle of Old Florida and the Southwest.* New
    Haven: Yale University Press, 1921, 1948. Albuquerque: University of New Mexico
    Press, 1996.

_____. *Spanish Exploration in the Southwest*, 1542–1706. New York: 1916.

Brown, Jonathan C. *Oil and Revolution in Mexico*. Berkeley: University of California Press, 1993.

Bunson, Margaret and Stephen. *Faith in the Wilderness: The Story of the Catholic Indian Missions*. Huntington, Indiana. Our Sunday Visitor Pub. Div., 2000.

Candelaria, Antonio Serna. *The Valley of Peace*. Privately printed. No date.

Carr, Barry. *Marxism and Communism in Twentieth Century Mexico*. Lincoln: University of Nebraska Press, 1992.

Cave, Dorothy. *Beyond Courage: One Regiment Against Japan, 1941–1945*. Las Cruces, New Mexico: Yucca Tree Press, 1992, 1996; 3rd Revised Edition, Santa Fe: Sunstone Press, 2006.

Chapman, Charles E. *The Founding of Spanish California: The Northwestward Expansion of New Spain, 1687–1783*. New York: 1916.

Chavez, Fra. Angelico, OFM. *Coronado's Friars*. Washington, DC: Academy of American Franciscan History, 1968.

Churchill, Winston S. *The Second World War*. Vol. 3: *The Grand Alliance*. Houghton Mifflin, 1950, 1951, 1953.

_____. *The World Crisis: 1911–1918*. New York: Free Press, 2005, revised from 1931 edition.

Colton, Ray C. *The Civil War in the Western Territories: Arizona, Colorado, New Mexico, and Utah*. Norman: University of Oklahoma Press, 1959, 1984, 1985.

Cremony, John C. *Life Among the Apaches, 1850–1868*. San Francisco: A. Roman & Co., 1868. Reprint Glorieta, New Mexico: Rio Grande Press, 1969.

Cummings, Billy Charles Patrick. *Frontier Parish: Recovered Catholic History of Lincoln County, 1860–1884*. Lincoln County, New Mexico: Lincoln County Historical Society Publication No. 4, 1995.

Curry, George. *George Curry, 1861–1947: An Autobiography*. Edited by H. B. Hening. Albuquerque: University of New Mexico Press, 1958.

Dawes, Gavan. *Prisoners of the Japanese: POWs of World War II in the Pacific*. New York: William Morrow & Co., 1994.

Domínguez, Fray Francisco Atanasia. *The Missions of New Mexico, 1776*. Translated and edited by Eleanor B. Adams. Albuquerque: University of New Mexico Press, 1956.

Emerson, Dorothy. *Among the Mescalero Apaches: The Story of Father Albert Braun, O.F.M.* Tucson: University of Arizona Press, 1973.

Englehardt, Father Zephyrin, OFM. *The Missions and Missionaries of California*. Vol. 2: *Upper California*. 2nd Revised Edition. Santa Barbara: Old Mission Santa Barbara, 1930.

Estergreen, M. Morgan. *Kit Carson: A Portrait in Courage*. Norman: University of Oklahoma Press, 1962.

Flanagan, General E. M., Jr. *Corregidor: The Rock Force Assault*. Novato, California: Presidio Press, 1988.

Fulton, Maurice G. *Lincoln County War*. Edited by Robert N. Mullin. Tucson: University of Arizona Press, 1968.

Geiger, Maynard J. *The Life and Times of Junípero Serra, O.F.M.: The Man Who Never*

Turned Back, 1713–1784. Washington, DC: Academy of American Franciscan History, 1959.

Gilbert, Beth. *Alamogordo: The Territorial Years, 1898–1912.* Albuquerque: Starline Printing, 1988.

Gonzales, Michael J. *The Mexican Revolution, 1910–1940.* Albuquerque: University of New Mexico Press, 2002.

Gonzales, Luis. *San José de Gracia: Mexican Village in Transition.* Translated by John Upton. Austin: University of Texas Press, 1994.

Granjon, Henry, Bishop of Tucson. *Along the Rio Grande.* 1903. Reprint Albuquerque: University of New Mexico Press, 1968.

Grew, Joseph C. *Ten Years in Japan: A Contemporary Record Drawn from the Diaries and Private and Official Papers of Joseph C. Grew, United States Ambassador to Japan, 1932–1942.* New York: Simon & Schuster, 1944.

_____. *The Turbulent Era: A Diplomatic Record of Forty Years, 1905–1945.* Boston: Riverside Press, 1952.

Haley, James L. *Apaches: A History and Cultural Portrait.* Norman: University of Oklahoma Press, 1997.

Hewlett, Richard and Francis Duncan. *A History of the United States Atomic Energy Commission.* Vol. 2: *Atomic Shield, 1947–1952.* University Post and London: Pennsylvania State University, 1969.

Horgan, Paul. *Great River: The Rio Grande in North America.* 2 Vol. New York: Rinehart & Company, 1954.

Hull, Cordell. *Memoirs of Cordell Hull.* New York: MacMillan, 1948.

Hunt, Frazier. *MacArthur and the War Against Japan.* New York: Scribner, 1944.

Hunter, Kenneth E. *The War Against Japan.* Washington, DC: Office of the Chief of Military History. Department of the Army, 1952.

Ind, Allison. *Bataan: The Judgment Seat.* New York: MacMillan 1944.

Jackson, Colonel Calvin D., MD. *Diary: Kept during World War II, 1941–1945.* Ada, Ohio: Ohio Northern University, 1992.

James, D. Clayton. *The Years of MacArthur.* 3 Vols. Boston: Houghton Mifflin, 1970– 1985.

Jimbo, Colonel Nobuhiko. *Dawn of the Philippines.* Privately printed. No date.

Jolly, John Pershing, Adjutant-General New Mexico. *History of the New Mexico National Guard, 1606–1963.* New Mexico National Guard, 1964.

Katz, Friedrich. *The Secret War in Mexico: Europe, the United States, and the Mexican Revolution.* Chicago: University of Chicago Press, 1981.

Keleher, William A. *The Fabulous Frontier.* Albuquerque: University of New Mexico Press, 1962.

_____. *Turmoil in New Mexico, 1846–1868.* Albuquerque: University of New Mexico Press, 1952, 1982.

Kelley, Francis Clement. *Blood-Drenched Altars: Mexican Study and Comment, with Documentation and Notes by Eber Cole Byam.* Milwaukee: Bruce Publishing Company, 1935.

Kerr, E. Bartlett. *Surrender and Survival: The Experience of American POWs in the Pacific,*

1941–1945. New York: William Morrow & Company, 1985.

Kessell, John L. *Kiva, Cross, and Crown: The Pecos Indians and New Mexico, 1540–1840*. Albuquerque: University of New Mexico Press, 2nd ed., 1987.

Knight, Alan. *The Mexican Revolution, 1910–1920*, 2 Vols. Cambridge: Cambridge University Press, 1986.

Knowlton, Robert J. *Church Property and the Mexican Reform, 1856–1910*. DeKalb: Northern Illinois University Press, 1976.

Krauze, Enrique. *Mexico: Biography of Power: A History of Modern Mexico, 1810–1996*. Translated by Hank Heifetz. New York: Harper Collins, 1997.

Lawton, Manny. *Some Survived: An Epic Account of Japanese Activity During World War II*. Chapel Hill, North Carolina: Algonquin Books of Chapel Hill, 1984.

Layton, Rear Admiral Edwin T., USN Retired. *And I Was There*. New York: William Morrow, 1985.

Leahy, William D. *I Was There: The Personal Story of the Chief of Staff to Presidents Roosevelt and Truman, Based on His Notes and Diaries Made at the Time*. New York: Whittlesey House, 1950.

Lee, Bruce. *Marching Orders: The Untold History of World War II*. New York: Crown Publishers, Inc., 1995.

Lilienthal, David E. *The Journals of David Lilienthal*, Vol. 2, *The Atomic Energy Years*. New York: Harper & Row, 1964.

Lockwood, Frank C. *The Apache Indians*. New York: MacMillan Co., 1938. Reprint, Lincoln: University of Nebraska Press, 1990.

MacArthur, Douglas. *Reports of General MacArthur*. 5 Vols. in 4 Parts. Prepared by his General Staff. Edited by Charles A. Willoughby. Department of the Army. Washington, DC: GPO, 1966.

Mallonee, Richard C. *The Naked Flagpole*. San Rafael, California: Rafael Presidio Press, 1980.

Manchester, William. *American Caesar: Douglas MacArthur, 1980–1964*. Boston: Little, Brown & Company, 1983. Reprint by Dell Publishing, 1978.

Marshall, S. L. A. *World War I*. New York: American Heritage Press, 1985.

McGee, John H. *Rice and Salt: A History of the Defense and Occupation of Mindanao During World War II*. San Antonio, Texas: Naylor Company, 1962.

McLoughlan, Emmett. *People's Padre: An Autobiography*. Boston: Beacon Press, 1954.

Melzer, Richard. *Coming of Age in the Great Depression: The Civilian Conservation Corps in New Mexico, 1933–1942*. Las Cruces, New Mexico: Yucca Tree Press, 2000.

Meyer, Jean A. *The Cristero Rebellion: The Mexican People Between Church and State, 1926–1929*. Translated by Richard Southern. Cambridge University Press, 1976. (Translation and Revision of the French edition published 1975 under title *La Christiade*.)

Miller, Darlis A. *The California Column in New Mexico*. Albuquerque: University of New Mexico Press, 1982.

Moorman, John. *A History of the Franciscan Order: From the Origins to the Year 1517*. Chicago: Franciscan Herald Press, 1988.

Morris, Eric. *Corregidor: The End of the Line*. New York: Stein and Day, 1981.

Morison, Samuel Eliot. *The Rising Sun in the Pacific, 1931–April 1942*. Vol. 3 of the series *History of United States Naval Operations in World War II*. Boston: Little, Brown & Company, 1948.

Morton, Louis. *United States Army in World War II: The War in the Pacific: The Fall of the Philippines*. Office of the Chief of Military History. Department of the Army. Washington, DC: GPO, 1953.

Noggle, Burl. *Teapot Dome: Oil and Politics in the 1920s*. Baton Rouge: Louisiana State University Press, 1962.

Olson, John E. *O'Donnell: Andersonville of the Pacific*. Privately printed. 1985.

100 Years: The Franciscans and St. Mary's Basilica. Privately printed. No date.

Owen, Gordon R. *The Two Alberts: Fountain and Fall*. Las Cruces, New Mexico: Yucca Tree Press, 1996.

Quezon, Manuel. *The Good Fight*. New York: Appleton, 1946.

Reich, Peter Lester. *Mexico's Hidden Revolution: The Catholic Church in Law and Politics Since 1929*. New York and London: University of Notre Dame Press, 1995.

Rhodes, Richard. *Dark Sun: The Making of the Hydrogen Bomb*. New York: Simon & Schuster, 1955.

Robinson, Sherry. *Apache Voices: Their Stories of Survival as Told to Eve Ball*. Albuquerque: University of New Mexico Press, 2000.

Romolo, Carlos P. *I Saw the Fall of the Philippines*. Garden City, New York: Doubleday, Doran, 1943.

Royer, F. *Padre Pro*. New York: P. J. Kennedy & Sons, 1954.

Ryan, John P. *Fort Stanton and its Community, 1855–1896*. Las Cruces, New Mexico: Yucca Tree Press, 1998.

Sandoval, R. Jack. *History of St. Francis de Paola Church, 1862–1983*. Tularosa, New Mexico: St. Francis de Paola Church, 1983.

Scholes, France V. *Troublous Times in New Mexico, 1659–1670*. Albuquerque: University of New Mexico Press, 1942.

Schultz, Duane. *Hero of Bataan: The Story of General Jonathan M. Wainwright*. New York: St. Martin's Press, 1981.

Short, William J., OFM. *The Franciscans*. Religious Order Series, Vol. 2. Collegeville, Minnesota: 1990.

Simmons, Marc. *The Last Conquistador: Juan de Oñate and the Settling of the Far Southwest*. Norman: University of Oklahoma Press, 1991.

Sonnichsen, C. L. *The Mescalero Apaches*. Norman: University of Oklahoma Press, 1958, 1973.

_____. *Tularosa: Last of the Frontier West*. New York: Devin-Adair, 1960; reprint University of New Mexico Press, 1980.

Stokes, Bernard H. *The Franciscan Province of Saint Barbara, 1915–1965*. Serra Press, 1965.

Stout, Joseph A., Jr. *Border Conflict: Villistas, Carrancistas, and the Punitive Expedition, 1915–1920*. Texas Christian University Press, 1999.

Stratton, David H. *The Memoirs of Albert Bacon Fall*. Southwestern Studies, Vol. 4, No. 3. El Paso: Texas Western Press, 1966.

_____. *Tempest Over Teapot Dome: The Story of Albert B. Fall*. Norman: University of Oklahoma Press, 1998.

Sulzberger, C. L. *World War II*. New York: American Heritage, 1985. Distributed by Houghton Mifflin.

Taylor, Vince. *Cabanatuan: Japanese Death Camp*. Waco, Texas: Texian Press, 1987.

Thomas, Alfred B. *The Mescalero Apache, 1853–1874*. New York: Garland Publishing Company, 1974.

Toland, John. *But Not in Shame*. New York: Random House, 1961.

_____. *Infamy: Pearl Harbor and its Aftermath*. New York: Doubleday & Company, 1983.

_____. *The Rising Sun: The Decline and Fall of the Japanese Empire, 1936–1945*. New York: Random House, 1970.

Truman, Harry S. *Memoirs*, Vol. 2: *Years of Trial and Hope*. Garden City, New York: Doubleday & Company, 1956.

Uttley, Robert M. *Frontiersmen in Blue: The United States and the Indian, 1848–1865*. Lincoln: University of Nebraska Press, 1967, 1981.

Wainwright, Jonathan. *General Wainwright's Story: The Account of Four Years of Humiliating Defeat, Surrender, and Captivity*. Edited by Robert Considine. Garden City, New York: Doubleday, Doran, 1946.

Watson, Mark Skinner. *Prewar Plans and Preparation, United States Army in World War II*. Office of the Chief of Staff. Washington, DC: GPO, 1943.

Weinstein, Alfred A. *Barbed Wire Surgeon*. New York: MacMillan Company, 1947.

Williams, Denny. *To the Angels*. Presidio of San Francisco, California: Denson Press, 1985.

Wright, John M., Jr. *Captured on Corregidor: Diary of an American P. O. W. in World War II*. Jefferson, North Carolina: McFarland & Company, 1988.

ARTICLES

Ball, Eve. "Father Braun to Observe Golden Jubilee August 15." *El Paso Times*, 8 August 1965.

Beard, Betty. "Long Standing Memory." *Arizona Republic,* 5 August 1995.

Bolton, Herbert Eugene. "The Mission as a Frontier Institution in the Spanish American Colonies." *American Historical Review*. Vol. 23, No. 4 (October 1917).

Braun, Father Albert, OFM. "The Baptism of 'Kisspus.'" *The Indian Sentinel*. Vol. 1, No. 13 (July 1919).

_____. "Building as the Old Padres Built." *The Indian Sentinel*. Fall 1927.

_____. "War Time Chaplain Winning Apache." *The Indian Sentinel*. Winter 1929–30.

Bucher, Father Marcian, OFM. "A Priest to All God's Family." *Homiletic and Pastoral Review*. November 1984.

_____. "I Come to Mescalero." *The Indian Sentinel*, November 1945.

Burke, Janet. "Father Albert: Love with a Little Salt." *Alive*, March 1972.

Davis, Ann Pence. "Apache Debs." *New Mexico* Magazine. Vol. 15 (April 1937).

Geiger, Maynard J., OFM. "The Arrival of the Franciscans in the Californias, 1768–

1769." *The Americas*, Vol. 8 (October 1951).

_____. "Santa Barbara Through the Years. The Settlement of Santa Barbara: The Founding of the Presidio in 1782." *Provincial Annals* 6 (October 1944).

Gleichauf, Justin. "The Hero Priest of Corregidor." *VFW* Magazine, January 1984.

Hammond, George P. "Pimería Alta after Kino's Time." *New Mexico Historical Review*, 4 (July 1929).

Joel, Kenny. "All-American Padre." *Friar*, September 1967.

Jones, Arthur. "Grace with the Cross in Las Cruces, N.M." *National Catholic Reporter*, 10 February 1989.

Jones, Emadair Fall. Letter, *Ruidoso Times*, 26 November 1987.

Katz, Friedrich. "Pancho Villa and the Attack on Columbus, New Mexico." *American Historical Review* 83, No. 1 (February 1979).

Marsteller, Jeanne de Lue. "From Whence the Workers." *The Way of St. Francis*, November 1953.

McGary, David D. "Educational Methods of the Franciscans in California." *The Americas*, 6 (January 1950).

Meadows, John P. "The Round Mountain Fight of 1868." *Alamogordo News*, January 30, 1936.

Mitchell, Father Brendan, OFM. "Albert Braun 1889–1983: The Man Who Never Quit." *Westfriars*, April 1983.

Morton, Louis. "Germany First: The Basic Concept of Allied Strategy in World War II." *Command Decisions*. Kent Roberts Greenfield, Editor. Office of the Chief of Military History. Department of the Army. New York: Harcourt Brace, 1959.

Nicholas, Dan. "Mescalero Puberty Ceremony." *El Palacio*, Vol. 46 (September 1939).

Ortiz, Father Ferdinand, OFM. "The Maidens' Dance: Mescalero Indian Reservation, New Mexico." *The Indian Sentinel*, July 1920.

Scholes, France V. "Church and State in New Mexico, 1610–1650." *New Mexico Historical Review* 11 (January, April, July, October 1936); 12 (January 1937).

Schwartz, David. "Closed Church to Reopen Christmas." *Arizona Republic*, 25 December 1991.

Yost, Barbara. "Hero Priest Recalls Bad, Good Days." *Phoenix Gazette*, 30 November 1981.

INDEX

and nurses on Corregidor, 304, 308, 309
at Old Mission San Luis Rey, 167-68, 170, 171, 173-75
at Omori prison camp, 334-42
and Operation Sandstone, 376-80, 384
optimism of, 204, 310, 321
ordination of, 43
on ordination of women, 467
and Oregon school problem, 158
at Parker, Arizona, 459-61
and Pastor Overman, 143
patriotism of, 93, 147, 189, 254, 302, 386, 490, 496
postwar depression of, 368-69, 373, 375
President Reagan's tributes to, 486-487
is promoted to Lt. Colonel, 355, 384
receives Purple Heart, 113
and Quezon, inauguration of, 291-92
is recalled to active military duty, 259, 261
is recommended for Distinguished Service Cross, 113
on rectories, 84, 450
and respect for Indian culture, 82-83, 94, 97
retires from army, 355, 386
as Retreat Master, Casa de Paz y Bien, 446-50
return of from World War II, 342-48
in Sacred Heart Nursing Home. *See* Little Sisters of the Poor
sails for France 1918, 105
sails for Manila 1941. *See* Braun, USS *George Washington*
at St. Anthony's Seminary, Santa Barbara, 34-35, 36-37, 40-41
at St. Elizabeth's Friary, Oakland, California, 41-42
and St. John's Indian School, Komatke, Arizona, 163, 164, 166-67, 170, 182, 210, 357, 359, 394, 428-30, 431, 448, 458-59
with St. Mark's parish, Phoenix, 408, 409-31
at St. Mary's High School, 393, 395-408 *passim*
in St. Mary's parish, 391-98, 400-408
in Salome-Aguila area, 459, 462
says covert masses as POW, 313, 314, 318, 324, 340
services on death of, 490-93
Silver Stars awarded to, 113, 293, 360, 373-74
smuggles food and medicine into POW camps, 315-17, 325, 328, 332
stubbornness of, 128, 167, 356, 361, 397-98, 464, 481, 495, 497
studies European church buildings, 114, 123
swims in icy pond, 149-50
temper of, 34, 128, 350-51, 452-53, 497
terrible driving of, 99, 128, 238, 269, 381, 442, 463, 493, 497
testifies at Albert Fall trial, 195, 196
secures title for land at Mescalero, 182, 183
and tower at San Luis Rey, 177-78, 180
in Trier, Germany, 118-21

Byrnes, Archbishop Edwin, 382, 383

religion, deities and spirits, 83; Dutch Reformed Church, influence on, 232, 367-68; early Catholic influence on, 84; similarities to Christianity, 83

reservation, 71

Metzger, Bishop Sidney, 349, 353, 357, 367, 479, 491

Meuse-Argonne offensive, 107, 108, 109-15, 116

Mexico, sub rosa trips into. *See under* Braun, Fr. Albert

Mexico, Church and State warfare, 148, 158, 198, 221-22, 416

    clergy, persecution of, 159, 160-61, 168, 169-70, 178-79, 229, 234

    Díaz presidency, 159-60

    Marxist revolution, 158-61, 168-70, 197, 438

    rebellion of Cristeros, 179-80, 208-09, 212-13

Michoacán, Mexican province, 180, 183, 204, 215, 216, 217, 365

Migeon, Fr. Lucien, 60, *65*, 84-85, 90, 143

Miller, Blasa Telles (Mrs. Samuel Miller), 63-64, 76, 87, 91, 99, 162, 182, 264, 349

Miller, Katherine, 64, 88, 91, 162, 182, 349. *See also* Mackey, Katherine Miller

Miller, Samuel, 60, 63-64, 76, 87, 91, 162

Mindanao, 285, 310, 321, 328, 332. *See also* Braun at Davao

Miranda, Fray Pedro, 52

Mitchell, Fr. Brendan, OFM, 174, 175-76, 324

Momsen, Dunnigan and Ryan Hardware Co., 220, 248

Moncrief, Fr. Justin, OFM, 462, 490, 491

Moore, Gen. George E., 272, 277, 306, 307

Mora y Del Rio, Archbishop José, 178

Mori, Shigeji, 313-14, 315, 316

Morones, Luís, 160, 161, 169

Morrett, Capt. John J., 321

Moser, Fr. Ildefonse, OFM, 247, 251

Mounier, Fr. Hubert, OFM, 439-40, *440*

Mutter, Fr. Lawrence, OFM, 173, 174

N

Nagasaki, 341, 377, 380

Naiche, Chief, 72, 85-86, 132, 501

Nana, Chief, 72, 73, 85

Nava, Fr. Bonaventure, OFM, 'Boni,' 148, 162, 166, 167, 180, 181, 182, 183, 211, 212, 233, 234, 461

Navajo Indians, 54, 58, 69, 70, 73

'New Deal,' 225, 231-32

New Mexico National Guard, 269

New York, Braun in, 184, 216-17, 346

Nimitz, Adm. Chester W., 329

92nd Coast Artillery, 272

92nd Garage area, 311-13

Nomura, Kichisaburo, 271, 277, 278-79

North Atlantic Treaty Organization (NATO), 378

O

Oblasser, Fr. Bonaventure, 156

Obregón, Alvaro, 160, 161, 168, 169, 212

O'Brien, Bishop Thomas, 495

Ogori, Sergeant, 339, 341

'Old Ladies' Village,' 77

Old Mission San Luis Rey. *See* Braun as Guardian of

Old Mission Santa Barbara, 37, 42, 240, 241, 249, 470, 481

'Old Tony.' *See* Leyva, Antonio María

Olsen, Col. Kenneth S., 324, 328, 330-31

Omori POW camp. *See* Braun as Japanese POW

Oñate, Juan de, 38, 50

Operation Sandstone, 376-80, 382

Order of Friars Minor (OFM). *See* Franciscan Order

Ordoñez, Fray Isidro, OFM, 50

Orlando, Vittorio E., 118

Orozco y Jimenez, Archbishop Francisco, 208-09, 220, 221-22

Orozco, Pascual, 160

Ortega, Fray Pedro de, 51

Ortega, Paul, 75, 232, 367-68

Ortiz, Fr. Ferdinand, OFM, 49, 63-4, 65, 78, 85, 87, 89, 93, 94, 95, 97, 120, 132, 140, 148, 149, 246, 392, 426

Ortiz y Pino, Concha, 228-29, 238, 240-41, 457

Ortiz y Pino, Don José, 228-29, 240-41

Overman, Pastor, 143

P

Padilla, Fray Juan de, 49-50

'Padre Sambrano.' *See* Tafoya, Fr. Jose Sambrano

Pala Mission, California, 175, 177

Palmer, Ignatius, 491, *492*

Papakeikus, Chris, 111

Parker, Arizona, 438, 459-61

Parker, George M., 294, 295, 299

Pearl Harbor, 28, 148, 262, 271, 279, 281, 285, 286

Peñalosa, Diego, 52

Pensacola convoy, 280, 286, 287, 295

Peralta, Don Pedro de, 50

Perea, Fray Esteban de, 51-52

Pershing, Gen. John J., 59, 103, 105, 107, 108, 109, 114, 115, 118

Philadelphia, Braun in, 129, 130-32, 183

Philippine Islands, 263, 265, 266, 267, 271, 272, 276, 277, 281, 282, 285, 294, 299, 333, 336, 346, 391, 413, 419, 442, 499, 501

Portolá, Gaspar de, 38-39

Posada, Fray Alonso de, OFM, 52

Pozos, Fr. Agustín, 166, 211-12, 216, 217

Puberty Ceremony. *See* Mescalero Apache tribe

Pueblo Revolt 1680, 53-54, 240

Q
Quezon, Manuel, 267, 287, 288-89, 291-92, 298, 301
Quivira, 49-50

R
Raab, Fr. Felix, OFM, 262, 265-66, 268, 269, 275-76, 278, 279, 356, 426
Radosevich, Capt. Joseph R., 354
Ramsey, Adm. Dewitt C., 386-87
Ramirez, Fray Juan, OFM, 52
Ramirez, Bishop Ricardo, 490, 491
Rauch, Bishop James S., 484-85, 490
Reagan, Ronald, 381, 486, 487
Red Cross packages, 321, 326, 328, 330, 337
Redmon, Fr. Francis, OFM, 262, 353, 356, 365-66, 367, 372
Resendiz, Fr. Domingo, OFM, 183, 184-85, 200, 212, 213, 215, 216, 217, 224, 233, 234
Reyes, Lulu, 323, 324, 450
Rhodes, Fr. Joseph, OFM, 140
Richardson, Adm. James O., 262
Rio Grande, 50, 57, 68, 69, 238
Roak, Capt. Jack, 383, 386
Rockwell, Adm. Francis, 288, 289
Rodríguez, Fray Agustín, OFM, 50
Romagna, Meuse District, 112, 114
Roman Chiquita, 82, 87, 193
Roosevelt, Franklin Delano, 259, 260, 262, 267, 270, 271, 272, 276-77, 278, 279, 282, 286, 287, 292, 298, 299, 300
Rosas, Luís de, 52
Round Mountain, Battle of, 61-2
Rubio, Pascual Ortiz, 213
Russell, Cecil, 241, 359, 493
Russell, Marie DuPuy, 241, 359, 493
Russia, 92, 93, 104, 118, 121, 270, 271, 272, 341, 368, 377, 382, 396
Ryan, Thomas Fortune, 195, 460

S
Sacramento Mountains, 56, 63, 77
Sacred Heart Center, 420, 431, 452
Sacred Heart Chapel ('La Capilla'), 409
Sacred Heart Church (Sagrado Corazon), 422, 427, 431, 438, 422, 423, 441, 444, 446, 448, 446, 451, 452-53, 458, 459, 461, 463, 469, 480, 498, 501
Sacred Heart Community. See Corazon community
Sacred Heart Nursing Home. See Little Sisters of the Poor
Sacred Heart parish, 422, 441-42, 482
Sacred Heart School, Phoenix, 432-33, 434-35, 440, 442, 495
Sagrado Corazon community. See Corazon community

Santa Rosa Center, 402-03, 405, *405*, 407
Santa Rosa settlement, 401-04, 409
San Xavier del Bac Mission, 237, 245, 464
Satler, Mary Brown, 31, *45*, 355, 469
Sayre, Francis B., 287, 288
Schlokum, Bro. Benedict, OFM, 177, 226-27, 238
Schnautz, Henry, 501
Schneider, Fr. Thomas, OFM, 410, 415
Schola Cantorum, 502
Schuler, Bishop Anthony, SJ, 54-55, 77, 87, 93, 95-97, 99, 128, 138, 140, 141, 152, 162,
    166, 171, 172, 173, 180, 183, 197, 199, 201, 202, 204, 206, 209, 210, 213-14, 216,
    223, 242, 249-50, *250*, 260, 306, 349
Schwartz, Fr. Alban, OFM, 167, 170, 177
Second, Frank, 155
seminarians at Mescalero, 186-99, *187*, *188*, 192
Serna, Mary, 503
Serra, Fray Junípero, OFM, 38-40, 41, 168, 355-56, 444, 495
Shanta Boy, 78, *79*, 79-80, 162, 192-93, 194, 349
Shanta clan, 91, 192, 205
Shanta Community, Three Rivers, 78, 79, 192
Shanta, Ruth, 162, 194
Shanta, Virginia, 80, 163, 182, 193, 194, 343, 347, 364. *See also* Klinekole, Virginia Shanta
Sheehy, Celine Henrion, 200, 202, 346, 381, 463. *See also* Henrion, Celine
Sheehy, Oliver, 122, 123-24, 200, 202, 346
Shosh, Margaret, 155-56, *157*
Sierra Blanca, 63, 67, 77, 79, 85, 100, *194*, 501
Silva, Agapito, 332
Sinclair, Harry, 147-48, 206
Singapore, 271, 282, 285, 299, 301
Sister Michael, 484, 489, 490
60th Coast Artillery, 290
Smith, Fr. John, 204, 233, 234, 238, 240, 247, 260, 262
Soto, Fr. Gabriel, OFM, 218, 229, 230, 233, 234, 236, 237, 260
Spottedbird, Tommy, 502
Stalin, Josef, 259, 270, 376
Stanton, Henry Whiting, 67
Stanton, William, 131-32, 183, 210, 249, 250
Stark, Adm. Harold, 271-277
Steck, Dr. Michael, 68
Stimson, Henry L., 277, 287
Storff, Fr. Hugolinus, OFM, 43, 93, 104, 108, 124, 127, 128, 129, 142, 148, 225
submarine warfare, 92, 104, 260, 270

T
Tafoya, Fr. José Sambrano, 84
Teapot Dome. *See* Fall, Albert Bacon
Tejeda, A., 178, 179

CPSIA information can be obtained at www.ICGtesting.com
Printed in the USA
LVOW11s2159021016

507112LV00001B/101/P